WHERE ARE THEY BURIED?

WHERE ARE THEY BURIED?

HOW DID THEY DIE?

Fitting Ends and Final Resting Places
of the Famous, Infamous, and Noteworthy

TOD BENOIT

REVISED & UPDATED

BLACK DOG
& LEVENTHAL
PUBLISHERS
NEW YORK

Black Dog & Leventhal Publishers
Hachette Book Group
1290 Avenue of the Americas
New York, NY 10104
www.blackdogandleventhal.com

Printed in the USA

Cover design by Katie Benezra
Interior design by Cindy LaBreacht

LSC-C

First revised edition: March 2019

10 9 8 7 6 5 4 3 2 1

Originally published in hardcover by Black Dog & Leventhal Publishers in May 2003.

Black Dog & Leventhal Publishers is an imprint of Hachette Books, a division of Hachette Book Group.
The Black Dog & Leventhal Publishers name and logo are trademarks of Hachette Book Group, Inc.
The Hachette Speakers Bureau provides a wide range of authors for speaking events. To find out more, go to www.HachetteSpeakersBureau.com or call (866) 376-6591.
The publisher is not responsible for websites (or their content) that are not owned by the publisher.

LCCN: 2018951380
ISBNs: 978-0-7624-6681-8 (trade paperback);
978-0-7624-6680-1 (ebook)

DEDICATION

This book is dedicated to the memory of Don Schellhammer, Sr., who died in November 2001 after a lengthy illness. At 58, Don was buried at St. Anne's Cemetery in Sturbridge, Massachusetts.

APPRECIATIONS

For their invaluable contributions, the author is sincerely grateful to the following folks: Brian Benoit for joining in the epic Seattle–to–San Diego run of 1996; Meryl Brodsky for her labors as research librarian extraordinaire; Becky Koh for all of her generosities, including introducing my work to Black Dog & Leventhal; Laura Ross and Lisa Tenaglia, the discerning editors whose unflagging enthusiasm provided light at the end of the tunnel; Sid Roberts for mountaintop lodging; Art Dol for accommodations Down Under; and Chris Shepherd for his enthusiastic and tireless shilling of the finished product.

I'm also indebted to J.P. Leventhal and the staff and freelancers of Black Dog & Leventhal, including Cindy LaBreacht, Kylie Foxx, Michael Driscoll, Sara Cameron, Dara Lazar, Gregory Hurcomb, and True Sims. Their combined efforts have lent a quality to this work that I never could have envisioned.

Finally, kudos to all of the nameless hundreds of people, from town clerks and funeral home directors to cemetery staff and priests, who've gone well out of their way to help this cause.

ABOUT THE AUTHOR

After earning an engineering degree at the University of Massachusetts, Tod Benoit spent 10 years incarcerated in Corporate America, profoundly disturbed that his biography might someday mirror that of Ivan Ilych's, as told by Leo Tolstoy. In 1997, he redirected his efforts and spent the next decades on assorted far-flung adventures, from mountainbiking the Continental Divide to hitchhiking the wilds of South America, while alternately mooring everywhere from New Hampshire to New Zealand. Tod is eager to address any comments or criticism emailed to him at todbenoit@usa.net.

CONTENTS

INTRODUCTION

Tomorrow is the most important thing in life.
Comes into us at midnight very clean.
It's perfect when it arrives and it puts itself in our hands.
It hopes we've learned something from yesterday.
—JOHN WAYNE'S EPITAPH

AS I RECALL, the seasonably cool morning of December 9, 1980, became bitterly cold, for me anyway, right around ten o'clock. I think that's when all this started, more or less.

I took my seat in an English class, nothing new there, and when the bell rang moments later, Chris Lozier bounced to her place directly in front of me. She was bright and cheerful, and in those days her arrival was a highlight.

"Can you believe that about John Lennon?" she asked.

"What, did he make a disco record or something?"

"No, he's dead. Someone shot him last night."

And so it was. The quick flash of a gun had claimed another victim. John Lennon hadn't been the first popular figure to pass on, and he wouldn't be the last, but the senselessness of his death, and the starkness of its brutality against the kindhearted way of his life, struck a particularly heartfelt chord. While a generation that had been raised to a Beatles soundtrack contemplated its own mortality, the world mourned. At school a few months later we were treated to a rendition of Lennon's "Imagine" by a most unlikely singer, a fellow student named John Wood. He sang it during an assembly and when he finished, the student body clapped reverentially. Though the pall of Lennon's death lingered, the pieces were picked up and everyone got over it. There was nothing else to be done.

During the mid-1980s, I attended university in Lowell, Massachusetts, swallowing whole the indoctrinations of the town's famous literary son, Jack Kerouac, an exhilarating drunk whose ruminating mind tended toward the exploration of society's underbelly. In an untimely fashion in 1969, Jack drank himself to death, and the buzz in some circles was that he was buried in a nearby cemetery. As friends and I had frequented his old barroom haunts, a pilgrimage to his grave seemed fitting.

The visit proved to be more complicated than I had anticipated. There are numerous cemeteries in Lowell and nobody seemed to know in which one Jack was buried. I finally learned the name of the cemetery by tracking down his obituary, but then had to figure out how to get there. Upon our arrival, my plan was again confounded: The office was closed, there was no directory, and Jack's grave could be anywhere among the thousands of stones. After wandering the cemetery's rows for a few hours I gave up the search, but returned a few weeks later with John Macolini, a college roommate and fellow Kerouac devotee. Together we eventually located Jack's grave, but I knew there had to be an easier way to find such landmarks.

The locations of famous graves, and especially the puzzle of exactly how to find them, appealed to me as a kind of offbeat treasure hunt, but responsibilities beckoned and I put the matter on the back burner. Then, in 1992, the death of Sam Kinison, a sublimely deranged comedian, prompted me to pursue a quirky mental exercise: I began to compile a list of the famous deceased who mattered to me, or who might matter to someone else. Personalities like Babe Ruth and James Dean came to mind quickly and, once the most obvious individuals had been collected, I ferreted out additional notable folks from library reference sources. "Year in Review" issues of magazines were especially useful, and they yielded many more obscure and/or unconventional famous people, such as Dian Fossey, Jim Fixx, and Oskar Schindler. After compiling a list of several hundred famous deceased, I was the proud owner of an apparently worthless pile of information. Filing it away, I moved on.

But in 1994, I chanced upon a newspaper article concerning John Lennon's slaying. Across the street from the Dakota apartment building in New York City where he was shot, a section of Central Park had been dedicated to his memory and named "Strawberry Fields." More than a dozen years after John's death, a steady stream of visitors continued to arrive there in order to commune with John's spirit, their captivation showing no sign of abating. The article was a concise digest of this curious phenomenon, though, at its most fundamental level, the reporter didn't quite understand it. But I did.

Humans are unique in the cognizance of their own mortality. Though some may cling optimistically to the concept of a joyous hereafter, most acknowledge our granular contribution to the infinite beach of time and, by default, concede that the ultimate substance of our individual lives is largely irrelevant. But while we accept that all things must pass and nobody lives forever, we still strive to achieve a singularity, a legacy by which we might be remembered. This very human desire to "live on" is affirmed by the importance and elaborateness of our cemeteries, our penchant for visiting and caring for them, and the universally accepted notion of "respect for the dead." Every tombstone, a kind of waypoint between life and death, confirms individuality. "I was somebody," they seem to say.

Nearly 7,000 "somebodies" die in the United States every day, their passing mourned by survivors who keep the flame of their memory burning until joining them in ashes and dust. Though most passings are recognized by relatively small circles of family and friends, some deaths are more publicly mourned because, for better or worse, these people made a lasting imprint on the fabric of our society's culture. That culture includes all of us, and when John Lennon, or any famous or infamous person, is raised in memory, it's for the purpose of acknowledging and celebrating his or her unique and lasting stamp on our lives.

In the fall of 1994 I retrieved my list of famous deceased and the next step became obvious: It was time to find and document the resting places of our cultural heroes—and I was just the guy to do it. The project was ideally suited to my interests in history, travel, and research and, furthermore, I saw it as an opportunity to make the world just a little bit more fair. It somehow didn't seem equitable that some of our national icons, like John F. Kennedy and Elvis Presley, basked in the adoration of those who made the journey to the location of their well-documented monuments, while other worthy folks were relegated to the margins, cast off and all but forgotten.

I've since cataloged the locations of more than 1,000 famous graves, over 500 of which are described in this book, and believe me, it's been an enormous undertaking. There were multiple frustrations in locating many of the graves, and I pursued countless dead ends (no pun intended). However, that which did not kill me made me stronger, and I'm now grateful for my original ignorance: Had I comprehended the scheme's ultimate dimensions, I most certainly would have come up with a different hobby, and you'd be channel surfing right now.

Nonetheless, though there were innumerable disappointments and setbacks, it seemed that I was always rewarded for my persistence. Every blundering pitfall was supplanted by an equally elevating triumph. At a California cemetery, I suffered the wrath of some wasps whose nest I had inadvertently disturbed, but that misadventure resulted in a friendship with the groundskeeper. Later, I tapped out parts of this manuscript at his lofty Sierra Nevada mountain retreat. There were problems with rental cars: One particularly unlucky Taurus suffered a late-night collision with a near-sighted owl and, 20 minutes later, while I peeked through the new pattern of cracks in the windshield as we glided along a foggy stretch of Wisconsin blacktop, a suicidal skunk ambled into the car's path. The skunk never knew what hit him, but I'll bet the friendly Hertz staff in Minneapolis still cringes at the memory of that car's return. At another point, I accidentally deposited my vehicle's keys into a Long Island mailbox, but my idiocy was rewarded when it turned out that the mailman who arrived to retrieve them had known Mario Puzo personally. The helpful public servant showed me Mario's current digs and, with lukewarm Bud Lights retrieved from under the seat of his government-issue jeep, we saluted the progenitor of the fictitious Corleone crime family. In Texas, I lost a few pages of notes during a horrific windstorm but, a few days later in the lonely outpost of Picacho, New Mexico, I felt compensated when I was asked to serve as a sort of impromptu pallbearer for a forgotten pauper. I never knew what might be around the next bend in the road, and for that I'm thankful. It was an adventure.

I have one last anecdote to share. It's a little lengthy, but it's interesting, it's true, and it swings us full circle.

In October 1997 I was visiting famous graves in the Deep South, cutting a swath from Nashville to New Orleans when, on a dark stretch of Mississippi pavement, I came upon a traffic jam. There had been an accident and the road was temporarily closed to traffic in both directions. The midnight air was chilly so most people stayed in their idling vehicles, but I pulled to the side, slipped on my coat, and walked up to the crash site. It was gruesome—a pickup truck had clocked a bridge, and a dozen solemn bystanders gave the rescue team plenty of room. Unbelievably, I recognized the man who stood next to me in a dungaree shirt and cream-colored, flat-brimmed hat. I had to look twice, not quite trusting my eyes, but—sure enough—it was Bob Dylan. An hour earlier he had performed in concert at Mississippi State University, but he now stood anonymously in the shadows, exchanging short remarks with his personal bodyguard, a tough-looking Asian man nearly as thick as he was tall.

I casually sidled up to Dylan and offered commentary on the crash, but he was wary. His rugged sidekick eyed me suspiciously, no doubt concerned that his boss might end up like his old friend John Lennon. My mind working at hyperspeed, I desperately sought a dialogue a notch above the typical tongue-tied, starstruck blather that Dylan most certainly detested. Knowing that he was a fan of boxing, I ventured to share a chuckle with him over the recent Mike Tyson ear-biting debacle, but the conversation quickly stalled. I dug deep. The previous day, in Montgomery, Alabama, I had visited the grave of Hank Williams and it just so happened that I knew that Dylan was a dyed-in-the-wool Hank fan. So I told him about it. And remarkably, he listened. For the first time, he looked at me while I spoke. There was something to this grave stuff after all.

The accident scene was almost cleared and the drivers that had been delayed grew anxious. Bystanders were now murmuring and pointing their fingers; Dylan had been recognized, and a state trooper interrupted us, asking for an autograph. The trooper went away satisfied, but the escort indicated that they should be returning to the tour bus. Dylan turned to leave and then paused. He asked me, "What was the name of that cemetery?"

I don't know that Bob Dylan ever paid a call to Hank Williams' grave, but I like to think that he did. In 1975 he had visited Jack Kerouac's grave in Lowell and, sitting cross-legged while Allen Ginsberg chanted along in double time, he strummed a guitar for the amusement of Jack's ghost. That was a fitting homage; such humble alms are precisely suited to the occasion of visiting a person's resting place, whether it's of someone famous or otherwise. My sojourns were never about being photographed in the presence of their notoriety or checking graves off in the style of a grocery list. I've conscientiously maintained a model of decorum and, should you choose to visit any of these sites, I trust you'll preserve the tradition.

In the grand scheme of things, I don't suppose that all of this talk about the deceased and their graves amounts to a hill of beans. Still, I choose to believe that keeping a flame of memory burning for them matters somehow, even if it's in some mystical way that we cannot fully grasp. For that reason, I uphold my end of that unspoken accord. Maybe now you will join me.

—TOD BENOIT

SPORTS HEROES

LOU ALBANO

JULY 29, 1933 – OCTOBER 14, 2009

COLORFUL AND KOOKY, crazed and charismatic, "Captain" Lou Albano was a larger-than-life pro-wrestling icon who helped turn what was once a fringe, low-rent sport into a pop culture phenomenon.

After a short stint in the Army ended in 1951, Lou's father had nearly convinced his hard-to-handle son to open an insurance agency with him, but after a chance meeting with a distant cousin Lou was persuaded that his fortune lay in the fledgling business of wrestling instead. Following a lackluster start as "Leaping Lou," Albano teamed up with Tony Altomare to form "The Sicilians," and the duo played up a sort of half-assed stereotypical Italian mobster shtick all the way to a WWF (then the World Wrestling Federation) United States Tag Team title.

Moving on to managing wrestlers beginning in the 1970s, he compiled a stable of some of the toughest and meanest heels in the business and, along the way, developed a unique persona as a ranting, hoarse-voiced blowhard. Under an unkempt mane he delighted in half-open Hawaiian shirts that revealed a generous portion of his flabby 310-pound physique, and he sported three rubber bands dangling from a pin on one cheek, a few others hanging from an ear, and yet another wrapped tightly around his wildly curly goatee. Portraying a streetwise bully, he challenged his rivals' manhood and hurled politically incorrect epithets at the gathered crowds. He was a jerk and a weasel, a guy willing to talk big who remained safely situated behind his various protégés. But while his cowardice infuriated the crowd, Lou saw himself otherwise: "Sure, I yell and holler a lot, but in real life? I'm a regular guy just trying to make a living."

Albano's career continued along this crowd-displeasing path until 1983 when he met then-hot pop star Cyndi Lauper on a flight to Puerto Rico. Perhaps seeing a kindred spirit in one another, the unlikely duo teamed up in her new video for "Girls Just Want to Have Fun," with Albano playing her domineering father. Soon he appeared in a string of her music videos and even briefly lured her into the wrestling world and, though the whole thing was just a logical business decision for Lou, the campaign pushed wrestling toward the mainstream. In short order there were wrestlers on talk shows and in commercials seemingly everywhere. Wrestling had been lurking in the shadows all along, but the Rock 'n' Wrestling movement made it inescapable and Lou, a sort of patron saint of the WWF, became its main benefactor as he was vaulted to show business fame.

But after just a few years, Lou's star was shadowed by younger personalities such as Hulk Hogan, though Lou seemed not to mind. "I've been married to the same woman for 32 years, and I've got four wonderful grown kids. Cyndi and I are lifetime honorary chairpersons for multiple sclerosis, and when I started doing charity work, for the first time people said, 'Hey, fat guy, you're not so bad after all.'"

At 76, Lou died in his sleep of a heart attack and was buried at Rose Hills Memorial Park in Putnam Valley, New York.

GRAVE DIRECTIONS: At 101 Mill Street, drive past the office and up the winding hill, staying straight at the four-way intersection. Head for and drive between the mausoleums at the top, parking at the end of the drive on the left. Walk into and through that mausoleum and then turn right. You'll find the Captain near the end of this outside walkway in the third row from the bottom.

MUHAMMAD ALI
JANUARY 17, 1942 – JUNE 3, 2016

AFTER HIS BICYCLE was stolen off a Louisville street, 12-year-old Cassius Clay Jr. began boxing in order to exact revenge on the thief. Though that day of retribution never materialized, eight Golden Gloves titles and an amateur record of 100-5 did, and in 1960 the talkative teenager returned from Rome an Olympic gold medalist, as well as a professional contender.

Vanquishing one opponent after another, and often even predicting in rhyming and comical verse how and when he'd send an opponent to the mat, boxing's new wonder boy soon developed a mass following. Courted by the most eminent promoters and agents, whom he quickly rejected, he found his direction in the Nation of Islam, a Muslim sect that rejected the pacifism of typical civil rights activism, and he secretly converted in 1963. After pummeling heavyweight champion Sonny Liston the following year, the vainglorious new champion renounced his Cassius Clay "slave name" and said he would be known from then on as Muhammad Ali.

In rejecting his birth name and adopting a seemingly subversive one, Ali came to represent a new kind of athlete, someone who created his own style in defiance of past traditions. Seemingly overnight, he went from a bubbly, boyish champion with a gift of gab to a quasi-revolutionary. Nonetheless, casual and unpredictable,

Ali was perfectly suited to television and became a talk-show and sports program fixture.

Despite the seeming contradiction of a boxer advocating nonviolence, in 1967 Ali refused military induction and was condemned as a draft dodger. "Why should they ask me to put on a uniform and go 10,000 miles from home and drop bombs and bullets on brown people in Vietnam, after so-called Negro people in Louisville are treated like dogs and denied simple human rights?" he asked. His boxing license and heavyweight crown stripped, convicted of draft evasion and sentenced to five years in prison, Ali still refused to serve and held firm to his principle of pacifism, maintaining that his Muslim beliefs forbade him from participating in the killing of others. His pronouncement outraged much of middle America, but as the war dragged on and the cultures of youth and black America surged, the national conscience stirred. Ultimately, the episode elevated Ali as an emblem of conscience and courage.

Though he never actually had to serve any prison time, as the conviction was reversed on appeal and his boxing license restored in 1970, Ali lost three years of his athletic prime. After two tune-up fights, the 29-year-old sought to regain his heavyweight title from the new champion, Joe Frazier, in a highly touted bout guaranteeing each man at least $2.5 million, the highest payday for any athlete up to that time. Frazier won the match by unanimous decision, and Ali suffered his first professional defeat.

Their slugfest ignited a decade-long golden era for heavyweight boxing. To the cadence of inimitable Howard Cosell commentary, Ali, Frazier, George Foreman, and Leon Spinks beat one another mercilessly in a series of celebrated international spectacles with names such as "Rumble in the Jungle" and "Thrilla in Manila." Ali regained the title in 1974, lost and then won it back again in 1978, and then, finally, after losing the title yet again in 1980, he retired.

Even before retirement, Ali was showing signs of slurred speech and general sluggishness, but in 1982 he was diagnosed with Parkinson's disease, a condition that slowly robbed him of both his verbal grace and his physical dexterity. As his health gradually declined, Ali threw himself into humanitarian work and was admired not just as a supreme athlete but as a symbol of understanding and hope. With his push for philanthropic causes and incessant crisscrossing of the globe, whoever he met with—heads of state, royalty, or the Pope—agreed that Ali was always the most famous person in the room.

Asked to share his personal philosophy near the end of his life, Ali's wife read what he'd written: "I never thought of the possibility of failing, only of the fame and glory I was going to get when I won....When I proclaimed that I was the greatest of all time, I believed in myself, and I still do."

After being hospitalized for a respiratory illness, Ali died at 74 of septic shock "due to unspecified natural causes" and was buried at Cave Hill Cemetery in Louisville, Kentucky.

GRAVE DIRECTIONS: Enter the cemetery at 701 Baxter Avenue and follow the green line that's painted in the road to Ali's grave.

ANDRE THE GIANT
MAY 19, 1946 – JANUARY 27, 1993

ANDRE RENE ROUSSIMOFF, of French heritage and better known as Andre the Giant, was a professional wrestler afflicted with a genetic disorder resulting in gigantism. In 1973 he made his American debut at Madison Square Garden and, proving fantastically successful, wrestled more than 300 days a year for the next 16-odd years, becoming one of the world's most famous professional athletes.

Though he was advertised as 7-foot-4, he was probably just under seven feet and tipped the scales at around 500 pounds. Andre's immense appetites for food and alcohol were legendary, and it was estimated he consumed 7,000 calories a day in alcohol alone.

In 1987, he played Fezzik, the gentle giant in the movie *The Princess Bride*, a role for which he was suited in both dimension and disposition, and it remained one of his most cherished achievements—he carried a video of the film with him when he traveled and held frequent screenings.

Unfortunately, as he grew older his size caused him frequent health problems and he became increasingly overweight and immobile.

In Paris, Andre attended his father's funeral and the following day died of a heart attack in a room at the Hôtel de la Trémoille. Just 46, he was cremated and his ashes scattered at his horse ranch in Ellerbe, North Carolina.

ARTHUR ASHE
JULY 10, 1943 – FEBRUARY 6, 1993

ARTHUR ASHE WAS the first African American man to win tennis' most prestigious tournaments: the U.S. Open and Wimbledon. He first learned to play tennis on a segregated playground, then parlayed

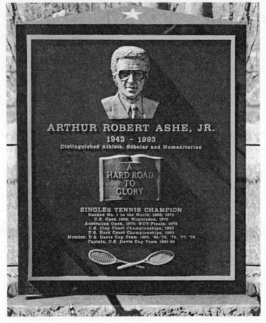

that into a 12-year career that included 33 singles and 18 doubles titles. He later became president of the Association of Tennis Professionals and captain of the Davis Cup team, which won two championships under his direction.

Though the titles and ensuing endorsement contracts made Arthur a millionaire, wealth didn't distract him from the social issues of the day. He became a civil rights activist, fighting for all minorities that were victims of exclusionary practices. He also served as the national campaign chairman for the American Heart Association, edited several books, and contributed generously to African American programs everywhere.

After Arthur disclosed that he had AIDS in 1992, he devoted himself to becoming a role model in the fight against the disease, and began a $5 million fund-raising effort on behalf of his namesake foundation.

At 49 Ashe died of pneumonia, a complication brought on by AIDS, and was buried at Woodland Cemetery in Richmond, Virginia.

GRAVE DIRECTIONS: Enter the cemetery at 2300 Magnolia Road, turn at the first left, and proceed for 100 yards. Arthur's grave is on the left.

Fans of Arthur's will also want to view the statue crafted in his honor on Monument Avenue. As a child, Arthur had not been allowed to play on Richmond's segregated tennis courts, but today his memorial stands tall in the heart of the Confederacy's capital city.

RED AUERBACH
SEPTEMBER 20, 1917 – OCTOBER 28, 2006

AFTER LEAVING THE Navy in 1946 where he'd directed the sports program at Norfolk Naval Base, basketball legend Red Auerbach signed on as coach for the Washington Capitols during the Basketball Association of America's first season. Four years later, Red moved over to the fledgling Boston Celtics franchise even though the future of the team and the entire NBA was hardly secure—by 1955 seven of the league's franchises had gone belly-up and more than once Red paid the Celtics travel costs out of his own pocket.

But six winning seasons drove Celtics ticket sales up and in 1956, through shrewd maneuverings, Red secured the services of gifted defensive center Bill Russell and that acquisition began the greatest basketball dynasty the country has ever seen. By the end of Red's 39-year coaching and general manager career—a tenure marked by him berating referees and pacing the sidelines with a rolled-up program in his clenched fist—the stocky and cantankerous Red had led the Celtics to 16 championships including a sure-to-be-unequaled eight straight from 1959 through 1966.

Defining his secret to coaching in his 2004 biography, *Let Me Tell You a Story*, Red said: "I teach my players not to accept the philosophy that being a sore loser is a bad thing. Only losers accept losing."

A longtime tradition of Red's had been to light and savor a victory cigar—his favorite was the Hoyo de Monterrey Excalibur—during a game's late moments as it became apparent that victory was at hand. The customary seat he occupied as elder statesman of the game in his later years at TD BankNorth Garden—Loge 12, Row 7, Seat 1—is devoid of any telltale burn marks, but to this day fans visit it briefly to have their picture snapped in the legend's chair.

At 89, Red died of a heart attack. In a casket lined in Celtic green, he was buried at King David Memorial Gardens in Falls Church, Virginia.

GRAVE DIRECTIONS: Enter the cemetery at 2725 Hollywood Road, turn right at the first drive, and stop at the top of this loop, immediately after the small grove of trees with a walkway. In the grass on your left, inside the loop, Red's flat bronze marker surrounded in marble is at Plot 15-137-3A.

WILT CHAMBERLAIN
AUGUST 21, 1936 – OCTOBER 12, 1999

THE 7-FOOT-1 WILT Chamberlain so dominated the game of basketball that, in direct response to his abilities, the NBA changed some of its rules in order to give everyone else a fighting chance. The lane under the basket was widened, the offensive-goaltending rule was implemented, and regulations regarding inbounding and free throws were revised. Though the changes served their purpose to some degree, Wilt "the Stilt" continued to be a heavy presence. By the time of his 1973 retirement, he'd set a number of records, two of which will probably never be broken. First, Wilt never once fouled out through 1,205 games. Second, in 1962 he scored an astonishing 100 points in a single game.

In 1991 it came out that Wilt also held one other pseudo-record, though it was somewhat nefarious and hard to verify. In his autobiography, *A View from Above*, the lifelong bachelor devoted an entire chapter to sex and there made the revelation that, if he had to count his sexual encounters, he'd be closing in on 20,000 women. "Yes, that's correct, twenty thousand different ladies," he wrote. "At my age, that equals out to having sex with 1.2 women a day, every day since I was fifteen years old." Some fans recoiled at Wilt's macho accounting and roundly criticized him, while others contemplated that, even if he was exaggerating by a factor of 10...

At 63, Wilt died of congestive heart failure. He was cremated and his ashes were entrusted to his family.

ROBERTO CLEMENTE
AUGUST 18, 1934 – DECEMBER 31, 1972

IT WAS A long journey to the Baseball Hall of Fame for Roberto Clemente, and sadly, the star outfielder and humanitarian never even witnessed his own induction ceremony. After learning the game on a muddy field in Puerto Rico where a tree branch was used for a bat, Roberto graduated to the Major Leagues in 1954, and, with the Pittsburgh Pirates, he became a cherished 12-time

All-Star who notched 3,000 hits and won 11 consecutive Gold Gloves.

But though his athleticism won him widespread admiration, Roberto's most genuine affection was earned well beyond the white lines of baseball diamonds. He sought to be an authentic role model, not merely a guy who could hit and catch a ball pretty well. To that end Roberto generously assisted charitable causes with hard cash, donated thousands of autographed pictures to juvenile facilities, and personally worked for the destitute during the off-season.

When a catastrophic earthquake hit Managua, Nicaragua, its neighbors and other organizations coordinated relief, but reports of Nicaraguan corruption resulting in the misdirection of supplies soon surfaced. Roberto was prompted to organize his own relief mission and, on the New Year's Eve of 1973, he boarded a donated DC-7 in San Juan, Puerto Rico, bound for Managua. Packed with five men and over 16,000 pounds of supplies, the airplane bobbed, bucked, and wheezed after takeoff. Moments later, an engine burst into flames and the plane took a nosedive into the ocean off Isla Verde beach.

Rescuers rushed to the scene but there was nothing to be done. There were no survivors, and Roberto's body was never found.

TY COBB
DECEMBER 18, 1886 – JULY 16, 1961

AS A DARING base stealer, hustling outfielder, and powerhouse slugger, Ty Cobb, "the Georgia Peach," is considered to be among the best all-around players of baseball. Lining up on a Major League diamond for the first time in 1905, he played 22 seasons for the Detroit Tigers while his last two years were spent with the Philadelphia Athletics. Ty's lifetime batting average of .367 still stands as a record, though most of the others he held have since been broken (due largely to the longer schedule now played). But despite an unparalleled desire to excel and win, Ty never played on a World Series champion team.

For all of his on-field heroics, Ty was never adored by his fans; they admired his athletic prowess, but the love affair ended there. This has been alternately attributed to the fact that much of Ty's career occurred before Babe Ruth ushered in base-ball's golden age, or that the Tigers were never a powerhouse team. But there's also a more accurate explanation: Ty Cobb was a self-centered, hot-tempered, overtly racist curmudgeon who seemed to delight in the controversy of contentious relations with other players, the press, and his own family.

In 1960, long after his playing days had ended, Ty contracted an up-and-coming sportswriter named Al Stump to write the "real story" of his life. Ty was dying, nobody gave a damn, and he now wished to counter for posterity what he felt was an inaccurate version of his life. Stump was happy to oblige but, soon enough, as Ty twisted the facts of every ugly incident to paint himself as the pitiful victim, it became clear to Stump that he was merely a hired gun; Ty, a bitter and unreasonable, cancer-ridden drunk who was deservedly lonely, was trying to use Stump as a shill to counter the "lies."

But Stump went along with it, writing Ty's biography the way Ty wanted it written, all the while secretly keeping notes about the real Ty on the side. In 1961 *My Life in Baseball: The True Record* told the story of Ty's life, and Ty went to his grave content that his "truths" had been established. Then in 1994, after a curious 33-year procrastination, Stump released *Cobb: The Life and Times of the Meanest Man Who Ever Played Baseball*, offering less antiseptic and sentimental insight into the baseball great.

Ty was shrewd off the field as well; he invested heavily in General Motors and Coca-Cola and, when he died, was worth millions. But his death was emblematic of his life. Instead of having friends and family at his side, a handgun and a fortune in stock certificates were on the nightstand next to his hospital bed. Only three former baseball colleagues attended his funeral, and there was no national mourning.

Not long before his death, when asked if he had any regrets, Ty replied, "If I had my life to live over again, I'd have done it a little different. I'd have more friends."

At 74, he was buried at the Rose Hill Cemetery in Royston, Georgia.

GRAVE DIRECTIONS: You won't miss Ty's big mausoleum in the center of the cemetery at 30 Burch Street.

HOWARD COSELL
MARCH 25, 1918 – APRIL 23, 1995

AMERICA'S MOST OUTSPOKEN sportscaster, Howard Cosell, of bad toupee and garish sports jacket fame, epitomized a holier-than-thou "New Yawk" know-it-all attitude and became the catalyst of countless arguments around office watercoolers as sports fans alternately loved or hated his brash, no-nonsense style and unqualified immodesty. Wordy harangues, punctuated by a signature catchphrase, "I just tell it like it is," dripped with an intonation of a Brooklyn-bile accent never heard at the highest levels of network television before or since. A social phenomenon and crusading journalist who broke the pretty-face, perfect-hair, former-jock mold of network sports personalities with his unique style and delivery, Howard was a lightning rod for criticism.

From the early 1960s when he first began to attract national attention, Howard, a lawyer by training, frequently tackled the toughest issues in sport; he allied with the then-controversial heavyweight champion Muhammad Ali and was the first to stand by him after Ali was stripped of his title for refusing induction into the Army during the Vietnam War. He was a vocal critic of baseball's reserve clause (which, before the advent of free agency, bound a player to one team), and he railed over the corruption in boxing, the cheating and academic abuses of college sports, and the rampant commercialism of the Olympic movement.

At the height of his popularity, Howard was alleged to be the most valuable property in sports as he alone was capable of promoting, reporting, and criticizing an event packaged and merchandised by his own network. In a sense, Howard triumphed by building a franchise around himself; his second greatest triumph, then, was *Monday Night Football*. In 1970 many believed putting a sports event on in prime time against entertainment programming would be a disaster, but ABC gambled that Howard could draw viewers to the telecast. Decades later *Monday Night Football* is still going strong, though the same can't be said for Howard. Nonetheless, his diatribes remain: "Arrogant, pompous, obnoxious, vain, cruel, verbose, a show-off, I have been called all of these. Of course, I am."

At 77, Howard died of a heart embolism and was buried at Westhampton Cemetery in Westhampton, New York.

GRAVE DIRECTIONS: At 21 Station Road, enter the cemetery at the rightmost drive, which is marked Drive J. About three-fourths of the way down this drive, find the Pasqualini stone on the left and four hedgerows farther, in the middle of the row, is the Cosell plot.

JAY "DIZZY" DEAN
JANUARY 16, 1911 – JULY 17, 1974

WITH A BLAZING Ozark fastball, Jay Hanna "Dizzy" Dean pitched himself right into the Baseball Hall of Fame. He did it by doing what came naturally, as he "was never taught to play base-ball and never had to learn."

After his playing days, Dizzy became an announcer and was revered as a folk hero for his great turns of the English language in the booth. One player looked "mighty hitterish" to Dizzy, another "slud into third," and one team's problem was that "they ain't got enough spart." Pressed for an explanation of that locution, Dizzy replied, "Spart is pretty much the same as fight or gumption. Like the *Spart of St. Louis*, that plane Lindbergh flowed to Europe in."

At 63 he died of a heart attack, and was buried at Bond Cemetery in Wiggins, Mississippi.

GRAVE DIRECTIONS: At 55 Murrey Avenue, Dizzy's grave is easy to find in the 11th row from the road.

DALE EARNHARDT
APRIL 29, 1951 – FEBRUARY 18, 2001

DALE EARNHARDT NEVER had any doubt about what he would do with his life. As a boy his weekends were spent watching his father, Ralph Earnhardt, race stock cars, and he later summed up his commitment to the sport thusly: "I can't remember anything but racing. I didn't want to go to school or anywhere else, I just wanted to be racing."

Dale left school after the eighth grade, dreaming of making a living among cars. By 18 he had succeeded; a service station attendant, he mounted tires and wielded wrenches to support himself and a young family. But that wasn't exactly the script he had dreamed of, and the aspiring, self-financed racer plugged away at his passion. In 1973 his father died of heart failure while working on his race car, and Dale resolved to make it big on the professional circuit for both of them.

In 1979 Dale took home NASCAR's Rookie of the Year award, and he won the Winston Cup series title the following year, becoming the only driver ever to win the rookie crown and series championship in consecutive seasons. His next title came in 1986, which began an incredible run of six championships in nine seasons. Winning every major NASCAR event at least once, he earned more than $40 million in purses as well as "the Intimidator" nickname.

But Dale's fortunes changed at the 2001 Daytona 500 in Florida. On the last lap of the prestigious race, Dale was running in an "interference" position while fellow teammates Dale Jr. and Michael Waltrip held the top two spots. As long as Dale could hold on to his third-place standing, the team would enjoy a podium sweep. However, between the third and fourth turns of that final lap, just seconds from the finish, Dale inexplicably crashed his car into the wall at a speed approaching 200 miles per hour. Though it seems he was killed upon impact, Dale wasn't pronounced dead until arriving at the Halifax medical facility less than a mile away. His was the first driver fatality in the 43-year history of the Daytona 500.

It was later determined that Dale's seatbelt had failed, which, of course, contributed to his death. But doctors also weighed in with their opinion that, had Dale been wearing a full-face helmet like that worn by virtually every other professional race-car driver, instead of the open-face helmet that his ego required, his injury pattern would've been different; Dale's chin struck the steering column in such a way as to fracture the base of his skull, and a full-face helmet may have saved his life.

At 49, Dale was buried on the grounds of his estate in Mooresville, North Carolina.

GRAVE DIRECTIONS: From I-77, take Exit 36 and follow Route 150 east for 2½ miles. Turn right on Route 136 and, after 4½ miles, you'll see a building that looks somewhat out of place on the left. (There is no sign.) That's the main workplace of Dale Earnhardt Incorporated, or DEI, as it's locally known.

In the front of this building are a small museum and a large gift shop wherein the public is cordially invited to shop for $29 coffee mugs and fashionably hideous $450 coats. That's as far as the public's invitation extends, however, and as a member of such, you'll not be allowed to cast your eyes upon Dale's resting place; he lies in a mausoleum within the confines of the estate behind the main DEI building.

JOE FRAZIER
JANUARY 12, 1944 – NOVEMBER 7, 2011

SMOKIN' JOE FRAZIER was the first man to defeat Muhammad Ali, yet he spent a lifetime playing second fiddle to his nemesis.

After winning Olympic gold in Tokyo in 1964 and then knocking out his first 11 professional opponents, Frazier set himself up as a challenger to Ali's heavyweight crown. But in April 1967, Ali declared, "I ain't got nothing against them Vietcong," refused to be drafted, and was stripped of his title. To fill the vacated position, heavyweight contenders participated in an eight-man elimination tournament and when it was over, Frazier was undisputed World Heavyweight Champion.

Eight months later, a court reinstated Ali's boxing license and the sports world salivated at the prospect of Frazier and Ali—neither of whom had ever lost a bout—squaring off in the ring. Touted as the "Fight of the Century," the Ali-Frazier showdown was given a political and social cast too. Ali came to represent rising black anger in America, while Frazier, who voiced no political views, was nonetheless depicted as the establishment's favorite. Calling him ignorant and a gorilla, Ali publicly humiliated Frazier with pre-bout banter and, unable to match Ali's charisma or gift for the provocative quote, Frazier stewed and ultimately came to detest Ali.

The time for talk ended at Madison Square Garden, where, with a ferocious brawling and slugging style, Frazier pummeled Ali mercilessly while ducking and weaving from opposing jabs. In the 14th round, Frazier landed perhaps the most famous left hook in history, devastating Ali's jaw and dropping him to the canvas like a lead weight. The new undisputed champion, Frazier left the ring declaring, "I always knew who the champ was."

In 1973, though, George Foreman stripped Frazier of his crown, knocking him down six times in just two rounds before the bout was stopped. Once Ali then took the title from Foreman, the stage was set for an Ali-Frazier rematch.

The "Thrilla in Manila" of 1975 is regarded as one of the greatest fights in boxing history. The Philippine ring was sweltering as hot lights overpowered the air-conditioning, but still

Frazier and Ali traded punches with a fervor unimaginable for heavyweights. It ended when a battered Frazier, one eye swollen shut, did not come out for the final round, his trainer telling him, "Sit down, son. It's all over. Nobody will ever forget what you did here today." Shortly after, at 32, Frazier hung up his gloves for good.

Frazier spent the rest of his life trying to fight his way out of Ali's shadow, a cast that darkened when he later struggled financially and ran a Philadelphia gym to make ends meet, while Ali became one of the most beloved people in the world. In an interview 30 years later, Ali apologized, saying, "I said a lot of things in the heat of the moment that I shouldn't have said. Called him names and I apologize for that. I'm sorry. It was all meant to promote the fight."

At a gala held on the 40th anniversary of Frazier's 1971 win, Smokin' Joe said he no longer felt any bitterness toward the man who by then was suffering from Parkinson's disease and was mostly mute. "I forgive him. He's in a bad way." That night the "Fight of the Century" remained fresh in Frazier's mind. "I can't go nowhere where it's not mentioned. That was the greatest thing that ever happened in my life."

Smokin' Joe died of liver cancer at 67 and is buried at Ivy Hill Cemetery in Philadelphia.

GRAVE DIRECTIONS: Enter the cemetery at 1201 Easton Road and stay on the main drive for a couple hundred yards. You won't miss Joe's magnificent stone in front of you at the second fork.

JOHN HEISMAN
OCTOBER 23, 1869 – OCTOBER 3, 1936

FOR 36 YEARS John Heisman coached college football, contributing numerous key innovations to the sport. He was responsible for legalizing the forward pass, he was the first coach to use the quarterback as safety on defense, and he promoted the division of the game into quarters and the scoreboard showing down, distance, time, and score. Heisman also introduced the center snap and the "hike" or "hep" count signals of the quarterback in starting play. Before that innovation, the center on an offensive line would roll the ball on the ground to the quarterback.

Between 1892 and 1927, he coached at eight different colleges including Clemson and Auburn, but it was his head coaching position at Georgia Tech that was most memorable. With the Yellow Jackets, Heisman introduced the "Heisman Shift," a feared offense used to compile an impressive 100-29-6 record over his 16-season tenure. In 1916, Heisman gave new dimension to the word "rout" when his Yellow Jackets stung Cumberland's Bulldogs, 222-0. That game, which has been called the Game of the Century, is still celebrated in Georgia Tech sports lore while Cumberland prefers to pretend it never happened.

After his death, the Downtown Athletic Club of New York City—of which John was the director—named its annual trophy in his honor. The Heisman Trophy is awarded each year to college football's outstanding player. Many of the trophy's past winners have gone on to lead illustrious professional football careers including such renowned players as Roger Staubach, Tony Dorsett, Tim Tebow, and, of course, O.J. Simpson.

After a bout of pneumonia, John died at 66 and was buried at Forest Home Cemetery in Rhinelander, Wisconsin.

GRAVE DIRECTIONS: At the corner of Coon and Newell Streets, enter the cemetery, bear left, then stop just before the next paved road on the right. Follow the grass path on your right for about 80 feet to the Donaldson stone. This is John's wife's family plot, and here you'll find John's flat marker as well.

BEN HOGAN
AUGUST 13, 1912 – JULY 25, 1997

BEN HOGAN STARTED in golf as an 11-year-old caddy and by 19 was a professional player. In those Depression-era years, a career as a professional golfer wasn't nearly as lucrative as it is today, and tour pros pooled their monies and traveled together. The monetary reward for being a superior player wasn't at that time evident and diligence on the practice range was somewhat of an oddity. Upon reaching the professional ranks, many players were content to let their skills plateau.

Ben, however, was a pioneer at refining his game. While his competitors succumbed to other distractions, Ben, who called learning a "daylight-till-dark process," dedicated himself to developing a "repeating swing" that could stand up under the pressure of tournament play. True, in those early years, Ben was almost winless, so perhaps he needed the practice more than anyone else, but it seems too that through the rote discipline of perfecting his swing and other particulars, Ben was able to create a more solid base of golfing ability that stayed with him through the stress of competition.

His skills also stayed with him during his military service during World War II, when there wasn't a lot of time to play golf, or any game for that matter. Indeed, upon his discharge from the Army, Ben resumed his place on the tour and almost immediately dominated the competition, butting heads with rival Sam Snead in the process, and winning 62 USPGA events, including nine majors between 1946 and 1953. The tremendous run of athletic excellence came despite a horrific 1949 car accident from which he suffered, among other injuries, some loss of vision in his left eye.

Nearly unbeatable, Ben was asked how he'd learned his trade. "I dug it out of the ground," replied the master.

At 84, Ben died of heart failure and now rests at Greenwood Mausoleum in Fort Worth, Texas.

GRAVE DIRECTIONS: At 3100 White Settlement Road, pull into the drive after the funeral home, and the mausoleum is the low marbled building in front of you. Enter the mausoleum through the second door on the right side of the building. Walk straight in, under the Yandell crypt, and 20 feet farther, on the left is Ben Hogan.

GORDIE HOWE
MARCH 31, 1928 – JUNE 10, 2016

FINALLY HANGING UP his skates after his hair had silvered and he'd become a grandfather, the tenacious right wing Gordie Howe played professional hockey longer and better than just about anyone who ever glided onto the ice. Signing his first pro contract in 1945 for the annual princely salary of $2,350, he played 1,767 games in a record 26 seasons and helped lead the Detroit Red Wings to seven straight regular-season championships.

Another of Gordie's hallmarks was roughness and he was notorious for delivering a crushing body check or a sharp jab with his elbow, or the end of his stick, to opponents who dared incur his wrath. Not invincible, however, he now and then got the worst of it and in his career endured some 300 stitches in his face. And never mind fussing over penalty *minutes*—nearly 30 *hours* of his career were spent in the penalty box. So frequently was he involved in fights that the Gordie Howe Hat Trick—a goal, an assist, and a fight in one game—is still part of the hockey vernacular.

Gordie left the Red Wings and seemingly retired in 1971, but two years later was back—this time teamed with sons Mark and Marty, before finally calling it quits six seasons later at age 52 with the Hartford Whalers.

An animated storyteller who good-naturedly mingled with fans and signed autographs for hours, Gordie reflected once on the key to his career longevity: "There is no doubt in my mind that it was my love for the game," he said. "To succeed, you've got to love what you're doing. I tell kids, if you don't love it, get out of the way for someone who does."

After being diagnosed with dementia and then suffering a series of strokes that impaired his speech and confined him to bed, his family announced that Gordie died "of old age" at 88. He was cremated and his ashes interred inside the base of his statue at the entrance of the SaskTel Centre Arena in Saskatoon, Saskatchewan, Canada.

"SHOELESS" JOE JACKSON
JULY 16, 1889 – DECEMBER 5, 1951

BY AGE NINE, Joe Jackson was working 12-hour days at a textile mill in South Carolina to help support his family. By 12 he was playing on the company's baseball team. In 1908, at 18, Joe joined the minor league Greenville Spinners. During one particular game, Joe wore a new pair of spiked baseball shoes, but they gave him blisters, so he finished the game in his stocking feet. Later, after belting a triple, he slid into third base and an opposing fan yelled "You shoeless son of a gun!" which led a sportswriter to dub him "Shoeless Joe."

Joe was soon promoted to the Major Leagues and after just two seasons with the Cleveland Indians he was revered as one of baseball's best players, always a threat with the bat and a dependable fielder with a strong and accurate arm. In 1915 he was traded to the Chicago White Sox and over the next four seasons became the city's favorite sports hero, often leading the league in a variety of hitting statistics.

In 1919, Shoeless Joe and seven teammates, the Chicago Eight, were implicated in the so-called Black Sox scandal that charged they had received cash payments in return for playing below their ability and allowing the Cincinnati Reds to win that year's World Series. "Say it ain't so, Joe," soon became a tag line of fans that hoped that their heroes had not betrayed them or the game.

After a year of high anxiety for the eight defendants and millions of sports fans, the prosecution's case crumbled when a transcript of grand jury testimony went missing. Nevertheless, after the 1920 baseball season the Chicago Eight were banned from baseball for life by Commissioner Kenesaw Landis. For the last

80 years, various baseball nuts have petitioned the league to reverse the ban against the players, and especially against Shoeless Joe, so that he might assume his place in Cooperstown.

To date, the ban has not been reversed, and for good reason, it seems. The "missing" transcript surfaced in 1923 and it demonstrates quite clearly that Shoeless Joe and three of the other players admitted to participating in the fix, albeit reluctantly. After being asked by the grand jury whether anyone paid him money to throw the series in favor of Cincinnati, Shoeless Joe replied, "They promised me $20,000 and paid me five [thousand]." Later, though, when asked whether he made any intentional errors on a particular day, Shoeless Joe replied, "No, sir, not during the whole Series." It appears that Shoeless Joe agreed to throw the game, then later had misgivings and played as well as he could, but his team lost anyway.

After their ban, none of the Chicago Eight played Major League baseball again, though a few may have surreptitiously played in other leagues, and Shoeless Joe retired to South Carolina, where he ran a liquor store and a pool hall.

Shoeless Joe died at 64 of a heart attack or, "coronary thrombosis caused by arteriosclerosis and cirrhosis of the liver," and he was buried at Woodlawn Memorial Park in Greenville, South Carolina.

GRAVE DIRECTIONS: Enter the cemetery at 1935 Wade Hampton Boulevard, turn at the first right, then bear left at the "Y." Stop 30 feet before the next intersection and look along the left-hand curb for the Landers plot in Section V. Shoeless Joe's grave is nine rows behind Landers, a flat marker punctuated with spare baseballs and shoes left by previous visitors.

JACK JOHNSON
MARCH 31, 1878 – JUNE 10, 1946

IN SOME AREAS of America during her history, impromptu bare-knuckled boxing contests between black fighters were an underground cultural staple held for the gambling entertainment of cajoling white spectators. In Texas during the late 1800s, the preeminent champion of these so-called "battle royales" was a powerful combatant named Jack Johnson.

Jack moved on to broader venues in 1897, fighting professionally in the heavyweight class where five years later he won California's Negro heavyweight championship. The title was a bit of a contrivance since blacks were not permitted to fight against whites in championship bouts, the main reason being the social ramifications in the event that a black man won. Excellence of a black over a white in a prestigious contest could not be chanced; decades after the Civil War, Jim Crow segregation was alive and well.

But a monkey wrench was tossed into this farcical situation in 1908 when Jack traveled to Australia and knocked out World Heavyweight Champion Tommy Burns—a white man. Johnson was crowned the new champion and the psyches of bigots from coast to coast were staggered. Keen on righting what was widely considered a horrific travesty of sport, a frenzied series of matches for a "Great White Hope" to dethrone Jack were undertaken, and he was forced to defend his crown seven times during the next 16 months. Finally, the mockery prompted former undefeated heavyweight champion James Jeffries from retirement as he announced, "I am going into this fight for the sole purpose of proving that a white man is better than a Negro."

In downtown Reno on July 4, 1910, the match billed as "The Fight of the Century" took place in front of 22,000 people. While the ringside band played a special composition titled "All Coons Look Alike to Me," Jack and Jeffries took their respective corners and began a slugfest that ended with Jeffries quitting during the 15th round. The outcome of the fight incited race riots across the country. Humiliated whites were in no mood for celebratory blacks during what was "supposed" to be their weekend of comeuppance, never mind that the whole affair occurred, not coincidentally, on the nation's most celebrated holiday.

Five years later, Jack Johnson lost his title to Jess Willard, suffering a knockout in the 26th round of a scheduled 45-round fight. Those were the golden days of boxing, indeed!

Jack spent his retirement enjoying the prestige of a celebrity athlete though there were limitations; after marrying a white woman in 1912, he and his bride fled to Canada and then France for a period after learning Jack was the target of a retaliatory lynching. In 1920, he surrendered to U.S. marshals and spent a year in Leavenworth on trumped-up charges related to violation of the Mann Act, though he was posthumously pardoned in 2018. At 68, he died in a North Carolina car crash, reportedly after angrily racing away from a diner that refused to serve him.

Jack is buried at Graceland Cemetery in Chicago, Illinois.

GRAVE DIRECTIONS: At 4001 North Clark Street, enter the cemetery and follow Main Avenue to Greenwood Avenue. Turn left and the Johnson family plot is a short distance on the left.

BOBBY JONES

MARCH 17, 1902 – DECEMBER 18, 1971

BOBBY JONES, ARGUABLY the most talented golfer of all time, accomplished in 1930 what no one had ever done before—and no one has done since. He achieved a grand slam, that is, victories in the United States and British Opens and in the United States and British Amateur championships within a single season.

Then, at only 28 years old and at the pinnacle of his career, Bobby turned his back on the game. Promptly and decisively retiring from tournament golf, he established a successful career in law and made contributions to the game in other ways; he co-founded the Augusta National Golf Club and the Masters tournament.

A nation that idolized him for his athletic successes found a new respect for him and for his decision to treat golf as a game rather than a way of life. As for Bobby himself, he seemed never to regret his retirement decision. "Golf is like eating peanuts," he once said. "You don't want to have too much."

At only 47 years old, Bobby was diagnosed with syringomyelia, a progressive and incurable paralysis that caused him to use a cane, leg braces, and, finally, a wheelchair.

He died at 69 and is buried at Oakland Cemetery in Atlanta, Georgia.

GRAVE DIRECTIONS: At 248 Oakland Avenue SE, enter the cemetery and turn onto the first paved drive on the right. Go to the end of this drive and stop. On the left is a brick walk. One hundred feet down this walk, on the right against the brick wall, is Bobby's grave.

TOM LANDRY

SEPTEMBER 11, 1924 – FEBRUARY 12, 2000

TOM LANDRY FLEW 30 combat missions and survived a crash landing as a bomber pilot in World War II. After the war, as professional football lurched forward, he became a star running back for New York teams in the old-school, black-and-blue version of the game. By 1956 he had moved away from playing and was the Giants defensive coach. Three years later, when Tom was offered the position of head coach for the new Dallas Cowboys expansion team back in his home state of Texas, he jumped on it.

The new outfit was awash in chaos and in that first year they were thoroughly trounced. But for one tie, they lost every single game. Dallas was the laughingstock of the league and it was seven long seasons before Tom fielded a winning team. But once he finally had one, he went ahead and had another and another, racking up 20 straight winning seasons. While the dogged pattern of 270 victories took shape, the Dallas Cowboys became "America's Team," steamrolling over opponents with a startling array of playbook gadgetry, and showcasing a parade of football personalities, including the eye-popping Cowboy cheerleaders, who gyrated incongruously behind Tom, the proper Christian coach who stoically paced the sidelines in his trademark business suit and fedora.

Over 29 seasons with the Cowboys, Tom made his mark through stunning innovations, seemingly completely out of sync with his personality, which unleashed an unpredictable but controlled havoc on the field. Ushering in the efficient modern era of pro football, Tom uncorked a mathematical approach to the game by charting opposing offensive patterns, and he was the first to overhaul defensive schemes on the fly with signals from the sideline.

In the mid-'80s, as his innovations were adopted league-wide, his aura of invincibility suffered and whispers suggested that perhaps the Cowboys no longer needed Tom. Indeed, he had preached that there were three important things in life: God, family, and football, and, as it seemed football had become an increasingly distant third on his list, it became obvious that Tom no longer needed the Cowboys either. In 1989, he was sacked as head coach and settled into a citizen emeritus role in Texas, appearing on the nostalgia circuit at charity dinners and golf tournaments.

At 75, Tom died of leukemia and was buried at Sparkman Hillcrest Memorial Park in Dallas, Texas.

GRAVE DIRECTIONS: At 7405 West Northwest Highway, enter the cemetery, bear right around the funeral home, then bear left at the next opportunity. After a short distance, you'll see a sign on the right for the Garden of the Cross section. Stop here. On the left, across from that sign, is a marker for the Crespis, behind which is the Landry plot.

VINCE LOMBARDI
JUNE 11, 1913 – SEPTEMBER 3, 1970

IN 1949 VINCE Lombardi left his $1,700-a-year high school teaching position to manage the defensive line of West Point's football team. Five years later Vince was in charge of offensive strategy for the New York Giants, channeling the talents of Frank Gifford from defense to offense and earning for himself a reputation as a steely-eyed visionary.

But by 1958, the 45-year-old Vince was tired of being an assistant and he jumped on an opportunity to prove himself, becoming head coach of football's perpetual losers, the sorriest team in the league, the Green Bay Packers. In 1959 he held the first of his notoriously intense training camps and made clear to his protégés that he expected obedience, dedication, and 110 percent effort from each man. "Dancing is a contact sport, football is a hitting sport," he told his Packers. "If you aren't fired with enthusiasm, you'll *be* fired with enthusiasm," he threatened. But Coach Lombardi also made his team a promise: If they obeyed his disciplines and observed his doctrines, they would be a championship team.

Three years later, the fiery coach's promise became a reality. At Lambeau Field in Green Bay on December 31, 1961, Vince watched proudly as his new Green Bay Packers defeated his old New York Giants 37-0 for the National Football League championship. When Vince retired as head coach in 1967, the Packers had put together nine phenomenal winning seasons and had dominated professional football, collecting five NFL championships and two Super Bowls (I and II), and acquiring a record of 98-30-4. The Packers had become the yardstick by which all other teams were measured.

Pacing the sidelines in his trademark wristwatch and button-down, short-sleeved white shirt, Vince had helped the men he coached live up to their innate abilities. He had commanded respect from his players: "When he says 'Sit down,' I don't even bother to look for a chair," one of them explained. Their efforts brought pride and victory. With the heavy-handed discipline of an all-knowing drill sergeant, he inspired complete trust. "Vince is fair. He treats us all the same—like dogs," said another player. Vince's legacy of perseverance had made his name synonymous with winning, and had turned him into an American icon that transcended his sport.

After retiring from the Packers, Vince soon realized that he still wanted to coach and accepted the head coaching position for the Washington Redskins in 1969. During that season, Vince upheld the Lombardi tradition and led the Redskins to their first winning record in 14 years.

But Vince would never lead another team to the Super Bowl. After one season with the Redskins he was diagnosed with intestinal cancer, and he died from the affliction at 57.

Vince was buried at Mount Olivet Cemetery in Red Bank, New Jersey.

GRAVE DIRECTIONS: Enter the cemetery across from 140 Chapel Hill Road, stay straight for a bit, then bear right and take the next left. Proceed for the length of a football field, and then, on the left in Section 30 next to the road, is the Lombardi plot.

JOE LOUIS
MAY 13, 1914 – APRIL 12, 1981

IN THE OPINION of many, Joe Louis, the plain, unobtrusive legendary Brown Bomber, was the best heavyweight fighter of all time. He held the world championship title for 12 years, defending it an amazing 25 times, including during a period of time beginning in December 1940 known as the "Bum of the Month" campaign, when he met challengers at the rate of one per month.

Many years after his career was over, Joe found himself in the public eye again when the IRS dogged him for more than a million dollars past due, which they eventually forgave as Joe was penniless and his earning days over. Despite all his money woes, Joe never considered himself broke. As his wife, Martha, described, "Joe is rich with friends. If he said he needed a dollar, a million people would send him a dollar and he'd be a millionaire."

At 66, just hours after attending a heavyweight championship fight at Caesar's Palace, Joe died of cardiac arrest and was buried at Arlington National Cemetery in Arlington, Virginia.

GRAVE DIRECTIONS: Park in one of the lots off of Memorial Avenue, get a map at the information booth, then walk to Roosevelt Drive, which is in front of the Memorial Amphitheater. Standing on Roosevelt looking at the Tomb of the Unknown Soldier, there is a walkway on the far right that winds up the hill. Joe's grave is along this walkway in Section 7A, Stone #177.

ROCKY MARCIANO
SEPTEMBER 1, 1923 – AUGUST 31, 1969

ROCKY MARCIANO WAS *the* world heavyweight boxing champion of the 1950s, and the crowning achievement in his brutal ring career is one that nobody else has yet matched: Rocky retired with a record of 49-0, the only world boxing champion to complete his professional career undefeated. To top it off, 43 of those wins were by knockout.

Rocky's boyhood was the typical sports-loving one and his professional athletic career actually started when he reported to the Chicago Cubs as a catcher. Released because of erratic throws to second base, Rocky then joined the Army where he discovered his real talents were in boxing.

He turned pro in 1947, and after strong victories over the heavy hitters of the day, Rocky earned the right to fight the heavyweight champion, Jersey Joe Walcott, in 1952. Marciano won by a knockout in the 13th round and over the next four years defended his title numerous times before retiring in 1956.

"No man can say what he will do in the future, but barring poverty, the ring has seen the last of me. I am comfortably fixed and I am not afraid of the future," Rocky said at his retirement. Indeed, he changed his focus, becoming very active in a wide range of charitable causes.

En route to a birthday party, Rocky and two others were killed when their Cessna Skyhawk airplane crashed into a wooded area as it approached the Newton Municipal Airport in Newton, Iowa.

At 45, Rocky was laid to rest at Forest Lawn Memorial Gardens in Fort Lauderdale, Florida.

GRAVE DIRECTIONS: Enter the cemetery at 499 NW 27th Avenue and park at the semicircular drive in front of the mausoleum. Enter the mausoleum, walk past the first reflecting pool, and continue to the second jaggedly shaped reflecting pool. Immediately before this pool, turn right and the Marciano crypt is on the right in the bottom row, the jagged pool pointing almost directly to it.

NEW YORK YANKEES

IN PROFESSIONAL SPORTS, the generational staying power of the New York Yankees and the team's ability to somehow emerge consistently and, for some people, frustratingly, victorious is unmatched. Since 1903, when the franchise was purchased for $18,000 and moved from Baltimore, its roster of over 1,200 players has produced 27 World Series championships and 41 Pennants, and the team that baseball fans alternately adore and despise has boasted many of the game's most memorable and remarkable players.

LOU GEHRIG
JUNE 19, 1903 – JUNE 2, 1941

IN 1925, A husky and young Lou Gehrig faced another day as backup first baseman on the New York Yankee bench. It was frustrating not starting because, in his entire life of baseball, playing from pockmarked New York City outfields to the fastidiously raked infield of Columbia University, he'd always been his teams' ace-in-the-hole. Lou yearned now to be back in the minors; at least he'd be playing.

A few weeks later, the team's starting first baseman was hit hard during batting practice and Lou was tapped to join the starting lineup. Trotting onto the field, the nervous but eager rookie promised himself he'd not blunder the opportunity, and he didn't; by game's end Lou had played rock-solid defense while posting three hits and an RBI.

On the strength of that performance, Lou earned the nod to start the next game, and the next, and the ... well, let's just say that, over the next 14 years, for 2,130 consecutive games Lou Gehrig was the *only* Yankee to play first base.

He was part of the notorious Yankees' "Murderers' Row" lineup of powerhouse hitters, he was first in the league to hit four home runs in a single game, and he was a big part of five World Series triumphs. Yet Lou's unassuming demeanor and quiet home life never generated headlines, and he never experienced the adulation that defined his flashier teammates. Lou had become an authentic American working-class hero; it just so happened that his workplace was Yankee Stadium. Even to his wife, Eleanor, "Lou was just a square and honest guy."

But by 1938, it was clear that something was wrong with this Rock of Gibraltar; pitches that Lou should've homered became routine fly outs, and his sprints between bases deteriorated to slow-motion scrabbles. With the opening of the next season, it was clear that the off-season's pause had had little effect on his decline and, upon recognizing that his presence hindered the team more than it helped, Lou removed himself from the lineup and ended his celebrated consecutive-game streak.

Six weeks later, Lou was diagnosed with a degenerative and fatal condition of the nervous and muscular systems, amyotrophic lateral sclerosis, today known as Lou Gehrig's disease. On the Fourth of July, 1939, 60,000 fans turned out for a Lou Gehrig Appreciation Day and said goodbye to their "Iron Horse." After some prodding, Lou stepped to the microphone and in a simple but eloquent two-minute speech consigned himself to immortality: "Fans, for the past two weeks you have been reading about a bad break I got. Yet today I consider myself the luckiest man on the face of the earth . . ."

Lou died two years later at 37, and was buried at Kensico Cemetery in Valhalla, New York.

GRAVE DIRECTIONS: At 260 Lakeview Avenue, enter the cemetery at the Commerce Street entrance and bear right onto Powhattan Avenue and then Ossipee Avenue. Halfway around the sweeping right-hand bend in Section 93, behind the Winkhaus stone, is the Gehrig plot.

GEORGE "BABE" RUTH
FEBRUARY 6, 1895 – AUGUST 16, 1948

THERE EXIST A dwindling number of people who have personally seen George "Babe" Ruth play. His speedy trot around the bases in old newsreels seems to belong to some faraway, distant time, yet Babe continues to exert an influence on our culture as his memory epitomizes the image of a larger-than-life sports hero.

George was the first of eight children, though only he and a sister survived to maturity. The family lived above his father's saloon in a dirty and crowded Baltimore neighborhood, but after the mischievous seven-year-old became too much of a bother, his parents signed custody of him over to an order of missionaries and he was sent to live at St. Mary's Industrial School for Boys.

St. Mary's was a combined juvenile detention center and orphanage, though he really belonged in neither type of facility; his parents just happened to be a couple of irresponsible drunks. George remained there for more than a decade and under its rigid structure he thrived, especially in athletics. At 19, he was offered a contract by the Baltimore Orioles, but because his parents had passed him to the missionaries he was bound to remain in their custody until the age of 21. To circumvent that legality, the manager of the Orioles actually assumed George's legal guardianship and it was then, as the youngest player on the team and the manager's adopted "baby," that the Babe nickname surfaced. The moniker stuck for the rest of his life—and then some.

After just a few months, though, in July 1914, his contract was sold to the Boston Red Sox, where Babe developed into a feared southpaw pitcher. Six seasons later, the Sox set the fabled "Curse of the Bambino" in motion by trading Babe to their New York Yankee rivals. At the time of the trade, the Yankees commanded zero respect and had never won a pennant. They didn't even have their own ballpark and instead rented space at the New York Giants' Polo Grounds. But after acquiring Babe from Boston they won seven pennants and four World Championships in 13 seasons. Meanwhile the "Curse" relegated the Red Sox to an 84-year cycle of disappointment while the Yankees went on to become the most dominant franchise in all of sports.

Because of his demonstrated prowess on the mound, Babe's acquisition had cost the Yankees the then-fantastic sum of $100,000, but the Yankees management boldly chose to disregard his pitching skills and instead started Babe as an outfielder to exploit his diamond-in-the-rough batting ability. Babe hit 54 home runs during his first year with the Yankees and in short order he was baseball's preeminent player. Excitement heightened with every mighty swing of the Sultan of Swat's bat, a golden age for baseball was ushered in, and the game became the quintessential American spectator sport. Fans packed ballparks in record numbers and the once-lowly New York Yankees built a tremendous new stadium, Yankee Stadium, which became known as "the House that Ruth Built." On its opening day in 1923, Babe slapped Yankee Stadium's first-ever home run.

Contrasting with Babe's on-field heroics was an exceedingly hedonistic off-field life, and detractors saw him as a loudmouthed, overeating, headstrong lout. But on the other hand, Babe was generous and charitable, especially to needy children, his philanthropy fueled by a breakneck endorsement-contract pace that saw him shill everything from underwear to shaving cream to shotguns.

By 1933, Babe's once-great talents began to diminish and he threatened to leave the Yankees unless given the opportunity to become a manager. The Yankees called his bluff and Babe left the following year to join the Boston Braves, who baited him with the promise of an eventual assistant-manager position. It shortly became obvious that the Braves wanted him only for his drawing power and had no intention of making him a manager, so Babe resigned from the team and made his last appearance as a player in May of 1935.

Upon his retirement he held 54 Major League records including two that were regarded as unbreakable: 60 home runs in a single season and 714 career home runs. In 1961 and in 1974, though, Roger Maris and Hank Aaron, respectively, broke Babe's records.

In 1946 Babe began suffering severe headaches and finally checked into a hospital after the left side of his face became so swollen he couldn't swallow. Doctors removed a tumor in his throat but were unable to excise the source of the growth. After 18 painful months, Babe died of throat cancer at 53. For two days, his body lay in state at the main entrance to Yankee Stadium while thousands of people paid their last respects.

He was buried at Gate of Heaven Cemetery in Hawthorne, New York.

GRAVE DIRECTIONS: Enter the cemetery at 10 West Stevens Avenue, turn right, and follow the main road up the hill. Turn right immediately before Section 25 and Babe's gravesite is 50 yards on the left.

THURMAN MUNSON
JUNE 7, 1947 – AUGUST 2, 1979

AFTER 99 MINOR-LEAGUE games, Thurman Munson was called up to the Yankees, and as their starting catcher was named the 1970 Rookie of the Year. Despite a well-deserved reputation as a surly and irritable curmudgeon, Thurman was named Yankee team captain in 1976—its first since Lou Gehrig—and he was a key element of the Yankees 1977 and 1978 World Series championships.

But one sunny Thursday afternoon, Thurman lost his life at the Akron-Canton airfield after crashing his Cessna Citation airplane 1,000 feet short of the runway while practicing touch-and-go landings. Upon hitting the ground, his plane burst into flames and, though his two passengers managed to extricate themselves, Thurman was paralyzed from the impact and died of asphyxiation. He was 32.

Following his death, the Yankees retired his number 15 uniform and dedicated a plaque to his memory on Yankee stadium's center-field wall. To this day, as a tribute, Thurman's locker remains unused.

He was buried at Sunset Hills Burial Park in Canton, Ohio.

GRAVE DIRECTIONS: At 5001 Everhard Road NW, enter the cemetery at the last driveway, next to the office, and follow that drive to its end at a turnaround. On the left you'll see Thurman's grave marked with a grand memorial.

ROGER MARIS
SEPTEMBER 10, 1934 – DECEMBER 14, 1985

IN 1953, FRESH out of high school, Roger Maris signed with the Cleveland Indians farm team, and he finally made his Major League debut on opening day in 1957. Roger went 3-for-5 that day, and on the next, he hit his first big league home run, a grand slam that won the game. In 1960 he was traded to the Yankees and, with Mickey Mantle off the injured list, the stage was set for a season-long Yankees slugfest.

During the 1961 season, Roger and Mickey played out a drama for frenzied fans as they each swung for the heavens to claim the American League home run title. By mid-season it became obvious that they were both on pace to threaten Babe Ruth's "impossible to beat" record of 60 dingers in a season and their friendly competition took on a new intensity. Sports pages were filled with daily updates of the sluggers' duel and rabid fans argued over the possibility of either slugger breaking the record. (Babe had set his record when the season consisted of just 154 games, and the season had since then been expanded to 162 games.)

Mickey fell off the pace after suffering an injury in September but Roger pressed on and tied the home run record during the

159th game of the season. Finally, in the season's last game, Roger hit his 61st home run, breaking the Babe's 34-year-old record, establishing a new benchmark that would itself stand for the next 37 years.

Of course, not everyone was delighted with Roger's accomplishment. Many of baseball's old guard scoffed at his feat because Roger's record was established after 162 games. Roger felt the hostility and he later commented, "They acted as if I poisoned their record books or something. As a ballplayer, I would be delighted to do it again but as an individual, I doubt if I possibly could."

The Yankees capped that magical 1961 season with a world championship but the season also proved to be Roger's last great one. The next year he hit "only" 33 home runs and by 1966 he was traded away to the Cardinals. Two seasons later he retired to run a beer distributorship and, at 51, Roger died of lymphatic cancer. He was buried at Holy Cross Cemetery in Fargo, North Dakota.

Despite his accomplishments, Roger is not a member of baseball's Hall of Fame.

GRAVE DIRECTIONS: At 1502 North 32nd Avenue, turn into the cemetery at the driveway after the metal garage. Go down the hill and Roger's black diamond-shaped stone is on the left just before the road bends.

BILLY MARTIN
MAY 16, 1928 – DECEMBER 25, 1989

ALFRED MANUEL BILLY Martin was a rough street kid who found an outlet for his aggression in baseball. After a couple seasons in the minors, Billy became a steady Yankee second baseman and got used to winning; in his seven seasons there, the Yankees won five World Series. Though Billy played with a scrappy ferocity, he really distinguished himself off the field, and his notorious late-night carousing culminated at the infamous 1957 Copacabana melée, after which the Yankees, having had had enough of his drinking blowouts, traded him to Kansas City.

Billy bounced around among six teams in the next four seasons and retired from playing in 1961. Over the next dozen years he developed a reputation as a boy-wonder genius, a manager who could turn any team into a winner. In 1975, the despotic George Steinbrenner tapped Billy to pilot his ailing Yankee team.

Thus began an infamous Bronx psychodrama, the clash of outsized egos that pitted Billy the firecracker manager against the meddling owner Steinbrenner. Over the next 10 years, Billy gained and lost his job managing the "Bronx Zoo" on five separate occasions. Though Billy's departures from the helm were the result of everything from vicious fistfights with marshmallow vendors, and even his own pitchers, to televised shouting altercations with Steinbrenner, Billy was always rehired because he really was a heck of a manager, perfecting a swashbuckling brand of baseball that came to be known as Billyball. Under his on-again, off-again tenure, the Yankees won two pennants and a World Series.

In 1986, Billy's beloved number 1 jersey was retired by the Yankees, and when Billy addressed the audience he told them, "I may not have been the greatest Yankee to put on the uniform, but I was the proudest."

In an interview, he once said, "As a manager, I demand only one thing of a player, hustle. It doesn't take any ability to hustle." Hustling home as a passenger in a pickup truck on a snowy road, Billy was killed on Christmas Day 1989, in a single-car crash in upstate Fenton, New York.

At 61, Billy was buried near Babe Ruth at the Gate of Heaven Cemetery in Hawthorne, New York.

GRAVE DIRECTIONS: Enter the cemetery, turn right, and follow the main road up the hill. Turn right immediately after Section 25 and the Martin plot is 120 feet on the right.

MICKEY MANTLE
OCTOBER 20, 1931 – AUGUST 13, 1995

MICKEY MANTLE'S SEMI-PRO baseball player father believed that the only way to excel in the Major Leagues was as a switch-hitter, and from a young age he taught his son to swing from both sides of the plate. The coaching paid off and, while still in high school, Mickey signed with the Yankees for the bargain price of $140 a week.

After two years in the minors, he earned a place on the team's 1951 big-league roster and, by the next year, became the primary focus of the New York media—Mickey had been the player chosen to replace the irreplaceable Joe DiMaggio. Mickey quickly adjusted to the majors and developed into a premier power hitter; one home run shot, later measured at 565 feet, might be the longest ever hit. Led by Mickey's talents, the Yankees again dominated baseball, and during his tenure, they won 12 pennants and seven World Series.

Mickey himself was named MVP three times and in 1956 he won baseball's Triple Crown with a .353 batting average, 52 home runs, and 130 RBIs. Though he was frequently sidelined with a recurring injury, by the time of his 1969 retirement he had amassed 536 home runs, a record 18 in World Series play.

Mickey's athleticism was impressive, but he was a flawed and reckless role model whose family life was marred by his alcoholism and well-publicized late-night pursuits. In the 1980s, Mickey became a sort of sports antihero and disgruntled many old fans by exploiting his fame in the burgeoning and tacky world of sports memorabilia shows.

In 1994 Mickey finally sought treatment for his alcoholism at the Betty Ford clinic. The following year, though, he learned that his irreparably damaged cirrhotic liver was on the verge of collapse, and that unless he received a transplant liver, he would soon die. Sympathy poured in, but Mickey's endgame was touched by controversy when, just 48 hours after his name went on a waiting list, he was chosen to receive a donated liver. Cynics criticized the apparent preferential treatment—Mickey had jumped ahead of more than 250 other Texans in the liver waiting line—but doctors maintained that he had received a liver so quickly because he was the sickest one on the list.

In any event, the transplant hardly benefited Mickey and he died of complications just two months later, at 63. He was buried at Sparkman Hillcrest Memorial Park in Dallas, Texas.

GRAVE DIRECTIONS: Enter the cemetery at 7405 West Northwest Highway, continue straight, and go all the way to the cemetery's rear, where the mausoleum is located. Park in the back of the mausoleum, enter through the rear door, and ahead 40 feet on the right, in the bottom row, is Mickey's crypt.

JOE DIMAGGIO
NOVEMBER 25, 1914 – MARCH 8, 1999

AFTER BABE RUTH retired, the fabled Joe DiMaggio filled the Yankee lineup's void with grace and superlative play, and he was rewarded with the sweeping idolatry of sports fans everywhere during an American era when baseball reigned supreme. The son of an immigrant Italian fisherman, Joe learned baseball skills by hitting balls with a broken oar, beat the odds to rise to the summit of the sport, and was even married, briefly, to the most glamorous of movie stars, Marilyn Monroe.

Living the quintessential dream of the American boy, his allure reached far beyond the baseball diamond, and even those who cared not a lick for sports cherished Joe as a cultural icon. Though Joe's appeal depended largely on his exceptional on-field abilities, it was his off-field composure that clinched his universal intrigue; with impeccable dress and tailoring, he was always proud to be a great American sports hero and was committed to living up to the image by comporting himself with a self-assured style that was uniquely Joe DiMaggio.

It's important to note that most of Joe's years as an athlete were spent without the benefit of television. The successes of his life and career were widely reported in the print media and his games were broadcast on radio, but he retired before television became a common household fixture. Whereas television often demythologizes heroes through overexposure, radio and print served to make Joe famous but not *too* familiar, and heightened the DiMaggio mystique.

Joe played 13 record-filled seasons with the Yankees, including the storied 1941 season, during which he hit safely in a still-unbroken streak of 56 consecutive games. At 37, with his game tapering slightly from the wonder years, Joe chose to leave baseball when it became obvious that, though the fans still adored him, he was failing to live up to the lofty New York expectations. Always elegant and inspiring, Joe retired in 1951, though he was offered enormous financial incentives to stay another year. Said DiMaggio's brother Dom, "He quit because he wasn't Joe DiMaggio anymore."

On March 8, 1999, Joe died of a lung infection at 84 and was buried at Holy Cross Cemetery in Colma, California.

GRAVE DIRECTIONS: Enter the cemetery at 1500 Mission Road, drive up the hill, and go past the stop sign. Turn left at the next drive, go a little more than halfway around the circle, and stop before the Moynihan mausoleum on the right. There on the right under the trees is Joe's grave.

JIM "CATFISH" HUNTER
APRIL 8, 1946 – SEPTEMBER 9, 1999

JIM "CATFISH" HUNTER was a centerpiece of pitching staffs, first with the Oakland A's and then with the New York Yankees. In a 15-year career, he was the foundation of five World Series champion teams, including three straight in 1972–74 with the A's. He

strung together five straight 20-victory seasons, and retired with 224 wins, one of which was a perfect game. Not surprisingly, Catfish landed in the Hall of Fame.

Catfish came up to the majors in 1965 with the A's and he was given his colorful nickname by the A's owner after he told him, in his inimitable country drawl, that he enjoyed "huntin'" and "fishin'." Catfish went along with the moniker and later even grew distinctive whiskers, completing the "Catfish" look.

But in 1974, after winning a third straight World Series with Oakland, Catfish was ready to become a baseball trailblazer. When the A's were late in paying a particular annuity clause in his contract, Catfish argued that he was no longer bound to the team and, after arbitration, he was declared a free agent. George Steinbrenner stepped to the plate with a landmark $3.75 million, five-year contract, and Catfish became a Yankee. In today's baseball economics, the contract was a small-change deal, but in 1974 it made him the highest-paid player in baseball history, and set the stage for full-scale free agency.

After signing on with the Yankees, Catfish became the team's workhorse. By 1977 they won the World Series championship for the first time since 1962 and the following year they won again. By 1979, though, after recurring arm trouble, Catfish finished his baseball career with the Yankees at just 33 and returned to his hometown farm.

In September 1998 Catfish learned he had, of all things, a disease most commonly known by the name of a fellow Yankee Hall of Famer, whom it had killed almost 60 years before: Lou Gehrig's disease. The disease, for which a cure is unknown, attacks nerves in the spinal cord and brain that control muscle movement, causing progressive paralysis leading to death.

While battling the disease, Catfish reflected on his days as an ace pitcher. "I would trade all of that for good health," he said. "I'd be a groundskeeper and have nobody know me."

On September 9, 1999, Catfish died of the disease at 53 and was buried at Cedarwood Cemetery in Hertford, North Carolina, just a few hundred yards behind the high school he attended and where he learned to play the game.

GRAVE DIRECTIONS: At 100 Jimmy Hunter Drive, you won't miss Catfish's grave opposite the flagpole.

On the way back from the cemetery, it's worth a stop in Hertford's tiny center; Catfish was a native son and the town is damn proud of him. On the lawn of the courthouse is a monument dedicated to his memory and, across the street, the Hertford Café displays Catfish memorabilia.

GEORGE STEINBRENNER
JULY 4, 1930 – JULY 13, 2010

DURING HIS TUMULTUOUS 37-year reign as owner of the New York Yankees, George Steinbrenner won from both players and fans equal amounts of admiration and contempt for his impulsive personnel moves and win-at-all-costs mentality—and also won two suspensions from Major League Baseball.

Son of a Great Lakes shipping tycoon, he entered the family business and was soon president of the American Ship Building Company. But from his early years, Steinbrenner longed to own a professional sports team and in 1960 he bought the Cleveland Pipers of the short-lived American Basketball League. After they went belly-up, he moved to acquire his hometown Cleveland Indians but his bid in that move was dead-ended. In 1973, though, Steinbrenner got the last laugh when he and a group of investors bought the Yankees from CBS for $10 million. By the time of his death the franchise would be worth some $1.6 billion.

When Steinbrenner took the reins of the club they were wilting, having been without a pennant since 1964 and enduring sagging attendance while the upstart crosstown Mets thrived. "I won't be active in the day-to-day operations of the club at all," he declared, "I'll stick to building ships." But just a few months later, one of the minority owners of the investment syndicate remarked that "nothing is as limited as being a limited partner of George's."

An overbearing perfectionist and disciplinarian, Steinbrenner quickly became immersed in every decision concerning almost anything about the team, even though, by most accounts, he knew nothing about baseball. With an obsessive dedication to detail, he meddled in everything from the brand of grass seed used in the outfield to the shade of paint that covered the walls of box seat suites. Fastidious about his own grooming, he insisted that his players shun unruly hair and beards. When he thought the club's parking lot was too crowded, Steinbrenner stood out of sight and watched a guard who checked every driver's credentials. Personnel were sent spinning through his revolving door at a dizzying pace; during his tenure, he had switched managers 23 times. Meanwhile, George ran into trouble far beyond the ball field.

In 1974 he was implicated in a campaign finance scandal involving President Nixon and, after pleading guilty to obstruction of justice, he was handed a two-year suspension from baseball. In 1990 his reputation worsened when it was learned that he had paid for damaging information on slugger Dave Winfield, in the hopes of blackmailing the former Yankees star into dropping a lawsuit against the team. For this offense, Steinbrenner was banned from baseball for life, although he managed to gain reinstatement in 1993.

In his later years Steinbrenner mellowed and spent time at his Florida stud farm, which entered horses in the Kentucky Derby six times. Nostalgic, he cried in public on several occasions, including the time a group of West Point cadets cheered him at a Yankees home opener. "This is a very important thing that we hold," he said of the Yankees, his voice cracking. "This is the people's team."

With impeccable timing, he died of a heart attack at 80, six months after the federal estate tax expired, saving his wife and children about half a billion dollars. He is buried at Trinity Memorial Gardens in Trinity, Florida.

GRAVE DIRECTIONS: At 12609 Memorial Drive, turn onto Community Drive and then make a left into the cemetery, where you won't miss George's mausoleum on the right.

YOGI BERRA
MAY 12, 1925 – SEPTEMBER 22, 2015

THE "YOGI" MONIKER with which Lawrence Peter Berra was afflicted came about after his teenage friends saw a newsreel in which a Hindu yogi sat cross-legged. The posture struck them as exactly the way Berra sat on the ground, and from that day on, he was Yogi Berra.

The summer after eighth grade, Yogi decided he'd had enough schooling and he never went back, instead toiling in a shoe factory and spending a year in the minor leagues before finding himself on a Navy gunboat during the D-day invasion of Normandy. In a later Allied assault named Operation Dragoon, he caught a bullet and a Purple Heart.

In 1946 he became a New York Yankee, and though he homered in his first big league game, his early years were often a struggle. "My first two years, I was awful, just terrible," he confessed. But Yogi's sure hands and strong arm blossomed, and he's now regarded as one of the finest catchers—if not the finest—to have ever played. Indeed, just a cursory glance at his stats underscores the high regard: Boasting 1,430 RBIs and 358 HRs, the power hitter whiffed only 414 times in more than 7,500 at bats, and threw out almost half the men who tried to steal a base against him. Named to 15 All-Star teams, he also played in 75 World Series games, including one in 1956 in which he caught Don Larsen's perfect game—the only one in series history. According to Larsen, he threw every pitch Berra called for, never once disagreeing.

But for all his on-field heroics, it seems Yogi Berra the Hall of Famer was perhaps eclipsed by Yogi Berra the character. Short and squat, with an awkward running gait, he looked out of place among his more imposing teammates, and that he consistently triumphed on the diamond in spite of his underdog appearance was certainly a source of his popularity. But his ungainliness also begat a humility that, coupled with down-home Yogi joviality and mannerisms, yielded a triumphant and original American rube with qualities to which fans could aspire. Epitomizing what it meant to be a selfless sportsman and big-hearted citizen, Yogi became a fast favorite. People might hate the Yankees, but they loved Yogi.

The Yogi caricature was forged too by his knack for tangled tidbits of wisdom, Zen-like epigrams somehow both nonsensical and wise that ended up in the American vernacular. To wit: "When you come to a fork in the road, take it"; "You can observe a lot just by watching"; "If you don't know where you're going, you might wind up somewhere else." As the list of "Yogi-isms" underwent variations and grew over the years, he finally declared, "I really didn't say everything I said."

At home in his sleep, Yogi died at 90 and was buried at Gate of Heaven Cemetery in East Hanover, New Jersey.

GRAVE DIRECTIONS: From the entrance at 225 Ridgedale Avenue, drive to Section 49, which is all the way in the rear. Yogi's brown stone is along the hedge, left of the gazebo.

JESSE OWENS
SEPTEMBER 12, 1913 – MARCH 31, 1980

DURING THE 1936 Olympic Games, Jesse Owens achieved the finest one-day showing in track history by winning an unprecedented four gold medals. What made his accomplishments even more memorable was that they unfolded directly in front of Adolf Hitler, in his own Nazi Germany capital, where it was expected that the Games would be a forum for his supposed Aryan supremacy. Instead, a black athlete named Jesse ruined Hitler's day by affirming that it was again only individual excellence, rather than race or national origin, that distinguishes one from another.

Upon his return to the States from that tremendous performance, Jesse was showered with accolades. But in those days athletes were not offered lucrative endorsement contracts, and Jesse needed to support his young family. Taking a position as a playground director in Cleveland, Jesse took his first step toward a lifetime of working with underprivileged children, and for the remainder of his life, he was tirelessly and continuously involved in the promotion of youth guidance activities. In 1976, Jesse was recognized for his efforts with our nation's Medal of Freedom award, the highest civilian honor.

Eighty years ago, the detrimental effects of smoking weren't as well-known, and certainly not as well-publicized, as they are today. Many professional athletes smoked, and some even appeared in print ads advocating smoking because they had been led to believe that it helped open the lungs. Jesse was one of those misinformed athletes but, by the time the dangers of tobacco were widely publicized in the 1960s, it was too late for Jesse; he was hopelessly hooked on cigarettes.

Jesse died of lung cancer at 66 and was buried at Oak Woods Cemetery in Chicago, Illinois.

GRAVE DIRECTIONS: Enter the cemetery at 1035 East 67th Street, turn right, then bear left at the "Y" onto Memorial Drive. After the lake, turn right and Jesse's grave is on the right.

WALTER PAYTON
JULY 25, 1954 – NOVEMBER 1, 1999

IN THE YEARS between Ernie Banks' retirement and Michael Jordan's emergence, Walter Payton took up the slack as sports-hungry Chicago's most beloved athletic hero. When the Chicago Bears picked him in the first round of the 1975 NFL draft, they had failed to compile a winning record for eight seasons, but with an aggressive running back destined for the Hall of Fame in their ranks, the Bears' fortunes changed quickly. After Walter's rookie year he posted the first of what would be 10 consecutive 1,000-yard seasons, and by his third year in the league he won the first of two MVP awards.

By the time of his 1987 retirement, Walter had played in 184 consecutive games and held the all-time rushing record with an incredible 16,726 yards—almost 10 miles! But, of most importance to the city of Chicago, Walter led the once lowly

Bears to a Super Bowl championship and gained them the status of respected adversary.

The team retired his number 34 uniform upon Walter's own retirement and he was elected to the Pro Football Hall of Fame in 1993.

In February of 1999, in an emotional press conference, Walter announced he was suffering from primary sclerosing cholangitis (PSC), a rare liver condition with no known cure but, if a suitable donor could be found, his life could probably be saved. While Walter languished with all the other waiting-list hopefuls, his liver condition deteriorated into a cancer, transplant became impossible, and he died at 45.

Walter was cremated and his ashes remain with his family.

STEVE PREFONTAINE
JANUARY 25, 1951 – MAY 30, 1975

AT THE UNIVERSITY of Oregon, track specialist Steve Prefontaine won four consecutive NCAA titles in the 5,000-meter event and later held every national outdoor track distance record above 2,000 meters.

At the 1972 Olympics, he was a relatively young 21-year-old, but still managed a fourth-place finish in the 5,000. Always a crowd favorite for his talent as well as his exuberance—after a win Steve would often take not just one, but two or three victory laps while shaking his fists—he was well on his way to becoming perhaps the greatest American distance runner ever and it was generally expected that Steve would win gold in the 1976 Olympics.

But fate intervened and Steve's life was cut short. His is a story of what might have been. Less than five hours after running the second-fastest 5,000 meters in U.S. history, Steve died in a single-car crash in Eugene, Oregon. In his MG convertible, driving alone with a blood-alcohol level of 0.16, he lost control and the car flipped and pinned him underneath, where he suffocated.

Steve was only 24 when he was buried at Sunset Memorial Park in Coos Bay, Oregon.

GRAVE DIRECTIONS: Enter the cemetery at 63060 Millington Frontage Road. Just 75 feet up the hill from the cemetery office, next to a small Alberta Spruce tree, is the flat stone marking Steve's grave.

BOBBY RIGGS

FEBRUARY 25, 1918 — OCTOBER 25, 1995

BOBBY RIGGS, ONE of tennis' most resourceful and calculating players, was at his best in 1939, when he won nine tournaments and went 54-5 in matches. It was that year that he also swept all three titles at Wimbledon, the only time he played there. An inveterate gambler, he said, "I scraped up every dime I could find," to take a London bookmaker's 200-1 odds against him winning the singles, doubles, and mixed-doubles titles. At tournament's end, Bobby pocketed $108,000. In the next decade he also won three U.S. open titles, but his enduring legacy is surely his "Battle of the Sexes" matches.

In 1973 Bobby seized center court by emerging from retirement claiming that any decent male player could defeat even the best female players. He challenged Margaret Smith Court, then the world's top-ranked female, to a winner-take-all Battle of the Sexes match on national television; Margaret accepted the challenge but lost. After the match, Bobby declared, "I want Billie Jean King . . . I want the women's lib leader." These were the early years of the women's movement, and Billie Jean King was an outspoken advocate and top-ranked player; such a match would transcend the boundaries of sport.

Like Margaret, Billie Jean gamely accepted the challenge and the contest attracted the attention of a broad spectrum of people. In a hyperbolic swell of promotion before the September 1973 event, Bobby brought sexist posturing to the level of self-parody, practicing in a "male chauvinist pig" T-shirt and vowing to jump off a bridge if he lost.

The "Libber versus the Lobber" match was broadcast live from the Houston Astrodome and in the circus atmosphere Bobby made his grand entrance in a gold-wheeled Chinese rickshaw pulled by six beautiful models, while Billie Jean was carried in on a red velvet-covered Cleopatra-style litter, held aloft by men clad in mini-togas. But once play began, the 29-year-old Billie Jean was all business, and she methodically overpowered the bespectacled Bobby, the pre-match favorite despite his 55 years, trouncing him in consecutive sets.

Bobby was humiliated before an estimated 40 million television viewers while Billie Jean was awarded the $100,000 prize, proving that female athletes could indeed excel in pressure-filled situations. The match, and especially Bobby's hype, inadvertently fueled an interest in women's tennis and helped make it the major spectator and money sport that it is today. Neither Bobby nor Billie Jean held any hard feelings and the two became good friends.

Bobby continued in the limelight as an over-the-hill hustler-player, and as women's tennis gained popularity, he abandoned his chauvinistic stance. At a gala marking the match's 25th anniversary, Billie Jean said, "After the fact he really understood he made a difference. He'd be thrilled to be around for all these things this year. And I really want people to appreciate him for being one of the top ten players in history."

In 1988, long out of the spotlight, Bobby was diagnosed with prostate cancer. After battling the disease for six years, he made his condition public during the opening ceremony of the Bobby Riggs Tennis Museum Foundation. In the last year of his life, Bobby worked to educate the public about the disease.

At 77, Bobby died of the cancer. He was cremated and, per his wishes, his ashes were sprinkled over a few of his favorite tennis courts.

JACKIE ROBINSON
JANUARY 31, 1919 – OCTOBER 24, 1972

BRANCH RICKEY
DECEMBER 20, 1881 – DECEMBER 9, 1965

ON APRIL 15, 1947, Jackie Robinson, grandson of a slave, crossed the white chalk line at Ebbets Field to play first base for the Brooklyn Dodgers and broke Major League Baseball's rigidly enforced color barrier. It's true that if not he, then some other black player would have integrated the national pastime eventually, but it was Jackie who did it, and because he did it so incredibly well, he became a near-mythic figure.

After a four-sport college career at UCLA and a stint as the top player in the Negro League, Jackie was asked by Branch Rickey, general manager of the Dodgers, to play for one of their farm teams. At first Jackie was disbelieving, not even interested, but Branch persisted and Jackie signed on. Many owners, sportswriters, and fans were against the integration, claiming that it would destroy the game, but Branch ignored his detractors and added Jackie to the team's roster. The Brooklyn Dodgers instantly became the favorite team of African Americans nationwide.

It's now been more than 70 springs since that day when Jackie first walked onto Ebbets Field and today it's difficult to appreciate the full weight of the event; it would be eight years before Rosa Parks would refuse to move to the back of a Montgomery bus and no one had ever yet heard of Martin Luther King Jr.

While black fans huddled around radios and crowded together in the bleachers to delight in Jackie's achievement, Jackie himself suffered lonely indignities; pitchers took pleasure in picking him off, base runners tried to spike him, fans mocked him, and he was subjected to a steady stream of racial insults and hate mail. But Jackie let his playing do the talking. He was named Rookie of the Year and just two seasons later won the Most Valuable Player award. Renowned for his daring steals of home, Jackie came to be one of the sport's most exciting players, and baseball fans both black and white filled ballparks to see him in action. The Dodgers set new attendance records, he led them to the World Series six times, and by 1950 he was the highest-paid player on the team.

He retired in 1957 and during his induction into the Baseball Hall of Fame five years later, Jackie asked Branch Rickey to stand with him onstage as he accepted the honor; time hadn't eroded his appreciation for the opportunity that Branch had afforded him and all others of his race.

For all of his strength and athletic prowess, Jackie's health deteriorated at a relatively young age and, nine days after throwing out the ball to open the second game of the 1972 World Series, he succumbed to complications from diabetes at 53.

Jackie was buried at Cypress Hills Cemetery in Brooklyn, New York. His epitaph reads: *A life is not important except in the impact it has on other lives.*

GRAVE DIRECTIONS: Enter the cemetery at 833 Jamaica Avenue, turn right, and drive past the office. After the road's left-hand bend, turn at the first right, then take the next left. Drive up the hill to Memorial Abbey and Jackie is buried across the drive from the abbey, next to the Sluter tomb.

Four years after bringing Jackie into the majors, Branch Rickey quit the Dodgers' front office and became general manager of the Pittsburgh Pirates. Concerned about players getting struck in the head by errant pitches, Branch presented the idea of a batting helmet to tinkerer Ralph Davia. In 1953 the Pirates' batters were obligated to don the new protective headgear and within three years batting helmets were a league-wide requirement. To meet demand, Branch formed the American Baseball Cap Company and today, ABC thrives as a leading manufacturer for a variety of baseball equipment.

While addressing a meeting of businessmen, Branch suffered a heart attack at 83 and died a few days later.

He was buried at Rushtown Cemetery in Rushtown, Ohio.

GRAVE DIRECTIONS: At 4757 McDermott Pond Creek Road, enter at the second drive, approaching so that the cemetery is on the left. Branch's off-white stone is at the top of the hill in the first section on the left.

WILMA RUDOLPH
JUNE 23, 1940 – NOVEMBER 12, 1994

WITH THE CARDS stacked against her from birth, Wilma Rudolph was an unlikely Olympic hero. Besides being born with polio and wearing a steel leg brace until she was 11, she was also stricken with double pneumonia and scarlet fever.

At 14, though, after years of intensive therapy began to affect her legs positively, she began participating in track meets and, incredibly, only two years later, at just 16, Wilma Rudolph was named to the 1956 Olympic team. That year, she failed to qualify for the 200-meter event but did run on the bronze-winning relay team. Four years later, at the 1960 Games in Rome, Wilma shocked the world by becoming the first American woman to win three gold medals at a single Olympics.

After her Olympics career ended, Wilma graduated from Tennessee State University and held a succession of positions as teacher, coach, and community service leader. In 1977 her autobiography was published, and it later became a television movie. Her story has served as an inspiration to handicapped youths ever since.

At 54, Wilma died of brain cancer and was buried at Edgefield Baptist Church Cemetery in Clarksville, Tennessee.

GRAVE DIRECTIONS: Enter the cemetery between the brick pillars at 1400 Paradise Hill Road, and Wilma's grave is in the center loop of the drive.

SAM SNEAD

MAY 27, 1912 – MAY 23, 2002

SAM SNEAD WAS the son of a Virginian backwoods farmer and, though he caddied at the local resort to help his family, his dream was to become a football star. After a back injury put an end to his football dream, Sam chose to pursue golf, and by his early twenties he was a club pro. After working his way through local and regional tournaments, he pursued the tour full-time beginning in 1937 and at his second event, claimed his first professional victory.

In that rookie year, Sam went on to win four more events and, over the next 23 years, won at least one tournament every year on tour except one. His biggest season was in 1950, when he won 11 times. No one has won that many since. At age 52, he was the oldest player to win on the PGA Tour and he remained a threat well into his sixties. In 1979, at 67, Snead became the youngest player to shoot his age—and if that wasn't enough, he shot a 66 two days later. Though some players steeled themselves to win particularly prestigious events, Sam was never that fussy. "I don't give a damn what tournament it is," he said. "If you play it, you want to win it."

Despite 84 career victories on the American tour and another 80 worldwide, the U.S. Open always eluded him, though he was runner-up four times. But the Masters was a different story. It was his playground, and at Augusta Sam won three green jackets over a six-year stretch, finishing in the top five on six other occasions.

Beginning in 1983, Sam was the Masters Tournament honorary starter and he did it with style; wearing a straw hat and a cocky grin, he'd make a quick jaunt to the first tee and thunder a drive with his flawless swing, then retreat to the sidelines and tell golfing stories flavored with an inimitable brand of homespun humor and folksy wisdom. "The sun doesn't shine on the same dog's tail all the time" was a favorite Sam Snead maxim.

But in 2002, Sam had been ill before the Masters Tournament and, though lesser men might have politely bowed out of the engagement, Sam never considered passing on the tradition of hitting the first drive. Still, that Masters appearance was more ceremonial than any ever before; someone else teed up Sam's ball and his shot flew into the gallery, striking a fan in the face and breaking his glasses.

Six weeks later, Sam died at home at 89, passing away in his bed while holding hands with his son and daughter-in-law.

Sam was buried at his estate in Hot Springs, Virginia.

GRAVE DIRECTIONS: The Snead estate is on the west side of Route 220, about 13 miles north of the big paper mill in Covington. This estate, though, is very private property. The Snead family still lives there, you can't see Sam's grave from the road, and I don't recommend showing up without an invitation.

WILLIE STARGELL
MARCH 6, 1940 – APRIL 9, 2001

WILLIE STARGELL, KNOWN affectionately to Pittsburgh Pirates fans as "Pops," was a powerhouse hitter who crushed 475 soaring and majestic home run shots. Batting cleanup for most of his 21-season career, he rattled the confidence of pitchers by pinwheeling the bat in rhythm with their delivery and, once he connected, his sheer power was unmatched; Willie once held the record for the longest homer in nearly half of the National League parks and still remains the only person to have ever hit a ball out of Dodger Stadium. Later, as if to prove it was no fluke, he did it again.

Upon teammate Roberto Clemente's death in 1972, Willie stepped up to lead the team, and in 1979, he became the oldest player ever, at 39, to win the Most Valuable Player award. In 1988, he was elected into the Hall of Fame at Cooperstown in his first year of eligibility.

For the Pirates and their fans, opening day 2001 promised to be particularly memorable—the day would also mark the official opening of their brand-new PNC Park field, which had been built to replace the aged Three Rivers Stadium of Willie's glory days. But for all the pomp surrounding Pittsburgh's 2001 opening, the sunny April celebration turned out bittersweet. That morning, just hours before the first pitch was thrown, home run–king Willie died after a long battle with kidney disease. Fittingly, in a style of which Willie is assuredly proud, the very first hit at the new stadium was a home run.

At 61, he was interred at Oleander Memorial Gardens in Wilmington, North Carolina.

GRAVE DIRECTIONS: Enter the cemetery at 306 Bradley Drive, and immediately after the white, fenced bridge, turn left and drive up the hill to the mausoleum. At the mausoleum, Willie's crypt is on the right-hand wall, second row from the top.

JIM VALVANO
MARCH 10, 1946 – APRIL 28, 1993

THE PEOPLE AND fans of North Carolina were simply not prepared for what hit them, and their ears, when Jim Valvano took over as head coach of the North Carolina State Wolfpack basketball team in 1980. The fast-talking coach made himself into the state's most audible character, appearing almost incessantly on a statewide radio hookup, accepting speaking engagements, and cheerfully promoting soft drinks and fast food.

But whatever misgivings his ubiquitous activities may have engendered were generally swept away by what happened at the end of the 1983 season. Finishing the regular season in a tie for third place in the Atlantic Coast Conference, the team did not lose again. They won a bid to the NCAA tournament and upset higher-ranked teams to reach the final.

Their opponent in the final was top-ranked Houston, which had won 26 straight and, for all its postseason flair, Jim's Wolfpack wasn't given a chance. But in that final game, Jim demonstrated his mastery as a coach, slowing the tempo of the game to frustrate Houston's charging style. In the final minute, with the Wolfpack trailing by a slim margin, he ordered his team to commit fouls to capitalize on their opponents' weak free-throw skills. The Wolfpack erased the deficit and after a few wild seconds of bedlam basketball at game's end, won 54-52, claiming the national championship in outlandish, Cinderella style. In the ensuing triumphant pandemonium, Jim Valvano lent himself to sports-reel immortality and defined the emotion of victory, leaping off the bench with a whoop and running madly down the court looking for someone to hug.

After being forced from his job six years later by a recruiting and admissions scandal, Jim started a career as a commentator, but in 1992, he was diagnosed with a cancer, adenocarcinoma, and given a year to live. Jim spent the remainder of his life establishing his own V Foundation as a money-raiser for the fight against cancer, which to date has awarded research grants totaling more than $170 million.

At 47, Jim was buried at Oakwood Cemetery in Raleigh, North Carolina.

GRAVE DIRECTIONS: Enter the cemetery at 701 Oakwood Avenue, turn right, and go under the archway at the office. Then bear left twice, onto Elm and then Walnut Drive, proceed past the maintenance shed, and bear left onto Locust Drive. After 100 feet, Jim's stone is near the curb on the left.

TED WILLIAMS

AUGUST 30, 1918 – JULY 5, 2002

WHEN THE BOSTON Red Sox brought Ted Williams up to the majors in 1939, he didn't exactly look like a home run hitter. But young Ted, "the Kid," smacked .327 with 31 homers during that rookie season and, most impressively, he drove in a mind-boggling 145 RBIs as well. In a 19-season career, he batted .344 and swatted 521 home runs, but his numbers could have been even higher if not for his Marine Corps service in World War II and the Korean War.

Throughout much of Ted's career, New York Yankee Joe Di Maggio was his archrival and when the Kid hit his fabled .406 in 1941, his feat was overshadowed by DiMaggio's 56-game hitting streak. That summer rightly belonged to both players and, in the 70 years since, no one has come within 12 games of DiMaggio's streak or 12 points of Ted's average. But, although Ted's career was longer (19 seasons to 13) and more productive (521 homers to 361), DiMaggio seemed to get more publicity, probably because he was a regular World Series champion. Like all Red Sox players from 1919–2003, Ted never won a World Series ring.

Nonetheless, his statistics are undeniable, and they make a fair case that Ted achieved the goal he set for himself when he came up to the big leagues. He merely wanted, he said, people to look at him one day and say, "There goes the greatest hitter ever to play the game." But he had other qualities that made him a compelling figure and was an athlete who did not believe that the world owed him a living. Instead, he preferred a kind of isolation from the adulation of the crowd and the attentions of the media. His brother Danny had died of leukemia and, for over 50 years, Ted was willing to go anywhere and do anything that cancer funds asked him to do, as long as there were no cameras around to record him doing it. Single-minded and stubborn, he was stoic and solitary in an age when ballplayers were becoming whiners and exhibitionists.

Considered by many to be the greatest hitter in baseball history, Ted fittingly ended his 19-year career in 1960 by smacking a homer in his final at bat. John Updike wrote about that moment: "He didn't tip his cap. He hid in the dugout. Gods do not answer letters." Nor, apparently, do they harbor any nostalgia; a few years after retiring Ted told a reporter, "I'm so grateful for baseball, and so grateful I'm the hell out of it."

After a series of strokes and congestive heart failure over several years, Ted died of cardiac arrest at 83.

After his death, Ted's body was taken to the Alcor Life Extension Foundation's cryogenic facility in Scottsdale, Arizona, though his will stated that he wanted to be cremated and have his ashes scattered at sea off the Florida coast. The change of plans came about when it was revealed that in November 2000, Ted, his son John Henry, and his daughter Claudia entered into a pact to freeze themselves after their deaths, according to a note that was filed in court. The handwritten pact, signed by all three parties, read: "JHW, Claudia, and Dad all agree to be put in Bio-stasis after we die. This is what we want, to be able to be together in the future, even if it is only a chance."

For reasons that are unclear, Ted's oldest daughter, Bobby-Jo, was not included in the pact, and she challenged its veracity, arguing it invalid as it was made "in a tender moment before surgery" when Ted likely wasn't thinking straight. Nonetheless, an accord was eventually reached and, at this very moment, Ted is hanging upside-down at minus 325 degrees in one of Alcor's liquid nitrogen–filled cryogenic tanks where it's expected he'll be chilling for a very long time.

DENTON "CY" YOUNG
MARCH 29, 1867 – NOVEMBER 4, 1955

HIS NICKNAME ARISING from the shortened "Cyclone" moniker given him by a sportswriter, Denton "Cy" Young was an anatomical pitching marvel whose arm seemed never to tire. Over 22 seasons he started more than 800 games, finishing with more wins, more innings, and more complete games than any other hurler. One hundred years later, his records remain unchallenged.

Cy's Major League debut came in 1890 with Cleveland, where he stayed until 1898. After a two-year stint for St. Louis, he ended up in Boston and remained there until retirement. During that time, Cy pitched the first perfect game in American League history, threw three no-hitters, and was honored to throw the first-ever pitch in a World Series. Finishing his career with 511 wins, Cy retired to his native Ohio in 1911.

At home, seated in his favorite armchair, Cy suffered a fatal heart attack at the age of 88 and was buried at the Church Cemetery in Peoli, Ohio.

GRAVE DIRECTIONS: Fifty feet left of the twin cedar trees, Cy's stone is easy to find at this cemetery on the south side of Route 258.

Baseball didn't forget about Cy Young and in 1956, when an award program to recognize the outstanding pitcher of the Major Leagues was established, it was named the Cy Young Memorial Award. In 1967 the award was expanded to recognize two pitchers each year—one from each league—and today the award is the game's most-coveted pitching honor.

TELEVISION
& FILM
PERSONALITIES

ABBOTT & COSTELLO

LOU COSTELLO
MARCH 6, 1906 – MARCH 3, 1959

WILLIAM "BUD" ABBOTT
OCTOBER 2, 1895 – APRIL 24, 1974

THROUGH THEIR CLEVERLY crafted routines featuring an unlikely pair bantering back and forth in complete misunderstanding of each other, Bud Abbott and Lou Costello became one of the most successful comedy teams in Hollywood history. Abbott played the insulting, "I am not amused" straight man, while Costello was the boisterous "baaaaad boy" and buffoon—a short and round innocent who perpetually suffered his partner's berating and won the audiences' sympathies amid howls of laughter. The quick-tongued tandem found fame in vaudeville, radio, Broadway, television, and perhaps most famously, on the silver screen.

Their official teaming was in 1936, and the duo soon landed on radio's *The Kate Smith Hour*. It was on this program that their classic signature skit "Who's On First?" came to national attention, and Abbott & Costello rocketed to fame. By 1939 they'd signed a movie deal with Universal Pictures. Their first few films, including *Buck Privates*, were smash hits, but the team's most popular films were yet to come. In 1948, the duo developed a comedy-horror genre with the hilarious *Abbott & Costello Meet Frankenstein* film, which ushered in the *Abbott & Costello Meet...* era. Over the next eight years the pair made a series of beloved films in which they "met" the Invisible Man, the Mummy, and Dr. Jekyll and Mr. Hyde, among others.

When Bud and Lou dissolved their partnership in 1956, the tabloids went into overdrive speculating about bad blood between the two comedians. But the truth seems to be that theirs was a completely amicable parting; at 60, Bud had grown noticeably weary of the spotlight, while Lou welcomed a change of pace and had other aspirations as a talk-show host and as a dramatic actor.

But just over two years later, any such inclinations of Lou's were put on permanent hold when he suffered a heart attack. Lou was ordered to go on bed rest, and he obliged, but a few days later the funny guy suffered a more massive coronary and died at 52.

Lou rests at Calvary Cemetery in Los Angeles.

GRAVE DIRECTIONS: Enter the cemetery at 4201 Whittier Boulevard, then bear left and drive to the big mausoleum on the hill. Inside the mausoleum is a chapel with three short halls that extend to the right. Lou's crypt is in the top row of the middle hall, and is marked with his given name, Louis Francis Cristillo.

In 1961, Bud suffered a sort of epileptic fit while aboard an airplane, and in 1965 he had a mild stroke. Bud was never quite the same after those calamities, but he did survive for nearly a decade, and even provided the voice for his own character in the short-lived *Abbott & Costello Cartoon Show*. At 78, Bud died of cancer.

He was cremated and his ashes scattered in the Pacific Ocean.

ALL IN THE FAMILY

CARROLL O'CONNOR
AUGUST 2, 1924 – JUNE 21, 2001

JEAN STAPLETON
JANUARY 19, 1923 – MAY 31, 2013

IN 1971, AN adaptation of the British sitcom *Till Death Do Us Part* made its stateside debut as the *All in the Family* television sitcom. The show starred Carroll O'Connor as a middle-aged, bigoted, word-mangling dockworker named Archie Bunker, while Jean Stapleton portrayed Edith, his daffy yet wise, kindhearted, homemaking wife. Rounding out the regular cast was their outspoken feminist daughter, Gloria, and her overeducated, chronically unemployed, bleeding-heart husband, whom Archie called "Meathead." The show marked a sharp departure from the bland comedies viewers were accustomed to being force-fed, and at first audiences did not quite know what to make of its uncommon storylines and content. Ultimately, though, the show changed not only American television, but America itself.

In the post–civil rights era, the series became a forum for social commentary and unabashedly confronted subject matter that had formerly been taboo. Controversial topics of the day—racism and feminism, intolerance and draft dodging, affirmative action and integration—were addressed through the eyes of Archie Bunker, a befuddled but strong-willed, somehow likable blue-collar guy who was trying his best to get along in a world that was changing way too fast, as well as through the ears of Edith, whose unexpected bursts of truth regularly defused Archie's bluster.

The blockbuster show ran for nine seasons and in that time, anyone who was even peripherally involved with the program received piles of awards. When it was all over, both Edith's and Archie's prized living room chairs were installed in the Smithsonian Institution.

In 1979, Jean decided to bow out of the series and, though she did appear in a few episodes the following season, Edith was soon written out completely in a touching episode wherein viewers learned she had died of a stroke. Left to mourn her loss, Archie bought his favorite neighborhood bar and carried on for three more years in the less popular show *Archie Bunker's Place*.

Afterward, beginning in 1988 and continuing for seven seasons, Carroll starred as Chief Bill Gillespie on the well-received drama *In the Heat of the Night*, frequently alongside his only child, Hugh O'Connor, whom Carroll had adopted during the 1962 filming of *Cleopatra* in Italy. Hugh endured a long battle with drugs, though, and his addiction culminated in suicide at 32. He was cremated and his ashes interred at a private crypt in Rome.

After Hugh's death, Carroll became a teary advocate urging parents to help their children abstain from drugs. At 76, he died of a heart attack and was buried at Westwood Village Memorial Park in Los Angeles.

GRAVE DIRECTIONS: Enter behind the office complex at 10850 Wilshire Boulevard, turn left at the office, and on the right, the second grave past the chapel is Carroll's.

After *All in the Family*, Jean purposely sought out roles that would separate her from the character of Edith, and in so doing led a less celebrated performing life. Off Broadway, she played Julia Child in the mini-musical *Bon Appetit!*, while on television she sang with the Muppets and made several television movies, including *Eleanor, First Lady of the World*.

At 90, Jean died of natural causes and was cremated.

MILTON BERLE

JULY 2, 1908 – MARCH 27, 2002

AS MILTON BERLE'S father was never able to provide for his family very well—they lived in an assortment of crummy flats and brownstones in the Bronx and upper Manhattan—his mother was determined to make one of their progeny a star. She chose Milton, and after winning a tin cup at a Charlie Chaplin look-alike contest, Milton became the boy in the Buster Brown shoe ads. Aided by the tireless promotion of his mother, by 16 Milton was already a vaudeville veteran and had appeared in several silent films.

Through the 1930s and '40s, Milton was a popular master of ceremonies, performed nightclub comedy routines, was heard on a few radio programs, and appeared 553 times in the Ziegfeld Follies. The radio shows weren't particularly successful for Milton; his style was too visual: the raised eyebrow, a turned head and a wink, a tap of the ever-present Cuban cigar. But in 1948 he received an offer to do the radio show *Texaco Star Theater* and, though what Milton really wanted was to break into the new medium of television, he accepted the radio offer.

The show was a hit, and its success led Texaco to sponsor an hourlong television version that fall. While some of his radio competitors were reluctant to risk flopping on the tube, Milton jumped at the opportunity and was the first of the big-name comedians to get his feet wet in television.

The immensely popular *Texaco Star Theater* television show was basically vaudeville on video (vaudeo, if you will), and in 1954 it was renamed *The Milton Berle Show.* For eight years the manic energy of "Uncle Miltie" permeated the Tuesday night airwaves with wacky skits and zany tunes, flying acrobats and full-bosomed showgirls, and, of course, the no-holds-barred emcee Miltie, beaming with a Cheshire Cat grin, dressed in drag and getting pies in the face.

Milton's success spawned many imitators, the show's ratings eventually waned, and in 1956 it was canceled. Milton was all but washed-up as a major television personality, and for the remainder of his years was relegated to guest spots, limited comedy tours, and appearances on talk shows and award programs. With time on his hands, Milton also put his energies into the Friars Club, a high-profile, who's-who watering hole legendary for its honorary, good-natured "roasts." As Abbot of the Friars' Hollywood chapter, Milton presided over its jocular celebrity members for almost 30 years.

The position seemed to fit. "I think laughter is imperative and it's the important part of my life, making people laugh so they can forget their problems," Milton said. "A good laugh is better than anything."

After years of failing health, including colon cancer, Milton died in his living room at 93 while taking a nap. He was buried at Hillside Memorial Park in Culver City, California.

GRAVE DIRECTIONS: At 6001 West Centinela Avenue, drive straight into the park and loop almost all the way around the hill on which the big mausoleum is located. As you reapproach the park's entrance, on the left you'll see a mural of a rabbi officiating at a wedding. Uncle Miltie lies in a crypt immediately to the right of the mural, third row from the bottom.

MEL BLANC
MAY 30, 1908 – JULY 10, 1989

MEL BLANC ENTERED radio acting in 1933 and later gained fame as "the Man of 1,000 Voices," supplying the vocals for hundreds of popular and beloved animated cartoon characters, including Bugs Bunny, Woody Woodpecker, Daffy Duck, and Porky Pig. Though Mel was virtually never seen on the silver screen during the golden era of *Merrie Melodies* cartoons, the myriad permutations of his acrobatic vocal cords have remained instantly recognizable by children of all ages around the globe for more than 75 years. Among the many lines he repeatedly uttered were "Eh...what's up, Doc?" through the wiseacre hare, Bugs Bunny; "I tawt I taw a putty tat," from the tart-tongued canary Tweety; and, of course, the stutter-strewn meanderings of Porky, the wistful pig.

"You know, my wife talks to me a lot about retiring," he once told an interviewer. "I say to her, 'What the hell for?' I never want

to stop. When I kick off, well, I kick off." Or, as Porky said over those many years: "That's all, folks!"

Mel died at 81 of heart disease and is buried at Hollywood Forever in Los Angeles, California.

GRAVE DIRECTIONS: Enter the cemetery at 6000 Santa Monica Boulevard, stay straight, and then stop about 150 feet past the second drive on your left. There at the curb on your left is Mel's grave.

HUMPHREY BOGART
DECEMBER 25, 1899 – JANUARY 14, 1957

WHILE THE IMAGES of other cinematic luminaries of Hollywood's bygone golden era have faded, the legend of Humphrey Bogart still looms large. With a trademark lisp, dangling cigarette, and world-weary cynicism, Humphrey wove his "Bogie" persona into an untouchable archetype of the reluctant but romantic anti-hero possessing a touching vulnerability.

As Sam Spade in *The Maltese Falcon*, he became a bankable action star, but it was his role opposite Ingrid Bergman in *Casablanca* that made him into a full-fledged leading man. In 1944 he married the 20-year-old actress Lauren Bacall (it was his fourth marriage) and together they made such memorable features as *To Have and Have Not* and *Key Largo*. In 1951 Humphrey was showcased as an unkempt riverboat captain opposite Katharine Hepburn's strait-laced missionary role in the universally loved *African Queen*.

Humphrey made his final film in 1956, the gritty boxing drama *The Harder They Fall*, and shortly after its release he underwent surgery to remove a cancerous growth from his esophagus. A few months later in November, he went under the knife again to have some scar tissue in his throat removed, but Humphrey never quite recovered from that surgery. One afternoon, Lauren found him comatose in his wheelchair, and he died the next morning at 57.

Humphrey was cremated and his ashes interred at Forest Lawn Memorial Park in Glendale, California.

GRAVE DIRECTIONS: Enter the park at 1712 South Glendale Avenue, get a map from the information booth, and make your way up to the Gardens of Memory. Humphrey's ashes are in the Columbarium of Eternal Light, which is located within the Garden section just left of the statue of David. However, these gardens are locked and admittance "is restricted to those possessing a Golden Key of Memory, given to each owner at time of purchase." Still, sometimes you can get lucky and an owner will let you in.

If you're really determined to get into these gardens but don't want to hang around until a property owner with a key shows up, here's what you can do: Go to the park before it officially opens at eight o'clock and, though there may be placards in the driveway stating that it's closed, drive past them and proceed up to the Gardens of Memory like you own the place. This is the time of day when new guests are being interred and the maintenance staff is scurrying everywhere. The doors to the private sections are sometimes propped open by work crews or, if that's not the case, you'll at least have a good chance of persuading one of the maintenance people that you've forgotten your "Golden Key of Memory" and should be allowed entry.

SALVATORE "SONNY" BONO

FEBRUARY 16, 1935 – JANUARY 5, 1998

BEFORE HE WED Cherilyn Sarkisian in 1964, Sonny Bono bumbled along as a songwriter, penning such hits as "Needles and Pins." But in 1965, the upbeat songs he cranked out became unexpected hits when he and his wife performed them as Sonny and Cher, topping the charts with "I Got You Babe" and "The Beat Goes On."

In 1971, Sonny shed his Depression-era roots and became a born-again flower child when he and Cher landed their own

television show, *The Sonny and Cher Comedy Hour.* Donning suede-fringed vests and bell-bottoms, Sonny played the lovable goofball with a droopy mustache opposite his stunningly slender, sharp-tongued wife, Cher, who teased audiences in outrageous sequined outfits. Millions tuned in for their memorable onstage bickering and the show proved to be a hit. But in 1974, as Sonny and Cher's marriage faltered, the show ended.

While Cher went on to a successful music and acting career, unpretentious Sonny took another direction and morphed into Citizen Bono. He opened two restaurants and, after a disagreement with City Hall over some building plans, Sonny ran for and was elected mayor of Palm Springs. In 1992 Sonny ran for the U.S. Senate and bottomed out in the primaries, but redeemed himself in 1994 with election to the House of Representatives.

On a sunny Monday at Heavenly Ski Resort with his wife, Mary, and their two children, Sonny skied off alone while Mary tended to one of the kids who had fallen, and he was never seen alive again. Mary reported him missing and he was found that evening, dead of a head injury near the Orion ski trail. As Sonny was wont to do, he had veered from the groomed trail in order to ski the deep powder of a wooded area, and was killed when he lost control and struck a tree. Though he was in an unmaintained area of the ski mountain, the section was not considered closed or off-limits to skiers.

An autopsy concluded Sonny was not under the influence of alcohol or drugs. On average, 30 people die in ski accidents annually, and Sonny just happened to be one of them.

At 62, Sonny was buried at Desert Memorial Park Cemetery in Cathedral City, California.

GRAVE DIRECTIONS: Enter the cemetery at 31705 Da Vall Drive, turn right, and then follow the drive to the Fountain Court waterfall. Sonny's grave is right there in the grass, just 10 feet from the base of the flagpole.

MARLON BRANDO
APRIL 3, 1924 – JULY 1, 2004

IN THE 1950S, a handsome and hypnotic Marlon Brando ruled Hollywood. Amid both his peers and his public, the brooding and lusty star was considered to be among the world's best actors. Yet by the end of his life, Marlon, who on separate occasions had summited as the wild one, the Godfather, and the could-a-been contender, had devolved into a self-parody of obesity and bizarre behavior.

Raised in Nebraska by alcoholic parents, Marlon, after being expelled from a Minnesota military school in 1943, moved to New York and worked as a department store elevator boy. He debuted onstage after a brief stint in acting school, and three short years later made theatrical history with a brutish yet complex performance as Stanley Kowalski in Tennessee Williams' *A Streetcar Named Desire*, which he later recaptured on film.

Accolades poured in over the next decade for performances in *The Wild One*, *Julius Caesar*, and *On the Waterfront*, making Marlon *the* symbol for rebellion against stuffy American conformity of the era. But, by the 1960s, he didn't seem to stand for anything, appearing in one ludicrous bomb after another while gaining a reputation of being deliberately unreasonable, going as far as wearing earplugs to avoid hearing direction on the set. And Marlon didn't seem to care either. "I get excited about something, but it never lasts longer than seven minutes," he said. "Seven minutes exactly. That's my limit."

In 1972, though, Marlon experienced an unexpected renaissance for his role as Mafia boss Vito Corleone in *The Godfather*. His delivery of "make him an offer he can't refuse" joined other timeless catchphrases of his career, including "I coulda been a contenda" and his tortured cry of "Stella! Stella!" Marlon was nominated for a Best Actor Academy Award for his role as Corleone but refused to appear at the ceremonies and instead dispatched a former Miss American Vampire named Maria Cruz to read a Brando indictment of policies hostile toward Native Indians.

In 1979 came another high-water mark as Marlon nailed the role of Army Col. Walter E. Kurtz, a shaved-headed symbol of madness in *Apocalypse Now*. However, for the better part of 40 years, Brando viewed acting as a lark and, not surprisingly, his personal setbacks and erratic behavior comprised the majority of news about him.

In 1990 his oldest son, Christian, killed the lover of Marlon's daughter, Cheyenne. Christian was sentenced to 10 years in prison, and Cheyenne eventually committed suicide. In 1995 Brando sought Irish citizenship because Tahitian gangsters had supposedly put a contract on his life for his role in the financial destruction of a particular atoll he'd purchased. The public read about the bitter breakups of three marriages, his 13 children with at least six women, and the disintegration of his physique as he ballooned to more than 350 pounds. Odd behavior included kissing TV host Larry King on the lips during an interview before signing off with, "Goodbye, darling." Before it was even released, he ridiculed his movie *The Freshman* as the biggest turkey of all time. In his last years, Marlon lived as a recluse, his refrigerator reportedly padlocked so he wouldn't eat himself to death.

"I've had so much misery in my life, being famous and wealthy," he told an interviewer in 1990, and explained that he'd withdrawn under the stress of being constantly in the public eye. "But I am myself, and if I have to hit my head against a brick wall to remain true, I will do it."

At 80, Marlon's numerous health problems got the best of him. He was cremated and his ashes spread in Tahiti and Death Valley.

CHARLES BRONSON
NOVEMBER 3, 1921 – AUGUST 30, 2003

ONE OF 15 children born to destitute Lithuanian parents in a hard-scrabble Pennsylvania coal-mining town, Charles Buchinski was no stranger to abject poverty and hard times; at six years old he once attended school in a sister's hand-me-down dress, and by 15 he worked 14-hour days clawing coal from the mines for $1 a ton.

"Rescued" by World War II, he became a B-29 tail gunner based in Guam, and after the war he surfaced in California as an out-of-work would-be actor. Lining up day after day with other acting hopefuls at Paramount Studios' front Bronson Gate entrance, Charles got the bright idea of changing his ethnic family name to Bronson and, as the story goes, his career soon soared.

Credits for the craggy-faced actor include supporting roles in such blockbusters as *The Magnificent Seven*, *The Valachi Papers*, and *The Great Escape*, as well as accolades for a number of European films where he came to be known as Il Bruto, that is, The Ugly One. In the 1970s, his series of *Death Wish* films sealed his typecast tough-guy fate, and Charles came to symbolize vigilante justice for his role as an everyman who, prompted by the rape and murder of his wife, extracts violent revenge against the thugs and hooligans that haunt darkened city streets.

Bronson died of pneumonia at 81 and was buried at Brownsville Cemetery in West Windsor, Vermont.

GRAVE DIRECTIONS: At the cemetery located at the intersection of Route 44 and Brownsville-Hartland Road, Charles' big flat tablet with bookend plant pots and a wrought iron bench is easy to find at the top of the hill.

GEORGE BURNS & GRACIE ALLEN

GRACIE ALLEN
JULY 26, 1902 – AUGUST 27, 1964

GEORGE BURNS
JANUARY 20, 1896 – MARCH 9, 1996

GEORGE BURNS' EARLY showbiz attempts were not very successful. He played "lousy little theaters that played lousy little acts—and I was one of them," he said. Often the performances were so bad that he'd have to change the name of his act in order to be booked for a second engagement. "I was what you call a disappointment act," George later explained. "If an act got sick, I'd take their place."

But in 1923 George met a soft-spoken dancer, Gracie Allen, and, after a little coaxing, she agreed to team with him in a comedy act. They specialized in the humor of illogical logic; Gracie played the daffy but unflappable wife, while George was the unruffled but confused straight man whose simple questions elicited her nitwit answers. The combination was magical and for the next 35 years, including the 20-year run with their *Burns and Allen* radio show, the first-class comedy pair delighted audiences with their hilarious homespun routines. George himself described their act as "having more plot than a variety show but not as much as a wrestling match."

In ill health, Gracie retired in 1958 and she died of a heart attack in her sleep six years later, at 62. George was devastated upon the death of his "Googie," the love of his life, and he retreated from romance, never to remarry. He later allowed that he'd kept the light on at her side of the bed for three years and, for the remainder of his life, he visited her grave once a month. "I just talk to her and tell her what has happened. I don't know if Gracie can hear me, but it certainly does me a lot of good," he said.

Throughout the 1960s, George tried to revive his Burns and Allen act with Carol Channing and a few others, but the chemistry was never the same. George's career was finally revitalized when he costarred in *The Sunshine Boys*, winning an Academy Award in 1975. Soon, George was a fixture of television and film, and he adopted the role of raconteur, telling funny stories that he maintained were true but had been embellished over the years. Using his cigar for punctuation, George was a master of one-liners and sardonic wit: "Too bad all the people who know how to run the country are busy driving taxi cabs or cutting hair," he noted.

As George approached his 100th birthday, the media clamored around, asking the comic his secret to longevity. "Fall in love with what you do for a living," he said, taking a sip of a martini and a light puff of his cigar. "I don't care what it is. It works."

More than three decades after Gracie passed away, George curled up in their bed and died of natural causes at 100.

According to his butler Daniel Dhoore, he was buried in a dark blue suit with a light blue shirt and a red tie. Dhoore continued, "We put three cigars in his pocket, put on his toupee, put on his watch that Gracie gave him and his ring. And, in his pocket, his keys and his wallet with ten hundred-dollar bills, a five, and three ones, so wherever he went to play bridge he'd have enough money."

In a companion crypt, George and Gracie lie together at Forest Lawn Memorial Park in Glendale, California.

GRAVE DIRECTIONS: Enter the park at 1712 South Glendale Avenue, stop at the booth for a map of the cemetery's roads, then drive to the Freedom Mausoleum. Walk in the front entrance of the Freedom Mausoleum, proceed down the hall on the right, then turn left into the Sanctuary of Heritage. On the right at eye level is the companion crypt that George and his Googie share.

JOHN CANDY
OCTOBER 31, 1950 – MARCH 4, 1994

JOHN CANDY JOINED the famed Chicago-based Second City improvisational comedy troupe in 1977 at Dan Aykroyd's urging, and from there success was just around the corner. In 1980 he appeared beside Aykroyd and his hilarious partner in crime, John Belushi, in the soon-to-be-famous film *The Blues Brothers*. That role led to plenty of others and John became an audience favorite for playing genial losers and big-hearted chumps with a touchingly human and genuine sincerity in such films as *Stripes*, *Uncle Buck*, and *Planes, Trains, and Automobiles*. John worked tirelessly during the 1980s, which allowed him to go from, as he put it, "macaroni and cheese to macaroni and lobster."

His exceptional girth was key to the Canadian-born comic's success, and though John often reacted to unexpected references to his size with self-deprecating jokes, he struggled behind the laughs with a succession of diets. Attending the Pritikin Longevity Center, John exercised on treadmills and stationary bicycles, but was never able to control his weight—or his cigarette addiction, for that matter.

By 1994, when John traveled to Durango, Mexico, to shoot the movie *Wagons East*, he was tipping the scales at 375 pounds. Eager to finish shooting as scheduled, they sometimes filmed for 12 hours in the stifling heat. On one particular morning, John's bodyguard rang him up but the phone went unanswered. A short while later, the guard let himself into John's accommodations and found John, dressed in a black and red checkered nightshirt, expired in his bed of a massive heart attack.

At 43, John was interred at Holy Cross Cemetery in Culver City, California.

GRAVE DIRECTIONS: Enter the cemetery at 5835 Slauson Avenue, and drive to the mausoleum at the top of the hill. Walk through the front entrance and proceed down the hall on the right. On the right-hand side is Room 7, and in there John's crypt is on the right.

JOHN CAZALE
AUGUST 12, 1935 – MARCH 13, 1978

THE ACTOR JOHN Cazale is known most famously for his role as Fredo Corleone, the vulnerable and cheerless misfit who was passed over in favor of his younger brother, Michael (played by Al Pacino), in *The Godfather*. After the astounding success of that Francis Ford Coppola masterpiece, John's career found its legs. In 1974 he reprised his Fredo role in *The Godfather Part II* and co-starred alongside Gene Hackman in what would prove to be a lost classic, *The Conversation*.

In 1975 John and Pacino (who, interestingly, had been friends since their teen years) paired up for *Dog Day Afternoon*, a fact-based drama about two dysfunctional crooks that rob a bank to pay for the sex-change operation of Pacino's character's lover. After an emotional performance in which he said more with his face than he did with dialogue, John's acting status accelerated further and he was soon offered and accepted the role of "Stosh" in the provocative Vietnam War epic, *The Deerhunter*.

However, unbeknownst to the film production company, John had been diagnosed with terminal bone cancer just weeks before

filming began. When Universal Studios learned of his condition, they moved to nullify his contract but Meryl Streep, his costar in the movie and real-life fiancée, petitioned for his retention and the studio eventually relented; the shooting schedule was rearranged and John's scenes were shot first.

John did not live to see the release of the film, and thus never learned that every feature movie in which he starred has received an Academy Award nomination for Best Picture, a distinction that no other actor in the history of cinema shares.

At 42, John was buried at Holy Cross Cemetery in Malden, Massachusetts.

GRAVE DIRECTIONS: Enter the cemetery at 175 Broadway, turn right at the fifth paved drive, and immediately stop. The Cazale marker is the tallish soapstone-colored one along the road on your left.

CHARLIE CHAPLIN
APRIL 16, 1889 – DECEMBER 25, 1977

IN 1915, CHARLIE Chaplin was told to wear something funny to the set of his first film, *The Tramp*, so he showed up in a grab-bag costume consisting of pants belonging to Fatty Arbuckle, size-14 shoes worn on the wrong feet, a tight coat and derby, a prop cane, and a false, square mustache. Coupling all this ridiculousness with a splayed, shuffling walk, Charlie gave rise to his Little Tramp character, who in some 80 silent films elevated popular slapstick to an artistic realm. Chaplin's films were so revered that even as the silent era drew to a close in the late 1920s and "talkies" became the rage, his silent films remained among the top-grossing for another decade.

But moviegoers weren't the only ones to take an interest in Charlie. Proud to retain his British citizenship, he refused an offer of U.S. citizenship in 1924. That, coupled with his left-of-center political views in films like 1921's *The Idle Class*, brought him unwanted attention from paranoid federal officials who began compiling a file on the curious, baggy-pants actor. By the time Charlie had released *Modern Times*, a pointed commentary on the alienation of capitalism, and *The Great Dictator*, a satire of Hitler whose humor was lost on the sober and staid director of the FBI, J. Edgar Hoover, Charlie was a marked man and fingered by Hoover as a Hollywood "parlor Bolsheviki."

Accusing him of "un-American activities," the feds were unsuccessful in an attempt to revoke his residency so, instead, Hoover had Charlie's reentry visa invalidated when he left the States for a brief London trip in 1952. It seems that if Charlie had challenged their underhanded move he'd have certainly regained entry, but he instead turned bitterly around and moved to Switzerland.

Charlie got revenge, of sorts, with a satirical look at the House Committee on Un-American Activities in the 1957 film *The King in New York*, but he was still clearly broken by what he rightly perceived to be a snubbing by America. Charlie and America made brief and strained amends in 1972, when he returned to receive a special Academy Award for "the incalculable effect he has had in making motion pictures the art form of this century." In 1975, after many years of self-imposed exile from his native England, he was knighted Sir Charles Chaplin.

At 88, on Christmas Day 1977, Charlie died of "old age" at his estate in Switzerland and was buried overlooking Lake Geneva. But not for very long.

Kidnapping is a risky business, and it can be difficult to keep the struggling victim from escaping while the ransom payment is arranged. In March 1978 two enterprising would-be criminal geniuses circumvented that quandary by kidnapping a dead victim: Charlie Chaplin. A few weeks after his coffin, with him in it, was dug up and spirited away, Charlie's widow, Oona, received a ransom demand of $600,000 for its safe return. She refused to consider the ransom but, with police at her side, bargained with the grave robbers over a tapped telephone. Two men, a Pole and a Bulgarian, were captured and charged with, among other things, "disturbing the peace of the dead." The Pole, regarded as the brains of the operation, was jailed for four years while the Bulgarian was given a suspended sentence.

After being dug out of a cornfield 10 miles away, Charlie was reinterred in the small town cemetery of Corsier-Sur-Vevey, Switzerland, but, this time, in a concrete vault.

IRON EYES CODY
APRIL 3, 1904 – JANUARY 4, 1999

IN A PUBLIC service announcement that aired on the first-ever Earth Day in 1971, Iron Eyes Cody paddled his canoe up a polluted stream past a belching smokestack and walked to the edge of a busy highway strewn with trash. As the camera moved in for a closeup, a single tear rolled down his cheek as a narrator said, "People start pollution, and people can stop it."

That tear proved to be more eloquent than any words, and viewers were moved to dedicate themselves to preserving the beauty of the American landscape. The ad is still remembered by millions and was recently named one of the best commercials of all time. For Iron Eyes, "the crying Indian," the spot proved to be a career zenith and it alone lent him more notoriety than did his 60 years of acting work in almost a hundred Westerns.

But as Iron Eyes gained celebrity and his brethren swarmed to champion his Native American roots, a petty issue nagged: Iron Eyes, it turned out, wasn't an Indian after all.

Instead, his true heritage lay in Kaplan, Louisiana, where records at Holy Rosary Catholic Church confirm he was baptized Espera DeCorti, the second son of Italian immigrants who toiled as replacements for freed slaves. Around 1925, Espera—or Oscar, as everyone called him—and two brothers struck out for California. They changed their surname to Cody, and Oscar "turned 100 percent Indian," as his half sister May Abshire put it. "He had his mind all the time on the movies." Even as a youth, she recalled, Oscar would dress up as an Indian and lead neighborhood boys in outdoor games. "He always said he wanted to be an Indian. If he could find something that looked Indian, he'd put it on."

The Iron Eyes Indian guise became a comfortable escape from his unsettling past and proved to be a ticket to Hollywood fame besides. But his was not a short-lived masquerade, or one that was donned and doffed whenever expedient. As Iron Eyes Cody, he seldom left home without his beaded moccasins, buckskin jacket, and braided wig; he married an Indian woman, Bertha Parker, and adopted two Indian boys. He spoke of how his Cree Indian mother and Cherokee father raised him in Oklahoma and he generously pledged time and money to Native American causes.

For their part, the Native American community accepted the plain evidence that Iron Eyes was not an Indian, but they continued to honor him, pointing out that his charitable deeds trumped his non-Indian heritage. But Iron Eyes never made apologies. "You can't prove it," he said. "All I know is that I'm just another Indian."

After a series of strokes, he died at 94 and rests at Hollywood Forever in Hollywood, California.

GRAVE DIRECTIONS: There are a number of famous people residing at Hollywood Forever, and the cemetery encourages visitors. They sell a guidebook in the flower shop, and even just a simple map of the grounds will set you back a sawbuck. But you won't need those.

Enter the cemetery at 6000 Santa Monica Boulevard, turn right after the information booth, then make a left and stop in front of the Hollywood Forever Mausoleum (sometimes referred to as the Abbey of Psalms), which is the huge building on your right. Walk into the mausoleum and turn right into the Sanctuary of Memories hallway. Iron Eyes is three-fourths of the way down this hall, on the left-hand side in the third row from the floor, at number 3301.

BOB CRANE
JULY 13, 1928 – JUNE 29, 1978

FROM 1965 TO 1971 Bob Crane played Colonel Hogan on *Hogan's Heroes*, an improbably popular television comedy set in a Nazi prisoner-of-war camp. It featured a wily group of World War II prisoners who each week outsmarted their German captors, Colonel Klink and Sergeant Schultz.

Before *Hogan's Heroes*, Bob had been a drummer with the Connecticut Symphony Orchestra and a radio disc jockey, but after the show's cancelation he turned to dinner theater. His new travel schedule enabled him to pursue his desperate sexual compulsion on a more or less full-time basis, and Bob slept with hundreds of women, recording the encounters in still photography and then, once the technology was available, on videotape. That extravagantly promiscuous and meticulously documented sex life seems to have, at the least, been a contributing factor to his death, and his subsequent tabloid notoriety has eclipsed his rerun celebrity.

At 49, Bob was found savagely beaten to death in a Scottsdale, Arizona, apartment. Though his swinging video-technician friend, John Carpenter, was a prime suspect, the police were never able to assemble a solid case. In 1994, realizing that the passage of time was jeopardizing their already tenuous case, the authorities decided to proceed with the circumstantial evidence and Carpenter was charged with Bob's murder. But Carpenter was acquitted and Bob's murder remains unsolved.

Bob is buried at Westwood Memorial Park in Los Angeles.

GRAVE DIRECTIONS: Behind the office complex at 10850 Wilshire Boulevard, Bob's marker is in the cemetery's central lawn. Counting from the drive bordering the top of the lawn, it's in the fifth row, approximately in the middle.

JOAN CRAWFORD
MARCH 23, 1906 – MAY 10, 1977

JOAN CRAWFORD WAS a Broadway chorus-line dancer and progressed to Hollywood, where she found success in silent films. In 1928 she starred in *Our Dancing Daughters* as a flapper—that liberated, devil-may-care, flirtatious, high-society creature of the period—and the role catapulted her to major stardom.

She easily made the transition to "talkies" and the next two decades brought Joan a string of successes playing socialites and rags-to-riches shopgirls opposite many of the biggest male leads of the day. Her personal life mirrored her roles in some ways; Joan's love affairs and public breakups with the likes of Douglas Fairbanks Jr. and Clark Gable made gossip headlines. Perhaps her most brazen and scandalous tryst was with Franchot Tone, an involvement that found her in a love triangle with Bette Davis. Both women fancied themselves the sole object of Tone's affections, yet Joan emerged victorious and married him. Marked by two miscarriages and frequent beatings, the marriage lasted just four years, with Joan finally divorcing Tone after she caught him and a young starlet in a compromising position.

Through the '50s, Joan's career slowed and she was relegated to more menial roles, until 1962 when she starred with her arch-rival Bette Davis as a pair of nutty sisters, showbiz has-beens living in a decaying Hollywood mansion, in *Whatever Happened to Baby Jane?* The popular black comedy brought brief new life to each of their waning careers, afforded gossip journalists a field day, and reignited their old feud as well, prompting a remark from Davis that Joan had "slept with every male star at MGM except Lassie."

The last years of Joan's life were devoted to Christian Science and vodka, and she died of cancer at 71.

She is interred at Ferncliff Mausoleum in Hartsdale, New York.

GRAVE DIRECTIONS: Enter the cemetery at 280 Secor Road, bear left, and park toward the left-hand side of the main mausoleum. Enter the mausoleum through the front bronze doors and turn left, right, left, left, and right. Joan is in Alcove E on the right in the Steele crypt, which was her married name at the time of her death.

BETTE DAVIS
APRIL 5, 1908 – OCTOBER 6, 1989

IN SOME 90 films, most of them unmemorable, Bette Davis played an unusually wide range of characters with a brassy but controlled edge, from drunks to glamour queens to retiring old maids and lunatics. Filmgoers loved her portrayals of these fiercely independent characters that usually suffered nobly but, in her real life, she acquired an often-justified reputation as bellicose and impossible to work with. Bette herself once said, "I adore playing bitches . . . there's a little bit of bitch in every woman, and a little bit of bitch in every man."

Bette's acting debut came in 1929, and three years later Warner Bros. signed her to a long-term contract. In 1935 the studio began giving her decent parts, and that year's release of *Dangerous* established her, after 22 forgettable films, as a major actress. Bette won her first Academy Award and quipped that the statue's backside resembled her husband's, Oscar Nelson, which some say led to its nickname "Oscar."

By the end of the '30s, Bette was the industry's top-ranked female draw, but her popularity peaked in the early '40s and began to sag under the weight of weak pictures by the end of the decade. By the '50s her career was seriously faltering, but in 1962, after a pairing with her nemesis Joan Crawford in *Whatever Happened to Baby Jane?*, Bette found a new audience and worked steadily thereafter on the big screen, as well as in theater and on television.

A survivor of four unhappy marriages, a heavy drinker, and a five-pack-a-day chain-smoker, Bette suffered from numerous ailments in her later years and succumbed to cancer at 81 while in France.

In a large white crypt inscribed, *Bette Davis—She did it the hard way,* she rests at Forest Lawn Memorial Park in Hollywood Hills, California.

GRAVE DIRECTIONS: Enter the park at 6300 Forest Lawn Drive, stop at the booth, and after getting a park map, go to the Courts of Remembrance. In the grass on the front left is her resting place.

JAMES DEAN
FEBRUARY 8, 1931 – SEPTEMBER 30, 1955

THE HANDSOME AND brooding actor James Dean had one of the most spectacularly brief careers of any screen star. In just more than a year and in only three films, James created a sensation and became an instantly recognizable image with his blue jeans, dangling cigarette, and characteristic slouch, personifying the restless American spirit of 1950s youth. Immortalized through at least a dozen biographies and songs, fan clubs, and a postage stamp, he's deeply etched into American pop culture.

After growing up in Indiana's farm country, James relocated with his father and stepmother to California in 1949 and attended Santa Monica City College, majoring in pre-law. But the only class in which James shone was drama, and he left after two semesters to live precariously as a parking-lot attendant, chasing auditions wherever they were available. After a few television commercials and bit film roles, young James took the advice of an actor's workshop and in 1951 moved to New York in pursuit of a career. While earning a living as a busboy, he appeared in several television shows and landed parts in two Broadway plays.

The New York exposure paid off. In 1954, James won the role of troubled adolescent Cal Trask in the screen adaptation of John Steinbeck's *East of Eden*, which shortly led to the swaggering James being cast in a new but similar role as the angst-ridden Jim Stark in 1955's *Rebel Without a Cause*.

In March 1955 James celebrated the universal praise he was enjoying for his *East of Eden* role by purchasing his first Porsche, a 356 Super Speedster convertible. By June, he was an aspiring race-car driver, with three amateur road race events under his belt. When *Rebel* finished up that month, he met up in Texas with fellow cast members Elizabeth Taylor and Rock Hudson to shoot his third film, *Giant*. Again, James was directed to be charming but restless, this time as the tough, half-genius ranch hand, Jett Rink.

The day before filming was completed in September, James bought another Porsche, a silver 550 Spyder, and had the nickname he had earned on the set of *Giant*, "Little Bastard," hand painted on its back end. Now with a bit of free time on his hands, James anticipated racing his new car and, at the end of the month, he and his mechanic, Rolf Wutherich, jumped in the Porsche and headed from Los Angeles to a race in Salinas.

But they never got there. James delighted in his new vehicle and along the way, he intermittently goosed the high-performance car up to its speed comfort zone. At 3:30 p.m., his driving caught the attention of a patrol officer who pulled the star over for driving in excess of 80 mph and warned him to slow down. But 2½ hours later, when James was traveling west on Route 466 just before the city of Cholame, he was speeding again when a Ford Tudor driving in the opposite direction with Donald Turnupseed at the wheel made a left turn onto Route 41 in front of him. The impact was direct and the Porsche was demolished. Rolf suffered serious injury and Donald walked away with only superficial harm, but James was dead on arrival at Paso Robles Memorial Hospital.

Less than a month later, *Rebel Without a Cause* opened in New York City, and the James Dean legend was born.

At just 24, James was buried at Park Cemetery in Fairmount, Indiana.

GRAVE DIRECTIONS: Pull into the cemetery on North Main Street at the entrance after the culvert, bear right at the fork and take the next right. At the crest of the hill, James' grave is on the right.

WALT DISNEY
DECEMBER 5, 1901 – DECEMBER 15, 1966

FROM HIS FERTILE imagination and factory of drawing boards, Walt Disney, himself only a mediocre artist, turned animation into an art form and in Mickey Mouse and Donald Duck fashioned the most enduring stars ever to come out of Hollywood. His film company became *the* provider of family entertainment, and from the base that Walt built, Disney Studios has grown into one of the most successful film companies in the world.

Walt first scored big in 1928 when he and longtime associate Ub Iwerks developed Mickey Mouse. The first two Mickey shorts were silent and for the third, which featured sound, Walt himself provided Mickey's squeaky voice. With *The Three Little Pigs* he was the first to gamble on Technicolor's expensive new three-color system and, after testing animation's appeal in a full-length format with *Snow White and the Seven Dwarfs*, he quickly followed with *Pinocchio, Dumbo*, and *Bambi*. Every film required the creation of new, lovable, and unsophisticated cartoon characters and Walt created nearly all of them.

In the '50s, Walt diversified from animation and produced live-action films like *Treasure Island* and *Old Yeller*. Later, his visionary and wildly successful amusement parks perpetuated the Disney magic.

In November 1966, Walt's cancer-ridden left lung was removed but, within a month, at 65 he succumbed to the disease anyway. Walt rarely attended funerals and no announcement was made for his own, which was attended only by relatives. The secrecy initiated a rumor that Walt, instead of being buried, was encased in a deep-freeze cryogenic vault to await a cure for his lung cancer, at which time he'd be thawed and resume living. But such stories are pure fantasy. Walt was cremated and his ashes interred at ground temperature at Forest Lawn Memorial Park in Glendale, California.

GRAVE DIRECTIONS: Enter the park at 1712 South Glendale Avenue, stop at the booth for a map of the cemetery's roads, then drive to the Freedom Mausoleum. Walt's plot is in the garden just to the left of the Freedom Mausoleum's main entrance. His marker, you'll see, is quite cleverly positioned and visible only when you're standing on the mausoleum's front steps.

DIVINE
OCTOBER 19, 1945 – MARCH 6, 1988

HARRIS GLENN MILSTEAD, better known by his stage name and alter ego, Divine, was a drag queen and a high-profile character in the overwrought gay culture of the '60s and '70s. With Divine as the star and neighborhood pal John Waters directing, a series of films that crossed every taboo and charted an exceedingly bizarre course of self-expression bred a distinctly new genre that, even by underground standards, was intensely offbeat.

Dreamland Studios, the production company that Waters operated out of a basement, churned out about a dozen shorts and features that quickly enjoyed the status of cult classics. Perhaps their crowning achievement was 1972's *Pink Flamingos*, the premise of which is that Divine, as Babs Johnson, is in a competition of sorts to prove she is the dirtiest person alive. Film history is made in the final scene when Divine eats dog feces on camera—straight from the dog, without any edits.

By 1988 Divine and Waters had toned their work down a few notches and the mainstream release, *Hairspray*, won critical acclaim. Divine, however, failed to enjoy this breakthrough as he died in his room at the Regency Hotel in Los Angeles of an enlarged heart caused by obesity.

At 42, Divine was buried at Prospect Hill Cemetery in Towson, Maryland.

GRAVE DIRECTIONS: Pull into the cemetery at 701 York Road, follow the drive to the lower area, and stop when you see on your left an old set of stairs that lead back to the upper area. Opposite those stairs, in the lawn on the right and about 30 feet off the pavement, is Divine's grave.

PETER FALK
SEPTEMBER 16, 1927 – JUNE 23, 2011

ACTOR PETER FALK rose to fame in a rumpled raincoat as the polite and absentminded, dumb-as-a-fox, one-eyed detective who outwitted high-society murder suspects at their perfect-crime game for some 35 years on the television program *Columbo*.

The glass eye was the result of a cancerous tumor when he was just three years old, but despite the missing eye Peter was a standout on his high school baseball team. After bouncing around at a few colleges and serving a stint with the Merchant Marines after WWII, he went to work as an efficiency expert for the State of Connecticut, though on his first day of work he couldn't find his building so his boss had to retrieve him at the local post office. "Oh, I was some efficiency expert," he recalled.

It was in Hartford that he began acting, joining an amateur troupe called the Mark Twain Masqueraders, and in short time moved to New York to pursue the craft full-time. On Broadway he was cast as the bartender in a revival of *The Iceman Cometh,* and his first on-screen splash was as Abe Reles, a vicious mob hit man in the film *Murder, Inc.* for which he earned an Oscar nomination for best supporting actor.

In 1968, Bing Crosby turned down the role of Columbo in the television film *Prescription Murder,* and fate came knocking for Peter, who delivered a unique spin to the character. "I was attracted to the idea of playing a character that housed within him two opposing traits," he said. "On the one hand he was a regular Joe Six-Pack, the neighbor like everybody else. But at the same time, he's the greatest homicide detective in the world." Besides the lead character, the other appeal of the show was that its structure was unlike that of any previous mystery program. In traditional "whodunits," the audience works side by side, gathering clues in tandem with the sleuth, but the *Columbo* creators showed both criminal and crime in great detail during the opening scenes. It was then up to Columbo to stumble on the scene and figure out how it had happened—something viewers already knew. "What are you hanging around for?" Peter, addressing viewers, wrote in his memoir. "Well, just one thing—you want to know how he gets caught."

When filming began, Peter selected a battered Peugeot convertible from the studio motor pool. Rejecting the fashionable attire laid out by the costume shop, he chose instead a raincoat from his own wardrobe and matched the rest of his character's clothes to its shabbiness. He completed the character with a mass of quirks and peculiarities: the quizzical squint, the mild speech impediment that gave his dialogue a breathy quality, perpetually patting his pockets for a light for his signature stogie, and constantly referring to a variety of relatives who were identified in shorthand—a cousin who operated the Los Angeles Dodgers scoreboard, say, or an aunt whose homemade quilt was on display at the state house. Typically too he would string his suspects along, flattering them, apologizing profusely for continuing to trouble them with questions, appearing to have bought their alibis, and, just before making an exit, nailing them with a final, damning query that he unfailingly introduced with the innocent-sounding, "Just one more thing." It was the signal to viewers that the jig was up.

In 2008, Peter, suffering from Alzheimer's disease, was found disoriented and in his bathrobe on a Beverly Hills street. His daughter soon filed for conservatorship and a doctor testified that his condition had been worsening and the actor could no longer even remember *Columbo*. At 83, the disease claimed Peter and he was buried at Westwood Memorial Park in Los Angeles, California.

GRAVE DIRECTIONS: Behind the office complex at 10850 Wilshire Boulevard, enter the cemetery and turn left at the office. Proceed down this walkway just about to the end, where you'll find Peter's grave on the right.

FAMILY AFFAIR

TELEVISION SITCOMS SEEM to have an affinity for single-parent households and, if that's the recipe for comedy, then *Family Affair*, which lifted the one-parent theme to the next stratum, should have been hilarious.

The show's premise was that six-year-old twins Buffy and Jody (Anissa Jones and Johnny Whitaker), along with their 16-year-old sister, Cissy (Kathy Garver), were orphaned when their parents were killed in a car wreck. Their uncle Bill (Brian Keith), a wealthy and swinging bachelor, had a bombshell dropped on him when the children showed up on the doorstep of his luxurious Fifth Avenue pad needing a place to live. Although reluctant at first, the gruff-but-lovable Uncle Bill and his fastidious butler, Mr. French (Sebastian Cabot), acquiesced and the show's story-lines followed the new family's predictably sweet and tame crises.

After five seasons, when the "six-year-olds" looked as if they might be soon driving their own cars to the set, everybody involved with the program, especially the viewers, seemed to have had enough. The show was canceled in 1971.

ANISSA JONES
MARCH 11, 1958 – AUGUST 28, 1976

ANISSA JONES WAS 13 when *Family Affair* ended and, after unsuccessfully auditioning for the part of Regan MacNeil, the possessed head-spinner in *The Exorcist*, she promptly quit show business and enrolled in public high school. Her parents had divorced acrimoniously years earlier and they still wrangled over Anissa's custody. Eventually, she began rebelling against both of them through drugs and alcohol. Anissa moved in with a friend at 16 and, at 18, she finally was able to tap into a $75,000 trust fund that had been set up during her acting days. She spent some of the money on long-pending bills, but the remainder of it financed cars and apartments and, especially, partying supplies for herself and her friends. Sadly, within just a few months the money was gone and Anissa resorted to working at a doughnut shop. After a day of partying in Oceanside, California, Anissa died alone, only five months after turning 18. Her death from an overdose of drugs was ruled accidental, though the coroner stated that Anissa's was the most massive overdose he'd ever seen.

Anissa had no funeral but was cremated and her ashes scattered over the Pacific Ocean.

SEBASTIAN CABOT
JULY 6, 1918 – AUGUST 23, 1977

THE VERY ENGLISH Sebastian Cabot got his start as an actor in British stage and films in the late 1930s. Older folks recall him as the criminologist on the 1960s TV drama *Checkmate*, while the younger generation recognizes his voice as the narrator of Disney's *Winnie the Pooh* cartoons. At 59, Sebastian died of a stroke. He was cremated and his ashes interred at Westwood Memorial Park in Los Angeles, California.

GRAVE DIRECTIONS: Enter the cemetery behind the office complex at 10850 Wilshire Boulevard. Across the drive from the park office is a cluster of small markers for cremains. In the top row, you can find Sebastian's marker.

BRIAN KEITH
NOVEMBER 14, 1921 – JUNE 24, 1997

DURING WORLD WAR II Brian Keith was a Marine fighter-pilot hero, and after the war he played secondary roles in a few dozen films. It appeared his acting career might peak with *Family Affair*, but Brian was able to parlay his popularity as Uncle Bill into many other roles, including three seasons as the cranky Judge Milton

"Hardcase" Hardcastle in the somewhat popular action series *Hardcastle and McCormick* during the mid-1980s.

By 75, Brian was suffering from lung cancer and emphysema, and was overwhelmingly distraught by the gunshot suicide of his daughter, Daisy. Two months after her death, Brian shot himself to death inside his home. After cremation, his ashes were interred with Daisy's at Westwood Memorial Park in Los Angeles, California, the final residence of his old friend Sebastian Cabot.

GRAVE DIRECTIONS: Enter the cemetery, turn left at the office and, after the chapel, walk down the ramp into the new Garden of Serenity section. Turn left before the triple fountain and, 15 feet along the wall on the left, in the top row, are Brian and Daisy's remains.

FARRAH FAWCETT

FEBRUARY 2, 1947 – JUNE 25, 2009

AFTER FARRAH FAWCETT was voted one of the "10 most beautiful coeds on campus" at the University of Texas in 1968, a Hollywood publicist urged her to quit school for a career in show business. Although reluctant to leave college, she soon found work in commercials for toothpaste and shampoo and landed small guest roles in a few TV shows, including four episodes of *The Six Million Dollar Man,* whose star, Lee Majors, she married in 1973.

But in 1976, Farrah's fortune was forever changed when the idea of a poster of her was pitched to her agent. Farrah agreed, and a photo shoot at her home was arranged; she styled her own hair, did her own makeup, and heightened her blonde highlights with a squeeze of lemon juice. Searching for a backdrop for Farrah in her one-piece red swimsuit, the photographer grabbed an old Navajo blanket from the front seat of his pickup. From 40 rolls of film, Fawcett herself selected her six favorite pictures, which were narrowed to the one that made her famous.

The resulting pinup poster of Farrah in that bathing suit with a perfect smile and girl-next-door charm amid a halo of impossibly buoyant curly hair entered her into the dreams of adolescent boys everywhere. Women thronged to hair salons to copy her feathered "Farrah hair," which remained in vogue throughout the decade. The poster sold some 12 million copies—more than twice as many copies as Marilyn Monroe and Betty Grable ever sold combined. No poster since has achieved anywhere near its popularity and, arriving before the Internet era, in which now the most widely disseminated images are digital, it seems it will have been the last of its kind.

Farrah's pinup fame led the producers of a new television show, *Charlie's Angels,* to cast her as Jill Munroe, one of three beautiful private detective "angels" of an unseen boss named Charlie, who, in order to bring an evildoer to justice, often ordered his angels into decoy roles that put them in skimpy outfits and provocative situations. *Playboy* magazine called the show "the first mass visual symbol of post-neurotic fresh-air sexuality" but Farrah put it more plainly: "When the show was number three, I figured it was our acting. When it got to be number one, I decided it could only be because none of us wears a bra."

After just one season, though, Farrah left the show to pursue a film career, reinventing herself in a niche portraying vulnerable or troubled women in made-for-TV dramas such as *The Burning Bed* and *Small Sacrifices.*

In 2006 came a cancer diagnosis, Farrah's battle against which was played out in public, the tabloids fixating on the ravages suffered by her face and physique. Her cancer fight also became her last project, *Farrah's Story,* a prime-time documentary showing both the ugly and uplifting sides of her struggle, juxtaposing video of the actress vomiting and shaving her head with scenes of her dancing and jumping on furniture during times when her health was up.

At 62, Farrah succumbed to the disease and was buried at Westwood Memorial Park in Los Angeles, California.

GRAVE DIRECTIONS: Enter the cemetery behind the office complex at 10850 Wilshire Boulevard, turn left at the office and, just a short walk after the chapel on the right, you'll see Farrah's stone along the drive.

ERROL FLYNN
JUNE 20, 1909 – OCTOBER 14, 1959

THE CHARMING ACTOR Errol Flynn was a well-to-do Tasmanian who, after being expelled from several fine schools in Australia and England, had his share of adventures before making Hollywood his playground. A natural athlete and a rugged outdoorsman, Errol managed a New Guinea tobacco plantation, sailed the Southern seas, took a turn as a gold prospector, and, for a gold-mining company, he "recruited" unwilling natives to toil in the depths as slaves.

After rave performances on English stages, the gallant Errol and his irresistible accent headed for Hollywood in 1935. In his first film, *The Case of the Curious Bride*, he played a corpse, but in the more than 20 movies following, Errol usually starred as a swashbuckling, quick-witted, romantic hero. Women were instantly attracted to his virility and dashing good looks, while male moviegoers admired his vigor, devil-may-care attitude, and witticisms. There was a native intelligence behind his affable, sometimes even self-deprecating disposition, and Errol parlayed his unusual appeal into a spectacular Tinseltown success story. His crowning achievement came in 1938 with the stupendous hit *The Adventures of Robin Hood*. When Westerns became the rage in the 1940s, Errol looked rather silly outfitted as a cowboy, but audiences didn't seem to mind and continued to flock to his films.

By the 1950s, though, Errol's offscreen life began to take a physical toll. That which made him a lovable, drink-sloshing knave on film transformed him into a bloated drunk in real life. The same passion with which he embraced assorted celluloid bombshells enflamed his fiery offscreen affairs. Barely 15 years after capturing movie audiences with his dashing portrayal in *Captain Blood*, his best swashbuckling days were behind him. Errol tried more dramatic roles with little success until 1957, when he was cast as an aging alcoholic in Hemingway's *The Sun Also Rises*, in a bit of real-life typecasting that hit its mark.

Worn out at 50, Errol died in Canada under dubious circumstances, supposedly while having sex with a teenage lover.

Before Errol was buried at Forest Lawn Memorial Park in Glendale, California, friends slipped a bottle of whiskey into his coffin.

GRAVE DIRECTIONS: Enter the park at 1712 South Glendale Avenue, stop at the booth, get a map, drive to the Freedom Mausoleum, and walk up to the courts. Errol's grave is in the Garden of Everlasting Peace, opposite the garden's entrance, in the grass near the wall.

REDD FOXX
DECEMBER 9, 1922 – OCTOBER 11, 1991

THE CANTANKEROUS REDD Foxx is best remembered as the irascible junk dealer Fred Sanford in the 1970s television series *Sanford and Son*. Before he made it on television, though, Fred had a long career as a very "blue" stand-up comedian. In the tell-it-like-it-is style that hallmarked his personality, he was one of the first to broach the taboo topics of sex, race, and religion on more than 50 of his own "party records"—spoken comedy with no music—a genre he originated in 1956.

As Fred Sanford he often feigned heart attacks, so when he collapsed of a real heart attack while filming a new series named *The Royal Family*, the people on the set initially thought he was joking. It was no joke—Redd was dead at 68 and is buried at Palm Memorial Park in Las Vegas, Nevada.

GRAVE DIRECTIONS: Enter the cemetery at 7600 South Eastern Avenue, and immediately on your left will be an island, a drive, and a lawn area, the Garden of Devotion. From the drive, count 19 rows into the lawn and there, 50 yards from Eastern Avenue, is Redd's grave.

CLARK GABLE & CAROLE LOMBARD

CAROLE LOMBARD
OCTOBER 6, 1908 – JANUARY 16, 1942

CLARK GABLE
FEBRUARY 1, 1901 – NOVEMBER 16, 1960

CLARK GABLE AND Carole Lombard epitomized the picture of marital bliss, two famously gorgeous people sharing the world as their oyster in the fullest and most fortuitous time of their lives.

Carole's start in show business came when she was 12; a natural rough-and-tumble tomboy, she played a mischievous spitfire in a 1921 silent film. By 16, she had seven credits on her silent film resume but after suffering extensive facial injuries in a near-fatal 1926 automobile accident, her film contract was canceled. Within two years, scar tissue on her face had lightened considerably and, with a lot of camouflaging makeup, she returned to the big screen.

Meanwhile, across town lived Clark Gable, a struggling actor with big ears and little visible talent who for a dozen years had honed his craft in minor roles, dreaming of the day he'd make it big. After working together briefly in 1932 on the set of *No Man of Her Own*, Clark and Carole began a friendly and eventually romantic offscreen relationship while, during those Depression-era years, both of their careers raced for the stratosphere.

Clark found his springboard to superstardom in 1934 with an Oscar-winning role in the comedy *It Happened One Night*. Carole, a more natural and steady talent, earned her fan base through a long string of solid performances. In March 1939 Clark and Carole were wed during a break in the filming of Clark's latest movie, *Gone with the Wind*.

The newlyweds settled in the relatively rural San Fernando Valley and balanced high-profile public appearances with a country-style personal life. Following the entrance of the United States into World War II, Clark was made chairman of the Hollywood Victory Committee and he arranged for Carole to headline a War Bond rally. But on a cold January night, the 33-year-old Carole, her mother, Elizabeth, and 21 others were killed when their airplane crashed into Mount Potosi, 30 miles outside of Las Vegas. Clark drove to the crash site and, after a search for his beloved's body, Carole and Elizabeth were interred at Forest Lawn Memorial Park in Glendale, California.

Clark was devastated and felt absolute responsibility for Carole's death as he had arranged the tour. Perhaps to blunt his grief and guilt, he enlisted in the Army Air Corps and served out his time as a tail gunner. After the war, he returned to Hollywood to make a number of undistinguished films and in 1960, Clark signed on to the making of a "modern Western," *The Misfits*. During filming, he performed several grueling stunt scenes with wild horses that perhaps proved too much; just two days after completing the film, Clark died of a heart attack. At 59, he was interred alongside Carole and her mother.

GRAVE DIRECTIONS: Enter the park at 1712 South Glendale Avenue, get a map at the information booth, and make your way to the Great Mausoleum. Except for a small area where the public is invited inside to view a slide show, this enormous mausoleum is closed to the public. But as it turns out, that inch of invitation yields just enough of a toehold for you to see where Clark, Carole, and Elizabeth lie.

Walk into the mausoleum, tell the woman at the booth that you'd like to see the Last Supper slide show that's offered at regular intervals throughout the day, and she'll direct you to the area where it's shown. Once there, you'll see an entrance on the right that leads into the Columbarium of Prayer. If you look in there you can see the Sanctuary of Trust. There will be a sign in the entrance that states the area is restricted to property owners so at this point, you're on your own. Clark, Carole, and Elizabeth are in that Sanctuary of Trust, on the left wall at waist height about halfway into the first room.

Remember, this is private property and there are cameras around. Really, it's not worth it to trespass and there's not much to see anyway, just three plain nameplates.

GRETA GARBO
SEPTEMBER 18, 1905 – APRIL 15, 1990

THE PHOTOPHOBIC AND reclusive Greta Garbo began her career as a model for a department store, then moved into film during its silent era, in her native Sweden. In 1925, Mauritz Stiller, an acclaimed director who had been mentoring Garbo, was offered a Hollywood contract by MGM that he accepted on the condition that the unproven and inexperienced Garbo be offered a contract as well, so taken was he with her talent. MGM agreed and at just 19 Garbo came to the States.

In 1925 Garbo began shooting her first MGM film, *The Torrent*, and with breathtaking incandescence, revealed to the studio's executives the exciting qualities that Stiller had recognized. The camera loved her from any angle, and she projected an intoxicating eroticism. Stiller, though, was finished. MGM replaced him and he returned to Sweden, where he died two years later.

After a few more silent films, Garbo debuted in a "talkie" in 1930, *Anna Christie*, for which she was nominated for an Academy Award. She was thrilled that she'd successfully made the transition to sound in a language not even her own. During the next several years, Garbo's work was distinguished by increasingly intense performances and in 1935 she gave the performance of her life in *Anna Karenina*, playing the title role of a woman torn between her lover and her son.

Never a publicity hound, Garbo defied Hollywood convention by refusing to sign autographs or grant interviews. In fact, she would not even attend her own premieres and her studio never managed to obtain her telephone number. She never married (she once stood up John Gilbert at the altar), her sexual orientation was ambiguous, and Garbo herself may have deliberately fed the rumor mill by juxtaposing torrid affairs with her leading men with whispered liaisons involving beauties of her own gender. Of course, the more reclusive the actress became, the more her public wanted to know about her private life—but Greta was unyielding.

By 1941, though, it was all over. Greta's last film was *Two-Faced Woman*, a domestic comedy that flopped. The Swedish Sphinx gradually withdrew into an isolated retirement. In virtual seclusion for the next 50 years, she painted, gardened, wrote poetry, followed a daily exercise routine, and most determinedly, perpetuated the Garbo mystique from her Manhattan home. Appearance and interview requests never let up, but Garbo never wavered.

At 84, Garbo died of natural causes and was cremated. Her cremains were buried at Woodland Cemetery (Skogskyrkogarden) in Sweden, which is on the southern city limits of Stockholm. Marked by a beautiful and elegant, sandstone-like slab simply inscribed, "Greta Garbo," her ashes are eternally alongside her parents.

AVA GARDNER
DECEMBER 24, 1922 – JANUARY 25, 1990

THE DARK AND sultry Ava Gardner was a popular actress of the 1950s and '60s and her catalog includes memorable roles in 61 classic movies including *Mogambo*, *The Sun Also Rises*, and *Showboat*.

But despite her accomplishments as an actress, Ava was better known for her offscreen whirlwind marriages and high-profile romances with the day's most coveted men, not all of them single. At just 19 she wed Mickey Rooney, but they divorced within a year. Two years later, Ava and bandleader Artie Shaw went to the altar, but with Artie as with Mickey, a year together proved to be plenty and the couple split up. Ava's next romance made for wonderful tabloid fodder as whisperings of a torrid affair with the then-married Frank Sinatra eventually proved true. Sinatra divorced his wife and married Ava, but after three years of tumult and three years of separation, this union also ended.

Ava moved to Madrid in 1958. She had discovered Spain's allures while filming *The Barefoot Contessa* in 1954, and at her new retreat she dated high-profile playboys and matadors. Ava's last major film was *The Night of the Iguana* in 1964, and in 1968, Ava moved to London. She lived the remainder of her life there, only occasionally returning to the U.S. to act in one minor role or another. A notable but short-lived role of that era was as Ruth

Galveston, the manipulative matron on *Knot's Landing*, a popular 1980s nighttime soap opera.

Ava suffered a stroke in 1989, and the next year died of pneumonia at 67.

She was buried at her family's plot at Sunset Memorial Park in her hometown of Smithfield, North Carolina.

GRAVE DIRECTIONS: Enter the cemetery at 700 West Market Street and at the "T" make a left turn and stop. On the right is a cement walk, and at the end of this walk is Ava's plot.

JACKIE GLEASON
FEBRUARY 26, 1916 – JUNE 25, 1987

GROWING UP IN a downtrodden Brooklyn neighborhood, Jackie Gleason hung with the Nomads, an "athletic club" one knife fight away from being a street gang, and there he developed a keen flair for rough verbal play, sharp dress, and virtuoso pool playing. When he was orphaned at 16, during the Depression, those street smarts were his sole asset, and he used them to finagle himself a position as master of ceremonies at a vaudeville house. That gig led to others, and for the better part of the next 20 years Jackie jumped from one opportunity to another in a continuous search for a berth that might perfectly suit his professional persona. He worked as an emcee, a carnival barker, and a bouncer; he was a house comic and a disc jockey; he landed bit roles on Broadway and minor parts in Hollywood films; but by 1950 he'd plateaued and was at a crossroads.

Jackie was in his mid-thirties and just when he needed a stroke of fortune, he got one: He was signed as host of the *Cavalcade of Stars*, a comedy-variety television program that perfectly suited his talents; the show's format required that the host be able to move seamlessly between sketches and Jackie's years of emceeing had made him a master of the segue. Television close-ups captured the extravagant mugging and grandiose gestures that were often lost when he worked onstage.

Jackie was so successful that within two years he headlined his own show, *The Jackie Gleason Show*, over which he was given full authorial control and a lavish budget. There, he honed the formula that had worked so well for him and developed his signature opening routine. Asking the bandleader for "a little travelin' music," Jackie danced wildly across the screen and froze stage right to announce, "And awa-a-ay we go," which led

viewers into an hour of sketch comedy and guest appearances by top musical acts.

The Honeymooners was the show's most popular sketch and the pairing of Jackie as a nervous and quick-tempered Ralph Kramden with his dim-witted upstairs neighbor Ed Norton (Art Carney) yielded one of television's first great original comedy teams. During the 1955–56 season, Jackie repackaged the sketch into a filmed half-hour situation comedy of 39 episodes, and they became one of the most successful commercial properties in show business history. Unlike other popular series, those 39 episodes of *The Honeymooners* were all that were ever made, and they have run countless times each, gathering new generations of fans. Jackie explained that "the excellence of the material could not be maintained, and I had too much fondness for the show to cheapen it."

Perhaps the most remarkable and little-known aspect of Jackie's showbiz career was in the record business. He composed many songs, including the theme songs for both *The Honeymooners* and *The Jackie Gleason Show.* Because he could not read a note of music, Jackie would hum the melodies for transcribers. He also recorded what he called "pure vanilla music," popular songs with moody, string-laden orchestrations. In 1955 he assembled an orchestra and, personally wielding the baton, recorded his own lush arrangements of old standards. That first release, *Music for Lovers Only*, sold more than half a million copies and Jackie followed with 36 more.

Now a television superstar, Jackie's services were in high demand for feature movies too. In 1961, he was cast opposite Paul Newman in the film *The Hustler* as the legendary pool player

Minnesota Fats and performed his own pool shots; the role earned him an Academy Award nomination. In the 1970s he played the cantankerous, drawling redneck lawman Buford T. Justice in the *Smokey and the Bandit* series, and in 1985 he reunited with Art Carney for the television movie *Izzy and Moe*.

"Life ain't bad, pal," Jackie once told an interviewer. "Everything I've wanted to do I've had a chance to do."

Jackie died of colon and liver cancer at 71 and is buried at Our Lady of Mercy Catholic Cemetery in Miami, Florida.

GRAVE DIRECTIONS: At 11411 NW 25th Street, enter the cemetery and proceed to the "T" at the flagpole. Make a left and park at the circle at the end of this drive. On your right, 150 yards across the lawn, you won't miss the large white memorial that marks Jackie's plot.

ANDY GRIFFITH
JUNE 1, 1926 – JULY 3, 2012

WHEN HE WAS a teenager, Andy Griffith bought a Sears and Roebuck trombone and wheedled lessons out of a local pastor. Then he became interested in singing, and for a while thought he might be an opera singer. Later he decided he wanted to be a Moravian preacher and enrolled as a pre-divinity student at the University of North Carolina, where he became involved in drama and musical theater, finally graduating with a degree in music. Next came the frustration of teaching high school music and phonetics, which he left after three years because as he explained, "First day, I'd tell the class all I knew and then there was nothing left to say for the rest of the semester."

After assembling a traveling variety show routine with his wife, Barbara, he eventually caught the attention of entertainment agent Richard Linke, who secured Andy a semi-regular spot as a monologist on *The Ed Sullivan Show*. That led to a role as Will Stockdale in the Broadway play *No Time for Sergeants*, which got Andy nominated for a Tony Award. But it was a guest appearance as a small-town mayor on the sitcom *Make Room for Daddy* that in 1960 led CBS to give him his own sitcom, *The Andy Griffith Show*. The show, in which he played the gentle and philosophical small-town Sheriff Andy Taylor of the make-believe town of Mayberry, imagined a reassuring world of ice cream socials and rock-hard family values. Among the show's delightful yet oddball characters were Andy's jittery sidekick, Deputy Barney Fife, and a simple-minded gas station attendant named Gomer Pyle. Andy Taylor, a widower, often philosophized with his young son, Opie, at local fishing holes. The show was a quiet reprieve from a decade that grew progressively tumultuous and it consistently ranked among the most popular sitcoms during the entirety of its run. After the run ended with episode 249, the show lived on in spinoffs, endless reruns, and even Sunday school classes organized around its rustic moral lessons.

In 1983 Andy was suddenly stricken with Guillain-Barré syndrome, a crippling muscular disease that left him partially paralyzed. After six months of private rehabilitation, he made a full recovery and returned to acting, making a triumphant return to TV stardom as Matlock, a crafty and rumpled but good-natured defense lawyer in the series of the same name.

To viewers, Andy's portrayals seemed so effortless they presumed he was simply playing himself. He wasn't, he insisted; he was always acting, but took that misimpression as a compliment to his artistry. "You're supposed to believe in the character," he said. "You're not supposed to think, 'Gee, Andy's really acting up a storm.'"

At 86, Andy died of a heart attack at home. He was buried at the Griffith family cemetery on his Roanoke Island ranch in North Carolina. The private estate is not amenable to visitors.

FRED GWYNNE
JULY 10, 1926 – JULY 2, 1993

THE LUMBERING 6-FOOT-5 Fred Gwynne followed a complicated path to his destined role as the fumbling and sweet-tempered Herman Munster.

The son of a successful stockbroker, Fred was packed off early to a prestigious Massachusetts preparatory school and, after graduation, he enlisted in the Navy and served on a World War II sub chaser. Later, Fred spent a year at a design school developing his dormant drawing talents and then entered Harvard University on the G.I. Bill. At Harvard, he presided over and contributed cartoons to *The Harvard Lampoon* and after a few performances in the Hasty Pudding Club's farcical productions, Fred decided that his future was onstage.

Most casting directors found Fred too tall or unattractive, but he did manage to appear in a few Broadway plays and even had a bit part in *On the Waterfront*, though work as a commercial artist was really paying the bills. Finally, in 1961, he was hired to costar in the TV sitcom about two hapless cops, *Car 54, Where Are You?* and upon its cancelation three years later, Fred finally found a tailor-made role in *The Munsters* as Herman Munster. Actually, Fred wasn't completely perfect for the part—he had to wear five-inch-high platform soles—but he was right at home as a lovable Frankenstein, and audiences adored him.

The Munsters flashed only briefly and after its demise Fred found to his chagrin that the Herman role had typecast him for life. But eventually, as his hair thinned and his facial features became patriarchal, he returned to Broadway and film, usually as a booming, authoritative character. Fred's career took on new zest in 1992 when he played an autocratic Southern judge in the comedy film *My Cousin Vinny.*

But Fred decided to go out while he was still on top and, even as the accolades for *My Cousin Vinny* poured in, he withdrew and purchased a farm in rural Maryland. After just a short period of tranquility, Fred was diagnosed with pancreatic cancer. Surgery and chemotherapy followed, but the cancer continued to spread. He died at 66.

Fred was buried at Sandymount United Methodist Church in Sandyville, Maryland.

GRAVE DIRECTIONS: At 2101 Old Westminster Pike, walk into the cemetery behind the church and near the back is a distinctive brown Shannon stone. About 20 feet in front and to the left of the Shannon stone, Fred is buried in a grave that, but for the grass covering it, has no marking of any kind.

JIM HENSON
SEPTEMBER 24, 1936 – MAY 16, 1990

AS A CHILD, Jim Henson was fascinated by television, and in the summer of 1954 he learned that a local station needed someone to perform with puppets on a children's show. Jim wasn't particularly interested in puppets, but he did want to get on TV, so he and a friend made a couple of puppets, and they were hired. That show ended quickly but, within a few months, Jim landed a new program on a local NBC-affiliate station and called it *Sam and Friends.*

Having realized that it was necessary for television puppets to have "life and sensitivity," Jim's proto-Muppets on *Sam and Friends* were much different from traditional puppets. Kermit the Frog was there right from the start, and he looked and sounded much as he always would (until his death, Jim provided the voice and animation of Kermit); even at this early time he had a face that was pliable, he could move his mouth in synchronization with his speech and could gesticulate in ways that were impossible for a marionette.

Throughout the early 1960s, Jim's creations made appearances on variety and talk shows, but it was on *Sesame Street,* the public television program for preschoolers that first aired in 1969, that his Muppet crew won the hearts of a generation. With wit that also appealed to adults, Oscar the Grouch, innocent Big Bird, considerate Bert, fun-loving Ernie, and the rest of the lovable gang helped youngsters learn about everything from numbers and the alphabet to birth and death.

But despite the Muppets' success on *Sesame Street* and their demonstrated appeal to adults as well as children, no U.S. network would give Jim a show of his own. Finally in 1976, after a British producer offered Jim the necessary financing, *The Muppet Show* was born. It ran until 1981, when Jim decided to end it lest its quality begin to decline. Later, Jim turned to the big screen and produced three box-office hit Muppet films.

At 53, Jim died suddenly of an especially aggressive bacterial infection known as streptococcus pneumonia. He arrived at a New York hospital suffering from an inability to breathe and was immediately treated with high doses of antibiotics but, despite the aggressive regimen, the infection overwhelmed his body. Within 20 hours of walking into the hospital, Jim died of uncontrollable bleeding into his lungs. Before contracting the illness, Jim had been in excellent health and had never even had a personal physician.

He was cremated and his ashes were scattered at his ranch outside Santa Fe, New Mexico.

KATHARINE HEPBURN
MAY 12, 1907 – JUNE 29, 2003

THE STRONG-WILLED MOVIE characters portrayed with a trademark feisty spirit and often-imitated voice of a well-bred New Englander made Katharine Hepburn a beloved film heroine for most of the twentieth century. With a no-nonsense manner, she gained standing as a unique independent who rejected the phony Hollywood façade. By declining roles she didn't like and refusing to be fawned over by the press, her rebellion gained her a reputation for being ornery and snobbish, though she viewed it as a byproduct of strict adherence to absolute honesty.

Katharine became a movie star quickly and by just her third movie, 1933's *Morning Glory,* had earned the first of her four Academy

Awards—though she never showed up to collect any of them. But, after a number of flops over the next few years, her status declined almost as meteorically as it had risen. Katharine took charge of her situation in a way few women dared in those days. After earning "free-agency" status by buying out her contract with RKO Pictures, she persuaded sometimes-beau Howard Hughes to help purchase the rights to the hit play *The Philadelphia Story*. Katharine then shrewdly sold the property to MGM with stipulations that she would play the lead and have ultimate control of casting. Once Cary Grant and Jimmy Stewart signed on, the movie was destined for greatness and she never lost control of her career again.

On the set of *Woman of the Year* she began a romantic relationship with Spencer Tracy and it was this pairing that, perhaps, most fascinated her fans. Tracy remained married for the duration of their tryst, which lasted through nine films together and 27 years. It was a mystery why she remained with him since, besides the fact he was married, he was given to drinking binges and violent outbursts. "I honestly don't know," she said, long after his 1967 death. "I can only say that he was there and I was his."

As the years advanced and her health declined, Katharine one day considered the future from the solitude of her Connecticut oceanside estate. "I think people are beginning to realize I'm not going to be around much longer. And you know they'll miss me, like an old monument. Like the Flatiron Building."

Katharine expired of old age at 96 and was buried at Cedar Hill Cemetery in Hartford, Connecticut.

GRAVE DIRECTIONS: Drive straight into the cemetery at 453 Fairfield Avenue, stay left at the flagpole, and bear right at the next fork. Then, at the funky five-way intersection, stay more or less straight and

Section 10 will then be on your left. About halfway around this section, the Hepburn plot is between two big spruce bushes.

BENNY HILL
JANUARY 21, 1925 – APRIL 20, 1992

THE BRITISH COMEDIAN Benny Hill worked as a radio performer during the 1940s and for the next two decades appeared on a variety of programs in that medium as well as on television. In 1969, writing nearly all of his own material, Benny began making a series of sketch comedies for Thames Television and, when 111 half-hour-long compilations of the sketches debuted on American television as *The Benny Hill Show* in 1979, he achieved international cult status.

Benny was a master of the double entendre, and his sketches featured skimpily clad women, sight gags, a lot of cross-dressing, and a healthy dose of *The Three Stooges*. With his own uniquely comic twist, he turned ordinary slapstick into something entirely new. A typical Benny skit might find Benny and a pretty young woman walking arm in arm along a path when they come to a puddle. Like a gentleman, Benny removes his coat and lays it over the water so his lady might cross without wetting her feet. But, of course, the water is deeper than expected and the woman is immersed up to her neck.

Critics said his humor too often crossed the line from good fun into sexism but Benny was never bothered by the complaints. "I use a pretty girl the way Henny Youngman uses his violin—as a bridge between one laugh and the next," explained Benny. Bemoaning the treatment he received at the hands of feminists, Benny answered them by pointing out that he had never chased a woman on-screen in his life—they had always chased him.

On Benny's 50th birthday he told his small, bald sidekick, Jackie Wright, that he had had a very good life, that he'd been lucky, and that he would not mind if he died the next day. However, even with the astounding success that Benny would enjoy in the subsequent decade, it is hard to see his life as anything other than sad and lonely.

Benny lacked confidence in the medical profession as a whole and, in a case of life imitating art, he entrusted his health to a gynecologist with a pathological obsession with pinching women's bottoms. Despite his wealth, he shied from the responsibility he associated with property ownership, and instead lived in a series of rented flats, each one sparsely furnished and scattered with cardboard boxes. Rejected by both women to whom he'd proposed, Benny never married and, it seems, may have died a virgin.

In the spring of 1992 Benny's neighbors sensed a particularly pungent odor emanating from Benny's apartment and, realizing they hadn't seen the funnyman for a few days, called the police. Their fears were soon realized; Benny had died very much as he had lived his life, alone. In front of his television, he was slumped on the couch, surrounded by cardboard boxes, unwashed crockery, empty glasses, and piles of videotapes.

At his death of heart failure at 67, Benny left no survivors and was buried at Hollybrook Cemetery in Shirley, Southampton, England.

GRAVE DIRECTIONS: Enter the cemetery at 110 Dale Valley Road and, from the main gate, turn left at the chapel and Benny's black marble tomb is the first grave in the seventh row.

After Benny's death, his will was contested by a few parties and, since Benny wasn't particularly trusting of traditional financial vehicles, the actual disposition of some of his fortune was unclear. (It became rumored that some had been buried with him.) In October 1992, grave robbers unearthed Benny, but only they know whether or not his coffin hid anything; when officials peered into his open grave the next day, there was no treasure to behold. Since then, a solid slab of granite has been laid across the top of his grave.

ALFRED HITCHCOCK
AUGUST 13, 1899 – APRIL 29, 1980

IN 1919 ALFRED Hitchcock joined London's Paramount studio as a lowly title designer, but he quickly moved up the ranks. Within six years he was directing and, over the course of the next 50 years, Alfred spun a remarkably consistent thread of suspense-thrillers, a genre he virtually invented. He deftly wove sex and humor into his stories in a steady demonstration of the eternal symmetry of good and evil and, as a brilliant technician, he developed a stock of subtle techniques and clever camera tricks that inspired his contemporaries and all who came after.

Just a year after his 1925 directorial debut, he launched his breakthrough film, *The Lodger*, a prototypical example of the classic Hitchcock plot: An innocent protagonist is falsely accused of a crime and becomes involved in a web of intrigue. This was also the first film in which he appeared as an extra. Such cameo roles would later become another of his trademarks, and spotting him would become a passion among fans. In his first "talkie," *Blackmail,* in 1929, he introduced a "selective sound" technique; a young woman's anxiety was emphasized by gradually distorting all but the word "knife" in a scene with her neighbor. In *Murder!,* released the following year, he first made explicit the link between sex and violence. Through the remainder of the 1930s, Alfred was the leading director in Britain and garnered international acclaim as well for a series of spy thrillers, including *The Man Who Knew Too Much.*

In 1939 he moved to Hollywood where he continued his prodigious output: *Notorious, Shadow of a Doubt, Spellbound,* and *Lifeboat* exemplify his work of the next decade. The 1950s, however, turned out to be Hitchcock's decade of personal inspiration and his three masterpieces of that period, *Rear Window, Vertigo,* and *North by Northwest,* lifted the typical manifestations of evil to a new plane. Employing subtle male-female relationships, witty symbolism, and dramatic film techniques and scores, he expanded classic Hitchcock to something sleeker and faster-paced and, ultimately, more entertaining. By contrast, 1960's *Psycho,* which has been held aloft as a classic of shot selection and editing, may have, in the end, only served to inspire the slasher genre.

Though Alfred seems to have had a few favorite actors—Cary Grant, Grace Kelly, James Stewart—he was also famous for his general disregard for the acting profession, and when his celebrated comment, "Actors are cattle," stirred up protest, he issued a correction and said, "I have been misquoted, what I really said is: Actors should be treated as cattle." Not surprisingly, performers weren't very enamored with him either. His meticulous planning of every shot and complete refusal to improvise or deviate from his shooting schedule ruffled plenty of feathers, but complaints to studio heads always fell on deaf ears; the strength of Hitchcock's directorial feats and his popularity guaranteed him the last word.

Though he was nominated for an Academy Award on six different occasions, he never won one. Instead, in a gesture that seemed prompted by the common knowledge that his time was drawing near, Hitchcock received a Lifetime Achievement award six months before his death.

Severely arthritic and suffering from kidney failure for a year, Alfred expired of heart failure at 80.

He was cremated and his ashes were scattered, though no one seems to know where.

BOB HOPE

MAY 29, 1903 – JULY 27, 2003

MAKING A VAST fortune out of the one-line-gag, Bob Hope's career spanned eight decades and the applause on which he thrived seemed to be the source of his youthfulness. His historic show business career began at the age of 10, when he won a Charlie Chaplin imitation contest and soon after, he learned how to tap dance, joined a road-show musical, and performed in blackface. Bookings for stage theatrics as well as comic emceeing followed and he honed his wit with his own radio program during the 1930s. But Bob wasn't a bona fide star until he appeared in his first of more than 50 movies, *Big Broadcast of 1938*, in which he sang the signature tune that would become his theme song, "Thanks for the Memory."

In 1940, he teamed with Bing Crosby for the first of their seven "Road" flicks and in a string of pictures beginning with 1941's *Caught in the Draft*, he tended to play would-be ladies' men that almost never got the girl. In 1950, Bob debuted on television, but wisely declined a weekly show and instead opted for semi-regular specials featuring musical skits by a bevy of entertainers and appearances by athletes and other celebrities. All the action invariably came after an opening monologue chock full of quips and *The Bob Hope Specials* became ratings blockbusters airing more than 300 times.

During World War II, Bob attempted to enlist but was told his talents would be better served as an entertainer to build morale and in that capacity his enduring portrait of compassion and humanitarianism was revealed. With a touring show of performers, this Ambassador of Goodwill, or G.I. Bob as the soldiers called him, became a staple of USO shows covering almost every overseas base and boosting the morale of more than 10 million troops.

As the years rolled along and his thousands of friends and associates from a life well-lived passed on by the hundreds, it seemed that Bob's time too would be near—but Bob had the last laugh. In 1998, while eating breakfast one morning he was surprised to see members of Congress paying tribute to him on live television; a pre-written obituary had been released and media organizations picked up the story before the mistake was corrected.

Two years later, Hope attended the opening of the permanent Bob Hope Gallery of American Entertainment in the Library of Congress, which includes 88,000 handwritten jokes as well as letters, photos, and other mementos. "His career pretty much parallels the history of American entertainment," said a spokesman. "The gallery is both a history of Bob Hope and a history of American entertainment."

At his death at 100, Bob was laid to rest at San Fernando Mission Cemetery in Mission Hills, California.

GRAVE DIRECTIONS: From the entrance at 11160 Stranwood Avenue, follow the signs to Bob Hope Memorial Garden and there you'll see the beautiful architecture and landscaping of his final resting place.

DENNIS HOPPER
MAY 17, 1936 – MAY 29, 2010

DENNIS HOPPER'S ACTING career began in 1955 with a role credited as "Goon," one of the high school gang members who menace James Dean in *Rebel Without a Cause*. He flowered in art films like *The Trip* during the next decade, and later specialized in psychotic villains in such films as *Blue Velvet* and *Speed*. But it was his role as the long-haired, pot-smoking biker named Billy opposite Peter Fonda's character, Wyatt, or "Captain America," in the 1969 counterculture film classic *Easy Rider* that gave Dennis his most enduring claim to fame.

The made-on-the-fly movie, which he directed and costarred in, was an anti-establishment tale of two disenchanted chopper-riding hippies, who, thanks to some drug money scored from a cocaine sale, embark on an ultimately tragic odyssey from Los Angeles to New Orleans. "A man went looking for America and couldn't find it anywhere," went its famous tagline. The low-budget film's exploration of the hippie counterculture and its reaction to the Vietnam War paved the way for the New Hollywood of the 1970s, vindicating Dennis' generation. Dubbing it his "state of the union" message, he said, "None of our crowd had ever seen themselves portrayed in a movie. At every love-in across the country people were smoking grass and dropping LSD, while audiences were still watching Doris Day and Rock Hudson."

Easy Rider catapulted him into the pantheon of countercultural celebrities and he was soon surrounded by groupies and acolytes, which, for someone who had already been lolling in the deep end of excess since he was 18, became his undoing. Tales of hard drinking and drug taking often blighted Dennis' private life, but now, his lifestyle became the stuff of Hollywood legend—or nightmare. He became the bad-boy sheriff of Hollywood, often carrying a gun and knife when he wasn't running around the streets of Los Angeles—literally—in the nude like a madman. He was married five times, once for just seven days. He spent time on a commune firing machine guns and taking stimulants, his daily intake including 30 beers, half a gallon of rum, and a few grams of coke. His descent reached a low point in 1982, while making a film in Mexico. "I ended up walking off into the jungle, naked, in the middle of the night," he said. "I was convinced they were listening to my mind and my friends were being gassed." Hallucinating on the flight home, he tried to jump out of the plane and was committed to a psychiatric ward.

After rehab, his career experienced a renaissance and he earned a 1986 Oscar nomination for his role as an alcoholic basketball-team manager in *Hoosiers*. That same year, he received critical acclaim for his chilling performance as the sadistic brute in *Blue Velvet*. By his sunset years, golf, the Atkins diet, and trips to Fashion Week with his new wife replaced boozing and drugs. Dennis was also an outspoken, if unlikely, Republican in Hollywood. He regretted his wasted years, saying, "The alcohol was awful. I was a terrible alcoholic and I was only doing the coke so I could drink more. I was looked on as a maniac and an idiot and a fool and a drunkard."

At 74, Dennis lost a long battle with prostate cancer. After a service at the chapel of the San Francisco de Asis Church, his funeral procession proceeded to Jesus Nazareno Cemetery where he was laid to rest in an Indian-style burial mound, his simple wooden coffin covered in a jumbled mound of rocks and gravel. The cemetery is located in Ranchos de Taos, New Mexico.

GRAVE DIRECTIONS: Off La Canada Road, near where it intersects Espinoza Road, a drive next to a low-slung adobe-colored building will deliver you to the cemetery, though there is no sign. After a couple hundred yards, there is a dirt area big enough to turn around in on the right, and immediately in front of that is Dennis' grave.

ROCK HUDSON
NOVEMBER 17, 1925 – OCTOBER 2, 1985

AFTER A STINT in the Navy during World War II, Roy Harold Scherer Jr. worked as a vacuum cleaner salesman and a truck driver in Hollywood while awaiting his big break. It arrived in 1948 when he was offered a role in the film *Fighter Squadron*, and Roy, never one to squander an opportunity, delivered his one line flawlessly after just 38 takes. His effort went uncredited.

After his agent persuaded him to have his teeth capped and change his name to Rock Hudson, he appeared in dozens of films during the 1950s, most notably alongside James Dean and Elizabeth Taylor in *Giant*, but Rock's defining role came opposite Doris Day in the following decade. The pair starred in a series of comedies with suggestive titles like *Pillow Talk* and *Lover Come Back*, Rock epitomizing the comely and charismatic, perpetually aroused ladies' man, while Doris flustered as a professional virgin. In 1966 he starred in *Seconds*, a psychological thriller that was panned at the time but has since become a cult classic.

For decades, females fawned over Rock's rock-solid good looks, fabulous physique, and imperial grace, but Rock obliged only one time, marrying his agent's secretary in 1955 and divorcing her three years later. He afterward engaged only in the most private of trysts and, in 1984, Rock seemed to confirm 30-year-old suspicions that he was a homosexual when he announced he was dying of AIDS, a disease that, up to that point, was mostly limited to the gay community.

The following year, at his death at 59, Rock became the first public casualty of the disease. He had no immediate survivors, but a lover, Marc Christian, successfully sued his estate for $14.5 million in actual damages on the grounds that Rock had kept his AIDS diagnosis a secret and caused him "enhanced fear" that he might contract AIDS. In 1989, Christian, who was never diagnosed with the disease, was awarded an additional $14.5 million in punitive damages.

Rock was cremated and his ashes scattered along the Pacific Coast, but 10 years later friends honored his memory by having his name inscribed in the Tower of Memories at the Palm Springs Mortuary and Mausoleum in Cathedral City, California.

GRAVE DIRECTIONS: Enter the mortuary at 31705 Da Vall Drive and park in the office lot on the left. Then walk back across the lane that you just drove in on, proceed past the fountain, and on the right is the Tower of Memories, just before the restrooms. There's a checkerboard pattern of tiles on this wall and Rock's name is engraved on the tile that's third from the top and third from the left.

I LOVE LUCY

DESI ARNAZ AND Lucille Ball created the situation comedy *I Love Lucy* in 1951 and the show quickly achieved unprecedented popularity. The program featured Lucille's antics as Lucy, the wacky, high-spirited wife of a struggling Cuban bandleader named Ricky Ricardo, played by Desi. Meanwhile, their good-natured landlords and best friends, Fred and Ethel Mertz, played by William Frawley and Vivian Vance, came along for the laughs. Every Monday night during its six-year run, millions of people across America gathered in front of what was usually the first television set in the house to watch their continuing comedic adventures.

Desi and Lucy weren't just a couple on-screen, they were married in real life as well. In 1953 when Lucy Ricardo was seen going to the hospital to give birth to "Little Ricky" (who was actually Lucille's real son, Desi Arnaz Jr.), it was a sort of national occasion. Nonetheless, all things must pass and, after illuminating the direction for years of future television programs, *I Love Lucy* ended its run in 1957, only to begin a new run of worldwide syndication.

WILLIAM FRAWLEY
FEBRUARY 26, 1887 – MARCH 3, 1966

ORIGINALLY A VAUDEVILLE and then Broadway stage actor, William Frawley was later known for playing supporting roles, usually as a gruff but likable character, in over 100 films. Because of a reputation as a hard drinker, his contract with *I Love Lucy* stipulated that he'd be fired if he had more than three days of unexplained absence or if he ever showed up drunk. Bill agreed to the stipulation and for $350 a week joined the cast as landlord Fred Mertz.

Offscreen, Bill made no bones about his dislike for Vivian Vance, who played his on-screen wife, Ethel, once remarking, "She's one of the finest gals to come out of Kansas, and I often wish she'd go back there." Likewise, Vivian often expressed her disgust at having to play opposite a curmudgeon who was 25 years her senior.

After *I Love Lucy* went off the air, Bill appeared as Bub the housekeeper on *My Three Sons*. In 1966, he suffered a heart attack while walking down Hollywood Boulevard and, a few minutes later, died in the lobby of a nearby hotel.

At 79, Bill was buried at San Fernando Mission Cemetery in Mission Hills, California.

GRAVE DIRECTIONS: Enter the cemetery at 11160 Stranwood Avenue, turn left, and stop where you see a statue of Jesus on the lawn to the right. Here, five rows from the curb, is Bill's grave.

VIVIAN VANCE
JULY 26, 1912 – AUGUST 17, 1979

IN THE SUMMER of 1951 Vivian Vance was a stage actress at the La Jolla Playhouse. At the urging of *I Love Lucy's* director, Desi went to see her performance and, after the show, she was cast as Ethel Mertz, the Ricardos' landlady and Lucy's best friend. After *I Love Lucy*, she joined Lucy as Vivian, not Ethel, on *The Lucy Show* for three seasons and later retired to Connecticut.

In 1979 Vivian succumbed to bone cancer at 67. She was cremated and her ashes scattered by family and friends.

DESI ARNAZ
MARCH 2, 1917 – DECEMBER 2, 1986

LUCILLE BALL
AUGUST 6, 1911 – APRIL 26, 1989

THOUGH MARRIED JUST 20 years, the lives of Desi Arnaz and Lucille Ball are inextricably linked. After marrying in 1940, they continued their own careers; Lucy was in radio and "B" movies, while Desi was a touring big-band musician. With Desi constantly on the road, the marriage was problematic from the beginning and when CBS proposed that Lucy take her popular radio program, *My Favorite Husband*, to the new medium of television, she saw a chance to save their failing marriage and agreed to the program on the condition that Desi play her husband.

CBS agreed but balked at their next demand: Lucy and Desi proposed filming their show and then beaming it to audiences at a later time. In 1951, before the perfection of videotape, nearly all television shows were live productions, fed from the East Coast because of time-zone differences. CBS agreed to their proposal on the condition they take salary cuts to cover the increased expenses, and Lucy and Desi granted that concession providing Desilu, a company they'd created, would own the programs after the initial broadcast. A few years later, the couple sold the films back to CBS for more than $4 million, a sum that provided the economic base for building what became the powerful Desilu production empire.

The couple divorced three years after *I Love Lucy* ended and, after Lucy bought Desi's half of Desilu for $3 million, he soon retired to gambling and alcohol and only rarely made public appearances again. But Lucy wasted no time: She reformatted the old show into a new series called *The Lucy Show* and later, *Here's Lucy*, which ran on prime time through 1974.

In 1986, at 69, Desi Arnaz died of lung cancer at his home in Del Mar, California. He was cremated, his ashes reportedly scattered.

A week after undergoing open-heart surgery, Lucy suffered a ruptured aorta and died at 77. She was cremated and her ashes are interred at Lakeview Cemetery in Jamestown, New York.

GRAVE DIRECTIONS: Drive straight into the cemetery at 907 Lakeview Avenue and after a couple hundred yards, turn right and go up the hill. Across the drive from the grand Sheldon monument you'll easily find the Ball stone where Lucy lies with her parents.

BORIS KARLOFF
NOVEMBER 23, 1887 – FEBRUARY 2, 1969

BORN THE SON of a wealthy British diplomat, Boris Karloff enjoyed the privileges customary to the family of an agent of the Crown in late Victorian England. His childhood included private schooling, exposure to art and theater, extensive travel, and, finally, enrollment at London University in preparation for a career in his country's foreign service. But at 21, Boris promptly abandoned the aristocracy and eloped with the first of his five wives to Canada.

To support himself, Boris worked as a farm laborer in Ontario and joined a touring theater company. Though he became known as a skilled character actor, often donning heavy makeup and playing men many years older, he was divorced and penniless at 30 and left to find work in Hollywood. Boris had fantastic success working in Hollywood—in a dozen years he made 80 film appearances—but the quantity of work dwarfed both his monetary compensation and critical recognition for all the effort.

Finally, in 1931 Bela Lugosi refused to take a role in which he would have his face hidden by makeup and have no lines, the role of the creature in *Frankenstein*, and so the part went to Boris, who had no vanity or misgivings about his work in the horror genre. The picture became a classic and 70 years later, Boris' is the only name readily associated with it, though he was not even credited in the original release, receiving just a question mark.

Over the next 25 years Boris reigned as the King of Horror and made countless movies in that vein—in his career he had more than 200 film credits—but by the late 1950s he abandoned the hectic pace as his health faltered. Still, he didn't give up making movies entirely and, in the last decade of his life, though he suffered from severe emphysema and was forced to use a wheelchair and an oxygen mask between scenes, his appearance remained familiar to television viewers and moviegoers.

At 81, Boris died at his home from complications of his emphysema. He was cremated and his ashes buried in the Garden of Remembrance at Mount Cemetery, which sits high on a hill above Guildford, England.

ANDY KAUFMAN
JANUARY 17, 1949 – MAY 16, 1984

AFTER SCORING A zero on the draft board's psychology test, resulting in a 4-F deferment, Andy Kaufman pursued a career as a comedian of the most unorthodox variety. His act tested the audience's discomfort threshold and during performances he alternately read passages from *The Great Gatsby*, ate potatoes, sang religious songs, and even took an extended onstage nap. Nonetheless, Andy's mainstream potential became evident in 1975 when his "foreign guy" character was showcased on *Saturday Night Live*'s inaugural broadcast. The heavily accented, nonsensical character was the genesis of Latka Gravas, a goofy Latvian mechanic, and beginning in 1978 Andy played him to the hilt during the hit television show *Taxi*'s five-year run.

Andy was a frequent guest player on *Saturday Night Live* but his bizarre offstage antics eventually alienated fans and in a November 1982 phone-in poll, he was voted off the show by viewers, 195,544 to 169,186. The conflict had arisen after Andy took the show's humorous Inter-Gender Wrestling Champion role to a bizarre extreme and turned it into his own alter ego on the professional wrestling circuit. In the guise, Andy lobbed insults at the audience and baited women with a $1,000 prize if one were able to pin him. More than 60 accepted the challenge, and Andy won all the bouts, but the dirty fights garnered him few allies. In this time spent out of his element, Andy somehow developed a weird vendetta against pro-wrestler Jerry Lawler, and the whole grotesque affair promptly ended after Jerry pile-drove Andy into the hospital with a damaged cervical vertebrae.

In November 1983 Andy developed a nagging and hacking cough. After it persisted, then worsened, he was subjected to a battery of medical tests and it was finally determined that he had a rare, large-cell carcinoma in his lungs. The cancer was in its advanced stages, inoperable and incurable. Andy had never smoked and he was a strict health-food fanatic, so when this news became public, many believed that the whole thing was another cleverly crafted performance piece. The news was all too real for Andy, though, and in a search for a magic cure, he even traveled to the Philippines for help from shamans.

But Andy eventually succumbed to the cancer and, because faking his own death seemed to be the apotheosis of his bad taste, some arrived at his funeral expecting a reception from him in one or another of his personas. But instead, they found Andy's lifeless body and, hoping that this was his strangest put-on of all, many poked him when they thought no one was looking, to be certain that he really was gone.

At 35, Andy was buried at Beth David Cemetery in Elmont, New York.

GRAVE DIRECTIONS: Enter the cemetery at 300 Elmont Road and go past the office. Make a right onto Lincoln Avenue, then turn left onto Brandeis Avenue. At Autumn Avenue turn right and stop at its end. The Kaufman plot is just to the left.

SAM KINISON
DECEMBER 8, 1953 – APRIL 10, 1992

SAM KINISON WAS a high-flying, patently outrageous performer who was simultaneously loved and hated from the time he found success as a comedian in 1985 with an appearance in Rodney Dangerfield's *Back to School* until his death seven years later. On one side of the fence, gays, feminists, and conservatives howled in protest against Sam's poisonously rude and bitter jokes, while an adoring legion of equally vocal fans thrilled at his shocking, high-decibel outbursts. Often appearing in a trademark beret and overcoat, the former Pentecostal preacher's pitch-black routines, delivered in loudmouthed, wildman style, were surpassed only by his real-life offstage excesses. An avid substance abuser, Sam lived a reckless life filled with drugs, alcohol, women, and controversy.

By 1992, though, Sam had revamped his comedy act to direct it toward a more lucrative mainstream television audience. He made frequent appearances on *Saturday Night Live* and *In Living Color*, and starred as Charlie Hoover on the short-lived sitcom of the same name. It was ironic then that, after years of hard partying followed by a renewed commitment to cleaning up his abusive habits, Sam was killed—while sober—in a traffic collision caused by a driver who had been drinking.

Having just returned from their Hawaii honeymoon, Sam and his new wife, Malika Souiri, a Las Vegas dancer, were traveling in Sam's new Pontiac Trans Am to a sold-out Friday evening show in Laughlin, Nevada. Meanwhile, in the other direction, two

teenagers in a pickup truck littered with beer cans swerved into oncoming traffic near Needles, California. In the ensuing head-on impact, Sam met his demise. In the moments after the horrific crash, Sam seemed to be fine, according to his brother Bill, who witnessed the tragedy from his own car following behind. With relatively minor cuts on his face and forehead, Sam wrenched himself free of his mangled vehicle, but then lay down by the side of the road.

Sam's face had no color and he kept saying, "I don't want to die, I don't want to die." Bill cradled Sam's bleeding head in his arms while Sam had what seemed to be a conversation with somebody else. "But why?" Sam asked. It was like he was talking to somebody upstairs. "Then I heard him say, 'Okay okay, okay,' and the last 'okay' was so soft and at peace like whatever voice was talking to him gave him the right answer, and he just relaxed with it. He said it so sweet, like he was talking to someone he loved," Bill related.

Sam hadn't been wearing his seatbelt and an autopsy revealed that when Sam's body struck the steering wheel, his internals had decelerated so quickly that his aorta had been ripped from his heart. On the side of Highway 95, while his older brother comforted him helplessly, Sam died of a broken heart at 38.

Sam was buried in his family's plot at Memorial Park Gardens in Tulsa, Oklahoma.

GRAVE DIRECTIONS: Enter the cemetery at 5111 South Memorial Drive and follow the yellow line to the chapel. There you'll see the Lakeside Mausoleum off to your right, in front of which is Section 28, Garden of the Apostles, where Sam is buried.

Section 28 is divided into quadrants by four walkways, and the Kinison plot is in the southeast quadrant. (When standing in Section 28 and looking at the mausoleum, north is to your left, so the southeast is to your right front.) Within the southeast quadrant, Sam's grave is seven rows east of the walk and about two-thirds of the way north.

STANLEY KUBRICK
JULY 26, 1928 – MARCH 7, 1999

AS A YOUNG adult, Stanley Kubrick had the opportunity to attend many film screenings at New York's Museum of Modern Art and later said that seeing so many bad films gave him the confidence to do better. "I was aware that I didn't know anything about making films, but I believed I couldn't make them any worse than the majority of films I was seeing," he once said. "Bad films gave me the courage to try making a mediocre movie."

After a couple forgettable noir thrillers, the aspiring director found his center and established himself as a filmmaker to be reckoned with by releasing *Paths of Glory* in 1957, a devastating antiwar indictment of military duplicity. Two years later came the high-budget Roman epic *Spartacus* followed by the erotic *Lolita* in 1962, but the first of his true masterpieces was the nuclear-age comic satire *Dr. Strangelove or: How I Learned to Stop Worrying and Love the Bomb*, which imagined nuclear Armageddon as a macabre joke culminating with Slim Pickens riding an H-bomb like a bucking bronco.

The public and critical acclaim for *Dr. Strangelove* earned Stanley the rare freedom of absolute control over his projects and, though the reclusive artist would shoot just six more films in the 35 years preceding his death, nearly all of them have their place in screen history. From the visual grandeur and dazzling special effects of *2001: A Space Odyssey* to the emblematic images of man as a primordial beast evident in *The Shining*, *A Clockwork Orange*, and *Full Metal Jacket*, all of his films have an overpowering feel of perfectionism, and the Kubrick innovations and imaginations lent to his coldly brilliant films ensure that he'll remain in our cultural consciousness for a long time to come.

Four days after the final screening of what would be his last film, *Eyes Wide Shut*, Stanley died of a heart attack at 70, though, according to some fanaticists, things may have been a little less tidy than the newspapers reported. Apparently, because his swan song film broached the decadent and kinky underbelly of the rich and famous and served merely as a thinly veiled vehicle for exposing and embarrassing a secret "Illuminati" society concerned with One World Order, Stanley paid for the transgression with his life. He was snuffed. You can read all about it online, just below the stories about children raised by wolves.

Stanley is buried on the grounds of his own 200-acre estate, Childwickbury Manor near St. Albans, England. Marked by an indigenous smooth and weathered stone inscribed "Here lies our Stanley," his grave is in a little garden under the shade of a 150-year-old monkey puzzle tree. The stately fortress-like home and grounds, ringed by three sets of electric gates and a blizzard of notices warning of closed-circuit cameras and stiff prosecution, is not open to the public.

CHARLES KURALT

SEPTEMBER 10, 1934 – JULY 4, 1997

AT 25, CHARLES Kuralt was CBS' youngest-ever correspondent, and during the 1960s he cut his teeth on such choice assignments as Vietnam and Latin America, covering stories for which most hard-nosed reporters yearned. But, weary of hawks and doves, after just eight years Charles turned his attention to his own country and took to the road in a quest to tell the story of Smalltown, U.S.A. Eventually his poetic storytelling and curiosity led to the creation of *On The Road*, a leisurely TV news magazine that followed his travels.

As television's Everyman, he was gifted with the ability to see poetry where others saw the prosaic, ferreting out the stories from a motor home and logging up to 50,000 miles a year. Charles got the ideas for his quirky vignettes from viewers, or he found the items himself in snippets buried in rural newspapers. He was genuinely interested in the people he profiled, even the kookiest, and spoke with them without the slightest hint of condescension.

The balding and pudgy reporter was anything but intimidating and the persona helped him get to the heart of such stories as a high school basketball team that lost 127 straight games and a gas station that doubled as a poetry factory. Charles interviewed a country-song-singing dentist, a 93-year-old bricklayer, and a paraplegic auto mechanic. From unicyclists and professional wrestlers to lumberjacks, whittlers, and horse traders, Charles' stories celebrated America and its everyday people.

Too, Charles' patriotic love of America was readily apparent and, when he passed away at 62 of complications of lupus, it was fitting that he departed on the Fourth of July.

But after Charles' death, it emerged that the best oddball story might have been one he never told. For 29 years while his wife remained at their home in the concrete canyons of New York City, Charles maintained a second family in the wild canyons of Montana. He had met Patricia Shannon, the woman of his dreams, just a year after starting his *On The Road* travels, and he visited for two or three days every few weeks. He bought Shannon a $50,000 cottage in Ireland, put her children through college, gave her $400,000 to start a London business, and together they purchased acreage and a cabin along the Big Hole River and backpacked in the neighboring mountains.

Charles' infidelity came to light when Shannon instigated a court action against Charles' legal wife, Suzanna Kuralt, claiming that Charles had intended for her to keep a second Montana property. Suzanna died in October 1999 (and is faithfully buried alongside Charles) but Charles' daughters continued the court battle, which they lost in December 2000. Adding insult to injury, a judge ruled that the daughters were required to pay the estate taxes on the second Shannon property, even though it was ultimately awarded to Shannon.

Charles and Suzanna are buried at the Old Chapel Hill Cemetery, on the campus of the University of North Carolina in Chapel Hill, North Carolina.

GRAVE DIRECTIONS: At 351 South Road, enter the cemetery at the third entrance and walk 50 yards up the path. You'll see the Kuralt plot on the left.

LAUREL & HARDY

OLIVER HARDY
JANUARY 18, 1892 – AUGUST 7, 1957

STAN LAUREL
JUNE 16, 1890 – FEBRUARY 23, 1965

IN 1919 OLIVER Hardy, the fat one, began working as an all-purpose comic for the Hal Roach studio. In 1926 he was teamed with Stan Laurel, and a 30-year comedic partnership was initiated. In short time, the boys were hailed as the newest comedy sensation, and they eventually made more than 100 films. Their act was brilliantly simple: Hardy was an incapable buffoon, and Laurel was so exceedingly dumb that, in his eyes, Hardy was a genius.

The pair easily made the transition to talkies, as there never was a lot of dialogue anyway, and in 1932 Laurel and Hardy won an Academy Award for their short subject *The Music Box*. In that film, they struggled to deliver a piano to the top floor of a house on a hill only to have it topple down after they both let go of it to wipe their brows. A sort of film history was made when, instead of getting the laughs from the visual of a falling piano, the audience was treated to a prolonged close-up of their faces as they listened to the piano

STAN LAUREL
1890 – 1965
A MASTER OF COMEDY
HIS GENIUS IN THE ART OF
HUMOR BROUGHT GLADNESS
TO THE WORLD HE LOVED.

exaggeratedly crashing downward. Though the fare's premise seems painfully slight by the standards of today, film comedy had to start somewhere.

Oliver Hardy suffered a massive stroke in 1956 that left him partially paralyzed and never again able to speak. After a year in bed, he died at 65. Oliver was cremated and his ashes interred at Valhalla Memorial Park in North Hollywood, California.

GRAVE DIRECTIONS: Enter the park at 1061 Victory Boulevard, turn right, and proceed toward the fountain. On the right, before you get to the fountain, there is a low, stone wall called the Garden of Hope. On the opposite side Oliver's ashes are interred, and there is a plaque dedicated to his memory attached to the wall.

In 1965 Stan Laurel died at 74 after suffering a heart attack. It's reported that he was in bed and said to his nurse, "I wish I was skiing," and she asked, "Oh, Mr. Laurel, do you ski?" to which Stan replied, "No, but I'd rather be skiing than doing what I'm doing." And then he died.

Stan was cremated and his ashes buried at Forest Lawn Memorial Park in Hollywood Hills, California.

GRAVE DIRECTIONS: Enter the park at 6300 Forest Lawn Drive, get a map from the information booth, and drive to the Gardens of Heritage, which are across the drive from the Old North

Church. Bolted to the second wall, two levels behind the statue of Washington, is a white plaque that marks Stan's resting place.

HEATH LEDGER
APRIL 4, 1979 – JANUARY 22, 2008

BEFORE DANCING AND smirking his way through the teen comedy *Ten Things I Hate About You* and being feted worldwide for his performance as a lip-locking gay cowboy in *Brokeback Mountain*, Heath Ledger had worked hard at becoming a substantial actor.

He'd come from a well-to-do Perth family of high romantics and was named after Emily Brontë's Heathcliff. After picking up the game of chess at the all-boy Guildford Grammar Academy, Heath won Western Australia's junior championship at age 10. He soon switched gears and opted toward more physical endeavors such as skateboarding and surfing and, with the guiding hand of his race-car-driver father, won several go-kart champion titles.

Beyond all this, there was art, and at 11 Heath took the lead in a theater production of *Peter Pan*. Idolizing Gene Kelly, he taught himself to dance like his hero and at 15 choreographed a 60-strong Guildford team to the first all-boy victory at the Rock Eisteddfod Challenge, a national dance competition. During his teens, Heath acted in a series of forgettable Australian productions but one astute casting director finally took notice and in 1997 Heath had his big breakthrough as Conor, a loincloth-clad Celtic prince, in the medieval fantasy *Roar*. A strong performance as a low-grade hustler in *Two Hands* led to an audition for the lead part opposite teen-of-the-moment Julia Stiles in *Ten Things* and, as that high school romp took flight, so too did Heath's star power.

Scripts came pouring in for film's newest heartthrob but, instead of cashing in with a series of brainless teenage frolics, Heath assumed an uncompromising stance and waited out Hollywood for offers of more serious productions. The move paid off and in quick succession came prime roles in *The Patriot, Monster's Ball, A Knight's Tale*, and *Ned Kelly*. In 2007 Heath was one of six actors who embodied different aspects of Bob Dylan's life in *I'm Not There*. Predictably, Heath had become big news around town and high-profile flings with a variety of prospects including Heather Graham and Naomi Watts stoked the tabloid fires. Nonetheless, after *Brokeback Mountain*, Heath settled down with his on-screen wife from that film, Michelle Williams, though they were separated after just a couple years of matrimony.

In 2007 Heath locked himself away in a London hotel for a few weeks to develop the subtleties of the iconic twitches and cold-blooded laugh for his character impersonation of a murderous clown, The Joker, for the latest big-budget *Batman* sequel, *The Dark Knight*. Though it would turn out that he wouldn't survive even to see its release, his performance was the talk of audiences and he posthumously won both a Golden Globe and an Oscar for his efforts.

On a winter afternoon at his Manhattan apartment, Heath's masseuse found him cold and unresponsive on the floor near his bed and reacted in a fairly unusual manner—she called actress Mary-Kate Olsen in California. Olsen herself then phoned a New York–based security guard while, presumably, the masseuse madly searched for the phone book to find the number for 911. In any event, her failure to respond to the situation appropriately didn't matter as Heath was already a long time gone. Autopsy would demonstrate he'd suffered accidental "acute intoxication" from the combination of two strong painkillers.

At 28, Heath was cremated and his ashes scattered near his grandparents' gravesite in Karrakatta Cemetery, Perth, Australia.

BRUCE & BRANDON LEE

BRUCE LEE
NOVEMBER 27, 1940 – JULY 20, 1973

BRANDON LEE
FEBRUARY 1, 1965 – MARCH 31, 1993

WHILE HIS PARENTS were visiting the States, Li Jun Fan was born in San Francisco and, after claiming his American birth certificate, the happy family returned to Hong Kong. Obsessed with martial arts and bodybuilding, Li spent his adolescence turning his small body into a weapon and he appeared as a child actor in 20 movies. As he approached 18, his mother shipped him back stateside to keep him from fraternizing with his violent gang buddies and, after taking the name Bruce Lee, he got a job teaching the Wing Chun style of martial arts in Seattle. In 1964, at the first major American demonstration of kung fu, Bruce, an unknown, decimated his competitors and recast the martial arts culture.

After landing a role as Kato in the television series *The Green Hornet*, he attracted students like Steve McQueen and Kareem Abdul-Jabbar. By 1968 he had become the patron saint for the era's cult-of-the-body devotees; Bruce took vitamins and steroids, tortured himself with isometrics, experimented with electrical muscle stimulation, brewed ginseng teas, ate raw eggs, and drank beef blood. But despite his readiness to promote and embrace all that was American, Hollywood wouldn't embrace him, and Bruce soon returned to Hong Kong to make films.

By 1973 Bruce had made three kung fu flicks, *The Big Boss, Fists of Fury,* and *Way of the Dragon*, which, played back-to-back, can almost be mistaken for a single, eternally long exhibition of spin-kicks and flying leaps. On this side of the Pacific the films were roundly panned. One critic wrote that they make "the worst Italian western look like the most noble achievement of cinema," but they set box-office records in Asia, and Hollywood approached Bruce for a strictly American version.

Lest the producers change their minds Bruce cobbled together *Enter the Dragon* in a couple of months featuring the same tired sequences; a few dozen enemies attacked Bruce only to die as soon as he karate-chopped them. But three weeks before the film opened, Bruce died in Hong Kong at the apartment of actress Betty Ting Pei, who had a role in his next movie, *Game of Death*, which they were then filming. Bruce was at her apartment "discussing the script," as the story was later spun, and after he complained of a headache, Betty gave him a prescription painkiller, Equagesic. Bruce went to lie down in the bedroom, Betty was later unable to rouse him, and he died at the hospital later that night.

The coroner determined that Bruce had died of a "cerebral edema," a brain aneurysm, possibly prompted by an allergic reaction to the Equagesic. But of course Bruce's fans would have none of this. It was impossible for superhumans of Bruce's ilk to drop dead from a mere allergic reaction, or even an aneurysm, for that matter, and it was obvious, to them anyway, that his death was the result of some conspiracy. A choice motive was that Bruce had been murdered for flouting his traditional ancestors and giving away ancient fighting secrets to Westerners. For this, Bruce had been killed either by an undetectable Oriental poison or, by "the vibrating hand," a mysterious death touch that kills two years after it's applied.

In any event, at 32, Bruce was buried at Lakeview Cemetery in Seattle, Washington, and, 20 years later, his son, Brandon, met his own peculiar end.

Following in his father's footsteps, Brandon became a player in martial arts films, though by the time Brandon surfaced the genre had matured into a form that even viewers who weren't karate-chop aficionados could enjoy. His first role was in 1986's *Kung Fu: The Movie* and, after a handful of similar roles, filming for *The Crow* began in 1993.

A particular scene in that movie called for Brandon to be shot. The scene began and actor Michael Masee fired a gun containing a dummy bullet at Brandon, who collapsed to the floor exactly as the scene specified. But as the other actors continued playing out the remainder of the scene, it became apparent that Brandon's writhing on the floor was more than an act. Brandon really had been shot and he died of his wound the next day.

After an investigation, the accident was determined to have unfolded this way: For an earlier close-up scene that required the gun to be filmed being loaded, the gun was loaded with a dummy bullet. That is, the bullet had a slug (a projectile) for visual effect, but the bullet's casing had no gunpowder. However, when that dummy was taken out of the gun, its slug was dislodged from its casing, and the slug remained unnoticed within the gun's firing chamber. Next, a different kind of dummy bullet, the exact opposite of the previous dummy, was put into the firing chamber. This dummy bullet consisted only of a casing holding gunpowder for sound effect—it had no slug. The gunpowder of the second dummy bullet propelled the slug left behind by the first dummy bullet and, in effect, the two dummies conspired to produce one very smart, lethal bullet.

At 28, Brandon was buried alongside his father in Seattle.

GRAVE DIRECTIONS: At 1554 15th Avenue East, enter the cemetery and go to the top of the hill, where there is a circular road. Near this road's curb, on the side closer to the entrance, is the Lee plot.

VIVIEN LEIGH
NOVEMBER 5, 1913 – JULY 7, 1967

IN 1937 PRODUCER David Selznick began searching for an actress to play the part of the impetuous Southern belle, Scarlett O'Hara, in the film adaptation of Margaret Mitchell's epic love story, *Gone With the Wind*. After passing on hundreds of starry hopefuls, including Katharine Hepburn, Bette Davis, and Joan Crawford, Selznick became so frustrated that he started filming without a Scarlett. At the same time, the doe-eyed, British sweetheart Vivien Leigh was campaigning across town for the role of Cathy in *Wuthering Heights*, opposite leading man Laurence Olivier, with whom she was carrying on an affair. But Vivien was turned down for the role because she was unknown in America at the time. It became the ultimate irony that Vivien was instead cast as Scarlett O'Hara in *Gone With the Wind*, which premiered alongside *Wuthering Heights*, and completely eclipsed it at the Academy Awards for 1939. Upon *GWTW*'s premiere in January 1940, Vivien became America's newest darling and captured the Academy Award for Best Actress.

It was also in 1940 that Vivien and Laurence married, after they left their respective spouses. The couple acted together onstage and in films but, after miscarrying in 1944 and battling tuberculosis in 1945, Vivien became manic-depressive and their marriage became strained. As was customary for those times, Vivien underwent electroshock therapy to ease her depression, but the treatment seemed only to worsen her condition.

Vivien never really shook the tuberculosis, and it plagued her repeatedly, recurring to varying degrees for the remainder of her life. By 1960, when Laurence was long gone, her condition had substantially worsened and she developed a persistent, hacking cough. But even then, perhaps due to the breakup of her marriage, Vivien tried to rejuvenate her stage career. Her illness, however, changed her from the Scarlett O'Hara audiences expected to see, and her coughing prompted numerous absences. In May 1967, Vivien suddenly began to lose weight and cough up blood. Her tuberculosis had advanced considerably and she was ordered on bed rest. Finally, Vivien was found on her bedroom floor, dead of the disease that had drowned her lungs in fluid.

At 53, Vivien was cremated and her ashes scattered over the waters of the mill pond at her estate, Tickerage, outside of London in Blackboys, England.

JACK LEMMON
FEBRUARY 8, 1925 – JUNE 27, 2001

JOHN UHLER LEMMON III was born in an elevator; his mother went into labor during a bridge match and the closest she got to the delivery room was the hospital lift. Jack's father had high hopes that his anxious progeny would follow him into the doughnut business, but Jack was more interested in "the theayatuh," as he called it.

After a stint in the Navy, he graduated from Harvard University in 1947, and immediately took off for the bright lights of New York, where he supported himself mainly by playing piano in a local saloon. Seven years later Jack nabbed his first Hollywood role in *It Should Happen to You* and, after an exceedingly steep learning curve, he played the anxious-to-please Frank Pulver in *Mister Roberts* the next year and won the Oscar, firmly establishing his career. Next came a string of 15 comedies, including *Some Like It Hot* and *The Apartment*, but Jack ached to show what he could really do and, in 1962, he did; after his harrowing portrayal of an anguished, alcoholic husband in 1962's *Days of Wine and Roses*, roles were Jack's to pick and choose.

Though fans still seemed to love him most in comedic romps as one or another neurotic in anxious conflict with his better instinct, Jack's style matured and he particularly found his center in 1973 when he portrayed the desperately cornered garment maker, Harry Stoner, in *Save the Tiger*. After Jack played the lead in *The China Syndrome* in 1979, he was universally admired. After he nailed the part of the washed-up real-estate hotshot Shelly "The Machine" Levene in the brilliantly dark *Glengarry Glen Ross*, he became a vivid and permanent part of American pop culture.

Jack's vulnerability and wounded grace mirrored an uneasy generation's passage from eager upward mobility to embittered confusion borne of age and social upheaval. His public identified with his dubious characters that crossed the line, and it's hard to find anyone who flatly disliked him. His biographer summed it up nicely: "Everybody likes Jack. Attacking him would be like pulling a chair out from under your mother."

Of complications from cancer, Jack died at 76 in the company of his family.

He was buried at Westwood Memorial Park in Los Angeles, California.

GRAVE DIRECTIONS: Behind the office complex at 10850 Wilshire Boulevard, enter the cemetery, turn left at the office and, just after the chapel on the right, you'll see Jack's stone along the drive.

THE LONE RANGER & TONTO

JAY SILVERHEELS
MAY 26, 1918 – MARCH 5, 1980

CLAYTON MOORE
SEPTEMBER 14, 1914 – DECEMBER 28, 1999

CLAYTON MOORE AND Jay Silverheels are infinitely better-known by their on-screen names: the Lone Ranger and Tonto from the long-running television series, *The Lone Ranger*. The show debuted in 1949 as a descendant of a hit radio program of the same name, and it was one of the first shows to be filmed exclusively for television. Its premise was that the Lone Ranger was the sole Texas Ranger to survive an ambush by the vicious Hole-in-the-Wall gang. With his identity protected by a mask and his loyal American-Indian sidekick Tonto by his side, the Lone Ranger exhibited unparalleled integrity and bravery as a maverick ridding the Old West of its outlaws.

Clayton was offered the lead role after a stint as a high-flying aerialist in a circus troupe and working his way through the acting ranks into afternoon serials. Jay also had an athletic background; the full-blooded Mohawk Indian from Ontario had been a runner-up Golden Gloves boxing champion and played on the Canadian national lacrosse team. Upon landing in Hollywood in 1938, he secured work as a stuntman and extra, most of his roles earning him credit solely as "Indian."

The Lone Ranger ran for eight years and after its 1957 cancelation, Jay made occasional film appearances until he died of a heart attack in 1980, at 61. He was cremated and his ashes spread over the Six Nations of the Grand River Reserve near Brantford, Ontario.

Clayton never really gave up the role of the Lone Ranger when the series was canceled. For the rest of his days, Clayton thrived on a self-made Lone Ranger cottage industry, making countless appearances in the famous black mask championing the TV character's merits. In 1975, Jack Wrather, who actually owned the Lone Ranger rights, sued to prevent Clayton from making such personal appearances because a new Lone Ranger feature movie was in the works and Clayton no longer personified the youthful hero. In a court compromise, Clayton was forbidden from wearing the mask and he instead resorted to equally ridiculous mask-like sunglasses. The movie bombed and 10 years later, Clayton went back to wearing the real trademark mask.

In 1999, Clayton died of a heart attack at 85 and was buried at Forest Lawn Memorial Park in Glendale, California.

GRAVE DIRECTIONS: Enter the park at 1712 South Glendale Avenue, get a map at the information booth, and proceed to the area of the Freedom Mausoleum. In front of the mausoleum is the walled Garden of Everlasting Peace. Walk into this garden and you'll find Clayton's grave in the top row of the big grass area in front of the Morgenroth statue.

BELA LUGOSI
OCTOBER 20, 1882 – AUGUST 16, 1956

BELA LUGOSI WAS a serious and successful stage actor in his native Hungary for almost two decades before he moved to America in pursuit of a silent film career. In 1927 Bela garnered the lead in the Broadway production of *Dracula*, and three years later, Universal Pictures bought the rights. As the first huge horror hit of the sound era, the film *Dracula* was an instant sensation and the role made Bela, with his black cape, dark menacing eyes, and velvet voice, a star.

The next year Bela passed up an offer to play the lead role in *Frankenstein* and, unwittingly, gave Boris Karloff his big chance. From then on, the two actors were rivals for the public's attention as heir to the horror genre throne that had been vacated with the passing of Lon Chaney. Over the next 20 years, Bela appeared in dozens of horror films, from *White Zombie* to *Abbott and Costello Meet Frankenstein*. While plenty of them had very questionable scripts, others were just downright awful.

In 1953, after Bela's affinity for an occasional morphine hit had switched into full-on addiction and Hollywood wanted nothing to do with the 70-something-year-old has-been, he met up with the transvestite schlock director Edward D. Wood Jr., who today is ignobly known as the worst director of all time. Bela appeared in several of Wood's films, including 1955's *Bride of the Monster*, but after Bela's death, Wood cobbled together miscellaneous footage and made what is often called the worst film of all time, *Plan 9 from Outer Space*. For scenes in which Wood was unable to find pertinent footage of Bela, he employed his wife's chiropractor as Bela's double, his face completely obscured by the ridiculous cape.

In these later years, Bela had become increasingly strange and began taking his horror image rather seriously. He often gave interviews while lying in a coffin. In April 1955 Bela committed himself to a hospital to kick his morphine addiction and left in August, supposedly clean as a whistle. But Bela's days were numbered anyway and, just a few months after marrying his fifth wife, he died of a heart attack—a wooden stake or silver bullet wasn't necessary after all.

Bela was buried at Holy Cross Cemetery in Culver City, California, and, as he requested, he's wearing his Dracula cape. He died a pauper, but, supposedly, Frank Sinatra wrote a check to provide him a decent burial.

GRAVE DIRECTIONS: Enter the cemetery at 5835 Slauson Avenue, turn left, and start up the hill. A hundred yards on the left is the Grotto lawn and altar and, four rows from the altar, is Bela's grave.

JAYNE MANSFIELD
APRIL 19, 1933 – JUNE 29, 1967

JAYNE MANSFIELD TOOK her place in Hollywood as a caricature of the blonde stereotype starlet. Though a married mother at just 17, she parlayed her 40-22-34 curves into bit television parts, but superstardom on the order of Marilyn Monroe was her real goal and much of her career was an unending campaign of self-promotion.

During one memorable ploy, Jayne was "stranded" on a desert island. But her most successful gimmick was a carefully designed scheme that unfolded at a press junket to promote a new Jane Russell film, *Underwater*. On that day she "fell" into the pool while sunbathing, causing her bathing suit strap to break. Upon coming up for air her endowment was captured by the scrambling press. "I worried about becoming famous first, then an actress," Jayne later confessed in an interview.

Though her stunts were successful to a degree—she eventually secured a contract with Twentieth Century Fox—moviegoers never really went for Jayne's limited acting ability, and her resume is fleshed out with a string of flops. Her striking looks did help sell merchandise, however, and she promoted an array of products ranging from maple syrup to nylon sweaters to electric switches. Her ample proportions were not lost on *Playboy* magazine either, and Jayne was one of the first stars to take it off for the monthly.

Jayne later toured the country with a burlesque nightclub act that featured show tunes and comedic skits and climaxed with a striptease routine. In the early morning hours after she'd performed the act at the Gus Stevens Supper Club in Biloxi, Mississippi, Jayne and three of her children, plus her boyfriend and a driver, glided along a narrow country road (now Highway 90) on the way to New Orleans. The road became obscured by the white haze of a mosquito fogger and, unable to discern its presence, the 20-year-old driver slammed the Buick Electra into and under the slow-moving truck. The three adults in the front seat were killed instantly, but Jayne's three children asleep in the back were spared serious injury.

After a blonde bouffant wig was photographed lying on the ground at the accident scene, it became contemporary lore that Jayne had been decapitated but, for the record, though her death was gruesome, she was not actually beheaded. Her death certificate notes a "crushed skull with avulsion (forcible detachment) of cranium and brain," which in layman's terms means that her skull was cracked open and a piece of it and her brain were separated. Her "death car" has been exhibited in several far-flung museum collections.

At only 34, Jayne was buried at Fairview Cemetery in Pen Argyl, Pennsylvania.

GRAVE DIRECTIONS: At 1160 Middletown Road, enter the cemetery at the second entrance and go around the U-shaped drive. Two hundred feet before the stone pillared exit, you'll see Jayne's heart-shaped grave on the right.

GROUCHO MARX

OCTOBER 2, 1890 – AUGUST 19, 1977

AFTER CONQUERING BROADWAY in the 1920s, Groucho Marx and his four brothers moved to Hollywood and became a veritable comedy attack force, slinging a wild and anarchic style of humor at movie audiences, the likes of which had never been seen. With his trademark swallow-tailed coat, greasepaint mustache, and rolling, leering, depraved eyes, the intensely verbal Groucho was the key to the brothers' success in a legendary series of movies highlighted by such pictures as *Animal Crackers* and *A Night at the Opera*.

After the brothers broke up in 1949, Groucho became host of the radio and TV series *You Bet Your Life* and he elevated his quick wit into an art form. On one occasion, he asked a contestant her age and she replied, "I'm approaching 40," to which Groucho shot back, "From which direction?" On another program, a contestant developed stage fright and was unable to utter a word, to which Groucho delivered the now-infamous comment, "Either this man is dead, or my watch is stopped."

Groucho died of pneumonia at 86 and, after cremation, his ashes were interred at Eden Memorial Park in Mission Hills, California.

GRAVE DIRECTIONS: At 11500 Sepulveda Boulevard, enter the park, turn at the first right, and park your vehicle. Up the hill on your left is a large mausoleum that is divided into three sections. On the left-hand side of the middle section is the door to a columbarium and inside, at about eye level, are Groucho's cremains.

His brothers Chico, Gummo, and Harpo are buried at Forest Lawn Memorial Park in Glendale, California. In 1979, death took the last surviving Marx brother, Zeppo, and he was cremated.

WALTER MATTHAU

OCTOBER 1, 1920 – JULY 1, 2000

GRADUATING FROM HIGH school during the Depression, Walter Matuchanskavasky took a series of government jobs—as a forester in Montana, a gym instructor for the WPA, a boxing coach for policemen—before enlisting in the Army Air Corps and serving as a radio cryptographer during World War II. One of the senior officers on the base was none other than Jimmy Stewart and, after sneaking in to watch Jimmy do a morning briefing, Walter decided that he wanted to become an actor.

After the war, Walter took some acting lessons and, after a stint on Broadway, by 1955 was sharing film credits with some of the great stars of the day, including Burt Lancaster in *The Kentuckian* and Kirk Douglas in *Lonely Are the Brave*. But Walter really hit his stride in 1966 as an unscrupulous lawyer trying to win an insurance settlement opposite Jack Lemmon in *The Fortune Cookie*, for which he won an Oscar for best supporting actor.

That collaboration also marked the first of many memorable teamings with Lemmon. The duo, whose banter was as playful offscreen as on, worked together on some of Hollywood's funniest flicks, usually featuring Walter's character mercilessly tormenting Lemmon's. In addition to *Fortune Cookie*, the duo appeared in *The Front Page*, *Buddy, Buddy,* and *Grumpy Old Men*. But their most memorable face-off was in the 1968 movie version of Neil Simon's classic *The Odd Couple*, with Walter playing the disheveled sportswriter Oscar Madison to Lemmon's anal-retentive Felix Ungar.

"Every actor looks all his life for a part that will combine his talents with his personality," Walter once said. "*The Odd Couple* was mine. That was the plutonium I needed. It all started happening after that."

Despite professional triumphs, Walter faced trials in his personal life. He publicly admitted that his struggle with compulsive gambling had cost him an estimated $5 million over the years and he agreed with physicians that the strain of his gambling and heavy smoking had contributed to a heart attack suffered while filming *The Fortune Cookie* in 1966. Though he gave up his three-packs-per-day smoking habit, coronary bypass surgery came in 1976, he was hospitalized with double pneumonia in 1993, and in 1995 he underwent surgery to remove a non-malignant colon tumor. In typical form, Walter attributed his maladies to his bad eating habits: "If you eat only celery and lettuce, you won't get sick.... I like celery and lettuce, but I like them with pickles, relish, corned beef, potatoes, peas. And I like Eskimo Pies."

Despite health issues, Walter continued to work steadily, playing his trademark codger, an irritable ailing father, in his final film, *Hanging Up*.

Following a heart attack, America's favorite grumpy old man died at 79.

He was buried at Westwood Memorial Park, Los Angeles, California.

GRAVE DIRECTIONS: Behind the office complex at 10850 Wilshire Boulevard, enter the cemetery and turn left at the office. Pass the chapel, pass Jack Lemmon's grave, and, on the right after a few more plots, you'll see Walter's stone along the drive.

SAL MINEO
JANUARY 10, 1939 – FEBRUARY 12, 1976

SAL MINEO BECAME a teen idol after his breakout role in 1956's *Rebel Without a Cause*. By playing Plato, the switchblade-wielding juvenile delinquent cloaked in an aura of smoldering boyishness, Sal was transformed from a Bronx gang member and parochial-school dropout to an Academy Award nominee who received some 4,000 letters a week from adoring fans.

The next few years were lucrative for Sal; he had plenty of offers and appeared in numerous films, most notably *Exodus*, for which he was nominated for another Oscar. But once he matured from teen idol status, his best film offers were behind him and Sal was relegated to scraping out a living on stages in Los Angeles.

Late one evening after parking in the carport outside of his West Hollywood apartment, Sal was stabbed in the heart and, at 37, died on the sidewalk before the paramedics even arrived. With the absence of any apparent motive, the slaying went unsolved for two years until an inmate in a Michigan prison bragged that he'd killed Sal and that "it had been easy." In 1979 Lionel Williams was sentenced to 51 years, though he was released after just 18.

Despite a barrage of tabloid theories that the motive for Sal's murder was everything from a bad drug deal to a homosexual lovers' quarrel, the reason behind the killing has never been established, and now it's generally believed Sal was just the unlucky victim of a robbery gone wrong.

Sal is buried at the Gate of Heaven Cemetery in Hawthorne, New York.

GRAVE DIRECTIONS: Enter the cemetery at 10 West Stevens Avenue, turn right, and follow the main road up the hill. Bear left at the fork, make a right just before Section 2 (toward the stone tower), then turn right again at the next drive. A couple hundred feet on the right, Sal's grave is marked with a flat stone in front of the Donofrio mausoleum.

MARILYN MONROE
JUNE 1, 1926 – AUGUST 5, 1962

THE MOVIES HAVE lent a millennial shelf life to Marilyn Monroe's most perishable qualities of youth and beauty. Had she been born before the cameras rolled, she may have existed as only a Helen of Troy legend but, thanks to celluloid, her bumping and cooing will be here to greet the Second Coming. Media stars live forever, and Marilyn is their torchbearer.

Marilyn came into this life named Norma Jean, the daughter of a film cutter who flirted with insanity. Due to her mother's assorted delusions, Norma Jean spent most of her childhood in foster homes. At 16, when her then–foster family planned to move and could not take her with them, they arranged for her to marry a family friend, the 21-year-old James Dougherty. Before James left to serve during World War II, he secured Norma Jean a job at Lockheed and she became part of the home-front war effort, working in a division that made target planes.

At some point, a magazine team visited the plant to take inspiring propaganda shots and a bright-eyed, curly haired, brunette named Norma Jean Dougherty soon found herself on the magazine's cover. She quit her job, had corrective dental work, went on a diet, and had her dark, wool-tight curls straightened and platinumed. She divorced her husband, who had been absent for almost the entirety of their marriage, and Norma Jean became a popular photographer's model, her likeness gracing pin-up posters, advertisements, and pulp magazine covers.

Encouraged by success, Norma Jean aimed for a career in motion pictures. Despite her lack of acting experience, she found work and bounced from studio to studio, filling out the visual landscape of lightweight comedic romps as the fresh-faced Marilyn Monroe. After nude calendar photos of her emerged, Marilyn's star appeal soared and she participated fullbore in the promotion of her sex-symbol image. In 1953, she secured a place in media history when she graced the premiere issue of *Playboy* magazine. That sensation propelled Marilyn to the stratosphere.

Marilyn laid bare her life and begged the public to love her, and they did. Movie studios competed for Hollywood's newest sex kitten, and the deals came in fast sequence. Predictably, Marilyn most often played the hopelessly irresistible home-wrecker or the warm-hearted floozy in a series of romantic farces whose titles—*The Seven-Year Itch, Gentlemen Prefer Blondes*—predicated the storylines. But, because she wasn't a trained actress, the improbabilities of her movies' plots perfectly complemented her provocative bravado. In other films, particularly 1959's acclaimed *Some Like It Hot*, in which she played the lovelorn singer Sugar Kane, Marilyn's patent grandiosity and inimitable breathy singing style made an indelible mark.

In contrast to her successful professional career, Marilyn's affairs were unsteady, to say the least. Three heavily flashbulbed marriages and divorces, including those to Yankee clipper Joe DiMaggio and literary icon Arthur Miller, left her personal life a shambles, while tabloid tell-alls burst with abortions and off-duty trysts involving Frank Sinatra and multiple Kennedys. After her last two film releases flopped, a 30-something Marilyn must have wondered how much longer her sex-kitten status would last and, perhaps, she decided that stardom had become too much of a burden.

By August 1962 Marilyn was increasingly dependent on medication and was getting prescriptions from at least two doctors. Her housekeeper, Eunice Murray, had been sleeping at Marilyn's Brentwood home at the request of Marilyn's psychiatrist and, one evening, Eunice found Marilyn dead in bed. Though the coroner declared her death a suicide from ingestion of nearly 50 Nembutal sleeping pills, as well as a quantity of another sleeping potion, chloral hydrate, Marilyn's death has since been otherwise variously attributed to accidental overdose, political necessity, and a mob hit.

After more than 300 biographies, countless documentaries, and a postage stamp, the debate over the "real" Marilyn and her untimely death has yet to be resolved. Meanwhile, adoring fans cling to the memory of the beloved actress who may have gotten some of what she wanted but not all of what she needed.

Marilyn was laid to rest at Westwood Village Memorial Park in Los Angeles, California.

GRAVE DIRECTIONS: Enter behind the office complex at 10850 Wilshire Boulevard. As you stand in the cemetery yard and look toward the cemetery office, on your far left is a series of small rooms with crypts. Marilyn's crypt is several yards to the left of the Room of Prayer.

DUDLEY MOORE
APRIL 19, 1935 – MARCH 27, 2002

AFTER LEAVING OXFORD University in 1958, Dudley Moore performed as a cabaret pianist and toured widely before founding the Beyond the Fringe comedy revue with partner Peter Cook.

The troupe's antics opened the door to television, which, in turn, led to a screen debut in *The Wrong Box* in 1966. Dudley wrote, starred in, and composed the score for his next film, *30 Is a Dangerous Age*, two years later.

In 1979 Dudley found a wider audience when he played a composer grappling with a midlife crisis in the hit movie *10* and, with his diminutive stature, he became one of Hollywood's most unlikely stars. Afterward he appeared in a string of comedies and is best remembered as the lovable, drunken playboy in the 1981 box-office smash *Arthur*. Prompted by some fans to consider more serious fare, "Cuddly Dudley" once remarked, "I would love to do serious roles, but I'm just not built that way."

In the early 1990s Dudley seemed to become unreliable and began having trouble remembering lines. It was widely believed that he was spiraling downward due to alcoholism or a drug problem and in 1995, fed up with his inconsistency, Barbra Streisand fired him from the movie *The Mirror Has Two Faces*.

In 1997 Dudley had an extended hospital stay after a stroke and open-heart surgery, and it was then discovered that his erratic behavior didn't stem from substance abuse after all. Instead it had been caused by a rare and incurable condition called Progressive Supranuclear Palsy (PSP), similar to Parkinson's disease. In the last years of his life, the disease slowly robbed Dudley of his faculties; his vision became hazy, his motor control was impaired, and his speech slurred. Eventually, even swallowing became difficult.

At 66, Dudley died of pneumonia, a complication of PSP, and was buried at Hillside Cemetery in Scotch Plains, New Jersey.

GRAVE DIRECTIONS: Enter the cemetery at 1401 Woodland Avenue and continue past the office. Bear left and shortly you'll see Section D3 on your left, where Dudley's proud stone is easily found.

AUDIE MURPHY
JUNE 20, 1924 – MAY 28, 1971

AUDIE MURPHY WAS the most decorated American combat soldier of World War II. He received 28 medals, including the Medal of Honor and three Purple Hearts, and later parlayed his war-hero status into a Hollywood career.

But in deference to the untold millions who also dedicated themselves to that war, it's important to point out that Audie Murphy wasn't the bravest or most courageous—he was the most decorated. He was exactly like everyone else who gallantly fought for his country but he lived to tell about it, unlike many of his fellow patriots, and he even gained celebrity from it. By that measure, then, we should say that Audie Murphy was a brave and courageous soldier, but if we wish to apply a superlative, then perhaps we should say only that he was the luckiest.

After the war, *Life* magazine ran a cover story on Audie's exploits and actor James Cagney became convinced that Audie's looks and persona, as well as his status as a war hero, could make him a star. Audie was invited to Hollywood and, after a few lean years, Cagney's hunch proved right and Audie's career took off. His earliest films were war movies but by the 1950s he moved from the genre, barely, and the majority of his roles were in Westerns.

Critics generally agree that Audie's best film performance was in Stephen Crane's Civil War epic, *The Red Badge of Courage*, but the most popular of his 44 films was his autobiographical *To Hell and Back*. The movie was so popular in fact, that after its release by Universal Pictures in 1955, that studio did not have a higher-grossing picture until 1975's blockbuster film *Jaws*.

With varying success, Audie branched into other arenas as well. Horse racing gained his attention, especially its gambling aspects, and he eventually became a racehorse owner and breeder. Remarkably, Audie also had a talent for songwriting, and his songs have been recorded by such renowned performers as Dean Martin, Charley Pride, and Roy Clark.

Plagued with insomnia and depression, Audie suffered from what is now called post-traumatic stress disorder. The condition was then known as "battle fatigue," which implied that its effects would wear off with time and rest. But decades after WWII had ended, many veterans, including Audie, could find no respite. In his celebrity, Audie was candid about his battle-fatigue problems and made a public call for the United States government to study the emotional impact of war and to address its effects.

At 46, Audie and five others died when their plane crashed into the side of a mountain near Blacksburg, Virginia. Contrary to popular belief, Audie was not the pilot of that plane. Although he did hold a pilot's license and once owned his own plane, on that tragic day he was merely a passenger on a chartered flight.

Audie was buried at Arlington National Cemetery in Arlington, Virginia.

GRAVE DIRECTIONS: Park in one of the lots off of Memorial Avenue, get a map at the information booth, and then walk to

Memorial Drive. With the Tomb of the Unknown Soldier behind you, Audie's grave is in front of you in Section 13.

THE NELSONS
OZZIE NELSON
MARCH 20, 1906 – JUNE 3, 1975

RICKY NELSON
MAY 8, 1940 – DECEMBER 31, 1985

HARRIET NELSON
JULY 18, 1914 – OCTOBER 2, 1994

IN 1952 THE eight-year-old radio program *The Adventures of Ozzie and Harriet* debuted as a television show and over the next 14 seasons and 435 episodes, the Nelsons became America's ideal nuclear family. The most remarkable aspect of the slow-paced, light comedy was that the on-screen Nelson household was portrayed by the real-life Nelson family, which comprised the husband-and-wife team of Ozzie and Harriet, and their two sons, Ricky and David. Viewers especially took to the boys, who, before the viewers' very eyes, bloomed through pubescence, dated lucky teenage girls, and eventually married and had children of their own, all while the cameras kept rolling.

From his first appearance, the wisecracking kid brother, Ricky, was the show's most popular character, and his trademark line, "I don't mess around, boy," became a catchphrase. On a 1957 telecast, Ricky sang the popular Fats Domino hit "I'm Walkin'," which became a real-life million-seller, and Ricky began a new chapter of his career as America's first "teen idol," the phrase coined by *Life* magazine.

Ricky's new popularity was, of course, engendered by the show, but it turned out that he actually was possessed of some genuine talent. Over the next half-dozen years he had a number of teen-angst, rockabilly-flavored pop hits, including "Travelin' Man," "Lonesome Town," and "Hello, Mary Lou," but the Beatles soon stole Ricky's fans, and his career ebbed during the mid-'60s. Moving into a smoother form of country rock, in October 1971 he gigged a bill at Madison Square Garden with a number of other 1950s acts. But he was booed practically off the stage by a crowd that wanted to hear oldies; they didn't pay to see a long-haired, rockin' Ricky Nelson in bell-bottoms. Devastated, he reflected on the experience with a new track, "(I Went to a) Garden Party," which became a Top 10 hit. Ricky's talents were ultimately legitimized in 1987 when he was inducted into the Rock & Roll Hall of Fame, albeit posthumously.

In 1983 Ricky purchased a vintage DC-3 that had been previously owned by Jerry Lee Lewis, and was dubbed the "flying bus" because of its sluggishness and its propensity for mechanical failure. After leaving Alabama for a New Year's Eve concert in Dallas, Ricky, age 45, his new fiancée (fortunately for viewers, Ricky's divorce from his first wife had occurred after the TV series was canceled), and four members of the Stone Canyon Band were killed when the plane caught fire and was forced to crash-land in DeKalb, Texas. Upon landing, the passengers were trapped by a fire that raced through the cabin, and they all perished in its flames, though the pilot and copilot managed to escape through the cockpit window. Early press reports suggested that drug usage, specifically the free-basing of cocaine, might have played a role in the airplane's fire, but the National Transportation Safety Board conclusively determined that the fire was caused by a malfunctioning gas heater.

After *The Adventures of Ozzie and Harriet* ended its run in 1966, Ozzie and Harriet retreated from the limelight and made only occasional benefit appearances. At 69, Ozzie died after a bout with cancer, and Harriet passed away at 80 of congestive heart failure.

Ozzie, Harriet, and Ricky are all buried at Forest Lawn Memorial Park in Hollywood Hills, California.

GRAVE DIRECTIONS: Enter the park at 6300 Forest Lawn Drive, get a map from the information booth, and drive to the Revelation section. Across from where Crystal Lane intersects Evergreen Drive, walk up the grass hill and count 13 rows to find Ozzie's and Harriet's markers. Ricky's marker is two rows farther up the hill and it's engraved with his given name, Eric Hilliard Nelson.

PAUL NEWMAN
JANUARY 26, 1925 – SEPTEMBER 26, 2008

IN CONTRAST TO the defiant and sullen rebel as defined by James Dean or Marlon Brando, Paul Newman re-created the American male as a likable renegade, a strikingly handsome, high-spirited figure of steely blue-eyed sincerity. Through dozens of roles, from the self-destructive convict in *Cool Hand Luke* and the amicable bank robber just trying to get along in *Butch Cassidy and the Sundance Kid* to the well-heeled, middle-aged liquor sales-man in *The Color of Money* and, finally, as an affable yet deadly gangster boss in *Road to Perdition*, Paul achieved what most of his peers found impossible: remaining a charismatic major star well into old age even as he redefined himself as more than a Holly-wood celebrity. Paul abhorred the majesty of fame and especially mocked his sex-symbol status, maintaining that his personality was actually closest to the vulgar, second-rate hockey coach he played in *Slap Shot*.

Teamed at one time or another with virtually every other great actor and director of the last 50 years, Paul on occasion also worked with his wife and fellow Oscar winner, Joanne Woodward, with whom he had one of Hollywood's rare long-term marriages. "I have steak at home, so why go out for hamburger?" he famously commented when asked if he was tempted to stray.

But even the movies, occasional stage role, and all the ce-lebrity weren't enough for him. As an amateur race-car driver, albeit one with particularly deep pockets, he won several Sports Car Club of America national driving titles and even competed at Daytona as a 70th birthday present to himself. Stumping for liberal causes, he earned a spot on Richard Nixon's enemies list and wryly classified the distinction as "the highest single honor I've ever received."

In 1982, he and his neighbor started a company to market a salad dressing Paul had created and bottled for friends at Christmas. Thus was born Newman's Own, a multimillion-dollar brand that's since expanded to include lemonade, pop-corn, spaghetti sauce, pretzels, and wine, to name a few. All of the company's profits, some $490 million to date, have been donated to charity including a significant amount for Newman's so-called Hole in the Wall Gang Camps, which provide free summer recreation for children with cancer. Several years before the establishment of Newman's Own, Paul's only son, Scott, died at 28 of a drug overdose, and Paul's charitable monument to him is the Scott Newman Center, which seeks to prevent drug abuse through education.

At 83, Paul died of cancer. He was cremated and his ashes remain with his family.

DANA PLATO

NOVEMBER 7, 1964 – MAY 8, 1999

AT 13 YEARS old, Dana Plato won the role of Kimberly Drummond, the daughter of a wealthy New York businessman who takes in two disadvantaged boys on the sitcom *Diff'rent Strokes*. Written out of the program six years later when she became pregnant, Dana hoped to return after giving birth, but the show was canceled before she was able to make her comeback.

Having sampled fame, Dana wanted more and was dismayed that she was unable to find new acting work. Dana spent the next 15 years chasing an ever-elusive dream, and the tragedy of her life was the self-destructive path she took in her quest to get back to her fame. After *Diff'rent Strokes*, Dana appeared in low-budget films like *Bikini Beach Race*, and to shed what she felt was her teenage girl image, shed her clothes for *Playboy* magazine in 1989. By 1991, battling alcohol and drug problems, Dana was handed a five-year probation sentence after an armed robbery of a Las Vegas video store; the following year she was arrested again for forging Valium prescriptions.

The truth is, Dana was never a very good actress, and once her arrests and substance-abuse problems became tabloid fodder, an acting career was highly unlikely. Everyone seemed to know that except for Dana, and she continued to languish on the fringes, always seeking a reentry point. Finally, after she starred in a lesbian soft-porn movie in 1997, any hopes of a legitimate acting career were gone, and, soon, so was her life.

In 1999 Dana and her fiancé, Robert Menchaca, were living in a Florida RV park when Dana, still hoping for an acting comeback, secured an appearance on Howard Stern's radio program. After that, she flew to Robert's parents' home in Oklahoma, where Robert was waiting for her with the Winnebago. The next evening, Robert, seemingly distraught, called 911 to report that Dana had retired to the Winnebago to take a nap but was now unresponsive. Paramedics arrived but it was too late. Dana was dead at 34.

In an odd twist it was learned that Robert had actually taken pictures of Dana as she lay dying because he thought she was "snoring funny." Family members requested that Dana be autopsied to find out if perhaps foul play was involved—after all, it didn't seem that someone's death rattle could be mistaken for an odd snore. An autopsy and an investigation were conducted but authorities found no evidence of foul play.

Dana's death was ultimately ruled a suicide by multi-drug intoxication.

She was cremated and her ashes scattered in the Pacific Ocean.

ROBERT REED

OCTOBER 19, 1932 — MAY 12, 1992

ROBERT REED WAS a classically trained actor whose early credits included starring roles in a number of Broadway productions, most notably *Barefoot in the Park*. His TV acting debut came in 1961, playing a young attorney in the courtroom drama *The Defenders*.

As part of Paramount's stable of contract players, in 1969 Robert was cast as quintessential family man Mike Brady in the sitcom *The Brady Bunch*. But as a dramatic actor, he often lacked enthusiasm for the role and wasn't always comfortable with the show's gags and gimmicks. Still, *The Brady Bunch* and its syrupy, albeit charming, view of suburban family life enjoyed a successful, five-year run. It was canceled when the Brady child actors physically outgrew their roles but since then, through endless syndication, the popularity of the series has swelled to a phenomenal level.

Few were aware of it but, as loving husband Mike Brady, Robert was a bit out of his element. "I'm not a family man," he once confessed.

Indeed. When Robert died of colon cancer at 59, television's tawdry sleuth Geraldo Rivera obtained a copy of his death certificate and learned that AIDS had been a "significant condition contributing to (Robert's) death." Geraldo tracked down a few of Robert's longtime confidants, including a bartender who waited on Robert for 30 years at a gay nightspot and, on his *Now It Can be Told* tabloid television show, Geraldo announced that Robert had been gay. Some called Geraldo's tactics unconscionable and others made comments that can't be reprinted here, but finally it all made sense.

Convinced that his career would be ruined if it became known that he was gay, Robert had lived a lonely life of one-night stands with sex-for-hire partners. Remote and standoffish, he became an expert at small talk and effortlessly deflected innocent inquiries about his personal life. Robert so effectively kept his homosexuality a secret that even most *Brady* cast members were blindsided by the development.

At 59, Robert was buried at Memorial Park Cemetery in Skokie, Illinois.

GRAVE DIRECTIONS: Enter the cemetery at 990 Gross Point Road, turn left after the office and follow this drive for several hundred yards. On the right you'll see the Memento Mori Chapel and then, on the left, is a sign marking the "1-9 Annex" section. Turn left just before this section and look for the Ayersman stone on your right. Robert's grave is nine rows behind the Ayersman plot.

CHRISTOPHER REEVE
SEPTEMBER 25, 1952 – OCTOBER 10, 2004

DANA REEVE
MARCH 17, 1961 – MARCH 6, 2006

THE TALL SQUARE-JAWED actor Christopher Reeve was perfectly suited for his big-screen role as the "Man of Steel" and millions of fans will always remember him as cinema's modern-day Superman. But to countless others, Christopher is renowned more for real-life heroics and inspiration, a powerful proponent who encouraged scientists and politicians to work together in developing cures for neurological disorders.

After graduating from Cornell and studying at Juilliard, where he roomed with Robin Williams, Christopher made his Broadway debut as Katharine Hepburn's grandson in *A Matter of Gravity*. Soon came an offer of a screen test for the starring role in a big-screen revival of what would prove to be the blockbuster movie of 1978, *Superman*. Nailing the test, the relatively unknown actor won the part and, by the time of the third sequel in the chart-busting series nine years later, the strapping actor had become a major box-office draw. Maturing immeasurably, he won audiences' respect not only for his role as the famous action hero, but also for work between *Superman* sequels, most particularly as a love-struck time-traveler opposite Jane Seymour in the cult classic *Somewhere in Time*.

By the late 1980s Christopher had grown weary of the Hollywood lifestyle and relocated to Massachusetts, closer to his roots. There he met a singer named Dana Morosini and they were wed in 1992.

A superb athlete, Christopher was an accomplished sailor, skier, and scuba diver and, after earning his pilot's license at 24, flew solo across the Atlantic twice in a small plane. By the 1990s, horses had become his passion and, in May 1995, he was taking part in a jumping competition when his horse, Eastern Express, balked and threw him. Christopher landed headfirst and his spinal cord was damaged high in his neck. The signals to keep his body alive were instantly cut off; he couldn't move his limbs, feel his body, or breathe. Prompt medical attention saved his life, but he was now a quadriplegic.

In the days after the accident he contemplated suicide but was dissuaded by Dana and together they turned the tragedy into a legacy, crisscrossing the country advocating for the disabled. Especially wrenching were Capitol Hill appearances in which the wheelchair-bound former athlete pleaded for the use of embryonic stem cells in research so that, just maybe, he and others like him might walk again.

Later, as Christopher's condition stabilized, he returned to work, directing 1997's *In the Gloaming* and starring the following year in a modern remake of the Hitchcock thriller *Rear Window*. Dana caught the performance bug again too. She co-hosted the daily talk show *Lifetime Live* and earned acting credits on *Law & Order* and *All My Children* as well.

After developing a systemic infection from a pressure wound, which is a common complication for people living with paralysis, Christopher died of cardiac arrest at 52.

In a heartbreaking twist of fate, less than a year after Christopher's passing, Dana publicly announced that she had been diagnosed with lung cancer despite having never smoked a day in her life. Though a sympathetic public rallied around Dana and she wore a brave face in spite of her grim prognosis, it seems too that perhaps she had grown weary of the calamities that befell her family: "It's another journey," she said. "And I'm ready to be finished with the journeys." Seven months later her journey finished. Dana and Christopher were each cremated and their ashes remain with their families.

GEORGE REEVES
JANUARY 5, 1914 – JUNE 16, 1959

THOUGH GEORGE REEVES was an accomplished film and play actor, he's certainly best known for his role as the original Superman during the six-season run of the 1950s television series. But unlike the invincible hero he portrayed, George was mortal and, at 45 years old, just three days before he was to be wed, he was killed by a single gunshot wound to the head. His death has been the subject of endless speculation because, though police have always considered his demise a suicide, there are a number of puzzling factors.

On the evening of his death, George was entertaining his fiancée and a few friends in his lavish Hollywood home when he reportedly felt tired and went upstairs by himself to his bedroom. After about 30 minutes, the guests heard a gunshot and George was found dead, sprawled nude on his bed with a bullet hole in his right temple. The death was ruled a suicide because the houseguests could provide no other explanation, and there was no sign of an intruder or forced entry.

However, no suicide note was found and, when George was lifted from the bed by authorities, the bullet's shell casing was found to be *under* him. Furthermore, the gun was found on the floor between his feet, and no fingerprints were found on it. There were no powder burns on his head wound, implying that the gun was held at least several inches from his head at the time it was fired, which is unusual for a suicide, and the police were not called for at least a half an hour after the death.

George was cremated and his ashes interred at Mountain View Cemetery in Altadena, California.

GRAVE DIRECTIONS: Enter the cemetery at 2400 North Fair Oaks Avenue, bear right, and, at the first opportunity, turn right again. Park in the lot and walk into the Pasadena Mausoleum, then turn immediately left into the columbarium. George's ashes rest in the seventh niche on the right, at about waist height.

JOHN RITTER
SEPTEMBER 17, 1948 – SEPTEMBER 11, 2003

BORN INTO SHOW business as the son of singing cowboy star Tex Ritter and actress Dorothy Fay, the student body president and class clown of Hollywood High School spent his summers touring fairgrounds and rodeos where his father performed.

Graduating from university in 1971 with a degree in drama, John first earned household familiarity with his role as the minister on *The Waltons*. In 1977, though, his star arced when he won a lead role as Jack Tripper, a goofy, closet-heterosexual bachelor with an uncanny knack for pratfalls in the *Three's Company* sitcom. With Ritter's character amid two great-looking, curvy roommates living downstairs from their leering landlord and his sex-starved wife, some found the show an empty-headed waste of time but, as a vehicle for sexual innuendo and temptation, it skyrocketed, becoming one of the highest-rated programs in television. John regularly rose above his material and carved an identity, prompting movie roles including *Sling Blade* and

Problem Child. In 2002 his career enjoyed a major resurgence as he played the starring role of Paul Hennessey in the family sitcom *8 Simple Rules for Dating My Teenage Daughter*.

One day on the set, John felt nauseous and light-headed so he relaxed in his dressing room for a while. Feeling worse a few hours later, and now vomiting too, he was rushed to the hospital across the street—in fact, the very hospital where he had been born almost 55 years earlier. Tests showed abnormalities consistent with a heart attack and doctors ordered anticoagulants and planned a cardiac catheterization. But John's condition only worsened and it was then learned he had suffered an aortic dissection, a tear in the heart's chief aorta. A "Code Blue" was sounded and, though doctors worked feverishly, they ultimately were unsuccessful in saving the actor's life.

He was buried at Forest Lawn Memorial Park in Hollywood Hills, California.

GRAVE DIRECTIONS: Enter the park at 6300 Forest Lawn Drive, get a map from the information booth, and drive to the Gardens of Heritage, which are across the drive from the Old North Church. Walk up two levels behind the statue of Washington, turn right, and go through the door in the stone wall into the next garden. Around the other side of the low stone wall on your left, John's grave is in the lawn at Number 1622.

GENE RODDENBERRY
AUGUST 19, 1921 – OCTOBER 24, 1991

AS A DECORATED B-17 pilot who flew 89 combat missions during World War II, Gene Roddenberry's stories and essays written during spare moments in the South Pacific were published in newspapers and magazines. After the war, Gene studied literature at Columbia University and became a commercial airline pilot for Pan Am. But in 1948, after an engine fire forced Gene to crash-land into the Syrian desert, killing 38 of the craft's 46 passengers, he decided to pursue writing full-time. Gene moved to Los Angeles and, supplementing his initially meager income by working for the LAPD as department spokesman, Gene eventually attracted interest in his screenplays.

By 1953, Gene had left the LAPD and was writing full-time. He sold scripts for numerous television productions, including *Dragnet* and *Goodyear Theatre* and, as head writer for *Have Gun Will Travel*, Gene won an Emmy. For four years beginning in 1960, Gene produced *The Lieutenant*, which spawned the wildly popular boy's doll G.I. Joe. Despite all these accomplishments, though, Gene will be forever remembered for taking generations of viewers on a journey into "space, the final frontier" as creator and producer of the television series *Star Trek*.

As a science-fiction devotee, Gene saw similarities between space explorers and American pioneers, and he envisioned a science-fiction television series that would feature continuing characters just as the popular *Wagon Train* Western series had. In 1966, Gene presented his idea of a "wagon train to the stars" to a culture whose schoolchildren practiced nuclear attack drills and whose World's Doomsday Clock was set at just 12 minutes to midnight. *Star Trek* initiated the notion that anything was possible, fearsome technologies had righteous worth, man was inherently noble, the future was full of hope, and both the horizon and our destiny were infinite.

Star Trek's optimistic view of the future found an adoring mainstream audience while it's fanatical cult faction took on a life all its own. Aboard the *Starship Enterprise*, the dauntless Captain Kirk and his pointy-eared comrade, Mr. Spock, became cultural icons that spawned a major entertainment industry. Legions of zealots known as "Trekkies" inspired a cottage industry, flocking to conventions dressed as out-of-this-world travelers to socialize with other intergalactic pilgrims and debate the merits of such futuristic hardware as "transporter beams" and "phaser guns."

The magnitude of the *Star Trek* phenomenon surprised everyone. And today, after four sequel television series, numerous feature films, dozens of books, and countless other forms of merchandising, it shows no signs of slowing. Even Gene never imagined such a future. Instead, he wished merely to "demonstrate that television need not be violent to be exciting. Neither promiscuity, greed, or jealousy have a place in *Star Trek*."

Gene died of a massive blood clot and heart attack at 70.

He was cremated and, in April of 1997, a bit of his ashes, along with those of Timothy Leary and 22 other space enthusiasts, were blasted into space from Vandenberg Air Force Base in the world's first space funeral. Celestis, a Texas-based company, organizes such ventures and piggybacks the ashes, sealed in lipstick-sized capsules, aboard commercial satellites. On May 20, 2002, after 28,132 orbits around the earth, the capsules reentered the atmosphere over Papua New Guinea and burned up in a fiery finale.

FRED ROGERS

MARCH 20, 1928 – FEBRUARY 27, 2003

FOR 30 YEARS, Fred McFeely Rogers came through his front door and into our living rooms singing, "It's a beautiful day in the neighborhood," as the unlikely television star of his easy-paced children's program *Mister Rogers' Neighborhood*. Despite a complete lack of animation on Mister Rogers' part, and "action" that consisted of either a tour through the Neighborhood of Make-Believe on a cheesy little trolley or maybe, if you were lucky, a low-budget puppet show, the program won the hearts of millions, and today, one of Mister Rogers' signature sweaters hangs in the Smithsonian.

The key, of course, was Fred Rogers himself, a caring fatherly figure who always has time for children in spite of an increasingly busy world outside. And when Mister Rogers addressed his young viewers with his safe and moderated voice, they responded in kind and flocked to their unhurried cardigan-clad mentor. From the security of his comfortable little home, he taught children simple, soothing lessons about life's ups and downs including the importance of sharing, how to conduct yourself if you happen to get angry, and even why it's silly to fear the bathtub, assuring the kids they'd never be washed down the drain.

And by all accounts, Fred's persona was no act. There are no stories of him turning into a raging tyrant behind the scenes and it seems that off the air he really was the same soft-spoken and

earnest person that millions of children, and not just a few adults, admired. Though he was an ordained minister, Fred was careful never to introduce religious beliefs into the show, though he did genuinely believe his lot was to be part of the drama of loving and serving people. *Mister Rogers' Neighborhood* became the vehicle for teaching kids how to love themselves and others, and for learning the lesson that compassion and kindness never fall out of style.

Admittedly, it all sounds kind of schmaltzy, but it seems he really was onto something. After his death from stomach cancer, thousands and thousands of heartfelt condolences arrived in the mail from viewers young and old, and I think this right-to-the-point note from a seven-year-old offered the best summation of good old Mister Rogers: "You taught me to be nice to others and to hang up my coat."

At 74, Fred was buried at Unity Cemetery in Latrobe, Pennsylvania.

GRAVE DIRECTIONS: Enter the cemetery at 114 Chapel Lane, turn left at the chapel, and then take the second right. At the next intersection you'll see the Given mausoleum on the corner and, though you can't enter it, you can sneak a peek at Mister Rogers' hiding place by peering inside.

ROY ROGERS & DALE EVANS

ROY ROGERS
NOVEMBER 5, 1911 – JULY 6, 1998

DALE EVANS
OCTOBER 31, 1912 – FEBRUARY 7, 2001

DURING THE 1940S, '50s, and '60s, the Roy Rogers and Dale Evans husband-and-wife, cowboy-cowgirl entertainment team was the most recognized anywhere. They made some 400 recordings and 27 films together, had a hit television program, and their personas were immortalized on everything from Western wear to lunch pails. But even before their union, both Roy and Dale had separately enjoyed their own successes.

As Leonard Franklin Slye, Roy got started in the music business by playing at square dances with his cousin Stanley. In 1937 he became Roy Rogers and his big break came the following year when he was cast to replace Gene Autry in a film following a contract dispute. With his trusty palomino Trigger under him and his dog Bullet at their side, Roy made scores of films and gained an enormous following for his gallant exploits in the then-popular musical-Western genre that romanticized the Old West.

As Frances Smith, Dale took a more indirect route to show-biz, but ultimately her singing and songwriting abilities were recognized. Pregnant at 14, she eloped with an older school-mate and, after their son's birth, took a secretarial position at a Memphis radio station. Upon discovering she could sing, the station manager put her on the air and she eventually ended up as Dale Evans, a jazz singer in Chicago supper clubs during the music's heyday.

After a stint as a USO trouper, she found herself a California agent and repackaged the Dale Evans persona for the Hollywood publicity machine. Seven years were shaved off her age, she no longer wore a wedding band, and her selfless devotion to her teenage brother, Tommy, was extolled. (He was, of course, actually the son she'd had at 14.)

In 1944 Dale was offered a role alongside Roy in *The Yellow Rose of Texas*, and the Western film showcased an irresistible chemistry between them. The on-screen chemistry quickly spilled over to an offscreen friendship and romance and, after Dale divorced her third husband and Roy's wife, Arlene, died following complications from childbirth, the two were married on New Year's Eve 1946.

As the "King and Queen of the Cowboys," Roy and Dale became emblematic of all-American family values and domestic solidarity and found great success in film and records. *The Roy Rogers Show* aired in 1951. It ran until 1957 and was then revamped and reintroduced in 1962 as *The Roy Rogers and Dale Evans Show*. Dale was an especially prolific songwriter—she claimed more than 200 credits in her lifetime—and she penned the show's theme song, "Happy Trails."

In contrast to the couple's blissful professional life, their family life was marked by tragedy; the only child they had together died from complications of Down Syndrome before her second birthday and though they eventually adopted four other children, one died in a 1964 church bus accident, and the following year another choked to death.

As an active Evangelical lay minister, Dale was inspired by the tragedies to write moving motivational books, and her first, *Angel Unaware*, was applauded for raising acceptance of retarded children in an era when most were institutionalized their entire lives. She wrote a total of 20 inspirational and religious-themed books and they led to a Christian program, *A Date With Dale*, that she hosted until her death.

Roy died of congestive heart failure at 86 in 1998, and Dale followed him three years later at the age of 88.

They are buried at Sunset Hills Memorial Park in Apple Valley, California.

GRAVE DIRECTIONS: Enter the cemetery at 24000 Waalew Road and Roy and Dale's plot is immediately on the left beside the reflecting pools.

TIM RUSSERT
MAY 7, 1950 – JUNE 13, 2008

A POWERHOUSE OF broadcast journalism, Tim Russert made interviewing both an art form and a contact sport. After attending Woodstock "in a Buffalo Bills jersey with a case of beer," and putting himself through law school by whatever means required (including earning a small score by booking a 1975 Bruce Springsteen concert at his alma mater, John Carroll University), this son of a Buffalo garbage collector worked as special counsel for New York senators and governors. In 1984 he was hired to work on special news projects for NBC, gaining a reputation quickly for arranging an appearance by Pope John Paul II on the *Today* program the following year.

It soon became apparent that Tim had a gift for making complex political machinations understanding and compelling. And in 1991, entirely on the strength of his political banter among colleagues during conference calls, Tim was tapped as the new moderator of *Meet the Press* despite the fact that he had never hosted a program or, for that matter, had never even once *appeared* on television. Reformatting the then-43-year-old news show's sleepy reputation, Tim ditched its long-winded encounters between reporters and political hacks and instead compiled an issue-dense program focused on in-depth interviews with high-profile guests. A stickler for extensive preparatory research, Tim gained renown as a formidable super-informed interviewer inclined to pressing his guests with their past statements and positions that were in

direct contradiction to their present-day talking points. Yet however rugged the exchanges, the stout-faced Russert arched his thick eyebrows and ended with the same gentlemanly closing: "Thank you for sharing your views."

At the offices of WRC-TV in Washington where he was recording voiceovers for a Sunday edition of *Meet the Press*, Tim collapsed after uttering his last words, "What's happening?" as a greeting to an arriving associate. Co-workers immediately began CPR and paramedics, arriving a few minutes later, attempted to defibrillate his heart three times to no avail. Forty minutes later he was pronounced dead at a local hospital. An autopsy showed the journalist had an enlarged heart and that cholesterol plaque ruptured an artery, causing coronary thrombosis.

At 58, Tim was laid to rest at Rock Creek Cemetery in Washington, D.C.

GRAVE DIRECTIONS: This cemetery, located at 201 Allison Street NW, is a maze of confusing drives and pathways and you'd do well to get a map at the office. Otherwise, proceed as straight as possible, stay left at the chapel, pass the line of mausoleums, and then, at the intersection near the pond, make a right and stop. On your left in Section C, Tim's six-foot-tall monolith is often adorned with empty Rolling Rock bottles, reportedly his favorite beer.

SATURDAY NIGHT LIVE

THE FREEWHEELING TELEVISION program originally titled *NBC's Saturday Night* first aired October 11, 1975, showcasing zany comedy sketches by the "Not Ready for Primetime Players." Representing a bold leap for television, the show was an immediate hit, and within just a couple years—its name by then having been changed to *Saturday Night Live*—it was the highest-rated late-night show in America. In the 40-plus years since, it's hardly looked back.

Over the years, regular players have come and gone while the show's main elements have remained the same: a celebrity host and a musical guest, comedy sketches, commercial parodies, and a news segment. *Saturday Night Live* has proved to be a springboard for the careers of many previously unknown talents including, to name just a few, Bill Murray, Eddie Murphy, Julia Louis-Dreyfus, Mike Myers, Chris Rock, Jimmy Fallon, Seth Meyers, and, of course, the four entertainers profiled here.

JOHN BELUSHI
JANUARY 24, 1949 – MARCH 4, 1982

JOHN BELUSHI WAS an original member of the *Saturday Night Live* troupe, and he quickly became an audience favorite for his maniacal style, luxuriating in a comedic netherworld a tick away from categorical insanity. For six years, John delighted in his uniquely manic and belligerent characters on the show, portraying everything from a Samurai warrior to a Greek luncheonette hamburger-slinger.

John quickly parlayed his popularity into a spate of comedy films. His biggest hit was 1978's crowd-pleaser for the college set, *Animal House*. In it, he starred as the classic crude, flunking, frathouse drunk, Bluto, who bashed beer bottles over his head and incited riots. Later, John and his partner in crime, Dan Aykroyd, developed personas as the Blues Brothers, decked-in-black blues singers who caused havoc everywhere they went.

In March 1982 John was staying in Bungalow Number 3 at the Chateau Marmont on the Sunset Strip in Los Angeles. After partying it up at the nightclub On The Rox, John returned home where, for a short time, a few friends, including Robert DeNiro and Robin Williams, joined him. When everyone left, John, always needing a little more action, had his friend Cathy Evelyn Smith shoot him up with a drug concoction called a speedball, a mixture of heroin and cocaine.

After John had seemingly passed out, Cathy left the room. A few hours later it was discovered by another of John's friends that he was no longer just passed out, but was quite dead. The cause of death was classified as a drug overdose and, after Cathy related her story to a tabloid, she was arrested for supplying the drugs and served 30 months in prison.

Atop his motorcycle, Dan Aykroyd led the funeral procession to Abel's Hill Cemetery in Chilmark, Massachusetts, where John was buried at 33. However, the story doesn't end there.

Weary of disrespectful fans on mopeds or with beers in hand trashing the cemetery grounds looking for John's grave, the cemetery installed a large boulder engraved *Belushi* at the entrance in 1985, while his original skull-and-crossbones marker was removed from his actual plot near the rear of the cemetery. It's up for debate, though, whether John himself was actually moved to this spot (popular consensus is that he wasn't) or instead was left to enjoy some peace and quiet in his original, but now unmarked, grave a few hundred feet away. In any event, in 2006 the old-school tombstone resurfaced and was installed near the boulder.

Meanwhile, in 1996, after John's widow remarried, another stone dedicated to John was installed at his family's plot at Elmwood Cemetery in River Grove, Illinois. Possibly, since John's tenuous ties to Martha's Vineyard were effectively broken once Judith remarried, his family elected to inter him alongside his deceased parents. But cemetery officials unequivocally maintain that his body was not interred there, and this author is inclined to believe them.

So where is John? Well, the people who *really* know aren't saying, and that's their prerogative. Some like to believe his spirit is everywhere so, wherever you choose to salute him, I hope you'll send my regards.

DIRECTIONS TO GRAVE IN MASSACHUSETTS: At 322 South Road, you'll see John's memorials surrounded by a split-rail fence.

DIRECTIONS TO GRAVE IN ILLINOIS: Enter the cemetery at 2905 Thatcher Avenue and continue straight until you see the Manof mausoleum. Make a right there, then a left at the "T," then take the next right. After the road winds a little bit, you'll see Section 7 on the right, and the Belushi plot is there near the drive.

GILDA RADNER

JUNE 28, 1946 – MAY 20, 1989

AS A CHILD, Gilda Radner was severely overweight, had a speech impediment, and few friends, and she later attributed her keen sense of humor to these setbacks. After majoring in drama at the University of Michigan, she landed a job playing a clown on a Canadian children's television show and in 1973 began performing with an improvisational troupe at Toronto's Second City comedy club. Gilda later joined Dan Aykroyd and John Belushi on the *National Lampoon Radio Hour* and, after answering Lorne Michaels' casting call, in October 1975 the trio debuted on the new program that would come to be known as *Saturday Night Live*.

Gilda developed a number of memorably beloved and zany characters on the show, many of which contributed catchphrases to the slang lexicon. There was "It just goes to show you, it's always something," from the prickly mock-news commentaries of squinty-eyed, fright-wigged Roseanne Roseannadanna. The near-deaf, inept, spinsterly media analyst Emily Litella ended her tangents with "Never mind," and schoolgirl geek Lisa Loopner coined "That was so funny I forgot to laugh."

Gilda left *Saturday Night Live* in 1979 and moved on to Broadway, starring in a one-woman show that she co-wrote, *Gilda Radner: Live From New York*, and the next year she married *SNL* guitarist G.E. Smith. By 1982 things seemed to be going great for Gilda, but privately, she was suffering from nervous exhaustion, her marriage was crumbling, and she was battling bulimia, which she had overcome once before. Nonetheless, Gilda teamed with Gene Wilder in the comedic adventure *Hanky Panky* that year and, during filming, the two became romantically involved. They were married two years later.

In 1985 Gilda suffered chronic fatigue and mysterious bouts of unexplained illness and pains that her doctors dismissed as the flu or overwork, but the following year she collapsed and was found to have been suffering from advanced ovarian cancer. Through nearly three years of treatment, Gilda retained her sense of humor and when she lost her hair during radiation therapy, she opted to wear her gravity-defying Roseanne Roseannadanna wig. Her last able days were spent penning her memoir, *It's Always Something*, and bolstering the spirits of other cancer patients with impromptu visits.

Though her spirits never seemed to fail, her physicality did, and with Gene at her side, she died at 42 and was buried at Long Ridge Cemetery in Stamford, Connecticut.

GRAVE DIRECTIONS: Along 156 Erskine Road, about two-thirds of the way down the cemetery's length, you'll see a few old stairs that lead into the cemetery. Just about 50 feet directly behind these stairs, near a small bench, Gilda's grave is marked with a flat stone.

CHRIS FARLEY

FEBRUARY 15, 1964 – DECEMBER 18, 1997

AFTER GRADUATING FROM Marquette University, Chris Farley studied at the Improv Olympic theater school and was performing at Chicago's Second City when he was discovered by *Saturday Night Live* producer Lorne Michaels. In 1990 Chris became a regular *SNL* player and his boisterous, fat-guy schtick quickly won him wide appeal.

One of Chris' most hilarious characters was a giddy and flabby Chippendale's strip-club dancer who competed in an audition against Patrick Swayze, his jiggling gut spilling over his waistband. But his signature bit was the sweaty, tightly-wound motivational speaker Matt Foley whose identity was predicated on Chris' foghorn voice and whose vein-popping speeches invariably ended with him smashing through the furniture in a froth, his polyester leisure suit bursting at the seams.

After he left *SNL* in 1995, Chris hammed his way through a string of starring roles as the same kind of lovable, bumbling slob in such movies as *Tommy Boy* and *Beverly Hills Ninja*. But though Chris' hilarious on-screen routines garnered him professional triumph, his offscreen lifestyle propelled him toward disaster. For years Chris had battled against compulsions to overeat and overindulge in drugs and alcohol, and by 1997, those forces had conspired in a manner that was anything but funny.

It troubled the 300-pound, 5-foot-8 comic that he'd never had any meaningful girlfriends, and he often indulged in prostitutes to help ease the pain. Chris bought an apartment on the 60th floor of Chicago's John Hancock tower and after a December day spent doing hard drugs with a call girl named Heidi, they ended up at his place. Around 3:00 a.m., Heidi went to depart when Chris collapsed onto the floor, wheezing, "Don't leave me." Ten hours later, Chris' brother found him still lying on the floor, but no longer wheezing.

In an interview Chris had once confessed that he "dreamed of being John Belushi. I wanted to follow him," but unfortunately, he never realized how far he would follow him. Just like his idol, Chris died at 33 of an accidental overdose of heroin and cocaine.

GRAVE DIRECTIONS: At 2705 Regent Street, there is a chapel on Resurrection Cemetery's grounds in Madison, Wisconsin. Walk into the chapel and you'll find Chris' crypt on the top left, just behind the altar.

PHIL HARTMAN

SEPTEMBER 24, 1948 – MAY 28, 1998

AFTER CO-WRITING *PEE-WEE'S Big Adventure* with Paul "Pee-Wee Herman" Reubens, Phil Hartman joined *Saturday Night Live* in 1986. Though best known for his dozens of over-the-top impersonations, including Frank Sinatra, Ted Kennedy, and Bill Clinton, he also excelled at nailing treacherous and weaselly characters with his insincere grin and smug demeanor.

Phil left *SNL* in 1994 and got himself a new job as the arrogant, egotistical news anchor Bill McNeal on the sitcom *News Radio*. Phil also lent his memorable baritone to a number of characters on *The Simpsons*, including attorney Lionel Hutz and spokesman Troy McClure.

One balmy Wednesday night Phil's wife, Brynn, who had a history of substance abuse and instability, went out partying with a few friends. For reasons known only to Brynn, upon returning home around 2:00 a.m. she executed Phil while he lay sleeping in their bed, shooting him in the head, neck, and arm.

In a panic she fled the house, leaving the couple's two school-aged children sleeping in their beds, and went to the house of a friend, Ron Douglas. Brynn told Ron, "I shot Phil," but because she was so wired and her story so outlandish, he didn't believe her. Later, while Brynn dozed, Ron found and confiscated a revolver from her purse. Together they went back to the Hartman residence but, upon arriving, Brynn grabbed a second gun and locked herself in the master bedroom with Phil's body.

Ron called 911 and, just after 6:00 a.m., as the police who had arrived were escorting the couple's still-sleeping children from the house, a shot rang out. As Phil lay dead beside her, Brynn had put the gun's barrel into her mouth and pulled the trigger while officers struggled to break in through one of the bedroom windows.

At 49, Phil was cremated and his ashes scattered around Emerald Bay at Catalina Island, California.

TELLY SAVALAS

JANUARY 21, 1924 – JANUARY 22, 1994

OVER THE COURSE of his 30-plus-year acting career, Aristotelis "Telly" Savalas appeared in dozens of movies, from *The Greatest Story Ever Told* to *The Dirty Dozen* to the James Bond flick *On Her Majesty's Secret Service*. But it was his personification of the tough-talking but big-hearted Lieutenant Theo Kojak in the *Kojak* television series that brought real celebrity to Telly. Fans adored him as the lollipop-addicted detective with a shiny, shaved head and trademark line "Who loves ya, baby?" and the show enjoyed a six-season, award-winning run.

Reflecting on the recognition that the *Kojak* role brought him, Telly said, "Before *Kojak*, I made 60 movies with some of the biggest names in the business and people would still say 'There goes what's-his-name.'"

Telly died of prostate cancer at 70 and is buried at Forest Lawn Memorial Park in Hollywood Hills, California.

Either Telly or his survivors attempted to incorporate the writings of Aristotle (Telly's namesake) into his epitaph but, embarrassingly, the chosen quote actually contains the last words of Socrates, as recorded by Plato.

> *The hour of departure has arrived,*
> *and we go our ways.*
> *I to die and you to live.*
> *Which is the better God only knows.*

GRAVE DIRECTIONS: Enter the park at 6300 Forest Lawn Drive, get a map from the information booth, and drive to the Gardens of Heritage, which are across the drive from the Old North Church. Enter the Gardens at the stairs that are to the left of the statue of Washington, walk up four short flights, then turn left. Telly lies 40 feet to the left, around the side of the Chu plot.

JESSICA SAVITCH

FEBRUARY 1, 1947 – OCTOBER 23, 1983

YOUNG JESSICA SAVITCH was a diligent Philadelphia newscaster whose big break came when she got national exposure during coverage of the 1975 Ford/Carter presidential debate. Within a year, she held the Senate news beat for NBC, and while old-school broadcasters were unimpressed with Jessica's starlet style and follow-up remarks that sometimes displayed a lack of background knowledge, viewers loved her and she parlayed that into becoming one of the most prominent women in network news.

But as her professional career zoomed, Jessica's personal travails became tabloid fodder. There were reports of the usual celebrity problems—screaming off-camera rants, cocaine binges, and promiscuous weekends—but other peculiar gossips surfaced as well. Jessica married the wealthy socialite Mel Korn, 30 years her senior, and after a quick divorce she then married her gynecologist, Donald Payne. During the marriage to Donald, Jessica carried on an affair with reporter Ron Kershaw (who reportedly beat her, resulting in bruises that makeup artists weren't always able to conceal), and a distraught Donald hung himself in her basement with the leash of her dog, Chewy.

By 1983 Jessica's on-camera persona had become increasingly unreliable and her popularity waned. As other bright newswomen emerged, the competition for a finite number of anchor positions intensified and Jessica's on-screen time was reduced. In one of her final spots, she humiliated herself with a slurred and confused newsbreak delivery.

After dinner at Odette's Restaurant in New Hope, Pennsylvania, with Martin Fischbein, vice president of the *New York Post*, Jessica and Martin (and her infamous dog, Chewy) drowned after Martin accidentally drove the car into a canal bordering the restaurant's parking area. In poor visibility due to an evening downpour, Martin had drifted left off of the pavement and once the driver's side wheels went over the edge, the whole car plunged upside down into the canal. Though the canal held just four feet of water, knee-deep mud sealed the doors shut and the two were trapped inside. Nobody had seen the accident and it was about four hours before the car was found. By that time, Jessica and Martin were long dead. Neither drugs nor alcohol was determined to have been a factor in the accident.

At 36, Jessica was cremated together with her dog, Chewy, and their ashes were scattered in the ocean surf near Atlantic City.

ROD SERLING
DECEMBER 25, 1924 – JUNE 28, 1975

ON THE DAY he graduated from high school, Rod Serling enlisted in the Army. During the invasion of the Philippines he was wounded by shrapnel and awarded the Purple Heart and, when Rod was discharged from the Army, he was "bitter about everything and at loose ends." For the remainder of his life, in flashbacks and nightmares, Rod was troubled by the hypocritical experiences of the war and by the ultimate dimensions of mankind's assault on its own humanity.

After the war, while attending Antioch College on the G.I. Bill, Rod began writing and acting for a local radio station and, by 1952, he was writing for television full-time. Rod won three Emmys during television's golden age: for *Patterns* in 1955, *Requiem for a Heavyweight* in 1956, and *The Comedian* in 1957. Though he was very successful, many scripts Rod wrote contained social commentary or touched on weighty issues, and corporate sponsors in 1950s America were unwilling to underwrite anything that might clash with the time's apple-pie outlook.

But Rod also realized that advertisers might approve scripts with potentially controversial material as long as they took place in a fictitious world. ("I found that it was all right to have Martians saying things Democrats and Republicans could never say.") From this awareness came *The Twilight Zone* in 1959, and, with its instantly recognizable opening theme music and Rod as the charismatic host, the program achieved a permanent place in American popular culture as well as, it seems, permanent syndication. And, much to Rod's gratification, its out-of-this-world vignette format lent him license to skewer dozens of formerly untouchable social issues including bigotry, religious zealotry, capital punishment, aging, and sexism.

After production of *The Twilight Zone* ended in 1964, leaving Rod "tired and frustrated," he began to concentrate on movie scripts; his most acclaimed screenplay was the adaptation he cowrote with Michael Wilson of Pierre Boulle's book, *The Planet of the Apes*. Later, Rod was enticed back to television, writing episodes of the 1970s anthology series *Rod Serling's Night Gallery*, a kind of *Twilight Zone* stepchild.

A lifelong smoker, Rod died at 50 of complications after a coronary bypass operation. He was buried at Lakeview Cemetery in Interlaken, New York.

GRAVE DIRECTIONS: Enter the cemetery at 3660 County Road 150 and bear right at the first two forks. Go past the concrete holding house on the left, turn right at the four corners, and stop at the twin cedar trees on the left. A hundred feet farther left is Rod's flat stone marker.

JIMMY STEWART
MAY 20, 1908 – JULY 2, 1997

IN 1932, UPON graduating with a degree in architecture from Princeton University where he had served on the cheerleading squad, the stammering, "aw-shucks" actor Jimmy Stewart promptly got into theater. After some summer stock and barnstorming stage work, he headed to Hollywood and for a few years languished as a bit player in everything from murder mysteries to musicals. But in 1938 Jimmy scored in the romantic comedy *You Can't Take It With You*, and the next year he received an Oscar nomination for *Mr. Smith Goes to Washington*. In 1940 Jimmy won an Oscar for his performance as a smitten reporter in *The Philadelphia Story*.

In his 50-year career, Jimmy often played the earnest and bashful hero, slow to anger but possessed with bottomless reserves of perseverance. In an age of elegant, handsome matinee idols, lanky Jimmy was more the average-looking guy next door who embodied the small-town values of decency and moral courage, both on the screen and off. While he served in the Air Force as a bomber pilot he refused all the publicity the military tried to pour on him, insisting instead on being treated like any other serviceman. He continued as a reservist after the war, retiring as a brigadier general in 1968. Jimmy sometimes returned to help his family's small-town Pennsylvania hardware store where his best actor Oscar was displayed in the window for 20 years. Jimmy was married just once, for 45 years, and he and his wife lived quietly, generally avoiding the Hollywood social whirl.

Of course, he's best known for his role as a suicidal businessman who finds redemption in the 1946 Christmas classic *It's a Wonderful Life*, but Jimmy also starred in the great Alfred Hitchcock films *Vertigo* and *Rear Window*. In these roles Jimmy set a precedent that actors profit from today. Trading his flat salary for a percentage of the movie profits, he benefited handsomely when the films went on to become box-office hits. But Jimmy even refuted credit for that idea, saying, "There's too much praise for small things. I won't let it get me, but too much praise can turn a fellow's head if he doesn't watch his step."

Suffering respiratory problems and mourning the recent death of his wife, Gloria, he quietly expired at home. Jimmy's last words were "I'm going to be with Gloria now."

At 89, he was buried at Forest Lawn Memorial Park in Glendale, California.

GRAVE DIRECTIONS: Enter the park at 1712 South Glendale Avenue, start driving up the hill, and turn at the first left. As the road winds around in a wide, right-hand curve, on the right is the Taylor memorial, which is a statue of a crouching archer. Stop here, walk up the hill, and orient yourself so that the archer is aiming directly at you. Then, six rows from the memorial's base, you can find Jimmy's grave.

ED SULLIVAN
SEPTEMBER 28, 1901 – OCTOBER 13, 1974

STRAIGHT OUT OF high school, Ed Sullivan became a stringer reporter and sports columnist for New York's Hearst-owned newspapers, and in 1932 seized an opportunity to replace rival reporter Walter Winchell as the reporter for the *New York Daily News* Broadway gossip column, "Little Old New York." As a leading entertainment columnist for the next 42 years, he was wooed by celebrities from all walks of media and his access to the glamorous world of stars made him a luminary himself.

Frequently exploiting his column contacts to enlist celebrity guests for charity galas and parties, Ed finally took full advantage of his unique situation in 1948 and debuted his *Toast of the Town* variety show on CBS. The network gave Ed just $375 to secure his guest lineup for the opening show, but even with that paltry budget he was able to produce a half-dozen acts, including the little-known comedy team of Dean Martin and Jerry Lewis.

As a host, Ed Sullivan had a strange drawl, awkward mannerisms, and a deadpan delivery style—but whatever he lacked in stage presence, he compensated for in his outstanding eye for talent. Temperamental and controlling, he choreographed each act's staging and edited their material, but as the popularity of the show grew, it was understood that Sullivan was a certified star maker and few argued with his demands, lest they be denied their "big break." From Elvis Presley and the Beatles to Sammy Davis Jr. and Phyllis Diller, the show was a hit. After being renamed *The Ed Sullivan Show* in 1955, it ran until 1971 for a total of 1,087 shows, while Ed continued his tenure as newspaper gossip columnist throughout.

Ed died of heart failure at 73 and is interred at the Ferncliff Mausoleum in Hartsdale, New York.

GRAVE DIRECTIONS: Enter the cemetery at 280 Secor Road, bear left, and park toward the left-hand side of the main mausoleum. Enter the mausoleum through the front bronze doors and turn left, right, left, left, and right. Then go to the end of the last hall and Ed's crypt is along the wall near the elevator.

SHARON TATE
JANUARY 24, 1943 – AUGUST 9, 1969

SHARON TATE WAS a Texas homecoming queen who aspired to be a movie actress. After a number of insignificant appearances in film and television, Sharon landed the more visible role of Jennifer North in 1967's *Valley of the Dolls* and gave a breakthrough performance. By the time of her marriage to the director Roman Polanski the following year, Sharon's star was on the rise.

At her Los Angeles estate one warm summer evening, while Roman was away finishing a project in London, an eight-months-pregnant Sharon and her four houseguests, Abigail Folger, Wojciech Frykowski, Steve Parent, and Jay Sebring, were stabbed, shot, beaten, and strangled to death by unknown assailants. The gruesome murder scene included cryptic expressions written in blood, while a rope fastened around Sharon's neck snaked through the bloody pools.

Not surprisingly, the murders made headlines but, before authorities were able to even catch their balance, the killers struck again the following night, slaughtering grocer Leno LaBianca and his wife, Rosemary, in equally grisly fashion. Hysteria gripped Los Angeles, sales of guard dogs and home alarms boomed, and, though a number of theories for the seven apparently motiveless murders were put forward, it later turned out that the actual motive was even more grotesque than, perhaps, the murders themselves.

Charles Manson was a deranged, self-styled guru who presided over a gaggle of equally troubled disciples at his squatters' manor, an isolated and abandoned movie ranch in the desert mountains. Through some perverse twist of illogic, Manson came to believe that a kind of apocalyptic racial war in which black men would prevail and oversee the demise of every white was imminent. While the conflict raged, however, Manson and his "family" would be living safely inside the earth, only to emerge and seize power from "the black man" to rule the world.

Manson was obsessed with this vision. The only other thing that intrigued him equally was the Beatles because, as Manson considered himself the fifth angel, Jesus Christ, the Beatles were the other four angels. In 1969 the Beatles released what became known as the *White Album*. (How much of a clearer signal could they send Manson?) The recording was interpreted by Manson as a message from his angels that the time for the race war was nigh, and he adopted the title of one of its feature songs, "Helter Skelter," as the name for his imagined Armageddon. In his mind, the Helter Skelter war was to be initiated by indiscriminate killings of whites by blacks, but when the blacks failed to act, Manson became frustrated and decided it was his responsibility to get things moving.

To that end, Manson handpicked a few of his apostles and instructed them to select a house within a distinctive neighborhood and massacre its white occupants, while making it somehow look like the crime was committed by blacks.

Manson and four of his followers were convicted of the murders and sentenced to death. When California abolished its death penalty, their sentences were changed to life terms. Every few years they are each eligible to apply for parole, though to date they've been repeatedly denied it.

As for Sharon, she was 26 at her death and now resides at Holy Cross Cemetery in Culver City, California.

GRAVE DIRECTIONS: Enter the cemetery at 5835 Slauson Avenue, turn left, and start up the hill. One hundred yards on the left is the Grotto Lawn and an altar and to the left of the altar is another level, St. Ann's Garden. Sharon's grave is in that garden, third row from the top.

ELIZABETH TAYLOR
FEBRUARY 27, 1932 – MARCH 23, 2011

IN A CAREER of some 70 years and more than 60 films, the violet-eyed actress Elizabeth Taylor was synonymous with Hollywood glamour. First appearing on-screen at age 10, she grew up there and was a star her entire life. In one quick leap from *National Velvet* to *A Place in the Sun,* and from there to *Cleopatra,* Elizabeth was indelibly transformed from a vulnerable child actress into a voluptuous film queen.

Ms. Taylor's popularity endured throughout her life, but critics were sometimes reserved in their praise of her acting. In that sense she may have been upstaged by her own striking beauty. Could anyone as lovely as Elizabeth Taylor also be talented? The answer, of course, is yes. By her own estimation, she "whistled and hummed" her way through her early films. But that changed in 1951, when she starred in *A Place in the Sun,* playing her prototypical role as a seemingly unattainable romantic vision. The film, she said, was "the first time I ever considered *acting* when I was young." Given her lack of professional training, the range of her acting was surprisingly wide. She convincingly played predatory vixens and wounded victims, while her melodramatic heroines would have been at home on soap operas.

One prominent, perhaps surprising, dissenter about her looks was Richard Burton, who was twice her husband. The notion of his wife as "the most beautiful woman in the world is absolute nonsense," he said. "She has wonderful eyes," he added, "but she has a double chin and an overdeveloped chest, and she's rather short in the leg." Of her seven husbands, it seems he may have been the love of her life and Elizabeth said that had he not died she probably would have married him a third time. Long after his death, she kept a copy of his last letter in her bedside drawer.

Pursued by paparazzi and denounced by the Vatican, Elizabeth existed for the public and her life was played out in print: miles of newspaper and magazine articles, a galaxy of photographs, and a shelf of biographies, each one painting a different portrait. But behind the sometimes-scandalous behavior was a woman with a sense of morality: She habitually married her lovers. People watched and counted, with vicarious pleasure, as she became Elizabeth Taylor Hilton Wilding Todd Fisher Burton Burton Warner Fortensky—enough marriages to be certified as a serial wife.

"I've been lucky all my life," she said just before turning 60. "Everything was handed to me. Looks, fame, wealth, honors, love. I rarely had to fight for anything." But she suffered misfortune as well. Burton died before his time and her third husband, Michael Todd, perished at 48 in a plane crash. In later years Elizabeth struggled with alcohol while an overeating problem made her fodder for late-night TV comics. Playing five doctors against one another, she managed hundreds of antidepressant and painkiller prescriptions resulting in a prolonged rehabilitation at the Betty Ford Center. According to one chronicler, she suffered more than 70 incidents that required hospitalization, including an appendectomy, an emergency tracheotomy, a punctured esophagus, a hysterectomy, dysentery, an ulcerated eye, smashed spinal discs, skin cancer, a brain tumor, hip replacements, and a half a dozen back surgeries. In her later years she had to use a wheelchair because of osteoporosis and scoliosis.

Long after she faded from the screen, she remained a mesmerizing figure and turned to business, cannily peddling her own Passion perfume for $165 an ounce. In 1985, Elizabeth became the most prominent celebrity to back what was then a most unfashionable cause: AIDS, for which she would eventually raise nearly $300 million. For that work, in 2000, Queen Elizabeth II made her a

Dame Commander of the Order of the British Empire, an honor on the level of knighthood. Upon entering Buckingham Palace in a wheelchair, she told the media, "You can now call me Dame Elizabeth, though I've been a broad all my life."

At 79, she passed away of congestive heart failure. At her request, the funeral began 15 minutes after it was scheduled to begin. As her representative told the media, "She even wanted to be late for her own funeral."

Elizabeth was buried at Forest Lawn Memorial Park in Glendale, California.

GRAVE DIRECTIONS: Enter the park at 1712 South Glendale Avenue, get a map at the information booth, and make your way to the Great Mausoleum. Walk in its front entrance to the Hall of Memory and there you'll see a 12-foot-high, Michelangelo-like carved statue of an angel with arms outstretched, beneath which is the crypt of Elizabeth Taylor.

DANNY THOMAS
JANUARY 6, 1914 – FEBRUARY 6, 1991

BEGINNING HIS LIFE as Muzyad Yakhoob, Danny Thomas was an enduring television entertainer whose comedic talents were surpassed only by his shrewd production activities and his well-known philanthropy. He began his career as the stand-up comic Amos Jacobs, developing his storytelling shtick into a familiar routine of lengthy narratives peppered with a blend of Irish, Yiddish, and Italian witticisms. Quite often these routines tended toward sentimentality, only to be rescued in the end by what he called the "treacle cutter," a one-liner designed to undercut the mushy sentiments with irony.

After a USO tour with Marlene Dietrich, Danny was cast in his first film, *The Unfinished Dance*. He refused to surgically alter his trademark nose, a decision that may have contributed to the short-lived nature of his film career, but he performed to good reviews for his appearance in 1951's *The Jazz Singer*, and a costarring role in *I'll See You in My Dreams*.

Meanwhile, Danny anxiously pursued a television series. He soon got one, *Four Star Review*, but its fast-paced sketches were ill suited to his expository style. In 1953 Danny came up with the autobiographical premise of *Make Room for Daddy*, which revolved around the absentee-father dilemmas of a traveling singer-comic named Danny Williams. Incorporating Danny's singing and storytelling talents, the show became one of television's most successful comedies.

Danny had an enormous impact upon the growing medium of television; he invented the concept of a "spinoff" series and his off-camera stand-up routines for the studio audience were imitated and institutionalized as the now commonplace "warm-up." With Sheldon Leonard, he established Thomas-Leonard Productions and the powerhouse company became responsible for a multitude of successful series including *The Andy Griffith Show, The Dick van Dyke Show, Gomer Pyle*, and, in 1965, *The Danny Thomas Hour*.

And of course, Danny was renowned the world over for his humanitarianism. While his television career skyrocketed in the 1950s, Danny assembled fund-raisers and benefits for a new children's hospital that would become his legacy. In February 1962, the St. Jude Children's Research Hospital opened in Memphis, and Danny told the crowd that had gathered for the dedication, "If I were to die this moment, I'd know why I was born." For the remainder of his life, he organized and performed at fund-raising events for St. Jude, a world leader in research and treatment of childhood disease.

Danny died of a heart attack at 77 and now rests in his own Memorial Garden at his beloved St. Jude Children's Research Hospital in Memphis, Tennessee.

GRAVE DIRECTIONS: From I-40, take Exit 1B and follow the signs on Danny Thomas Boulevard to the hospital. Just inside the gate, on the left past the guard shack, is the beautiful courtyard that contains his tomb.

THE THREE STOOGES

THE ACT THAT was to become television's *The Three Stooges* started in 1922 as a vaudeville act. In 1930 came the trio's big-screen debut in *Soup to Nuts* and, four years later, the Stooges were offered a contract by Columbia to make their knockabout-style, slapstick comedy shorts, of which they eventually made about 200 in all, setting a record for the longest-running comedy series in Hollywood. Their humor, tasteless and repetitive, was punctuated by pokes, grunts, screeches, and various bits of bedlam, and it was also liberatingly funny. Moe was the know-nothing, know-it-all leader who committed cheerful acts of mayhem against his partners that magically never seemed to harm them; Larry was the innocent with a porcupine hairdo who just wanted to get along; and Curly was the bald, round, wacky, "nyuck-nyuck" wild man with a hilarious habit of reducing to rubble everything he touched.

The team, with four different Curlys over the years, enjoyed a quarter-century of success before finally being released by Columbia in 1958. But shortly afterward, a whole new generation discovered the trio and, in the twilight of their lives, the Stooges were hotter than they had ever been. A cult of sorts was spawned, complete with marathon film festivals, fan clubs, lunch boxes, and coffee mugs, and the Stooges cashed in with personal appearances and a few feature films. Failing health finally shut down their act but the shows are in endless syndication on television.

Though the most familiar incarnation of the trio consists of Larry Fine, Moe Howard, and his brother Jerome Howard as Curly, the part of Curly was also played by Moe's older brother, Shemp, by Joe Besser, and finally, by Joe DeRita.

JEROME HOWARD
OCTOBER 22, 1903 – JANUARY 18, 1952

REPLACING HIS BROTHER Shemp in 1932, Jerome shaved his head for the mundane purpose of looking starkly different from Moe and Larry, and he became the first Curly with that look. He constantly forgot his lines and his "woo-woo-woo-woo" trademark was originally an improvisation for when he was stuck for words. It stuck.

During the filming of the Stooges' 97th short in May 1946, Jerome suffered a stroke while on the set. He recovered enough to get married again and have a daughter but he didn't return to acting. After a few more strokes, he died at 48 and was buried at Home of Peace Memorial Park in Los Angeles.

GRAVE DIRECTIONS: Enter the park at 4334 Whittier Boulevard, bear right, take the next right and the next left. Stop on this drive about 100 feet before it makes an abrupt left. On the curb to the right are markings for the Western Jewish Institute. Jerome's stone can be found five rows back.

SHEMP HOWARD
MARCH 17, 1895 – NOVEMBER 3, 1955

SHEMP WAS THE original Curly and seems to be the favorite of many Stooge aficionados, if there could even be such a thing. He was there at the beginning of their run, but in 1932 he left the act to pursue a solo career, only to return in 1946 after Jerome suffered a stroke. Over the next nine years Shemp made 73 shorts with the Stooges but his run came to a quick end in 1955 when he suffered a fatal heart attack while riding in a car with friends. At 60, Shemp was interred at Home of Peace Memorial Park in Los Angeles, like his brother Jerome, though they are in completely different areas of the cemetery.

DIRECTIONS TO SHEMP'S GRAVE: Enter the park, bear right, then turn left and park in front of the mausoleum. Walk inside through the pews and turn left at the Corridor of Benevolence. Then turn right at the Corridor of Eternal Life and Shemp's crypt is on the right, second row from the bottom.

LARRY FINE
OCTOBER 5, 1902 – JANUARY 24, 1975

BEFORE BECOMING THE happy-go-lucky Stooge, Larry was a professional violinist. Keeping a low profile, always trying to keep the peace, and almost never delivering funny lines, he was considered insignificant by some fans, but it's doubtful the show would have gone anywhere as *The Two Stooges*. When Larry suffered a stroke in 1970, the Stooges' act finally ended forever.

Larry died five years later at 72 from complications of his stroke, and he lies at Forest Lawn Memorial Park in Glendale, California.

GRAVE DIRECTIONS: Enter the park at 1712 South Glendale Avenue, stop at the booth, get a map, and drive up to the Freedom Mausoleum. Walk in the front entrance, make a left, and go down the stairs. At the bottom of the stairs, turn right and then right again. The last hall on the right is the Sanctuary of Liberation. It's where you'll find Larry's crypt.

MOE HOWARD
JUNE 19, 1897 – MAY 4, 1975

IN 1922 MOE, his brother Shemp, and friend Ted Healy ad-libbed a hilarious stage act that was, though they didn't know it, the first incarnation of the Three Stooges. Moe later sold real estate for a time (would you buy a house from this man?) and, as the only

Stooge with any business experience, he handled all of the business particulars for the group.

After completing his memoirs in May of 1975, Moe succumbed to lung cancer at 77. He's lying quite peacefully at Hillside Memorial Park in Los Angeles.

GRAVE DIRECTIONS: Enter the park at 6001 West Centinela Avenue, make a left after the flagpole, then drive about 100 yards and stop. Walk down the stairs of the Court of Love, which is on your left. Across the court is the Alcove of Love, where Moe rests in Crypt C-233.

JOE BESSER
AUGUST 12, 1907 – MARCH 1, 1988

JOE WAS NAMED as Shemp's replacement in 1956 and he certainly had his own style; he was the only Stooge who dared to hit Moe back with any regularity. But after only 16 comedies, Columbia canceled *The Three Stooges* and Joe was cast back into the real world.

At 80, Joe died of heart failure and, like Larry, he lies at Forest Lawn Memorial Park in Glendale, California.

GRAVE DIRECTIONS: Joe is buried in the grass outside the Freedom Mausoleum, across the drive in the Dedication section. His grave is directly across from the Williamson plaque and nine rows down the hill from the curb.

JOE DeRITA
JULY 12, 1909 – JULY 3, 1993

AFTER THE STOOGES comedies were released to television in 1958, their newfound popularity provided opportunities to make films, but the fact that Joe Besser had to care for his ailing wife left them one Stooge short. That's when Joe DeRita stepped in, helping them make six feature films during the 1960s including *It's a Mad, Mad, Mad, Mad World.*

You'd think that out of the six different comics that made up the Stooges, at least one of them would have had an interesting or funny parting from this world. But it seems that relatively pedestrian passings are the theme here. When Joe died of

pneumonia at 83, an era ended: His passing marked the demise of the last Stooge.

Joe was buried at Valhalla Memorial Park in North Hollywood, California.

GRAVE DIRECTIONS: Drive through the gate at 1061 Victory Boulevard, turn right, and stop 50 feet after the road bends to the left. Joe is buried in the grass on the right, close to the road.

THE TONIGHT SHOW

ORIGINATING IN 1951 as a Los Angeles radio show, *The Tonight Show* moved its variety-show format to television three years later and it now lays claim to an incredible 60-year run in delighting late-night American audiences. Though the show's skits and comedy routines seem to fall flat as often as they soar to hilarity, the show's strength has always been in the lively conversation of its jocular hosts with a rainbow of celebrities and interesting people from all walks of life. In that vein, the show's reach can hardly be overstated when it's considered that over six decades, there may hardly be a single mainstream famous person— everyone from Katharine Hepburn to Janis Joplin and Henry Kissinger to Rodney Dangerfield—who has *not* appeared on *The Tonight Show*. Nonetheless, without pleasant banter from a hard-working, quick-thinking, likable host, celebrity interviews can quickly devolve into drone-fests, so the show's success is also a testament to the skills of the following three hosts and one lovable emcee.

STEVE ALLEN

DECEMBER 26, 1921 – OCTOBER 30, 2000

AS A CONGENIAL radio-show host since 1946, Steve Allen caught the eye of television producers working to bring *The Tonight Show* to network and it eventually debuted in 1954 with Steve as its wisecracking host. Though the producers had a vision for the general format of the show, Steve's witty monologues, jocular ad-lib high jinks, comical skits, and engaging interviews with both celebrity guests and the "man on the street" gently expanded the staid 1950s norms and he ended up earning credit as the person responsible for creating much of the successful late-night formula. After laughing it up for two years, Steve handed the reins over to Jack Paar and hosted his own prime-time variety show, *The Steve Allen Show,* which ran until 1964 and launched the careers of a generation of comedians and personalities.

Though he is best remembered for his intelligent and informal comic style, Steve was also a gifted musician, seasoned author, and a part-time actor. An accomplished pianist who never learned to read music, he is listed in the *Guinness Book of World Records* as the most prolific composer of modern times, credited with some 7,000 tunes including such hits as "This Could Be the Start of Something Big" and "Impossible." He wrote newspaper columns and plays, published some 50 books on everything from poetry to social criticism to humor, and a dozen novels. Steve appeared in Broadway shows and on soap operas, and he even starred as the King of Swing in the 1956 movie *The Benny Goodman Story.*

When Steve died at his home at 78, newspapers dutifully reported that he'd suffered an apparent heart attack. However, most newspapers ignored the more interesting aspect of his death, which came to light with the release of his autopsy report two months later.

Steve had actually died due to a hemopericardium, a hole in the heart that leaked blood into the surrounding sac. On the day of his death, he had been in a minor traffic accident in which another driver backed his vehicle into Steve's car. The fender-bender bruised Steve's chest and ruptured tissue in his heart, which wasn't too healthy in the first place. The rupture caused a blood leakage and, when Steve dozed off after dinner, he simply never awoke.

He was cremated at 78 and his ashes remain with his family.

JACK PAAR

MAY 1, 1918 – JANUARY 27, 2004

REMARKABLY, FOR SOMEONE who eventually made his living talking and mostly without the benefit of written material or rehearsal, Jack Paar grew up a persistent stutterer. Equally remarkable, he overcame the affliction on his own. Feeling embarrassed and ill at ease around others, Jack spent much of his childhood alone with books and one day read a story about Demosthenes, a Greek orator who cured himself of stammering by putting pebbles in his mouth and loudly reciting passages from books over the roar of the sea. Willing to try anything, Jack filled his mouth with buttons from his mother's sewing box and spent hundreds of hours reading magazines over the drone of a radio turned up loud. It worked, and Jack's speech so improved that he confidently began pursuing his dream of becoming a radio broadcaster at just 16.

His first job in the industry consisted mainly of custodial duties, but the powers soon relented, allowing him to read the call letters: "This is station WIBM, Jackson, Michigan." In time, Jack was spinning records and reading commercials in a kind of trademark "hemming and hawing" style he developed that helped keep his stammering at bay.

After service in World War II, Jack turned to television, hosting quiz shows and game shows, and in 1957 took over from Steve Allen the reins of *The Tonight Show,* which would prove to be the defining role of his career. Jack's style was to simplify the format a bit—the sofa-and-desk set that remains a fixture to this day was his idea—and his own persona was shaped around witty and knowledgeable conversation. Instead of uncomfortably participating in zany sketches for which he had no talent, Jack employed a salon of eccentrics including professional hypochondriac Oscar Levant and British raconteur Peter Ustinov, and provided a nurturing ground for such young comedic talents as Bill Cosby, Bob Newhart, and the Smothers Brothers.

Under Jack's tutelage *The Tonight Show* became a staple of American culture, but after just five years at the helm, in 1962, after confessing that "his creative field was running dry," he left the show. A short-lived variety series of his own followed, and thereafter Jack eschewed the limelight, choosing instead to buy and run a small Maine television station and rarely making public appearances.

After undergoing triple bypass surgery and suffering a stroke, Jack died at his home at 85. He was cremated and his ashes given to his family.

JOHNNY CARSON

OCTOBER 23, 1925 – JANUARY 23, 2005

AT AGE 12, Johnny Carson sent away for a magic kit and shortly thereafter began his show business career, billing himself to private parties as "The Great Carsoni" magician and ventriloquist. After a stint in the Navy during World War II, Johnny chased the new medium of television to Los Angeles, where he hosted a handful of low-budget comedy series, conducting phony interviews and performing skits and characters. The material was quirky and occasionally naughty, yet homespun enough to hit home with the heartland. Although he was popular, the shows weren't, so he took a new job writing jokes for Red Skelton where he eventually graduated to substitute hosting Red's show. In 1962 Johnny took the reins of *The Tonight Show* from a "bone-tired" Jack Paar and, with the dependable sideline chortles of Ed McMahon and easy banter of gaudy bandleader Doc Severinson filling in the rough spots, Carson hosted the show for 30 years—an astonishing 4,531 episodes.

In what became America's late-night televised cocktail lounge, Carson combined his casual innocence and cosmopolitan wit with a well-stocked supply of facial expressions to become the acknowledged master at lampooning the pretentious and salvaging the boring all while keeping his finger on the pulse of the mainstream's moods, attitudes, and concerns. He exploited politics but only for quick one-liners, and though Johnny was the star of the show, it was never about him. Whether he listened to a guest curiously or cavalierly shrugged off their eccentricities, the audience followed his cue. The result was a cornucopia of memories that fill the national psyche:

There was the scared marmoset that crawled onto Johnny's head and peed on him, and the time Jimmy Stewart teared up while reading a poem about his dog. One night a man rendered the national anthem by making flatulent noises with his hands, while on another a loaded Dean Martin secretly tipped cigarette ashes into the cocktail of an oblivious George Gobel. An eccentric old lady presented her beloved collection of potato chips shaped like faces of celebrities and when Carson blithely munched a chip, the poor lady nearly suffered a heart attack, until he revealed a separate bag behind his desk.

In private life, Johnny was almost the opposite of his spontaneous, charming onstage personality. He was married four times, was private to a fault, and was reputed to be rather calculating in his dealings with others; after close friend Joan Rivers briefly competed against him with her own nightly program, the chill behind Johnny's twinkle became ice-cold and he never spoke to her again. Nevertheless, a brilliant Mr. Middle America who changed late-night television is the man who will be remembered and, indeed, on his retirement in 1992 he was regarded as a national institution.

More than 50 million people tuned in to witness Johnny's swan song. "And so it has come to this. I am one of the lucky people in the world. I found something that I always wanted to do and I have enjoyed every single minute of it," Carson said to close his final show. "I bid you a very heartfelt goodnight."

In the early days of *The Tonight Show*, Johnny could often be spotted holding a cigarette behind his desk and eventually they caught up with him. At 79, clinging to this world by the grace of a life support temporarily fending off the consequences of emphysema, he opted to have the machine turned off and died within hours. Johnny was cremated, and his ashes remain with his family.

ED MCMAHON
MARCH 6, 1923 – JUNE 23, 2009

ED MCMAHON, JOHNNY Carson's boisterous and outgoing second banana sidekick, made his first "showbiz" appearance calling bingo games at age 15. Next came a few spare years chasing carnivals and fairs throughout New England followed by a radio station broadcasting job. Later, when World War II broke out, the affable opportunist finagled himself into a choice slot in a Marine Corps flight school, and though he received orders in July 1945 to report to the Pacific Fleet, they were quickly rescinded as Japan surrendered three weeks later.

Ed then studied drama at Catholic University on the G.I. Bill and on the weekends sold vegetable slicers on the Atlantic City boardwalk to make ends meet. An opportunity to work as a clown on a Philadelphia variety show presented itself, and within weeks Ed was hosting the program. Soon he had become "Mr. Television" around Philadelphia, laughing his way through a dozen different programs during the 1950s including a cooking show, a quiz show, and even a breakfast-hour program called *Strictly for the Girls.*

Finally, in 1958, Ed met a rising young comedian who would forever alter his career and fortunes: Johnny Carson. "Johnny didn't look as if he was dying to see me," Ed said of their first meeting that was, as he put it, "about as stimulating as watching a traffic light change." Nonetheless, Johnny hired him to be the announcer on his afternoon comedy quiz show and when Johnny became *The Tonight Show*'s host in 1962, he took Ed with him.

Ed quickly became "Big Ed," the good-time guy who did the audience warmups and commercials and performed in sketches, but his primary job was to be Carson's comedy foil and straight man or, most commonly, just sit on the couch and laugh uproariously at his jokes. "I was there when he needed me, and when he didn't, I moved down the couch and kept quiet," Ed once explained.

Long before Johnny's final *Tonight Show* on May 22, 1992, Ed capitalized on his "feel-good fever" and made a name for himself as a first-class pitchman; at one point he was hawking everything from Budweiser to Breck Shampoo while being a spokesman for more than 20 different banks. For years he served as the spokesman for American Family Publishers' national sweepstakes, his friendly mug famously informing Americans "You may already have won $10 million!" With Dick Clark he hosted 16 years of *TV's Bloopers & Practical Jokes,* made 41 appearances on the Jerry Lewis Telethon, and spent a dozen years hosting *Star Search.*

One would think that with working so much in what seems to be a lucrative field, Ed would have had no financial worries, but in 2008 it was reported he was in arrears on his Beverly Hills home and his lender had filed a notice of default. "If you spend more money than you make, you know what happens, and it can happen," he said. "You know, a couple of divorces thrown in, a few things like that."

At 86, Ed's multitude of medical problems—including a fractured neck suffered in a fall, evils brought on by an allergy to a mold, pneumonia and, ultimately, bone cancer—caught up with him and he died in his sleep. In keeping with what seems to be a tradition with *The Tonight Show* hosts, Ed was cremated and his ashes given to his family.

RUDOLPH VALENTINO
MAY 6, 1895 – AUGUST 23, 1926

RUDOLPH VALENTINO WAS the greatest Latin lover of the silent screen era. At 18 he left Italy and, after arriving in New York aboard the steamer *S.S. Cleveland,* Rudolph was soon the star tango dancer at Maxim's, a high-class New York cabaret from which he moonlighted as a gigolo. After a particular married woman with whom he was having an affair killed her husband, Rudolph conveniently left town in 1916 with the Masked Model touring tango group and ended up in Hollywood.

Blessed with hypnotic eyes and a dashing charm, Rudolph was an instant star, mainly in the role of the romantic "Sheik" in a series of desert melodramas. From his days as a dancer, he had learned to move with a sort of grace and finesse unfamiliar to moviegoers of the day, and he enchanted audiences with his exotic appearance and unconventional mannerisms. In the seven years before his untimely death, Rudolph appeared in 14 major films, including *The Four Horsemen of the Apocalypse* and *The Eagle*, and female moviegoers openly swooned over his extraordinary sex appeal.

By 1926 the Great Italian Lover's second marriage had collapsed, and he set off newly single again. In the morning after an all-night party thrown in his honor, Rudolph went to the hospital with severe stomach pain. Doctors immediately performed surgery to repair a perforated ulcer and remove his ruptured appendix. However, uremic poisoning had already swept through his body and penetrated the wall of his heart. Six days later, Rudolph was dead.

Widespread hysteria among his idolizers ensued. At the Funeral Church at 67th Street and Broadway in New York, Rudolph was laid out in a silver-bronze coffin with a plate-glass barrier so fans could look at, but not touch, the man who had been the world's greatest lover. At one point, the frenzied throng broke through the church's front window and dozens of people were injured in the ensuing chaos. Eventually, some 80,000 people filed past the dead Sheik.

At 31, Rudolph was buried at Hollywood Forever in Hollywood, California.

GRAVE DIRECTIONS: At 6000 Santa Monica Boulevard, enter the cemetery, turn at the second left, drive straight through the next intersection, and park in front of the Hollywood Cathedral Mausoleum on the right. Walk in the mausoleum's main entrance, turn left at the second corridor, then right at the last corridor. Rudolph's crypt is on the left at the end.

For a period of years, a mysterious "Lady in Black" faithfully visited Rudolph's tomb on the anniversary of his death. Theories about her identity circulated endlessly until a movie house admitted to creating the event as a stunt intended to stoke interest in the Valentino mystique.

HERVE VILLECHAIZE

APRIL 23, 1943 — SEPTEMBER 4, 1993

THE 3-FOOT-9 ACTOR Herve Villechaize was best known for his TV role as Ricardo Montalban's sidekick, Tattoo, on the popular *Fantasy Island* program. Every episode opened with a planeload of guests arriving at the island to realize their fondest dreams, and in his role Herve would excitedly exclaim, "Boss! De plane! De plane!"

Over a salary dispute, Herve quit *Fantasy Island* the year before it was retired in 1984, and perhaps his absence hastened its cancelation. But the show seemed to have crested a few seasons earlier, anyway. Herve's next project was a lengthy unemployment streak broken only by an appearance in a doughnut commercial where he resurrected his infamous line in the context of his pastry preference: "De plain! De plain!" That's show business.

Born with undersized lungs and suffering from ulcers and a spastic colon, of all things, Herve's despondency over his health problems, and other personal issues too, culminated in his suicide. He shot himself to death behind his garage at age 50.

Herve was cremated and his ashes scattered off Point Fermin in California.

JOHN WAYNE
MAY 26, 1907 – JUNE 11, 1979

AFTER ATTENDING THE University of Southern California on a football scholarship, Marion Morrison appeared in over 50 feature films and serials, mostly Westerns, during the 1930s. At some point in that early career, an executive did him the favor of a lifetime by unceremoniously changing his name to John Wayne, simply because he didn't like his real name. Nonetheless, John Wayne appeared to be doomed to a role as a leading player in low-budget films.

But in 1939 John was cast in the lead role of John Ford's *Stagecoach* and the film proved to be a turning point in his career. Although it took time for him to develop his rugged, American image, within a decade John was a top box-office draw and even today, he is one of the most popular actors of all time. Though the majority of his roles in the next 75 films were as an archetypal, no-nonsense hero in classic Westerns such as *The Searchers* and *The Man Who Shot Liberty Valance*, John also personified the hard-as-nails patriot in war films like *Sands of Iwo Jima* and *The Green Berets*.

After four decades of Hollywood stardom, John and his fans suspected that the 1978 film *The Shootist* would be his last hurrah. John had lost a lung to cancer back in 1964 and, after studio press agents tried to conceal the nature of the illness, he'd gone before the public and shown that the disease was no match for John Wayne. But now the disease had invaded his internal organs and everyone, especially John, was cognizant of the awful, impending reality; the selfless hero on-screen was being done in by a selfish villain offscreen. When he died in the final shootout scene,

everybody knew they'd seen the last of both John Waynes, the real and the imaginary.

John died of stomach cancer at 72 and was buried at Pacific View Memorial Park in Corona del Mar, California.

GRAVE DIRECTIONS: Enter the park at 3500 Pacific View Drive, bear left, and go up the hill toward the Lagunita Hill mausoleums. Across the drive from the mausoleums, find the "578" curb marking and John's grave is six rows down the hill.

LAWRENCE WELK
MARCH 11, 1903 – MAY 17, 1992

WHO COULD EVER have imagined that an uneducated, heavily accented, dirt-poor farm boy from North Dakota would preside over one of the longest-running shows in television history? Lawrence Welk attained that distinction by blending his folksy charm and his orchestra's easy-listening music with such traditional entertainment forms as tap and ballroom dancing, ragtime piano, jazz accordion, and mellow singing acts.

After a quarter-century of crisscrossing the country and leading his band everywhere from Yankton, South Dakota, to Newport, Oregon, to Hackensack, New Jersey, Lawrence scored a television show in 1955. *The Lawrence Welk Show* was an immediate success and it popularized his "champagne music," a term coined by a Pittsburgh radio announcer that succinctly characterized his sparkling and light, middle-of-the-road sound.

As the years wore on and the day's popular music continually reinvented itself, Lawrence stayed true to his muse; he made no pretense of being even remotely hip, and he refused to vary his basic recipe: Play what the people understand, keep it simple so the audience feels like they participate, and, when in doubt, return to a composition that puts the girl back in the boy's arms. The show's banality became the butt of jokes, and detractors considered it tinkly Mickey Mouse music dispensed to geriatrics, but legions of fans adored the sentimentality as a reassuring time capsule of a simpler and happier time. And Lawrence continued to be popular long after his contemporaries faded, suggesting that perhaps he was onto something after all.

In 1971 *The Lawrence Welk Show* was canceled, but Lawrence shrewdly signed up some 250 independent television stations and kept the program going for another 11 seasons. In sum, there were 1,542 "wunnerful, wunnerful," Lawrence Welk-hosted, champagne music broadcasts.

At 89, Lawrence Welk died of pneumonia at his Santa Monica beachfront condo.

He was buried at Holy Cross Cemetery in Culver City, California.

GRAVE DIRECTIONS: Enter the cemetery at 5835 Slauson Avenue, drive up to the mausoleum on the hill, and to the right of the mausoleum you'll see a flower shop. Lawrence's grave is about 175 yards diagonally behind and to the left of the flower shop in Plot 110-T9.

ORSON WELLES
MAY 6, 1915 – OCTOBER 10, 1985

ALTHOUGH HE WORKED on the stage for more than 50 years, gave countless radio performances, starred in more than 60 films—many of which he both wrote and directed—and had a hand in another hundred or so motion pictures, Orson Welles' fame rests primarily on two projects he completed before he was barely 25 years old. By Orson's own admission, he "started at the top and worked my way down."

The public became aware of Orson with his chillingly realistic 1938 radio dramatization of *War of the Worlds*, complete with news bulletins and field reports of a supposed Martian landing and invasion in New Jersey. The radio play caused a panic among thousands of listeners; some even armed themselves and fled for the hills.

Orson was also the boy genius that co-wrote, directed, and starred in the film *Citizen Kane*, an extraordinary epic that some consider to be the greatest movie ever made. The film won Orson accolades and Academy Awards as well as numerous offers to direct many other films. After *Citizen Kane*, though, Orson's directorial work was inconsistent and he was eventually unable to find work as a director. Orson resorted to acting, just for the money, it seems, as his primary ambition was to acquire necessary financing for a number of his other dream projects. The next decades of his life were a cycle of bad movies, grandiose projects that inevitably failed, and then more acting work to acquire more funds. After years of acting in truly terrible films (with the exceptions of *Jane Eyre* and *A Man for All Seasons*), and decades of relentless panning by critics, Orson had fallen from grace in Hollywood.

In the twilight of his life, Orson enjoyed a new acceptance within the show business mainstream and, even though he still could not attract the funding to direct motion pictures, he became a frequent talk-show guest and commercial pitchman.

In his latter years, Orson was obese and suffered a number of weight-related ailments. Seated at his typewriter working on the next day's script changes for his movie, *The Other Side of the Wind*, Orson suffered a heart attack and died at 70.

He was cremated and his ashes shipped to the retired bullfighter Antonio Ordoñez, an old friend, in Ronda, Spain. Orson's cremains were placed into an old brick well at Ordoñez's country house, which was then sealed and, per Orson's request, no designation of any kind marks the spot.

MAE WEST
AUGUST 17, 1892 – NOVEMBER 22, 1980

MAE WEST LEFT formal education behind at age 12 to join a professional stock company, and by 14 was consistently drawing crowds to the vaudeville stage. With tight-fitting clothing and provocative comments delivered in a throaty voice, Mae soon gained a bawdy reputation and throughout her career never squandered an opportunity to heighten this risqué allure or, better yet, use it to advantage.

In 1926 she wrote a play entitled *Sex*. It was popular on Broadway, but after 41 weeks of performances the entire cast was arrested and Mae was found guilty of corrupting the morals of youth. Later plays, *The Drag, Pleasure Man*, and *Constant Sinner* also became the targets of censors and some were forced to close after just one performance.

Tired of censorship struggles, Mae moved to Hollywood in 1931, confident that a career in film would afford more artistic freedom. Already popular onstage, she immediately won a contract with Paramount and enjoyed an enormous streak of success at the box office. Opposite many of the biggest actors of the day, Mae played diverse roles, from lion tamers to gangsters' girlfriends, with the haughty sexuality that had become her trademark.

By the 1940s though, Mae's age began to show and as her allure slipped, so did her popularity. Mae attempted to return to the stage but, beyond writing and starring in the risqué play *Catherine Was Great*, her revival was not well received. In the early 1950s Mae tried again to revive her career, this time creating a nightclub act, complete with bodybuilders in loincloths, that portrayed her as a sultry siren, though she was now over 60.

Apparently, Mae never heard the word "quit," because in the 1960s she was back again—this time with an album that featured her singing Bob Dylan and Beatles songs. In 1977, at 84, Mae made one last movie, *Sextette*, which even her die-hard fans agree was her worst ever.

In her final years, Mae became increasingly interested in paranormal events and insisted she was in contact with a pet monkey who had died. Mae herself expired at 88 after suffering a stroke and lies at Cypress Hills Cemetery in Brooklyn, New York.

GRAVE DIRECTIONS: Enter the cemetery at 833 Jamaica Avenue, turn right, and go past the office. After the road's left-hand bend, turn at the first right and then the next left. Go up the hill and Memorial Abbey will be in front of you. In this Abbey, which is generally locked, is the West family tomb.

ROBIN WILLIAMS
JULY 21, 1951 – AUGUST 11, 2014

BEFORE ATTAINING A full scholarship to study acting at New York's Juilliard School, Robin Williams was an unknown funnyman who performed as a mime on Manhattan street corners. He left the school during his junior year on the advice of John Houseman, the founding director of the school, who, recognizing that the school's conservative and classical environment wasn't a fit for Robin, told him he was wasting his time and there was nothing more Juilliard could teach him. Unable to find work, Robin moved back home to the San Francisco area to attend "a comedy workshop that was in the basement of a church that had lesbian poetry and stand-up."

Thereafter Robin quickly established a local reputation for his wacky stand-up comedy, and that led to a bit of TV work, which eventually resulted in a guest spot playing a character named Mork on the *Happy Days* sitcom. Response to that appearance was so strong that the network parlayed Mork into the spinoff *Mork & Mindy*, a zany yet endearing fish-out-of-water tale in which Robin played an alien from the planet Ork. By the time the series ended in 1982, Robin had firmly imprinted a fully formed idiosyncratic comedy style onto the public consciousness. His madcap monologues, chock-full of unexpected accents and non sequiturs and peppered with uniquely screwball, off-the-cuff impersonations and a whirlwind of free-association riffs and gags delivered at a startling speed, had become his trademarks, and he was recognized as one of the brightest new comedians as well as a perennial favorite of late-night television talk-show audiences.

All the exposure earned Robin the leverage to expand his craft into film, and though there was considerable skepticism over whether or not he was a one-trick pony who might be capable only of "Mork from Ork" types of characters, he ended up surprising the doubters with a slew of successful film roles that showcased both his comedic ability and what turned out to be an all-star talent for serious fare as well.

Among his most notable roles were the high-octane disc jockey Adrian Cronauer in *Good Morning, Vietnam*, freethinking teacher John Keating in *Dead Poets Society*, the troubled homeless man Parry in *The Fisher King*, a creepy photo developer in *One Hour Photo*, and, of course, the hilarious cross-dressing Mrs. Doubtfire. Even when not pictured on-screen, Robin had a tendency to become the center of attention, including a celebrated turn as the voice of the nutty genie in the animated film *Aladdin*.

After returning from a Minnesota alcoholism treatment center, sleeping in a different room from his wife due to restlessness and anxiety, and suffering from depression and a general despondency, at 63 he chose to take his own life. Found "cold to the touch" in his bedroom by his personal assistant, Robin had asphyxiated himself with a belt slung from a closet door. Superficial cuts on the inside of his left wrist were found along with a pocketknife that had his dried blood on it. An autopsy revealed no alcohol or illegal drugs in his system, and while prescription medications were present, their concentrations were found to be at therapeutic levels. Examination of his brain tissue also confirmed that the comic was suffering from Lewy body dementia, a degenerative disorder whose primary feature is cognitive decline and hallucinations. Doctors agreed that this condition "was the critical factor" in his suicide.

Robin was cremated and his ashes scattered around his beloved San Francisco Bay.

FLIP WILSON
DECEMBER 8, 1933 – NOVEMBER 25, 1998

ONE OF 18 children born to a poor New Jersey household, Clerow "Flip" Wilson lied about his age and joined the Air Force at 16. With a lively sense of humor, he excelled in the service and it was his fellow servicemen who branded him "Flip," for his "flipped-out" personality. After leaving the Air Force at 21, Flip worked as a bellhop and moonlighted as a stand-up comedian. In 1965 he was invited to appear on *The Tonight Show*, and after that exposure, his star rose meteorically. Within a few years he had his own television show, *The Flip Wilson Show*.

The variety comedy show received only a tepid response at first, but wide-eyed Flip quickly drove the show to the top of the ratings with his keen wit and a collection of stock characters to which he brought comedic life with his hysterical body fluidity: Geraldine Jones was the sassy and swinging liberate who "don't take no stuff." There was the lecherous and slightly less-than-honest Reverend LeRoy of the Church of What's Happening, and Sonny the White House janitor was the "wisest man in Washington."

In 1974, after four award-winning seasons, the show's time was up and, strangely enough, so was Flip's. Though he'd exhibited that he could draw audiences, his career immediately lost its momentum and, except for an occasional guest spot, Flip vanished from show business.

At 64, Flip died after surgery to remove a malignant tumor on his liver. He was cremated and his ashes given to his family.

THE WIZARD OF OZ

IF *THE WIZARD of Oz* had been released in almost any other year but 1939, it more than likely would have swept the Academy Awards. However, 1939 was one of the greatest years in movie history and *Oz* competed against such acclaimed films as *Mr. Smith*

Goes to Washington, Of Mice and Men, Wuthering Heights, and *Gone With the Wind*. Opposite such strong competition, *Oz* won just two "Ozcars."

It did establish a new Hollywood benchmark of excellence for family musicals, but *The Wizard of Oz* didn't receive its deserved recognition until it debuted on television, almost 20 years later, to an audience that was very different from the Depression-era movie patrons who had celebrated its first release.

In 1956 MGM sold the *Wizard of Oz* rights to CBS. It debuted on television in November of that year and, because their agreement stipulated that *Oz* could only be aired once a year, CBS presented the film with all the pomp and circumstance afforded a precious jewel, causing a substantial lifting of the film's cultural status in the opinion of viewers. For the next 30 years, the annual showing of the *Wizard of Oz* was a can't-miss event for children of all ages because, if you did miss it, there was a one-year-long wait until Dorothy would again click her heels together. As a result, though *The Wizard of Oz* is certainly secure on its own merits as one of the best films ever made, the pageantry that surrounded its airings has indelibly branded *Oz* into the psyche of Baby Boomers who link it to the warmth and security of an innocent time long gone. Indeed, there's no place like home.

L. FRANK BAUM
MAY 15, 1856 – MAY 6, 1919

ORIGINALLY FROM A wealthy family in the castor oil business, Lyman Frank Baum took turns as a small-town journalist, a chicken breeder, and an actor before failing as the proprietor of a South Dakota general store. Finally, at 40, Frank settled into writing and in the course of his remaining days turned out 30 books, from fairy-tale collections to window-dressing manuals. But, of course, Frank's most celebrated book is *The Wonderful Wizard of Oz*.

The book was immediately popular upon its release in 1900 and two years later, it became a musical stage production. Soon Frank's life revolved around everything *Oz*; he wrote 13 *Oz* sequels, published a periodical, *The Ozmopolitan*, and built a home in California that he called "Ozcot." But for all his enthusiasm for his progeny, Frank would not live to enjoy its greatest celebrity.

At 62, 20 years before his *Wizard of Oz* appeared in Technicolor, Frank died of a congenital heart defect. He directed his last words to his wife, saying, "Now we can cross the shifting sands," a reference to the boundary that separates this world from the Land of Oz.

Frank was buried at Forest Lawn Memorial Park in Glendale, California.

GRAVE DIRECTIONS: Enter the park at 1712 South Glendale Avenue, get a map at the information booth, and drive over to Section G, which is in a maze of lawns behind the funeral home. In the middle of the section you'll see the white Peters stone, and just 20 feet left is the big and blocky Baum stone.

TOTO
1932 – 1945

CONTRARY TO POPULAR belief, the little Cairn terrier who played Toto in *The Wizard of Oz* was not named Toto, until *Oz* became so popular that almost everyone forgot what her original name was. Like all of the other cast members, she had a character name, Toto, and a real name, Terry. She may have been the best player on the set too, because, without even the benefit of makeup or a costume, Terry the girl dog played Toto the boy dog.

Terry's owner and trainer, a guy named Carl Spitz who ran the Hollywood Dog Training School, adopted her in 1933 but had no plans for little Terry to become a movie star. Her original owner had left her to be trained but never returned. Later, when the casting director put out a call for a dog that looked like the one in the illustrations in *The Wonderful Wizard of Oz*, Carl knew right away that they needed a Cairn terrier, and he brought Terry to the studio.

Terry was hired on the spot and she immediately began living the high life, which meant two weeks at Judy Garland's house and a $125-a-week salary. But life in the spotlight wasn't always glamorous. Terry didn't like being in the basket, she cowered when the set's wind machines were switched on, and she suffered a sprained foot after being stepped on accidentally by one of the Witch's guards. But Terry recuperated, and she returned a few weeks later to film the Munchkinland scenes, as good as new.

After *Oz*, Terry's name was officially changed to Toto and she appeared in another half-dozen films. In 1945, Toto died at 13 (that's 91 in dog years) and was buried somewhere in Carl's backyard, somewhere in Hollywood, California.

VICTOR FLEMING
FEBRUARY 23, 1883 – JANUARY 6, 1949

STARTING IN HOLLYWOOD as a chauffeur, Victor Fleming eventually finagled a position as an assistant cameraman. Later, as President Woodrow Wilson's official cameraman, he filmed the signing of the Treaty of Versailles, which marked the end of World War I. Armed with those credentials, Victor returned to Hollywood in 1919 and made his directorial debut, launching a three-decade-long career with MGM Studios.

Victor had a talent for spectacular action movies but, though *The Wizard of Oz* may have been a bit of a departure from his usual directorial duties, the film certainly doesn't seem to have suffered. Remarkably, *Oz* wasn't the only blockbuster that Victor directed in 1939; when George Cukor quit as director of *Gone With the Wind*, Victor took over the job and, for two months until the shooting for *Oz* finished, he directed them simultaneously. When Academy Awards were passed out in February 1940, it was no surprise that a frazzled Victor walked out with the award for best director, though it was for his *Gone With the Wind* work.

At 65, Victor died of a heart attack and now lies at Hollywood Forever in Hollywood, California.

GRAVE DIRECTIONS: Enter the cemetery at 6000 Santa Monica Boulevard, turn right after the information booth, then make a left and stop in front of the Hollywood Forever Mausoleum, which is the huge building on your right. Victor is inside this mausoleum in the Sanctuary of Refuge. Walk inside, turn left, and, about halfway down this hall, on the right-hand side and second row from the floor, is Victor's crypt at number 2081.

FRANK MORGAN
JULY 1, 1890 – SEPTEMBER 18, 1949

WHEN CASTING BEGAN for *The Wizard of Oz*, MGM executives searched for a famous comedian to fill the title role. But their first choice, W.C. Fields, wanted too much money and Ed Wynn turned down the part because he felt it was too small.

Finally, one of the studio's own character actors who already had an Academy nomination under his belt, Frank Morgan, auditioned for the part of the befuddled Wizard. He was perfect. In fact, Frank landed not just one part but five: Frank also played Professor Marvel, the Emerald City gatekeeper, a cabby, and a soldier.

After *The Wizard of Oz*, Frank continued acting and earned another Oscar nomination for *Tortilla Flat* in 1942. Away from Hollywood, he tended to his 550-acre California farm.

At 59, Frank died in his sleep and was buried at Greenwood Cemetery in Brooklyn, New York.

GRAVE DIRECTIONS: Enter the cemetery through the elaborate gates at 500 25th Street, bear left up Battle Avenue, and drive up the hill. Turn left onto Border Avenue, keeping the city street and fence to your left, until you reach Sassafras Avenue. Turn right, then make a left onto Grape Avenue and, immediately before Lychnis Path, you'll see the Wupperman plot on the left. (Wupperman was Frank's given surname.)

CHARLIE GRAPEWIN
DECEMBER 20, 1869 – FEBRUARY 2, 1956

BY THE TIME Charlie Grapewin was offered the role of kindly old Uncle Henry in *The Wizard of Oz*, he'd already spent nearly 40 years in the movie business and was thinking about getting out of it for good. But when casting began for the movie, Charlie was the first choice to fill the role, in no small part because he appeared in the original *Wizard of Oz* stage musical back in 1902. For old times' sake, he postponed his retirement and accepted the role.

Apparently, Charlie enjoyed his one week of filming because he forgot his retirement plans and appeared in another two dozen movies after *Oz*, most notably as Grandpa Joad in *The Grapes of Wrath*.

At 86 Charlie died of natural causes. He was cremated and his ashes interred at Forest Lawn Cemetery in Glendale, California.

For directions, see Clara Blandick's profile. Her ashes happen to be interred in the same mausoleum as Charlie's, though his are kept at Niche 14639 in the Columbarium of Inspiration.

CLARA BLANDICK
JUNE 4, 1881 – APRIL 15, 1962

CLARA BLANDICK ENJOYED a 40-year career as a stage and film actress but, as Auntie Em on the film that would immortalize her, she worked for just one week. And she's almost forgotten there; for some reason, Clara's name doesn't appear in the film's opening credits and she is billed last in the closing credits, right below Pat Walshe, who was the chief winged monkey. Perhaps MGM felt that the $750 Clara received for her appearance was payment enough.

After *The Wizard of Oz*, Clara continued acting and most often appeared as an archetypal maternal character or kindly spinster until her retirement in 1950.

In 1962, after years of surviving as a near-blind arthritic, Clara had had enough. Following a Palm Sunday service, Clara returned to her room at the Hollywood Roosevelt Hotel, dressed in her finest clothes, and penned a suicide note that began, "I am now about to take the great adventure . . ." Clara then ingested a number of sleeping pills, secured a plastic bag around her head, and died.

At 80, Clara was cremated and her ashes interred at Forest Lawn Memorial Park in Glendale, California.

GRAVE DIRECTIONS: Enter the park at 1712 South Glendale Avenue. If you'd like, you can stop at the booth, get a map of the grounds, and make your way over to the Great Mausoleum where Clara's remains are interred, but it probably won't do you any good. The Great Mausoleum is open only to property owners and there's a gatekeeper at its entrance that keeps everyone honest. But if you do manage to schmooze your way in, Clara's niche is Number 17230 in the Columbarium of Security.

BERT LAHR
AUGUST 13, 1895 – DECEMBER 3, 1967

LIKE MOST OF his *Oz* costars, Bert Lahr, the Cowardly Lion, got his start in burlesque theater and vaudeville. He met his wife, Mercedes Delpino, on the circuit and by 1925 they were listed as a Keith-Albee All-Star Act. By the 1930s Bert's career was firing on all cylinders but Mercedes' mental health was deteriorating and she was soon committed to a sanitarium. Bert spent the next years mugging and gagging his way through film roles but, personally, he anguished over Mercedes.

Within a few years it was apparent that Mercedes' situation was hopeless, and Bert became involved with another woman, Mildred. But Bert was unable to annul his marriage to Mercedes and, in the meantime, Mildred married someone else. By the time filming for *The Wizard of Oz* began, Bert was beside himself, constantly anxious, unable to sleep, and suffering from a variety of imagined illnesses—just like the Cowardly Lion.

The boundless energy that made Bert the perfect lion made him difficult to cast in other films and after *Oz*, Bert retreated back to the stage. Bert was finally offered a role in the nostalgic 1967 film *The Night They Raided Minsky's*. But unfortunately, he died of a hemorrhage resulting from cancer complications during the film's production, forcing the producers to finish the film with a different actor in several scenes.

At 72, Bert was buried at the Union Field Cemetery of Congregation Rodeph Sholom in Ridgewood, Queens, New York.

GRAVE DIRECTIONS: At 11 Cypress Avenue, proceed down the road that's directly behind the office. After it bends to the left, watch for path markings on the curb and stop at number 5 on the right. A short way down this path, Bert is buried on the right-hand side.

JUDY GARLAND
JUNE 10, 1922 – JUNE 22, 1969

WITH HER OVERAMBITIOUS stage mother prodding her along, 13-year-old Judy Garland reported to MGM as a contract player in 1935 for $100 a week. Judy attended school on the studio lot with other future stars Ava Gardner and Mickey Rooney and, except for appearing in a handful of unremarkable movies, Judy was more or less just another teenager until 1939, when she lost herself and found Dorothy Gale, the forever-young, celluloid image of magnetic warmth blessed with a beautifully strong, tremulous singing voice. Later, when Dorothy became more than just a film personality to Judy's fans, the innocent teenager named Judy disappeared forever.

In the decade after *Oz*, superstar Judy was a moneymaking machine for MGM and she made films at a breakneck pace. Judy married twice, began smoking heavily, and rode the roller coaster of drug and alcohol abuse. When the pace became unbearable in 1950, Judy escalated her troubles by slitting her own neck with a piece of glass. Within a few years, though, life for Judy turned more agreeable; MGM canceled her contract, her domineering mother died, and she married Sid Luft. It was Sid's idea that she sing in concerts and the 1950s turned out to be some of Judy's best years. While dazzling sell-out crowds with concerts that invariably included her lifelong theme song, "Over the Rainbow," Judy also returned to the silver screen and gave a knockout performance in *A Star Is Born*.

But by the early '60s, the screw had again turned and she accelerated toward her tragic destiny. Hanging out with the Rat Pack exacerbated her drinking problem, and *The Judy Garland Show* was canceled after she appeared on it drunk and disoriented once too often. Although she was brilliant in *Judgment at Nuremberg*, she was fired from other movies. Her personal life was again a shambles; she lived in hotels, was constantly in and out of hospitals for substance-related illnesses and, not surprisingly, her fourth marriage was disintegrating. By the late 1960s the prematurely aged Judy was performing onstage again, but her voice was shot, and she would often slur her way through her concerts.

In 1969 Judy was living in London with her fifth husband, Mickey Deans. He awoke one morning to a phone call for Judy and, seeing that she wasn't in bed, called for her in the bathroom. Getting no answer and finding the door locked, Mickey climbed onto the roof to look in the bathroom window and, there on the toilet, he saw Judy slumped over dead at 47.

The coroner determined she had died "of an incautious self-overdosage of sleeping pills," though others saw her death in less clinical terms. Ray Bolger, the Scarecrow, said, "Judy didn't die of anything except wearing out. She just plain wore out."

In the silver lamé gown she'd worn at her most recent wedding, Judy was interred in a crypt at the Ferncliff Mausoleum in Hartsdale, New York.

GRAVE DIRECTIONS: Enter the cemetery at 280 Secor Road, bear left, and park toward the left-hand side of the main mausoleum. Enter the mausoleum through the front bronze doors and go up the stairs on the left. At the top of the stairs turn left, go to the end of the hall, and turn left again. Then make the next right, walk up the four stairs, and turn at the next right. Judy is in Alcove HH on the left bottom wall.

BILLIE BURKE
AUGUST 7, 1884 – MAY 14, 1970

BILLIE BURKE, THE delightful redhead cast as Glinda the Good Witch in *The Wizard of Oz*, was named after her father, Billy Burke, a Barnum and Bailey circus clown.

After establishing herself as a stage actress in London, where she spent her formative years, Billie moved to the States in 1908 and duplicated that success in the New York theater. In 1919 Billie married Florenz Ziegfeld, the producer whose dazzling *Ziegfeld Follies* revues featuring glitzy costumes and lavish sets epitomized the theatrical excesses of the Roaring Twenties. With money no longer an issue, Billie retired from show business to have a family, but the stock market crash of 1929 financially devastated their household and Billie was forced to return to work. Three years later, Florenz died of a stress-related heart attack.

Billie was 55 when she was cast as Glinda in 1939, and, as she was under contract to MGM, she didn't receive any more compensation for the blockbuster movie than her regular paycheck. By the time she played her last role in 1960, Billie had appeared in almost 70 films, usually as a daffy and scatterbrained lady of society. Highlights include *Dinner at Eight*, *Father of the Bride*, and *Merrily We Live*, the last of which earned her an Oscar nomination.

Ten years after she retired for good, natural causes sent Billie over the rainbow at 85.

She rests alongside husband Florenz at Kensico Cemetery in Valhalla, New York.

GRAVE DIRECTIONS: At 273 Lakeview Avenue, enter the cemetery at the Commerce Street entrance and then cross over to Powhattan Avenue. Follow it to the circle and there on the left, in Section 78 behind the Roth mausoleum, lies Billie Burke.

JACK HALEY
AUGUST 10, 1899 – JUNE 6, 1979

JACK HALEY, THE Tin Man who wanted a heart, used to say that the first five years of his life were a waste because he didn't yet know what he would do with his life but, at six, he attended a play and resolved to become a dancer. After a run in vaudeville, Jack became a contract player at Fox and he appeared with Judy Garland in her very first feature film, *Pigskin Parade*, in 1936. But like the rest of the cast, it was his *Oz* role that brought Jack immortality.

Buddy Ebsen was MGM's original choice for the Tin Man, but after he suffered a nearly fatal allergic reaction to the makeup, Fox lent Jack out for the role. Jack later recalled that his days on the *Oz* set were among his most miserable because of the costume. Two hours a day were spent in the makeup chair, and once he had his costume on, he could not sit or lie down.

In 1974, an oddly personal bond was forged between Judy Garland and Jack; the Tin Man's real-life son, Jack Haley, Jr., married Dorothy's real-life daughter, Liza Minnelli.

Ironically, after wanting for a heart in *Oz*, it turned out that Jack's real-life ticker failed him. At 79, he died of a heart attack and was buried at Holy Cross Cemetery in Culver City, California.

GRAVE DIRECTIONS: Enter the cemetery at 5835 Slauson Avenue, turn left, and start up the hill. A hundred yards on the left is the Grotto lawn and altar, and six rows down the hill from the altar is Jack's grave.

MARGARET HAMILTON
DECEMBER 9, 1902 – MAY 16, 1985

MARGARET HAMILTON, WHO was a kindergarten teacher before landing her first movie role in 1933, played the cackling Wicked Witch of the West. And, like Jack Haley, the Tin Man, Margaret wasn't the studio's original choice for the role of the Wicked Witch.

The producers originally wanted the Wicked Witch of the West to be slinky and glamorous, like the wicked queen in Disney's *Snow White*, and they cast star actress Gale Sondergaard, envisioning her in a tight-fitting black sequined dress. But when it was decided that the witch would instead be ugly and hateful, Sondergaard backed out of the film and Margaret got the nod.

When Margaret Hamilton stepped onto the set she was already experienced in the role, having played it twice in community theater productions. After suffering through the makeup routine, Margaret's withering scowl and screeching chortle further enhanced the character's identity and audiences believed her to be very old. But in fact, Margaret was just 36, while Billie Burke, as Glinda the Good Witch, was 55.

After *Oz*, Margaret continued to act in a variety of media and in the 1970s she appeared in commercials as Cora, the shopkeeper who sold only Maxwell House coffee.

At 82, Margaret died of a heart attack. She was cremated and her ashes remain with her family.

RAY BOLGER
JANUARY 10, 1904 – JANUARY 15, 1987

WHILE RAY BOLGER'S portrayal of the Scarecrow made him one of the most beloved characters in *The Wizard of Oz*, Ray seemed to love *Oz* fans just as much. He was one of the few *Oz* actors who lived long enough to enjoy the movie's success after it became a television phenomenon, and he faithfully made *Oz*-related appearances, signed autographs, and sat for interviews.

Starting in vaudeville, Ray Bolger was half of a dance team called Sanford and Bolger. By 1936 Ray had secured a contract with MGM and when casting began for *The Wizard of Oz*, he was delighted to be included, then horrified to find out that he had been cast as the Tin Man. Knowing his dance style was better suited to the rubbery-legged straw man, he fought for the Scarecrow role and eventually wore down studio executives, who agreed to a switch.

The slow pace of moviemaking took its toll on high-energy Ray and, a month after finishing *The Wizard of Oz*, he asked to be released from his MGM contract. Ray then returned to his comfort zone on Broadway stages, though he reunited with Judy Garland in *The Harvey Girls* in 1946 and with Margaret Hamilton in *The Daydreamer* in 1966. He had his own television sitcom in 1953, *The Ray Bolger Show*, and later made the rounds on talk shows. In 1985, Ray took an affectionate look back at his 50-year career in a *That's Dancing* film extravaganza that was sentimentally co-hosted by Judy's daughter, Liza Minnelli, and directed by her ex-husband Jack Haley Jr., who was the son of the Tin Man from *Oz*, Jack Haley.

Three years later, Ray died of bladder cancer and he bequeathed a $2.5 million trust in his name to the UCLA School of Theater, Film, and Television.

At 83, Ray was laid to rest at Holy Cross Cemetery in Culver City, California.

GRAVE DIRECTIONS: Enter the cemetery at 5835 Slauson Avenue, drive to the mausoleum at the top of the hill, and enter it through the front door. Proceed straight into the chapel and you'll see Ray's crypt alongside the pews, the sixth one on the bottom left.

NATALIE WOOD
JULY 20, 1938 – NOVEMBER 29, 1981

NATALIE WOOD WAS only four years old when she began her Hollywood career, and this little darling became one of the very few child actors who made a successful transition to adult stardom. Born Natasha Gurdin to Russian parents, Natalie made her mark as a nine-year-old costar in *Miracle on 34th Street*. After struggling through adolescence on a television series called *Pride of the Family*, she broke out for good as a young adult opposite James Dean in *Rebel Without a Cause*.

In 1961, the success of *West Side Story* vaulted petite and doe-eyed Natalie to superstar status and so began an insatiable public appetite for Natalie. The reports of her flamboyant lifestyle, huge salaries, and romantic escapades, her mansions and yachts, midnight swims, motorcycle rides, celebrity parties, and night life fueled the aura surrounding Natalie Wood. Heightening the mystique further, many of her films' titles during this era were suggestive and controversial and, even though most were not critical successes, her films were consistent box-office hits because of her star power.

Natalie was wed three times, including twice to the same guy, actor Robert Wagner. At 19, she married him for five years and then, at 30, she married British producer Richard Gregson, with whom she stayed for four years and had a daughter. In 1973, when she was 35, Natalie and Robert married for the second time, but several years later the marriage again began to crumble.

One night in November 1981, after a swordfish dinner and a lot of wine at a posh restaurant on California's Catalina Island, Natalie and Robert, along with actor Christopher Walken, returned to the couple's yacht, anchored offshore. Walken had been romantically linked to Natalie and he was costarring with her in *Brainstorm*, a science-fiction film that would be released posthumously. Around midnight, Natalie excused herself and went to bed while the two drunken men carried on, sometimes arguing.

Unable to sleep because the dinghy kept bumping into the vessel, it seems that she went out on the deck to tie it more securely but, inebriated from the night's refreshments, she accidentally slipped into the water. The Coast Guard found Natalie wearing bed socks and a short tartan nightie, wrapped in a waterlogged red duvet, floating face down in the water offshore near Catalina's lava caves.

Robert and Walken, as well as the yacht's captain, who had been sleeping in his cabin, were separately interrogated, and their testimony was found to be fairly consistent. Bruises found on Natalie's arms and hands were believed to have been a result of her struggles to climb back aboard the vessel. Though her death was ruled an accidental drowning, the three men's versions of the night's events never quite jibed, and many believe that one of them has been less than completely truthful. Forty years on, some look askance at Wagner, cautiously suspicious of a more nefarious role he may have played in Natalie's untimely death.

Robert had named their yacht *Splendor* after the 1961 movie *Splendor in the Grass*, for which Natalie was nominated for an Oscar. It was an odd gesture since, during its filming, Natalie had fallen for the routine seductions of costar Warren Beatty, which led to the breakup of her first marriage with Robert. Even more ironic, in *Splendor in the Grass* Natalie played a girl who tried to drown herself.

Natalie was 43 and was buried at Westwood Memorial Park in Los Angeles.

GRAVE DIRECTIONS: Behind the office complex at 10850 Wilshire Boulevard, Natalie's marker is in the central lawn of the cemetery. Counting from the drive bordering the top of the lawn, it's in the fifth row, approximately in the middle.

ORIGINAL
WOMEN

MAYA ANGELOU

APRIL 4, 1928 – MAY 28, 2014

MAYA ANGELOU PUBLISHED more than 30 books in her lifetime, rising to fame in 1969 with the publication of her landmark work, *I Know Why the Caged Bird Sings*, an exploration of her childhood and teenage years through the lens of race, family, community, and the collective past.

She lived an itinerant childhood, alternately raised by her mother in St. Louis and her grandmother in a rural Jim Crow–plagued hamlet of Arkansas. Though Maya's grandmother's general store "in the heart of the Negro area" made the family relatively well-off, they nonetheless suffered the ugly everyday casual racism endemic to such communities in the 1930s. As she wrote in the acclaimed memoir, she was sexually assaulted by her mother's boyfriend at age seven, and after she testified against him, he was tried and convicted for the crime but was jailed for just one day. Upon his release, the man was beaten to death, probably by her uncles, and the ordeal caused Maya to cease speaking for years. "My seven-and-a-half-year-old logic deduced that my voice had killed him, so I stopped speaking for almost six years," she said. She later wrote that her love of literature helped restore language to her, and the experience helped her find the lyrical and searing voice that punctuated her later writing.

Delving into her struggles with the rape, racial identity, and sexism, *I Know Why the Caged Bird Sings* is her story up to age 17, when she quit high school to support her son as a single mother. In following volumes, Maya chronicled the struggles and triumphs of her remarkable and varied life: winning a scholarship to a San Francisco arts school; working as a shake dancer in nightclubs, a cable car conductor, a fry cook in hamburger joints, and a laborer in a mechanic's garage; and supporting herself with short-lived stints as a prostitute and a madam. The works go on to recount her three marriages and alternate brief careers in Egypt and Ghana, where she worked as an editor and journalist. In the 1950s she toured the world as a featured dancer in a production of *Porgy and Bess* and released an album, *Calypso Lady*.

Settling in New York at the age of 31, she became active in the Harlem Writers Guild, helped Malcolm X set up the Organization of Afro-American Unity, and became coordinator of the New York office of the Southern Christian Leadership Conference. Later she sang at the Apollo, earned a Tony Award nomination for her role in the Broadway production of *Look Away*, portrayed Kunta Kinte's grandmother in the television series *Roots*, and appeared in feature films including *How to Make an American Quilt*. In 1993, she read the poem "On the Pulse of Morning" at the swearing in for President Bill Clinton, the recording of which won a Grammy.

Her writing career took off when a dinner companion urged her to memorialize her captivating childhood stories in print. When she wrote, Maya stuck to a rigid set of rituals. She wrote in hotel rooms, going so far as to rent one near her home if she was writing there. Stretched out on the bed with yellow notepads, an ashtray, a deck of cards, a dictionary, a thesaurus, and a Bible next to her, she relaxed by playing solitaire until her muse came to her. Though she cited Poe, Shakespeare, Frederick Douglass, and Thomas Paine as her literary influences, she credited herself too. "I created myself," she said. "I have taught myself so much."

At 86, Maya died of natural causes at her North Carolina home. She was cremated and her ashes remain with her family.

ERMA BOMBECK
FEBRUARY 21, 1927 – APRIL 22, 1996

AS AMERICA'S FIRST lady of household humor, Erma Bombeck turned her views of daily life in the suburbs into satirical newspaper columns and 14 best-selling books, including *I Lost Everything in the Post-Natal Depression* and *The Grass Is Always Greener Over the Septic Tank*.

Erma began a career in journalism but left the profession in 1953 to start a family. At 37 she realized she was "too old for a paper route, too young for Social Security and too tired for an affair," and started writing a weekly column for a local paper. The column, "At Wit's End," was a showcase for her repartee and observations on such drudgery as dirty laundry, uncooperative pets, nosy neighbors, and her blossoming, know-it-all children. She was master of precise witticisms, to wit: "No one ever died from sleeping in an unmade bed"; "Never go to a doctor whose office plants have died"; and "It goes without saying that you should never have more children than you have car windows." Erma's banter raised the spirits of housewives and, within a year, her column was syndicated, eventually appearing in more than 600 papers.

In 1991 Erma was diagnosed with breast cancer and underwent a mastectomy shortly thereafter. Two years later she began a daily routine of dialysis as polycystic kidney disease took hold and, in April 1996, Erma received a kidney transplant. For the first time, Erma discussed her disease in a column to her readers, writing about illness and compassion, and her faithful, adoring readers responded by the thousands with moving sympathy for their adored spokeswoman.

Three weeks after the operation, Erma died of complications from the transplant at 69.

At her funeral service, one eulogist reminded mourners of a final Erma quotation: "When I stand before God at the end of my life, I would hope that I would not have a single bit of talent left and could say, 'I used everything you gave me.'"

She was buried at Woodlawn Cemetery in Dayton, Ohio.

GRAVE DIRECTIONS: Enter the cemetery at 118 Woodland Avenue and, after about 150 yards, to the left you'll see a bench with two derby hats sculpted into it (dedicated to the Wright Brothers). Behind this bench is a jagged boulder that was trucked from her Arizona home, and behind that lies Erma.

JULIA CHILD
AUGUST 15, 1912 – AUGUST 13, 2004

DURING WORLD WAR II, Julia Child found work with the Office of Strategic Services and her first successful recipe was for a shark repellent that prevented underwater explosives from being prematurely jostled and detonated by sharks. Remaining in France after the war with her high-ranking military husband, who was an erudite culinary expert, she attended the prestigious Le Cordon Bleu culinary academy and proved fearless in her willingness to try new techniques, from filleting a fish to gutting a chicken, and later opened her own informal school teaching the intricacies of French cuisine to fellow ex-pats.

In 1961, Julia's 734-page book (in collaboration with French chefs Simone Beck and Louisette Bertholle) *Mastering the Art of French Cooking* was published and soon topped the bestsellers list, lauded for its precise attention to detail and for making fine cuisine accessible to ordinary folk. Later that winter at an appearance to promote the book, Julia brought an omelet pan, a whisk, an apron, and a dozen eggs to liven up the televised interview and chattily whipped up an omelet in front of the cameras. A star was born.

Showcasing a *sui generis* persona, her own television series named *The French Chef* (which would become the longest-running program in the history of public television) soon debuted, and she eventually headlined eight more shows while penning nine additional cookbooks. As America's new gastronomic guru, Julia Child found no equal, and in a warbling and encouraging voice she elevated the nation's culinary standards. She taught that food and wine should be relished as a way of appreciating life's bounty and her *joie de vivre*, ability to explain techniques, and what-me-worry approach to mistakes made serious cooking fun. If she dropped a potato pancake while flipping it, she scraped it up and went on. Sipping wine and tasting liberally while cooking, Julia concluded every show with a cheery "Bon Appétit!"

At 91, Julia died in her sleep and was cremated. Her final meal was French onion soup.

DIANA, PRINCESS OF WALES

JULY 1, 1961 – AUGUST 31, 1997

DAUGHTER OF AN earl in one of the most aristocratic British families, Diana Frances Spencer was the perfect candidate to marry Prince Charles, heir to the throne. Their courtship began after her older sister Sarah's nine-month relationship with Charles ended and, at 19, Lady Diana Spencer became an object of fixation for the national media. She soon cultivated a bashful but charming smile for the cameras that earned her the nickname "Shy Di."

In February 1981, Charles proposed to Diana, and the couple appeared together in public for the first time at the official engagement announcement. They were married in the wedding of the century on July 29, 1981, at St. Paul's Cathedral. The couple smiled blissfully from the balcony at Buckingham Palace and kissed dutifully. To the adoring public, Diana and Charles appeared to be the perfect royal couple, especially when they produced William and Harry, an "heir and a spare."

Reports that their marriage was steadily unraveling leaked from the palace in the late 1980s, and the relentless press speculated that both Charles and Diana were having extramarital affairs. Indeed, Charles had resumed a liaison with a darling from his bachelorhood, Camilla Parker-Bowles, while Diana carried on with a cavalry officer, James Hewitt. In December 1992 it was announced that Charles and Diana were separating and a year later, Charles admitted in a television interview that he'd had an adulterous relationship with Camilla. Diana responded with her own admission of adultery and expressed her desire to be "queen of people's hearts."

In a February 1996 letter, Queen Elizabeth II urged the couple to divorce and by the end of the year their decree was officially granted. Under the terms of the divorce agreement, Diana shared custody of William and Harry, received a lump-sum payment of $26.5 million, and was allowed a Kensington Palace apartment. Diana was also stripped of her honorific "Her Royal Highness"; she would instead be known as Diana, Princess of Wales.

Though Diana maintained a hectic schedule of appearances, especially for her favorite charity causes—AIDS, breast cancer, child abuse, and land mines—as a new divorcée unencumbered by stodgy royal protocols, she began to live on her own terms and soon splashed into a romance with debonair Egyptian-born businessman Dodi Fayed.

Only five weeks into their whirlwind relationship, Diana and Dodi were killed in a car crash in a tunnel under the Seine River in Paris. Her death shocked the world and precipitated an outpouring of condolences that no one could have predicted. Anger was directed toward the paparazzi, which supposedly had been pursuing the fleeing Diana and her entourage, indirectly causing the crash. (It was later determined that the driver of their car, Henri Paul, who was also killed, was legally drunk at the time of the crash.) The report further stated that both Diana and Dodi would have survived the crash had they been wearing seatbelts.

Donations flooded the newly established Diana, Princess of Wales Fund, which was set up to serve her favorite charities, and Elton John earmarked future royalties from his song "Candle in the Wind," which he'd reworked to eulogize Diana, to the trust. After an extravagant service at Westminster Abbey, Diana was laid to rest on a leafy island in the center of a tranquil ornamental lake known as the Oval at the Spencer family's Althorp estate. The estate is open to the public during the summer months, but if you wish to see Diana's grave, save your money. Access anywhere near her resting place is restricted.

PHYLLIS DILLER
JULY 17, 1917 – AUGUST 20, 2012

THE RAPID-FIRE STYLE of Phyllis Diller's stand-up comedy was activated when, as a poor and dissatisfied 30-something mother of five, she regaled like-minded women at the local laundromat with hilarious accounts of her home life and habitually unemployed husband. Word spread about the sassy and screeching cutup and, after gaining confidence from an empowering self-help book that she read more than a dozen times, Phyllis was soon delighting audiences with barbed accounts of harried domestic life at any gathering that would have her—Christmas banquets, PTA meetings, retirement parties—wherever and whatever it took.

Her professional debut, at a nightclub called the Purple Onion in 1955, elicited only a lukewarm response, so Phyllis set to honing an outrageous stage persona. She dyed her hair platinum blonde and teased it into an electrified flyaway frenzy; wore short, shapeless dresses and long velvet gloves to accentuate her out-of-proportion toothpick limbs and flat chest; and carried a candy cigarette in a garish holder from which she continually flicked imaginary ashes. She sashayed precariously, her feet pointed penguin-style in stiff and outsized rhinestone-studded, high-heeled, knee-high laced shoes. Finally, Phyllis's thin, overlong features and wide-open eyes conspired with her shrill voice and menacing cackle to complete a unique sort of court-jester-meets-Wicked-Witch-of-the-West identity.

It all worked, and audiences delighted in Phyllis' flamboyant and crazed yet calculated style. Honing her barrage of rapid-fire self-deprecating jokes, the zany comedienne morphed into the ultimate domestic demon and with a straight face regaled howling audiences with madcap tales of how she prepared garbage soup and buried her ironing in the backyard. Of her husband she offered, "His finest hour lasted a minute and a half," and of her oversized mother-in-law Phyllis snickered, "If you get in an elevator with her, well, you better be going down." Within seven years Phyllis was selling out Carnegie Hall.

In the 1970s Phyllis became one of the first celebrities not just to have cosmetic surgery but also to acknowledge, publicize, and even brag about it. Keeping a plastic surgery "resume" on her person at all times, she would present it to anyone who asked. In two decades she underwent more than a dozen operations, including two nose jobs, three face lifts, chemical peels, cheek implants, eyeliner tattoos, a tummy tuck, and bonded and straightened teeth. Her candor about her surgeries earned her an award from the American Academy of Cosmetic Surgery as "the first person to have the courage to proclaim her surgery and show her results publicly."

After 47 years in stand-up, Phyllis played her last show at age 85. Asked later if she missed performing she said, "I don't miss the travel. I miss the laughter. I do miss the actual hour…that hour is a high, it's as good as you can feel."

Passing away "peacefully in her sleep with a smile on her face" at 95, Phyllis was cremated.

DIAN FOSSEY
JANUARY 16, 1932 – DECEMBER 27, 1985

IN 1967, DIAN Fossey established the Karisoke Research Center in Rwanda's Volcano National Park, and from this primitive and isolated rainforest camp, she studied mountain gorillas for almost 20 years. Dian's methodology was not to study the apes from afar, but rather to ingratiate herself into their society as a peripheral quasi-member. Thus, she put together a firsthand chronicle of the elusive apes' world.

By the 1970s, though, poachers had uncovered markets wherein gorilla babies could be sold for exhibition, and they were also able to command high black-market prices for the trophy heads, hands, and feet of adults. The appendages were made into ashtrays, of all things. Recognizing the threat posed to the gorillas' fragile population, Dian fought against the poachers. Rwandan authorities, however, did not consider poaching a priority, nor did they have adequate resources to control it.

Fears for the safety of her own gorilla "family" were justified in 1978 when her most darling gorilla, Digit, was killed. His hands and feet had been hacked off and other members of his family killed too. Dian buried the massacred gorillas in a cemetery she built by her camp and steeled herself to become a vigilante of sorts, engaging in an all-consuming, unconventional war against the poachers. Circulating stories that she was a sorceress who could curse her enemies, she played the role of a witch around suspected poachers and fueled the notion that she had the power to damn them. She organized antipoaching patrols and placed bounties on poachers' heads. On one occasion, she abducted the child of a local woman suspected of stealing a gorilla baby and offered to exchange hostages. Meanwhile, her Western colleagues wondered if Dian had gone insane.

Animosity between Dian and the poachers reached a boiling point and finally, at age 53, Dian was found dead at her tent compound, her body hacked to death by machete. No arrests were ever made, but conventional wisdom suggests that the killer or killers likely came from the poachers' ranks.

Fittingly, she was buried in her own Gorilla Graveyard near her beloved friend, Digit.

Dian's headstone summarizes her life:

Dian Fossey 1932-1985
No one loved gorillas more . . .

Deep within Africa's Virunga Mountains, the Karisoke Research Center and its Gorilla Graveyard lie in Rwanda, south of the base of Mount Visoke and Volcanoes National Park, two miles from the border with the Democratic Republic of the Congo (formerly Zaire).

In the 1990s a civil war and genocide wracked the Rwandan countryside and Virunga National Park filled with refugees, some of whom killed gorillas for food, while Dian's camp was completely looted and largely destroyed. Later, illegal logging decimated large areas of the park, but despite such adversity Dian's Gorilla Fund International soldiered on and, remarkably, the population of mountain gorillas in the park has today more than doubled from its low point of 255 in 1981.

BETTY FRIEDAN
February 4, 1921 – February 4, 2006

THROUGH 400 PAGES of impassioned yet clearheaded analysis of the issues that limited women, in her acclaimed 1963 manifesto *The Feminine Mystique* the egalitarianist and activist Betty Friedan tore open society's fabric to lay the groundwork for the modern feminist movement.

After training as a psychologist, Betty had turned down a research fellowship from Berkeley because the physicist she was dating felt overshadowed by her success. After marrying and moving to New York, she reported for a succession of labor union publications. But in 1952, upon becoming pregnant for a second time, she was dismissed, and for a handful of years, though she occasionally freelanced magazine articles, Betty's life centered on a vacant drudgery of cooking and mopping and laundering and shopping.

While conducting a survey for a reunion of her Smith graduating class in 1957, Betty discovered she wasn't alone in the dissatisfaction of her supposed suburban idyll. Unaccountably

BETTY FRIEDAN

February 4, 1921 · February 4, 2006

אִם לֹא עַכְשָׁיו אֵימָתַי

If not now, when?

tired, distraught, and impatient, many survey respondents described painfully limited existences and a craving for something that neither charity work nor bridge, nor therapy or tranquilizers or even an extramarital affair, could satisfy. Betty would famously categorize this widespread and troubling inclination as "the problem that has no name," a phony bill of goods that left women unfulfilled.

Cataloging their collective despair in a 7,000-word article, she found that no women's magazine would publish it, so Betty steeled herself to write her book. Identifying precisely why women were miserable, it hit like a veritable firebomb. Asserting that women should aspire to separate identities as individuals, that husbands and babies weren't everything, and that women needed to be treated as equals and freed to become themselves, Betty's ideas branded her as a revolutionary.

Book reviews ran the gamut from bewildered to outraged to laudatory, but it was the avalanche of letters from grateful housewives that convinced Betty she was onto something big and that much more than words was needed. To better the condition of women's lives she co-founded the National Organization for Women, and with the wind of legions of loyal sisters behind it, the movement campaigned on such issues as sex-neutral help-wanted ads, equal pay and promotion opportunities, maternity leave, and national daycare, while lobbying for the enforcement of inalienable constitutional rights for women.

Though Betty was hailed as a chief architect and impetus for the sweeping social upheaval and liberation victories won by feminists over the next decades, she was by no means universally beloved, even by members of her own movement. Famously abrasive and overbearing, she insisted on continually holding the floor and, running roughshod over assistants and claiming undue credit, she alienated many. Loathing political correctness and gender politics, she made unnecessary enemies with her sharp tongue, while she also fell from favor with the bra-burning, militant fringe of the movement who sought all-out war while Betty coached an incremental approach. In later years, as her focus turned to ageism and family issues, some even accused her of reversing the revolution, while others dismissed her work as outmoded. "It isn't that I have stopped being a feminist, but women as a special separate interest group are not my concern anymore," she countered.

In any event, many routine aspects of modern life—from unisex help-wanted ads to women in politics, the clergy, and the military—are a direct result of the momentum begun by *The Feminine Mystique*, and perhaps no other single book has ever been responsible for such tumultuous social change.

On her birthday, Betty died at home of congestive heart failure at 85 and was buried in the cemetery of Temple Adas Israel in Sag Harbor, New York.

GRAVE DIRECTIONS: At 320 Hampton Street (Route 114), park along the road and walk under the white Chevra Kodetia archway. About 100 feet inside, Betty's grave is next to the Schwartz monolith.

SUSAN HAYWARD
JUNE 30, 1919 – MARCH 14, 1975

IN MORE THAN 50 films, Susan Hayward's inspirational roles made her a favorite of female movie fans, and during the 1950s she was one of the most sought-after stars in Hollywood.

Beginning her life as Edythe Marrener, Susan created an indelible impression of brassy charm, pert sexiness, and a spirit that met tragedy with defiance in movies like *I Want to Live!* and *Smash-Up: The Story of a Woman*. Her greatest impact was playing real women who dealt with heartbreak and struggle, and endured.

Susan's personal life mirrored her movies, with many ups and downs: A modeling career started with a lucky break—she walked in the door of an agency just as it received a call for a redhead; a director who saw her picture in a magazine offered her a screen test; she was rejected as costar in *Gone With the*

Wind; a bicycle accident cast her onto the lawn of an agent who created her lasting stage name. A gutsy appeal to a convention of film distributors set her career rolling, and she enjoyed public triumph, stardom, and an Oscar. But then, personal tragedy struck: an ugly divorce, a custody battle for her twin sons, and an attempted suicide. Finally, a happy marriage ended tragically when Susan was widowed.

In a final twist, it was discovered in 1973 that Susan had a brain tumor, the same affliction that befell her character in *The Stolen Hours*, and at 55 she died of the ailment.

Susan was buried at the Cemetery of Our Lady of Perpetual Help Catholic Church in Carrollton, Georgia.

GRAVE DIRECTIONS: At 210 Old Center Point Road, you won't miss Susan's grave in the Chalkey plot with the elaborate stone curved headwall.

BILLIE HOLIDAY
APRIL 7, 1915 – JULY 17, 1959

BILLIE HOLIDAY WAS born in the Baltimore ghetto, and at age six, when perhaps she should've been in school, she was instead working at Alice Dean's brothel, running errands and scrubbing floors for a living. At 10, she was raped by a neighbor and for that "offense" was sent to a home for wayward girls. By 13 Billie had surfaced in Harlem and was working as a part-time prostitute.

Fortunately, at around 16, it was discovered that she was a bit of a jazz singer, and Billie went from selling her physical talents to her musical ones. She became a fixture of the nightclub scene and in 1932, Columbia talent scout John Hammond (who years later discovered both Bob Dylan and Bruce Springsteen) heard Billie's wailings and arranged for her to record a few titles with Benny Goodman's orchestra.

Billie elevated her technique over the next few years and, despite having never received any technical training, her delicately wavering voice made her the outstanding jazz singer of her day. Billie came to be known as Lady Day, and between 1933 and 1944, she recorded over 200 "sides," though she never received royalties for any of them.

With trademark white gardenias in her hair, she turned second-rate love songs into jazz classics, and during the 1940s, though a demon knocked at her door, Billie was at an artistic peak. "Singing songs like the 'The Man I Love' or 'Porgy' is no more work than sitting down and eating Chinese roast duck, and I love roast duck," she wrote in a 1956 autobiography.

Billie's demon was heroin, and in 1947 her addiction landed her in a West Virginia prison for 10 months. Worse, because of the drug conviction, for the rest of her life she was ineligible for a New York cabaret license, which she needed in order to sing at the most popular clubs of the day.

By 1959, Billie was a physical wreck. She collapsed during a Greenwich Village performance after just two songs and was admitted to a city hospital in Harlem, suffering from cirrhosis and heart trouble. In those sad last days, she was arrested again for heroin possession, on her gurney, after a nurse said she found a foil package of the white powder near her bed. At 44, Billie's lungs became congested and her heart gave out. When she was removed from the bed, 15 $50 bills were found taped to one of her legs, an advance for some autobiographical articles.

Wearing her favorite pink lace stage gown and pink gloves, Billie was buried at St. Raymond's Cemetery in the Bronx, New York.

GRAVE DIRECTIONS: Enter the cemetery at 2600 Lafayette Avenue and, shortly after ahead on the right, not far from the main office, is the St. Paul section. Billie is buried there at Range 56, Plot 29. In this cemetery's parlance, the notation means Billie's grave is in the 56th row (every 15th row is marked), and her stone is the 29th from the road.

JANIS JOPLIN
JANUARY 19, 1943 – OCTOBER 4, 1970

JANIS JOPLIN GREW up in a relatively comfortable family and, though her siblings did not challenge their traditional way of life, Janis abhorred it. She left her Texas home at 17 and, after a few years as a country-and-western singer around Houston, hitchhiked to her destiny in San Francisco.

Soon she joined a new group called Big Brother and the Holding Company and everything fell into place. Until Big Brother, Janis hadn't done much rock singing but she found it to be a perfect outlet for her pent-up frustrations, while the band's exuberant and jagged sound complemented her raw vocals. Janis became a vibrating, explosive part of the songs, and with soaring screams and wails and almost animalistic abandon, she sang to sellout audiences up and down the West Coast.

Janis so overshadowed the group that it was only a matter of time before she went solo, and shortly after the band released

Cheap Thrills in 1968, she did. It turned out to be a miscalculation on her part. She assembled two different bands over the next two years but, though each was musically adept, there was little feel for Janis' undisciplined style, and the raucous excitement of her work with Big Brother was missing.

Busy on a new album in the fall of 1970, Janis was living in Room 105 of what is now the Highland Gardens Hotel in Hollywood. On her last Saturday, she called City Hall and inquired about getting a marriage license and, that night, recorded for *Pearl* until about eleven o'clock. After visiting a bar with friends, Janis returned to her room and shot heroin.

After Janis was a no-show at Sunset Sound Recorders the next day, her road manager found her dead on the floor beside her bed. Though many suspected suicide, the 27-year-old's official cause of death was "accidental heroin overdose possibly compounded by alcohol."

In accordance with her wishes, Janis was cremated and her ashes scattered from an airplane over the Marin County coastline.

Janis had a will that included the following bequests: $2,500 for two memorial gatherings for her friends in New York and in California; all rights and royalties for her work to be divided equally among her parents, her brother, and sister.

Three months later, *Pearl*, which included Janis' raspy and timeless heartfelt rendition of Kris Kristofferson's "Me and Bobby McGee," was released and quickly went gold.

FLORENCE JOYNER
DECEMBER 21, 1959 – SEPTEMBER 21, 1998

WHILE GROWING UP in the Watts ghetto of Los Angeles, Florence Joyner took up running through a local youth foundation. She later attended UCLA on a track scholarship and, the year after graduation, earned a Silver Medal in the 200-meter event at the 1984 Olympic Games. After the Olympics, Flo worked as a bank service representative during the day and as a hairstylist at night and, at one point, added almost 60 pounds to her previously superb athletic physique.

But by 1987, in a resolve to return to competition and qualify for the 1988 Games, Flo began training anew with her husband, Al Joyner, and her sister in-law, Jackie Joyner-Kersee, who had each already won their own gold medals. By the time of the Olympic Trials, Flo's comeback was on track and she shaved an astonishing 2.7 seconds from the women's 100-meter dash, a record that stands today.

At the games in Seoul, Flo's comeback was complete. Flashy and confident, she stunned the world's track community by claiming three gold medals for the 100-, 200-, and 400-meter races, as well as a silver medal for the 1,600-meter relay. During that summer of spectacular performances, Flo (or Flo-Jo, as she came to be known) also teased audiences by showing off her perfectly toned physique in signature one-legged racing outfits with low-cut tops. She made a further fashion statement with her lengthy and elaborately painted fingernails.

Not surprisingly, on the heels of her Olympic knockout performance, rumors swirled that Flo had been taking performance-enhancing substances. She always denied the accusations and never failed a drug test. She soon announced her retirement and lived comfortably on her endorsements of athletic gear and fingernail products. Later, Flo established the Florence Griffith Youth Foundation, a nonprofit program for disadvantaged youth.

On a September morning in 1998, Al Joyner awoke to find Flo unresponsive and not breathing. She had died during the night. A preliminary investigation suggested that she suffered some kind of cardiac problem, and the public's immediate assumption was that Flo had died of a heart attack instigated by the excessive use of steroids. However, an autopsy revealed that Flo had died of "positional asphyxia due to epileptiform seizure" caused by a brain abnormality known as "cavernous angioma." In layman's terms, a deviation in her brain had caused an epileptic seizure, though not of the common convulsing variety, and Flo had simply suffocated in her pillow. The Orange County coroner added that he knew of no connection between that condition and steroid use.

At 38, Flo was buried at El Toro Memorial Park in Lake Forest, California.

GRAVE DIRECTIONS: Drive straight into the cemetery at 25751 Trabuco Road and park on the right in front of the Zaki Abujudeh bench, just before the "Park Rules" signboard. Follow the concrete path so that all of the columbarium niches are on your left and, at the end of the path, walk into the grass on the right. There you'll find Flo's grave in front of the white Duncan bench.

ANN LANDERS & ABIGAIL VAN BUREN

(EPPIE FRIEDMAN LEDERER)

JULY 4, 1918 – JUNE 22, 2002

(POPO FRIEDMAN PHILLIPS)

JULY 4, 1918 – JANUARY 16, 2013

BE HONEST: DID you know that famed advice columnists Abigail Van Buren and Ann Landers were twin sisters? Well, okay, neither did I.

"Half of the same egg," as their parents liked to say, the sisters were given the synchronized names Pauline Esther Friedman and Esther Pauline Friedman, though throughout their lives they were known as Popo and Eppie. After dressing identically during their youth, attending college together (where each claimed the other "majored in boys"), and then dropping out to be married in a double ceremony followed by a double honeymoon, their twin-ness cracked in 1955 when Eppie beat out 28 other applicants to become the "Ann Landers" advice columnist at the *Chicago Sun-Times*.

At first, Eppie received help from Popo, who proposed replies to the cascade of letters that Ann Landers received. But in short time, Popo came to recognize she herself had a knack for witty and succinct responses and so pursued a column of her own. Suggesting to the *San Francisco Chronicle* that their current columnist's lovelorn advice was dull, she presented sample columns written in a breezy and modern style and was quickly hired. Originating the name Abigail Van Buren, Popo's Dear Abby column debuted in 1956 and was an immediate hit. The column was syndicated within just a few months and eventually became the most widely syndicated column of any type in the nation.

But as you may have guessed, not everyone was thrilled with Popo's newfound success as Abigail Van Buren, least of all her now-rival twin sister, Ann Landers. After they'd been teammates their entire lives, Abby betrayed her twin by covertly seeking a directly competing career. A familial rift was opened that took the better part of a decade to reconcile and, even then, tinges of discord and acrimony lingered for the remainder of their lives.

Oh well. Though it seems the sisters could themselves have benefited from some interpersonal advice, both Abby and Ann did the reading public an enormous favor as they moved their genre away from its previously prissy and moralistic forms. Adopting contemporary styles, their energetic columns became conversational clearinghouses for the prickly conundrums of modern life. Ann's responses were often more measured and homey, while Abby enjoyed wordplay and could wield a briskness too, occasionally cutting through absurdity or pettiness with dismissive but clever one-liners.

In 1966 Eppie secured the rights to the Ann Landers name and decreed that it wouldn't continue after her death. "There will never be another Ann Landers," she said. "When I go, the column goes with me." Sure enough, when Eppie "went" at 83 and was cremated, Ann Landers left the building for good.

As for Popo, or Abby if you prefer, died at 94 after a dozen years of Alzheimer's affliction and was buried at Minneapolis Jewish Cemetery in Richfield, Minnesota.

DIRECTIONS TO ABBY'S GRAVE: Enter the cemetery at 7032 Penn Avenue South and immediately on the left, in the section surrounded by black iron fence, is the gray tombstone of Pauline Esther Phillips, the original Dear Abby.

CHRISTA McAULIFFE
SEPTEMBER 2, 1948 – JANUARY 28, 1986

IN 1985 CHRISTA McAuliffe, a New Hampshire fifth-grade social studies teacher, was chosen by NASA to be the first "ordinary person" to fly into space. In the months leading up to the celebrated six-day mission, American classrooms around the nation tuned in to follow her experience and Christa, 38, endeared herself to the public at large. She was comfortable in front of a camera, well-spoken, and likable, and her "Reach for the Stars" history-making space shuttle mission was proving to be a public relations bonanza for NASA.

On a gorgeous Tuesday morning, Christa and her fellow astronauts Greg Jarvis, Ron McNair, Ellison Onizuka, Judy Resnick, Dick Scobee, and Michael Smith boarded the space shuttle *Challenger* and a spellbound nation watched with high expectations as their craft lifted cleanly off the launch pad at 11:38 a.m., leaving its typical trail, a blazing geyser of fire and smoke. But 73 seconds

into the flight, as the majestic spacecraft soared 13 miles into the deep blue sky above Florida, *Challenger* exploded in a ferocious fireball whose power was later described by NASA scientists as comparable to a "small nuclear weapon."

For a lingering moment there was stunned silence. As the pieces of wreckage traced slow-motion arcs out of the sky, the 1,200 well-wishers who had gathered around a giant television screen in Christa's hometown, prayed in hushed disbelief. At Cape Canaveral's VIP viewing room, families of the seven astronauts who'd perished before their eyes shared an inconsolable grief.

After being bombarded by countless scientific and not-so-scientific explanations, conspiracy allegations, and talk-show elucidations, the official cause of the accident was presented through the Report of the Presidential Commission on the Space Shuttle *Challenger* Accident in June 1986. The report concluded that there was a failure of an O-ring seal in one of the craft's solid rocket motors. The seal failed due to a sensitive design that was degraded by external factors including temperature and reuse.

It was assumed by the general public that all those aboard *Challenger* died the moment the external fuel tank blew up. Of course, NASA was initially careful not to disturb this opinion, but the agency later concurred with scientists and engineers who insisted that not everyone, and probably no one, aboard the *Challenger* died the second the tank exploded.

If the cabin depressurized immediately, the crew would only have lived for perhaps 15 seconds after the blast. But if the cabin remained pressurized, which is possible, they might have survived for the full 2 minutes and 45 seconds it took to fall 65,000 feet back to Earth. However, they could not have survived the crushing 207 mph impact into the Atlantic Ocean, which refutes the wilder tabloid stories that had them alive for hours, or even days, waiting under the sea for rescuers who failed to reach them in time.

Possibly the best clue to solving the mystery of how long the doomed crew survived lies in the four emergency air packs that were recovered. Three had been manually activated, which demonstrated that at least some of the crew realized something was amiss, but the remaining inactivated packs indicate that loss of consciousness was also occurring at the same time.

A complete understanding of exactly what transpired is elusive because NASA remains highly secretive about the specifics of the tragedy. Furthermore, the agency may not themselves know exactly what befell the crew members as the wreckage and bodies spent up to six weeks in the sea before being recovered. Even then, much of the debris was never found.

Christa's remains were buried at Calvary Cemetery in Concord, New Hampshire.

GRAVE DIRECTIONS: At 207 North State Street, enter the cemetery at the third entrance (the one with the granite archway). Bear right after the archway, take the next left, then go all the way to the back. Christa's gravesite is marked with a black headstone on the left.

Unfortunately, the identity of all the recovered remains could not be established and, in a private ceremony on May 20, 1986, the unidentified remains were placed in a single, common grave at Arlington National Cemetery in Arlington, Virginia. The site in Section 46 is marked with a single tablet dedicated to the memory of the seven *Challenger* astronauts.

GEORGIA O'KEEFFE
NOVEMBER 15, 1887 – MARCH 6, 1986

GEORGIA O'KEEFFE'S CATALOG is an embodiment of boldly original paintings encompassing a wide vision, from sensuous evocations of flowers to dramatic cityscapes to bleached bones stranded in the high desert. Though raised on a Wisconsin dairy farm, she settled in New York City with art impresario Alfred Stieglitz, whom she wed, though he was 25 years her senior. After his 1946 death, Georgia moved to an old adobe house in New Mexico that came to be known as her Ghost Ranch and from there, for four decades, she interpreted the region's ancient Spanish architecture, dramatic landscapes, and strident skies with brilliant multicolored hues that startle the senses.

But for a few major exhibits, Georgia withdrew from the public almost completely during her Ghost Ranch years, and in 1973 she also abandoned painting as her eyesight failed. A 27-year-old potter named Juan Hamilton who had started off pruning her hedges was soon helping her complete her autobiography and, upon her death of natural causes, Juan was sole heir to her $70 million estate.

At 98, as her ultimate destiny neared, Georgia confirmed her unflagging spirit: "When I think of death, I only regret that I will not be able to see this beautiful country anymore . . . unless the Indians are right and my spirit will walk here after I'm gone."

Georgia was cremated and her ashes scattered at Pedernal Mountain near Abiquiu, New Mexico.

SYLVIA PLATH

OCTOBER 27, 1932 – FEBRUARY 11, 1963

BY AGE FIVE Sylvia Plath was writing complete poems and when she was eight one of her works was published in the *Boston Herald* newspaper. Later, her short stories that appeared in teen magazines helped gain her a scholarship to Smith College, where she won poetry and fiction contests.

Under the textbook surface of sensitivity, intelligence, and perfectionism lay grave personal turmoil for Sylvia and after a stint as guest editor for *Mademoiselle* she attempted suicide. Electroshock and psychotherapy treatments followed, Sylvia was seemingly cured, and, resuming her pursuit of excellence, she graduated summa cum laude from Smith and then went to Newnham College in England on a Fulbright scholarship.

In 1956, Sylvia and the poet Ted Hughes married and, though Sylvia had committed herself to an honest run at happiness, Ted was not the ideal husband she imagined; he was moody and slovenly, flirtatious and adulterous, while Sylvia was blindly faithful. But their marriage was coming apart at the seams. By 1962 they had two children but their marriage nonetheless dissolved as Sylvia's suspicions were proven correct and Ted abandoned her for another woman.

Sylvia kept writing throughout these tribulations. Her talent was keenly displayed in 1960 in her book of poems, *The Colossus*, and again in 1963 in her loosely autobiographical novel, *The Bell Jar*. But the formal precision of these works only hinted at what was fermenting as her relationship with Ted disintegrated.

The winter of 1963 was furiously cold in London and, while Ted cavorted in Spain with his new maiden, Sylvia battled the flu with her children in a cold and dark London flat, mustering the courage to execute her final plan. Late one night, Sylvia left a little food and milk in the bedroom of her sleeping children, cracked open their window, and sealed their door with towels and tape. Downstairs in the kitchen, Sylvia ingested a handful of sleeping pills, sat on the floor, and rested her head inside the oven, its gas taps turned on full.

Sylvia's nurse found her in the morning. At her side, a suicide note read simply, "Please call Dr. Horder."

After Sylvia's death at 30, the poems over which she had toiled during the last chapter of her life were collected and released in three volumes: *Ariel*, *Crossing the Water*, and *Winter Trees*, each of which astonished the literary world. In these confessional poems Sylvia abandoned the restraints and conventions of her earlier work and unleashed graphically macabre verse full of ironic wit and hallucinogenic imagery.

"Dying is an art like everything else. I do it exceptionally well," she wrote in "Lady Lazarus."

"I am terrified of this dark thing that sleeps in me," read a passage in the poem "Elm."

It is upon these poems that Sylvia's literary reputation mainly rests and, because her divorce from Ted was never finalized, he won control of all their rights. In 1981, after Ted assembled some of them into *The Collected Poems*, Sylvia was honored with a posthumous Pulitzer Prize.

She was buried in the new cemetery adjoining the Church of St. Thomas Becket in Heptonstall, a small hilltop village above the town of Hebden Bridge in West Yorkshire, England. To find her grave, enter the cemetery from the entrance nearest the church and walk to the left along the second row of graves. Sylvia's unassuming stone is about two-thirds of the way down the row.

On her gravestone there is an inscription, from "Monkey," a story written by Wu Ch'eng-en about 1560: "Even amidst fierce flames the golden lotus can be planted."

MARGARET SANGER
SEPTEMBER 14, 1879 – SEPTEMBER 6, 1966

IN 1912 MARGARET Sanger was a public health nurse serving New York's poverty-stricken Lower East Side tenement families whose misery was mostly the result of unchecked childbirth. Her duties brought her into contact with many prematurely old and tired women, their bodies weakened by far too many pregnancies, and who, in panic at the thought of another child, customarily resorted to a self-induced or back-street abortion that too frequently ended in death. Others simply chose suicide directly. When women begged doctors for information on how to prevent future pregnancies, they were flippantly advised to "have their husbands sleep on the roof." Margaret attributed her own mother's premature death to her 18 pregnancies and, from all this despair, she launched a revolution that discarded age-old birth-control taboos and made it acceptable not only to the medical profession, but to the public at large.

Of course, Margaret faced obstacles in her fight to make birth control information available. One was ignorance: Not even the medical community knew much about contraception. Another was public opinion: Many people considered family planning immoral and perverted, and even the discussion of it unthinkable. But the main obstacle was the Comstock law, a federal statute that classified all contraceptive information as pornography and provided hefty fines and prison sentences of up to 45 years for its violators.

In 1914 Margaret established a newspaper, *The Woman Rebel*. In this radical monthly, the term "birth control" was coined and, though the newspaper contained no specific how-to information, Margaret was charged with violating federal law. Wanting the case to rest on more fundamental principles than the offenses of which she was accused, Margaret hurriedly distributed a pamphlet entitled *Family Limitation*, which included the forbidden contraceptive information, then fled overseas to avoid prosecution. After studying birth control in the more liberal European countries for a year, Margaret returned stateside better prepared to face the charges against her but was disappointed when the government backed down, reluctant to try a case that might lead to changes in the law.

In a desperately poor Brooklyn neighborhood, Margaret and her sister opened America's first birth-control clinic in 1916. Though it lasted only 10 days before being shuttered while the defiant sisters were hauled off to jail for a month, Margaret's court hearing yielded a clarification in a law that opened the door for doctor-staffed birth-control clinics.

Despite continuing legal harassment and strident opposition from religious groups, in 1923 Margaret opened another clinic, this time staffed by a physician who offered contraceptive counseling and instruction not only to women but also to other doctors. But this time when police stormed the clinic, physicians howled that the doctor-patient privacy relationship had been violated and all charges were dismissed.

Margaret formed the American Birth Control League, forerunner of the Planned Parenthood Federation, which persistently chipped away at legislative restrictions, and in 1936 the Comstock law finally crumbled. By 1940 the movement expanded worldwide, and by decade's end it had been generally accepted by medical professionals and the American public at large.

After four years in a Tucson nursing home, Margaret died of congestive heart failure at 86. Shortly before her death, she said that she hoped to be remembered for helping women because women take care of culture and tradition, they preserve what is good, and they are the strength of the future.

Margaret was buried at Fishkill Rural Cemetery in Fishkill, New York.

GRAVE DIRECTIONS: Enter the cemetery at 801 Route 9, go past the office, and stay on the paved drive after the bridge. Turn right between Sections G and R, turn right again at the "T" in the road, then stop after 30 feet. A dozen yards to the left is the Slee plot, belonging to her husband's family, and there Margaret is buried.

GERTRUDE STEIN & ALICE B. TOKLAS

GERTRUDE STEIN
FEBRUARY 3, 1874 – JULY 29, 1946

ALICE B. TOKLAS
APRIL 30, 1877 – MARCH 7, 1967

AFTER HER FORMATIVE years in San Francisco, Gertrude Stein became disillusioned while studying psychology at Johns Hopkins University and, in 1903, moved to Paris, where she would stay for the rest of her life. There, Gertrude soon established herself as a leading patron of avant-garde art and opened a salon with her brother Leo, who was himself an art critic and painter. As a result of Gertrude's notoriously sharp wit and formidable literary and artistic judgment, the salon became a gathering place for developing artists and writers including Henri Matisse, Ezra Pound, Pablo Picasso, F. Scott Fitzgerald, and Ernest Hemingway. It was Gertrude who coined the phrase, adopted by Hemingway, "the lost generation," to describe the expatriate writers living abroad between the wars.

In 1907 Gertrude met Alice B. Toklas and they settled into life as partners; Gertrude wrote while Alice juggled domestic duties, which happened to include proofreading and typing Gertrude's manuscripts. Though the arrangement of Gertrude fulfilling herself while Alice took care of her seemed to mimic an unfair aspect of an unpleasant heterosexual marriage, the women stayed devoted to each other and expressed contentment in their roles.

Strong-willed and boastful, Gertrude referred to herself as "the creative literary mind of the century," but her fragmented style was not well-received and for a time the duo lived almost solely off modest inheritances. Later came the more influential works *The Making of Americans* and *How to Write* and, in 1933, Gertrude came to real prominence for *The Autobiography of Alice B. Toklas*. (The work is actually a biography of Gertrude, written by Gertrude, told from Alice's perspective.) Further confusing the matter was the popular 1968 film *I Love You, Alice B. Toklas*, which had absolutely nothing to do with the book, Gertrude, or Alice.

After surviving France's Nazi occupation, Gertrude contracted cancer as the war wound down. Before undergoing surgery, she turned to a worried Alice and asked, "What is the answer?" Alice was silent and Gertrude continued, "In that case, what is the question?" These were among her last words; she died during the surgery at 72.

Alice lived another 21 years and tried her own hand at writing, contributing articles on cooking to magazines and compiling her memoirs in *What Is Remembered*. A reviewer called her "a woman who all her life has looked in a mirror and seen someone else."

When Alice died at 89, she was buried with Gertrude in a joint plot at the Père-Lachaise Cemetery in Paris.

MOTHER TERESA
AUGUST 26, 1910 – SEPTEMBER 5, 1997

IN 1928 AGNES Gonxha Bojaxhiu, Mother Teresa, by way of Ireland and Turkey, arrived in India where for the next twenty years she taught at a wealthy Christian girls' school. After a spiritual second calling, the Vatican granted her permission to begin a new kind of work, and in 1950 her Missions of Charity order, where the most abjectly poor and terminally ill would be served, received official status.

Mother Teresa needed immediately to secure a place where she could care for these desperate people and, remarkably, the first location offered to her for this Christian work was an empty "dormashalah"—a place on the grounds of a sacred Hindu Kali Temple where pilgrims rested after their holy journeys. There, the sisters rallied against the squalor and worked to fill the last days of the loneliest destitute with dignity. Their order's distinguishing garment—a simple white sari with sapphire blue bands—soon became a familiar identifier of the caretakers of Calcutta's most impoverished.

In 1953 Mother Teresa's first orphanage opened and four years later her mission began working with lepers. In 1959 the order expanded outside of Calcutta and today there are more than 500 Missions of Charity worldwide, all dedicated to service of the most indigent.

By popular consensus and in the wake of her 1979 Nobel Peace Prize, Mother Teresa was lionized by the public but nonetheless continued to strike an apolitical pose, refusing to take a stand on anything other than strictly religious matters. Never a social critic, she did not attack the economic or political structures of the cultures that were producing the people she served. Her role was only to provide constant love.

At 87, Mother Teresa left her physical body and was buried in the back courtyard of the Mother House of the Sisters of the Missionaries of Charity in Calcutta, India, on the street of Acharya Jagadish Chandra Bose.

Usually the canonization of a potential saint does not begin until at least five years after their death. But Pope John Paul II, who had a particular propensity for declaring saints, and in fact declared more than all of his predecessors in four centuries combined, allowed the process of her beatification to begin just two years after her passing. In September 2016, after the attribution of requisite miracles, she was canonized St. Teresa of Calcutta.

GREATS OF LITERATURE, PHILOSOPHY & THE ARTS

EDWARD ABBEY

JANUARY 29, 1927 – MARCH 14, 1989

THE NOVELIST AND essayist Edward Abbey was a man mightily threatened by the encroachment of technocracy upon the individual and his environment. In his books and articles he profiled the West the way it once was, the way it is today, and the way he feared it would become unless the intrusions of civilization and industrialization were curbed. In his role as defender of the southwestern landscape, Abbey attained the status of a modern-day folk hero for ecological subversives everywhere.

Of his 21 books, the 1968 nonfiction work *Desert Solitaire* made his initial reputation, but seven years later Abbey eclipsed it with the riotous *Monkey Wrench Gang*. In it, he depicts a small gang of "monkey wrenchers," a term he seems to have coined, as they sabotage road builders and others who would develop the desert.

At 62, Ed died of complications brought on by hepatic hypertension.

As per his wishes, he was buried by family and friends in an old sleeping bag deep in the Cabeza Prieta Desert of southwestern Arizona. His body was transported in the bed of a pickup truck and there was no undertaker, embalming, or coffin. The exact location of his grave remains a secret known only by a select few of his survivors.

ANSEL ADAMS

FEBRUARY 20, 1902 – APRIL 22, 1984

THE MAN RESPONSIBLE for the most majestic black-and-white landscapes of the American West liked to credit his photographs to luck, saying, "I get to places just as God is ready to have someone click the shutter." In reality, each of Ansel Adams' finished prints was the result of a painstaking effort to achieve an artistic result.

When he was 14, Ansel's family vacationed in Yosemite and, from that visit until his death, he maintained a love affair with the land and became an advocate for its conservation. The visit also marked the beginning of his involvement with photography. Armed with his father's Kodak Brownie box camera and with one of the country's most beautiful landscapes before him, young Ansel began taking photographs, and he simply never stopped.

Though he worked as a concert pianist during his twenties, Ansel's photography hobby eventually overwhelmed his musical aspirations and he began to articulate his ideas about photography as an art form. In 1927, with *Monolith, the Face of Half Dome*, Ansel first developed his unique photographic style, using a red filter to dramatically darken the sky while leaving the famous granite formation in clear and sharp focus. By the outbreak of World War II, Ansel's prominent standing and expertise gained him a position training the military's photographer historians.

Over the next decades Ansel produced most of the finest examples of the country's glorious and epic vistas. He received fellowships to record the national parks, was director of the Sierra Club for 37 years, and, by the 1970s, his prints accounted for half of the total dollar value of commercial photographic art sales in the United States. He was awarded the Presidential Medal of Freedom, the nation's highest civilian honor, and the humble visionary graced the cover of magazines. Indeed, Ansel always stressed the importance of vision, as distinct from gadgetry. "A picture," he said, "is only a collection of brightnesses and there is nothing worse than a brilliant image of a fuzzy concept."

After his death at 82, Congress designated more than 200,000 California acres as the Ansel Adams Wilderness Area and his family later scattered his ashes on its 11,760-foot mountain, which now bears his name.

DOUGLAS ADAMS
MARCH 11, 1952 – MAY 11, 2001

DURING A HITCHHIKING trip around Europe, British teenager Douglas Adams was lying in a field, a little bit drunk, thumbing a copy of *A Hitchhiker's Guide to Europe*, when it occurred to him that somebody should write a similar guide to the galaxy. As it happened, that "somebody" was Doug himself, and in 1979 *The Hitchhiker's Guide to the Galaxy* was published, though its life began the previous year as a BBC radio series.

The cult science-fiction comedy is a picaresque account of mild-mannered suburbanite Arthur Dent's travels through space with his friend Ford Prefect after the Earth is destroyed to make way for an intergalactic highway. The book blends Doug's witty philosophy with memorably named characters like Zaphod Beeblebrox and Marvin the Paranoid Android, and is a repository for all knowledge, including the answer to "the ultimate question of life, the universe and everything" which, as it turns out, is 42.

Spawning best-selling sequels including *The Restaurant at the End of the Universe* and *So Long, and Thanks For All the Fish*, as well as hit television and stage shows, the *Guide* became a huge success, and one for which Doug always claimed he was quite unprepared. "It was like being helicoptered to the top of Mount Everest," he said, "or having an orgasm without the foreplay."

Doug died of a heart attack at 49. He was cremated and his ashes were buried at London's East Highgate Cemetery.

GRAVE DIRECTIONS: At this historic and majestic cemetery off Swain's Lane, Doug's slate-gray stone is easy to find, located on the left, just a hundred feet past the entrance.

ISAAC ASIMOV
JANUARY 2, 1920 – APRIL 6, 1992

ISAAC ASIMOV WAS an amazingly prolific writer who churned out hundreds and hundreds of titles on a wide range of subjects. Though best known for elevating the science-fiction genre from pulp-magazine adventure to a higher intellectual level dealing with sociology and history, he was also prone to explore whatever happened to be his muse du jour and wrote critically acclaimed books about physics, biology, and astronomy, as well as Roman, Greek, and American history. There were textbooks and primers, a collection of limericks, a smattering of mysteries, a guide to Shakespeare, works about the Bible, and even children's books. And to top all of that in case you're not yet suitably impressed, Isaac contributed some 1,600 columns, essays, and short stories to magazines.

Explaining how he became a compulsive writer in the first volume of his autobiography, *In Memory Yet Green*, he wrote that his father owned a variety store that was open for a 19-hour stretch every day of the week. If young Isaac was even a few minutes late to the store after rushing from school, his father yelled at him for being a *folyack*, which is a Yiddish slang term for slacker. More than 50 years later, Isaac remained committed to his own 14-hour-day, seven-day-a-week routine and wrote: "I am still showing my father I'm not a folyack." Indeed, books and writing were Isaac's only interests; never once in his life did he swim or even ride a bicycle.

Teaching himself to read before he was five, Isaac skipped several grades, received his high school diploma at 15, and sold his first story when he was 18. Three years later in 1941, he sold a story called *Nightfall* to Astounding Science Fiction, then the top magazine in the field. Isaac got paid a penny a word for the story. "So for a 12,000-word story I expected $120. I got a check for $150 and thought they'd made a mistake," he recalled. "But when I called to tell them, they said the story had seemed so good to him they gave me a bonus of one-quarter cent a word." Almost 30 years after *Nightfall* was published, the Science Fiction Writers of America voted it the best science-fiction short story ever written.

After earning a Ph.D. in chemistry from Columbia University in 1948, Isaac accepted an offer from Boston University to teach biochemistry, though he "didn't feel impelled to tell them that I'd never studied biochemistry," he recalled during an interview. "But three years later I was writing a textbook on the subject, and it was then I realized the only thing I really wanted to be was a writer."

Isaac's science fiction won many accolades and his Foundation Trilogy, consisting of *Foundation, Foundation and Empire*, and *Second Foundation*, earned him a Hugo Award for Best All-Time Science-Fiction Series. In *I, Robot* he invented the Three Laws of Robotics governing the relation of robots to their human masters: Robots may not injure a human or, by inaction, allow a human to be harmed; robots must obey humans' orders unless doing so conflicts with the first law; robots must protect their own existence unless doing so conflicts with the first two laws. Among his nonfiction works, *Asimov's New Guide to Science* is considered one of the best books about science for the layman, though Isaac himself made no great claims for his work. "I make no effort to write poetically or in a high literary style," he said. "I never read Hemingway or Fitzgerald or Kafka and I have no doubt that it shows in my prose."

After contracting AIDS from a blood transfusion during a coronary bypass operation, Isaac died of the affliction at 72. His will stipulating there be "no permanent memorial of my existence," he was cremated and his ashes scattered.

AUTHORS' RIDGE

MOST AMERICANS HAVE heard of Concord, Massachusetts, and are aware of its historical significance during the Revolutionary War. Depending on one's interest level, anywhere from a few hours to a few days can be spent enjoying the area's historical landmarks and, if it's your inclination, be sure to include a visit to Sleepy Hollow Cemetery. The cemetery holds numerous Revolutionary-era heroes and, at the area of the cemetery known as Authors' Ridge, the four authors profiled below rest peacefully beside one another.

HENRY DAVID THOREAU
JULY 12, 1817 – MAY 6, 1862

ALTHOUGH HE LIVED in relative obscurity, the rugged individualist Henry David Thoreau has come to be considered one of the central figures of American thought. He celebrated Independence Day 1845 on his own terms by beginning a two-year, self-imposed exile at a hut near Walden Pond, a period he later described in his most famous work, *Walden; or, Life in the Woods*. The book is an unfulfilled plea for simplicity and deliberateness in everyday life and continues to haunt those who are cognizant of the distance between their ideals and our materially driven culture.

The use of the word "exile," by the way, is not wholly accurate. In actuality, Thoreau made frequent trips to Concord, welcomed occasional visitors, and entertained dinner guests. During this time, he even went to jail for refusing on principle to pay a poll tax and that one-night imprisonment was the catalyst for one of his most important political essays, "Civil Disobedience." In it, Thoreau exalts the law of conscience over civil law and implores citizens to nonviolent protest: "Unjust laws exist; shall we be content to obey them, or shall we endeavor to amend them, and obey them until we have succeeded, or shall we transgress them at once?" he wrote.

Finally, Thoreau is embraced by conservationists for his essay *Walking*, in which he celebrates the joys of the amble and pleads for conservation of the world's wild places. Published a month after his death, the work is recognized as one of the pioneering documents in the conservation and national park movement in America.

After suffering a prolonged case of tuberculosis, Thoreau died at 44.

If you journey to Concord, you may also want to see Thoreau's house—the yellow one at 255 Main St. It's now a private home, but I'm sure the residents are used to gawkers. Thoreau lived in its attic during the last third of his life and, in the parlor just to the right of the front door, he died.

GRAVE DIRECTIONS: Once in the cemetery at 134 Bedford Street, look for the stone signs that direct you to the parking area for Authors' Ridge. A walk up a small knoll delivers you to the ridge, and there you'll find the graves of Alcott, Emerson, Hawthorne, and Thoreau, each within a short distance of the others.

NATHANIEL HAWTHORNE
JULY 4, 1804 – MAY 19, 1864

IN 1842 NATHANIEL Hawthorne settled in Concord and, though he fraternized with the Transcendentalist crowd, he didn't share in their intellectual idealism. Instead, Nathaniel concentrated on the Puritan origins of American history, and on creating a distinctive literary style in two of the first truly great works of American literature, *The Scarlet Letter* and its companion, *The House of the Seven Gables*.

When Franklin Pierce became president in 1853, he appointed his old college buddy to an ambassadorship in England, and there Nathaniel wrote his last major work, *The Marble Faun*. In 1864 the two friends reunited for a pleasure trip to New Hampshire. In his sleep at the Pemigewasset House hotel in Plymouth, Nathaniel quietly expired at 59.

RALPH WALDO EMERSON
MAY 25, 1803 – APRIL 27, 1882

AFTER GRADUATING FROM Harvard in 1825, poet Ralph Waldo Emerson entered the ministry. He soon became an unwilling preacher, however, and, unable in good conscience to administer sacraments to his deceased 19-year-old wife, he resigned his pastorate in 1831. Soon he had settled in Concord, and in 1836 Emerson's ideas were collected in a volume of essays entitled *Nature*. The work prompted him to be considered, along with his contemporary

Henry David Thoreau, as a chief proponent of the new Transcendentalist philosophy and literature movement, a reaction against scientific rationalism. The central tenet was that everything in our world is a microcosm of the universe, "an infinitude of the private man." Transcendentalists tended to disregard external authority and to rely instead on direct experience. Emerson's motto, "Trust thyself," became the movement's watchword.

For the remainder of his life, in essays, poems, and lectures, Emerson preached these themes and encouraged audiences to trust instinct and pursue authentic self-discovery for a path toward an enlightened American culture.

At 78, Emerson died of pneumonia.

LOUISA MAY ALCOTT
NOVEMBER 29, 1832 – MARCH 6, 1888

LOUISA MAY ALCOTT began writing a series of popular melodramatic short stories under the pseudonym A. M. Barnard in the late 1840s, but the turning point of her career came with the publication of *Little Women* in 1869. Though the work now seems somewhat dated and moralizing, *Little Women* and its four sequels document 1800s New England life with touching accuracy. They were instrumental in changing the focus of juvenile literature to include more sensitive and realistic portrayals of young adults, they have undergone several film adaptations, and adolescents continue to flock to the works today.

After spending the last decades of her life working for women's suffrage, Louisa May died at 55 of the long-term effects of mercury in her system. At the time, mercury was a common treatment for the effects of typhoid fever, to which she'd been exposed as a child.

THE BEATS

THE BEATS WERE a group of carefree writers who emerged out of the strait-laced, post–World War II era to shake up the literary scene forever. Their refreshingly original approach advanced a reckless stance against the establishment, and their styles challenged the very notion of what constituted "literature," uprooting entrenched norms.

The word "beat" was itself a common localism for society's underbelly and was never meant to be elevating at all. It meant just the opposite, in fact—to be exhausted by existence. The word acquired historical resonance when Jack Kerouac, who would become the most cherished of the Beat writers, remarked to John Clellon Holmes, "I guess you might say we're a beat generation." Appropriating this conversation, Holmes brought the word into the mainstream in a November 1952 article, "This is the Beat Generation," in which he described it as "a feeling of being reduced to the bedrock of consciousness."

Writers soon began to invest the viewpoint of the defeated with a mystical perspective. Allen Ginsberg wrote, "the point of Beat is that you get beat down to a certain nakedness where you actually are able to see the world in a visionary way, which is the old classical understanding of what happens in the dark night of the soul." Through its literature, the Beat Generation outlived its historical moment, it survived its notoriety and the ensuing media blitz, and its works still inspire passionate ideals.

NEAL CASSADY

FEBRUARY 8, 1926 – FEBRUARY 3, 1968

RAISED BY AN alcoholic father in skid-row hotels, Neal Cassady was a car thief who developed the suave instincts of a charming con artist—though he never seemed to want to con anybody out of much more than a 10-dollar bill or a roll in the hay. He became one of the most vibrant members of the Beat movement and ultimately influenced Kerouac, Ginsberg, Ken Kesey, Tom Wolfe, and the Grateful Dead, among others.

Neal met Jack and Allen Ginsberg in New York in 1946. Allen, a homosexual, immediately fell in love with him, and Neal, ever the hustler, began a sexual relationship with Allen, balancing it with his numerous heterosexual liaisons. But Neal and Jack soon left New York and began racing aimlessly around the country on adventures that would become *On The Road*. Jack wrote about their exploits even as they unfolded, but Jack grew frustrated, unable to find a style that fit the content. Later, a series of letters from Neal gave Jack the idea of documenting the trips exactly as they had happened, without pausing to fictionalize or even think, and to write the book the way Neal talked, in a rush of mad, unpretentious ecstasy. This spontaneous approach worked, and *On The Road* became a sensation by replicating Neal's unconstrained voice.

Neal was in tune with America and he resonated along the same frequency as the currents that were giving rise to the hippies and their flower power. In 1964 Neal met Ken Kesey and before long, Ken's work was also showing the influence of Neal's optimistic ideals. Neal swayed the scene at Ken's "acid tests" while the Grateful Dead provided the soundtrack. Later, while his old friend Jack withdrew into alcoholism and early middle age, Neal began an entirely new series of road adventures as one of Ken's Merry Pranksters. A natural highwayman, he was the driver slinging abstractions in double time behind the wheel of their psychedelic bus, nicknamed "Furthur."

In San Miguel, Mexico, 20 months before Jack died, Neal wandered away from a Mexican wedding and, with a belly full of drinks and assorted recreational drugs, he decided to walk the 15 miles to the next town. Neal slipped into the chilly desert night wearing only a T-shirt and jeans, and the next morning was found comatose alongside a stretch of railroad tracks. He died later that day at 41.

Neal was cremated, and his ashes are kept by his son in an ornate box. On a scrap of paper stapled to the box's side are the fading, typewritten words: *Contiene Cenizas Del Sr. Neal Cassady Jr.*

JACK KEROUAC
MARCH 12, 1922 – OCTOBER 21, 1969

IF THERE'S A father of the Beat generation, his name is certainly Jack Kerouac. He came out of a broken-down New England mill town during the Depression and, as the star back on his high school team, won a football scholarship to Columbia University, from which he hoped to bring new prosperity to his blue-collar family. But things went wrong at Columbia and Jack dropped out. After being discharged from the Navy for having "an indifferent character," he ended up sailing with the merchant marines in 1942, and, when Jack wasn't sailing, he hung around New York with a new crowd of friends: a libertine Columbia student, Allen Ginsberg; a brilliantly bizarre literary inspiration, William S. Burroughs; and Neal Cassady, a joyful street cowboy from Denver.

Jack was already an author, but in 1951 he created something different. During a 20-day binge, Jack wrote a "stream of consciousness" manuscript on a continuous, 128-foot scroll of tracing paper that became his *On The Road* masterpiece. With a sharp edge of social comment, it's an autobiographical story of two friends, Sal Paradise (Jack) and Dean Moriarty (Neal), who spontaneously and exuberantly reject middle-class conventions and wander through America in search of respite from mundane conformity. Jack, who also incorporated his sometime-mentor Allen into the book as Carlo Marx, spent years trying to get the work published, carrying it around in a rucksack wherever he went, until finally it was released in 1957. The work was an immediate success, but was mostly panned by literary critics, who objected to its fast and mad style. (Truman Capote famously complained, "That's not writing, that's typing.") But it's now a basic text for disenchanted youths whose lives have become claustrophobic and oppressive. More important, the book was a catalyst for the unfettered Beat lifestyle.

But Jack didn't react well to his sudden celebrity. Trying to live up to the image he'd presented in *On The Road*, his penchant for drink considerably worsened. He pursued Zen Buddhism and moved to California, but his brightness dimmed and he aged prematurely. In the half-dozen years after *On The Road*, Jack published many similar books, including *The Dharma Bums* and *The Subterraneans*, but most had actually been written years earlier. He lost his momentum as a writer, though he continued to be an involuntary celebrity through the 1960s. But mostly, Jack drank.

Defeated and disconnected, in 1961 Jack moved in with his mother, watching television, playing solitaire, and retreating into an alcohol-induced mania. In 1967 he married Stella Sampas, a maternalistic childhood friend, and the remainder of his life was spent sharing a home with both women. At 47, Jack died of an abdominal hemorrhage—he had drunk himself to death.

He was buried at Edson Cemetery in Lowell, Massachusetts.

At his death Jack was destitute, but in 2001, his original *On The Road* manuscript was sold at auction for $2.43 million.

GRAVE DIRECTIONS: This cemetery is located at 1375 Gorham Street, and the main road inside the cemetery is called Third Avenue. Follow it to Lincoln Avenue, turn left, then stop 30 feet after Seventh Avenue. Forty feet into the lawn on the right, in the Sampas family plot, is the flat stone that marks Jack's grave.

ALLEN GINSBERG
JUNE 3, 1926 – APRIL 5, 1997

ALLEN GINSBERG AND Jack Kerouac greatly influenced each other's work. From Jack, Allen learned to write instinctively and impulsively and, in Allen, Jack found a tireless promoter for his labors. But during the 1960s their paths diverged. While Jack withdrew, Allen became more visible. In 1955, while television's married couples slept in separate beds, he released his declamation against the hypocrisy and silence of society's elders in his poem "Howl." But, unlike Jack, Allen stood publicly in defiant contrast to every kind of conformity.

Allen's detractors saw him as a drugged-up, blissed-out, left-wing pederast (which, of course, he was), but they failed to recognize that his relentless bombardment of the excesses of America's consumer-crazed culture was right on the money. The whole confused mish-mash of the nation's changing scene needed a point man, and Allen, never one to ignore any sloppy mainstream contradiction, gladly volunteered.

Away from poetry, he was a ringleader at be-ins and antiwar demonstrations and, in one particularly politically charged stunt, he even "exorcised" the Pentagon. He was at the acid tests, he was with the Dead and the Hell's Angels, and he supported Abbie Hoffman's high jinks at the 1968 Democratic Convention. Long before "coming out" was defined, Allen proudly pronounced his homosexuality. In music, he championed Bob Dylan as the electronic poet laureate and, later, songwriters from Patti Smith to Beck systematically took Allen's lyrical models to heart. He coined the term "flower power" and extolled the virtues of Buddhism, along with just about every inebriant or psychedelic drug that came his way. Wherever something "happened," it seemed, Allen Ginsberg was there.

At 70, surrounded by 40 family members and friends, Allen died of a heart attack related to his terminal liver cancer.

He was buried at B'nai Israel Cemetery in Newark, New Jersey.

GRAVE DIRECTIONS: On the west side of Mt. Olivet Avenue, park at the gate next to the brick shed and walk into the cemetery along the paved drive. From the circle, the Ginsberg family plot is 30 feet to the right.

The self-penned epitaph gracing his stone reads:

Father Breath once more farewell,
Birth you gave was no thing ill,
My heart is still, as time will tell.

WILLIAM S. BURROUGHS
FEBRUARY 5, 1914 – AUGUST 2, 1997

IN 1945 JACK and Allen shared a Greenwich Village apartment with William S. Burroughs, who, as the elder, published sage, introduced his juniors to the esoterics of literature and the lowlife haunts of the big city. William was the most colorful and curious of any would-be Beat. As the grandson and namesake of the inventor of the adding machine, he had turned his back on a life of privileged respectability to sample drugs and pass his life in an outrageous, self-destructive fashion.

When he was 13, William's short essay "Personal Magnetism," debunking control, was published. Two years later he somehow "learned to hate horses" at a New Mexico boys school. After graduating from Harvard University in 1936, he lopped off his left little finger and presented it to his analyst. By 1942 William was working as a New York City exterminator because "he knew where all the roaches were," but in 1946 William left the city after he and Jack were arrested for failing to report the murder of a quasi-friend. Although William, Jack, and Allen never again lived in proximity, Jack followed William to his various expatriate enclaves around the globe, and Allen later bluntly assessed William's impact on his writing by saying, "He showed me the world."

William got married and, after being a no-show for a New Orleans court appointment where he was to answer charges of drug possession, he and his wife, Joan, moved to Mexico City where William shot Joan dead in 1951 while trying to reenact the story of William Tell. He left Mexico before the incident could be investigated and, for the next 20 years, flitted about the globe more or less on the lam. Though he was spiraling into drug addiction, he was also writing again and, after Jack visited him in Morocco and helped him organize his "routines," *Naked Lunch* was published in 1959.

Though William's style mirrored that of his Beat buddies, the content of *Naked Lunch* came from some other distant netherworld. It's a torrent of nightmarish descriptions of bodily functions, sex acts, and grotesque medical procedures told under the influence of hallucinogenic addiction. It was praised as "a daring assault on conformity" by some quarters, while others dismissed it as "gibberish masquerading as social commentary." But, not surprisingly, it achieved cult status and William rode that success back to New York in 1974. Later, William began to write more conventional narratives, including *Place of the Dead Roads*, and with the renewed interest in the Beat movement during the materialistic 1990s, its stone-faced godfather gained new popularity as an avant-garde pioneer.

At 83, William died after suffering a heart attack and was buried at Bellefontaine Cemetery in St. Louis, Missouri.

GRAVE DIRECTIONS: Enter the cemetery at 4947 West Florissant Avenue and make an immediate right after the office, which is Fountain Avenue. The drive winds around a bit, up and down a hill, then becomes Lake Avenue. Turn left when you get to the "Y," and the Burroughs plot is immediately on the right, marked with a big, white, granite obelisk.

RAY BRADBURY
AUGUST 22, 1920 – JUNE 5, 2012

AS A CHILD, science-fiction writer Ray Bradbury was an inactive film buff who was romanced by the fantasy of Buck Rogers, Lon Chaney, and the World's Fairs. "When I was born, the auto was only twenty years old and radio and TV didn't exist. I was born at just the right time to write about all of these things," he said.

But with the fantasies came nightmares and Bradbury often spoke of night visions that left him sweating and sleepless. A visit to the carnival at 12 brought him face-to-face with Mr. Electrico, a magician who awakened Bradbury to the notions of reincarnation and immortality, catalysts that led him to become a writer. "He was a miracle of magic, seated at the electric chair, swathed in black velvet robes, his face burning like white phosphor, blue sparks hissing from his fingertips," he recalled. "He pointed at me, touched me with his electric sword and said, 'Live forever.' I decided that was the greatest idea I had ever heard and I knew something special had happened in my life. I stood by the carousel and wept." From then on, he spent at least four hours a day every day, unleashing his night visions in stories he wrote on butcher paper.

His stories began to appear in small genre pulps and in 1939 he started a mimeographed fan magazine called *Futuria Fantasia*, but Ray's big break came in 1950 when some of his Martian stories were collected into a volume titled *The Martian Chronicles*. The thematically linked stories celebrated the romance of space travel while condemning the social abuses that modern technology had made possible. Their impact was immediate, and critics who had dismissed science fiction as adolescent prattle praised them as stylishly written tales of morality set in a future that seemed just around the corner. Bradbury's follow-up bestseller, 1953's *Fahrenheit 451*, was written in the basement of the UCLA library, where he fed the typewriter 10 cents every half hour. "You'd type like hell. I spent $9.80 and in nine days I had *Fahrenheit 451*." An indictment of authoritarianism, it portrays a book-burning America of the near future, its central character a so-called fireman whose job it is to light the bonfires.

Bradbury's books, multi-layered and ambitious, offered a set of metaphors and life puzzles to ponder for the rocket age and beyond, and established him as an author of particular insight who urged readers to consider the consequences of their actions. "I'm not a futurist. People ask me to predict the future, when all I want to do is prevent it," he said. He was hardly the first science-fiction writer to represent science and technology as a mixed bag of blessings and abominations, but Bradbury differed from his contemporaries in that he eliminated the technical jargon for which mass audiences had no patience and packaged his troubling speculations about the future in an appealing blend of poetic metaphors. That subtle turn helped Bradbury step over the threshold from genre writer to mainstream visionary.

It seems the purists had a point because, though his dozens of books and 600 short stories predicted everything from ATMs to live broadcasts of fugitive car chases, Ray himself was actually reserved and cautious of scientific breakthroughs. With very strong opinions about what the future had become, he feared that in the drive to make their lives smart and efficient, humans had lost touch with their souls. Content to restrict his own adventures to the realm of imagination, he never even learned to drive and kept up his thousand-word-a-day writing schedule on an electric typewriter long after technology had passed it by. He long maligned computers and hated the Internet. Saying that e-books "smell like burned fuel," he refused to allow electronic versions of his works, only relenting on that point in what turned out to be the last year of his life. Instead, he lived to sniff the roses and, approachable and animated, could often be spotted out and about, a familiar figure with a wind-blown mane of white hair and heavy black-framed glasses browsing the stacks of bookstores, his bicycle leaning against a pole just outside.

Though his books became a staple of high school and college English courses, Bradbury himself disdained formal education and went so far as to attribute his success as a writer to his never having gone to college. "I'm an idea writer. I have fun with ideas and I play with them," he explained. "I'm not a serious person, and I don't like serious people." He added, "My goal is to entertain myself and others."

Credited with saying, "The problem with death is it's so damn permanent," Bradbury went to his permanence at 91, while asleep at his home. He is buried at Westwood Memorial Park in Los Angeles, California.

GRAVE DIRECTIONS: Enter the cemetery behind the office complex at 10850 Wilshire Boulevard, turn left at the office, walk into the Garden of Serenity adjacent to the chapel on the right, and there you'll see Bradbury's memorial stone.

PEARL S. BUCK

JUNE 26, 1892 – MARCH 5, 1973

BORN TO SOUTHERN Presbyterian missionaries, Pearl S. Buck was taken to China at the age of three months and lived there for 40 years. She became intimately familiar with the daily lives of China's poorest inhabitants, and the village where she lived provided the primary setting for her first stories, including her novel *The Good Earth*. Loved by millions of readers since its publication in 1931, it was one of the most popular novels of the twentieth century, won a Pulitzer Prize, and was made into an Oscar-winning film.

But Pearl's ambitions weren't sated by mere success as a best-selling author. Upon her return to the States, for 40 years she passionately represented a rainbow of humanitarian concerns including nuclear testing bans, the Equal Rights Amendment, and civil rights, while lending her own voice to those who couldn't be heard, including the disparate peasants of forgotten Third World countries and the handicapped and orphaned children of these shores. Selflessly contributing to those less fortunate, Pearl left a legacy far greater than her writings.

At 80, she died of cancer and was buried at her Green Hills Farm Estate in Dublin, Pennsylvania.

GRAVE DIRECTIONS: At 520 Dublin Road, enter the farm's main driveway and after about a hundred yards is a small paved pullout on the right. Stop and park here. Across the drive, follow the paved walk a short distance to Pearl's grave under an ash tree. She chose the gravesite herself and her tombstone, which she designed, does not record her name in English; instead, the Chinese characters representing the name Pearl Sydenstricker are inscribed.

Green Hills Farm is now a National Historic Landmark and houses the international offices of the Pearl S. Buck Foundation. The work of the privately sponsored foundation is to assist Amerasian children in their native countries, particularly abandoned offspring fathered by American servicemen stationed overseas.

MICHELANGELO BUONARROTTI

MARCH 6, 1475 – FEBRUARY 18, 1564

A FLORENTINE ART prodigy, by age 15 Michelangelo was living in the ruling Medici palace with Lorenzo de Medici acting as his sole patron. Lorenzo died in 1492, and when the French invaded under Charles VII two years later, Michelangelo fled Florence and eventually landed in Rome.

There, Michelangelo quickly returned to his art and by 1498 his reputation was cemented with the completion of a magnificently sculpted *Pietà* (a representation of Mary's mourning over Christ's body), which now stands in Saint Peter's Cathedral. Word of his talent spread and Michelangelo returned to Florence in 1501 to sculpt the marble *David* that now flanks the entrance to the Palazzo Vecchio. Upon *David's* completion, Pope Julius II summoned Michelangelo again to Rome to begin work on his tomb, which the master considered to be the low point of his career; by fits and starts, a scaled-down version of the colossally egoistic original was completed 40 years later.

While the tomb was in its early stages, Julius also commissioned Michelangelo to decorate the ceiling of the chief Vatican chapel, the Sistine. This would prove to be his masterpiece. Michelangelo and perhaps a half-dozen subordinates began the work in 1508 but, almost immediately, dissatisfied with his assistants' inability to meet his evolving demands, he sent them away and completed the monumental task single-handedly over the next four years. In a 1510 sonnet entitled "On Painting the Sistine Chapel Ceiling," Michelangelo offered a poignant account of his grueling task, painting while bent over backward: "My belly's pushed by force beneath my chin, My beard toward Heaven, I feel the back of my brain."

After the Sistine's ceiling came its huge *Last Judgment* altarpiece painting, followed by the completion of Julius II's tomb (the man, by then, had been dead some 30 years). Pope Paul III next appointed him to oversee the architectural design of Saint Peter's Cathedral, which stands today as final testimony of Michelangelo's grand vision.

He died at 89, and though the Pope desired his body buried in Saint Peter's, Michelangelo had requested that he rest in Florence. In the church of Santa Croce he was interred and may be visited whenever the church is open.

ALBERT CAMUS
NOVEMBER 7, 1913 – JANUARY 4, 1960

IN 1938 THE selective thinker and writer Albert Camus relocated from his Algerian homeland to France. History there overtook him, and he joined the resistance movement against Nazi occupation as a standout underground journalist. In the midst of the carnage that ravaged France in 1942, Camus put out his enigmatic novella *The Stranger*, his most hard-boiled work and the one for which he was awarded the Nobel Prize for Literature 15 years later. In this product of a five-year effort, Camus rendered his doctrine that the inevitability of death renders human life ultimately meaningless. Further, the individual cannot make rational sense of his life experience and is an insignificant victim of the absurd orthodoxy of habit.

In 1947, concluding that his journalistic activities were a response to the demands of the time, he retired from newspapers to concentrate on his fiction and essays. For the most part, Camus' later works were a continuation of his stringent search for moral order, and he expounded upon his philosophies most notably in *The Plague* and *The Rebel*. In 1970 the unfinished novel *La Mort Heureuse* was published posthumously, in which Camus succinctly announced, "All that matters really, is the will to happiness, a kind of enormous, ever-present consciousness. The rest is nothing but excuses."

In the winter of 1960, Camus was traveling to Paris in the front seat of a Facel-Vega sports car driven by his publisher, Michel Gallimard, whose wife and daughter were in the back. Thirty miles south of Paris, near a village named Petit Villemomble, the car slid off the wet road and hit a tree. Camus' neck was broken and he died instantly.

At 46, he was buried at Lourmarin Cemetery in Lourmarin, France, 30 miles north of Marseilles.

TRUMAN CAPOTE

SEPTEMBER 30, 1924 – AUGUST 25, 1984

THE CLUTTER FAMILY

DIED NOVEMBER 15, 1959

BORN TRUMAN STRECKFUS Persons to a 16-year-old beauty queen, Truman Capote was to become one of America's most controversial authors, partly due to his literary works, but perhaps even more as a result of his flair for publicity, his hunger for malicious gossip, and interest in his flamboyant lifestyle.

As a child, Truman was shuttled among a variety of relatives and, for a time, lived in Monroeville, Alabama. A close childhood friend there was none other than fair-haired tomboy Harper Lee, who in 1961 would become the Pulitzer Prize–winning novelist of *To Kill a Mockingbird*. Truman and Harper were inseparable—the entrepreneurial Truman charged other neighborhood children a nickel to use Harper's swimming pool—and she later modeled one of *Mockingbird's* central characters, Dill Harris, on Truman.

After a stint with the *New Yorker* magazine, Truman established himself as a serious author for his frank discussion of homosexuality in *Other Voices, Other Rooms*, and the provocative picture of himself on its cover stirred the gay community. In the 1950s, Truman's literary works lifted him to celebrity status, and he was the newest wonder boy of the jet set, a fixture of chic parties, and a notorious philanderer. For this, Truman was accused of frivolity, and his stock response—"I'm researching my next book"—was supported in 1958 by the release of *Breakfast at Tiffany's*, a sensational account of high society. The overwhelming success enjoyed by the book, as well as its celebrated 1961 film adaptation, assured Truman's position in the upper crust.

But Truman wasn't done yet. He became intrigued with the idea of writing a new kind of book, one that would blend journalism and fictional techniques to a previously untested degree and, in fact, Truman was looking toward a new art form—the "nonfiction novel." In November 1959 he read a small news item about the deaths of the Clutters, a Kansas family who were systematically and savagely murdered by point-blank shotgun blasts to the head, and decided he had found his ideal subject. Just three days after the murders, he traveled to Kansas and began a six-year, all-consuming writing project about the case. His intensive research included hours of interviews with the two killers, who were tried, convicted, and eventually executed.

Upon its release, the chilling masterpiece *In Cold Blood* was an instant success and won Truman glowing reviews, a good deal of money, a swarm of imitators, and an even greater measure of celebrity. He swiftly moved to his next novel, *Answered Prayers*, which was to be a bitingly honest portrayal of his high-flying world, but in 1975 when its first few chapters were released in *Esquire* magazine, a major scandal erupted. Truman had been too honest. He did "what people always tell writers to do, but [he] didn't wait till they were dead to do it."

The result was that Truman became ostracized from the world in which he was both working and living. He quickly declined into drug abuse and alcoholism, and the book was never finished. Shortly before his death Truman offered an apology of sorts by saying, "I am not a saint. I am an alcoholic, I am a drug addict, and I am a homosexual. But I am a genius."

The health of his liver compromised by hard living, Truman died of heart failure at 59, and today lies at Westwood Village Memorial Park in Los Angeles.

GRAVE DIRECTIONS: Enter the cemetery behind the office complex at 10850 Wilshire Boulevard and turn left. On the wall just left of the Sanctuary of Tenderness is Truman's crypt.

The subjects of *In Cold Blood*—Herbert, Bonnie, Nancy, and Kenyon Clutter—are buried at Valley View Cemetery in Garden City, Kansas.

GRAVE DIRECTIONS: Enter the cemetery at 2901 North Third Street and drive to the rear northwest corner, where you'll see a maintenance garage. The Clutter stones are in the sixth row of the section diagonally opposite the garage.

LEWIS CARROLL
JANUARY 27, 1832 – JANUARY 14, 1898

CHARLES LUTWIDGE DODGSON was the scholarly son of a vicar who at 18 entered Christ Church College at Oxford University and, in one capacity or another, stayed there until his death some 50 years later. A student of mathematics, he later wrote a number of weighty academic texts on the subject, but Charles is more commonly remembered, of course, for the children's stories he wrote under the pseudonym Lewis Carroll.

Lewis had personal issues that many historians neglect. He purported to be called to answer holy orders his entire life but, though he was ordained as a deacon in 1861, Lewis avoided the priesthood and sermonizing, probably because of his lifelong stuttering affliction. An exceedingly undemonstrative introvert who kept his hands hidden inside black gloves, he was uncomfortable around adults and never dated or married. All of his close friendships were instead with children, especially young girls, for whom he performed marionette shows and created puzzles and word games. Lewis was able to acquire a camera by 24 (no mean feat in 1856), and photography of children became his preferred pastime. Some of these pictures were undeniably erotic and featured young girls in stages of undress.

A particular muse of Lewis' was Alice Liddell, the 11-year-old daughter of the Christ Church College dean. During a rowboat excursion with Alice and two of her school-aged friends, Lewis wove for them a whimsical tale about a girl who went down a rabbit hole in search of a rabbit that was late for a tea party. He later expanded the story into a full manuscript and presented it as a gift to Alice entitled, *A Christmas Gift to a Dear Child in Memory of a Summer Day*. He also suggested to Alice's parents that he was interested in courting their daughter. By order of the Liddell parents, Lewis was forbidden from further association with Alice.

But they had to admit that he'd written quite a story, and they encouraged him to publish it. In 1865 Lewis self-published the story after renaming it *Alice's Adventures in Wonderland* and, seven years later, its *Through the Looking Glass* sequel came into print. *Alice's Adventures in Wonderland* has become one of the most widely translated and beloved children's stories ever written and, even after more than 150 years, it has never gone out of print.

Lewis died at 65 of a bronchial infection at his family's Chestnut estate in Guildford, England, and he lies at the nearby Mount Cemetery, his grave under a stately pine marked by a marble cross.

Many years after Lewis fantasized about his real-life Alice, there came a new interest in the storybook Alice from an unlikely quarter, the acid-test counterculture. In 1967 the Jefferson Airplane rock band's hit song "White Rabbit" graced the airwaves, and its lyrics revealed perceived drug allegories within the *Wonderland* story. That Alice's "trip"—in which she ingests potions that change her consciousness and lead to encounters with a cast of strange characters, including a Mad Hatter and a hookah-smoking caterpillar—might have been Lewis' allusions to an opium trip was not a new idea and had long been debated in literary circles. But the Jefferson Airplane song placed the debate squarely into the popular forum and, in short order, college students lined up for midnight showings of Disney's animated version of *Alice in Wonderland*, while hysterical libraries nationwide added the children's storybook to banned-book lists.

AGATHA CHRISTIE
SEPTEMBER 15, 1890 – JANUARY 12, 1976

THE 90-PLUS NOVELS and 14 short story collections produced by Dame Agatha Christie stagger even the most insatiable detective-fiction addict. Her works have been translated into 44 languages and have sold over 2 billion copies (recently exceeding Shakespeare and now surpassed by only the Bible). Even more astounding, perhaps, is that her murder-mystery play *The Mousetrap* has since its 1952 London premiere run continuously for some 27,000 performances. Wow!

Agatha introduced her eccentric Belgian detective, Hercule Poirot, in her first detective novel, 1920's *The Mysterious Affair at Styles*. In 40 books, the comic and amiable master-sleuth astutely observed a mountain of details that invariably led him, and the reader, to the identity of the murderer. Agatha later introduced another fictitious criminologist, the shrewdly inquisitive Miss Jane Marple, who was no less sensible than Poirot but relied more heavily on her feminine sensitivity and empathy to solve crimes. In fact, the perceptive methodologies of these characters were the key to Agatha's success. Readers were mesmerized by the unexpected twists that peppered her deliciously intricate plots until, in the end, they were surprised to find that they'd blindly ignored a vital clue that had been casually introduced hundreds of pages earlier. Her knack for consistently fooling her would-be detective readers in such works as *Murder on the Orient Express* and *Death on the Nile* earned Agatha her fans' allegiance.

Just a year after Agatha killed off Poirot in *Curtain: Hercule Poirot's Last Case* (which earned him a front-page obituary in the *New York Times*), Agatha herself died, though merely of natural causes.

At 85, she was buried at St. Mary's Churchyard in Cholsey, England, her grave marked by an ornate and broad headstone.

SALVADOR DALI
MAY 11, 1904 – JANUARY 23, 1989

INSPIRED BY PICASSO'S Cubism, Freud's interpretations of the dreamscape, and new attitudes toward sexuality in general, Europe's 1930s Surrealist painting crowd broke traditional constraints in their aim to represent the fantasies and visions of the deep psyche. Salvador Dali emerged as their torchbearer, and his *Persistence of Memory*—the painting with the dripping clocks—is probably the most recognized of the Surrealist movement.

Realistic and disturbing depictions of nightmarish images on vast and uninviting landscapes became his trademark. Dali claimed his work was a product of a "paranoiac critical method," a sort of self-hypnosis that allowed him to hallucinate freely, and that he himself was surprised by what appeared on his canvases.

Dali's reputation swelled worldwide and was based as much on his flamboyance and flair for publicity as on his prodigious output. He worked in several media, and his legacy includes poetry, fiction, and a controversial autobiography. His work in film includes credit for the dream sequence in Alfred Hitchcock's *Spellbound.*

By the late 1960s Dali's work was hampered by Parkinson's disease, but his personality had so captured the public's imagination that he continued to exert influence, if only as a source of ideas. In 1974 he championed the opening of his own museum, but the decade also found Dali mired in financial and strategic scandals, the worst of which was his reported signing of thousands of sheets of blank paper, falsely rendering anything later added to the paper a Dali lithograph. It was eventually estimated that collectors had been bilked for at least $750 million on phony Dali prints.

Dali's health, both physical and mental, deteriorated sharply after his wife's death in 1982, and the remainder of his life was spent in almost total seclusion.

He died at 84 of heart failure and respiratory complications, and is entombed in the basement of his own museum, Teatro Museo Dali, in Figueres, Spain.

CHARLES DICKENS
FEBRUARY 7, 1812 – JUNE 9, 1870

IN 1824 CHARLES Dickens' father and family were imprisoned for debt, while the 12-year-old Charles was put to work at a factory. This experience and his childhood of poverty and adversity haunted him for the remainder of his life, but also proved to be a source for his novels. His writings frequently delved into themes of alienation and betrayal, compassion for the lower classes, and Industrial Revolution–era social reform.

At 22, Charles joined a London newspaper and shortly thereafter began publishing monthly stories and sketches, the seeds of what would later become his novels. After the initial success of these stories, Charles embarked on a full-time career as a novelist and produced works of increasing complexity at an incredible rate, all the while continuing his journalistic activities.

In his novels—*Oliver Twist, A Christmas Carol, David Copperfield, A Tale of Two Cities,* and *Great Expectations,* to name a few— he created a Shakespearean gallery of characters, many of which later found life in film and theater, and all of which continue to enthrall the reading public today.

For most of his life Dickens lived in the village of Rochester, and his will stated his wish to be buried there with "no scarf, cloak, black bow, long hat band or any other revolting absurdity." But alas, he lies in the Poets' Corner of Westminster Abbey in London, while a lonely plaque at the Rochester graveyard states: "Charles Dickens wished to be buried here."

F. SCOTT & ZELDA FITZGERALD

F. SCOTT FITZGERALD
SEPTEMBER 24, 1896 – DECEMBER 21, 1940

ZELDA FITZGERALD
JULY 24, 1900 – MARCH 10, 1948

THE EARLY LIVES of the author F. Scott Fitzgerald and his wife, Zelda, epitomized the triumphs of the Roaring Twenties in affluence, accomplishment, and melodramatic love. Unfortunately, their fable reflected both sides of the dream, and they later suffered the common tragedies of intemperance.

Upon publication of *This Side of Paradise,* Scott married Zelda in an extravagant ceremony and the pair splashed into their roles as aspiring socialites. Balancing on the crest of success and relishing the perks of a new novelist's fame, their exploits, the trendiest fodder of popular society pages, included jumping fully clothed into the Plaza Hotel's fountains and arriving at glamorous soirées in an open car.

Their life together, though, lacked any semblance of order, and their wealth was something of an illusion. Scott, the overnight sensation, in fact earned very little for his work, and wrote for mass-circulation magazines to supplement his income. Though he endeavored to further his literary reputation, he was gaining common recognition only as an extravagant drunk. Meanwhile, Zelda struggled to maintain an identity, and her formerly charming, unconventional behavior became eccentric and bizarre.

After endless revision, *The Great Gatsby* was finally released in 1925 to critical praise, but even these sales proved disappointing, and the Fitzgeralds continued to live far beyond their means. As debts mounted, Scott plunged into alcoholism, and domestic rows triggered by drinking were frequent. Increasingly unstable, Zelda was institutionalized in 1930 and eventually diagnosed with schizophrenia. She would spend the rest of her life in and out of psychiatric hospitals.

After 1934 they would never live together again and soon Scott, hopelessly in debt, in poor physical health, and often incapacitated by excessive drinking, had what he described as his own "crackup." In 1937, almost in spite of himself, he won a contract as a screenwriter for MGM, fell in love with another woman and, after finding new spark in his writing, quit drinking altogether.

In 1940 Scott was living in Hollywood and working on a new novel, *The Last Tycoon*. In November he suffered a mild heart attack and was ordered to bed rest. He continued to work on his novel and, a month later, collapsed of a massive attack as he rose from a living room chair. At the time of his death at 44, all of his novels were out of print and he believed himself a failure. But by the 1960s, a Fitzgerald resurrection had occurred, and he's since achieved a secure place among America's acclaimed writers.

Zelda continued her unsteady course after Scott's death. In March 1948 she was staying at Highland Hospital in Asheville, North Carolina, in a room on the top floor, when a fire broke out in the middle of the night. She and eight others were killed, trapped behind the mental institution's locked doors.

At 47, Zelda was laid to rest alongside Scott at Saint Mary's Catholic Church Cemetery in Rockville, Maryland.

GRAVE DIRECTIONS: At 520 Veirs Mill Road, their graves are eight rows from the church.

IAN FLEMING
MAY 28, 1908 – AUGUST 11, 1964

IN ALMOST EVERY way, Ian Fleming's life mirrored that of his best-known fictitious progeny, the dashing man of intrigue and British secret agent, James Bond 007.

Hailing from an extremely wealthy Scottish family, after a childhood of privilege and exclusive schooling Ian sought a career in the foreign service. But he was rejected as an operative and turned to journalism instead, working for Reuters for a year before gaining an esteemed banking position in London. There he enjoyed the life of a playboy, entertained by high-stakes bridge games, elaborate meals, and carefree romances.

As Hitler's war machine steamrolled on in 1939, Ian was unexpectedly sent to Moscow to report on a trade mission for the *London Times* but, surreptitiously, he followed an ongoing espionage trial. Next, Ian was recruited by British Naval Intelligence to work with the super-secretive Ultra network, which, among other things, cracked the Nazi's Enigma code and ultimately changed the course of the war. But it wasn't until 10 years after his death that the extent of Ian's wartime intelligence work emerged and, even now, it's unclear exactly when he began working as an operative. Was it when he was in Moscow with the *Times*, or did his service begin while he was living as a banking playboy in London? It's now believed that Ian was never rejected as an operative in the first place and, from the time he went to work for Reuters, he was slyly working to establish an everyman guise.

At war's end, Ian built his Goldeneye estate on Jamaica's north coast, and he traveled there each winter to lounge in paradise and chase divorcées. However, one particular conquest turned out to be married, and after she ended up pregnant with his child, Ian decided it was high time he made some coin. In seven weeks he wrote *Casino Royale*, a spy thriller set in the tropics with a debonair, womanizing British secret agent named James Bond as its central character. Ian had woven his own elite existence, arrogance, and acid wit into the character and the resulting book was a smashing success. Ian penned 11 more Bond novels, including *Goldfinger*, *Dr. No*, and *From Russia with Love*, and the Bond hero, with vodka martinis "shaken, not stirred," became immortalized in celluloid and, ultimately, in popular culture.

In 1961, Ian suffered a heart attack and, recognizing that perhaps his time was near, put to paper an entirely different kind of story, a tale of a flying car with a bubbly personality, a story he had been carrying around in his head for years. Based on bedtime stories he used to tell his son, the children's classic, *Chitty Chitty Bang Bang*, was published just a few months before his death at 56 of heart failure. A year later, his final Bond thriller, *The Man with the Golden Gun*, was released, its last few chapters completed by a writer who remains anonymous to this day.

Ian's grave is in the churchyard of St. Andrew's, in the picturesque village of Sevenhampton, England.

His monument, a simple, four-foot-tall obelisk, contains the Latin inscription, "*omnia perfunctus vitae praemia marces*," from Lucretius, a Roman who wrote the words around 50 B.C. Translated, it means: "After enjoying the gifts of life, you lack ambition."

ROBERT FROST
MARCH 26, 1874 – JANUARY 29, 1963

BY HIS LATE thirties, a full-time aspiring poet and part-time New Hampshire chicken farmer named Robert Frost had not published a single book of poems. Taking a leap of faith, he sold the farm and dared to make a new start in London, where publishers might be more receptive. Finding almost immediate success with *A Boy's Will* and *North of Boston*, Frost fell into vogue in London and the sensation soon crossed over stateside.

In 1915 the Frosts returned to the States, an edition of the "new" poet's work became a bestseller, and Robert never looked back. He embarked upon a long writing career and received an unprecedented quantity of honors for his work, including four Pulitzer Prizes. Never before had an American poet achieved such rapid fame after such long delay.

In the twilight of his life, his political conservatism caused him to lose favor among literary critics, but his reputation as a major poet remains secure. He succeeded in realizing his life's ambition to write "a few poems it will be hard to get rid of."

Dying of a pulmonary edema at 88, Robert was buried at the Old Bennington Cemetery in Bennington, Vermont.

GRAVE DIRECTIONS: At Monument Circle, park in front of the Old First Church and follow the path on the left into the cemetery. On the far right and about a hundred yards behind the church is the Frost plot.

ZANE GREY

JANUARY 31, 1872 – OCTOBER 23, 1939

PEARL ZANE GREY attended the University of Pennsylvania on a baseball scholarship and after graduation, set up a dental practice in New York City while retreating to the Delaware River region on weekends. After meeting his future wife Dolly there, his first piece of writing, *A Day on the Delaware*, which Dolly had encouraged, edited, and presented to publishers, found publication in 1902. Three years later Zane and Dolly married and settled in the river valley, leaving dentistry behind as Zane pursued a full-time writing career financed by Dolly.

In 1906 the couple took a late honeymoon to Arizona and California and, during that trip, Zane's imagination was stimulated. Upon his return, he pioneered the new Western literary genre and, from his *Riders of the Purple Sage* to *The Last Round-Up*, he reinvented the public's conception of the West, presenting it as a moral battleground where the desperados and the righteous were alternately destroyed and redeemed.

Zane's books have since sold more than 40 million copies and been adapted into 112 films. Though even his most ardent admirers might admit to Zane's somewhat stilted style and rigid character development, there is broad consensus that he deserves recognition as a proto-environmentalist, custodian of the West's history, and interpreter of its rhythms.

Fulfilling their wish to rest together at the edge of the Delaware River, after Zane's death at 67 and Dolly's at 73, their ashes were interred at Union Cemetery in Lackawaxen, Pennsylvania.

GRAVE DIRECTIONS: In this small cemetery at 151 Scenic Drive, the Grey plot is easy to find on the right-hand side about three-fourths of the way to the rear.

ALEX HALEY

AUGUST 11, 1921 – FEBRUARY 10, 1992

WHILE SERVING WITH the Coast Guard during the Second World War, Alex Haley, a voracious reader, ran out of things to read, which prompted him to start writing. Alex toiled over his short stories for several years, suffering hundreds of rejections until one was finally accepted by a magazine in 1947. Taking notice of their budding author, in 1952 the Coast Guard promoted Alex to the rating of chief journalist for their public relations office. Later, upon his 1959 retirement from the service, Alex launched a new career as a freelance writer.

Alex wrote for *Reader's Digest* and then moved on to *Playboy*, where he initiated the magazine's trademark in-depth interview feature. One of the personalities he interviewed was Malcolm X, a meeting that inspired Alex's first book, 1965's *The Autobiography of Malcolm X*.

His conversations with Malcolm prompted Alex to search out his own genealogy, an endeavor that proved to be an exhaustive, 11-year odyssey. As Alex searched further and further back in time, he eventually landed in the village of Juffure in Gambia, West Africa, where a native oral historian, a *griot*, recounted to Alex seven generations of Mandinka tribal history. In the griot's account, Alex's early ancestor, 16-year-old Kunta Kinte, was wrested from the forest while searching for wood to make a drum, then sold into slavery.

Alex painstakingly chronicled his ancestors' passage from slavery to freedom and, in 1976, his acclaimed book *Roots: The Saga of an American Family* jolted America's conscience with its powerful affirmation of black history and shattering view of slavery. *Roots* became a phenomenon. The book became a number one national bestseller, the 12-hour television miniseries broke ratings records, lesson plans based on *Roots* were used in schools, and a new interest in African American genealogy was stimulated. Alex was awarded a special Pulitzer Prize, received honorary degrees, was lauded with a resolution by the U.S. Senate, and labeled a "folk hero" by *Time* magazine. *Roots* was indeed a cultural milestone, bringing the issues of slavery and racism to the forefront of American consciousness. It was groundbreaking and monumental but, unfortunately, it was also fiction.

In 1977 Harold Courlander filed a suit charging that *Roots* plagiarized his novel *The African*. In fact the history of Kunta Kinte closely resembled that of a character named Hwesuhunu as chronicled in Courlander's work, and several passages in *Roots* were copied almost verbatim from *The African*. After a threat of perjury from a trial judge, Alex settled out of court for $650,000.

And there were even more unsettling discoveries. Subsequent investigation of tapes in Alex's own archives revealed that Kunta Kinte was a historical imposter invented with the full cooperation of Gambian government officials. From a review of Alex's private papers, virtually every genealogical claim in Alex's story has been shown to be false. Even his attempt to re-create the Middle Passage experience

of enslaved Africans by sleeping on a "rough board between bales of raw rubber in the hold" of a transatlantic ship is fundamentally inaccurate; he sailed the *Red Star* from Dakar to Florida in 1973, but never stayed in the hold, according to the ship's first mate, Frank Ewers. "I had the keys to the hold and Haley never went down there at night. He would have died from the cocoa fumes."

In 1980 Alex wrote a television series called *Palmerstown, USA*, in 1988 published *A Different Kind of Christmas*, and *Queen: The Story of an American Family* was released posthumously. Unfortunately, none of these works had the impact of *Roots*. On its own merits, *Roots* is an astounding piece of culturally significant fiction, and if Alex had released it as such, with appropriate bibliographic footnotes, his reputation would be untarnished and permanent. As it is, his place in literary history stands under a shadow.

At 70, Alex died of a heart attack and was buried at his boyhood home in Henning, Tennessee.

GRAVE DIRECTIONS: At the corner of Haley Avenue and Church Street, you'll see Alex's marker in the front yard.

JOSEPH HELLER
MAY 4, 1923 – DECEMBER 12, 1999

AFTER TRAINING AS a B-25 bombardier in the Army Air Corps, Joseph Heller was shipped to Italy in 1944 and would later describe his 60 requisite combat missions as "largely milk runs." But they inspired him too, and the notes he kept of his adventures in the skies were the seeds of his masterpiece novel, *Catch-22*.

Returning to America in 1950, Joseph taught composition at Penn State and then wrote ad copy where his unusual creative process emerged: Find the first and last sentences of a story, then fill in the middle. The opening of his significant work hit like lightning but would take years to fully develop. "I wrote the first chapter in longhand one morning in 1953, hunched over my desk at the advertising agency." Accepting a $750 advance for his book, he took another five years to complete it. But it was well worth the wait.

A darkly comic novel, *Catch-22* became a universal metaphor not only for the insanity of war but also for the madness of life itself. The breathtaking satire centered on a pilot Yossarian, who tries to get himself declared crazy so he won't have to fly any more missions. But he is foiled by regulations, as Doc Daneeka explains: "Anyone who wants to get out of combat duty isn't really crazy." This absurdity, along with every other illogical aspect of war, was masterfully captured by Joseph, who then gave all of it the name Catch-22. "There was only one catch and that was Catch-22, which specified that a concern for one's own safety in the face of dangers that were real and immediate was the process of a rational mind. If he flew the missions he was crazy and didn't have to; but if he didn't want to, he was sane and had to."

The book was not an immediate success but, a few years after its 1961 release, as the reality of Vietnam set in, *Catch-22* was embraced and became required reading for the flower-power generation. Part of the genius of the book was that readers could grasp Yossarian's terror and cynicism even while believing that World War II was wholly necessary. But, when young Americans began to be drafted and to die by the tens of thousands during Vietnam, *Catch-22* became an allegory for a war that many felt was unnecessary. Succeeding first as a work of literary art, it had a forceful second life as a powerful political document.

Joseph later produced a half-dozen more novels but could never duplicate the satirical wit that defined *Catch-22*, and they were never met with much more than a lukewarm response. His wit always armed and ready, his sardonic answer to a query about never having written another book as successful as his first was "Who has?" Quizzed about his pastimes, he replied, "I hate sports. I also hate gardening and walking. I don't go to movies or the theater or watch television, but what I do like is lying down."

In 1981 Joseph was afflicted with Guillain-Barre syndrome and within days was in near-total paralysis. After a gradual recovery he divorced his wife of 36 years and married his nurse. Following his death of a heart attack at 76, he was buried at Cedar Lawn Cemetery in East Hampton, New York.

GRAVE DIRECTIONS: On Cooper Lane, turn into the last entrance on the left and then take the second right to Section P. Just after the second tree on the right, Joseph's military-style stone reminds us, "There was only one catch…"

ERNEST HEMINGWAY
JULY 21, 1899 – JULY 2, 1961

MARGAUX HEMINGWAY
FEBRUARY 16, 1954 – JULY 1, 1996

WHILE WORLD WAR I raged, young Ernest Hemingway tried to enlist in the Army but was rejected due to a vision problem. Eager for action, he instead took a job driving an ambulance for the Red Cross, and in that capacity found himself under fire on the Italian front. After being severely wounded by a mortar blast, then two machine gun rounds as he was being carried away on a stretcher, Ernest the war hero recovered at an Italian hospital and fostered a relationship there with a nurse. These experiences would provide the groundwork for one of his greatest novels, *A Farewell to Arms*.

Ernest married during a short stay in the U.S., and in 1921 the couple moved to Paris, flitting into an intellectual circle of expatriate authors and artists that included F. Scott Fitzgerald, Ezra Pound, and Gertrude Stein, who, at some level, Ernest accepted as a mentor. This "lost generation," a term that Stein coined but Ernest made popular in the epigraph of 1929's *The Sun Also Rises*, characterized a postwar generation that decried the false ideals that led naïve soldiers marching to their dooms for the gratification of carnal elders.

After Paris, Ernest traveled extensively for both work and pleasure, hunting in Africa and witnessing bullfights in Spain, where he returned in the late 1930s as a correspondent covering its Civil War. Again drawing from personal experience, Ernest wrote *The Snows of Kilimanjaro*, *Death in the Afternoon*, and his most ambitious novel, *For Whom the Bell Tolls*. In this period, he gained international acclaim for simple, straightforward prose sprinkled with unemotional but realistic dialogue.

During the Second World War, Ernest volunteered as a Caribbean submarine spotter using his own fishing boat, and it was then that he discovered the allure of Cuba, to which he's now inextricably linked. By 1950 the literary clique was whispering that "Papa" was finished, as for the last decade Ernest had been living in a small Cuban village, making no waves. But in 1952

Ernest unexpectedly set readers on their heads again with what many consider his most significant short work, *The Old Man and the Sea*, for which he was awarded the Pulitzer Prize and Nobel Prize in Literature.

After Castro's 1959 revolution, Ernest relocated to Idaho but by then his physical health was in sharp decline. Suffering from hepatitis and uncontrollable high blood pressure while increasingly confined to his home, Ernest found he was no longer able to conjure his writer's muse, initiating a downward spiral in his mental stability.

His wife, Mary, found him one morning holding a shotgun and staring out a window, and Ernest spent the next two months under heavy sedation at the Mayo Clinic. Upon his return home, Mary locked all the guns in the basement, but Ernest remembered where to find the keys. Two days later, while Mary slept, he chose a favorite shotgun he'd used many times to hunt birds and, with the magnificent view of the Sawtooth Mountains at his foyer's bay window, Ernest put the gun to his forehead and pulled the triggers of both barrels.

At 61, Ernest was buried at Ketchum Cemetery in Ketchum, Idaho.

GRAVE DIRECTIONS: On Route 75 a half-mile north of town, enter the cemetery, bear right, and proceed about 100 yards. On the right is a stand of three evergreen trees, under which is the marble tablet marking Ernest's grave.

The Hemingway family seemed to have an uncanny predilection for suicide. Ernest's father, Dr. Clarence Hemingway, shot himself to death with a revolver in 1928. In 1966, Ernest's sister Ursula did herself in with a deliberate drug overdose, and in 1982, his brother Leicester killed himself with a pistol. More than one wag has suggested that perhaps the Hemingway family's NRA membership should be revoked.

And then there was Margaux, Ernest's fresh-faced granddaughter who leveraged the Hemingway mystique to reserve a seat aboard the 1970s modeling and acting fun ride. But after appearing in one lackluster film after another, beginning with a dreary turn in her 1976 debut, *Lipstick*, Margaux's star dimmed and by 1980 her life was a slow-motion train wreck. Middle-child syndrome left her feeling unloved, dyslexia hindered the memorization of scripts, bulimia weakened her, depression encumbered ambition.

In 1987 Margaux admitted herself to the Betty Ford Clinic for alcoholism treatment and in 1990 came a last-ditch effort to jump-start her career with a *Playboy* photo spread. After attempting to allay her troubles with spiritual guidance from the Dalai Lama, she experienced difficulty separating reality from fantasy, and was soon hearing voices to boot. Rock bottom came in 1995 as Margaux filmed infomercials for the Psychic Friends Hotline.

After Margaux hadn't been seen for a few days, concerned friends asked the handyman of her Santa Monica apartment building to check her quarters. Upon entering, he was overwhelmed by a horrible odor; Margaux was quite dead. She was found covered up in her bed, wearing only a white T-shirt. On a coffee table was an altar of sorts, complete with salt at each corner, an arrangement of candles, a variety of pendants lined up alongside burned incense, a white horseman chess piece, and pieces of paper arranged in a heart-shape. On the papers, in her handwriting, was written, "Love, healing, protection for Margot forever."

An autopsy found Phenobarbital in Margaux's system at many times the recommended dosage, and it was concluded that she died in the Hemingway style, a suicide at 42.

After cremation, Margaux's ashes were buried alongside her grandfather. Her epitaph reads, "Free Spirit Freed."

WASHINGTON IRVING
APRIL 3, 1783 – NOVEMBER 28, 1859

WASHINGTON IRVING STUDIED law haphazardly and amused himself by writing essays on New York society and theater under a variety of pseudonyms, including Diedrich Knickerbocker. (The surname was a colloquialism for Dutch settlers but, after being used by Irving, it became slang for "New Yorker.") In 1809 he published *A History of New York*, which purported to be a scholarly account of the occupation of the New World but was really a satire. Today it is regarded as the first great American book of comic literature.

Washington traveled to Europe on three different occasions that, considering the period in which he lived, ranked him very highly within that elite category of the well traveled. His first two trips were in service of his family's durables business and, after the enterprise soured, Washington refocused his concerns. He arranged a collection of his stories and essays into *The Sketch Book*, publishing it in 1819 under the name Geoffrey Crayon. Within this compilation were two widely loved tales that would immortalize the Washington Irving name—"Rip Van Winkle" and "The Legend of Sleepy Hollow"—and their enthusiastic reception immediately promoted him to the status of best-known living figure in American literature.

By 1826, Washington had parlayed his credentials into an appointment as a diplomatic attaché at the American embassy in Madrid, and there he produced a number of other narratives and sketches, though none as popular as his previous work. Later, after serving as ambassador to Spain, Irving labored on a five-volume biography of George Washington, completing it just days before his death at 76.

For 137 years, Washington was buried in the village of North Tarrytown, New York, but, in November 1996, without ever having been moved, he was at once buried in the village of Sleepy Hollow. By referendum, the village's residents honored their beloved son by legally changing the village name to its traditional name, Sleepy Hollow, and Irving sleeps there now at the village's cemetery of the same name, in its Old Dutch Burial Ground section.

GRAVE DIRECTIONS: At 540 North Broadway, turn in at the main gate before the church, bear left at the "Y," and take the next left onto Crane Way. Surrounded by hedges, 100 yards on the right is the Irving plot.

KEN KESEY
SEPTEMBER 17, 1935 – NOVEMBER 10, 2001

RAISED IN A religious fire-and-brimstone household, Ken Kesey was an Oregon high school champion wrestler and voted "Most Likely to Succeed." While studying at Stanford, he worked to support his young family, which quickly grew to a three-baby affair, yet nonetheless managed to suitably impress the faculty for a Woodrow Wilson Fellowship to pursue a burgeoning writing bug.

While at Stanford, though, Ken's progress toward Young Republican of the Month changed course after he participated in experiments in the psychology department to earn extra money. The studies included the ingestion of chemicals, and the chemicals included lysergic acid diethylamide or, more commonly, LSD. The acid experiences certainly had an effect on Ken, well beyond any temporary color-hearing or psychedelic, out-of-body experience. His life's focus was altered, and though he never strayed too far from his familial responsibilities, Ken's crowd of friends shifted and he tuned in to the burgeoning San Francisco scene.

Around this time, Ken was also working as an orderly in the psychiatric ward of the Menlo Park Veteran's Administration hospital. In 1962 he released his first novel, which clearly showed the influences of his experiences, the critically popular and successful *One Flew Over the Cuckoo's Nest*. In 1974 Ken would sell its movie rights for just $5,000, and a film version would sweep the Academy Awards. In 1964 his *Sometimes a Great Notion* was published and, though it was well received, the book never approached *Cuckoo*'s success.

As the 1960s blossomed, Ken was at the forefront of the counterculture. He threw "acid test" parties around Palo Alto's bohemian community and became a patron of a local band called the Warlocks, later known as the Grateful Dead. In 1964 his band of proto-hippie friends, dubbed "the Merry Pranksters," loaded onto an LSD-fueled, Day-Glo–colored school bus nicknamed "Furthur" and, with Neal Cassady at the wheel (the real-life Dean Moriarty of Jack Kerouac's *On The Road*), Ken orchestrated the ultimate cross-country road trip. The journey immortalized the psychedelic sixties and was later chronicled in Tom Wolfe's *Electric Kool-Aid Acid Test*.

After a short jail term on marijuana charges in 1965, Ken moved to Oregon. He raised beef cattle, served on the school board, and coached high school wrestling while Furthur rusted away in a boggy pasture. Though he continued to write short fiction and the occasional magazine article, he found that it had become harder to write since he became famous. "Fame isn't good for a writer. You don't observe well when you're being observed," he said.

Before his death at 66 during a surgery to remove a spot of cancer on his liver, Ken had sensed the end could be nigh and penned a goodbye note to be released after his passing. Closing the message, he wrote, "Meanwhile, I've still lots of forms to fill out and they're looking for a bigger halo but durned if I'm going to play that harp. I'm holding out for the thunder machine. See you around. Kesey."

After a public memorial service in Eugene, his tie-dyed coffin was brought back to his Pleasant Hill estate and, there on the privacy of his farm, Ken was buried next to his son Jed, who'd perished in a 1984 van crash. There are no visiting hours.

LOUIS L'AMOUR
MARCH 22, 1908 – JUNE 10, 1988

IN 1923 THE LaMoore family was uprooted from its native North Dakota after a series of bank crises and, over the next 25 years, Louis wandered the world over. He skinned cattle in west Texas, sailed the world's seas as a merchant seaman, lumberjacked the great Northwest forests, hobo'd to New Orleans, biked across India, mined for silver in Nevada and, after attending Tank Destroyer school, commanded a platoon of fuel-supply vehicles in Europe during World War II. As if that weren't enough, during many of those years Louis complemented his erratic income by boxing on professional fight cards.

After the war, he concentrated on writing and nearly starved as he struggled to find a suitable genre, moving from adventure tales to detective yarns to sports stories. In 1950 Louis was hired to write Hopalong Cassidy novels as Tex Burns and there, in the sagebrush and box canyons, he found his home as a writer of Westerns. In 1952 Louis pitched his *Gift of Cochise* short story to Bantam Books and, though they were not enamored of his new surname (spelled as "L'Amour," which insinuated it'd be a "Western written in lipstick"), Louis was signed to a long-term contract. The next year *Gift of Cochise* was made into the feature film *Hondo*, starring John Wayne, and Louis' career skyrocketed.

Over the next three decades his historically accurate novels sold an astounding 200 million copies, confounding critics who denounced his work as pulp fodder with haphazard composition and stilted dialogue. Meanwhile, Louis remained unapologetic for any shortcomings, maintaining shortly before his death that "I don't give a damn what anyone else thinks. I know it's literature and I know it'll be read a hundred years from now." Indeed, he's on track—in the 20 years since his passing, another 65 million L'Amour sagas have been sold.

After being diagnosed with lung cancer, Louis began his long-postponed memoir, *Education of a Wandering Man*, and was editing the book the afternoon that he died.

At 80, he was buried at Forest Lawn Memorial Park in Glendale, California.

GRAVE DIRECTIONS: Enter the park at 1712 South Glendale Avenue, get a map at the information booth, and make your way to the Great Mausoleum. But don't go inside—Louis is buried outside near the mausoleum's Memorial Terrace entrance. His grave is against the wall on the right, just beside the white statue of Jesus Christ seated with children.

HARPER LEE
April 28, 1926 – February 19, 2016

NELLE HARPER LEE'S father was a tax attorney who took but one criminal case: In 1917 he defended a black father and son who were charged with murdering a white Alabama storekeeper. Found guilty, both men were hanged, and the remnants of this event seemed to contribute to the shape of Harper's 1961 Pulitzer Prize–winning book, *To Kill a Mockingbird*. One of the most cherished novels in modern American literature, it's a definitive and sobering tale of Deep South race relations during the Jim Crow era.

After earning a degree in English literature, Harper introduced her talent by submitting stories to a literary agent at the insistence of Truman Capote (a childhood friend who was the inspiration for Dill, the peculiar, tale-spinning boy in *Mockingbird*). Once the agent recognized her flair, he encouraged her to move to New York to mature it. Taking his advice, Harper struggled along in the big city working as an airline reservation agent by day, while passing her nights in the damp and cold confines of a cellar apartment, writing on a desk she fashioned from a door. But on Christmas morning 1956, her lot changed when two wealthy friends of Capote's, Michael and Joy Brown, presented Harper with an envelope containing a note with the promise of a large financial gift: "You have one year off from your job to write whatever you please. Merry Christmas." (Though Harper wrote about this gift in a 1961 *McCall's* magazine article, neither she nor the Browns ever disclosed their identity. In 2006 an unauthorized Harper biography broke the news and the Browns confirmed it six years later.)

With new freedom and confidence, Harper developed a portfolio of short stories and vignettes, which over three years she morphed into her fully formed masterpiece novel. Poignant and beautiful, it was a remarkable debut by a writer who had not yet turned 35.

From the moment *Mockingbird* was published to almost instant success, Harper consistently avoided public attention, finding the role of literary celebrity oppressive. Retreating totally into private life, she became a sort of literary Garbo, the gate to her existence kept closed by her lawyer sister, Alice, with whom she lived and who managed her affairs, while friends and neighbors closed ranks around her and fended off unwelcome attention.

In 1964, during one of her last public interviews, Harper talked of writing a series of novels describing the world she grew up in, which now seemed to be disappearing. The reading public waited for a sequel and was occasionally pacified by tantalizing hints that the second novel was in progress, but 50 years went by and… nothing. Like Margaret Mitchell, Harper had become a one-book literary wonder.

Then in 2015, *Go Set a Watchman*, a supposed follow-up that turned out to actually be a 1957 first draft of *Mockingbird* in which central character Atticus Finch is portrayed as a staunch defender of segregation, was released under dubious circumstances. Both the "rediscovery" of the draft and the timing of the novel's publication were quite suspicious, its announcement coming just 10 weeks after the death of sister Alice, the reclusive author's lifelong advisor and protector.

As for Harper, having spent the better part of the last couple decades dropping quarters into the clattering slot machines of an Indian casino, she was now confined to a nursing home, where her private security guard shooed away unwelcome visitors—and it was questionable whether she was competent to approve the new publication: A friend related that the last time she had visited Harper, "She just hollered out: 'I can't see and I can't hear!' So I just told her goodbye."

At 89, Harper died in her sleep. Adorned with a spray of red and white roses, her oak casket was delivered by a silver hearse to Hillcrest Cemetery in Monroeville, Alabama, where she was lowered into the ground beside her father and sister.

GRAVE DIRECTIONS: At 321 Pineville Road, enter the cemetery at the southern entrance and turn at the first left. Then turn at the third right, and after 50 feet the Lee plot is on the left.

JACK LONDON
JANUARY 12, 1876 – NOVEMBER 22, 1916

JACK LONDON DROPPED out of Berkeley to join the Alaskan Klondike gold rush in 1897, and of his brutal experiences there, and later at sea, he wrote vigorous tales of men and animals at odds with one another. Upon his return to San Francisco the following year, he published his first collection of stories, *The Son of the Wolf,* but it was his next adventure story, *The Call of the Wild*, that turned him into the most successful writer of his time.

Over the remainder of his life, Jack wrote another 45 books of fiction and nonfiction. Most of his work was in the adventure genre, but he occasionally strayed, most notably in the philosophical and politically tinged *The Sea Wolf,* and *The People of the Abyss.*

Always a heavy drinker, Jack probably died of physical ailments related to alcoholism, though some scholars believe he committed suicide.

In any event, Jack was cremated and his ashes, their location marked by a mossy boulder, were buried on his Glen Ellen, California ranch, which is today the Jack London State Historical Park.

GRAVE DIRECTIONS: The park is located at 2400 London Ranch Road, and signs directing you to Jack are located after the ranger's booth.

NORMAN MAILER
JANUARY 21, 1923 – NOVEMBER 10, 2007

NORMAN MAILER NEVER wrote the great American novel, but he proved himself a great American writer who provoked, thrilled, and enraged his readers. After bursting onto the literary stage at 25 with *The Naked and the Dead*, a bestseller based on his experiences as a Harvard-educated sergeant during World War II, his thick lifetime catalog of fiction zigzagged across genres. *The Gospel According to the Son* was an unauthorized "autobiography" of Jesus, *The Castle in the Forest* imagined Adolf Hitler as a boy—featuring narration by the devil, *The Executioner's Song* about murderer Gary Gilmore blurred the lines between literature and journalism in a style pioneered by Capote, while what started as spare notes of personal observations about his participation in a 1967 march on the Pentagon by antiwar activists evolved into *The Armies of the Night*, a Pulitzer-winning, full-blown self-portrait interlaced with shrewd political and social commentary.

His writing reflected the gamut of contemporary culture and often explored willful masculinity clashing with established authority, portraits more often than not mirrored in the pugnacious and high-living writer's real-life exploits. A drinker, fighter, and unabashed pot smoker, Norman divorced five wives and nearly stabbed one to death. At the height of the women's movement, he gained the scorn of feminists for, amongst other affronts during a reading at a YWCA, characterizing women as "low, sloppy beasts" whose sole substance was to bear children. As a New York City mayoral candidate, his platform consisted of New York City becoming the 51st state, and he later urged a referendum for "black ghetto dwellers" to set up their own government. In 1968, the self-described "old club fighter" broke actor Lane Smith's jaw with a right hook and bit Rip Torn's ear in another scuffle. In 1981 his sponsored parole of Jack Henry Abbott, a convict with literary ambitions, turned tragic after Abbott killed a man six weeks after his release.

In the end, though, his writing was what mattered most. When he died at 84 of acute renal failure, praise for his literary contributions came from every corner of the world. He was buried at Provincetown Town Cemetery in Provincetown, Massachusetts.

GRAVE DIRECTIONS: At 24 Cemetery Road, turn right into the second paved drive, proceed over the little rise, and stop just before the maintenance shed. Norman's stone is the chalk-white one with an angled face in the grass on your right.

KARL MARX
MAY 5, 1818 – MARCH 14, 1883

EXPELLED FROM GERMANY, France, and Belgium for radicalism, renowned socialist thinker Karl Marx lived most of his adult life in "a long, sleepless night of exile" as a stateless and penniless London journalist in poor health. In a crusade of "merciless criticism of everything existing," he published hundreds of articles and essays promoting revolutionary reformist ideas, but his reputation primarily rests with two works: *Das Kapital* (Capital) and *Manifest der kommunistischen Partei* (*Communist Manifesto*).

Marx's central tenet is that the materialistic conception of history involves two basic notions: First, the economic system at any given time determines the prevailing ideas; and second, history is an ongoing process predetermined by economic institutions and evolving in regular stages of thesis, antithesis, and synthesis. Thesis corresponds to the precapitalist period when there were no classes or exploitation. Antithesis corresponds to the era of capitalism and labor exploitation. Synthesis, or communism, would be the final product under which capital would be owned in common and exploitation could not exist.

To Marx, then, capitalism is the last stage of historical development before communism, and the proletariat is the last historical class. The two are fated to be in conflict until the proletariat inevitably establishes a transitional order into communism, or a classless society. In Marxism, the complete collapse of industrial capitalism and its replacement by communism is inevitable.

Based on these ideas, Marx was a revolutionary who sought to effect social change and, indeed, his mission in life was to contribute, in his own peaceable and intellectual way, to the overthrow of capitalist society. His most famous treatises, his copious militant pamphlets, his work in underground organizations in Paris, Brussels, and London, and, finally, crowning all, his founding of the International Working Men's Association in 1864 stand as testimony to his purpose.

Though Marx's analysis of capitalist economy and his theories of historical materialism, the class struggle, and surplus value have greatly contributed to an almost scientific understanding of social divisions, Marx's influence during his life was not great. But after his death, his ideas and theories gained more prominence as Marxism was adopted by the labor movement.

Marx's theories on the nature of the capitalist state and the road to power were of critical importance with respect to subsequent historical epochs. During the twentieth century a radical incarnation of Marx's doctrines became the core of Bolshevik theory and, under the mercilessly brutal hand of Vladimir Ilich Lenin, communist Russia was born. However, it should be made clear that the totalitarian, police-state style of Communist governments that led to the misery of millions in places like the Soviet Union and North Korea bears little resemblance to the social form that Karl Marx idealistically proposed.

In the last two decades of his life, Marx was tormented by a mounting succession of ailments. In January 1883 it became tremendously difficult for him to swallow after a tumor developed in his throat. Two months later, he died in his armchair at 64.

Marx was buried in London's Highgate Cemetery. This elegant Victorian cemetery is at the top of Highgate Hill on the north side of town, off of Swain's Lane.

Marx's grand monument is surrounded by a black iron fence and topped by his intimidating, bearded bust.

JAMES MICHENER
FEBRUARY 3, 1907 – OCTOBER 16, 1997

ABANDONED BY HIS parents shortly after birth, young James was adopted by a Quaker widow, Mabel Michener. In his memoir, *The World Is My Home*, he wrote that his wanderlust sprouted upon realizing that the road outside their home continued forever, to strange lands and adventures he could not even imagine. He went on lengthy hitchhiking trips before he was old enough to drive and, ultimately, James came to be the consummate traveler.

But it wasn't until he was in his thirties, when the Navy sent him to the primitive South Pacific islands to gather wartime information, that he found his calling as a writer. The visits later provided the backdrop for some of his most memorable novels, which were invariably laden with geographical and historical details. James himself once admitted that he wasn't a "stylist" and wasn't very good at composing dialogue, but he also knew he could "put a good narrative together." Perhaps because he never knew his own roots, foreign backgrounds intrigued him. "I feel myself the inheritor of a great background of people," he said. "I could be Jewish, part Negro, probably not Oriental, but almost anything else, so I can't afford to be scornful about anyone."

On his first try as a published author he won the Pulitzer Prize for his 1948 collection of short stories, *Tales of the South Pacific*. These were later adapted into *South Pacific*, a long-running Broadway musical and motion picture. For the next five decades James took readers on obsessively detailed journeys across time to the far corners of the planet. Many of his 44 works had simple, one-word titles like *Hawaii*, *Sayonara*, and *Poland* and, often for 600 pages, the epics entertained while arguing James' universal ideals: religious and racial tolerance, hard work, and self-reliance.

Beginning in 1993, James waged a battle against kidney failure and, three times a week in three-hour-long sessions, his blood was pumped out, cleansed, and pumped back into his body by a dialysis machine. His once-wide world was reduced to only the city of Austin, which he lamented as "my prison." He never quit working, saying, "as long as the old brain keeps functioning, I know the desire will always be there," but life eventually became too much of a burden. "For the first time I understand how a person could say 'the hell with it,'" he confided.

Finally, the globetrotter refused any more life-sustaining dialysis treatments, and he died of kidney failure two weeks later.

At 90, James was cremated and his ashes buried at Austin Memorial Park in Austin, Texas.

GRAVE DIRECTIONS: Enter the cemetery at 2800 Hancock Drive, turn at the first drive on the right, and follow it up the hill. The last section on the right is Section 11, and there next to the curb is the reddish-colored Michener monument.

MARGARET MITCHELL

NOVEMBER 8, 1900 – AUGUST 16, 1949

WHILE GROWING UP, Margaret Mitchell was regaled with stories of Confederate Atlanta by her father, who was president of Atlanta's Historical Society. By the time Margaret was 27, she had written over a hundred feature stories for the *Atlanta Journal* newspaper, but once she was confined to her home after breaking her ankle, her second husband encouraged her to change gears and pursue her fiction-writing aspirations. Night and day, Margaret labored over her Remington typewriter, and after three years, she had completed a draft of *Gone With the Wind*, a fictitious epic featuring the experiences of a beautiful and manipulative Southern belle, Scarlett O'Hara, and describing the secession, Civil War, and Reconstruction periods from the seldom-heard Southern point of view.

The next half-dozen years were spent perfecting the book's historical accuracy and, once it was finally published in 1936, Margaret's 1,037-page novel immediately broke all previous records, selling 2 million copies within a year. Many critics panned it for being "overly Southern" but, nonetheless, *Gone With the Wind* was awarded the Pulitzer Prize the next year, and Margaret soon sold the film rights for $50,000. In 1939, its archetypal celluloid adaptation starring Clark Gable and Vivien Leigh premiered. This too was a smash. The film broke box-office records and the catchphrases it spawned—"Frankly, my dear, I don't give a damn" and "Tomorrow is another day" (Margaret's original title for the book)—haven't fallen from favor some 70 years since.

Remarkably, Margaret never wrote again. *Gone With the Wind* was the only book she ever authored and she was very adamant that, as the story could stand on its own, no sequel was necessary. Though it brought her fame and fortune, the book seems to have yielded her little joy. Chased by the press and public, Margaret and her husband lived modestly and traveled rarely.

On a hot Atlanta night in 1949, Margaret and her husband went downtown to see a movie. After parking the car across the street from the theater, the couple hurried across Peachtree Street arm-in-arm when a car suddenly sped toward them. In a panic, Margaret ran without her husband back to the curb, but the speeding car skidded and struck her, breaking her pelvis and fracturing her skull. Never regaining consciousness, she died five days later at 48.

In her will, Margaret instructed her secretary to burn all of her letters and the original *Gone With the Wind* manuscript, save for a few pages preserved to prove her authorship. And so, shortly after her death, her secretary and the custodian of the apartment building in which Margaret had been living burned nearly all of her documents in the building's boiler.

Margaret was buried at Oakland Cemetery in Atlanta, Georgia.

GRAVE DIRECTIONS: Enter the cemetery at 248 Oakland Avenue SE and turn left at the first paved drive. Just after crossing another paved drive, as the road bends to the right, stop. On the left is a brick walk that extends in the direction from which you were just driving. Follow this walk and then, at the second walk, turn left. A short distance on the left, behind the Peel mausoleum, is Margaret's grave.

GEORGE ORWELL
JUNE 25, 1903 – JANUARY 21, 1950

IN THE LATE 1940s, British author George Orwell established himself as one of the most influential voices of the century with two brilliant satires attacking totalitarianism.

His first important work, *Animal Farm*, was a fantasy novella, a mocking allegory of the Russian Revolution played out by sentient animals, some of whom were declared "more equal than others." Later, in a prophecy of a world laid waste by warring dictators, *1984* offered a bitter protest against the nightmarish direction in which Orwell believed the modern world was moving, complete with Thought Police and professional History Revisionists. At their core, both works are concise illustrations of the manner in which the degradation of language and the suppression of free speech precede all other oppressions. These powerful works are required reading at many schools of higher learning.

Just four months after the publication of *1984*, Orwell died at 46 of complications arising from a chronic tuberculosis condition.

He was buried in the yard of the All Saints Church in Sutton Courtenay, England. The large village is just a few miles south of Oxford, and the early-fourteenth-century church is at the north end of the village square. Orwell is buried under his own name, Eric Arthur Blair, and there is nothing on his headstone to indicate his achievements.

LUCIANO PAVAROTTI

OCTOBER 12, 1935 – SEPTEMBER 6, 2007

AS A MAESTRO of classical music, Luciano Pavarotti was acclaimed for the clear-as-a-bell tone and terrific projection of his pristine tenor, but his more enduring legacy is for a Midas touch that he lent to opera, extending its presence far beyond the traditional limits.

Luciano dreamed of being a soccer star until the day his voice emerged. Thereafter, he devoted himself to a serious opera career, spending every spare moment studying the fine points of phrasing and repertoire, and by his thirties was regarded as the greatest male operatic voice of his generation. Expanding his franchise exponentially, he shared the stage with Placido Domingo and Jose Carerras for the Three Tenors project. Performing with rock stars as varied as Elton John and Jon Bon Jovi—even the Spice Girls!—at his Pavarotti and Friends charity concerts, he also earned renown with the MTV generation.

Raising money for international causes, he won new friends onstage and off. Joking on talk shows and cooking programs, riding horses on parade, and even playing an improbable sex symbol in the movie *Yes, Giorgio*, Luciano solicited his fans' adoration and they fell at his feet. But as he became increasingly celebrated, he spent less and less time preparing for his operatic roles or studying new ones and traditional opera aficionados became disenchanted. Rudolf Bing, onetime manager of the Metropolitan Opera, complained that "seeing that stupid, ugly face everywhere I go is getting on my nerves. It's all so unnecessary, so undignified."

Luciano ultimately allowed success to turn him into an Elvislike caricature of himself. Everything about him became outsized and, as his girth increased exponentially, along with a new air of self-importance and untouchability, even the trademark Hermès scarves he draped over his frame had to be supersized. In poor health and hardly able to walk, the maestro canceled appearances, and when he did perform, his presentation seemed remote. Controversy followed Luciano offstage as well; tax collectors dogged him for millions, and he left his wife of 37 years for his secretary, a woman 35 years his junior.

Despite mustering strength for a farewell tour, Luciano postponed the extravaganzas after just a handful of dates when a malignant tumor was found on his pancreas, and a performance at the opening ceremonies of the 2006 Winter Olympics turned out to be his last.

At 71, Luciano was claimed by pancreatic cancer and he was buried at Montale Rangone Cemetery in Modena, Italy.

PABLO PICASSO

OCTOBER 25, 1881 – APRIL 8, 1973

PERHAPS THE MOST influential artist of the twentieth century, Pablo Picasso almost singlehandedly created modern art. Not even Michelangelo has ever been as famous as Picasso was in his own lifetime, and it seems likely that none ever will be again. Picasso's audience, meaning people who'd heard of him or who knew of his work, was in the hundreds of millions and his efforts were the subject of unending analysis.

One of the more remarkable qualities of his career was the rapidity with which he invented revolutionary art styles. After his Blue and Red periods came a simplification of art that shocked the masses with his Cubist works featuring abstract and multi-angled dissection. Around 1912, with his contemporary Georges Braque, Picasso began experiments with *papier collé* that created a new form known as collage. Later, with the Surrealists of the 1920s, his efforts turned to the grotesque, and he formed figures endowed with several heads, displaced noses and mouths, and enlarged limbs. One of his most historically significant works, the masterpiece *Guernica*, expresses the fascist brutality of the Spanish Civil War, and its completion marked the final turning point of his career.

The last period of Picasso's life was itself a tapestry, a torrentially productive era lacking any semblance of quality control. Wallowing in unprecedented adoration as an artist and "national monument," in his final years Picasso indulged his celebrity and did exactly as he pleased: Fanning a vulgar and cynical image, he became the King Midas of art—everything he touched turned to gold. In the last 20 years of his life, the master deliberately marred his own reputation, producing shoddy "signed" lithographs by the thousands as well as throwaway amateurish pieces for the consumption of deep-pocketed "collectors" hungry for any piece of the restless legend.

Picasso once told a visitor who admired his vigor, "A painter never finishes. Whenever you stop, it's only because you've started again." By some terms, the manic and obsessive quality of those words, and his productions, almost imply that he expected the creative act to forestall his death, though it did not.

At 91, Picasso died of a pulmonary edema.

His grave, adorned with his own "Woman with the Vase" sculpture, is located on the terrace leading to the front entrance of his castle in Vauvenargues, France. You're welcome to visit this bucolic Provence village anytime you'd like, but Picasso's castle, its grounds, and his grave are closed to visitors.

EDGAR ALLAN POE

JANUARY 19, 1809 – OCTOBER 7, 1849

EDGAR ALLAN POE created the narrative mystery-thriller genre and, more than any other writer, deserves credit for elevating short stories from a disrespected anecdotal form to an honorable artistic genre.

Orphaned at three, Edgar was adopted by the wealthy Allan family and baptized Edgar Allan Poe. At 17, he entered the University of Virginia to concentrate on classical languages, but after running up a $2,000 gambling debt that his stepfather refused to cover, Edgar left school and enlisted in the Army, eventually landing at West Point. While there, his first book, *Tamerlane and Other Poems*, was published, and Edgar, uninterested in a cadet future now that his writing talent had been validated, neglected his responsibilities until he was dismissed for "gross neglect of duty."

Edgar took up residence in Baltimore with his aunt, Maria Clemm, and her daughter, Virginia, his first cousin, whom the 27-year-old married in 1836 when she was 13. He became editor of the *Southern Literary Messenger* and there published much of his own fiction, most notably "Berenice," but beyond his own contributions, his editorial attention was scant. As Edgar's only other focus seemed to be alcohol, he was soon asked to resign.

The pattern of Edgar's career now seemed prescribed, and his experience at the *Southern Literary Messenger* was mirrored at a variety of other publications in Philadelphia and New York over the next decade. Edgar contributed his best flawlessly constructed fiction, including "The Fall of the House of Usher" and "The Tell-Tale Heart," to an assortment of literary periodicals, but his endless literary feuding, his alcoholism, and his inability to get along with people irritated employers, ensuring that his various tenures were invariably short.

In 1845, after releasing "The Raven" to popular acclaim, Edgar was pleased to find he could generate on-the-spot income by reciting the verse to paying audiences. His household's financial situation improved to its best level ever, but just as it seemed that Edgar's star might finally be rising, his young wife, Virginia, died in 1847, and Edgar retreated to hard drinking.

On a trip from Richmond to New York, Edgar's steamboat made a stop in Baltimore and, six days later, in the middle of the day, he was found ill, lying half-conscious in the street by a printer who knew him. He was wearing clothes that probably were not his own and, in a delirious state, kept calling for a polar explorer of the day named Reynolds. Taken to a hospital, Edgar drifted in and out of consciousness for the next four days until he uttered his final words: "Lord help my poor soul," and passed on at 40. The cause of death was presumed to be related to his alcoholism, and his brief obituary reported that he had died of "congestion of the brain." As the literary community did not particularly like Edgar, his obituaries weren't very kind and one stated simply, "We hope he has found his rest, for he needed it."

Edgar was buried the next day in an unmarked grave but, in time, the literary world came around and a group of devotees purchased a suitable grave and monument for the neglected author. In 1875 Edgar and Virginia were reburied in Baltimore's Westminster Presbyterian Church Cemetery and, upon Aunt Maria's 1885 death, she joined them and the struggling family was reunited for eternity.

Since 1949, on the night of the anniversary of Edgar's birth, a mysterious stranger known as the Poe Toaster has left a half-empty bottle of cognac and three roses at the Poe monument. The significance of cognac is uncertain, as it does not figure in Poe's works, but it's presumed that the three roses are for the three persons whose remains lie beneath. At Baltimore's Poe House and Museum, several of the bottles of cognac from prior years are on display.

GRAVE DIRECTIONS: Walk into the churchyard at 519 West Fayette Street, and the Poe plot is immediately on the right.

MARIO PUZO

OCTOBER 15, 1920 – JULY 2, 1999

FOR 48 YEARS Mario Puzo basked in relative middle-class obscurity; he served in the Air Force during World War II and, through a variety of jobs, barely supported a wife and five children over the next couple of decades. In 1955 Mario's income was augmented by monies earned through the sale of a novel, *The Dark Arena*, and nine years later an autobiographical chronicle of the experience of Italian-American immigrants, *The Fortunate Pilgrim*. Both works were only moderately successful and Mario continued writing freelance book reviews, stories, and articles for newspapers and magazines.

But Mario's fortunes changed after he secured a $5,000 advance for a book about a different group of Italian-American immigrants. In 1969 he published a fictitious account of the Sicilian Corleone crime family, *The Godfather*. An instant smash hit, it has sold at least 20 million copies and became one of the best-selling books of all time.

The Godfather and its sequels were of course also adapted for the screen, and Mario wrote the screenplays as well. Today *The Godfather* films, directed by Francis Ford Coppola, are recognized as masterpieces, and are responsible for adding such phrases to the pop culture lexicon as "Make him an offer he can't refuse" and "It's not personal . . . it's strictly business."

Later, it was speculated that Mario himself must have been in the Mafia to have the depth of knowledge of its workings that is displayed in his books, but the author vehemently denied the allegation. "Where would I have had time to be in the Mafia? I starved before the success of *The Godfather*," he once said in an interview. "If I was in the Mafia, I would have made enough money so I wouldn't have to write."

Mario doesn't "sleep with the fishes." Instead, at 78, he was buried at North Babylon Cemetery in West Babylon, New York.

GRAVE DIRECTIONS: Mario is in the section of cemetery on the west side of 400 Livingston Avenue. As you enter the drive you'll see the big Christopher stone in front of you, and four rows behind is the Puzo plot.

276

AYN RAND
FEBRUARY 2, 1905 – MARCH 6, 1982

BORN ALYSSA ROSENBAUM, the celebrated author Ayn Rand lived through the Bolshevik Revolution and learned to hate her Russian homeland, a country she later described as "an accidental cesspool of civilization." Early on, she planned to escape to the United States and, after studying philosophy and history at the University of Petrograd, her opportunity came in 1926 when she was allowed to briefly visit relatives in America. She never returned.

Speaking little English and virtually penniless, the 21-year-old stayed with relatives in Chicago before changing her name and moving to Hollywood, where she eventually found work as a script evaluator at Cecil B. DeMille's studio. By tripping him on purpose, Ayn met the tall, handsome actor Frank O'Connor, and they married in 1929.

Ayn later became a screenwriter and, having developed into a passionate, communist-hating capitalist, she spent years laboring over an ambitious novel. Rejected countless times for being "too intellectual," *The Fountainhead* was published in 1943 and 14 years later, *Atlas Shrugged* followed. These two 1,000-plus-page bestsellers reflect Ayn's deep belief in a philosophy she termed "objectivism," which glorifies the pursuit of unbridled self-interest as the right thing to do from an economic standpoint, and a moral one as well. That is, she believed that unrestrained, even arrogant, capitalist pursuit does far more to lift the world's standard of living than does an altruistic life of self-sacrifice.

Critics consider *The Fountainhead* to be the better work, but *Atlas Shrugged* more pointedly propagates Ayn's philosophy. It reads like a mystery, but its premise is that innovators become so fed up with those who regulate and tax and otherwise feed off of achievers that the achievers withdraw their talents from the world and threaten to send us all back to the Dark Ages. After its 1957 publication, Ayn spent the remainder of her life espousing the objectivist philosophy through lectures.

In 1979, Ayn underwent surgery for a spot of cancer on a lung, and the remainder of her life was plagued by poor health. Five days after being released from the hospital for pneumonia, she died of heart failure in her New York City apartment. At her funeral, Ayn was laid out in a coffin next to a six-foot-tall dollar sign.

At 77, she was buried at Kensico Cemetery in Valhalla, New York.

GRAVE DIRECTIONS: At 260 Lakeview Avenue, enter the cemetery at the Commerce Street entrance, make a right onto Tecumseh Avenue, then a left onto Cherokee Avenue. Where Ossipee Avenue intersects Cherokee, 30 feet into the lawn is the Rand plot.

NORMAN ROCKWELL
FEBRUARY 3, 1894 – NOVEMBER 8, 1978

IN 1916 NORMAN Rockwell's spectacular career as America's favorite artist-illustrator was launched when the *Saturday Evening Post* first used one of his paintings on its cover. Thus began an association spanning 317 covers and 47 years. His warm and folksy paintings made Norman Rockwell a household name.

Painting eight hours a day, seven days a week, Norman took average America as his subject. Through wars, civil strife, and the Depression, Norman stuck to his easel and recorded the awkwardness of youth, the tribulations of romance, and the virtues of loyalty and compassion. His body of work yields an extraordinary visual history of the century, portrayed with benevolent affection.

In addition to his *Post* covers, Norman contributed 53 Boy Scouts calendars, illustrated the lives of everyone from Ben Franklin to Huck Finn, and did portraits of all the presidential candidates from Eisenhower through Carter. In 1943 he painted his famous "Four Freedoms" series, and when the originals went on tour they helped sell $133 million in war bonds.

He left the *Post* in 1963, feeling that it had changed from a family-oriented periodical to one of "sophisticated muckraking," and his work changed dramatically. Norman left the role of chronicler of nostalgic America and became a crusader. Instead of painting gentler scenes of peace and prosperity, he showed a strong social conscience and delved into such issues as civil rights, poverty, the generation gap, and the war in Vietnam.

In a survey of Americans, his painting of a young boy standing on a chair inspecting the doctor's diploma while preparing to receive a vaccination in the behind was chosen by a majority as the favorite of his entire catalog. But Norman himself steadfastly maintained that he had no favorite painting. He once said,

"Someone asked Picasso his favorite of all the pictures he ever painted and he replied, 'The next one.' I'll echo the master."

At 84, Norman died peacefully in his sleep and was buried at the town cemetery in Stockbridge, Massachusetts.

GRAVE DIRECTIONS: Enter the cemetery at the entrance between the stone pillars on Church Street, proceed down the corridor of pine and hemlock trees, and at the first drive, turn right and stop. The Rockwell plot is on the right, surrounded by a hedgerow.

While in Stockbridge, you'll certainly want to visit the warm atmosphere of the Norman Rockwell Museum, where a regular rotation of his paintings is on display. At any given time, the gallery is adorned with a few hundred of his works, but you'll have to return quite a few times before you've seen the approximately 4,000 that comprise Norman's catalog. The Four Freedoms series are the centerpiece of the museum and, when you look up to view them, the effect is a virtual cathedral to the American Dream.

To reach the museum, follow Church Street for another mile past the cemetery and watch for signs to the left.

CHARLES M. SCHULZ
NOVEMBER 26, 1922 – FEBRUARY 12, 2000

COMIC STRIP CARTOONING requires such a peculiar combination of talents that very few people are ever successful at it. Of those, Charles Schulz is in a league all his own. Reconfiguring and dominating the comic-strip landscape for fully half of its history, the importance of *Peanuts* to the genre, or even to popular culture, can hardly be overstated.

After seeing a "Do you like to draw?" advertisement, Charles took an art correspondence course, and from that dubious training created an indispensable cultural touchstone via a most unexpected medium: a comic strip called *Peanuts*. For 50 years, in an intensely personal effort, Charles himself wrote and sketched every one of the strip's panels; he even had a clause inserted into his contract preventing anyone else from releasing new *Peanuts* cartoons after his death.

The strip was introduced in 1950, at the height of the American post-war celebration, when being unhappy was considered an antisocial act rather than a personal emotion. *Peanuts* introduced to the world a group of children who told one another the truth. Charles dared to bring his own quirks, his lifelong sense of alienation, insecurity, and inferiority, into the strip—something new in a time when comics were dominated by action-adventure, melodrama, or slapstick gags.

His characters were contemplative, made smart observations, and broached with gentle humor and twinkling insight such previously taboo subjects as faith, depression, intolerance, loneliness, and despair. Charlie Brown became a real person with a real psyche and, when he first confessed, "I don't feel the way I'm supposed to feel," he spoke for people everywhere. Through the 1950s Charles provided unconventional commentary in the national margins, but in the next decade, *Peanuts* skyrocketed into a mainstream cultural powerhouse. As the politics of the 1960s intensified and nothing quite worked out, *Peanuts* became a refuge for people who were putting up with all they could take. With great deliberateness, the strip proved that you were not alone when you woke in the middle of the night, in the company of your failures, worrying that the world had gone mad.

In 1965, as the nation teetered, Charles soared to previously unknown heights of popularity when more than half the nation's television audience tuned in to his animated special, *A Charlie Brown Christmas*, the success of which confounded network executives. By then, the long-suffering Charlie Brown, high-spirited Snoopy, contemplative Linus, and domineering Lucy had already become revered international figures, but on that night, Charles reached a more diverse, and perhaps larger, audience than any other American artist in history.

Many of the *Peanuts* characters were based on real people in Charles' life. An uncontrollable childhood dog named Spike was behind Snoopy, and the little red-haired girl, Charlie Brown's

unrequited love, was based on a girlfriend who rejected Charles' 1950 marriage proposal. Charles maintained that Charlie Brown was born from a friendship he made through the art instruction correspondence school, but ultimately, it seems that Charles Schulz was Charlie Brown.

Despite his fantastic success, stoicism and insecurity became Charles' personal themes, and high anxiety dogged him all his life. Though the world begged him to move beyond gentle commentary to a role as a national observer, he had no itch to be a teacher or a guru. "I don't know the meaning of life," he once said, "and I don't know why we are here. I think life is full of anxieties and tears and it can be very grim. And I do not want to be the one who tries to tell somebody else what life is all about. To me it's a complete mystery." Instead, in his Santa Rosa studio at One Snoopy Place, every day for five decades, he kept on drawing. He drew with the same old crow-quill pens dipped in ink and used the same drawing table; he liked to say he would remain at his desk until he wore a hole clean through it.

Though Charles took professional pride in the achievements of the strip, it did not automatically override his early disappointments, and he struggled to believe he was worthy of the admiration showered on him. "It is amazing that they think that what I do was that good," his voice quavered in a 1999 interview. "I just did the best I could."

By December of that year, a battle with colon cancer and a series of small strokes forced Charles to announce his retirement.

Just hours before the final *Peanuts* installment appeared in newspapers around the world, a single-block Sunday strip featuring a reflective Snoopy typing Charles' farewell letter, Charles died in his sleep of a heart attack at home.

Charles was 77 at his death and was buried at Pleasant Hills Memorial Park in Sebastopol, California.

GRAVE DIRECTIONS: At 1700 Pleasant Hill Road, pull into the first entrance and park at the triple fountains on the right. The stone bench near the top fountain marks Charles' grave.

Back when the strip peaked in popularity with 355 million regular readers, the branding of everything *Peanuts* became an enormous business. In fact, the strip almost single-handedly created that form of merchandising. Worldwide, more than a quarter million different products have been licensed based on the strip's characters and their carefree images can be found on everything from shoelaces to underwear, wind chimes to candles, and cookie jars to clocks. After tallying his hundreds of sources of income (don't forget advertising rights and even a Broadway production!), Charles' personal income rivaled that of the Beatles and Elvis Presley. As of 2018, his "lifetime" income is approaching $1.2 billion because, after all, he posthumously makes a lot of money—in 2016 alone, Charles' paychecks exceeded $30 million.

DR. SEUSS
MARCH 2, 1904 – SEPTEMBER 24, 1991

RETURNING FROM EUROPE by boat in 1936, Theodor Geisel amused himself during the long voyage by putting together a nonsense poem to the rhythm of the ship's motion. He later drew pictures to illustrate the rhyme, and after being rejected by either 23 or 28 or 38 publishers, depending on whom you ask, the resulting children's book, *And to Think That I Saw It on Mulberry Street*, made it into print the following year. Ted released the book under the name Dr. Seuss—a pseudonym he arrived at by inserting a "Dr." in front of his middle name—because he intended to keep his surname for more serious work. But when he later got around to doing a grown-up book, *The Seven Lady Godivas*, in 1939, he found that adults did not seem to care for his humor. So he went back to writing for children, and became famous and wealthy in the process.

The outbreak of World War II forced Seuss to devote his talents to the war effort and, working with the Information and

Education Division of the Army, he made documentary films for American soldiers. His film *Hitler Lives* won an Academy Award, a feat Seuss repeated with *Design for Death*, a documentary about the Japanese war effort.

In 1954 a magazine article argued that children were having trouble learning to read because their Dick and Jane primers were pallid and idiotic. The charge inspired Seuss' publisher to challenge him to write a book using no more than 250 words derived from a scholastically approved vocabulary list, which was the publisher's idea of how many words a first grader could absorb at one time.

Seuss responded with the zany classic *The Cat in the Hat*, an iconoclastic story in rhyme that presented an impelling incentive to read. Using just 223 words and considerable repetition, its short, choppy sentences reassured beginning readers and provided a lively alternative to the wooden dullness of the "See Spot run" learners. Its enthusiastic reception cemented Seuss' reputation, and led him to found Beginner Books, a publishing company specializing in easy-to-read books for children. A whole line of ridiculously logical storybooks was launched—all written by Seuss, and for the most part illustrated by him as well—that forever changed the world of children's books.

Seuss created modern classics from *Green Eggs and Ham*, which managed in a vocabulary of just 50 words to explain the need to try new experiences, and *Fox in Socks*, a series of increasingly boisterous tongue twisters, to *The Lorax*, about environmental preservation. Though some adults developed an occasional aversion to Seuss' books by reading them aloud one too many times, admirers were drawn to the unflagging momentum and breathless pace of his highly inventive vocabulary, and the way in which he championed virtue and goodness, while still managing to keep things lively. Seuss was one of the few authors of children's books who could get away with moralizing.

Dr. Seuss claimed his ideas started with doodles. "I'll doodle a couple of animals and if they bite each other, it's going to be a good book." Certainly those doodles aided his phantasmagoric imagination in the creation of persnickety Loraxes and fractious Sneetches, not to mention indescribable Zubble-wumps and ooey-gooey green Ooblecks. And Sam, of course.

At 87, Dr. Seuss expired in his sleep and was cremated.

WILLIAM SHAKESPEARE
APRIL 23, 1564 – APRIL 23, 1616

RELATIVELY LITTLE IS known about William Shakespeare's life and, though his works, considered the greatest in the English language, have been meticulously examined for flecks of autobiography, interpretations have fallen short. In any event, we know that words came easily to the playwright and that he had an incalculable influence on literature. "The Bard" converted the hitherto stiff verse meter into an instrument capable of expressing every facet of human emotion and intellect. And, through a brilliant array of characters, he explored the nature of man through astounding dramas that have never been equaled.

It's believed that Shakespeare spent the years 1580–82 as a teacher, then moved to London to become an actor. When the theaters were closed in 1592 due to plague, he turned to writing and, by the time the theaters opened again in 1594, Shakespeare had emerged as a rising playwright. Around 1598 Shakespeare became "principal comedian" of the King's Men acting troupe and it was during this time that he penned comedies such as *A Midsummer Night's Dream*. Likewise, when he became "principal tragedian" around 1603, works such as *Hamlet*, *Macbeth*, and *King Lear* were the result. Later came the romances, *Romeo and Juliet* among them.

Though the profession of playwright was not particularly noble or well paying, successful and prosperous actors were relatively respected and Shakespeare was able to live well as such. In 1596 he applied for a coat of arms for his family, in effect making himself into an aristocrat. Around 1610, he returned to his hometown where he had a house built and lived out the remainder of his years as a country gentleman.

Shakespeare died at 52 and was buried in the sanctuary of the Collegiate Church of Holy Trinity in Stratford-on-Avon, Warwickshire, England.

It seems ludicrous to question the authorship of the works of William Shakespeare but, in the centuries since his death, his legacy has indeed been debated. A number of respected books, particularly the 1908 work by George Greenwood, *The Shakespeare Problem Restated*, suggest that credit has been given to the wrong man and that someone other than the man we know as William Shakespeare is the author of his credited volumes. According to *Shakespeare Problem* proponents, there isn't a shred of hard evidence to prove that he wrote even one of his dramas. To the contrary, they argue, there is considerable evidence that he couldn't possibly have been the true Bard. Some who share this conviction regard Francis Bacon as the "real" author, while others champion Christopher Marlowe.

One of the lesser reasons that *Shakespeare Problem* partisans disregard him is that, in contrast to the passing of other distinguished literary folk of the era, Shakespeare's death was not an event. In fact, they say, "as far as anyone can know and can prove," Shakespeare wrote only one poem during his life, and his authorship of it stands undisputed. That one poem is the epitaph that he commanded be engraved upon his tomb. He was obeyed, and it remains there to this day. It reads:

> *Good friend, for Jesus' sake forbeare,*
> *To digg the dust enclosed heare!*
> *Blese be ye man yt spares these stones.*
> *And curst be he yt moves my bones.*

MARY SHELLEY
AUGUST 30, 1797 – FEBRUARY 1, 1851

GIVEN HER FAMILY legacy (both her parents were influential authors and propagandists), it seemed inevitable that Mary Shelley was to make a significant contribution to literature. Her mother, Mary Wollstonecraft, was an early (*very* early) feminist who authored the radical tome, *A Vindication of the Rights of Women*, which is still read today. Mary's father, William Godwin, was a celebrated liberalist whose goal was to translate France's Enlightenment into an English context, though his once voguish radicalism fell out of favor after the bloody excesses of the French Revolution.

The Godwin-Wollstonecraft relationship was intellectually based; the two even kept separate households until just before Mary's birth on the principle that women had the right to independence. When her mother died days after her birth, Mary was left to be reared by her father, an undemonstrative, self-absorbed, and cerebral man.

By the time she was 10, Mary was a student of her mother's oeuvre, and often retreated to the tranquil comfort provided by her mother's grave for study. At 16 she eloped with poet Percy Bysshe Shelley, a peer of her father's. As Mary was by now herself a writer, the couple immersed themselves in their own brainy relationship and enjoyed impulsive poetically inspired European jaunts.

In July 1816 they visited Lord Byron's Villa Diodati home near Geneva and fell to reading each other ghost tales. After they were joined by Gothic author John Polidori, the talent in the Villa superseded the stories being read and Byron suggested a kind of contest to see which of them could write the best supernatural tale; 18-year-old Mary's effort became *Frankenstein: or, the Modern Prometheus*.

In more than 40 *Frankenstein* film adaptations, the general spirit of the story has been significantly shifted to the shallow horror of a grunting, bolt-headed monster and his mad-scientist creator. But in fact, the *Frankenstein* story is largely a sympathetic narrative of a creature embittered after being unloved and deserted by his creator, and it reflects the net effect of Mary Shelley's life: a motherless child with a distant father. In any event, though she wrote five more novels, Mary's reputation rests with her "hideous progeny," the Creature created by Dr. Victor Frankenstein.

Mary Shelley died in her sleep at 53 and is buried alongside her parents at Saint Peter's Churchyard on Hinton Road in Bournemouth, England.

Prior to her death, Mary's poet husband, Percy, drowned off the coast of Italy in 1822, and his body was burned there in a beachfront funeral pyre. During the immolation, his friend Edward Trelawny retrieved Percy's heart from his body and later presented it to the newly widowed Mary, who must have been delighted by his thoughtfulness. Until her own death she kept it with a copy of his poem "Adonais," at which time both the poem and heart were buried with her.

JOHN STEINBECK
FEBRUARY 27, 1902 – DECEMBER 20, 1968

THE FACT THAT John Steinbeck spent his formative years in California—where migrant fruit pickers of the San Joaquin valley toiled the hard land while shiftless and carefree drifters camped together in shanties along Monterey Bay—was extremely influential on the budding writer.

After a short stay at Stanford University, a couple of lost years in New York, and two undistinguished novellas, Steinbeck refocused his writing efforts and in 1935 released *Tortilla Flat*, a sometimes-comical but affectionate story of rootless Mexican-American drifters. It was Steinbeck's first popularly successful work and it was followed quickly by the similarly acclaimed *The Red Pony* and *Of Mice and Men*.

In 1936 Steinbeck began hanging around the camps of farming refugees who had been stripped of their Midwestern livelihoods and displaced to California by the Dust Bowl hardships. Three years later Steinbeck released *The Grapes of Wrath*, the saga of one Okie family's struggle along Route 66 on the way to the promised land, and the family's subsequent pains at the hands of exploitive farm owners. It was an American masterpiece.

As is usually the case, not everyone was ecstatic about the work, and Oklahoma's governor characterized it as "a lie, a black, infernal creation of a twisted and distorted mind." But the following year, Steinbeck was redeemed when he received the Pulitzer Prize.

Steinbeck spent 1941 collecting marine life in Mexico with his marine-biologist friend Edward Ricketts, and the two men collaborated in writing *Sea of Cortez*, a study of the fauna of the Gulf of California. During World War II he took various war-correspondent assignments abroad and later etched more sentimental novels like *Cannery Row* and *The Pearl* while contributing the story for Alfred Hitchcock's film *Lifeboat*. Steinbeck's last work was *Travels with Charley*, a 1962 chronicle of his tour around America in a camper with his wife's poodle.

At 66, John died in bed at his Sag Harbor home and was cremated. A few days after his funeral, where Henry Fonda read a eulogy, John's family scattered some of his ashes along a rugged stretch of Monterey coastline overlooking Whalers Bay while sea otters played in the surf. The remaining ashes were buried at the Garden of Memories Cemetery in Salinas, California.

GRAVE DIRECTIONS: Enter the cemetery at 850 Abbott Street, turn right at the flagpole, and go past the mausoleum. Turn at the next right and, halfway down this drive, you'll see a "Steinbeck" sign and an arrow pointing left. John's ashes are interred 100 feet across that lawn in front of the Hamilton stone.

ROBERT LOUIS STEVENSON
NOVEMBER 13, 1850 – DECEMBER 3, 1894

IN 1867, ROBERT Louis Stevenson entered Edinburgh University with the tacit understanding that he'd follow his father and become a civil engineer. But Robert enjoyed a more romantic nature, and he instead spent his time studying literature and history. As a compromise, he switched to law and, though he was called to the Scottish bar in 1875, Robert never actually practiced. Instead he devoted himself to writing travel sketches and short stories for magazines.

Suffering from tuberculosis since childhood, Robert took advantage of his newfound adult freedom and jockeyed from place to place with the seasons to ease his respiratory discomforts. His rambles soon blossomed into wanderlust. "I travel for travel's sake," he wrote. "The great affair is to move," and the wanderlust, in turn, rendered inspiration for romantic adventure novels.

In 1878, his first book, *An Inland Voyage*, was published, and by 1883 he was held in high regard for *Treasure Island*. In 1886, after writing *The Strange Case of Dr. Jekyll and Mr. Hyde*, which was based on a dream and written and printed in a 10-week blizzard of activity, and *Kidnapped*, which recounted the tale of his ancestor David Balfour, Robert looked up from his notebooks to find he'd became the most popular author of the day.

Dogged by his flagging health, Robert and his family set sail for the South Pacific in 1888, and the following year he bought an estate in Samoa where he hoped to live happily ever after. The climate suited his respiration, the people were neighborly, and, more importantly, the island had a reasonably functional postal system. The Stevenson estate boasted a dozen Samoan servants who called Robert "Tusitala" ("the teller of tales") and in his time there he pounded out an impressive number of works, though none rivaled the popularity of his earlier successes.

But Robert's blissful experience on Samoa was short-lived. One evening while chatting with his wife, he suffered a cerebral hemorrhage. At 44, he was buried atop Mount Vaea on his own 300-acre Vailima estate in Apia, Samoa.

Robert's grave marker is graced by his own words:

Here he lies where he longed to be;
Home is the sailor, home from the sea,
And the hunter home from the hill.

HUNTER S. THOMPSON
JULY 18, 1937 – FEBRUARY 20, 2005

HUNTER S. THOMPSON'S ATYPICAL writing career began when he contributed to an Air Force newspaper, a service he had entered as part of a parole agreement after a particularly wild youth, and one which he exited, by his own account, with "totally unclassifiable status." Following the military stint he embarked on a career path that was rocky, to put it mildly; at *Time* magazine he was fired for spending his time typewriting entire F. Scott Fitzgerald works to better understand the author's writing style; at the *Middletown Daily Record* in New York, he was let go after a violent altercation with the company's candy machine; his tenure at a Brazilian media publication was terminated due to gross discrepancies on expense reports; and in 1961 he was canned from a treasured caretaking job at Big Sur Hot Springs after publishing a controversial piece about the area's hard-drinking, pot-smoking subculture.

Hunter inevitably gravitated to the drug and hippie culture of San Francisco where he fell into living and partying with the notorious Hell's Angels biker gang as a sort of hanger-on whom they tolerated. Their toleration turned to admiration once his 1965 magazine feature of their exploits hit the newsstands, but then devolved into contempt, as Hunter sought to further capitalize on their dead-end lifestyle by extrapolating the piece into a full-length book, *Hell's Angels: The Strange and Terrible Saga of the Outlaw Motorcycle Gang*. Oblivious to their rising displeasure, Hunter remained in their midst as he struggled to script a climactic final scene for the book's ending. Finally, tensions burst at a California roadhouse and his subjects demonstrated to him their idea for the last chapter by beating him within an inch of his life.

With the success of *Hell's Angels*, Hunter and his wide-open writing style became highly sought after and, in 1970, he inadvertently upped the ante and ended up casting an entirely new genre—a mad journalistic style in which the correspondent himself plays a central role in the story. With his mind blown out on assorted recreational inebriants and the heat of a deadline for a piece about the Kentucky Derby bearing down, Hunter resorted to merely delivering torn-out pages from his notebook. "I was sure it was the last article I was ever going to do for anybody," he recalled. Instead, the piece drew raves and was labeled a breakthrough in journalism, an experience the soon-to-be counterculture hero likened to "falling down an elevator shaft and landing in a pool of mermaids." Gonzo journalism was born and Hunter's heyday arrived.

In the next decade he perfected his acerbic mix of nonfiction writing and inserted himself into countless rambling essays and a handful of books that savagely chronicled the underbelly of American life and politics. In raw and sprawling satires such as *Fear and Loathing in Las Vegas* Hunter portrayed himself as a snarling maverick narrator whose beat was "the death of the American Dream." Extending the Dr. Gonzo image to his real life, it became apparent that there may not have been too much embellishment in his published exploits; perpetually wearing sunglasses and a baseball cap while a cigarette dangled from his lips, the independent outlaw showed up late, if at all, and defied norms and conventions via a claim to intimate familiarity with a variety of mind-altering chemicals, homemade explosives, and guns. "I hate to advocate drugs, alcohol, violence, or insanity to anyone . . . but they've always worked for me," he wrote.

By the 1980s fans and critics complained that he was merely regurgitating past glories without adding anything new and Hunter confirmed their protests by retreating to his Colorado compound. But for his weekly "Hey Rube" ESPN sports column, the increasingly grumpy and vitriolic writer either failed to complete assignments or flat-out rejected them in the first place for most of the rest of his life.

One fine day at his Woody Creek fortress, on the phone with his wife and with his son and daughter-in-law in the next room, Hunter blew his brains out while seated in front of a typewriter. His suicide note entitled "Football Season Is Over" read: "No More Games. No More Bombs. No More Walking. No More Fun. No More Swimming. 67. That is 17 years past 50. 17 more than I needed or wanted. Boring. I am always bitchy. No Fun—for anybody. 67. You are getting Greedy. Act your old age. Relax—This won't hurt."

After his death, friends remembered that on several occasions Hunter had mentioned he'd like his ashes to be shot from a cannon. Per his wishes, a field gun the size of the Statue of Liberty was assembled on his property and, while Bob Dylan's "Mr. Tambourine Man" blared from oversized speakers and well-wishers clinked glasses of whiskey, Dr. Gonzo's mortal remains were blasted over the Rocky Mountain peaks.

J.R.R. TOLKIEN
JANUARY 3, 1892 – SEPTEMBER 2, 1973

UPON HIS 1915 graduation from Exeter College, John Ronald Reuel Tolkien immediately took up a commission as a second lieutenant on the front lines of the raging Great War. In time, though, he was sent back to England to recover from a case of trench fever and he joined the English Dictionary staff (writing entries in the w's) at Oxford University. Around this time, Tolkien's enthusiasm for the myths and languages of northern Europe caught fire through his membership at a literature club, and the groundwork for his stories about Middle-earth was laid.

Tolkien conceived of a Middle-earth fantasy world as the setting for his visionary tales, and its creation occupied him for 20 years. The details of the realm were derived from Celtic and Germanic sources whose common traditions were reworked to reflect Tolkien's belief in the importance and perfectibility of man. Though its most striking creatures are the elves and dwarves, goblins and dragons, and wizards and demons, the most important race in Middle-earth is men and, free to choose their own destinies, they run the gamut from goblin-like evil and depravity to elf-like purity and integrity.

Tolkien also composed stories for his own children and, about 1930, began one with the idle sentence "In a hole in the ground there lived a hobbit." As the story evolved, it became clear to Tolkien that this adventure of one Bilbo Baggins took place in the same Middle-earth, though at a much later time. In 1937 this story, *The Hobbit*, was published as a children's book to critical and popular acclaim.

Bolstered by his success, Tolkien immediately began work on his next book, *The Lord of the Rings*, a longer, intense, and more intricately themed adult version of *The Hobbit* and, after years of painstaking revision, it was published in 1954. The work secured him a standing as an unequaled writer of imaginative literature, and Tolkien spent the rest of his life polishing and refining his vision. Leaving the original stories relatively untouched, he embellished their context with genealogical tables, historical speculations, and theological explications, all designed to clarify the meaning of his creation.

At 81, Tolkien died of a chest infection and was buried at Wolvercote Cemetery in Wolvercote, England.

Wolvercote is a picturesque parish of Oxford that overlooks the Thames River. The cemetery is off of Five Mile Drive, and the Tolkien grave is fairly elaborate. The main headstone is flanked by two smaller headstones for Tolkien and his wife, Edith, and they are engraved with flower patterns based upon those found in a posthumous work, *The Silmarillion*.

LEO TOLSTOY
AUGUST 28, 1828 – NOVEMBER 20, 1910

THE RUSSIAN AUTHOR Leo Tolstoy was of a noble family dating back to the fourteenth century. His father, Count Nikolay, had a passion for gambling and, though he exhausted the family wealth, he was able to recover by marrying an heiress of the Volkonsky fortune that included 800 serfs and a 4,000-acre estate, Yasnaya Polyana, where Leo was born.

As man of the house in his twenties, Leo contracted heavy gambling debts himself, and he lost the estate's 42-room mansion to a man named Gorokhov, who dismantled the structure as payment. After losing the main house, the family moved into one of the mansion's remaining wings, while Leo and his brother meandered to the southern Caucasus Mountains, volunteering for service in the Crimean War. Drawing material from his self-lacerating diary entries, he began to write during the long lulls between fighting, and by 1857 had published the trilogy *Childhood*, *Boyhood*, and *Youth*.

Leo once said, "The one thing that is necessary, in life as in art, is to tell the truth." An entry in his wife's diary for October 1863 reads: "Story about 1812, he is very involved with it," and indeed, Tolstoy was intent upon telling his truth through the historically accurate masterpiece *War and Peace*. Tolstoy was convinced that philosophical principles could only be understood in their concrete expression in history, and in his vast canvas of five families against the background of Napoleon's invasion of Russia, Tolstoy espoused that all is predestined, that we cannot live unless we imagine that we have free will. In his attention to the social matrix and psychological truth of his characters, Tolstoy reached the apogee of world literature.

No sooner did Tolstoy complete one masterpiece than he started another, and in 1877 he finished *Anna Karenina*. In this work he juxtaposed the crises of family with the quest for love. Tolstoy considered *Anna Karenina* his magnum opus. He later renounced all his earlier works, confessing, "I wrote everything into *Anna Karenina*."

The idolization that Tolstoy enjoyed during the 1880s caused him to see himself as a moral prophet, and the ethical quest that tormented him drove him to abandon all else in order to seek meaning. As Tolstoy took up cobbling and obsessed over Chinese philosophies, his family relations became increasingly strained, especially as he played with the idea of giving all his wealth to charity. But in 1884 he compromised with his wife, Sonya, and assigned her the estate and all copyrights. Still, he continued to write and especially noteworthy is his powerful 1886 story, "The Death of Ivan Ilyich," which affirmed his belief in the primacy of individual conscience over group-collective morality.

At various times in his life, Tolstoy had tried to live as a sort of wandering ascetic, returning home only to leave again on extended pilgrimages. Finally, after a quarrel with Sonya, he set out on what would be his last pilgrimage, dying of pneumonia days later in the stationmaster's house at a remote railway junction named Astapovo.

At 82, he was returned to his Yasnaya Polyana estate near Tula, Russia, and buried on a leafy overlook above a ravine.

Years after his death Sonya remarked, "I lived with Leo for 48 years, but I never really learned what kind of man he was."

MARK TWAIN

NOVEMBER 30, 1835 – APRIL 21, 1910

SAMUEL LANGHORNE CLEMENS, better known as Mark Twain, so hated school that he quit at 12 to become an apprentice printer at *The Hannibal Journal*. Immersed in the paper, he was soon contributing frontier humor essays and at 18 left to work as a Philadelphia journalist.

A few years later he jumped from the news business when an opportunity to work steamboats on the Mississippi River arose, and by 23, he was a licensed river pilot. From that experience came the pen name he'd later employ, which related to the distance between the steamboat's bottom and the riverbed; when a depth of two fathoms was detected, the leadsman sounded an alert: "By the maaaark, twain!"

Steamboat traffic dried up with the commencement of the Civil War's river blockade, and Mark, whose sympathies in those days were with the South, hurried to Hannibal and enlisted with a company of rangers. But, after a few cheerless weeks, and with no one yet to fight, Mark deserted and, along with thousands of others avoiding the War, moved west. Landing in San Francisco, Mark returned to journalism for the duration of the war.

By 1866, he was in New York City working as a correspondent aboard the *Quaker City* steamer, which was departing for a voyage to Europe, Russia, and the Middle East. Before he left, he compiled his writings from his western days and arranged for

the publication of his first book, *The Celebrated Jumping Frog of Calaveras County and Other Sketches*. Mark returned from the eight-month trip to find that *Calaveras* had been a success, and the next year he published a book of his travel letters from the *Quaker City* voyage, *The Innocents Abroad*.

Between 1873 and 1889, Mark settled in Hartford for a period of concentrated writing. These were his most productive years and he completed seven novels, including the classics *The Adventures of Tom Sawyer*, *Life On the Mississippi*, and his masterpiece, *Adventures of Huckleberry Finn*. In these novels, in which he wove colloquial language through socially intimate storylines, Mark Twain captured the era's rhythms and soon stood among the greatest character writers in the literary world.

For most of his final decade, having outlived his wife and three children, Mark resided in New York City in the company of dignitaries, usually appearing in his trademark white linen suit. Though he continued to write for the remainder of his life, none of his subsequent works ever approached the popularity of his Tom Sawyer and Huck Finn tales.

Mark had been born with Halley's Comet clearly visible in the heavens, and he predicted he'd "go out with the comet." While it streaked through the skies almost 75 years later, Mark slipped into a coma and died of angina pectoris. He was buried at Woodlawn Cemetery in Elmira, New York.

GRAVE DIRECTIONS: Enter the cemetery at 1200 Walnut Street and turn at the second right. Then turn at the second left and stop. The Twain plot is on the right.

VINCENT VAN GOGH
MARCH 30, 1853 – JULY 29, 1890

THOUGH PAINTER VINCENT van Gogh's work became an important bridge for modern painting between the nineteenth and twentieth centuries, he was almost wholly unknown during his brief lifetime and, of his more than 1,500 paintings and drawings, he sold just one of them.

The son of a Protestant minister, Vincent alternately worked at his uncle's art dealership, clerked at a bookshop, studied theology at the University of Amsterdam, and served as a lay missionary until he was 27. Then, in 1880, Vincent attended a Brussels school and chose art as a vocation, which he considered to be his spiritual calling.

Interested in the poor and dispossessed, Vincent concentrated on depicting miners and peasants in his so-called Dutch period, between 1880 and 1886. But, except for one picture, *The Potato Eaters*, his works from that period display few hints of the talent that was growing within.

By 1886 Vincent was drawn to the bohemian life and artistic activity of Paris and went to live there with his brother, Theo, who directed a small gallery in the city. Through contacts provided by Theo, he met the leaders of impressionism—Monet, Pissarro, and Gauguin. Under their influence, Vincent was persuaded to adopt more brilliant hues and change his subject matter to more typical impressionist themes such as the cafés and cityscapes reflected in works like *Restaurant de la Sirene at Asnieres.*

Wearying of Paris after just two years, Vincent left for Arles in the South of France, where he worked feverishly capturing the region's rustic tempo. With colors applied in simplified yet highly saturated masses, his images became more virile and incisive and, among others, the time yielded his masterpieces *Still Life with Sunflowers* and *Night Café.*

Recognizing van Gogh's genius, Gauguin moved to Arles so as to work more closely with him, but by this time Vincent had begun to experience maddening blackouts and seizures, and the friends often fell into violent disagreements. Finally, in one particularly celebrated irrational fit, Vincent mutilated the lower portion of his left ear with a razor and presented the severed lobe to a woman at a local brothel. Apparently having had his fill of the "genius," Gauguin split for Paris and the two never met again.

By May 1889, some of the citizens of Arles had become alarmed by Vincent's increasingly bizarre behavior and, when it was suggested that perhaps he should be confined, Vincent agreed and relinquished his freedom. At the St. Remy asylum, Vincent soon resumed painting at his feverish pace and in this period was drawn to natural objects under stress, such as whirling suns and twisted cypress trees. His colors lost their intensity, his lines became restless, and he applied the paint more thickly and violently, as in one of his best-known works, *Starry Night,* an obsessively beautiful exercise in circularity.

A year after being admitted to St. Remy, Vincent left to live near Theo again, this time in Auvers. Here he produced his last painting, *Wheat Field with Crows,* a disturbing struggle of savage brush strokes supercharged with crows, a universal symbol of death. A few days after its completion, Vincent set out his easel and painting materials in a wheat field and shot himself in the chest. The bullet did not kill him, however, and he staggered back to his room and collapsed in bed. Two days later, Vincent died in Theo's arms.

Vincent and Theo were very close, even for brothers, and corresponded constantly through letters. These letters form a uniquely human biographical record, and the 700 of them authored by Vincent provide a vivid historical account of his hopes and disappointments as his physical and mental states fluctuated. Six months after Vincent's death at 37, Theo, the grief-stricken brother, died at 33.

Now, you may well be wondering where did the brothers then Gogh? Theo was buried in Utrecht in the Netherlands, but, almost 25 years later, his wife had him reinterred alongside Vincent. They now both rest at the cemetery of Auvers-sur-Oise, France, a sleepy little town just north of Paris.

ANDY WARHOL

AUGUST 6, 1928 – FEBRUARY 22, 1987

THE CREATOR OF so-called Pop Art, Andy Warhol mass-produced paintings and prints of movie stars or even ordinary consumer goods, which, coupled with his keen talent for mischief and publicity, earned him regard as one of the most influential artists of his era.

During the 1950s, Andy worked in New York as a commercial artist but by the following decade he had hung up his brush and turned exclusively to the silk-screening of ready-made images, a medium that he pioneered. Such depersonalized depictions became the Warhol trademark but merely producing a portrait of cans of Campbell's soup wasn't his only radicalism; he also advanced a means of producing the images en masse, resulting in a consumer art that mimicked consumer culture.

Although himself shy and quiet, Andy attracted dozens of disciples who were anything but introverted, and their energy combined with his genius to produce a number of notorious events throughout his career. His Manhattan studio, the Factory, became a chic hangout for like-minded artists, musicians, fashion mavens, and movie stars, as well as the usual hangers-on and groupies who flocked to the new jet-set scene. Andy also produced underground films, some of which attempted to redefine our ideas of boredom and repetition; one showed 33 minutes of someone having his hair cut and another featured a follower, Edie Sedgwick, talking about herself through out-of-focus frames. Later, a rejected disciple shot Andy, who was momentarily declared dead, but Andy the survivor recuperated and thrived for two more decades.

Andy died of complications after a gallbladder operation and at 58 was buried at St. John the Baptist Byzantine Catholic Cemetery in Bethel Park, Pennsylvania.

GRAVE DIRECTIONS: At 1050 Connor Road, behind the office, up the hill, and six rows from the chain-link fence is Andy's grave. (Andy's surname was Warhola, but after a magazine misspelled it in 1949 he opted to make the change permanent, though his gravestone reverts to the original.)

E.B. WHITE
JULY 11, 1899 – OCTOBER 1, 1985

KNOWN MORE COMMONLY by his initials than by his given first name, literary stylist Elwyn Brooks White graduated from Cornell University in 1921 and soon joined the staff of the newly established *New Yorker* magazine. In a crisp and graceful style, E.B. churned out hundreds of essays advocating respect for nature and a simple life, detailing the complexities and failures of technological society, questioning the merits of organized religion, and celebrating internationalism. He married the magazine's literary editor, Kathryn Sergeant Angell, and continued to contribute to the publication for the remainder of his life.

With *Is Sex Necessary?* in 1929 E.B. first gained wide recognition, but it was his children's books that brought him the most accolades; in 1945 his orphaned mouse adopted as a child became the charming yet independent *Stuart Little*; a few years later came *Charlotte's Web* and its cast of barnyard friendships, and in 1970 a mute swan found a voice in *The Trumpet of the Swan*.

In 1939 E.B. moved to a farm in Maine and continued writing without the responsibilities of a regular job. He never stopped loving New York, calling it "a riddle in steel and stone," but he also foresaw the vulnerability of the city when he wrote in 1949's *Here is New York*, "A single flight of planes no bigger than a wedge of geese can quickly end this island fantasy, burn the towers, crumble the bridges, turn the underground passages into lethal chambers, cremate millions. Of all targets New York has a certain clear priority in the mind of whatever perverted dreamer might loose the lightning."

In 1978 E.B. was awarded a special Pulitzer citation for his body of work and he died from complications of Alzheimer's disease a few years later. At 86, he was buried at the Brooklin Cemetery in Brooklin, Maine.

GRAVE DIRECTIONS: Enter the cemetery on Route 175 next to the fire department and all the way in the back near the maintenance sheds are E.B. and Kathryn's twin gray tombstones.

WALT WHITMAN

MAY 31, 1819 – MARCH 26, 1892

BORN TO AN undistinguished Long Island family, Walt Whitman had almost no formal education but, by self-teaching through immersion in Shakespeare and Dante, he became a schoolteacher at 17. By his early twenties Walt moved into journalism and, though he published some of his writings, by his thirties he had still not displayed the slightest hint of any unique talent or vision.

It's difficult, then, to account for Walt's sudden transformation from hack writer into revolutionary poet. But, somehow, at 36, Walt distinguished himself when he self-published a slim volume of poetry, *Leaves of Grass*, in 1855. The 12 poems in his first edition were plain and simple celebrations of the explosive joy of living, and they seemed to have come from nowhere. Their style was connected to nothing else being written at that time or any other; Walt had turned his back on literary models of the past and virtually ignored meter and rhyme. Stressing the rhythms of native American speech, Walt delighted in colloquial and slang expressions. His ideas were as sexually frank as diary entries.

Walt received little attention and even less money for his groundbreaking *Leaves of Grass*. But by the time he added 20 more poems for its second issue, and an additional 146 that appeared in his "new Bible" third printing, he had created controversy for readers, whose attentions had by then turned to the Civil War's battlefields. Walt was enormously impacted by the war, and he published his reminiscences in a publication he called *Drum-Taps*. With aesthetic simplicity, these poems captured the conflict's horror and anguish, and they too were later folded into *Leaves of Grass*, which by the end of Walt's life had been issued in nine different editions.

By his last years, Walt received the homage due an exceptional literary talent as *Leaves of Grass* had been widely translated and he gained reputation worldwide. His emphasis on native idiom, his frank approach to muses hitherto thought unsuitable to poetry, and his divergence from approved structural precepts have all contributed to his reputation as having had a profound influence on modern poetry.

I believe a leaf of grass is no less than the journeywork of the stars,
And the pismire is equally perfect, and a grain of sand, and the
egg of a wren.

After suffering a series of strokes, Walt died of complications at 72 and was buried at Harleigh Cemetery in Collingswood, New Jersey.

GRAVE DIRECTIONS: Enter the cemetery at the second gate on 1640 Haddon Avenue, turn left in front of the office, then take the next right. After a short distance you'll see Walt's tomb on the left, before the pond.

LAURA INGALLS WILDER
FEBRUARY 7, 1867 – FEBRUARY 10, 1957

ENTICED BY THE free land offered to homesteaders during the 1870s, the family of Laura Ingalls Wilder moved west from Wisconsin and settled in what is now South Dakota. From those earliest childhood days, Laura persevered through a simple but arduous life on the American frontier. She was alternately a teacher and a farmhand and occasionally submitted small pieces to newspapers through those difficult days. By her forties, Laura secured a position at the *Missouri Ruralist* newspaper, eventually becoming its editor.

At 60 years old, Laura began to write her memoirs in a manuscript entitled *Pioneer Girl.* The concept of this book, which was essentially the entire series in one, led to the start of the *Little House* string of books, which featured stories drawn from her family's experiences as pioneers in the mid-1800s. Written with a folksy common sense, the books celebrated a peculiarly American spirit and good humor, and the eight-part series became children's classics. Later, the books enjoyed a revival as the basis for the *Little House on the Prairie* television series.

As Laura's family moved frequently, a number of enterprising wind-swept towns have managed to turn her assorted homesteads into a bit of a cottage industry. There are no less than six different Wilder museums and historic sites scattered among the Midwest and Great Plains.

Laura died in her sleep at 90, and was buried at Mansfield Cemetery in Mansfield, Missouri.

GRAVE DIRECTIONS: At the northern terminus of Lincoln Street, enter the cemetery at the second gate and stop after 100 feet. About 30 feet away, on the right, you'll see the Wilder plot.

TENNESSEE WILLIAMS
MARCH 26, 1911 – FEBRUARY 25, 1983

BY SHOWCASING THE Old South's gentility by way of tormented and unforgettable stage characters, Thomas "Tennessee" Williams created a series of powerful portraits of the human condition, earning respect as one of the greatest playwrights in the history of American drama. His emphasis on the irrational and desperate nature of individuals in many ways mirrored his personal experience and, indeed, Tennessee confessed, "If I did not write, I'd go mad."

Though he hailed from a prestigious Tennessee family that boasted the state's first governor and senator, his immediate family was a bit less distinguished; Tennessee's distant and abusive father traveled for business, his anomalous mother was never quite accepted by the genteel society she pursued, and his sister spent most of her life in mental institutions. After attending three different universities and working briefly alongside his father at a shoe company (an experience Tennessee called "a living death"), he moved to New Orleans in 1938.

In the Big Easy, he seemed to reinvent himself, starting with his name, which he legally changed to Tennessee. Having struggled with his sexuality all through his youth, Tennessee embraced the city's liberal attitude and, with a new name, a new home, and his developing talent, fully entered gay life. After struggling for a few years, Tennessee began to write about what he knew and, after mining his past for inspiration, the pristine tenderness of *The Glass Menagerie* propelled it into a Broadway hit, making 1945 a turning point for Tennessee. The next 15 years were his most productive: *A Rose Tattoo*, *Baby Doll*, and *Night of the Iguana* were well received by critics and popular with audiences. But it was two other works in that period, both Pulitzer Prize–winners, that sealed Tennessee's reputation as a supreme dramatist: *A Streetcar Named Desire* traced the decline of a sensitive woman at the hands of her brother-in-law; while *Cat on a Hot Tin Roof* tracked the moral decay of a Southern family, its Big Daddy character modeled after Tennessee's own father.

But the '60s and '70s were less kind and, after his longtime companion and steadying influence, Frank Merlo, died in 1961, Tennessee began a long downward spiral. Suffering from depression, he lived in fear that he would go insane like his sister. He became dependent on drugs, especially alcohol, and though he owned homes in New Orleans and Key West, he often lived as a sort of wealthy gypsy, moving frequently among hotels. Tennessee was terribly insecure, and as the quality of his work declined as a result of his personal difficulties, he got caught in a desperate and vicious circle of self-pity and violent jealousy of younger playwrights.

A monumental hypochondriac, Tennessee was obsessed with sickness and death. He worried that his heart would inexplicably stop beating and, in desperation, took pills that he didn't need. His death at 71 came in a way he probably never expected; after a night of heavy drinking, Tennessee choked to death on a bottle cap at the luxurious midtown Hotel Elysée in New York City.

Tennessee's will stipulated that he wished to be "buried in St. Louis," which was particularly curious since he had no connection whatsoever to that city. However, there is a historic cemetery in New Orleans, named St. Louis Cemetery, and its ornate marble tombs hold the remains of the French Quarter's high society movers and shakers from days long past. Unfortunately, executors of Tennessee's estate were unaware that this was the St. Louis where he wished to be buried so they did the next best thing: They buried him in St. Louis, Missouri, at Calvary Cemetery.

GRAVE DIRECTIONS: Located at 5279 West Florrisant Avenue, the grounds of Calvary are very large and the roads within are numerous and mazelike, so you should stop at the office and get a map. Tennessee is buried in Section 15 and, though Section 15 comprises three smaller sections, his plot is easy to find in the northernmost area. It is the pink-tinted stone near the road.

FRANK LLOYD WRIGHT

JUNE 8, 1867 – APRIL 9, 1959

FRANK LLOYD WRIGHT is considered one of the great figures in twentieth-century architecture. After just a few years of apprenticeship, he started his own Chicago firm in 1893, and from there espoused his philosophy of "organic architecture" whose central principle—"form and function are one"—demands that a structure be developed out of its natural surroundings.

Frank's Prairie House residential concepts were distinguished by low-pitched rooflines, deep overhangs, and uninterrupted walls of windows merging the horizontal home into the landscape. The interior space was maximized by eliminating attics, rooms flowed into one another with half-walls, and centralized stone fireplaces, translucent ceilings, and garden areas provided environmental oneness. His 1937 Kaufmann House (now known as Fallingwater and open to the public in Pennsylvania) is a later example of Frank's residential style.

But he was also a bold revolutionary in industrial design and departed from the lifeless arrangements favored by his contemporaries. He introduced numerous innovations, such as steel-reinforced concrete, all-glass revolving doors, indirect lighting, air conditioning, and even metal furniture. One of Frank's more remarkable engineering developments was an earthquake-proof design that featured a cantilever construction atop a floating foundation. With a shape reminiscent of a snail's shell, New York City's Guggenheim Museum is an example of a Wright work that mimics a design found in nature.

In Wisconsin, Frank converted his own Taliesin home into a school and workshop for apprentice visionaries, but in 1914, tragedy struck. One night while Frank was away on business, an employee of the school went berserk and burned Taliesin to the ground. Worse, before setting the complex ablaze, he nailed the exterior doors shut except for the lower half of a Dutch door. By the time the inferno was extinguished, seven people were dead, five of whom had been bludgeoned with an ax by the deranged employee as they tried to escape through the bottom of the Dutch door.

Frank rebuilt Taliesin and later remarried. In 1938, he built Taliesin West, a winter home and school situated atop a central Arizona mesa. The 37,000-square-foot country estate includes living quarters, offices, and farm buildings that are subtly distinguished from their environment. The 600-acre complex still functions as the winter campus for the Frank Lloyd Wright School of Architecture.

At 91, Frank died at Taliesin West after complications arose following an operation for an intestinal obstruction. Per his instructions, he was buried at the original Taliesin in Spring Green, Wisconsin, alongside the confessed love of his life, his mistress Mamah, who had been killed on that terrible night in 1914. However, it seems that Frank's second wife, Olgivanna, had her own idea about how Frank should spend eternity. Upon Olgivanna's death in 1985, her will stipulated that Frank be exhumed and cremated, his cremains mixed with her own, and the combined remains kept in an urn at Taliesin West.

Olgivanna's wishes were fulfilled and the urn holding their ashes is kept in Scottsdale. At the moment the urn is not available for public viewing, and is instead tucked safely away "in storage."

HEROES OF
ROCK &
BLUES MUSIC

THE ALLMAN BROTHERS

DUANE ALLMAN
NOVEMBER 20, 1946 – OCTOBER 29, 1971

GREGG ALLMAN
DECEMBER 8, 1947 – MAY 27, 2017

AFTER DUANE AND Gregg Allman's father was shot to death in 1949 by a drinking acquaintance in Virginia, their mother uprooted her boys to a Tennessee military school before eventually moving with them to Daytona Beach. With money saved from a paper route, 14-year-old Gregg bought a guitar from Sears and Roebuck, which his dropout brother, Duane, shortly appropriated. Duane's natural ability with the instrument was soon apparent and, to Gregg's annoyance, Duane uncompromisingly played his kid brother's guitar while its owner slogged his way through high school.

Eventually they both owned guitars and after stints with a variety of local bands, their Allman Joys band hit the road and developed their licks at seven-night-a-week blues bars. Later they settled in as the Allman Brothers Band, and in 1969 their self-titled debut album introduced a musical template of extended improvisational sound that jam bands adhere to even today. It took them just a couple years to perfect that fusion of earthy American blues with British rock, and their flair was confirmed in the follow-up albums *Idlewild South* and *Eat a Peach*. Nearly 50 years on, more than a dozen of their signature songs still hold up, including "Blue Sky," "Melissa," and "Midnight Rider."

But their hallmark was live shows and, weaving sophisticated melodic formations in an undercurrent of aggression and invention and sweat, the band earned every inch of their adulation. Having rightfully assumed the lion's share of guitar duty, Duane's playing encompassed a distillation of range from classic wailings to eloquent phrasing and riffs. At stage left, Gregg positioned himself behind a percussive Hammond B-3 organ and provided a chuffing counterpoint to his bandmates' heated musical interplay, his articulate yet down-home voice by turns anguished, brooding, and brawly.

But half of the brothers' magic spilled out at dusk on a Friday afternoon, at the intersection of Hillcrest Avenue and Bartlett Street in Macon, Georgia, when Duane laid his motorcycle into a parked vehicle. At the hospital, a doctor told Duane's girlfriend, "We brought him back up for a minute or two, but he's gone." At the funeral, with his guitar leaning on the casket, Duane's bandmates played "The Sky Is Crying" and "Stormy Monday" for their fallen brother.

Just about a year later and only a few blocks from where Duane lost his life, the band's bass player, 24-year-old Berry Oakley, was killed when he drove his motorcycle into the side of a bus.

Nonetheless, more or less, for the next 40 years the band played on. But the union wasn't always pretty—two extended breakups yielded an eight-year hiatus—and when matters came to a head they generally had to do with Gregg, who used a wide range of drugs, though at first the drugs may have been useful. About psilocybin, a favored mushroom derivative, Gregg wrote, "There's no question that taking psilocybin helped create so many spontaneous pieces of music."

Gregg also enjoyed an intermittent career as a solo artist, his recordings under his own name typically more subdued and his tone that of a soulful singer-songwriter. Sobering up in time to enjoy the music, Gregg re-formed the group in 1989, marking a renewal of band prosperity. Releasing two acclaimed albums in quick succession, the band was reborn as a live act too, and annual tours woke a new generation to their intricate and spontaneous synthesis. Their last-ever show was a four-hour-long jam played out at the Beacon Theatre in Manhattan in 2014, a venue they'd played 238 (!) times previous.

Three years later, the band's drummer, Butch Trucks, killed himself with a pistol shot to the head while arguing with his wife. "I've lost another brother, and it hurts beyond words," Gregg said. With the Allman Brothers Band from its very beginning, Butch had liked to recount how his Baptist parents only allowed him to be in a band because he'd promised to never play anywhere liquor was served. Butch was cremated at 69.

After the last Beacon show, Gregg decided it might be a good time to grow closer to his children—married seven times (including a turbulent three-year effort with Cher), he had five kids, each with a different mother—and retreated to his riverside ranch in Georgia, ostensibly to concentrate on family. But not for long, it turned out, as solo tours and projects soon beckoned the consummate music man.

In 2010 Gregg underwent a successful liver transplant after contracting hepatitis C, supposedly from a dirty tattoo needle, and six years later he was diagnosed with liver cancer anew, though he kept the news private. At 69, he died at home and was buried near Duane and Berry in Macon's historic Rose Hill Cemetery.

GRAVE DIRECTIONS: Enter the cemetery at 1071 Riverside Drive and proceed to the end of the cement drive. Turn right, parallel to the train tracks, then turn right at the next paved drive and go up the hill. Halfway up the hill, off to the left, the twin polished tombs of Duane and Berry are surrounded by a black iron fence, while Gregg is opposite them alongside the cement walkway.

THE BAND

BEGINNING AROUND 1960, four Toronto-area musicians plus one more from America's Deep South slowly came together as the Hawks to supply the backing sound for American rockabilly singer Ronnie Hawkins. Their music wove the old sounds of country blues with the new spirit of rock and roll, and the result was a distinctly new, listenable, and catchy style. Their talents quickly catapulted them beyond the roadhouse circuit, and in 1965 they backed Bob Dylan on his infamous, boo-filled tour that marked the former folkie's "going electric."

After the tour they took to calling themselves The Band and had holed up near Woodstock, New York, in a crash pad they affectionately dubbed Big Pink. In the basement of Big Pink, guitarist and chief-songwriter Robbie Robertson, bassist Rick Danko, pianist Richard Manuel, organist Garth Hudson, and drummer Levon Helm honed their unique lyrical and pastoral style, mentored by Dylan, who dropped by after crashing his motorcycle. Their harmony-filled debut album, *Music From Big Pink*, was released in 1968 and became the fulcrum for country rock.

A succession of albums and tours followed and The Band became a firm fixture in the rock aristocracy. But less than a decade later they had had enough and officially called it quits with a celebratory final concert at San Francisco's Winterland Ballroom on Thanksgiving Day 1976. The concert featured an unprecedented all-star lineup including the likes of Muddy Waters, Neil Diamond, Eric Clapton, and Van Morrison, and was documented by Martin Scorsese in his film *The Last Waltz*. Many consider it the finest concert film of all time.

RICHARD MANUEL
APRIL 3, 1943 – MARCH 4, 1986

THE RICH BARITONE and lonesome falsetto of pianist Richard Manuel helped the Band's rise to success, but by the time the bandmates regrouped in 1983, an unexplained weariness and despondency had settled over Richard. After a sold-out reunion show in Winter Park, Florida, Richard hanged himself in a motel bathroom while his wife lay sleeping.

At 42, Richard was buried at Avondale Cemetery in Stratford, Ontario, Canada.

GRAVE DIRECTIONS: Enter the cemetery at 4 Avondale Avenue, turn right, and proceed down this drive to where it bends hard to the left. After the hard left, count three more roadways on your left, then stop. On your left is Range 23A, and Richard is buried in this lawn at plot number 193.

RICK DANKO
DECEMBER 9, 1942 – DECEMBER 10, 1999

AFTER *THE LAST Waltz*, bassist and part-time lead singer Rick Danko continued his musical pursuits and was a mainstay of the tour circuit for the remainder of his life. His talent shone in his 1978 debut solo album, *Rick Danko*, and in the late 1980s he toured as part of Ringo Starr's All-Starr Band. In 1993 Rick spearheaded the release of a long-awaited new album by The Band, the acclaimed *Jericho*, and the next year they were all inducted into the Rock & Roll Hall of Fame.

At 57, Rick died in his sleep of a heart attack and was buried at Woodstock Cemetery in Woodstock, New York.

GRAVE DIRECTIONS: At 33 Rock City Road, drive all the way to the cemetery's rear and, along the back road, you'll find a reddish, double heart-shaped stone for the Cooks. Rick lies two rows behind the Cooks.

LEVON HELM
MAY 26, 1940 – APRIL 19, 2012

IN THE BAND, lead vocals changed from song to song, sometimes even within songs, and harmonies were elaborately communal. But when lyrics turned mystical or to tales of the American South such as in "The Weight" and "The Night They Drove Old Dixie Down," the group turned to the weathered voice of their drummer Levon Helm, who managed to sound desperate, ornery, and amused all at the same time.

Growing up on a cotton farm outside of Turkey Scratch, Arkansas, Levon's father often took the family to see traveling music shows at tents in Memphis just across the river where, unbeknownst to him, Levon literally witnessed the birth of rock 'n' roll. Smitten by musicians of every stripe, nine-year-old Levon played guitar in a rock duet with his sister called the Jungle Bush Beaters and learned a variety of other instruments as a teen before joining Ronnie Hawkins' rockabilly band after high school. He hoped music would be a way out of Arkansas, and it was. "I was praying that it was," Levon said. "Because I was a terrible cotton farmer and didn't have the heart for it. Sometimes I would look up and see a plane going across and wonder if it was going to New York or something."

When the Hawks left Hawkins and became The Band, Levon more or less assumed the role as the group's linchpin, though he never really called attention to himself. After *The Last Waltz,* he continued working at every opportunity, performing with a partly reunited Band, with his own band Levon Helm and the RCO All-Stars, with Ringo Starr's All-Starr Band, and even appearing in movies as an actor, most notably playing Loretta Lynn's father in *Coal Miner's Daughter.*

But in the late 1990s a pair of personal crises threatened to end his career and his life: A fire destroyed his home and studio, and then he was diagnosed with throat cancer, which required dozens of radiation treatments, leaving him hardly able to speak, let alone sing. The cost of these calamities nearly drove him to bankruptcy, so to help pay the bills he reinvented himself as a sort of roots-music patriarch, hosting in his barn eclectic, down-home concerts called Midnight Rambles.

Though the Rambles had been intended as a one-off "rent party," the interest from fans, and every musician from Elvis Costello to Kris Kristofferson who dropped in to play with him, was so widespread that the late-night jam sessions became an almost-weekly event leading to tours and Grammy-winning albums. "If I had my way about it, we'd probably do it every night," Levon said. "I never get tired of it." The hoedowns took precedence over nearly anything else in his life and in 2008 he even skipped the presentation of a Grammy Lifetime Achievement Award with The Band to host a Midnight Ramble instead.

In 2012 the cancer came back and Levon lost that battle at 71. Like his buddy Rick, Levon is buried at Woodstock Cemetery.

GRAVE DIRECTIONS: Enter the cemetery and drive to the top of the hill. On the right, notice the section of chain-link fence that has wooden boards attached to it, and that's where you'll find Levon.

THE BEACH BOYS

DENNIS WILSON
DECEMBER 4, 1944 – DECEMBER 28, 1983

CARL WILSON
DECEMBER 21, 1946 – FEBRUARY 6, 1998

IN 1961 BRIAN Wilson, with brothers Carl and Dennis, cousin Mike Love, and friend Alan Jardine, formed the Beach Boys. Though they only knew how to play three songs at their first concert, endless airplay of their feel-good pop tunes—"Surfin' USA," "Good Vibrations," and "Fun, Fun, Fun," among dozens of others—later lifted the Beach Boys, and each band member individually, to esteem as the epitome of California's carefree spirit.

The Beach Boys also elevated surfing itself, and the arcane pastime soon became a preoccupation among teenagers who lived far from any ocean. Their thickly layered wall of sound was best when it stayed within the bounds of that "surfing sound," but Brian, the group's visionary, contrived a new direction for his musical vision, and in 1966 the complex composition of harmonies and instruments of *Pet Sounds* raised the bar for musical artistry and

The Heart and Voice of an Angel

♥ CARL DEAN WILSON ♥

DEC. 21, 1946 - FEB. 6, 1998

The World is a Far Lesser Place Without You

inspired the Beatles to weave their own masterpiece the following year with *Sgt. Pepper's Lonely Hearts Club Band.*

The Beach Boys were later eclipsed by groups with harder sounds and rougher images and, though they pressed on over the next decades in various incarnations, they ceased to be a consistent rock music force after the 1960s.

Dennis was the only surfer of the bunch. Always at the beach instead of practicing, his mother had to later advocate for his inclusion in the band, which led to Dennis being the drummer by default. Though regarded as the least talented of the brothers, Dennis was a musician in his own right; he contributed a few songs to the Beach Boys' albums and in 1977 had an acclaimed solo release, *Pacific Ocean Blue.*

But with substance abuse slowing his creative momentum, by 1983 Dennis was nearly broke, a victim of excess. A few days after Christmas, while friends watched from the dock, he repeatedly dove into the chilly waters of the empty slip that once held his boat, the *Harmony,* in Marina del Ray, California. Each time Dennis emerged from the depths, he proudly displayed mud-clad treasures that had been tossed or dropped from his boat in the years before: drinking tumblers, a framed photo of him and his wife Karen. Back to the bottom he went again and again, until at last he failed to resurface. After a frenzied search, the 39-year old Dennis was found an hour later, drowned in the depths where he'd spent his last moments happily searching for his own sunken treasures.

Dennis' widow insisted that a burial at sea had been his desire but, as such a burial is reserved for deceased naval personnel, a special dispensation permit had to be requested from the U.S. government. The permit was granted and Dennis was so interred.

After Brian drifted into seclusion from the Beach Boys and Dennis died, brother Carl became the last active Wilson in the band.

Carl had always been overshadowed by his brothers' attention-grabbing lifestyles, and his lead guitar, which drove the band's concert sound, was consistently underrated. But with the departures of Brian and Dennis, Carl earned his deserved prestige. With his guitar, his melodic anchoring vocals, and his diplomatic presence, he led the band through an endless parade of sun-and-surf Beach Boy nostalgia tours during the '80s and '90s.

In February 1998 Carl died of lung cancer at age 51, and was buried at Westwood Memorial Park in Los Angeles, California.

GRAVE DIRECTIONS: Behind the office complex at 10850 Wilshire Boulevard, enter the cemetery, turn left at the office and, after about 50 feet, you'll find Carl's marker five rows into the grass on the left.

THE BEATLES

WHEN THE BEATLES made their U.S. debut on the *Ed Sullivan Show* in February 1964, playing their infectious new form of rock and roll, an entire generation realized that nothing would ever be the same again. And it wasn't. Over the next six years the Beatles—John and Paul, George and Ringo—dominated the culture and translated their style and music into new cultural trends in self-expression, appearance, attitude, and, of course, music. No group before or since has had a lasting effect on pop music and culture even approaching that of the Beatles.

John Lennon and, to a slightly lesser degree, Paul McCartney were generally regarded as the group's backbone. Under their direction the Beatles tirelessly evolved and ignited revolutions at every new creative pinnacle. Each of their key albums—*Rubber Soul, Revolver, Sgt. Pepper's Lonely Hearts Club Band, Magical Mystery Tour, The White Album, Abbey Road*—was an increasingly honed masterpiece and introduced new areas of musical exploration and penetrating lyrical introspection. Public appearances by the band elicited a hysterical response that came to be known as Beatlemania. The hysteria became so tiring to the band members, and created such a barrier to any semblance of a "normal" performance, that the Beatles concert of August 1966 in San Francisco became their last, just 2½ years after the *Ed Sullivan* debut.

The band started to come apart after their manager, Brian Epstein, died in April 1967. They suffered a protracted, slow-motion breakup, and had totally disbanded by the autumn of 1970. John,

Paul, George, and Ringo each pursued his own solo career with varying degrees of success, though none ever reached the popular heights enjoyed by the group as a whole.

STUART SUTCLIFFE
JUNE 23, 1940 – APRIL 10, 1962

STUART SUTCLIFFE WAS a friend and fellow art student of John Lennon at the Liverpool Art College when John suggested that Stu buy a bass guitar and join his band—never mind that he couldn't play. Stu bought a bass and became a sort of pseudo-band member. (George, Paul, and drummer Pete Best were already in the band and Stu's services weren't absolutely essential.) Nonetheless, Stu played with them for about a year at a number of Liverpool engagements, during a brief May 1960 tour of Scotland, and at some nightclub gigs in Germany.

Stu is generally credited for naming the band; it was he who suggested "Beetles" as a play on Buddy Holly's Crickets. Stu's girlfriend Astrid Kirchherr is generally credited for the Beatles "mop-top" hairstyles; she first cut Stu's and then George's hair in the distinctive style, and the other band members soon adopted it.

When the band went back to Liverpool after an extended 1961 booking at a nightspot in Hamburg, Stu stayed in Germany with Astrid, effectively bowing out of the Beatles. The day before the Beatles were to arrive back in Hamburg for a round of shows, Stu died of a brain hemorrhage at 21. He was buried at Huyton Parish Church Cemetery on Stanley Road in Liverpool, England.

BRIAN EPSTEIN
SEPTEMBER 19, 1934 – AUGUST 27, 1967

IN THE FALL of 1961, while running his parents' North End Road Music Store on Whitechapel Street in Liverpool, Brian Epstein began getting an inordinate number of requests for records by the Beatles, a local band with just one single that had been released in Germany. His curiosity was piqued. Epstein went to see the band at a basement hall called the Cavern Club, and a month later Brian offered to manage them. Intrigued by Brian's straightforwardness, John agreed on the spot and on January 24, 1962, the Beatles and Brian signed a contract.

Brian's first order of business was to get the band a recording contract, and he used whatever clout he could muster from his family's small chain of record stores to get meetings with British record companies. Brian and the band had plenty of rejections, but he finally secured them an agreement; in June 1962, two months after Stu Sutcliffe's death, George Martin signed them to Parlophone, a division of EMI. Martin later admitted that though he felt the Beatles had promise, he signed them in large part because of Brian's boundless enthusiasm.

John, Paul, and George next asked Brian to sack their drummer, Pete, and replace him with one Richard Starkey (who went by the name "Ringo Starr"). Then Brian set to smartening up the Beatles' stage appearance. He put them in matching mohair suits and encouraged a rather theatrical synchronized bow at the conclusion of each song.

The Beatles were now complete, and during their almost six years with Brian as manager, they enjoyed the greatest success that any popular artists had ever achieved, and, it seemed, without a single reversal of fortune. Upon his death, however, they lost the one person who had been capable of resolving their differences and, after a tangle of artistic conflicts and personal jealousies, the Beatles broke up three years later.

Brian had suffered bouts of depression and he often took pills to help him sleep. On August 27, 1967, from what was ruled an accidental overdose of the sleeping pill Carbitol, he died at 32 and was buried at Kirkdale Jewish Cemetery on Long Lane in Liverpool, England.

JOHN LENNON

OCTOBER 9, 1940 – DECEMBER 8, 1980

THROUGH PERSONNEL AND name changes during the 1950s and early '60s, John Lennon's band evolved from the Quarrymen, to Johnny and the Moondogs, to the Silver Beatles, before arriving at their final namesake, the Beatles. With co-helmsman Paul McCartney, John, the most blunt but thoughtful Beatle, steered the band that became a touchstone for their generation.

A year before the Beatles broke up, John married Yoko Ono and they began collaborating both creatively and as activists. He became an outspoken advocate of peace, even staging a flamboyant "Bed-In for Peace" protest with Yoko. In 1971, John again topped the music charts with his solo album *Imagine*, and through the decade he recorded with Yoko *Shaved Fish* and his final record, *Double Fantasy*.

Leaving their apartment in New York City's Dakota building on a Sunday afternoon, John and Yoko were approached by several autograph seekers. John obliged and among the autographs he signed was one on the cover of a *Double Fantasy* album for a Mark David Chapman.

The Lennons returned to the Dakota at about 10:50 p.m. When they exited their limousine, Chapman, who'd been waiting in the shadows, called out, "Mr. Lennon." He then fired four pistol shots, all striking John, who staggered to the concierge room, said, "I'm shot," and fell down. Police arrived within two minutes to a surreal scene. While John lay bleeding to death and a hysterical Yoko and passersby helplessly comforted him, Chapman stood calmly where he had fired the shots, the gun on the ground at his feet. John was put in a police car, and as they raced to Roosevelt Hospital an officer asked, "Are you John Lennon?" The voice of a generation's final word was breathed in a soft moan: "Yeah."

At 40 years old, John was dead on arrival, and the medical examiner later announced that no one could have lived more than a few minutes with such injuries. As word of his death spread, horrified fans grappled with the seeming impossibility that their generation's idol was forever gone in the quick flash of a gun. Later that evening, a statement was issued on Yoko's behalf: "John loved and prayed for the human race. Please do the same for him."

After John's death, people from around the globe spontaneously gathered at the Dakota in a sort of communion and, naturally, they spilled into the lawns of Central Park across the street. This became *the* place to eternalize the singer and, in a 1985 ceremony, a particular two-acre patch was dedicated to his memory as "Strawberry Fields." Located at the intersection of 72nd Street and the west side of Central Park, the triangularly shaped garden's focal point is a beautiful circular mosaic of inlaid stones from countries the world over. The mosaic's center spells a simple plea: IMAGINE.

At every hour of every day, fans of John's music and message meander about Strawberry Fields and, on the anniversaries of his birth and death, impromptu services pay homage.

John was cremated and his ashes given to Yoko Ono, who sprinkled some of them in John's hometown of Liverpool, England, and some at Strawberry Fields.

GEORGE HARRISON
FEBRUARY 25, 1943 – NOVEMBER 29, 2001

A MEMBER OF the Beatles since its very earliest Quarrymen days, George Harrison was the solid lead guitarist known as "the quiet one." Though George's presence was generally overshadowed by the songwriting talents of John and Paul, and by Ringo's antics, he was certainly a remarkable musician in his own right, and contributed a number of songs to the Beatles' catalog. Interested in Eastern culture, he traveled to India in 1965 to study with musician Ravi Shankar and the influence is obvious on the following year's "Norwegian Wood." George later contributed "While My Guitar Gently Weeps" and "Here Comes the Sun," among others.

After the Beatles ceased working together, George released *All Things Must Pass* in 1971, a three-record work in which he demonstrated his affinity for mixing rock and religion. Later that year he organized concert fund-raisers for Bangladeshi famine victims that featured himself and such artists as Eric Clapton and Bob Dylan, and the concerts resulted in another release, *The Concert for Bangladesh*. George's solo career seemed to peak then, and he later retreated from the public eye entirely.

In 1977, George got brief, though unwanted, attention when his marriage dissolved; his wife left him for his close friend Clapton, whom she would later marry. In 1987, George resurfaced as one of the all-star musicians in the Traveling Wilburys, and he followed that with *Cloud 9*, a solo work that included "When We Was Fab," a nostalgic tune recalling the Beatlemania heyday.

In a bizarre December 1999 episode, an intruder broke into his home wielding a knife. George said he shouted "Hare Krishna, Hare Krishna!" in an attempt to disorient him, but the crazed intruder attacked and plunged the knife four times into George, puncturing a lung. At that moment, George believed he'd been fatally wounded and a "personal memory" of a similar incident, perhaps Lennon's murder, flashed through his mind. George's wife beat the intruder with a brass poker and then a lamp, and moments later staff and police arrived.

Eighteen months later, reports trickled in that George was battling cancer and, after radiation treatment at a Staten Island hospital, he died of brain cancer at the Los Angeles home of a friend.

George was 58 at his death, and, in keeping with his Eastern faith, he was cremated and his ashes scattered on the River Yamuna in India, which runs through the area of his favorite spiritual retreat.

MARC BOLAN
SEPTEMBER 30, 1947 – SEPTEMBER 16, 1977

MARC BOLAN AND his band T. Rex were an important part of the glitter-rock scene that in many ways prefigured punk rock. Inspired by the work of J.R.R. Tolkien—unicorns and gnomes figured prominently in their song lyrics—the band was originally a hippie acoustic duo with percussionist Steve Took and Marc on guitar. But in 1970 the band expanded to a quartet and went electric, and success beyond their wildest dreams ensued. T. Rex became huge in England, logging 11 consecutive Top 10 hits, most of them from the albums *The Slider* and *Electric Warrior*.

Later, as the mania surrounding T. Rex ebbed, the band struggled through a few incarnations and, though Marc became disillusioned at times, he remained committed to the band even as he developed other interests; by the mid-'70s he was writing a weekly column for an English music magazine and hosting his own TV talk-variety show as well.

One evening, Marc and his girlfriend Gloria Jones went out for dinner and a few rounds of assorted adult refreshments. When it was finally time to head home around 3:30 a.m., they jumped into her purple Mini 1275 GT (Marc had never learned to drive) for what should have been an unremarkable drive. But along the way, Gloria lost control of the car, its passenger side was smashed into a sycamore tree, and Marc was killed instantly. He was 29.

Marc was cremated at Golders Green Crematorium in London and is remembered there with a rose bush and a bronze plaque. He shares the site with his parents, under the Feld name (his legal surname), and you can find it at the Keats rose bed, plot number 46087.

By the way, Steve Took, T. Rex's first drummer, choked to death on a cherry pit in 1980, and is buried nearby in Kensal Green Cemetery.

JOHN BONHAM
MAY 31, 1948 – SEPTEMBER 25, 1980

BONZO, AS JOHN Bonham was affectionately known, was an icon of the 1970s rock and roll scene, known for his thundering drumming in the hard-rock band Led Zeppelin.

Led Zeppelin itself had come together after the Yardbirds' rapid breakup left guitar-hero Jimmy Page in a bind; he was contractually obliged to perform 10 concerts, but he no longer had a band. So Page called a few friends together—drummer John, frontman Robert Plant, and bassist John Paul Jones. The 10 gigs were quite well received and the foursome decided to stick together. After a half-dozen smash albums and a few hit singles, including the rock anthem "Stairway to Heaven," Led Zeppelin was the hottest rock act anywhere. But it wouldn't last.

Besides being renowned for his drumming talents, John was also known as an avid consumer of daunting quantities of alcohol, and this proved his undoing. During a night of heavy partying at Page's home, legend has it that John consumed some 40 shots (!)

of vodka, then passed out. In his extravagantly inebriated state, John failed to rouse even as his stomach ejected its contents. Consequently, in the plainest terms, John choked to death on his own vomit.

John was buried at the bucolic Saint Michael's Church Cemetery in Rushock, England. He was 32.

DAVID BOWIE
JANUARY 8, 1947 – JANUARY 10, 2016

IN 1958 A precocious 11-year-old player of the ukulele and piano named David Jones was enrolled at a junior high school near London. Curiously, one of his early friends there was the art teacher's son, Peter Frampton. At 14, when David had already morphed into a hip and aspiring saxophonist, a punch to his left eye resulted in a permanently dilated pupil that conveniently added to an ethereal appearance he'd begun to cultivate. A couple of years later David was singing in a succession of local bands, and soon after was calling himself David Bowie to avoid confusion with Davy Jones of the Monkees. Intrigued by musical theater, he joined an avant-garde troupe, which introduced him to the unnatural body movements he later carried to his own stage routines. At 20, after a few weeks at a Buddhist monastery in Scotland, he put out a folky self-titled album, which flopped. Already, there seemed hardly a dull moment for young Bowie.

Just days before real astronauts landed on the moon, Bowie released *Space Oddity*, its melodramatic title track featuring a fictitious and disillusioned astronaut, Major Tom, who chooses to remain "sitting in a tin can, far above the world," rather than return to Earth. Major Tom ignited David's rock-star career and persona, which whiplashed through chameleon-like transformations for nearly five decades. Looking fiercely forward, his series of edgy alter egos invited listeners to explore the darkness of outsiders, to face the strange and misfit, and to champion a sort of clandestine insurgency against the norm.

Bowie's unparalleled showmanship and theatrical charisma mesmerized the alienated, who, it seems, recognized his over-the-top construct as being more sincere and saying more than could any naturalism. And in the same way that his scavenged visual style was hardly classifiable, so too was his music, though both were instantly identifiable as pure Bowie. A blend of rock, cabaret, and jazz that he called "plastic soul," his records influenced glam rock, disco, new wave, funk, punk, and electronic dance.

After the psychedelia of *The Man Who Sold the World* came Ziggy Stardust, an androgynous, rogue, glam-rock alien with an orange spike-topped mullet, platform boots, and bodysuits who belted out "Starman" and "Suffragette City." In 1975 an about-face came on *Young Americans* as David distorted into the Thin White Duke, a cabaret-ready, impeccably dressed, aristocratic maestro whose elastic vocals melded funk and disco into the creative rock sounds of "Fame" and "Golden Years." Alternating through the artsy, drugged-out rocker of his Berlin albums, the pop-rocking hit maker of *Let's Dance*, and the techno-enthusiast and jazz impressionist of his later works, his flair for speedy change often caught listeners off guard. "My policy has been that as soon as a system or process works, it's out of date," he said.

By the '90s Bowie had settled down a bit and married the model Iman. As the century turned, he assumed the role of elder rock statesman, a part that seemed to mildly amuse him, and, after suffering a heart attack backstage during a 2004 tour, he took a decade-long break. Just two days before liver cancer took David at 66, he released his last album, *Blackstar*, on which, backed by an explosive jazz quartet, he contemplated lust, spirituality, and, as always, transformation.

Per his request, Bowie had no funeral and was cremated.

JAMES BROWN
MAY 3, 1933 – DECEMBER 25, 2006

WHEN JAMES BROWN entered the world in a one-room, Deep South, Depression-era shack, midwives thought he was stillborn. But, they noticed, he stayed warm and he was revived 10 minutes later, according to James himself, who oughta know. Four years later he was dropped off to live at his aunt Honey's den of gambling, moonshine, and prostitution, where he earned pennies buck-dancing for soldiers and shining shoes. Predictably, James became a delinquent of the streets, which culminated in a jail sentence from which he was paroled after three years with a condition of release being that he leave the city and never return. Essentially, he was exiled, and more than 20 years later had to apply to have the probation terms nullified so he could hold a hometown concert. The city fathers changed their tune and, today, in the middle of Augusta's Broad Avenue, stands a bronze monument to the Godfather of Soul.

A singer, songwriter, and center stage attraction, James sold an incredible 500 million records over the years and produced some 119 singles including "Papa's Got a Brand New Bag" and

"I Feel Good." But even more important than his dozens of lusty and wild hits, James formed the entire musical idiom of funk, which became the foundation for disco, R&B dance, and hip-hop worldwide. Never one to be modest, the Minister of Super Heavy Funk, this Soul Brother Number One, bragged in his autobiography, "I taught them everything they know, but not everything I know."

As irresistible as Brown's powerful voice and percussive groove was, his stage act was perhaps even more extraordinary. With his twirling and flowing cape, tight pants, highly polished shoes, eye makeup, and impeccably coiffed helmet of hair, the "hardest working man in show business" transformed dance. His moves—the spins, the quick shuffles, the knee-drops, and splits—were imitated and adopted most famously by Mick Jagger and Prince, while they were admired from afar by many millions of others who chose not to try to duplicate them. Long, frenzied crescendos and a trademark routine of collapsing onstage, having a cape thrown over him and tossing it away for one more reprise, left delirious audiences shouting for more.

Though he maintained a breakneck touring schedule, James still managed to squeeze in a particularly tumultuous personal life. Fathering at least 14 children with no less than eight mothers (four of which he married), his child support obligations at one time approached $60K per month. On multiple occasions the IRS auctioned prized possessions for unpaid taxes. Confused, hallucinating, and brandishing a shotgun while high on PCP in 1987, he burst into a business seminar and then led police on a 12-mile car chase, which netted a three-year jail term. Arrested four times for charges of assault against his third wife, James was arrested yet again for the same infraction against a fourth wife.

At 73, James died of congestive heart failure. After being laid in a gilt coffin wearing a blue suit, white gloves, and silver shoes, James was paraded through the streets of Harlem atop a horse-drawn carriage while well-wishers by the thousands danced and sang his hits in tribute. As Brown lay in state for two days on the Apollo Theater stage where he made his 1956 debut, thousands of fans marched solemnly past (including Michael Jackson, who offered the corpse a kiss on the lips) while Al Sharpton reminded everybody, "James stood for us, the common people."

Because of legal disputes and a series of paternity claims, which held up his burial while trustees waited for courts to order DNA samples (two additional children were confirmed by the tests), James laid in a climate-controlled room for 73 days before being entombed in a crypt at the Beech Island, South Carolina, estate of his daughter, Deana. The word on the street is that someday he'll either be moved to a more public location, or the estate will be opened into a Graceland type of attraction. Until either of those scenarios plays out, I'd recommend keeping your distance from Deana Brown's crib unless you're all about big dogs with sharp teeth and bad tempers. Ouch.

HARRY CHAPIN

DECEMBER 7, 1942 – JULY 17, 1981

HARRY CHAPIN WAS one of America's best-loved troubadours, and he wove poignant tales of common people, lost opportunities, and life's cruel ironies and hypocrisies. He had only two pop hits, "Taxi" and "Cat's in the Cradle." Both were in his self-described "story song" style, a narrative form of songwriting similar to talking blues.

Though widespread commercial success always eluded him, it doesn't seem that he was ever in it for the money anyway. A charitable performer who pioneered the idea of benefit concerts—half of his shows were for charitable causes—Harry's principal commitment was to end world hunger.

While driving near Exit 40 on the Long Island Expressway one sweltering Friday afternoon, Harry turned on his emergency flashers and was slowing and changing lanes when his car was struck from behind by a tractor-trailer rig. The collision set his Volkswagen on fire and, though the truck's driver dragged an incapacitated Harry from the flaming wreckage to safety, Harry was pronounced dead at a hospital a short time later. Though it was generally reported that Harry died of his burns or other injuries suffered in the collision, his burns were superficial and his injuries were not life threatening. Instead, Harry actually died of a heart attack, which is what prompted him to slow his car and attempt to pull to the side of the highway.

At 38, he was buried at Huntington Rural Cemetery in Huntington, New York.

GRAVE DIRECTIONS: Enter the cemetery at 555 New York Avenue, bear right at the office, continue straight through the four corners, then go left up the hill. Turn at the next two lefts, then stop when the road bends to the right. On the right is Section 6L and Harry's grave, marked with a large boulder, is in the middle of this section. This boulder was transported from Harry's boyhood home where he practiced guitar while sitting on it, or so the legend goes.

CLARENCE CLEMONS
JANUARY 11, 1942 – JUNE 18, 2011

DURING THE EARLY 1960s Clarence Clemons attended what is now the University of Maryland on scholarship for both music and football, and he excelled at both. But when he crashed his Buick Riviera into a tree and badly injured his knee the day before a scheduled tryout with the Cleveland Browns, his pro football aspirations were permanently squelched. Over the next few years he spent his days working as a youth counselor for troubled kids, while at night he perfected his rich and soulful saxophone style at bars up and down the Jersey Shore.

In 1971, he became part of Bruce Springsteen's backing band, though they weren't yet known as the E Street Band, and the duo's first encounter became part of the band's lore. In most tellings, on a night that a terrific thunder-and-lightning storm was crashing onto Asbury Park's boardwalk, Clarence entered a bar where Bruce, an unknown and struggling musician, was holding court on an improvised stage with his guitar. The wind caught the door and (both of them swear this part is true) it was blown from its hinges and tossed down the street. Bruce was startled by the towering shadow at the door but nonetheless motioned for Clarence to come up and play along, and they immediately clicked. "I swear I will never forget that moment," Clarence recalled years later. "I felt like I was supposed to be there. It was a magical moment. He looked at me, I looked at him, and we fell in love. And that's still there."

For the better part of the next four decades, Clarence played a central part in Springsteen's music, providing a tapestry and a texture that shaped it. Complementing the group's electric guitar and driving rhythms with muscular yet melodic saxophone hooks, he stamped his horn's signature wail on dozens of Bruce classics including "Rosalita" and "Born to Run." Clarence's massive size, equally huge personality, brotherly relationship with Springsteen, as well as onstage role as the straight man, helped the Big Man, as he later came to be known, evolve into one of rock and roll's most beloved and recognizable sidemen.

Clarence extended a charisma mixed with eccentricity offstage too. Wherever the band played, he made his dressing room into a shrine he called the Temple of Soul. By many accounts, including his own, he was a champion partier and he enjoyed telling a story of once playing pool with Fidel Castro. He could be a womanizer too, married five times and divorced four. He also released several solo albums, most notably 1985's well-received *Hero*. He occasionally sat in with the Grateful Dead, owned a rowdy New Jersey nightclub called Big Man's West, and, surprisingly, even shot a music video with Lady Gaga. In 2009, Clarence published his memoir, *Big Man: Real Life & Tall Tales*.

Clarence died after suffering a stroke at 69. He was cremated and his ashes remain with his family.

KURT COBAIN
FEBRUARY 20, 1967 – APRIL 5, 1994

WITH THE 1991 groundbreaking release *Nevermind*, Kurt Cobain and his inventive band, Nirvana, produced in one deft stroke a new stepchild of rock and roll—alternative rock—and pulled rock away from the processed, synthetic, and stale sounds of the 1980s back to something more sincere. *Nevermind*'s signature song, "Smells Like Teen Spirit," was adopted by a disaffected generation as an anthem of discontent and cynicism, "grunge" was added to the national vocabulary, and thrift stores enjoyed a run on tattered flannel shirts.

But as an intense loner, superstardom never interested Kurt, and as the band skyrocketed, this reluctant guitar hero's personal life became a roller coaster. He was plagued by a chronic stomach condition that caused him a tremendous amount of pain and Kurt resorted to medicating himself with heroin. His 1991 marriage to Courtney Love, the brassy leader of the punkish group Hole, brought him some security but rumors of the couple's drug abuse were rampant; after a *Vanity Fair* article in which Love admitted using heroin while she was pregnant, child welfare authorities investigated and forbade the couple from being alone with their baby daughter for a month.

Just three years and three hit albums after Nirvana's breakthrough, Kurt's mental health had plunged and his already pronounced angst heightened. While on tour in Europe in March 1994, an overdose settled Kurt into a 20-hour-long coma. Even though 50 doses of a Valium-like prescription drug called Rohypnol were found in his stomach, the couple called the overdose "an accident." They returned home to Seattle, but matters only worsened.

At the end of March, Kurt checked into a Los Angeles drug rehabilitation clinic and, while he worked on dislodging the monkey from his back, Courtney settled into a hotel across town to work on an album. But Kurt sneaked away from the clinic and returned to their empty home. Barricading himself inside a greenhouse above the garage, Kurt shot some heroin, and then a shotgun. Three days later, an electrician who had arrived to work on the home's security system discovered a very dead body. It was presumed to be Kurt, and he was ultimately identified through his fingerprints.

Kurt left a note, but therein lies a minor controversy. Kurt's suicide note reads like the draft of a speech announcing a retirement from the music business—only in the last four lines is there any allusion to the idea that he might also be retiring from life—and here's the kicker: The lines were added after his signature, and are written in a hand that's similar, but different. Of course, through a short leap of logic, some now believe that Kurt was murdered and that his ruthless killer, finding Kurt's retirement address, simply added a few lines to turn it into a suicide note.

But it's all pretty unlikely. It seems quite clear, instead (to this writer anyway), that the note may have been originally intended as a retirement speech but, when it came time to end his life, Kurt figured that the draft could serve as a serviceable suicide note as well. In his tormented state of mind just before killing himself, perhaps while strung out on smack, he scribbled a few personal lines to his family and was done with it.

The note is readily available online and you're free to draw your own conclusions. They never do just fade away, do they?

At 27, Kurt was cremated. It's since been reported that his ashes have been scattered, well, almost everywhere.

EDDIE COCHRAN & GENE VINCENT

EDDIE COCHRAN
OCTOBER 3, 1938 – APRIL 17, 1960

GENE VINCENT
FEBRUARY 11, 1935 – OCTOBER 12, 1971

NO ONE PERSON "invented" rock and roll. Rather, over the years it worked its way out of the blues, and in the 1950s its development accelerated due to the imagination and innovation of a couple dozen pioneers. Eddie Cochran and Gene Vincent were two such pioneers; they recognized rock's potential and, for a while anyway, helped develop the foundations of a new cultural phenomenon. Though Eddie only had a couple of hits, most notably "Summertime Blues" in 1958, his influence was considerable in terms of musical arrangements, the role of the drums, and, indeed, the very deliberate and wild sound and attitude that he lent to rock music. Gene's sole hit was "Be-Bop-a-Lula," but it added fuel to the fiery excitement of the time, and his frenzied and energetic performing style was copied by his contemporaries.

For the first few months of 1960, Eddie teamed with Gene for a tour of England, successfully pacing the rock and roll mania that gripped the country's youth. After their last show at the Hippodrome Theatre in Bristol, Eddie, his girlfriend Sharon Steely, and headliner Gene caught a taxi back to London from where Eddie and Sharon planned to catch a plane. Zooming through the night along winding country roads, the taxi driver lost control at Rowden Hill in the village of Chittenham, and the Ford MKII was destroyed as it slammed into a lamp pole. Gene suffered a few broken bones and Sharon's pelvis was shattered, but Eddie went through the windshield and died of massive head injuries 10 hours later.

At 21, Eddie was buried at Forest Lawn Memorial Park in Cypress, California.

GRAVE DIRECTIONS: At 4471 Lincoln Avenue, drive past the gates and stop after about a hundred yards. Eddie's big, flat stone is on the left, 15 rows back.

By promoting his rebel image, Gene had become one of Britain's biggest draws by the time of his tour with Eddie. But by 1964 he'd lost favor with English audiences who were instead flocking to their homegrown bands, the Beatles and the Rolling Stones. He returned to the States but failed to stage a comeback. In 1971 Gene's alcoholism spurred a bleeding ulcer, and he died in his mother's arms at 36.

Gene was buried at Eternal Valley Memorial Park in Newhall, California.

GRAVE DIRECTIONS: Enter the cemetery at 23287 Sierra Highway and make an immediate left up the hill. Stop on the left after about 50 yards, perhaps 30 feet past the yellow water spigot. In the grass along the curb, find Lilard Rainbolt's marker and Gene's grave is just two rows farther into the lawn.

JOE COCKER

MAY 20, 1944 – DECEMBER 22, 2014

JOE COCKER WAS the gravelly-voiced, blue-eyed, and blues-drenched English soul singer who stormed onto the international music scene at the 1969 Woodstock festival with his riveting and uniquely spasmodic interpretation of the Beatles' song "With a Little Help from My Friends." Even by the loose standards of rock music in the late 1960s, Joe's stage moves—including air-guitar simulations and contortions that at times suggested he was having a seizure—seemed from another world. But for Joe, it was simply the way he felt music and his contortions were how he thought he'd move if he could play an instrument, a talent that escaped him. Nor was he conventionally handsome, and his vocals too were ragged, yet in his writhing and tortured style Joe telegraphed extraordinarily soulful interpretations of some of the most highly regarded songs of the era.

As a teen Joe formed his first group, the Cavaliers, who together stomached an early humility: Not only did they fail to get paid for their inaugural gig at a local youth club, but he and his bandmates actually had to pay admission to enter the hall. Joe later bounced around as a pub performer under the adopted handle of Vance Arnold with a variety of "skiffle" groups—free-form clusters of eclectic musicians who tended to improvise with offbeat instruments. The following year he began a long on-again, off-again partnership with the Grease Band, and with their rousing accompaniment through hundreds of hard-driving, pay-your-dues performances, Joe and the band attained renown.

Buoyed by the recognition gained after his amped-up stage freneticism at the Woodstock festival, Joe mounted the fabled Mad Dogs & Englishmen Tour with pianist Leon Russell. The massive ensemble, a fluid juggernaut of up to three dozen musicians, embarked on a legendarily dissolute series of dates, the group's indulgences serving as a template for rock's "sex and drugs" arc. Nonetheless, the tour, which hammered through 65 performances in just 57 days, made a bona fide star of Russell, while Cocker's career was left on the ropes due to escalating alcohol problems. In one infamous incident he threw up onstage during a show at the Roxy.

But while similar demons led to the early deaths of some of his peers during the 1970s, Joe embodied and even thrived during the times' hedonistic excesses and kept right on recording and performing his anguished hit interpretations of selections such as "Delta Lady," "Feelin' Alright," "She Came in Through the Bathroom Window," and "You Are So Beautiful." His biggest hit came in 1982 with

"Up Where We Belong," a duet with Jennifer Warnes featured in the movie *An Officer and a Gentleman.*

In 2013 Joe admitted that his hard-living ways nearly did him in, as he did "just about every drug imaginable. . . . If I'd been stronger mentally, I could have turned away from temptation," he said. "But there was no rehab back in those days. Drugs were readily available, and I dived in head first. It's not any fun having people tell you about things that you can't remember yourself."

By the year 2000, Joe had cleaned up his act for good, crediting his wife, Pam, with bringing him back from the abyss. Retreating to their 240-acre Mad Dog Ranch in Colorado, the couple grew tomatoes, fly-fished, and walked the dogs while Joe maintained his status as a solid concert attraction.

At 70, Joe died at the ranch after a protracted battle with lung cancer. He was cremated and his ashes scattered to the wind.

CHRIS CORNELL
July 20, 1964 – May 17, 2017

WHEN GRUNGE ROCK soared from the Seattle music scene to usher in a new era of rock around 1989, the culture-changing movement was in no small part launched by the angst-ridden anthems and grinding guitars of Soundgarden. Featuring a dirty and aggressive sound in a "Sabbath-influenced punk" style, as the band's lead guitarist liked to say, Soundgarden's soul emanated from their mesmerizing frontman, Chris Cornell. With penetrating blue eyes and an unapologetically throaty voice, Cornell played rhythm guitar but was best known for the gloomy yet gorgeous verbosity of his songs, his delivery of which guaranteed him status as the band's focal point, no matter what musical mayhem unfolded behind him.

Despite dominating rock radio for nearly a decade with a string of hits such as "Spoonman," "Black Hole Sun," and "Burden in My Hand," the band broke up in 1997 and Chris founded the short-lived supergroup Audioslave. After putting out four albums on his own, Chris then reunited Soundgarden and they picked up where they'd left off with an acclaimed release called *King Animal* in 2012.

Chris struggled with loneliness and depression throughout his life. Confessing to being "a daily drug user at 13," and a "pioneer" in the abuse of the opiate OxyContin, after nearly 30 years of on-and-off-again use, Chris cleaned himself up through rehab in 2006. Unfortunately, though, the depression lingered.

On tour in 2017, Soundgarden played the Fox Theatre in Detroit and during the show's final song, "Slaves and Bulldozers," Chris improvised the lyrics of a traditional gospel song, "In My Time of Dying," into the encore. "In my time of dying, want nobody to mourn / All I want for you to do is take my body home," he sang.

Less than an hour later, from Suite 1136 at the MGM Grand Hotel, Chris called his wife, Vicky, who was home in California. The two had a troubling conversation in which Chris ranted and became mean before repeatedly slurring his words, saying, "I am just tired" and abruptly hanging up. Vicky then frantically called Chris' bodyguard, told him what had transpired and her concerns, and urged him to check on Chris, breaking down his door if necessary. But in a delay of time wherein the bodyguard first unsuccessfully pleaded with hotel security to unlock Chris' door, and then finally broke open both the main and bedroom doors of the suite himself, Chris had already hanged himself with a red exercise band looped through a carabiner he'd attached to a hinge of the bathroom door. Dressed in a torn gray T-shirt and black underwear, he left no note.

At 52, Chris was cremated and his ashes buried at Hollywood Forever Cemetery in Los Angeles, California.

GRAVE DIRECTIONS: Enter the cemetery at 6000 Santa Monica Boulevard, then stop in front of the Grass mausoleum, which is on the right at the next intersection. In front of the pond, Chris' flat stone is 15 feet to the right of Johnny Ramone's guitarist statue.

JIM CROCE
JANUARY 10, 1943 – SEPTEMBER 20, 1973

YOU KNOW HIS songs—everybody does. You sing along with "Bad, Bad Leroy Brown" in your car and hum along to the Muzak recording of "Time in a Bottle" in elevators. But few actually remember Jim Croce, a mustachioed and cigar-smoking, working-class folk artist who struggled for years to break into the mainstream.

In 1969, with his wife, Ingrid, he cut an album titled *Ingrid and Jim Croce* and they remained on the New York City coffeehouse circuit for a couple of years before eventually tiring of city life. Moving a little west to Pennsylvania, Ingrid learned to bake bread and can vegetables while Jim worked low-paying odd jobs, pursuing music more as a hobby than a profession. But by 1972 Jim had penned a number of catchier pop ballads and that year he put out a solo album, *You Don't Mess Around With Jim*, which was an instant success. As his songs played on radios and turntables across America, Jim became a club and concert headliner.

After an appearance at Northwestern State University in Natchitoches, Louisiana, Jim and the four members of his band boarded a small, chartered airplane. On takeoff, the plane clipped a pecan tree at the end of the runway and went down, killing all on board. After Jim's death, sales of his music tripled and his signature songs became mainstays of classic-rock stations. The lesser tragedy is that Jim never lived to enjoy this broad popularity, and we can only hope that he's somehow basking in it now.

At 30, Jim was buried at Haym Salomon Memorial Park in Frazer, Pennsylvania.

GRAVE DIRECTIONS: Enter the park at 200 Moores Road and Jim rests about 50 yards off to the right, almost in front of the office. His is a flat stone shaded by a pine tree.

THE DAY THE MUSIC DIED

BUDDY HOLLY
SEPTEMBER 7, 1936 – FEBRUARY 3, 1959

RITCHIE VALENS
MAY 13, 1941 – FEBRUARY 3, 1959

J.P. "BIG BOPPER" RICHARDSON
OCTOBER 24, 1930 – FEBRUARY 3, 1959

BUDDY HOLLY PLAYED violin and piano as a child, but was a teenager before he adopted his signature guitar. By the time he teamed up with the Crickets at just 20, he'd already released a few records with Decca (the label accidentally dropped the "e" in his last name), and had introduced a unique songwriting style characterized by a blues-heavy lyricism.

In these very early days of rock and roll, Buddy Holly and the Crickets began recording at a New Mexico studio, and by May 1957 had nailed "That'll Be The Day," its title lifted from a line uttered by John Wayne in *The Searchers*. The song raced up the charts and they went on tour in its support, and by November "Peggy Sue" and "Not Fade Away" had joined the first hit. With the Crickets, Buddy appeared on *The Ed Sullivan Show* twice in those few short months and the limelight inspired a decidedly cosmopolitan shift in Buddy's appearance and manners; he began to wear stylish New York suits and donned the thick, black eye-glasses that he became known for.

In autumn of 1958, because of managerial and royalty disagreements, Buddy parted from the Crickets and their manager. He shortly assembled a new backing band, including future country-star Waylon Jennings on bass, and joined the Winter Dance Party tour, an assemblage of acts that would tour the upper Midwest.

The acts included Ritchie Valens, a hot, young artist known for his rock and roll version of the old Mexican standard "La Bamba," and Jiles P. "Big Bopper" Richardson, a Texas deejay-turned-rocker who found success with the song "Chantilly Lace." Buddy would headline, and Dion and the Belmonts rounded out the list of performers.

The 24-stop tour hit its 11th stop at the Surf Ballroom in Clear Lake, Iowa, and the performers arrived cold, tired, and disgusted. Since they'd set out 10 days earlier they had been traveling between venues in the bitter cold of a Midwest winter on a bus with a spotty heater. Dreading the 400-mile trip to Fargo, North Dakota, Buddy asked Carroll Anderson, manager of the Surf Ballroom, to arrange a charter flight instead. Carroll found a plane, a three-passenger Beechcraft from Dwyer Flying Service, and Buddy informed bandmates Waylon Jennings and Tommy Allsup that they wouldn't have to ride on the bus to Fargo after all.

However, during the concert at the Surf, Waylon Jennings gave his seat on the plane to the Big Bopper, whose stocky frame was a poor fit in the narrow and uncomfortable bus seats, and who was suffering from the flu, to boot. After the switch, Ritchie Valens began begging Tommy Allsup to give up his plane seat too. Tommy finally agreed to let a coin toss settle it; Ritchie called "heads," winning the toss and a seat on the plane. After the concert, Carroll drove Buddy, J.P., and Ritchie to the airport in nearby Mason City and bid them goodbye. With his wife and son, Carroll watched the plane take off and circle around as it took up its course. Nothing appeared out of the ordinary, and Carroll and his family went home.

By the next morning, though, it was clear to Jerry Dwyer, the plane's owner, that something was wrong. He hadn't yet heard from the pilot, Roger Peterson. After checking for Peterson by telephone at airports along the way to Fargo, Dwyer set out on an aerial search and soon spotted the plane's wreckage in a stubbled corn-field 5½ miles from the Mason City airport. Except for a solitary wing that was relatively undamaged, the plane was hardly distinguishable. Its three passengers were scattered around the field and the pilot was still trapped inside the wreckage; all four were dead.

Authorities could never find a reason for the crash; the pilot was experienced and competent, the navigational equipment was functioning properly and set for a course to Fargo, the aircraft was properly maintained and in good condition, and, contrary to some reports, the weather was favorable for flying; the night had been clear with just trace amounts of snow in the air. All appearances are that, for some unexplained reason, perhaps disorientation or inattention, the pilot flew the plane into the ground.

For teenagers of the period the crash was certainly devastating, but for the general public the news was not terribly significant. Buddy's clean-cut image and scandal-free life, coupled with the young ages of the three rockers, made the story all the more poignant. But rock and roll was new and not taken very seriously in those days, and Buddy Holly became a largely forgotten figure.

Then in 1971 a little-known singer-songwriter named Don McLean released a seven-plus–minute song called "American Pie." Its narrative is a rhyming allegorical history of rock and roll structured around the hook "the day the music died," a direct reference to Buddy's first hit "That'll Be The Day." Since then, Buddy has gotten his deserved credit and recognition, and in 1986 he was inducted into the Rock & Roll Hall of Fame.

Buddy was 22 at his death and was buried at the City of Lubbock Cemetery in Lubbock, Texas.

GRAVE DIRECTIONS: Enter the cemetery at 2011 East 31st Street and turn right. After about 100 yards there are two silver posts on the left side of the road. Another 30 feet beyond these posts, alongside the curb, is Buddy's grave.

Ritchie Valens was just 17 when he died in the plane crash, and he was buried at San Fernando Mission Cemetery in Mission Hills, California.

GRAVE DIRECTIONS: Enter the cemetery at 11160 Stranwood Avenue and park in front of the flower shop. Ritchie is buried across from the flower shop between curb numbers 235 and 247 in the third row from the drive.

At his death, Jiles P. "Big Bopper" Richardson was 28. He was buried at Forest Lawn Memorial Park in Beaumont, Texas.

GRAVE DIRECTIONS: After entering the cemetery at 4955 Pine Street, the Lilypool Garden lawn is immediately to the left and there near the curb in Lot 31 is the Big Bopper.

Waylon Jennings, who gave his plane seat to J.P., enjoyed a very successful career in country music. He died in 2002 and is profiled within these pages as well. Years after losing the coin toss for his plane seat to Ritchie Valens, Tommy Allsup opened Tommy's "Head's Up" Saloon in Dallas, Texas.

BO DIDDLEY
DECEMBER 30, 1928 – JUNE 2, 2008

IN THE FURNITURE-MAKING shop of his vocational high school in Chicago, a young Bo Diddley built himself a guitar along with a violin and an upright bass and, after dropping out of the school at 15, he played his instruments on street corners for spare change. Within a short while he had formed a rough-edged blues group called the Langley Avenue Jive Cats and become a fixture of the city's blues club scene. In 1954 Diddley cut a demo of two of his original songs, "Uncle John" and "I'm a Man," but instead of adhering to the traditional restrained blues brand of his contemporaries, he showcased the influences of a frenzied Pentecostal church congregation that he frequented. Those exultant and frenetic stylings are considered to be some of the very beginnings of rock and roll.

The next year his single, "Hey Bo Diddley," with its instantly recognizable rhythm of three-stroke/rest/two-stroke, or bomp-da-bomp-da-bomp, da-bomp-bomp, raced to the top of the charts. This "jungle beat," as he called it, had been around in various incarnations since time immemorial, including in the children's game hambone, but ever since Bo laid it on vinyl it's been a foundation of rock music.

After imprinting his trademark style on the world, Bo blitzed the charts throughout the 1950s with pile-driving performances, his guitar distorted with a bubbling tremolo and his booming

voice loaded with echo, all roped together around his spine-rattling rhythms. Yet his sound was only one element of Bo's musical charisma. In an age of apple pie and Chevrolet, his lyrics were radically playful, wisecracking and full of slang, mother wit, and sexual cockiness. And his live performances, where he usually sported a black cowboy hat, a loud plaid suit, and thick-rimmed glasses while coaxing out-of-this-world effects from a weird-looking rectangular guitar, were trancelike ruckuses. A wild performer who jumped and lurched and balanced on his toes while shaking his knees as he wrestled his instrument, Bo's high-kicking, hip-wiggling, swaggering stage repertoire and panache preceded Mick Jagger and James Brown. Playing his "ax" behind his head or with his teeth while using amped-up electric effects that included reverb and distortion was a breakthrough for music, especially once Jimi Hendrix and others took his inventions to extremes.

By the early 1960s new artists emerged using the sound he invented, and Bo quickly began to sound quaint. Searching for a hit, his record company had him make albums to capitalize on the Twist and surf and dance music, but the picture only worsened. These were low times for Bo. Completely disillusioned with the music business, he moved to New Mexico in 1971 and for two years served as deputy sheriff in the town of Los Lunas. Now that's a career change!

Despite flirtations with synthesizers, religious rock, and hip-hop in later decades, Bo's recording career never picked up again. But that wasn't even the worst of it: Throughout his life Bo was embittered about both his musical legacy and being exploited by the music industry. He felt that his standing as a father of rock and roll was never properly acknowledged and it frustrated him that he could never earn royalties from the songs of others who had borrowed his beat. "I opened the door for a lot of people, and they just ran through and left me holding the knob," he said. Despite all his hits, he enjoyed zero financial success from any record company, receiving not even a single dollar in royalties until 1989. "I am owed," Bo commented darkly. "I never got paid. I tell musicians, 'Don't trust nobody but your mama, and even then, look at her real good.'"

On a hot summer night, with his death imminent, family and friends surrounded Bo and together they sang the gospel song "Walk Around Heaven." Bo gave a thumbs-up and died minutes after his last words, a barely audible, "Wow, I'm going to heaven."

At 79, he was buried at Rosemary Hill Cemetery in Bronson, Florida.

GRAVE DIRECTIONS: On Route 24 just east of its intersection with Route 27, situated proudly under an old Spanish moss tree, Bo's stone can be seen from the car window while cruising past the cemetery.

RONNIE JAMES DIO
JULY 10, 1942 – MAY 16, 2010

WITH HIS POWERFUL, almost operatic vocals and doom-laden but often poetic lyrics, Ronnie James Dio, the "Man on the Silver Mountain," was an iconic heavy metal frontman who became one of the best-loved figures of the genre.

Born Ronald Padavona, he released his first record in 1958 with the group Ronnie and the Red Caps, and it was a few years later that he adopted his stage name, supposedly inspired by a New York mobster named Johnny Dio. By the 1970s, Ronnie was known in the then-limited heavy metal circle as a purist with a wide range of vocal prowess and a devilish stage persona, and in 1975 when Ritchie Blackmore left Deep Purple and hired Ronnie to front his new band, Rainbow, metal fans rejoiced and Ronnie's talents gained their first wide exposure. After four landmark albums with that band, personal differences drove him to leave and in short order he was filling Ozzy Osbourne's vacated shoes in Black Sabbath. Ronnie rejuvenated Sabbath's creative slump with gusto and their first album together, *Heaven and Hell,* went gold, as did its follow-up, *Mob Rules,* in 1981. But in rock, and especially in heavy metal, the only thing that's constant is change; after just a couple years Ronnie left Sabbath to start his own band named, aptly enough, Dio.

The cover art of Dio's first album, *Holy Diver,* an immodest and cartoonish painting of a red-eyed demon whipping a drowning priest, succinctly encapsulates the band's over-the-top style and the group became a symbol of both the glories and the silliness of heavy metal. Drawing heavily on medieval imagery, the theme of Dio's catalog of songs on 10 albums over the next 20 years revolved around the struggle between good and evil. Onstage, medieval theatrics abounded including swords and goblets and thrones and dragons, while Ronnie wailed about devils and defiance, punctuating his points with gale-force vibrato. Meanwhile in the audience, throngs of sweaty disciples rocked in unison, one hand upraised in the "devil's horn" hand gesture—index and pinky fingers up, everything else clenched in a fist—as a symbol of metal's occult-like worship of everything scary and heavy. Ronnie is widely credited with popularizing the hand gesture and claimed to have gotten it—the "malocchio" or "evil eye"—from his Italian grandmother. In any event, fans loved and embraced it—and him. Rock on, indeed.

At 67, Ronnie lost his battle with stomach cancer and was interred at Forest Lawn Cemetery in Hollywood Hills, California.

GRAVE DIRECTIONS: Enter the park at 6300 Forest Lawn Drive, get a map from the information booth, and drive to the Courts of Remembrance. Walk up the long sidewalk in the middle, up the two sets of three stairs each, and through the archway. After the archway, diagonally to the right is a painting of three children, in front of which is Ronnie's white sarcophagus.

CLARENCE LEO FENDER
AUGUST 10, 1909 – MARCH 21, 1991

IN THE 1930s musical instruments functioned much as they had for years: Drums provided the beat, horns performed the melody, and, because they couldn't be heard very well, string instruments were relegated to the background. But then a new invention changed modern music—and popular culture as well—the electric guitar.

By rudimentary physics, a vibrating metal object—a guitar string, for instance—moving in a magnetic field creates a signal that can be picked up by a wire coil. In 1931 an inventor named George Beauchamp applied this principle to his guitar hobby and, on his dining room table, built a crude version of the world's first electric guitar.

For the first time, a guitar could hold its own against the horn section, and guitarists could pick out melody lines instead of just strumming the rhythm. By the time Beauchamp finally got a patent in 1937, the electric guitar had been introduced to the jazz world, was redefining swing orchestra ensembles, and several companies were making their own electric guitars. After a few technical headaches were overcome and some stylistic changes were advanced by Les Paul and other pioneers, radio-repairman Leo Fender jumped onto the scene in 1945.

Leo advanced a solid-body guitar with a better pickup and tone controls but, most important, his guitar was cheap. Leo revolutionized the scene by mass-producing the instrument, beginning with his 1950 Telecaster, a guitar for the masses. The tools of the revolution that would soon become rock music were now in the hands of America's youth, and the culture would never be the same.

Leo died at 81 after a battle with Parkinson's disease and was buried at Fairhaven Memorial Park in Santa Ana, California.

GRAVE DIRECTIONS: Enter the cemetery at 1702 Fairhaven Avenue, turn left after the office, and from that point stay as parallel as you can with Fairhaven Avenue. Turn right when you finally reach a pronounced "T," then stop after 20 feet. In the grass on the right, Section J, count 11 rows to find Leo's grave.

And later on, check your attic. Though Leo offered his Telecaster for $75, such an early original can today fetch $60,000.

TOM FOGERTY
NOVEMBER 9, 1941 – SEPTEMBER 6, 1990

THE ECONOMICAL STYLE of rock and roll promoted by Creedence Clearwater Revival was a long way from rock's mainstream in the late 1960s, but these guys hit it big anyway. Featuring the growling vocals and rhythmic guitars of brothers Tom and John Fogerty, the band's recipe of three-minute songs earned them eight gold singles in just three years and Creedence seemed destined for greatness and longevity. But conflicts arose because of John's totalitarian attitude, and Tom left the band in 1971 to pursue a solo career.

In December of 1980 the original band reunited onstage for the first time in nine years during Tom's wedding, but this proved to be their last performance together. Tom released eight solo albums but never found much commercial success, and at 48 died of respiratory failure due to tuberculosis.

He was cremated and his ashes scattered in Hawaii and around California's Half Moon Bay.

Tom and John never fully reconciled and remained estranged even as Tom lay dying. The animosity between John and the other band members continues and, when Creedence was inducted into the Rock & Roll Hall of Fame in 1993, John declined to play with his ex-bandmates.

MARVIN GAYE
APRIL 2, 1939 – APRIL 1, 1984

MARVIN GAYE WAS a charter member of that generation of soul artists that skyrocketed to fame under the Motown label, and his songs—unique blends of soul music and old-time gospel—cut a wide swath from torrid sexual abandon to impassioned social rectitude.

The son of an iron-fisted Pentecostal minister, Marvin was still quite young when it became obvious to anyone within earshot that he could *really* sing and the boy became a church fixture, leading the congregation through hymns between his father's sermons. Eventually, the protracted religious discourses and his father's inflexibility induced an animosity that worsened through Marvin's teens. Still, though Marvin's lifestyle later drifted light-years away from the strictures of Pentecostalism, he was always quick to credit his father for instilling in him the faith he felt was central to his success.

After enlisting in the Air Force and then mutually parting ways with the service prematurely, Marvin gained a Motown solo recording contract and in 1966 hit pay dirt in a duet with Kim Weston titled "It Takes Two." The smash hit opened the floodgates and for the next decade both Marvin and Motown cashed in.

After a string of hits, including "Can I Get a Witness?" and "How Sweet It Is to Be Loved by You," Marvin released 1971's *What's Going On?*, an album of outspoken social commentary that surprised fans who'd come to expect danceable love songs. The album was nonetheless a Motown milestone, demonstrating that some of the label's artists might be more than mere dance-steppers. This was followed by a Grammy nomination for 1973's *Let's Get It On*.

Later in the 1970s, Marvin struggled with substance abuse, his marriage disintegrated, and he fell deeply into debt. Fleeing his demons via a three-year self-imposed European exile, Marvin returned with a new vitality and in 1982 released *Midnight Love*, a modern quilt of electronics woven through an imperfect reggae beat that some hailed as a masterpiece. Marvin won two Grammys for his efforts with the single "Sexual Healing," which became a radio standard.

Though Marvin's professional life seemed to be back on track, his personal life was a runaway train; the IRS dogged him for back taxes, he succumbed to cocaine addiction, romantic relationships imploded, and he was becoming ridiculously paranoid. After a tempestuous tour following the *Midnight Love* album, Marvin retreated to the Los Angeles home that he'd bought for his parents. But Marvin and his father had never addressed their 25-year-old animosities, and now, living together but apart (Marvin spent his days alone in his room), their conflicted relationship worsened.

One morning, after an argument and an altercation concerning Marvin Sr.'s inability to locate a letter from an insurance agency, the string finally broke. Without saying a word, Marvin Sr. entered his son's room and shot him while he sat on his bed. Marvin Jr. slumped to the floor, his father fired again, and his wife, Alberta, screamed to the heavens for her son. Marvin Sr. then went outside, threw the gun onto the front lawn, and waited on the porch for the police. Later that afternoon, on the day before his 45th birthday, Marvin Gaye Jr. was pronounced dead.

After a service at which Stevie Wonder sang, Smokey Robinson spoke, and 10,000 people passed by his open casket, Marvin was cremated and his ashes scattered in the Pacific Ocean.

BILL GRAHAM
JANUARY 8, 1931 – OCTOBER 25, 1991

WHILE MOST OF his family members died at the hands of the Nazis, Wolfgang Grajonca was able to escape their grasp, and at 12 he landed in New York City. At the onset of the Korean War he was drafted into the Army and there he changed his name, Bill coming from the English equivalent of Wolfgang, and Graham being closest to Grajonca in the phonebook. Bill served until 1953 and, after being awarded a Bronze Star for valor, was awarded United States citizenship.

Bill fell into organizing gigs for theater troupes and, quickly sensing a larger business opportunity, was soon arranging larger and more elaborate community events, which then morphed into providing legitimate venues for San Francisco's strange new counterculture. His purchase of the Fillmore Auditorium caused it to become ground zero of the burgeoning music scene, and Bill rounded out his hall's already bursting schedule with "acid tests" and "love-ins."

In 1968 Bill opened the Fillmore's spinoff in New York City, the Fillmore East, and, with his bookend auditoriums, became the leading promoter of rock music, hosting hundreds of turbulent performances. A stickler for quality and detail, Bill invested heavily in sound and lighting, and the revolutionary music shows he presented became a yardstick against which all his competitors were measured.

As rock music's popularity steamrolled worldwide, Bill led the movement with his shrewd business acumen. His production company, Bill Graham Presents, pioneered the rock concert as a social statement with events for charitable causes; he directed monster-sized tours for supersized groups, and he was the catalyst for the industry's booming merchandise business. In short, Bill amassed an untold fortune from the flower-power phenomenon and its progeny.

At 60, Bill died when the helicopter that was returning him from a Huey Lewis concert he'd promoted hit electrical lines and crashed near Vallejo, California. His company later put on a massive free concert in his honor at San Francisco's Polo Field and, in remembering him, Neil Young commented, "He always made all of us look good."

Bill was buried at Eternal Home Cemetery in Colma, California.

GRAVE DIRECTIONS: Enter the cemetery at 1051 El Camino Real, turn left, and park at the second circle. Bill's grave is six rows from El Camino and a dozen stones from the north wall.

GRATEFUL DEAD

IN 1963 JERRY Garcia formed his first band, Mother McCree's Uptown Jug Champions, with some friends, including guitarist Bob Weir and keyboardist Ron "Pigpen" McKernan. Neither Jerry nor anyone else could ever imagine the ultimate outcome of that modest inauguration. By 1965 bassist Phil Lesh and drummer Bill Kreutzmann had joined in the fun and, along with lyricist Robert Hunter, they took to calling themselves the Grateful Dead, a moniker of a reluctant corpse based on an old English fable that Jerry stumbled across in the dictionary.

Just as the poets at coffeehouses gave way to rock bands at dance halls, the Dead invented a spacy, extended performance style that made for perfect background music for the burgeoning hippie counterculture of "acid tests" and free love. The band members soon moved into a communal house at 710 Ashbury St. in San Francisco and rose to the top of the heap of psychedelic bands. The year 1967 marked their debut album, *The Grateful Dead*, but it was on their fifth and sixth albums, released just months apart in 1970, that the band hit full stride. On *Workingman's Dead* and *American Beauty*, the Grateful Dead created a watershed in rock music history. The songs on these albums, most notably "Truckin'" and "Casey Jones," exposed the band to a much wider audience, while cuts like "Ripple," "Uncle John's Band," and "Friend of the Devil" became cornerstones of the band's performance-based career, inspiring a supremely "deadicated" cult following.

Despite tempting fate with both its name and its lifestyle, the band somehow managed, for the most part, to avoid the type of ugly incidents that plagued many of their rock and roll contemporaries. For the next quarter-century, with only occasional changes in the lineup, the group concentrated on their music and toured endlessly. In a sea of tie-dyed attire, enchanted "Deadhead" fans dutifully followed the band around the world, from Japan to Vermont to the pyramids in Egypt, though most ordinary folks who were out of the loop never quite understood all the hubbub. Jerry tried to sum it up for them in 1981, saying, "Our audience is like people who like licorice. Not everybody likes licorice, but the people who like licorice, really like licorice."

RON "PIGPEN" McKERNAN
MAY 7, 1946 – MARCH 8, 1973

BEDECKED IN A leather jacket and bandanna, Ron "Pigpen" McKernan was beside Jerry from the very beginning. It was through his persistence that their jug band became an electric rock and roll band, and it was his dusty voice that handled the lead in those earliest days. Pigpen later mostly stuck to the keyboards and harmonica, only occasionally fronting during live shows, and even less often in the studio. Pigpen also developed an intensive audience-interactive rap session that became a highlight of Dead shows.

By 1968 Pigpen had become unreliable due to severe health problems resulting from his intoxicating vices, and the band added another keyboardist, Tom Constanten, to help take up some of the slack. In the summer of 1971 Pigpen was diagnosed with cirrhosis of the liver and, after detox, he never drank again. But the change did not come soon enough. Too ill to maintain the pace of touring, Pigpen retreated shortly after the Dead's 1972 tour of Europe. His general health continued to decline, and finally Pigpen died of a gastrointestinal hemorrhage.

At 26, Pigpen was buried at Alta Mesa Memorial Park in Palo Alto, California.

GRAVE DIRECTIONS: Enter the cemetery at 695 Arastradero Road and bear left after the office. Then make a hard right at the second opportunity and stop about three-quarters of the way down this drive. Ron's flat marker is on the left, third row from the curb.

KEITH GODCHAUX

JULY 19, 1948 – JULY 23, 1980

IN OCTOBER OF 1971, keyboardist Keith Godchaux joined the Dead after Pigpen's original replacement, Tom Constanten, left. Two months later, Donna, Keith's wife, joined the band as a vocalist and, though they remained aboard for seven years, some Dead aficionados felt (and feel) that the two never quite seemed to fit. In February 1979, agreeing that it might be best if they left, they did.

Keith and Donna assembled a new act called the Heart of Gold but, after just a single concert, Keith was killed in a California car accident. At 32, Keith was cremated and his ashes scattered off the coast of Marin County.

BRENT MYDLAND

OCTOBER 21, 1952 – JULY 26, 1990

PICKING UP WHERE Pigpen and Keith left off in the revolving-door keyboard spot, Brent Mydland joined up in 1979 and remained with the Dead through the '80s. In this period when the band became a full-blown cultural institution, Brent initially seemed a little overwhelmed, but he gained confidence after studio releases included some of his own songs, among them "Just a Little Light" and "Hell in a Bucket," which he co-wrote with Bob Weir. Eventually Brent was singing lead and trading verses on a number of songs.

Three days after the summer tour, Brent died at home of "acute cocaine and narcotic intoxication."

At 37, he was buried at Oakmont Memorial Park in Pleasant Hills, California.

GRAVE DIRECTIONS: Enter the cemetery at 2099 Reliez Valley Road, drive up the hill past the office, then, at the top of the hill, loop left around the Lesher mausoleum before the Garden of Meditation. Turn at the next right, go straight through the next intersection (the Garden of Hope will be in front of you), then bear left. After another hundred yards, stop at the "Always In Our Hearts" bench on the left in the Garden of Remembrance. Brent's grave is in the row above this bench, 18 markers to the left.

JERRY GARCIA

AUGUST 1, 1942 – AUGUST 9, 1995

IN THE SPRING of 1960, after just nine months of association, the Army and Jerry Garcia had had enough of each other, and the two parted ways. An aspiring musician, Jerry next embarked on a hand-to-mouth existence with future Dead lyricist Robert Hunter, and the two lived out of their broken-down cars, which were stranded next to each other in a Palo Alto parking lot. To make ends meet in the barest way, Jerry was filling in at a music store and giving guitar lessons whenever he could find a willing victim. Eventually, however, after a few lean years that included gigs at pizza parlors, things started to fall into place. By 1965 Jerry was frontman of his Grateful Dead progeny and, as the house band for the "acid tests" of Ken Kesey's "Merry Pranksters," the band played what would be the soundtrack for everything '60s, while Jerry himself came to be known as "Captain Trips," the personification of all that was groovy.

As his band steamrolled through the 1970s, Jerry also pursued an array of side projects, including the bluegrass group Old And In The Way, guest spots with a number of popular artists, solo efforts, and touring with his own Jerry Garcia Band in the lulls between Dead tours. In the next decade, though, Jerry's solo output slowed as he battled heroin addiction, and in 1986 Deadheads were spooked when Jerry went into a diabetic coma, from which he emerged seemingly unscathed five days later.

By the time the 1990s rolled around, the Dead was a cultural powerhouse and a concert phenomenon that couldn't misstep; even a line of Jerry-designed ties netted a few million dollars. But Jerry was still addicted and in the summer of 1995 checked into a California drug-rehab facility named Serenity Knolls. During a routine bed check Captain Trips was found dead of a heart attack there, expiring in a very spartan room that contained little more than a dresser and a closet. Witnesses said, "it looked like he just went to sleep."

At 53, Jerry was cremated. Some of his ashes were scattered in the Pacific Ocean and others were placed in the Ganges River near the town of Rishikesh, India.

WOODY GUTHRIE

JULY 14, 1912 – OCTOBER 3, 1967

BORN OF OKLAHOMA hardscrabble people, Woody Guthrie had almost no formal education, his father died drunk, and his sister died after she set herself on fire. But out of that heartache and adversity, and as a caustic witness to the impasses that mark the psyche of America's everyman—oil field busts, labor union lock-outs, Depression and Dust Bowl despair, World War horror, and Cold War paranoia—Woody bequeathed his inimitable folk songs and colloquial prose.

At 18, long after his family had broken up and the oil prosperity of Woody's hometown went bust, he began a journey that he never entirely abandoned. By 1933, he was married with three children and living in Texas but, while the Great Depression had made it hard to scrape together an existence, the Dust Bowl that hit in 1935 made it nearly impossible. Leaving his family behind, Woody and his guitar embarked on a Steinbeckian odyssey, joining the mass migration of Okie refugees who plodded westward in search of opportunity.

By the time he arrived, hungry and broke, in California in 1937, Woody had suffered the scorn of the outsider, a badge he wore the rest of his life. After walking into a Los Angeles radio station, he became a regular, performing his corpus of "people's songs": "I Ain't Got No Home," "Talking Dust Bowl Blues," and "Hard Travelin'," among dozens of others. The radio gig provided Woody a pulpit for commentary on everything from unionists to legislators, from Jesus Christ to John Dillinger. Not surprisingly, he railed against the establishment; he even abdicated his own rights in a songbook of lyrics: "This song is copyrighted for a period of 28 years, and anybody caught singin' it without our permission will be mighty good friends of ourn, cause we don't give a dern. Publish it. Write it. Sing it. Swing to it. Yodel it. We wrote it, that's all we wanted to do. W.G."

Never comfortable in one place for too long, Woody hitch-hiked east in 1940 and, along the way, wrote, "This Land Is Your Land," inspired by Irving Berlin's "God Bless America." In New York, Woody was embraced for his "authenticity," and cultural anthropologist Alan Lomax recorded him in a series of conversations and songs that are today's folk music touchstones. Then, in what seemed to be a departure from his philosophies, Woody accepted an obligation from the Bonneville Power Commission to write songs for a film promoting the development of the Columbia River and its newly constructed Grand Coulee Dam. The resulting *Columbia River Songs* was yet another remarkable collection.

Amidst all this activity, Woody remarried and, in a period of relative domestic stability, completed a semi-autobiographical account of the Dust Bowl, *Bound for Glory*. While World War II raged, he had four children with this second wife, but even they were not enough to exempt him from the draft, and he served until 1946.

Returning home to Coney Island, Woody formed the Weavers with Pete Seeger, which became the most successful folk group of its era. But after just a few years, restless and disillusioned with New York's "sissified and nervous rules of censorship," he rolled out again and, in California, married a third time. Around this time, Woody's behavior became unpredictable and his guitar-playing erratic. Confused about his condition, he took the only reasonable course of action and hit the road yet again, eventually tracing a path back to New York.

After being mistakenly diagnosed with everything from alcoholism to schizophrenia, in 1954 Woody admitted himself to a New Jersey hospital. It was later learned that he suffered from Huntington's chorea, a degenerative disease of the nervous system that would slowly steal from him every physical and mental capacity. Upon learning that the affliction is inherited maternally, Woody realized that it had also been responsible for his sister's death.

For the next dozen years, Woody deteriorated in a shuffle among various infirmaries, while his hundreds of songs were made popular by the newest folk revival. Finally unable to sit up or even speak, Woody died at 55 at a hospital in Queens, New York.

Woody was cremated and family members, including his son, Arlo (yes, *that* Arlo Guthrie), threw his container of ashes into the ocean. Waves soon tossed it back onto the beach, so for a second attempt, the container was opened to prevent floating and, while the wind whipped some of the ash back into their faces, the ghost of Woody Guthrie slipped beneath the Atlantic surf.

BILL HALEY

JULY 6, 1925 – FEBRUARY 9, 1981

BILL HALEY LED country-and-western bands around the Philadelphia area beginning in 1942, but by the early 1950s he had morphed the style of his band, the Comets, into a new sound that would eventually become rock and roll.

In fact, it can be fairly argued that Bill is the true father of rock music, which he bore at around 4:30 p.m. on April 12, 1954, in a Manhattan sound studio. From the moment when the studio's silence was broken by drummer Billy Gussak's two sharp rim shots, music would never again be the same. After the drum opening, Bill Haley shouted out the inspired and immortal words, "One-two-three o'clock, four o'clock ROCK!" and the song "Rock Around the Clock" became the international anthem of rock music. The song was perfect and, though it's since been covered by hundreds of artists, none has ever captured the special magic of Bill Haley and the Comets on that spring day in New York City.

Though "Rock Around the Clock" went to the stratosphere, the song proved to be Bill's highwater mark and, throughout the remainder of his life, he was content to release just the occasional recording and tour with various rock and roll revival shows.

At 55, Bill died in his sleep of a heart attack at home in Harlingen, Texas. He was cremated and his ashes remain with his family.

RICHIE HAVENS
JANUARY 21, 1941 – APRIL 22, 2013

RICHIE HAVENS LANDED in Greenwich Village when he was 17. He spent his days crouching his 6-foot-6 frame in front of an easel, painting portraits of tourists to make a spare living during the day, while he perfected his earthy music style at night, playing engagements at clubs with names like The Fat Black Pussycat. A couple of albums, including 1967's *Mixed Bag*, gained him limited recognition but it was when he opened the 1969 Woodstock music festival that he strummed himself into rock music immortality.

It wasn't supposed to be that way. Richie was scheduled to be the fifth act onstage but when the equipment of other artists got stuck in traffic on the New York Thruway, opportunity banged on his dressing room door in the form of organizers who pressed him to start the show. "It was five o'clock and nothing was happening yet," he remembered. "I was supposed to sing forty minutes, which I did, and from the side of the stage they go, 'Richie, four more songs?' I went back and did that, then it was, 'Four more songs...' and that kept happening 'til it was two hours and forty-five minutes later I had sung every song I knew."

As he sat on a stool and strummed his openly-tuned acoustic guitar in a fervent but rhythmic style, his booming, gravel-road voice mesmerized the hippie crowd. But the most majestic moment of the set actually came as he began to run out of material. Reminiscing many years later, Richie said he remembered "that word I kept hearing while I looked over the crowd in my first moments onstage. The word was: freedom." Chanting that word over and over, backed by his second guitarist and conga player, he eventually segued into the song "Sometimes I Feel Like a Motherless Child," which he had heard in church as a kid. The combined, surging medley wasn't just a crowd-pleaser; it later became a highlight of the *Woodstock* movie, which immortalized Richie and his orange dashiki.

In the years after Woodstock, Richie maintained his momentum with a score of albums, but onstage is where he was most in his element. Touring constantly, he claimed that he never planned his shows beyond the opening and closing songs.

"Many times people have come up to me after and they'd go, 'I wrote these songs down for you to sing and you sang 'em all in a row!' That's the kind of communication that happens, you know," he said. "It's like if you let the audience lead, then you are the audience."

At 72, Richie died of a massive heart attack. He was cremated and his ashes scattered at the site of the original Woodstock festival in Bethel, New York.

JIMI HENDRIX
NOVEMBER 27, 1942 – SEPTEMBER 18, 1970

JIMI HENDRIX'S CAREER and life were tragically brief, but his impact on music has spanned generations. The marriage of blues and rock that he initiated was a direct precursor to music as diverse as that of The Who and Prince, his guitar innovations set the stage for the heavy metal movement, and he inspired guitarists from Jimmy Page to Eddie Van Halen.

Jimi was of mixed heritage, black and Cherokee Indian, and after a shy and quiet adolescence he quit school and served in the Army for three years as a paratrooper. In 1964 he moved to New York and formed a band called Jimmy James and the Blue Flames, and after two years of playing Greenwich Village coffeehouses, Chas Chandler, the former Animals bassist, recognized Jimi's talent and moved him to London.

There, in 1967, the Jimi Hendrix Experience was born. Within six months, aided by the release of their epochal debut album, *Are You Experienced?*, and a ferociously climactic performance at the Monterey Pop Festival, the band had become one of the biggest rock acts on either side of the Atlantic.

The next two years saw the release of two more albums, each as successful as the debut, but by that time Jimi's life had devolved into confusion as disagreements among managers and bandmates created a revolving door of personnel. Some fans, not content to just let Jimi stand and play guitar, pressed him to take a political stance and make a public commitment to his roots.

It was easy for Jimi to lose his direction, and as he did, drinking and drugs became an increasingly larger part of his routine. While his girlfriend lay beside him, Jimi died at 27 of "suffocation due to inhalation of vomit during a heavily intoxicated sleep."

He was buried at Greenwood Memorial Park in Renton, Washington.

GRAVE DIRECTIONS: Enter the cemetery at 350 Monroe Avenue NE and you won't miss Jimi's 20-foot-high granite dome trimmed with rainbow marble.

JOHN LEE HOOKER

AUGUST 22, 1917 – JUNE 21, 2001

JOHN LEE HOOKER was the son of a sharecropping Baptist minister who discouraged his child's musical bent, but John's stepfather later taught him to play guitar, and by the time he was a teenager, John was performing at local fish fries and dances. Looking for work, he landed in Detroit, and in 1948 recorded his first hit, a foot-stomping guitar boogie called "Boogie Chillen."

John soon quit his janitorial job to pursue music full-time. He melded the country blues of his native Mississippi Delta with electric guitar, and his hypnotic, one-chord jams—which often included no intelligible words, just a discord of humming and mumbling in a mysterious, stream-of-consciousness growl—became John's hallmark. Over the next five decades, his foot-stomping songs, including "I'm In The Mood" and "Crawling King Snake," cemented his reputation as a key shaper of the modern blues and, by default, rock music.

Interestingly, as much as John was the quintessential Mississippi bluesman, he didn't succumb to the ills that often plagued his peers. He never had serious bouts with alcohol, drugs, or the law, and he didn't die broke. In his later years, John enjoyed his success by tooling around in his fleet of expensive cars and, occasionally, dropping in unannounced to tear through his catalog of hits at smoky music joints.

Toward the end of his life, when his legacy was sealed as a grandfather of music, John remained confounded by his success and confessed, "People say I'm a genius but I don't know about what."

At 83, John died of natural causes at home in his sleep, and now rests at the Chapel of Chimes Mausoleum in Oakland, California.

GRAVE DIRECTIONS: Enter the building at 4499 Piedmont Avenue through the glass doors toward the rear of the parking lot. Go to the end of the hall, turn left and then right, then take the elevator to the third floor. Out of the elevator, turn left and then right, and John's crypt is on the left, on the bottom after the French doors.

RICK JAMES

FEBRUARY 1, 1948 – AUGUST 6, 2004

WITH LONG HAIR styled in cascading braids and glistening Jheri curls, Rick James found his fortune with a seminal triple-platinum album released in 1981 called *Street Songs*. The album catapulted Rick to the forefront of his new "punk funk" style and its gritty and sexually explicit content bolstered his bad-boy reputation to a new zenith. Its biggest hit, "Super Freak," featured a female subject who was "the kind you don't take home to mother" but, as far as boys go, he may well have said the same thing about himself.

Interestingly, though the album sold dozens of times more copies than the relatively minor releases he had scored earlier, its success actually led to a parting between Rick and Motown as the label felt his graphic themes conflicted with the company's more conservative approach.

The album and the Motown parting saddled Rick with a rep that was tough to live down, and the 1980s found him kicking the party boundaries further and further in an attempt to bust himself and other players out of any ordinary existence he called "L Seven." Heavy involvement with methamphetamines and cocaine led to legal problems, health troubles, and, as one might expect, jail. In 1991 prosecutors said James and his girlfriend tied a woman to a chair, burned her with a hot crack pipe, and forced her to perform sex acts during a drug-induced binge at his home. While free on bail for those charges (of which he was eventually acquitted) he was arrested again, this time for punching a woman repeatedly in the face, and Rick ended up serving two years in Folsom Prison.

At 56, Rick was found dead in bed and he officially died of pulmonary/cardiac failure, with diabetes, an earlier stroke, and a pacemaker all listed as contributing factors. Later toxicology tests confirmed nine recreational drugs in his system which, it would seem to me, also affected his life circumstance negatively.

After some 6,000 well-wishers filed past Rick, who was smartly clad in a black suit with yellow shirt and two gold neck pendants, the cover to his casket was closed forever and he was interred at Forest Lawn Cemetery in Buffalo, New York.

GRAVE DIRECTIONS: Enter the cemetery at 1411 Delaware Avenue and bear left at three consecutive intersections. Then, when the drive begins sweeping hard to the right, stop, and in Section 10 on your left you won't miss Rick's gravestone reminding you that "God Is Love."

ROBERT JOHNSON
MAY 8, 1911 — AUGUST 16, 1938

IT'S GENERALLY ACCEPTED that the blues were born out of the hard times and suffering endured by Mississippi Delta blacks at the start of the twentieth century, and they've been called "a solo recitation of misery." Robert Johnson, were he alive today, would probably agree, as his songs certainly sprang from a life of poverty and squalor.

Born into the large family of a sharecropper, he learned to play the harmonica and guitar in the conventional "country blues" style, but it was his later development of guitar techniques that earned him the respect of modern musicians. Robert, it seems, was the first to play a guitar in the "finger-picking" style, a complex melody technique that allows one guitar to do the work of two by placing a treble-string melody over a constant bass-string accompaniment. And, though he didn't invent the bottleneck style in which a bottle is placed on the little finger of the fretting hand to yield that distinctive metallic *glissando* effect that's commonly heard in Hawaiian music, he certainly popularized and perfected it. Later, the bottleneck, or slide effect, as it's more commonly called, figured prominently in the works of artists such as Duane Allman and Jimi Hendrix.

Though Robert's lyrics were simple and colloquial, touching on the common themes of a longing to be somewhere else or of fleeting love, his compositions were fully developed and the language articulate. This was a significant departure from the traditional oral

improvisation common to his day's music. Further, he defined a song structure—instrumental, several verses, instrumental, verse, and end—that is used in rock music almost without variation today.

Robert Johnson recorded only 32 songs and never received a cent in royalties. In true blues fashion, his demise was dramatic: He was poisoned with strychnine-laced whiskey provided by a jealous husband. After three days of torturous agony, lolling madly on a makeshift cot amid the relentless humidity of a Mississippi summer, Robert died of his poisoning at 27.

He was buried at Little Zion Missionary Baptist Church Cemetery in Greenwood, Mississippi.

GRAVE DIRECTIONS: Three miles north of town on Route 518 is the cemetery, in the middle of which Robert rests in the shade of a pecan tree.

BRIAN JONES
FEBRUARY 28, 1942 – JULY 3, 1969

IF BRIAN JONES couldn't achieve rock immortality through the musical talent that burst from his seams, it seems he resolved to attain notoriety by virtue of the four different palimony suits that hung over him by age 24. But in the end, Brian was prematurely martyred as another rock-music casualty.

A sort of wandering and shiftless jazz and blues man, Brian eventually found his balance and drifted toward the new rock trends. By the end of 1962 Brian had formed his own band, the Rolling Stones, its lineup highlighted by guitarist Keith Richards and frontman Mick Jagger, while Charlie Watts thudded out the drum beats and Bill Wyman plucked bass lines. Through 1966, Brian was the leader of the band, nurturing them from ragtag anonymity to regal pop stars with a series of hit singles including "Ruby Tuesday," "Time Is on My Side," and "Heart of Stone."

By 1967, though, manager Andrew Oldham was increasingly developing the Jagger-Richards songwriting partnership to more effectively compete with their Lennon-McCartney rivals, and Brian, who had become the group's most substantial consumer of assorted recreational pharmaceuticals, was relegated to its margins. By the time of the *Beggar's Banquet* recording sessions in 1968, Brian's contributions were almost nil, and in June 1969 he officially departed the band citing musical differences.

All but forgotten a month later, Brian's status skyrocketed after newspaper headlines screamed he'd been found at the bottom of his swimming pool, dead at 27. A postmortem revealed that both his heart and liver were grossly enlarged due to long-term alcohol abuse, and traces of "an amphetamine-like substance" were found in his urine. However, no appreciable quantity of any other drugs was found in Brian's system and the final analysis handed down by the coroner declared his death was "by misadventure, cause of death drowning."

A horse-drawn hearse carried Brian to his neatly groomed grave near the chapel at Priory Road Cemetery in Prestbury, Gloucestershire, England.

HUDDIE "LEADBELLY" LEDBETTER

NOVEMBER 20, 1885 – DECEMBER 6, 1949

BORN ON A Louisiana plantation and surviving as an itinerant musician and sometime–farm laborer, Huddie "Leadbelly" Ledbetter personified the Delta bluesman. In 1918 Leadbelly received a 7-to-30-year prison sentence after pleading guilty to shooting a man to death in Texas, and it's been endlessly romanticized that he was pardoned after the governor heard a song of his in which he pleaded for release. Though Leadbelly did write such a song, it's clear that he was let out for good behavior after serving the minimum time.

In any event, Leadbelly was back behind bars by 1930. A white man had insisted to Leadbelly that "niggers is supposed to walk in the road" instead of on the sidewalk and, though he may have been guilty of assault after a scuffle ensued, the prosecution added that Leadbelly had "intended to murder," and he received six to 10 years of hard labor.

While on a 1933 tour of the South to document Negro work songs for the Library of Congress archives, John Lomax recorded Leadbelly in a Louisiana prison. Lomax returned the next year and Leadbelly, who sincerely believed that his Texas prison release came about because of that earlier ballad, convinced Lomax to put a similar ballad on the flip side of a recording of one of his favorite songs, "Goodnight Irene." Lomax personally delivered the record to Louisiana's governor and this time, the song may indeed have been instrumental in gaining Leadbelly's release, though Lomax's elucidation of the trumped-up charges upon which Leadbelly had been convicted didn't hurt.

In 1935 Leadbelly followed Lomax to New York and recorded the majority of his work there, including "Midnight Special" and "Gallows Pole," over the next dozen years. While his legend preceded him, Leadbelly performed tirelessly and played the part of a subservient Southern black that curious white audiences expected to see. Passing the hat after appearances in which he always played his "pardon songs," Leadbelly became the cajoling dark minstrel: "Bless Gawd, dat's a dime! Where is all de quarters? Thank you, boss! Thank you, missy, thank you!"

During a series of performances in Europe, Leadbelly's extremities grew numb and he died six months later, penniless at 64, from what was believed to be a particularly aggressive form of Lou Gehrig's disease.

Leadbelly was buried at Shiloh Baptist Church Cemetery in Mooringsport, Louisiana.

GRAVE DIRECTIONS: At 10395 Blanchard-Latex Road, Leadbelly's grave is surrounded by a black iron fence.

LISA "LEFT EYE" LOPES
MAY 27, 1971 – APRIL 25, 2002

LISA LOPES, A feisty rapper, songwriter, and keyboardist, was the "L" in the multimillion-selling rhythm-and-blues group TLC as well as the catalyst and onstage focus of the trio. Her self-given "Left Eye" moniker came about because a boy once told her she had beautiful eyes, "particularly the left eye," which was slightly larger, and she celebrated her nickname by wearing glasses with a condom over the left lens, which was later toned down into a mere trademark stripe under the eye.

TLC's breakout 1991 album, *Oooooohhh...on the TLC Tip*, spawned the hit "Ain't 2 Proud 2 Beg" and the group found traction with their looks and wardrobe. Their 1994 album, *CrazySexyCool*, addressing safe sex and black-on-black crime, was an even bigger hit and became the best-selling album by an all-female group, with 4 million–plus copies sold.

From the start, the TLC trio presented themselves as independent women and on the second album Lisa named herself "Crazy." That was also the year she pleaded guilty to arson for burning down her boyfriend's Atlanta mansion; to avenge his infidelity and alleged abuse, she had set fire to his tennis shoes and things got out of control.

In 1995 the group declared bankruptcy, saying that a meager royalty rate had left them broke. After a court upheld their filing and invalidated their old contract, TLC shopped for a new and better deal and roared back with another multi-platinum album. Followers in the fickle world of hip-hop stayed loyal and TLC toured sold-out arenas.

In 2002, as Lisa awaited the release of her first solo album, *Supernova*, she traveled to Honduras for a 30-day spiritual retreat with family and friends. While driving a Mitsubishi Pajero minivan with seven passengers on a winding and rolling mountain road, Lisa lost control and the van went off the road, flipping several times. Thrown from the vehicle, Lisa died instantly of head injuries, the sole fatality of the mishap.

At 30, she was buried at Hillandale Memorial Gardens in Lithonia, Georgia. Here's a snippet of the 172-word headstone epitaph that hangs over her grave like a bubble of cartoon dialogue: "Who's to blame for tootin 'caine into your own vein? What a shame you're shootin' aim for someone else's brain."

GRAVE DIRECTIONS: Enter the cemetery at 6201 Hillandale Drive and park in front of the office. Walk onto the lawn oriented so that your back is to the street, and you'll see Lisa's grave overlooking the pond, topped with the biggest tablet marker on the block.

LYNYRD SKYNYRD

RONNIE VAN ZANT
JANUARY 15, 1948 – OCTOBER 20, 1977

CASSIE GAINES
JULY 5, 1948 – OCTOBER 20, 1977

STEVE GAINES
SEPTEMBER 14, 1949 – OCTOBER 20, 1977

ALLEN COLLINS
JULY 19, 1952 – JANUARY 23, 1990

LEON WILKESON
APRIL 2, 1952 – JULY 27, 2001

BILLY POWELL
JUNE 3, 1952 – JANUARY 28, 2009

IN THE SUMMER of 1964 Ronnie Van Zant and four friends formed a band called the Noble Five, and that December they played their first paying gig at an auto-parts store's Christmas party. At the end of the night they were handed a single, crisp $10 bill and, after chipping in for gasoline, they strutted home with $1.75 each.

With nowhere to go but up, the bandmates practiced incessantly. Their band's name evolved into the peculiar Lynyrd Skynyrd, a play on the name of a gym teacher, Leonard Skinner, whom they particularly disliked for his dutiful enforcement of the school dress code prohibiting sideburns and long hair. By 1973 the Southern-style, rebel-rock band had gained a tremendous following throughout Florida, landed a deal with MCI Records, and seen their debut album, *(Pronounced 'Lĕh-'nérd 'Skin-'nérd)*, released. After they were tapped to be the opening act for The Who's U.S. tour later that year, they never looked back. By 1975, with two more best-selling albums under their belts, Lynyrd Skynyrd was one of America's hottest and hardest-working rock and roll acts.

Predictably, the temptations of the road took their toll, and Lynyrd Skynyrd picked up a well-deserved reputation as a collection of hellbent, redneck, rock-star drunks. Despite the hard partying, they remained true to their music and churned out a string of incendiary guitar-driven singles, "Gimme Three Steps," "Sweet Home Alabama," and "Saturday Night Special," to name a few. In 1976 the band made personnel changes in order to fine-tune its sound, the most critical being the addition of guitarist Steve Gaines and a female backup vocal group, the Honkettes, of which Steve's sister Cassie was a member. Charging with excitement, in January 1977 the lineup hit the road in support of their new album, *Street Survivors*.

In Greenville, South Carolina, after the 70th concert of a planned 80-concert tour, the band and its 12-person entourage boarded their leased Convair 240 and headed for their next gig in Baton Rouge, Louisiana. At 6:42 p.m. on October 20, 1977, the pilot radioed from 6,000 feet over McComb, Mississippi, that his craft was dangerously low on fuel and, less than 10 minutes later, the plane clipped the tops of branches over a swamp, then cut an 800-foot path through the trees until it lurched to a halt within the dense thicket. Because the plane had run out of fuel, it didn't burst into flames, and 18 people emerged from the wreckage with assorted injuries, some more serious than others. Not everyone survived, however, and among those killed were the new guitarist, Steve Gaines, and his sister Cassie, as well as the frontman and founder Ronnie Van Zant, without whom the real Lynyrd Skynyrd band ceased to exist. Who else could ever justly imitate his introduction of the song "Freebird": "What song is it you want to hear?"

At 29, Ronnie was laid to rest wearing his trademark black Texas Hatters cowboy hat and his favorite fishing pole was placed inside his coffin. After his original grave was defaced, his family chose to move him to Riverside Memorial Park in Jacksonville, Florida.

GRAVE DIRECTIONS: Enter the cemetery at 7242 Normandy Boulevard and the Van Zant family plot is immediately on the left.

Steve and Cassie Gaines had originally been buried next to Ronnie but, after the vandalism, their family moved the siblings to a private and undisclosed location.

On the 10th anniversary of the plane crash, most of the surviving original members of Lynyrd Skynyrd reunited for the Tribute tour in which lead vocals were provided by Ronnie's younger brother, Johnny. Besides those killed in the crash, a former band member glaringly absent from the lineup was Allen Collins, who had been in the original incarnation of the Noble Five and who had distinguished himself as lead guitarist. But Allen had also been one of the band's most notorious substance abusers both before and after the plane crash.

In 1986 Allen crashed his car while driving drunk, killing his girlfriend and leaving him paralyzed from the waist down. He pleaded no contest to DUI manslaughter, and his sentence required that he make public service announcements warning others of the consequences of drunk driving. Before each concert of the Tribute tour, Allen would roll up to the microphone and explain to fans that he was no longer able to play guitar that night, or any other night ever, due to a decision he had made to drive drunk another time long ago. With that, the musician watched from his wheelchair on the sidelines as his bandmates took center stage.

His lung capacity reduced due to the paralysis, Allen died at 37 after a bout with pneumonia and is buried near his old buddy Ronnie.

GRAVE DIRECTIONS: Enter the cemetery and drive past the fountain. Stop after about 75 yards and you'll see on the left a cement walk leading into the Garden of the Cross. Eighty feet down this walk is a stone bench inscribed "Collins-John." (John is the maiden name of Allen's wife, Kathy, who died in 1980 from complications after a pregnancy.) Opposite the bench are the graves of both Allen and Kathy.

Featuring three original band members—bass player Leon Wilkeson, pianist Billy Powell, and guitarist Gary Rossington—who teased the prying eyes of fans who longed for the Lynyrd Skynyrd of yesteryear, the Tribute incarnation stayed together for good and, with nine albums to their credit, have become a beer-soaked summer concert staple.

After more than a decade of thumping along in the band's new incarnation, Leon died in his sleep in a Florida hotel room during a brief break between shows. A medical examination found that he'd suffered from diseases of the liver and lungs and, after toxicology tests came back negative, it was ruled that he died of natural causes. At just 49, he was buried in the same park as Ronnie and Allen.

Leon was buried at Riverside Memorial Park Cemetery in Jacksonville, the same park as Allen.

GRAVE DIRECTIONS: Leon's grave is across the drive from Ronnie's, near the fountain on the left.

Believe it or not, Billy Powell, the only Lynyrd Skynyrd member with any formal college training in music theory, actually started with the band as a roadie, schlepping amps and speakers for a year before being "discovered" by Ronnie Van Zant himself. While setting up at a prep school's prom for which they had been hired to play (these really *were* the early years!), Billy noticed a piano in the corner. "I sat down and played them my version of 'Freebird,'" he remembered years later. "Ronnie came up to me and said, 'You mean to tell me, you've been working for us for a year and you can play piano like that?' So, right then and there, Ronnie said, 'We need a keyboard player.'"

Billy was a perfect fit and his keyboard talents invigorated the band with a new fullness of sound, while his "Freebird" intro evolved into a trademark concert highlight that never failed to ignite a wave of audience exhilaration within seconds of him tickling its first few notes. For the remainder of his life, Billy would cherish the memory of those wonderful dream-like years when everything clicked for the tight-knit group of friends who shared the bill with such juggernauts as the Rolling Stones.

Though the plane crash changed everything, Billy was fortunate enough to "only" suffer extensive facial lacerations including an almost completely severed nose. The first to be discharged from the hospital, he was the sole member able to attend his bandmates' funerals.

After the accident, Billy pursued a few music projects with ex-Skynyrd members, including the bands Alias and Rossington-Collins. After embracing religion, he excitedly joined with the Christian-rock band Vision in 1985, but that connection ended prematurely as Billy's late-night, carousing lifestyle clashed with the dreary habits of his Bible-thumping bandmates. In 1987 Billy reunited with fellow Skynyrd survivors for the Tribute tour, and ended up remaining with the band's new incarnation right up to his death. After a heart attack at 56, Billy was cremated.

THE MAMAS & THE PAPAS

"MAMA" CASS ELLIOT
SEPTEMBER 19, 1941 – JULY 29, 1974

"PAPA" JOHN PHILLIPS
AUGUST 30, 1935 – MARCH 18, 2001

DENNY DOHERTY
NOVEMBER 29, 1940 – JANUARY 19, 2007

DURING THE 1960s the Mamas and the Papas burst out of the Southern California pop scene and bombarded the Top 40 with lushly harmonized folk-pop songs. The group was formed by John Phillips, the creative talent and hit-writing machine of the foursome, after he pulled up stakes and left New York when the folk music scene went electric. The group's other three members—alto Cass Elliot, John's longtime collaborator Denny Doherty, and John's second wife, Michelle Phillips—contributed to the radiant blended sound, while session musicians provided the bulk of the instrumentation.

Projecting diversity in colorful hippie garb, they released a string of hit singles, including "California Dreamin'" and "Monday, Monday," and reigned among the hip vanguard that typified the newest breed of groups to follow in the Beatles' wake. But it all came apart in just a few years, as the quartet's intertwining romantic entanglements and chemical excesses strangled their ability to work together. They broke up in 1968 and reunited briefly in 1971 to make one last album per a contractual obligation, but that album flopped, and the Mamas and the Papas became only a fond memory.

Mama Cass Elliot then enjoyed a fairly successful solo career, but while in London for a two-week engagement at the Palladium, she died in 1974, alone in an apartment. A popular legend holds that Cass choked to death on a ham sandwich, but it's not at all true. Instead, a ham sandwich that she hadn't yet touched was on the table next to her bed when she suffered a heart attack. After an autopsy discovered "fatty myocardial degeneration," her official cause of death was ruled as heart failure due to obesity.

At 32, Cass was cremated and her ashes buried at Mount Sinai Memorial Park in North Hollywood, California.

GRAVE DIRECTIONS: Enter the park at 5950 Forest Lawn Drive, go up the hill, and as the drive bends left, the twin Courts of

Tanach are on the right. Cass lies in the first court, in the grass in the far left corner, under her given name, Ellen Naomi Cohen.

After John and Michelle divorced, Michelle embarked on an acting career. Meanwhile, John's life went into a tailspin and he spent most of the 1970s under the influence of one drug or another, often getting high with his teenage daughter, Mackenzie, who was a star on the *One Day at a Time* television series. A drug bust finally pushed him into therapy and, once clean and sober, John formed a reunion version of the group with Denny and two new Mamas.

At 65, John died of a heart attack. He now resides at Palm Springs Mortuary and Mausoleum in Cathedral City, California, where his crypt is emblazoned "California Dreamin'."

GRAVE DIRECTIONS: Enter the mortuary at 31705 Da Vall Drive, then walk back across the entrance lane, proceed alongside the fountain, then turn at the first left and the next right. John's crypt is on the left, just past the Frink family fountain, four rows from the bottom.

After the group's brief revival in 1982, Denny retreated to his native Nova Scotia and pursued his acting career, playing the Harbor Master in a popular children's television show called *Theodore Tugboat*. In 2003 his off-Broadway show called *Dream a Little Dream: The Mamas and the Papas Musical*, which traced the band's early years, dizzying arc of fame, and breakup amid drugs and alcohol, was well received. But he found it emotionally draining. "There's a part of this thing that if I'm not careful, I'd be just a blob on the stage crying my guts out," he explained. "It's an exercise in staying in the moment and not getting maudlin about your friends dying."

At 66 Denny died of an abdominal aneurysm and was buried at Gate of Heaven Cemetery in Lower Sackville, Nova Scotia.

GRAVE DIRECTIONS: At 33 Old Sackville Road, enter the cemetery at the entrance next to the main office and drive straight up to Section 6G, at the top of the hill behind the maintenance shop. Denny's stone is eight rows from the drive in the middle of the section.

BOB MARLEY
FEBRUARY 6, 1945 – MAY 11, 1981

EVEN THOUGH BOB Marley never had a U.S. hit, he stands as one of the most warmly regarded figures in all of popular music. Within the loose framework of a reggae rhythm that seemed to command listeners to fall into its groove, Bob turned simple lyrics into sharp criticisms, and his outpouring of grief for his beloved but corrupt Jamaican homeland stirred consciences worldwide.

Born to a young black mother and an older white father, Bob grew up in a lush hamlet, high in the mountains of Jamaica. In 1962, at just 17, he cut his first single and, throughout the next decade, made a number of recordings for small Jamaican labels with his backing group, the Wailers. But commercial success eluded Bob and in 1969 he took a chance on a nine-to-five routine at a Wilmington, Delaware, auto factory.

Bob soon returned to Jamaica and, with a fresh focus plus the enthusiasm of a new producer and record company, recorded a landmark album, *Catch a Fire*, in 1973. The work, packaged and marketed like a rock album, was astutely promoted to rock audiences and once Eric Clapton covered "I Shot the Sheriff" the following year, the transition was complete; the gritty and unique blend of rock, blues, and West Indies folk caught on and Bob Marley and the Wailers became stars.

As Bob's patterned melodies and endless hooks ramped his success skyward, he also gained credibility as a social leader. But even as a national hero and the King of Reggae, he could not bring change to the tormented social landscape of Jamaica. Bob was a Rastafarian—a member of the religious movement that favors nature, simplicity, marijuana, and, above all, peace—and was committed to peaceful revolution. Unfortunately, Jamaica's government recognized only the sword. In December 1976, two days before he was to give a free "Smile Jamaica" concert aimed at reducing tensions between warring political factions, gunmen attacked him and his entourage. Nobody was killed, though bullets grazed both Bob and his wife, and the incident served only to further galvanize his political outlook. Later works, especially *Exodus* and *Survival*, featured an urgent militant bent.

In 1977 a cancerous growth was found on a toe that he had injured years earlier while playing soccer. By 1980 the cancer had invaded his vital organs, and Bob died at 36 of brain cancer at a Miami clinic the following summer.

Just steps away from the small stone house in which he was born, Bob lies in a white mausoleum surrounded by a fence splashed with the black, yellow, and green colors of Jamaica. On his birthday, which in 1991 was proclaimed a national holiday, performers celebrate his memory on a nearby stage. The site is in the tiny village of Nine Mile, 70 miles northwest of Kingston, accessible from the B3 road.

FREDDIE MERCURY
SEPTEMBER 5, 1946 – NOVEMBER 24, 1991

DURING THE INFANCY and coming of age of "manufactured sound" in the 1970s, the British rock band Queen took great pride in the fact that its music featured no synthesizers. The group instead emphasized electric guitars (albeit heavily mixed) layered over smooth vocal harmonies, while the shrill lead was provided by flamboyant frontman Freddie Mercury.

Born in the British colony of Zanzibar as Farrokh Bulsara, his Parsi family settled in England when he was 13. After obtaining a degree in graphic arts, Freddie flitted about London's eclectic underground during the 1960s, selling clothing and artwork at the Kensington market during the day and singing with a variety of fledgling groups by night.

He eventually joined the group Smile, and in 1971, when fellow songwriter John Deacon joined up, they changed the band's name to Queen. The group found success with a quick streak of well-received singles and in 1975 was catapulted to superstardom by the overwhelming response to their masterpiece album, *A Night at the Opera*. Record executives were initially reluctant to release "Bohemian Rhapsody" as the album's promotional single—with a playing time approaching six minutes, melodramatic élan, and striking tempo changes, it broke the traditional rules about what constituted a commercially viable song—but the band members persisted and the song raced up the charts. Further, a short film they cobbled together to help promote the song is credited with kick-starting the music-video age.

Over the next decade, Queen toured worldwide and Freddie became renowned for his odd stage mannerisms and outlandish outfits. During the late 1980s it appeared that Queen had topped out in the studio, and each of the members pursued solo interests, though the band never really disintegrated. Instead, it chugged along in a state of arrested development, existing, it seemed, only to drain concert-goers' pocketbooks.

Among other projects, Freddie recorded with Spanish opera star Montserrat Caballe and, at home, he found a passion for the exotic Japanese fish *koi*, which sell for many thousands of dollars each. "Excess is part of my nature. Dullness is a disease," he explained.

In the late 1980s it became a sort of open secret that Freddie was suffering from AIDS, but visual confirmation came only in May 1991, when the band released their "These Are the Days of Our Lives" video featuring a shockingly emaciated and sickly

Mercury. Six months later, he died at his Kensington home of AIDS-related bronchial pneumonia.

At 45, Freddie was cremated at West London Crematorium in Kensal Green, England. Nobody seems to be sure what became of his ashes. Some say they are kept by a lover, while others maintain they were dispersed over Lake Geneva in Montreux, Switzerland, where he owned a cottage.

JIM MORRISON
DECEMBER 8, 1943 – JULY 3, 1971

AS LEAD SINGER and lyricist of the Doors, Jim Morrison's theatrical shock tactics and poetic (though sometimes disturbing) hyperbole came to symbolize the temptations and excesses of rock and roll. Full of himself, loaded with charisma and antics, Jim overshadowed the other members of the Doors. To their credit, however, they always seemed content to stand back and let Jim take center stage while they played the swirling and eclectic psychedelic rock music that was, in effect, the soundtrack of Jim's life.

Jim grew up the son of a strict and authoritarian Navy rear admiral, and this might have been a source of his outlandish rebellion. He would often falsely claim that both his parents were dead. Jim enrolled in UCLA's film and theater program in 1964, but found drugs, particularly LSD, more interesting than his studies. In 1965 he drifted from school and, together with classmate Ray Manzarek, formed the Doors.

In the summer of 1967 when their first album was released, Jim was still a slightly tentative frontman, but as the group rose to prominence and flower-power rockers pulsed to the hypnotizing rhythm of its "Light My Fire" single, Jim quickly worked himself into his role in grand fashion. Their next album, *Strange Days*, solidified the group's success, and Jim's throaty baritone and onstage persona became anything but shy, delivering keenly suggestive lyrics in alternate turns as a sullen poet and a fevered lunatic. His onstage behavior became increasingly erratic and exceedingly bizarre. After barrages of profanity at a show in New Haven, Connecticut, Jim was arrested on obscenity charges; in Miami, mimicking sex put Jim behind bars for lewd and lascivious behavior. Jim's indulgence in every hedonistic excess offstage and his off-the-wall behavior onstage put the band's very stability and survival at risk.

After the riotous concerts of 1969, the band went back to their songwriting roots and released two albums over the next two years; it seemed that perhaps Jim's spirit for good old rock and roll might be rejuvenated. When tours to promote the albums were announced, everyone hoped the over-the-top discord was in the past, but again, the shows were marked by controversy. Prompted by Jim's reputation, local police were a constant and intimidating presence, and the magic of the Doors live performances was lost. Fed up with the pressures from every direction, Jim withdrew and, in March 1971, went to Paris to unwind and write poetry with his companion, Pam Courson.

According to Pam, at 5:00 a.m. one morning, she found Jim lying in the bathtub of their apartment at 17 rue Beautreillis in Paris, dead as a doornail. Oddly, only Dr. Max Vassille, who signed Jim's death certificate, and Pam actually saw Jim's corpse. No autopsy was done, but on the death certificate Vassille stated that Jim had died of a heart problem aggravated by the use of alcohol followed by an abrupt change of temperature. In short, while half in the bag, Jim plopped into his bath and the sudden temperature change prompted a heart attack. Yeah, the whole thing smells fishy to me too.

Due to the mysterious circumstances surrounding Jim's demise and subsequent burial, theories ranging from accidental heroin overdose to murder have been trotted out as the "true" cause of his death. Some believe Jim never even died but merely staged it to escape the chains of stardom.

Jim, or at least his coffin, was interred at Paris' Père-Lachaise Cemetery. Drawing a million visitors per year, Jim's tomb is the fourth most popular tourist stop in Paris, which says reams about Jim, and Paris for that matter.

GRAVE DIRECTIONS: This celebrated graveyard and Jim's personal space are marked by signs off the Boulevard de Charonne.

In June 1970, Jim and Patricia Kennealy, a practicing witch, were married in a Celtic ceremony. Still, Jim's one-page will was quite simple and clear: Everything was left to Pam. Less than three years after Jim's death, Pam died of a heroin overdose in her Hollywood apartment. Like Jim, she was 27.

Pam was cremated and her ashes interred at Fairhaven Memorial Park in Santa Ana, California. Her nameplate is engraved "Pamela Susan Morrison," though, by all accounts, she and Jim never wed.

ROY ORBISON

APRIL 23, 1936 – DECEMBER 6, 1988

ROY WAS AN introverted and subdued performer but, blessed with a clear tenor that soared into an angelic falsetto, his voice was riveting. In dramatic ballads of isolation like "Blue Bayou" and "Crying," Roy's songs received endless radio airplay during the 1960s. Later career forays into rockabilly and then rock and roll were well received by adoring fans as well.

After his wife died in a motorcycle accident and two children perished in a fire, Roy stopped writing songs, and his career ebbed for 15 years. But in the 1980s it was rejuvenated when contemporary rock artists—musicians he'd influenced—brought a new popularity to his original songs. Roy was inducted into the Rock & Roll Hall of Fame, was featured in a cable-television special, toured regularly again, and had aligned with an all-star cast of musicians who together released a smash album as the Traveling Wilburys. Roy's career was back on track when, at 52, he died of a heart attack.

Roy was buried at Westwood Memorial Park in Los Angeles.

GRAVE DIRECTIONS: This little cemetery is just behind the office complex at 10850 Wilshire Boulevard. Many folks seem to have a hard time believing or understanding it, but Roy is in an unmarked grave (as is Frank Zappa just 25 feet away). Walk from the office into the central lawn area and count up eight rows to Frank Tuttle's stone. Roy's grave is in the next patch of grass, just left of the water spigot.

GRAM PARSONS

NOVEMBER 5, 1946 – SEPTEMBER 19, 1973

GRAM PARSONS, BORN Cecil Ingram Connors III, never hit it big, but has nonetheless become something of a cult figure in musical circles. His groundbreaking style of rock music, a seamless acoustic weave with a decidedly country tilt that he labeled "Cosmic American," was a direct precursor to such bands as the Eagles, and Gram's champions firmly maintain, "If Gram had lived…"

In 1968 Gram befriended Byrds bassist Chris Hillman and, almost before he knew it, had become a Byrds bandmember and was sparring for leadership with Roger McGuinn. He spearheaded their country-influenced *Sweetheart of the Rodeo* album, but immediately after its release, Gram and Chris quit the Byrds and

formed their own group, The Flying Burrito Brothers, which met only limited success. In 1972 Gram put out a solo album, *G.P.*, and followed that with *Grievous Angel*, though he never lived to see its release.

A few weeks after completing the *Grievous Angel* sessions, Gram went with some friends to visit California's Joshua Tree National Monument, one of his favorite places. Much of the day was spent at a motel pool drinking, smoking, and injecting a variety of substances. By nightfall, Gram had had enough and went to his room to sleep. A few hours later Gram's friends found him in a particularly deep slumber and a coroner later determined he had died of "drug toxicity, due to multiple drug use." Even in death, though, 26-year-old Gram was denied the attention he deserved; coverage of his demise was eclipsed by Jim Croce's death the following day.

After Gram's stepfather was informed of the death, he arranged for Gram's body to be flown to New Orleans for burial, but then, things got weird.

When Phil Kaufman, Gram's manager, learned that Gram had died, he was immediately reminded of a pact he'd made with Gram: After one of them died, "the survivor would take the other guy's body out to Cap Rock (a promontory at Joshua Tree), have a few drinks, and burn it." Once he was sufficiently liquored up, Kaufman decided to make good on his promise and, after having ferreted out the shipping arrangements, he and another friend, Michael Martin, dummied up some paperwork, drove out to the airport in a borrowed hearse, signed the release "Jeremy Nobody," and made off with Gram's remains. The two drunken body-snatchers then drove 150 miles to Joshua Tree and by moonlight dragged the coffin as close to Cap Rock as they could. Kaufman pried open the lid, poured in gasoline, and tossed in a match. As a giant fireball rose from the coffin, the two headed back home.

The story of Gram's hijacked and burnt corpse got more coverage in the newspapers than did his life and death (just as it does here), and there was even speculation that the amateur cremation was "ritualistic." The police, of course, were looking for Kaufman and Martin, and in short order they turned themselves in. Since a corpse has no intrinsic value, the two were charged with misdemeanor theft for stealing the coffin and ordered to pay $708 in damages, and fined an additional $300 each.

Meanwhile, Gram's charred remains were sent back to his stepfather, who had them buried at the Garden of Memories Cemetery in Metairie, Louisiana.

GRAVE DIRECTIONS: Enter the cemetery at 4900 Airline Drive; turn at the second right and then again at the next right. After the hairpin left, you'll see a large sculpture of *The Last Supper* in the field on the right. Fifty yards in front of this sculpture are two large hardwood trees. Between these two trees a large rectangular bronze relief of Gram marks his remains.

CARL PERKINS
APRIL 9, 1932 – JANUARY 19, 1998

IN 1953 CARL Perkins worked as a baker by day, but his nights were spent performing hillbilly songs at Tennessee honky-tonks in a band with his brothers. After overhearing a boy telling his date not to step on his blue suede shoes, Carl wrote the words on a potato sack. They would become the refrain of his most famous song, and in March 1956 his "Blue Suede Shoes" stomped up the charts. But as the song rose to the top, Carl was involved in a near-fatal traffic accident and, in the hiatus while he recovered, an upcoming artist named Elvis Presley covered "Blue Suede Shoes" and capitalized on the popularity Carl had been building.

His thunder stolen by an unfortunate turn of events and, unable to pen another hit song to regain his momentum, Carl never conquered the world of pop, although his place in music history was assured. Though Carl was inducted into the Rock & Roll Hall of Fame in 1987, he confessed that his biggest thrill was getting a gold record for "Blue Suede Shoes." "After all those days, the dreams came true in a gold record on a piece of wood. It's in my den where I wear it out looking at it every day."

At 65, Carl died after a series of strokes and was buried at Ridgecrest Cemetery in Jackson, Tennessee.

GRAVE DIRECTIONS: At 200 Ridgecrest Road, enter through the entrance with the brick columns and drive directly to the cemetery's rear. You'll see two mausoleums and there, in the one on the left, approximately in the center and at eye level, is Carl.

TOM PETTY
OCTOBER 20, 1950 – OCTOBER 2, 2017

TOM PETTY WAS never much of a student, and after briefly meeting Elvis Presley in a "life-altering moment" when he was 11, about the only thing that was on his adolescent mind was getting himself in a band and getting the heck out of Dodge—or at least out of Gainesville, Florida. At 16 Tom said goodbye to high school and after a few spare years scrounging for gigs around the Florida bar scene, he packed up with his Mudcrutch bandmates and the quintet split for Los Angeles.

But that band broke up soon after reaching California, and it wasn't until 1976 that Tom found his rock and roll stride with the album *Tom Petty and the Heartbreakers*, especially on the strength of its lead single and perpetual concert jam favorite, "Breakdown." Subsequent singles from the group's follow-up effort, *You're Gonna Get It!*, such as "Listen to Her Heart" and "I Need to Know," cemented the band's durability. Over the next decades Tom wrote dozens of succinct and hardheaded yet sentimental anthems that melded radio-ready rock with a stubborn down-home heritage written for the workaday everyman. With a pronounced nasal drawl that yielded a grainy and unpretty voice by any classical measure, Tom spoke for tight-lipped underdogs and irritable outsiders, while his soundtracks by turns veered between ringing folk rock and twanging country rock, as well as an occasional clever and uncategorizable arrangement such as "Don't Come Around Here No More." Steering clear of elaborate showmanship in concert, Tom let loose his full quiver of crowd-pleasers, including "Free Fallin'" and "Learning to Fly" while tossing in extended psychedelia-tinged jams too.

Living alone after a divorce, during the 1990s Tom fell into heroin addiction, which he overcame through rehab before a second marriage that was presided over by none other than ordained minister rock star Little Richard.

Earning a marvelous freedom to do whatever he wanted with his career after a long and steady cycle of recording and touring, in 2008 Tom shocked everyone by re-forming Mudcrutch for a new album and tour. Then, back with the Heartbreakers in 2014, he brought the band to a surprising milestone when, finally, after nearly 40 years together, their new album, *Hypnotic Eye*, became their first number one release. Back on the road in 2017, Tom said, "I'm thinking it may be the last trip around the country. We're all on the backside of our sixties.... I don't want to spend my life on the road."

Tom died at 66 and it was first reported that a heart attack had done him in. But three months later, upon the release of the official findings of the medical examiner, it came to light that his death was due to an accidental drug overdose as a result of mixing medications, including opioids. Tom was cremated and his ashes remain with his family.

ELVIS PRESLEY
JANUARY 8, 1935 – AUGUST 16, 1977

BORN IN TUPELO, Mississippi, Elvis Presley had a childhood similar to many other poor whites in the South. His father was a laborer who earned barely enough for the family to live on, and nowhere did there seem to be any hope for or indication of the kind of fame Elvis would later find. The family moved to Memphis and, after graduating high school, young Elvis got a job as a $41-per-week truck driver, a respectable enough career. That is, until Sam Phillips came along.

Under Sam's direction at Sun Studios in 1954, the budding superstar recorded his first single, "That's All Right, Mama," and, with his sexy sneer, suggestive hip gyrations, and breathy vocals, Elvis was an instant phenomenon. As the eye of a musical hurricane, he turned the establishment on its ear with one hit after another, eventually recording more than 700 songs. By the time of his death, he had sold some 600 million records. Now, more than 40 years after his death, the number is beyond counting.

But Elvis' appeal wasn't just limited to his swiveling hips and rockabilly sound. He had personal charm and bedroom eyes that Hollywood could hardly ignore. After a two-year stint in the Army, fostering a clean, all-American image, he married the daughter of a military officer and gave up live concerts with the intent of leading a quiet family life. But Elvis was soon persuaded to sign a movie contract and he made a series of films, some of which are almost painfully unwatchable. In Elvis' defense, though, his charisma made a few of them, such as *Jailhouse Rock* and *Viva Las Vegas*, genuinely entertaining.

In 1968, aware that his music career was foundering, Elvis went back on the road and jumpstarted the beginning of his tragic end with a period that bordered on self-parody as the burlesque "Las Vegas Elvis." In rhinestone jumpsuits topped with sequined capes, an overweight, drowsy-looking, mumbling, and sweaty incarnation of his former vibrant self held onstage court over swooning fans in more than a thousand performances. At the start of this period, his returns to the stage were often exciting, over-the-top productions, but eight years later, he wallowed in the depths as a sagging, 275-pound caricature of "Elvis the Pelvis," a pitiful reminder of the pitfalls of fame.

A new round of performances was scheduled for August 1977 and, as usual, they quickly sold out. In the week before the concerts began, Elvis hung around his Graceland mansion; he read his Bible, swam in the pool, played with his daughter, ate cheeseburgers, played racquetball, and took his ungodly regimen of assorted pills. After a 10:00 p.m. visit to the dentist for two porcelain fillings, Elvis returned home and, unable to sleep, batted a racquetball around with his cousin, Billy Smith, until about 4:00 a.m. Elvis then joined his current girlfriend, Ginger Alden, in bed and reportedly read for a couple hours. She fell asleep around six and upon waking at nine saw that Elvis still hadn't slept. In his best blue pajamas, he excused himself to the bathroom with the book *The Scientific Search for the Face of Jesus*, and that's the last time the 42-year-old King of Rock and Roll was seen alive. Around two that afternoon, Ginger found a bloated Elvis, with the book beside him, slumped in a fetal position on the brown shag carpet of his bathroom floor, and he wasn't breathing. Elvis had left the building.

A medical examiner declared that Elvis had died of cardiac arrhythmia—in layman's terms, he had a heart attack—and there was no indication of drug abuse of any kind. However, when the laboratory studies of his autopsy specimens were finally completed by toxicologists at the University of Utah in January 1978, 11 drugs, all consistent with medical treatment, were found to be present in the singer's system at the time of his death. Four of the drugs, all commonly known sedatives, painkillers, and depressants, were present in significant amounts. The remaining seven drugs were said to be present in insignificant amounts and one of them, morphine, has been trotted out as supposed proof that Elvis overdosed. However, toxicologists maintain that the trace amounts of morphine found in his system were solely a byproduct of the codeine sedatives; Elvis never actually ingested morphine. Well, not immediately prior to his death anyway.

Although there were a host of drugs in his system, Elvis actually died of heart disease. Though he would have been better off if he had laid off the drugs, Elvis had a weak cardiovascular system, and what he really needed was to lay off the cheeseburgers and play a lot more racquetball.

Dressed in a white suit, Elvis and his $3,600 copper casket were interred in a crypt at Forest Hills Cemetery for a short time. But in October 1977, two deranged fans attempted some manner of body snatching, and Elvis was removed from Forest Hills and buried at his 14-acre Graceland estate across town.

GRAVE DIRECTIONS: Just get yourself to Memphis and follow the tour buses to Elvis Presley Boulevard and Graceland. You won't miss it.

At Graceland, everything Elvis is on display. But if you can do without the memorabilia sideshow, and wish only to pay respects at the King's grave, simply arrive before 9 a.m. to gain free entry. And later, with the $29 admission you saved, thrill your family and friends with garish mementos such as a shot glass or potholder available from the gift shop.

THE RAMONES

AFTER FRIENDS JEFFREY Hyman, Douglas Colvin, John Cummings, and Tom Erdelyi alternately graduated or flunked out of New York high schools in 1973, they formed a punk-rock band comprising fictitious brothers, the Ramones—Joey, Dee Dee, Johnny, and Tommy, respectively. The adopted Ramone surname was borrowed from Paul McCartney, who had used it for incognito travel, but any commonality between conventional rock stars and the Ramones ended right there.

The Ramones were musicians strictly in the academic sense; they owned instruments and used them to make sounds. Tommy spent just two weeks mastering the drums before the band played its first gig. Dee Dee freely admitted that he never actually learned the notes on his bass but just "thump(ed) away on one string."

Though the Ramones were the first punk act to score a record deal, they weren't soul-searching lyricists, heartstring-tugging balladeers, or memorable melody makers. In their catalog of almost 200 frenetically paced songs, the average ditty clocked in at 2:19, prompting one wag to comment that the sole purpose of a Ramones song seemed to be to finish it as quickly as possible. They released 18 albums but only twice grazed the U.S. Top 100, and they never scored a real hit. Nonetheless, the Ramones did something right and their remarkable success can be attributed to the sheer power of persistence.

A few personnel changes notwithstanding, they were a hard-working band and spent 20 grueling years together. In 1989 Dee Dee said, "People always ask why we're still together. It's because we don't have a hit single and we still gotta work for a living." Although they were increasingly relegated to the music fringes, and despite their lack of commercial success, the Ramones never retreated from their punk cause and remained true to their legions of rabid fans. Years into the gig, their cartoon-like distinction continued and they blazed through songs like "I Don't Wanna Be Learned," "Now I Wanna Sniff Some Glue," and "Gimme Gimme Shock Treatment" with the same fiery intensity. In 2002 the Ramones were inducted into the Rock & Roll Hall of Fame.

JEFFREY "JOEY RAMONE" HYMAN

MAY 19, 1951 – APRIL 15, 2001

FROM BEHIND A curtain of long and straight black hair, Joey, the wraith-thin frontman, ignited manic audiences with yelped chants like "Hey, Ho, Let's Go!" or the trademark "Gabba Gabba Hey!" for two decades. His grim, leather-clad image was what initially endeared Joey to discontented youth but it was his deadpan, no-nonsense approach that retained the fan base.

When the Ramones finally broke up in 1996 after more than 2,200 pile-driving live shows, Joey continued as an outspoken opponent of censorship. He made select appearances as a headline act and, as reigning king of the music underground, Joey frequently acted as a special host for music events and galas.

In 1998, inklings of a serious illness came to light and Joey was forced to cancel a series of Canadian dates. In the winter of 2001 he checked into a New York hospital for treatment of

acute lymphoma, but the disease won out and, in the presence of family and friends, Joey died at 49.

Joey (Jeff Hyman) was buried at New Mount Zion Cemetery, which is a part of Hillside Cemetery, in Lyndhurst, New Jersey.

GRAVE DIRECTIONS: Heading north at 40 Orient Way, enter the cemetery at the second gate. Drive straight in and, after a hundred yards, you'll see a pair of granite pillars on the right belonging to the New York Social Club. Joey's grave is three rows back and five rows to the right of these pillars.

DOUGLAS "DEE DEE RAMONE" COLVIN

SEPTEMBER 18, 1952 – JUNE 5, 2002

THOUGH MOST RAMONES songs were equally credited to all the band members, Dee Dee and Tommy were the poets behind the bulk of their works. Dee Dee was the original lead vocalist too, but Joey took over once it became apparent Dee Dee really couldn't sing and play bass at the same time. Though some contend that he was never guilty of really singing or playing bass separately either (heh), Dee Dee none-theless forever held responsibility for introducing each song's tempo in a signature machine-gun-fire cadence of "One-two-three-four!"

Dee Dee's departure from the band in 1989 signaled the end of an era, and for the next decade he fumbled through an assortment

of identities and gigs in forgettable fashion. A heroin addict and substance abuser for most of his adult life, he was found dead in his kitchen with various drug paraphernalia scattered about, his death ruled the result of an accidental overdose.

At 49, Dee Dee was buried at Hollywood Forever in Los Angeles, California.

GRAVE DIRECTIONS: Enter the cemetery at 6000 Santa Monica Boulevard, then stop in front of the Grass mausoleum, which is on the right at the next intersection. Dee Dee's stone is in front of a tree just right of the mausoleum.

JOHN "JOHNNY RAMONE" CUMMINGS
OCTOBER 8, 1948 – SEPTEMBER 15, 2004

DESCRIBING HIS YOUTH as a period of glue-sniffing delinquency, Johnny was relegated to menial construction laborer jobs before the Ramones formed. Though his onstage image directly contrasted with that of a business-minded conservative, he was recognized as the brains of the operation, an organizer and a peacemaker who kept his mates grounded and the band together through its many trials. The Ramones never canceled or arrived late to a show, largely thanks to Johnny's willpower, and he handled situations requiring professional manners with ease. Bucking his teenage rebel persona even further, he belonged to the National Rifle Association and, upon the Ramones' induction to the Rock & Roll Hall of Fame, the lifelong Republican closed

the band's acceptance speech with, "God bless President Bush, and God bless America."

In a signature knee-level stance with hard-to-imitate machine-gun speed, the rhythmist punished his ax with a primitive chording style that influenced a generation of musicians to strip the pomp and bravado from their sound. "I started doing up-and-down strumming, basically to keep time," he explained. "And then I started realizing other players couldn't do it."

In 1981 a love triangle infected the band when Joey's girlfriend left him for Johnny and the two later married. Johnny and Joey continued to perform together for 15 years but the two almost never spoke, and though the tension sometimes simmered, it never boiled over. "I would be upset at times, but I never thought about quitting. It's what I do," said Johnny. "What am I going to do, throw away the only opportunity I have?" Even when Joey lay dying in the hospital, Johnny never acknowledged him, saying that a reunion would have been hypocritical, not to mention futile.

Never a smoker and rarely a drinker, Johnny was diagnosed with prostate cancer in 1999. The disease killed him five years later at 55, and in the final painful weeks he bravely faced the ordeal naturally, refusing a morphine drip or painkillers right up to the end.

Johnny was cremated and a beautiful cenotaph to his memory was erected near Dee Dee's grave at Hollywood Forever. Overlooking a little pond, Johnny poses with his Mosrite Ventures guitar in sculptural eternity. On an attached plaque Johnny reminds us, "If a man can judge success by how many friends he has, then I have been very successful."

TOM "TOMMY RAMONE" ERDELYI

JANUARY 29, 1949 – JULY 11, 2014

DURING THE GROUP'S very beginnings, the Ramones were actually a three-man show; Joey was the drummer, while Tommy, who was employed by day as a recording engineer at the famed Record Plant studio, was manager of the band. But Joey shortly moved to lead vocals and a call was put out for a drummer. "We started auditioning drummers, but they just couldn't grasp the concept of the band—the speed and simplicity," Tommy recalled. "So I'd sit down and show them what we were looking for and the guys finally said, 'Why don't you do it?' So I gave it a try and that's when the sound of the band sort of solidified."

He played only on the band's first three studio albums and their live record, *It's Alive*, and as it turned out, his high-energy, hyperactive style became a signature aspect of the band's sound. He also wrote many of the band's songs, including most of its hits. Tommy left the group in 1977 to concentrate on producing and was replaced by Marc Bell, who took on the name Marky Ramone.

In 2001, when the first of the Ramones started dying at a young age, Tommy was as unprepared as anyone. "After Joey's passing, everything became just a shock," he said. "Dee Dee's was totally unexpected. After that, I was numb. Johnny, once he started getting really sick, we started to anticipate it. It was a long mourning, really. I compartmentalized the whole situation."

At 65, Tommy expired from cancer of the bile duct. He was cremated and his ashes remain with family.

OTIS REDDING

SEPTEMBER 9, 1941 – DECEMBER 10, 1967

THOUGH HE SEEMED to have the ability and aspirations to be a star, Otis Redding's early recordings were hampered by his reserved demeanor. But in 1961, Otis drove a few friends to a Memphis studio where they had booked recording time and, at the end of the day, they offered the remaining 20 minutes of pre-paid time to Otis. With a different sort of vigor and abandon he sang an original tune called "These Arms of Mine," and it proved to be a hit.

Otis won himself a recording contract and, when his series of releases over the next two years found favor with black record buyers, concert engagements followed. In 1965 he hit full stride with "I've Been Loving You Too Long," while Aretha Franklin hit gold with his "Respect." After enjoying a hugely successful European tour, then giving a knockout performance alongside Jimi Hendrix at the Monterey Pop Festival in 1967, young music fans in white markets became interested in Otis' sound and it seemed he was breaking out of the strict R&B format. At the end of 1967 he wrote and recorded "Dock of the Bay," which would become his biggest hit, but tragedy struck and Otis never lived to enjoy its success.

After two nights at a Cleveland club called Leo's Casino, and just three days after recording "Dock of the Bay," Otis and his touring band, the Bar-Kays, boarded a twin-engine Beechcraft bound for Madison, Wisconsin. The flight was unremarkable until, three miles from his landing approach, the pilot became disoriented in heavy fog and slammed the plane into the ice of Lake Monona, where it broke through and sank, killing everyone except a single bandmember.

At 26, Otis was entombed in a white marble mausoleum at his Big O Ranch in Round Oak, Georgia.

GRAVE DIRECTIONS: The entrance to the Big O Ranch is on Otis Redding Drive, a mile from Route 11. Visitors, however, are not welcome on the property. Otis' widow, Zelda, who still lives there, explained, "This is not Graceland, this is my home."

In September 2002, a seven-foot-tall bronze statue of Otis was unveiled at the trailhead of the new Ocmulgee Heritage Greenway at Gateway Park in Macon. The Ocmulgee River drifts slowly along behind the statue, an appropriate backdrop for a man whose life was washed away, but whose music rolls on.

RANDY RHOADS
DECEMBER 6, 1956 – MARCH 19, 1982

A FOUNDING MEMBER of Quiet Riot, guitarist Randy Rhoads joined Ozzy Osbourne's band in 1981 during Ozzy's *Diary of a Madman* period.

While on tour in support of the *Madman* album, Ozzy and his entourage were en route to a show in Orlando when their tour bus driver, Andrew Aycock, stopped at an associate's estate in

Leesburg, Florida. He had been at the wheel for 10 hours driving from the band's previous engagement in Knoxville, Tennessee.

While members of the band and entourage variously milled around the property or snoozed on the bus, Aycock, who had a pilot's license, took a Beechcraft Bonanza airplane without permission from a hangar on the estate and invited people to join him for a spin. Aycock went up in the airplane with two people and, upon landing without incident, Randy, along with Rachel Youngblood, the group's makeup artist and hairdresser, got in the plane to take a ride with Aycock. During this trip the plane began to fly low to the ground, even below tree level, and three times buzzed the tour bus. On a fourth pass, the plane's left wing struck the bus and the plane hurtled through a pine tree and crashed into a garage, immediately erupting into a fireball.

Ozzy Osbourne, who had been asleep on the bus, initially thought it had been involved in a traffic accident, but the truth was far worse. All three people on the plane were killed instantly.

At 25, Randy was buried at Mountain View Cemetery in San Bernardino, California.

GRAVE DIRECTIONS: Enter the cemetery at 570 East Highland Avenue, bear left, and Randy's mausoleum is immediately to the left.

TUPAC SHAKUR
JUNE 16, 1971 – SEPTEMBER 13, 1996

IN THE EARLY 1990s Tupac Shakur joined the rap group Digital Underground, but he soon outgrew the group and went solo. His debut album, *2Pacalypse Now*, went gold, and a 1993 follow-up, *Strictly 4 My N.I.G.G.A.Z.*, saw platinum. That same year, Tupac costarred in the popular movie *Poetic Justice*, which further fueled his celebrity.

Pages turned quickly in the next two turbulent years as Tupac revolved in and out of recording studios, as well as court and jail on sexual assault charges. And, during a robbery in which he was (surprisingly) not the perpetrator, he was shot five times. He was passing time behind bars for the sexual assault charges when his third album debuted at number one and, while his case was on appeal, Tupac was bailed out by the owner of Death Row Records, Suge Knight. Tupac's fourth release, *All Eyez on Me*, came under Suge's label in 1996 and also raced up the charts.

But the whirlwind ended abruptly when Tupac was gunned down in the passenger seat of Suge's BMW while stopped at a traffic light near the Las Vegas strip. Without regaining consciousness, he died six days later at age 25. He was cremated, and his ashes were scattered.

After Tupac's death, two people closely related to his murder were themselves killed. Yafea Fula, a member of Tupac's entourage and eyewitness to his murder, was gunned down in New Jersey. Later, Orlando Anderson, who with his Crips gang brothers had rumbled with Tupac's entourage hours before the singer was shot—and who had been fingered as a prime suspect in the killing—died in a California gang shootout. Tupac's murder remains unsolved.

JOE STRUMMER
AUGUST 21, 1952 – DECEMBER 22, 2002

JOE STRUMMER'S DISTINCTIVE and raw, Cockney-accented, bawling voice and choppy rhythm guitar were the centerpieces that extended an urgency to the Clash, the 1980s band that connected punk's rage to mainstream audiences. "If you ain't thinking about man and God and law, then you ain't thinking about nothing," Strummer declared.

Born in Turkey as John Graham Mellor, he lived in Egypt and Mexico before attending London's Central School of Arts and Crafts, where, when it became obvious that he would soon be failed out, he beat the masters to the punch and dropped out. Assuming the role of an itinerant squatter, he supported himself with gigs ranging from gravedigger to garbage hauler, and it was during this time, at Tube stations where he performed folk standards for spare change, that his Joe Strummer moniker took hold.

By 1974 Joe was a mainstay soul-influenced rocker of the London pub circuit, until the Sex Pistols sound "bashed any sense of rules" out of him and an energy of insurrection rooted into his core. Channeling England's working-class rage into a frenetic yet purifying noise, his new band the London SS— quickly renamed the Clash—embraced both the nose-thumbing attitude and fast blast sound of punk while infusing their music with undertones of reggae, ska, rockabilly, and even what is now hip-hop.

Joe's punk rock distilled the anger and depression of the times in socially conscious rants about apathy, tyranny, racial tension, and posers of all stripes. Best-selling albums *Give 'Em Enough Rope, London Calling* (named the best album of the

1980s by *Rolling Stone*), and *Combat Rock* yielded a catalog of what are today's classic rock radio hits, including "Train in Vain (Stand by Me)," "Rock the Casbah," and "Should I Stay or Should I Go."

For a half-dozen years the Clash were at the vanguard of punk, but Joe was indifferent to any of it. "The trouble with this interview is that you're interviewing me as though I'm a success, and I feel I'm a failure," he said. "I only see the disappointments. I'm angry because everything we do turns to ash." After a final album in 1985 the Clash disbanded.

Moving on to a diverse and fitful solo career, Joe wrote a few movie soundtracks, briefly filled in as frontman for the Pogues, hosted a radio show appropriately named *London Calling*, and recorded and toured as the leader of the Mescaleros, a joyful and eclectic band whose sound was a bountiful mishmash of Latin, African, Irish, and Indian, along with anything else that happened to be at hand.

After walking his dog one day, Joe died when a defective heart artery burst as he was sitting on his living room sofa. A medical examiner affirmed the defect was congenital and it could have given out at any time, anywhere. Joe was cremated and his ashes entrusted to his family.

STEVIE RAY VAUGHAN
OCTOBER 3, 1954 – AUGUST 27, 1990

PERHAPS THE LEADING rock and blues guitarist of his generation, the spellbinding Stevie Ray Vaughan rose from Texas obscurity to meteoric success in the early 1980s by virtue of a technical virtuosity not heard since Jimi Hendrix.

By the age of 10, Stevie was a fairly accomplished player and, at 16, left school with his guitar and trademark bandito hat to become a stage fixture in Austin's blues clubs. Stevie's first big break came when David Bowie hired him as lead guitarist for his 1982 *Let's Dance* album, which led to a record deal for Stevie and his band, Double Trouble. In quick succession, *Texas Flood* and *Couldn't Stand the Weather* were released, and the following years proved to be a roller-coaster ride for Stevie.

Rabid fans, contemporary guitar heroes, and even jaded music critics hailed the goateed musician as the electric guitar's newest champion. But although his professional status soared, Stevie fell deep into alcoholism and drug addiction and, after an extensive American tour in 1987, he checked himself into a rehab program. Stevie was clean by 1989 and he soon released *In Step*, his fourth

album and his most successful to date, which earned a Grammy and went gold within just a few months. Stevie was on top, professionally and personally, and the sky seemed to be the limit.

In the summer of 1990 Stevie and Double Trouble set out on a headlining tour and closed the night's show at the Alpine Valley outdoor amphitheater in East Troy, Wisconsin, with a blazing encore, highlighted by a who's-who of guitarists including Eric Clapton, Buddy Guy, Robert Cray, and Jimmie Vaughan, Stevie's older brother and early mentor. The last song they played was "Sweet Home Chicago."

After the musicians left the stage, Stevie jumped aboard a Bell 206B Jet Ranger, one of four waiting helicopters. The craft took off in fog around 12:40 a.m. but it never arrived in sweet Chicago. Instead, just a couple minutes after taking off, all aboard were killed when the helicopter suffered a "high-energy, high-velocity impact at a shallow angle" with the ground. Occurring on the far side of a nearby hill, the crash wasn't heard by anyone leaving the noisy concert site, and a search was initiated only when a Coast Guard station on the Great Lakes picked up the craft's emergency transmitter signal four hours later. At 7:00 a.m., searchers found the bodies of Stevie, the pilot, and three members of Clapton's entourage. Later that morning, Clapton and Jimmie Vaughan identified the bodies.

At 35, Stevie was buried at Laurel Land Memorial Park in Dallas, Texas.

GRAVE DIRECTIONS: At 6000 South R. L. Thornton Freeway near Exit 420 off I-35, pull into the parking lot of the funeral home and you'll see two entrances leading to the cemetery—one faces south, the other faces east. Enter through the easterly gate and proceed down that drive, continuing on as straight as possible. There will be a couple of jogs in the road but continue to head east. After a third of a mile you'll come to an intersection and an island. This island, just past Section 38, is called the Vaughan Estate and is where Stevie rests.

SID VICIOUS & NANCY SPUNGEN

NANCY SPUNGEN
FEBRUARY 27, 1958 – OCTOBER 12, 1978

SID VICIOUS
MAY 10, 1957 – FEBRUARY 2, 1979

WHEN THE SEX Pistols first surfaced on London's 1975 music scene, nobody was quite sure what to make of the band or its heart-attack-paced, anti-love songs. The pack of spiky-cropped, incompetent misfits purported to carry the musical flag for rebellion and anarchy, but it soon became clear that perhaps the only ones less interested in their "music" were the Sex Pistols themselves. In their first interview, frontman Johnny Rotten (his surname earned through the decrepit condition of his teeth) made clear the band wasn't "into music . . . we're into chaos," and he later expanded by declaring that money was their other key interest. The papers realized that the crew of castaways made for good copy and, buoyed by a stream of bizarre news clips, the band prospered.

By 1977 the Sex Pistols were the utter apotheosis of punk rock. In February the band's bassist was replaced by John Ritchie, better known as Sid Vicious, and the Sex Pistols metamorphosed into something else entirely. Little more than a criminally disturbed child possessed by a lust for fame, Sid personified all that the Sex Pistols purported to represent; he was cruel and self-destructive, doggedly pursued a heroin addiction, happily suffered through self-inflicted injuries, and lived his life in a brutally demented haze. But for Sid, sadly, none of this was an act. After Sid's death, Johnny Rotten even confessed that Sid "was nothing more than a coat hanger to fill an empty space on stage."

Remarkably, for a short time anyway, the Sex Pistols seemed to be on the verge of advancing from rock's greatest failure to its greatest success when, nine months after Sid's arrival, their much-anticipated album, *Never Mind The Bullocks—Here's The Sex*

Pistols, briefly topped the charts in spite of, or perhaps because of, the fact that many outlets refused to stock it. Despite that accomplishment, the band still managed to self-destruct within another year. After a glorious period of endless turpitude, at their sixth-ever U.S. concert Johnny Rotten declared the group finished.

After the Sex Pistols' 1978 demise, Sid, with groupie-turned-girlfriend Nancy Spungen, circulated as the wandering-soul fun couple of the year. A troubled junkie herself, former go-go dancer Nancy was Sid's most ardent fan, and her tempestuous relationship with him had started a year prior when she traveled to London with the sole intention of "bedding a Sex Pistol." The bedding turned into an extended gothic romance highlighted by drug-crazed dysfunctional debauchery, and after the couple moved into Room 100 in Manhattan's Chelsea Hotel, their relationship turned even stormier.

After two months at the hotel, during which time Nancy worked as a prostitute to support their lifestyle and drug habits, one morning Sid called the front desk to tell them he had awakened to find his girlfriend dead. When police arrived, they found Nancy, crumpled under the bathroom sink clad in blood-soaked bra and panties, with a single, deep stab wound to her abdomen inflicted by a hunting knife. Still in a drugged haze, Sid was charged with her murder and arrested, but a few days later was released when Virgin Records posted his $50,000 bail.

As authorities had confiscated his passport, Sid stayed in Manhattan but a fight at a disco shortly landed him back at Riker's Island prison, where he entered a seven-week detox program. Released clean and sober on a Friday afternoon, he fell right back in with his junkie friends—and the junk—and later that night climbed into his Chelsea bed. His mother, Beverly, had flown from England to care for her son and, ever fearful that Sid would be arrested in a drug buy on the street, she had bought a supply of heroin for him. He awoke sometime past midnight and, finding the heroin in his mother's purse, he used it and drifted off again—this time permanently. The next morning Beverly found him nude on the floor, "lying there quite peacefully." Sid's mother shook him until she realized "he was very cold and dead." Sid's death at 21 was ruled accidental. But it was not unexpected.

At 20, Nancy was buried at King David Cemetery in Bensalem, Pennsylvania.

GRAVE DIRECTIONS: At 3594 Bristol Road, turn left into the cemetery at the second entrance, which is a double-wide drive. Stop when this drive intersects the big circular drive and, on the right near the curb, you'll find a Goodman marker. Walk down the concrete path of Goodman and you'll find Nancy's plot at the 17th marker on the left.

Sid was cremated, and it's been widely reported that his ashes were either scattered or buried at Nancy's grave. That, however, seems a bit too romantic, and I'm sure the Spungen family would've protested, considering the circumstances. Besides, in a press conference announcing the Sex Pistols 1996 reunion tour, Johnny Rotten remarked that he "was going to put a funeral urn on the table in his [Sid's] place today but unfortunately his ashes were blown all over Heathrow Airport some time ago. I would have needed a Hoover."

MUDDY WATERS
APRIL 4, 1915 – APRIL 30, 1983

BORN TO A Mississippi Delta sharecropping family, McKinley Morganfield earned his Muddy moniker as a child for always playing in the mud, or so the story goes. In any event, by 13, Muddy was done with pattycake, as every free minute he could spare was spent practicing with a crude box guitar.

During a 1941 visit to the Delta region in search of artists to record for the Library of Congress folk-song archives, Alan Lomax found Muddy who, by then, had developed his own jagged bottleneck guitar-playing style. Prompted by Lomax, Muddy moved north to Chicago, where he soon went electric because "couldn't nobody hear you with an acoustic." That provided the boost that lifted him above his contemporaries; Muddy's earthy, traditional vocals layered over an urgently amplified sound touched off the modern Chicago-blues movement. Into the 1950s, Muddy refined his artistry in releases such as "Hoochie Coochie Man" and the anthemic "Got My Mojo Working," and his style ultimately shaped the development of rock and roll music.

As the 1950s gave way to the '60s, Muddy's sort of blues became less relevant to black listeners who were being wooed by Motown's soul. But no matter—by this time, Muddy had been taken up by a new audience, anyway: the young, white middle class that had been born of the folk music revival. The taverns and back halls in which Muddy had previously performed gave way to college auditoriums, jazz clubs, and festival stages where he was widely accepted by the rock community and accorded the respectful adulation given a founding figure. In the last decade of his life, Muddy made three of his best-selling albums, *Hard Again*, *I'm Ready*, and *King Bee*, and he

frequently performed with such acts as Eric Clapton and the Rolling Stones, who regarded him as their mentor.

Muddy died in his sleep at 68, and was buried at Restvale Cemetery in Worth, Illinois.

GRAVE DIRECTIONS: Enter the cemetery at 11700 South Laramie Avenue and park your car. Engraved with his given name, Muddy's tablet is in Section H, to the left of the office and three stones from the drive.

THE WHO

ONE OF THE most enduring and influential rock groups of all time, The Who, featuring frontman Roger Daltrey, lead guitarist and primary songwriter Pete Townshend, solemn bassist John Entwistle, and wild-man drummer Keith Moon, were originally called the Detours but, after discovering that another band of the same name already existed, changed the name to the ever-confusing moniker The Who.

The group first caught the public's attention around 1965 thanks to their energetic live show, which included a nightly on-stage destruction of guitars and drum kits that quickly ate up the band's profits. Royalties from early hits such as "Magic Bus" and "I Can't Explain" helped pay the bills, but their real breakout came in 1969 when the Townshend-penned "rock opera" *Tommy*, the story of a handicapped youth who finds salvation through pinball, remained on the charts for over two years. Over the next decade, through *Who's Next*, *Quadrophenia*, and *Who Are You?*, the foursome crashed its way through a haze of rock and roll excess, emphasizing their art via ear-splittingly loud concerts while punctuating their tours with hotel room-destroying "Whooliganism."

After Keith died in 1978, the band documented their 1982 "farewell" tour on the live album *Who's Last*, but The Who didn't really disappear. In 2017 they played their 550th show since the Farewell Tour, suggesting that, 35 years on, The Who still hadn't finished saying goodbye.

JOHN ENTWISTLE
OCTOBER 9, 1944 – JUNE 27, 2002

BECAUSE THE WHO has only ever had a single guitarist, Pete Townshend, it was always vital that bassist John Entwistle play loud and complex bass lines to compensate for the absence of a rhythm guitar. The result was that John's fills and counter-melodies, indeed all manner of his bass lines, stood out from The Who's music like no other rock band's, and he became acclaimed as one of rock's premier bassists.

But though John's musical mannerisms stood out, he did not. A tax clerk before joining the band, he was content to be the quiet one whose calm, anchoring presence contrasted with his bad-boy bandmates' energetic activities. John did, however, contribute a number of songs to The Who catalog, most notably "My Wife" and "Boris the Spider." And, though they were characteristically uneven, John also had a half-dozen solo works to his credit.

On the eve of the band's summer tour kickoff in Las Vegas, John died in Room 658 of the Hard Rock Hotel of a heart attack, the coroner stating that cocaine in his system was also a contributing factor. He was cremated at 57 and the ashes scattered about his Quarwood estate in Stow, England.

KEITH MOON
AUGUST 23, 1946 – SEPTEMBER 7, 1978

RENOWNED FOR HIS ferocious and frenetic drumming, Keith Moon destroyed more drum kits in his lifetime than most musicians have had the opportunity to play. Though he often did only a mediocre job of timekeeping, he was certainly one of the most exciting drummers from an audience's perspective, and his explosive rolls and frantic style contributed to the outrageous package that was The Who.

Though Keith liked to claim he'd never had drum lessons, he actually had, though the fib wasn't hard to believe, as discipline was certainly not one of his attributes. As one of rock's greatest drummers, Keith only played when he was with The Who, never practiced and, even after he was famous, never had a drum kit in any place that he lived. Instead, Keith's time away from the band was an endless party, his hedonistic lifestyle perpetually in full swing. His fans revere him for driving a car into a swimming pool, but (sorry) it never happened.

In 1978 Keith was living in Mayfair, London, with his girlfriend, Annette, at Harry Nilsson's pad at 9 Curzon Place—the same flat, Number 12 on the top floor, in which "Mama" Cass Elliot had died four years earlier. Keith had been taking pills that had been prescribed by his doctor to ease alcohol withdrawal. Before going to sleep at about three o'clock one morning, Keith took a handful of the pills. He awoke in a daze a few hours later, had a sizable meal, ingested another bunch of the pills, and returned to bed.

When Annette tried to rouse Keith later that afternoon, he wouldn't be disturbed. The ultimate party animal, the poster child of recreational drugs and debauchery, had died of an accidental overdose of the prescription drug Heminevrin.

At 32, Keith was cremated at Golders Green Crematorium in London, and his ashes were scattered there at Section 3P. There is no plaque or memorial; the section is merely a flower-filled field of remembrance.

JOHNNY WINTER
FEBRUARY 23, 1944 – JULY 16, 2014

THE TEEN YEARS are awkward in the best of circumstances, but when you're a rail-thin, cross-eyed albino and have just 20/400 eyesight in your "good" eye, well, that would be a recipe for some miserable times indeed. Such was the lot of virtuoso guitarist Johnny Winter, who once reflected, "I really got the bad end of the deal. People teased me and I got in a lot of fights." But he was of the belief that the alienation wasn't all for naught: It provoked his musical ability and furnished a kinship with black musicians he idolized because "we both had a problem with our skin being the wrong color."

Between 1969 and 1971, Winter released four acclaimed albums of both classic and original blues, *Johnny Winter, Second Winter, Johnny Winter And*, and *Live Johnny Winter And* (creativity in naming albums apparently wasn't one of his strengths), and his wild and fluid performance at the 1969 *Woodstock* music festival set concert-goers on their heads. Unfortunately, Johnny's set was excluded from the Woodstock film; his manager refused to allow it because "he thought we wouldn't make any money," Johnny drearily explained.

He toured relentlessly at niche joints around the world for decades, his lightning-fast finger work emphasizing a high-octane and almost hyperactive guitar-playing style, while a flowing mane

of chalk-white hair and inimitable, gravelly vocals completed Johnny's unique stage persona. But on top of his already unusual appearance, drug and alcohol addictions conspired to lend him an additionally prematurely frail and cadaverous manifestation. Emaciated, he sat in a chair for the entirety of performances for a dozen years. Finally, in 2005, knocking at death's door and barely tipping 90 pounds, Winter managed to shake his dependencies, put on some weight, and resume vigorously touring.

After the last date of a European tour, Johnny gave out in his sleep at a Zurich hotel. At 70, he was buried at Union Cemetery in Easton, Connecticut.

GRAVE DIRECTIONS: This old church cemetery is located at the intersection of Route 136 and Sport Hill Road. Enter at the Sport Hill driveway and Johnny's white traditional-style tombstone borders the drive, 75 feet up on the right.

WOLFMAN JACK
JANUARY 21, 1938 – JULY 1, 1995

DISC JOCKEY WOLFMAN Jack was the Elvis Presley of rock radio. He fine-tuned and repackaged work originated by black musicians, then became a phenomenon by feeding this music, in his own inimitable style, to a massive white audience hungry for something different and fresh.

During the early 1960s the airwaves were still more or less segregated, so Wolfman (whose real name was Bob Smith) created a shadowy wild-man alter ego to play the black rhythm-and-blues records that he so loved. By broadcasting from XERF-AM, a station based just over the border in Mexico that boasted a signal 10 times more powerful than any U.S. radio station, the Wolfman soon developed a national following. His trademark throaty voice and rough tongue, peppered with sporadic wolf howls and interjections of black slang, blanketed North America with a flavorsome stew of R&B, jazz, rockabilly, and rock and roll. The restless youth of America immediately embraced Wolfman Jack. Nobody else came close.

The national press eventually took notice, and stories about the Wolfman surfaced in major newspapers and magazines. Todd Rundgren and the Guess Who wrote chart-making songs about him, and his popularity skyrocketed. But the questions lingered: *Who is Wolfman Jack? Where does he come from? What does he look like (is he black or white)?* Only Bob Smith and a few others knew the answers, and they weren't talking.

Finally, though, the cloak was lifted in 1973 when George Lucas, remembering Wolfman from his own youth, wrote him into the screenplay that became his hit film *American Graffiti*. When *American Graffiti* was released, Wolfman Jack was already firmly enshrined as a part of rock history. But his star certainly shone brighter afterward, and the film transformed him into a media superstar. Wolfman Jack became one of rock and roll's premier spokesmen, engaging in countless personal and television appearances, and even hosting his own television show, *The Midnight Special*.

At 57, Wolfman Jack died of a heart attack and, believe it or not, was buried in the yard of his home in Belvidere, North Carolina.

GRAVE DIRECTIONS: You can find Wolfman at 1640 Belvidere Road. It's in the middle of nowhere, but easy to spot once you get there as it's the only house with a gravestone in the side yard. If you do visit, please use discretion as this is a private residence.

MAX YASGUR
NOVEMBER 11, 1920 – FEBRUARY 8, 1973

FOR 30 YEARS, Max Yasgur basked in anonymity as the operator of Yasgur Farms, a wholesale milk business in upstate New York. But in 1969, the Yasgur name leapt overnight to international prominence when Max leased his farmland to a music promoter and the sleepy community of Bethel, New York, was transformed into the site of the world's largest rock festival—Woodstock.

Woodstock is now legendary. Some 500,000 people attended the three-day festival that celebrated peace, love, and, above all, music. But in the eyes of some Bethel residents, the long August weekend was nothing more than an orgy of psychedelic experimentation and group sex played out under the umbrella of loud, god-awful music. They were furious that long-haired flower children overran their bucolic village, used recreational drugs in the streets, trampled their crops, and brought about enormous traffic jams.

After the event, Max was both blessed and scorned. Masses of thankful hippies applauded his generosity, while neighbors who had previously been his friends rebuked him. Seeking to clear the air between the generations, Max appeared on radio and television and eventually most of the townspeople came around to forgiving him, mindful that he'd probably done more good for the town than harm.

Tragically, not even four years after the festival that made his farm famous, Max died of a heart attack and at 52 was buried at Landfield Avenue Synagogue Cemetery in Monticello, New York.

GRAVE DIRECTIONS: On Thompsonville Road, just east of its intersection with Rock Ridge Drive, there is a series of small cemeteries. Turn into the third driveway—the one at the telephone pole marked 26-A—and stop halfway before its end. Climb over the three-rail fence on your left and Max's marker is in the third row of stones.

If you'd like to visit the site of either the 1969 or 1994 Woodstock Festivals while you're in the area, directions follow. (A 1999 event, wherein angry concert-goers lit bonfires, looted vendors, and assaulted women, is probably best forgotten.)

DIRECTIONS TO SITE OF 1969 WOODSTOCK: None of the Woodstock concerts actually took place in the town of Woodstock. The 1969 site is in Bethel, and at the intersection of Hurd and West Shore Roads a stone and a granite memorial commemorate the festival. But only if you close your eyes can you see the stage down the hill on the left or hear skinny-dippers splashing in the pond across the street.

DIRECTIONS TO SITE OF 1994 WOODSTOCK: The 1994 soirée took place in Saugerties, in the fields on both sides of the dirt Augusta Savage Road. Abandoned water and wash stations, now almost completely dissolved back into the earth, are the only clue to these hills' place in rock history.

FRANK ZAPPA

DECEMBER 21, 1940 – DECEMBER 4, 1993

FRANK ZAPPA WAS one of rock's most committed iconoclasts, blazing new trails in rock music. But Frank was too ambitious to stay within the relative confines of rock, and in his lifetime he embraced everything from doo-wop and heavy metal to big band and orchestral music. Whenever a new pop fad surfaced, he could be counted on to address the craze with a trademark sardonic response. Frank's songs were characterized by bizarre lyrics, and the musical directions he chose turned out to be almost unlistenable at times. But that wasn't really the point. His objective was to push the envelope into the recesses of every musical region, to find out what lay over the horizon, to let the chips fall where they may.

Frank's initial foray into music was as the drummer in his high school marching band, but that ended when he was kicked out for smoking under the bleachers while in uniform. Remarkably, Frank was able to recover from that setback, and in 1966 he and his band, the Mothers of Invention, released *Freak Out*, one of rock's first concept albums. That record was followed up quickly with *Absolutely Free* and *We're Only In It for the Money*, albums that, to some degree, became underground anthems for 1960s counterculture. Over the next 25 years, Frank released 60 more albums and produced several films. Though he developed a substantial catalog of music, his work was uneven—some maintain his first three albums were his best—and Frank was never particularly successful from a commercial standpoint. But that never seemed to be the point anyway.

Frank managed to offend numerous political and social groups with biting, satirical, and sometimes-lascivious lyrics that left little sacred. He ignored any criticism, but in 1985, when the Parents Music Resource Center recommended voluntary album content labeling, Frank became concerned that artists might be prevented from freely expressing themselves. He went to Capitol Hill to accuse a Senate committee of promoting censorship. Frank compared the proposed warning label tactics to "treating dandruff by decapitation," and, though he seemed victorious then, content labels are de rigueur today.

Frank was rewarded for his innovations by twice being rejected for induction into the Rock & Roll Hall of Fame. On the other hand, after recording two albums with Pierre Boulez and the

London Symphony Orchestra, he was honored along with other avant-garde musicians at the 1992 New Music Festival in Frankfurt. Later, though, clearer heads prevailed and in 1995 the rockers inducted Frank posthumously.

After a four-year battle, Frank succumbed to prostate cancer and at 52 was buried at Westwood Memorial Park in Los Angeles.

GRAVE DIRECTIONS: Enter the cemetery behind the office complex at 10850 Wilshire Boulevard, walk into the central lawn area, and count up eight rows to the flat bronze marker of Charles Bassler. Frank rests in the unmarked plot above Bassler.

WARREN ZEVON
JANUARY 24, 1947 – SEPTEMBER 7, 2003

WARREN ZEVON TURNED to music early and as a teenager was instructed in modern classical by his Los Angeles neighbor, Russian composer Igor Stravinsky. After high school, the budding star drove a sports car his professional-gambler father had won in a card game to New York in an attempt to make it on the folk circuit and, once that plan fizzled, he returned west and developed a Sonny & Cher–type gig called Lyme & Cybelle. But though big-time success blossomed everywhere on the burgeoning West Coast music scene, it skipped over Warren's backyard and the dejected artist spent most of the 1970s writing jingles and working as a sessions man because the only records his own commercial attempts set was the speed in which they found their way to the clearance rack.

In 1978 Warren's third album, *Excitable Boy*, was released and it changed his fortune overnight. The odd theme of cartoonish violence that wove through the work combined with the catchy riff and humorous tagline of "Werewolves of London" vaulted Warren to prominence as rock's macabre jester. According to Warren, the brutality of his songs was a mask to cover his other anxieties. "Sickness and doctors, they scare me, not violence and helplessness," he said.

On the strength of the *Excitable Boy* album, Warren toured consistently for the next two decades, fitting in especially well with New England and Rocky Mountain ski slope audiences where he became a seasonal fixture. An underlying struggle with booze affected him now and again, and more than once he lost control onstage. The temptations to which he succumbed probably had a hand in his string of somewhat irregular albums, though he still managed to maintain signature irreverence with songs like "Detox Mansion" and "Things to Do in Denver When You're Dead." In any event, Warren's eclectic musings kept his cult fandom satisfied and he never suffered for an audience.

Warren was a frequent guest and occasional substitute bandleader on the *Late Show with David Letterman*, but the October 2002 appearance in which he was the hour-long show's only guest was bittersweet. Diagnosed with incurable mesothelioma cancer, this was Warren's swan song, a last goodbye. Candid as ever, he confessed that he "may have made a tactical error in not going to a physician for 20 years," and offered trademark eclectic counsel for the living too: "Enjoy every sandwich." As the show ended, Warren presented Dave with a prized guitar, saying, "I want you to have this; take good care of it." The program reached peak poignancy and there wasn't a dry eye in the house.

Warren spent much of his remaining time working on a final album, *The Wind*, which featured an all-star cast of famous musician friends, and writing personal goodbyes to make one final point, which was, in his words, "This was a nice deal: life."

At 56, Warren was cremated and his ashes scattered in the Pacific Ocean.

POPULAR MUSIC ICONS

LOUIS ARMSTRONG

AUGUST 4, 1901 – JULY 6, 1971

MOST BABY BOOMERS remember Louis "Satchmo" Armstrong on variety shows as a smiling older uncle warbling his gravelly voice through "What a Wonderful World" and playing a bit of trumpet afterward. But jazz aficionados remember Louis differently and freely refer to him as a genius. According to Tony Bennett (who ought to know), Armstrong "practically invented jazz singing singlehandedly." Further, outside of jazz circles it's largely unknown that, as a young avant-garde musician, Louis' Hot Five and Hot Seven recordings of the 1920s spurred a musical revolution.

Louis' achievements are all the more remarkable given his early life of extreme poverty in a New Orleans slum. But he somehow turned that adversity into opportunity and, while in the Colored Waifs' Home for Boys after a brush with the law, Louis discovered the cornet and began making music. In 1922 Louis joined Joe Oliver's Creole Jazz Band and shortly thereafter made his own recordings, which many consider the Rosetta Stone of jazz.

Before those recordings, jazz musicians modestly limited their solos, but Louis' were longer and bolder, and he started improvising on the chord structure. With his rhythmic fluidity, he also began playing on and around the beat, heralding the swing style that emerged in the 1930s. Louis also pioneered a new style of singing, imitating the horn with his voice and substituting improvised nonsense syllables for the lyrics. With the passing of the big band era, he formed his All Stars, and they became goodwill ambassadors of jazz throughout the world, helping break down racial barriers wherever they played.

Louis never forgot where he came from and recognized that he was blessed twice, first with a sandpapery, distinctive voice and second with keen trumpet skills. Together, his talents helped him reap the rewards that eluded most of the influential creators of his era. The affinity he felt for his trumpet superseded everything else. As he reflected once, "Anything that'll get in the way of blowing my horn, out it goes. The trumpet comes first, before everything, even my wife."

Louis died in his sleep of natural causes and was buried at Flushing Cemetery in Flushing, New York.

At the turn of the century, no one paid much notice to the birth of an illegitimate black baby boy in New Orleans, and Louis, never knowing his real birthday, chose to celebrate it as July 4, 1900. A baptismal certificate listing his birth date as August 4, 1901, was finally discovered in 1989, making Louis 69 at his death, not 71, as is generally recorded.

GRAVE DIRECTIONS: Enter the cemetery at 163 46th Avenue and bear left, keeping 46th Avenue on your left. Count the paved drives on your right and park at the fourth one. Section Nine will be in front of you, and Louis' dark brown stone, easily recognizable with a trumpet engraved on its face, is a couple rows off the curb.

FLORENCE BALLARD
JUNE 30, 1943 – FEBRUARY 22, 1976

IN THE MID-1960S, the Supremes—a Motown vocal trio comprised of Florence Ballard, Diana Ross, and Mary Wilson—were America's number one recording act. Hailing from a Detroit housing project, they enjoyed a fantastic rags-to-riches fairy tale, regaling mobs of fans worldwide with blockbuster hits such as "Stop in the Name of Love." In those heady days the ladies were fashion magazine features, Florence drove a plum-rose Cadillac, and they even had a loaf of bread named after them. The Supremes struck gold.

But in the real world, fairy tales can have unhappy endings, and so it went for Florence, who, in 1967, just as the Supremes reached the peak of their popularity, either quit or was fired from the group, depending upon whose account you believe. Signing away all her rights for only about $100,000, Florence soon lost her home to foreclosure, ballooned to almost 200 pounds, and was living back in the Detroit projects on a $95-per-week stipend from the Aid to Dependent Children program. During that time, she said, "When I go to sleep at night, I have dreams of what it was like when Diana, Mary, and I worked great places like the Copa. Once I had it all. I was Supreme. Now? Now I have nothing."

Just a couple months after reconciling with her estranged husband and moving into his home, Florence became alarmed one evening as her hands and feet went numb. She checked into a hospital that night and died of heart failure the next morning at 32. Flo was buried at Detroit Memorial Park in Warren, Michigan.

GRAVE DIRECTIONS: Enter the gate at 4280 13 Mile Road and, 50 yards inside, at Plot 291A, Section D, you'll find Flo's marker engraved with her given name, Florence Glenda Chapman.

IRVING BERLIN
MAY 11, 1888 – SEPTEMBER 22, 1989

IRVING BERLIN, THE songwriter who set the tone and tempo for the music that America listened and danced to for much of the twentieth century, was of the opinion that there actually existed only six different tunes in the world. In any event, from those six tunes he somehow fashioned some 1,500 songs that were by turns romantic, tragic, sentimental, and sophisticated.

His was a classic American success story. His family arrived from Russia penniless when he was five, and three years later his father died. Irving took to selling newspapers to help support his family and this marked the end of his schooling, which totaled less than two years.

Irving married at 24, and his wife died of typhoid fever six months later. To express his grief, he wrote "When I Lost You," which sold more than a million copies. It was like a dam broke when he followed that effort with dozens of standards like "White Christmas," "Always," "Blue Skies," "Puttin' on the Ritz," and "There's No Business Like Show Business." Of course, Irving also wrote America's unofficial national anthem, "God Bless America."

Irving's lack of schooling left him illiterate and, curiously, he could never read or write music; he left it to arrangers to transcribe his melodies. Throughout his long life in the world of music, he never learned to play in any key but F-sharp, and to overcome this limitation he used a specially built piano that had a hand clutch to change keys. It now resides in the Smithsonian Institution.

Irving died in his sleep at 101, at home in Manhattan, just a few miles from the Lower East Side tenement where he had lived while hawking newspapers some 95 years earlier.

He was buried at Woodlawn Cemetery in the Bronx, New York.

GRAVE DIRECTIONS: At East 233rd Street and Webster Avenue, the Woodlawn Cemetery is enormous, with 350,000 guests on 400 acres. Stop at the booth at the front gate and get a map. Then follow the dashed line painted in the road to its intersection with Prospect Avenue. Turn left on Prospect Avenue and then, at the next intersection (Walnut Avenue), you'll see the mausoleum of a James Hill on the right. Irving's grave is a flat stone just left of the Hill mausoleum.

GLEN CAMPBELL
APRIL 22, 1936 – AUGUST 8, 2017

AS JUST ANOTHER scruffy child of a dirt-poor, cotton-farming family of 14, it was darned fortuitous that a four-year-old Glen Campbell got a Sears and Roebuck guitar in his hands. As it turned out, his were the hands of a guitar prodigy, and by age six Glen was performing on local radio stations. Then, once he tired of "looking at the southern end of a northbound mule," Glen left school at 14 and took off for New Mexico with his musician uncle.

By 17 he was married and had a child, and, after earning his chops at what he called the "fightin' and dancin' clubs" of Albuquerque, he left with his young family for California. With his friendly Southern nature opening doors and his guitar versatility and honeyed voice earning him credibility, in Los Angeles, Glen became an essential player on the 1960s recording scene, contributing to everyone from Frank Sinatra to the Monkees. "I did what my dad told me to do—'Be nice, son, and don't cuss. And be nice to people.' And that's the way I handled myself, and people were very, very nice to me," he reflected. In 1965 he even toured with the Beach Boys for 40 shows, filling in while a distressed Brian Wilson took a breather.

But for all his years of session work that ranged from blues to rock to jazz, for himself Glen never strayed far from country music, or "people music," as he called it, because it was rooted in earthy stories of everyday people. In 1967 Glen reached his stride with "Gentle on My Mind," a chart-topper that began a remarkable streak of seven consecutive hits including "By the Time I Get to Phoenix," "Wichita Lineman," and "Galveston." Those successes led to his own variety show, *The Glen Campbell Goodtime Hour*, as well as a role alongside John Wayne in 1969's *True Grit*. After cooling for a few years, the hit making was reignited with

1975's "Rhinestone Cowboy," which became the signature Campbell anthem.

But life in those years had a dark side too, and as Glen's attention gravitated toward cocaine and Glenlivet scotch, his easygoing character fell into sharp relief with a new rashness. There was a hit-and-run and a near-overdose in Las Vegas, plus a DUI and 10 days in jail, while the tabloids played up a messy affair he had shared with Tanya Tucker. Eventually, though, after being baptized at his childhood swimming hole, Glen announced, "I accepted Jesus Christ on December the 21st, 1981. I'm singin' a new song."

Releasing a series of gospel albums and touring often, he easily filled theater seats during the 1990s. But during his 2005 induction into the Country Music Hall of Fame he seemed shaky, and in 2011 his wife announced that Glen was suffering from Alzheimer's disease. Remarkably, she confirmed that not only was he recording a final album, called *Adiós*, but he would soon be embarking on a tour called the Goodbye Tour. What was envisioned as a five-week tour turned into 151 shows over 15 months, shortly after which Glen was moved into a long-term care facility.

At 81, Glen died and was buried at his family's own Campbell Cemetery in Delight, Arkansas.

GRAVE DIRECTIONS: A half mile north of Route 301 on the east side of Billstown Road (no, don't be tempted by the nearby Billstown Cemetery Road) are the homey Campbell burying grounds.

KAREN CARPENTER
MARCH 2, 1950 – FEBRUARY 4, 1983

DURING THE 1970s, silky-voiced Karen Carpenter and brother Richard comprised their own soft-rock group, the Carpenters, which proved to be a can't-miss, hit-making association. Their light, airy melodies were in direct contrast to much of the day's gaudy rock. While many of the musicians who ridiculed them have been mostly forgotten, the Carpenters' meticulously crafted singles have stood the test of time.

Early on Karen was the drummer, but when her vocal talents became obvious she focused on singing and her rich alto became a Carpenters hallmark. Richard described their emerging style as "a choral approach to pop," and they created almost two dozen hit singles including, "Yesterday Once More," "Close to You," and "We've Only Just Begun," the last becoming a popular choice for post-hippie weddings.

By the late 1970s, though, the Carpenters were disintegrating from within; Richard was often strung out on a variety of methamphetamines while Karen was short-tempered and constantly fatigued. Finally, at a November 1978 show in Las Vegas, Richard announced that the Carpenters planned an extended hiatus from touring. In fact, that engagement proved to be their last.

Karen's mysterious fatigue turned out to be caused by self-induced starvation; she suffered from anorexia nervosa. Over the next few years, her attempts to control the disease sent her body on a roller-coaster ride; psychological counseling would help her to gain a healthy amount of weight, but soon she'd be secretly fasting again. In February 1983 it seemed that Karen had finally turned the corner for good; she weighed 110 pounds and seemed to have reached a mental balance as well. But though her body looked well, it had been malnourished for almost a decade.

One evening, Karen went to a Bob's Big Boy restaurant with her mother and enjoyed a shrimp salad. Upon returning to her mother's home, she complained of being tired and retreated to her old bedroom, where she ended up spending the night. The next morning, Karen's mother heard her get out of bed and open her closet door. When Karen failed to come downstairs, her mother went up to the room and found Karen on the floor of her walk-in closet, eyes rolled back, not breathing. At 32, Karen was dead of heart failure.

She rests at Forest Lawn Memorial Park in Cypress, California.

GRAVE DIRECTIONS: Go through the main gate at 4471 Lincoln Avenue, turn right, and drive up to the Ascension Mausoleum. Park in front and enter through the glass doors on the left. Turn left at the first hall, which is the Sanctuary of Compassion, and the beautiful Carpenter crypt is at the end.

JUNE CARTER CASH
JUNE 23, 1929 – MAY 15, 2003

JOHNNY CASH
FEBRUARY 26, 1932 – SEPTEMBER 12, 2003

JOHNNY CASH LIKED to recount the story of the day his voice "broke." It was after a long day of cutting wood at his family's Arkansas farm. "I came in the back door singing, and my mama turned around and said, 'Who's that?' And I said, 'That's me.' She came over and hugged me and said, 'God's got his hand on you, son. Don't ever forget this gift.'" The rumble-voiced performer never forgot the gift, but for a time he threw it away when an addiction to alcohol and amphetamines landed him on the fast track to a short life.

By the 1960s Johnny had created a musical niche that fell in a not-quite-identifiable region between the bluntness of folk, the rebelliousness of rock, and the world-weariness of country. The immensely popular artist was performing his cache of hits, including "Folsom Prison Blues," "I Walk the Line," and "Cry, Cry, Cry" to sellout crowds internationally. But as his addictions took hold, they got him uninvited from the Grand Ole Opry for smashing a number of footlights and arrested in El Paso for smuggling drugs in his guitar case until, finally, everything culminated in a desperate suicide attempt at a place called Nickajack Cave. He conquered his addictions with the help and support of friends and June Carter, and after he proposed to June during a London concert they were married the next week.

June too had a successful showbiz career. As a member of the Carter Family country music team she sang, played guitar and autoharp, and imbued her own special talent into the road show—a highlight of every show was June's "Aunt Polly" comedy routine. As a solo artist, she'd found success with upbeat country tunes of the 1950s like "Jukebox Blues" and after attending acting classes, the willowy upstart wrangled a few minor television roles.

The celebrity couple collaborated on a succession of acclaimed duet recordings including *Jackson* and *Guitar-Pickin' Man*. By

the mid-1970s, Johnny, and especially June, retreated from the limelight and the two dove into devout Christian fundamentalism recording disposable albums chock-full of children's music, gospel, and Christmas tunes. Nevertheless, Johnny continued to be a popular concert performer while June frequently joined him during the encore. In 1983, Johnny briefly relapsed on painkillers after being seriously injured by a kick to the stomach from one of his farm-raised ostriches.

By the 1980s it was uncool to be a Johnny Cash fan as country radio favored more contemporary artists and the new generation didn't bother trying to fathom his appeal. But in 1993 Johnny signed with American Records and a series of albums, called *American Recordings*, revived his career and brought him in touch with a younger rock-oriented audience who soon discovered and embraced the breadth of his earlier works. Meanwhile, June's acclaimed 1999 solo album, *Press On*, earned her a Grammy.

At 73, June died of complications after heart surgery and Johnny attended her funeral in a wheelchair looking weary and beaten. Four months later he followed June to their own heaven and the two now lie side by side at Hendersonville Memory Gardens in Hendersonville, Tennessee.

GRAVE DIRECTIONS: Enter the gardens at 353 East Main Street and park in the second lot near the Chapel of Memories. Cross the drive and walk into the memorial garden. About 60 feet away, you'll see the twin black tablets marking Johnny and June's graves next to a bench dedicated to their memories.

RAY CHARLES

SEPTEMBER 23, 1930 – JUNE 10, 2004

CRISSCROSSING FLORIDA AND Georgia as a teenage musical sideman and solo act, Ray Robinson took to calling himself Ray Charles to distinguish himself from boxer Sugar Ray Robinson. At a school for the blind, he learned Braille and got formal piano lessons, but his mother died and the distraught young man left school at 15.

In 1947 Ray split for Seattle, formed the McSon Trio, and released his first single, "Confession Blues." Carefully imitating the stylings of Nat King Cole, the trio's singles topped the "race records" (later known as R&B charts), and Ray picked up an Atlantic recording contract in 1952.

"I've Got a Woman" became Ray's first national hit in 1955, and a string of bluesy, gospel-charged numbers followed. His seven-piece band was expanded to include the Raelettes, female backup singers who provided responses like a gospel choir, and they became a signature of his music. By the end of the decade, Ray had become the key architect of soul.

Despite his blindness and a nagging 15-year heroin addiction, it seemed there was nothing he couldn't do musically. Whether in a splashy barrelhouse style or a precisely understated swing, he alternately shook the rafters and tugged at the heartstrings of audiences. His playing was inevitably overshadowed by his voice and Ray could sound suave or raw, joyful or desolate, then leap into a falsetto or slip into an intimate whisper, and finally let loose with a resonating whoop. In a warm and gravelly croon, he mesmerized crowds one moment with "America the Beautiful" or "Georgia on My Mind" and then nearly swayed himself from his piano stool playing "Hit the Road Jack" the next. Claiming all of American music as his birthright, his influence will echo through generations of musicians for years to come.

Shortly before his death, Ray commented, "I got enough sense to know that I ain't going to live forever. But I also know it's not a question of how long I live, but of how well I live."

Ray died at 73 due to complications of liver disease and was buried at Inglewood Park Cemetery in Inglewood, California.

GRAVE DIRECTIONS: Enter the cemetery at 720 East Florence Avenue, turn left, and you'll see a long stone building called the Mausoleum of the Golden West. Enter it at the Cenotaph entrance and proceed down the Sanctuary of Hope. Then turn right at the Sanctuary of Reverence, left at the Sanctuary of Dreams, and right at the Sanctuary of Eternal Love. Ray is in this corridor, on the right at Crypt A-32.

DICK CLARK
NOVEMBER 30, 1929 – APRIL 18, 2012

WITH THE BOYISH good looks of a junior executive and a ubiquitous on-camera presence, Dick Clark was among the most recognizable faces in the world, even if what he was first and most famous for—spinning records and jabbering with teenagers—seemed a bit insubstantial.

After studying at Syracuse University, where he was a disc jockey on the student radio station, Dick got a job as a news announcer. By 1952 he had his own easy-listening afternoon radio show, *Dick Clark's Caravan of Music*, and a few months later the station's television affiliate began an afternoon show called *Bandstand*. In the summer of 1956, *Bandstand*'s host was fired and the station turned to the right man at the right time, young Dick Clark. "I was 26 years old, looked the part, knew the music, and was very comfortable on television," he recalled. "'They said, 'Do you want it?' And I said, 'Oh, man, do I want it!' "

By the following October, the show was being broadcast nationwide with a new name, *American Bandstand,* and every weekday afternoon as many as 20 million teenage viewers eagerly watched their peers cut the rug with the newest moves like the Twist, the Pony, and the Watusi while the day's hottest hits and newest singles blasted the studio room. At song's end, a breathless raver often rated a record in a brief interview, and "It's got a good beat and you can dance to it!" became a national catchphrase.

Handsome and glib, Dick Clark, the man who would become "the world's oldest teenager," was the music-savvy older brother host, and from that position of authority he presided over this grassroots revolution in American culture. *American Bandstand* was the first show to use television to spread the gospel of rock and roll and introduced audiences to acts as varied as Dusty Springfield, Buffalo Springfield, and Rick Springfield. It helped give rise to the Top 40 radio format, made rock and roll a palatable product for visual media, convinced advertisers of the influence teenagers could have on steering popular taste, and became a cultural touchstone for the Baby Boomer generation.

As much a businessman as a television personality, Dick was especially deft at packaging entertainment products for popular consumption. For more than half a century he built a juggernaut empire, Dick Clark Productions, from the shoulders of *American Bandstand,* though even he acknowledged that many of his products were more diverting than ennobling. There were redundant awards shows like the *American Music Awards,* compilation shows like *TV's Bloopers & Practical Jokes,* and painful-to-watch, campy television-movie dramas. "I owe my success to knowing the mind of the broad audience," he said. "I've often dealt with frivolous things that didn't really count. I'm not ashamed of that."

Beginning in 1972 he became synonymous with one of the biggest nights of the year. His *Dick Clark's New Year's Rockin' Eve* became a tradition, with Dick hosting the festivities, introducing the entertainment acts, and, of course, counting down to midnight as the ball dropped in New York's Times Square. But in 2004 he missed the festivities after suffering a major stroke that left him partially paralyzed with his speech affected. The following year he returned for an emotional appearance on the show, telling the audience of how the stroke impaired him and that his "speech is not perfect but is getting there."

Unfortunately, Dick's speech never again really "got there," though he continued taking part in the show in a diminished role. In 2006, Dick summed it up for us: "I accomplished my childhood dream, to be in show business. Everybody should be so lucky to have their dreams come true." Indeed.

At 82, Dick died of a heart attack following surgery to fix an enlarged prostate. He was cremated and his ashes scattered in the Pacific Ocean.

PATSY CLINE
SEPTEMBER 8, 1932 – MARCH 5, 1963

AFTER HER SOPHOMORE year, Virginia Hensley left high school to work the food counter at a Greyhound bus terminal and help support her dirt-poor Appalachian family. At local beer joints "Patsy" entertained as a singer in honky-tonk bands, and in 1954 was invited onto the *Town and Country* radio program. The appearance led to her first single, "It Wasn't God Who Made Honky-Tonk Angels," which in turn led to a series of 1957 appearances on the *Arthur Godfrey Talent Show*.

Persuaded to drop her cowgirl attire for a more courtly cocktail dress, Patsy delivered her own heart-stopping rendition of "Walkin' After Midnight" during her first appearance on Godfrey's show. That performance won her a record deal, and by 1960 Patsy was a permanent member of the Grand Ole Opry. She enjoyed success with the chart-topping hit "I Fall to Pieces," but it was "Crazy," a song penned by Willie Nelson, that became Patsy's signature tune. By 1962 Patsy was a certified star, having made landmark appearances in Las Vegas, Hawaii, and at Carnegie Hall.

After a March 1963 concert in Kansas City, Patsy and fellow Opry stars Cowboy Copas and Hawkshaw Hawkins were stranded by a storm that grounded all flights. After almost two days, the weather finally cleared, they boarded their manager's Piper Comanche, and, after a couple hours, stopped for fuel in Dyersburg, Tennessee. But in traveling east, they'd caught up with the same front that had plagued them in Kansas City. Pilot and manager Randy Hughes was emboldened by the uneventful flight he'd just completed and, though he didn't have his instrument-flying certification, he rounded up his passengers and took off eastward again. Caught in a thunderstorm 60 miles out, the plane plunged to earth, and all aboard were lost.

At 30, Patsy was buried at Shenandoah Memorial Park in Winchester, Virginia.

Ten years later, Patsy was elected to the Country Music Hall of Fame, its first female solo artist.

GRAVE DIRECTIONS: At the first pair of brick pillars, turn into the park at 1270 Front Royal Pike, then turn at the next right, toward the office. Stop after 80 feet and, on the right, you'll see a square, concrete pad; on the left is a stone bench. Patsy's grave is just to the left of this bench. There is also a bell tower erected in her memory at the park.

In 1996, a stone memorial with the names of those lost in the crash was installed at the accident site in Camden, Tennessee. About three miles north of town on Mt. Carmel Road is a sign directing the way to the monument.

NAT KING COLE
MARCH 17, 1919 – FEBRUARY 15, 1965

AS IS THE case of many African American musicians, Nat King Cole's early training came through gospel singing at church and hymns learned on a piano. By 16, he was an up-and-comer on the Chicago jazz scene known for his versatility on the piano; outside of his father's church, he'd never sung a note. A couple years later, in 1938, Nat landed in Los Angeles and formed the first of the Nat King Cole trios, soon becoming renowned as a swing pianist.

By 1940 the schoolboyish Nat had gained confidence in his own singing, and he developed into an outright crooner; in 1944 his trio had their first major hit with "Straighten Up and Fly Right," and, as it received heavy rotation on the radio, Nat began de-emphasizing his piano. By 1950, thanks in part to the success of his landmark recordings of "The Christmas Song" and "Mona Lisa," his smooth vocal style eclipsed his exemplary piano talents, and Nat emerged as one of the day's most celebrated pop artists.

Not everyone was enamored of Nat's success, though, and the ugly issue of race confronted the crooner. A 1954 concert in Birmingham was ended early by a group of Ku Klux Klan members. Later, as Nat mulled the purchase of a beautiful Hollywood home, an uptight community committee moved to block the sale. Telling Nat they didn't want any undesirables in the neighborhood, he famously replied, "If any move in, I'll let you know." Ultimately, restrictive covenants excluding home sales to Jews and Negroes were removed by the courts.

But in 1957, consistent with the civil rights movement that had begun to roil the nation, the issue reached a boiling point when Nat launched his own television program, *The Nat King Cole Show* on NBC, the first to feature a black host. The show became one of the most popular shows of the time, but not solely for its entertainment value; it was a social experiment too. Black viewers who were starved for positive television images flocked to the program even as the urbane and elegant Nat was cherished by white viewers. But affiliate Southern stations would not carry the show and, with the deepening racial tensions of the 1950s, it became increasingly difficult to attract corporate sponsors. After Nat outraged some white viewers by touching the arm of a white female guest, the show was canceled in 1958.

A heavy smoker, Nat's velvet voice and his health deteriorated rapidly in the early 1960s. At 45 he died of lung cancer. At his funeral, Jack Benny offered this epitaph: "Sometimes death is not as tragic as not knowing how to live. This man knew how to live and how to make others glad they were living."

Nat rests at Forest Lawn Memorial Park in Glendale, California.

CEMETERY DIRECTIONS: From Highway 2, exit at San Fernando Road and follow it 1¼ miles north to Glendale Avenue. Make a right and the cemetery entrance is on the right. Stop at the booth for a map of the cemetery's roads, then drive to the Freedom Mausoleum.

GRAVE DIRECTIONS: Walk in the front entrance of the Freedom Mausoleum, proceed down the hall on the right, then turn left into the Sanctuary of Heritage. On the right, along the top row, is Nat's crypt.

JOHN COLTRANE
SEPTEMBER 23, 1926 – JULY 17, 1967

APPRENTICING WITH MILES Davis and Dizzy Gillespie, the composer and improviser John Coltrane secured a lofty jazz throne many years before his modern jazz classics *Giant Steps* and *My Favorite Things* lent him widespread commercial success in the early 1960s. Later, John explored new territories in free jazz and collective improvisation and introduced Eastern music to the scene too.

But the ride to success was bumpy and, for a time, it seemed that John's personal troubles would derail his career. Those concerns were realized when Miles Davis, who had already beaten his own heroin addiction, fired John in 1956 for his assorted dependencies. But with the support of his Christian mother and his Muslim wife, John experienced a spiritual awakening the next year and he quit doing drugs. Still, though, John's personal life contrasted with his professional good fortune; in 1959 he

lost his front teeth due to the residual effects of his heroin addiction, in 1964 he was agitated by a divorce that was prompted by him twice impregnating pianist Alice McLeod, and in 1965 John began a struggle to control his weight.

By 1967 John and Alice were married and enjoyed a comfortable Long Island life with their three children, but John was not well; he was fatter than ever and a constant pain nagged in his side. After he collapsed on his front porch, doctors finally discovered that a cancerous tumor had attached itself to his grossly cirrhotic liver, and three weeks later John was dead.

At 40, John was buried at Pinelawn Memorial Park in Farmingdale, New York.

GRAVE DIRECTIONS: At 2030 Wellwood Avenue, enter the park at the main entrance, which is William H. Locke Drive. Turn at the second left after the office onto Walt Whitman Drive, then turn at the second right onto Oak Drive. After a hundred yards, park at the turnout on the right. Across the drive is a brick wall, and John's grave is 24 rows beyond the wall.

PERRY COMO
MAY 18, 1912 – MAY 12, 2001

AS A 20-YEAR-OLD barber, Italian-American Pierino Como grew tired of cutting the hair of western Pennsylvania coal miners, and instead struck out for Cleveland, where he had an offer to sing with a big band of the day. After the orchestra broke up in 1942, the young and charming Perry showcased his melodic baritone as the host of a regional radio show, *Supper Club*, which attracted recording executives from every label.

Perry began recording, and his watershed came in 1945 when his dreamy rendition of "Till the End of Time" from the film *A Song to Remember* spent 10 weeks at the top of the charts, making it the biggest hit of the year. Confessing that his relaxed style was a direct emulation of Bing Crosby, Perry competed with his mentor for recognition as the era's top crooner, and his songs became a mainstay of radio and jukeboxes. But throughout his life, he was never particularly impressed with his own success, and in fact seemed surprised by it. "I don't have a lot to tell the average interviewer. I've done nothing that I can call exciting. I was a barber. After that I've been a singer. That's it."

In 1948, Perry crossed over to the emerging medium of television with the *Chesterfield Supper Club,* one of the earliest variety programs. Perpetually tanned and bedecked in cardigan sweaters, the youthful-looking Perry soon switched networks for his own *Perry Como Show.* Perry later began to indulge in lighter novelty fare, the titles often comprising nonsense words like "Bibbidi-Bobbidi-Boo" and "Hot Diggity Dog Ziggity Boom." These songs cemented Perry's reputation as a king of middle-of-the-road pop. To his credit, Perry openly disdained the lightweight numbers but good-naturedly patronized audiences by continuing to perform them.

By 1960, as rock and rollers crowded out screaming bobby-soxers, the appeal of Perry's breezy songs began to wane. In 1963 he gave up his regular television show and retreated to gala appearances and Christmas specials. But he returned in 1970 with a world tour, and his single "It's Impossible" made it to the Top 10. Still, his ultra-mellow stage manner clashed with the day's popular music and he became an obvious target for critics. Perry's resurgence was short-lived.

In 1974 he retired to Florida with his wife of more than 60 years. One Friday afternoon, in 2001, after sharing ice cream with his daughter and grandson, Perry went for a nap and died of natural causes at 88.

Perry is buried at Riverside Memorial Park in Tequesta, Florida.

GRAVE DIRECTIONS: Enter the park at 19351 SE County Line Road and turn left at the flagpole. Past the two mausoleum buildings there is a section of upright granite headstones on the right, and that's where you'll find Perry. His stone is nearly at the halfway mark, and not far from the road.

HARRY "BING" CROSBY
MAY 2, 1901 – OCTOBER 14, 1977

HARRY CROSBY'S LIFELONG moniker, Bing, was adopted from a popular comic strip he enjoyed as a child, *Bingville Bugle*.

Before electric amplification, lung power and projection were nearly as important as the ability to carry a tune. But Bing was among the first to rely on a microphone, and the informal fireside style it afforded him tugged the heartstrings of millions. His crooning was a welcome reprieve for Depression-era audiences, and as WWII raged, his renditions of "Silent Night" and "White Christmas" pointedly highlighted the nation's sorrows and separations due to the war.

Soon Bing was a box-office attraction too. He appeared in more than 60 motion pictures, and among his most popular features were his "road" movies with Bob Hope, *The Road to Singapore* and *The Road to Zanzibar*, among others. Since he was still recording and performing—he recorded some 1,600 songs in his lifetime—Bing was at this time easily the number one star in show business. By the 1960s, though, Bing's brilliant career wound down as ballads gave way to rock and roll, the tastes of movie audiences changed, and the younger generation moved in.

As one of the best-paid entertainers in the country, Bing was also one of the shrewdest. Over the years he invested his show business fortune and amassed an even greater fortune through a wide range of business interests in everything from frozen orange juice to oil wells, from cattle and racehorses to prizefighters, and from professional baseball and hockey teams to banks.

By the 1970s Bing's health was a bit shaky; a tumor was removed from his lung in 1973, and he was later hospitalized for a month after falling headfirst into an orchestra pit. After a two-week engagement at the London Palladium, Bing, an expert golfer, traveled to Spain to play La Morajela golf course near Madrid. After scoring an 85 and defeating two Spanish pros, Bing sauntered toward the clubhouse and collapsed from a massive heart attack.

Like many of his contemporaries, throughout his professional life Bing conveniently adjusted his date of birth by a few years. He was 76 when buried at Holy Cross Cemetery in Culver City, California, not 72 or 73 as he'd led most to believe.

GRAVE DIRECTIONS: Enter the cemetery at 5835 Slauson Avenue, turn left, and start up the hill. One hundred yards to the left is the Grotto lawn and altar, and four rows from the altar is Bing's grave.

MILES DAVIS

MAY 25, 1926 – SEPTEMBER 28, 1991

AFTER COMING OF age in the bebop era, the fiercely independent Miles Davis followed no one and refused to settle into any particular style. Instead, every 10 years or so, the master instigated a new format—cool jazz, hard bop, modal, and fusion—each turn invariably instigating a short-term negative critical reaction quickly overcome by long-term critical acclaim.

Generally, Miles definitively declared his new phases with landmark works: *The Birth of the Cool* in 1949, *Milestones* in 1958, and *Bitches Brew* in 1969. This last work became the standard for the nascent jazz-fusion movement, and was an especially important milestone because its abrupt commingling of jazz, rock, and funk (not to mention its freaky cover art) crossed over to rock audiences; Miles was "discovered" by a new, far-out generation. Overtly influenced by Jimi Hendrix and leaning toward rock in the 1970s, Miles even went so far as to share a stage with the Grateful Dead.

Although he had created yet another musical genre, Miles left it in 1975 when he dropped everything and retired for five years. His battles against heroin and alcohol addiction, his unmerciful quest for perfection, and a relentless touring schedule had taken their tolls on his health, and Miles suffered from ulcers, throat nodes, and bursitis. He claimed not to have touched his trumpet even once in those years. But as fusion sputtered in the early 1980s, Miles emerged again to return to an approach that was successful during the 1950s bop years, bravely embracing and reinterpreting popular songs. In Cyndi Lauper's

"Time After Time" and Michael Jackson's "Human Nature," Miles reminded audiences that his piercing sound, more than any voice, could touch the soul.

Miles died of respiratory failure at 65 and was buried at Woodlawn Cemetery in the Bronx, New York.

GRAVE DIRECTIONS: At East 233rd Street and Webster Avenue, the Woodlawn Cemetery is enormous and, if there's someone in the booth at the front gate, you should get a map. Otherwise, just proceed past the booth and keep the fence on your left. At Robin Avenue, turn right, merge onto Knollwood, then turn left onto Heather Avenue. Miles is in the Alpine Section along Heather Avenue. You won't miss his stone adjacent to Duke Ellington's.

JOHN DENVER
DECEMBER 31, 1943 – OCTOBER 12, 1997

A FOLK-POP BALLADEER with a breezy voice and an almost childlike love of nature, Henry John Deutschendorf Jr., better known as John Denver, earned international acclaim as a singer, songwriter, and humanitarian. John's first big break came in 1967 while making the rounds on the lonely folk nightclub scene; Peter, Paul, and Mary took one of his singles, "Leaving on a Jet Plane," and turned it into a number one hit. John's songwriting abilities soon became obvious to music companies, he secured a record deal, and over the next decade was a *Billboard* mainstay for such hits as "Rocky Mountain High," "Country Roads," and "Sunshine on My Shoulders."

With his wholesome good looks, hippieish wire-rimmed glasses, and aw-shucks disposition, John was a natural star of the television era and there became a fixture, harmonizing with everyone from George Burns to Kermit the Frog to Jacques Cousteau.

John's musical passions provided him the monetary means to pursue another of his passions: flying. By 1997 John was a very experienced pilot and had turned from traditional Cessnas to more esoteric craft, including an experimental, fiberglass aircraft called the Long EZ. This plane had a fuel selection valve located inside the cockpit that allowed the pilot the choice of drawing fuel from either the left or right tanks. However, the valve was located behind the pilot's left shoulder, and the only way to manipulate it was for the pilot to release the flight controls, twist around to the left, and turn the valve with his right hand. Further, in order to twist around, it was necessary for the pilot to brace his right foot, which was very difficult to accomplish without pressing the right rudder pedal all the way to the floor.

On a Sunday afternoon, John practiced touch-and-go landings with his new Long EZ at Monterey Airport in California. After accomplishing a few go-rounds, he went for a spin down the coast. Minutes later, at an altitude of only 500 feet, the engine of his plane started sputtering, starved for fuel. As John reached around to turn the fuel valve, his foot pressed on the right rudder and the plane rolled to the right, obliterating itself in a full-speed nosedive into the choppy Pacific waters.

What remains could be recovered were cremated, and John's ashes were scattered at his ranch in his adopted hometown of Aspen, Colorado. He was 53.

ELLA FITZGERALD
APRIL 25, 1918 – JUNE 16, 1996

SLIDING EFFORTLESSLY FROM bebop to ballads and employing endlessly inventive vocal improvisations over three full octaves, Ella Fitzgerald thrilled audiences and was her generation's preeminent jazz singer.

A 1938 swing version of the classic nursery rhyme "A-Tisket, A-Tasket" was her first hit, after which Ella moved almost immediately to "scat" singing, a form she adopted to accommodate the spontaneity of Dizzy Gillespie's band. She spent the war years with various road shows, and in 1955 she recorded a series of songbook albums, each devoted to a particular composer, which are generally regarded as her best work. In an attempt to broaden her base in the 1960s, Ella embarrassed herself with a country album but quickly returned to jazz with a new vigor. By career's end, she had recorded over 2,000 songs and sold some 40 million albums.

The 1970s marked the decline of her beautiful voice and her health, and in her last years Ella was nearly blind and her lower legs had been amputated. From complications of diabetes, she died at 79 and is buried at Inglewood Park Cemetery in Inglewood, California.

GRAVE DIRECTIONS: Enter at 720 East Florence Avenue, turn right, and park at the Sunset Mission mausoleum. In the entrance on the front right, proceed down the El Sereno hall, go up the stairs, and turn left at the top. In this Sanctuary of Bells, Ella's crypt is on the right, second row from the bottom.

GEORGE &
IRA GERSHWIN

GEORGE GERSHWIN
SEPTEMBER 26, 1898 – JULY 11, 1937

IRA GERSHWIN
DECEMBER 6, 1896 – AUGUST 17, 1983

IN A CAREER tragically cut short by a brain tumor, the composer George Gershwin, who bestrode the realms of both pop music and concert music, proved himself to be one of the great songwriters of his extremely rich era.

George left school in 1913 and, combining his classical piano training with the popular ragtime style, he became a major figure in the Tin Pan Alley tradition, composing for Broadway shows under the pseudonym Arthur Francis during his teens. At 20 came his first real hit, "Swanee," and the same year saw his first Broadway musical, *La, La, Lucille.* During the next 18 years, George produced an impressive amount of music and, with lyrics written largely by his older brother, Ira, their songs came to define the 1920s and '30s while musicals like *Strike Up the Band* and *Of Thee I Sing* delighted Broadway audiences.

In 1924 George composed his first classical piece, *Rhapsody in Blue,* as a piano concerto for a popular band, and its success made George contemplate the wide gap between Tin Pan Alley's simple arrangements and classical music's serious offerings. To him, that void represented an unrestricted frontier. By that simple abstraction, George strove to unite commercial and classical genres, and the result was historic jazz-oriented concert works such as *Rhapsody in Blue* and *An American in Paris,* as well as the folk opera *Porgy and Bess.* Almost every one of his concert works has entered the theater, and the American psyche, and people with no interest in opera hum parts of his pieces without knowing where the material came from or even that it's part of something larger.

In the mid-1930s George and Ira had a successful run in Hollywood writing for Fred Astaire and Ginger Rogers but, for some reason, the normally athletic and cheerful George grew less enchanted with the parties and womanizing he used to enjoy. In February 1937 his mind went blank during a performance, though a few moments later he continued without interruption. Two months after that, he had a similar blackout in a barbershop and, each time, George said the lapse was accompanied by the smell of burning rubber.

By June, George was suffering painful headaches and was often confused, groggy, and irritable. Doctors could find nothing wrong with him and attributed his pains to stress. On July 9, George was too weak to get out of bed. He soon fell into a coma, and doctors finally diagnosed an inoperable brain tumor. George's condition deteriorated rapidly and he died two days later at 38.

Following George's death, Ira continued writing and made a successful living composing scores for films until his death from natural causes at 86.

Both George and Ira rest at Westchester Hills Cemetery in Hastings-on-Hudson, New York.

GRAVE DIRECTIONS: At 400 Saw Mill River Road, follow the main drive into the cemetery. The brothers are in the third mausoleum on the right. Though the mausoleum's primary marker is engraved "George Gershwin," Ira lies there as well.

DIZZY GILLESPIE
OCTOBER 21, 1917 – JANUARY 6, 1993

AS A PRIME architect of the 1940s movement from swing to bebop, jazz trumpeter Dizzy Gillespie set new standards for horn players and also wrote some of the era's greatest tunes, including "Groovin' High" and "A Night in Tunisia." Dizzy is also lovingly revered for his zany antics, the skyward bent bell of his horn, and the "happy clown" personality that begot the Dizzy moniker.

At first interested in the trombone, he gave it up after realizing his arms were too short to play it well and instead switched to trumpet, quickly earning local jazz notoriety as a talented and fun up-and-comer. Though his high-spirited disposition won him notice and opportunity, his antics lost him at least one opportunity too: Onstage in 1941, Dizzy "just nicked" the posterior of the equally silly zoot-suited bandleader Cab Calloway with a knife. The "nick" took 10 stitches to close, and closed the association between Cab and Dizzy to boot, though they later reconciled.

In 1953 Dizzy's stage appearance, which already featured black horn-rimmed glasses and a beret, was further peculiarized by his instrument itself, its bell bent at a heavenward 45-degree angle. The bend in his horn was originally accidental, caused by another musician falling on his trumpet during an episode of backstage roughhousing. Without another instrument available, Dizzy went onstage with his bent trumpet and was happy to find that he could hit some notes a little softer due to its slightly restricted airway. A trumpet manufacturer began bending Dizzy's trumpet bells upward and that, along with his impossibly bulbous cheeks, became his visual trademark.

In 1956 Dizzy became bandleader for a State Department jazz band that gave goodwill and diplomatic performances worldwide. Later he recorded and toured with other bebop legends and all-star groups, and in his final years, his clean lifestyle and entertaining audience rapport were rewarded as he basked in high regard as one of jazz's true elder statesmen.

After a bout with pancreatic cancer, Dizzy died at 75 and was buried at Flushing Cemetery in Flushing, New York.

GRAVE DIRECTIONS: Enter the cemetery at 163 46th Avenue, bear left, and stay left all the way to the back of the cemetery. At Section 30, look for the "Tassa" stone on your left, next to the curb. Dizzy lies 150 feet behind the Tassa stone, four rows from the back fence.

BENNY GOODMAN
MAY 9, 1909 – JUNE 13, 1986

STRUGGLING TO RAISE a family of 11 on sweatshop wages in Chicago's impoverished Jewish ghetto, Benny Goodman's father believed music might be a ticket out of poverty for his eldest sons. He enrolled them in the free music classes that were offered at a local synagogue when Benny was just 10 and, as his older brothers were given a tuba and a trombone, little Benny was handed a clarinet. For the rest of his life, he hardly let go of it.

Benny dropped out of school at 15 to establish himself as a professional musician and was soon a member of the Ben Pollack Orchestra. The Swing era was an exciting time for music in America. A stepchild of jazz, swing was characterized by very large, bass-heavy bands whose musicians took alternating solos, in contrast to group improvisation. The rhythms of big band swing jazz quickened the pulse of a generation determined to jitterbug their way through the Depression, and it initiated a culture of defiant dress and "hipster" attitude. Swing's frenzied followers, bobby-soxers, answered to no one except their own "King of Swing," who by the mid-1930s was clearly Benny Goodman.

With clarinet in hand, the tall, apple-cheeked Benny and his various bands were greeted with near pandemonium wherever they played. Through swing, Benny led jazz into the commercial mainstream, was the first major bandleader to put black and white musicians together onstage, and even introduced the common man's music to the sanctity of Carnegie Hall, blowing wide its staid walls with a performance whose live recording later became one of the best-selling jazz albums of all time.

But for all its excitement and spirit, swing jazz faded just as quickly as it had come into prominence, and by the 1940s big bands had been eclipsed by a new jazz form, bebop. Benny formed a small group that performed selected television engagements and toured throughout the 1950s and '60s and his life story, *The Benny Goodman Story*, became a celluloid box-office hit in 1955. Compared to his wildest days as the King of Swing, Benny was no longer in great demand, but there was still a place for his music; Benny's last days were spent as a goodwill ambassador at occasional musical engagements.

Tireless in a quest for impeccable music structure, Benny demanded excellence from band members who, at times, wearied of his meticulous temperament. After Benny's death, one of his pianists remarked, "With him, perfection was always just around the corner. I figured Benny would die in bed practicing that damn clarinet." As it turns out, he wasn't too far off. After rehearsing a Brahms sonata for an upcoming performance at Lincoln Center, Benny lay down on his couch and expired of a heart attack in his sleep.

At 77, Benny was buried at Long Ridge Cemetery in Stamford, Connecticut.

GRAVE DIRECTIONS: At 156 Erskine Road, Benny's grave is in the third row from the back, approximately halfway along the cemetery's length. It's marked with a flat stone and a small bench.

MERLE HAGGARD
APRIL 6, 1937 – APRIL 6, 2016

AS COUNTRY MUSIC legend Merle Haggard recalled, his schoolboy days consisted mainly of making up songs while staring out the window. That early creativity never flagged and for most of his life he composed wherever he went, all day, every day; decades later he guessed he may have written 10,000 songs. Though the gruff troubadour could find inspiration in everyday banality ranging from a rose to a road sign, some of his most beloved songs—the prison diaries of "Mama Tried" and "Sing Me Back Home" or the hard-living anthem "I Think I'll Just Stay Here and Drink"—were inspired by the pages of his life.

After his father died when Merle was nine, the rudderless boy became a troublemaker who rotated through reform schools. Finally, in 1957, his pages-long rap sheet inspired a judge to hand the young incorrigible a man-sized sentence and Merle was delivered to San Quentin for a 6-to-15-year visit. The next year, Johnny Cash performed at San Quentin for what was the first of a series of Cash concerts held at various prisons, and Haggard was in the audience. As Merle recalled, "When he walked away, everyone in that place had become a Johnny Cash fan. I saw the light. I realized what a mess I made out of my life, and I got out of there and stayed out of there. Never did go back."

After being paroled a couple years later, Merle did turn his life around and wasted no time unfurling his musical gifts. As one of the key architects of the revved-up and twangy Bakersfield sound, he produced an astonishing string of more than 100 hits, 38 of which were number one singles. Capturing the American condition in a rough and hard-edged rockabilly style, Merle's supple baritone championed the dignities of the flag-waving working class, the laments of the outsider, and the desolation of the heartbroken, in hits such as "The Fightin' Side of Me," "Workin' Man Blues," and "If We Make It Through December."

Though he was forever thankful for his life's favorable post-prison turn, he continued to live on the knife's edge: Merle made millions, but five marriages and four divorces helped send him to bankruptcy court, while drugs and drinking didn't do him any favors either. Later, as country music softened and morphed into something he called "bubble-gum," Merle was marginalized, his hits ebbed, and his audience shrank, though he and his band, the Strangers, hardly paused from touring. Labeling his life "a 45-year bus ride," in his later years he confessed to "a restlessness in my soul that I've never conquered, not with motion, marriages, or meaning. I've mellowed a lot, but it's still there to a degree. And it will be till the day I die."

On the morning of his 79th birthday, eight years after a lung cancer diagnosis necessitated the removal of part of a lung, Merle died of double pneumonia. He was buried on the grounds of his 168-acre Palo Cedro ranch in California, and there are no visiting hours.

WHITNEY HOUSTON

AUGUST 9, 1963 – FEBRUARY 11, 2012

WITH THE VOICE, looks, and pedigree of a superstar, Whitney Houston emerged as one of the 1980s' greatest vocalists. Showcasing her choir-trained and polished voice in a niche straddling pop and R&B, her debut album of sweet and catchy love songs, *Whitney Houston*, sold some 12 million copies and featured three number one singles: "Saving All My Love for You," "How Will I Know," and "The Greatest Love of All."

Cultivating the image of a fun-loving but ardent good girl while dressed in everything from formal gowns to T-shirts, Whitney enjoyed boundless popularity, which she soon parlayed into entry to the movie business. Her acting in 1992's *The Bodyguard* was strong and convincing, while her octave-stretching version of the soundtrack's "I Will Always Love You" became another of her calling cards. In quick succession, the movies *Waiting to Exhale* and *The Preacher's Wife* gave Whitney occasion for two more hit albums.

But by the mid-1990s, Whitney had become, as she told Oprah Winfrey, a "heavy" user of marijuana and cocaine. She married the singer Bobby Brown but their relationship—which was documented in a forgettable reality-TV series named *Being Bobby Brown*—was turbulent, marred by drug use and by his professional jealousies, and spoiled with psychological and physical abuse. The couple had a daughter in 1993, Bobbi Kristina Brown, and in 2007 they divorced.

By the 2000s Whitney was struggling. Her voice grew smaller, scratchier, and less secure, and fans grumbled of live performances that were less than stellar. New albums billed

as "comebacks" slipped quickly and quietly from the charts. Tabloids swarmed and *The National Enquirer* ran a photo of her bathroom showing drug paraphernalia. Still revered for her once-soaring and heavenly voice, she remained a cherished pop diva, but there were concerns.

As the music industry descended on the Grammy Awards in 2012, Whitney was found dead, submerged in the bathtub of Suite 434 at the Beverly Hilton. Police reported there were no signs of criminal intent, and two days later the coroner's office reported her cause of death as drowning due to the "effects of atherosclerotic heart disease and cocaine use." Later toxicology tests revealed the presence of Benadryl, Xanax, and marijuana in her system.

In 2015, Bobbi Kristina met a fate eerily similar to her mother's when she was found face down in the bathtub of her Georgia home. Though she was still alive and breathing, doctors determined her to have "global and irreversible brain damage." After languishing in a coma for nearly seven months Bobbi passed on at 22, the underlying cause of her death cited as "immersion associated with drug intoxication."

Both Whitney and Bobbi are buried at Fairview Cemetery in Westfield, New Jersey.

GRAVE DIRECTIONS: At 250 Gallows Hill Road, enter at the drive across from the Greek Orthodox church, make two quick rights, and then follow Memorial Drive around its sharp left-hand bend. After about 500 feet is a drive that intersects on the left—don't turn at that left, but at that point begin counting rows of gravestones on the right-hand lawn. In the 10th row, Whitney and Bobbi are side by side.

BURL IVES
JUNE 14, 1909 – APRIL 14, 1995

OVER THE COURSE of a long and diverse show business career, the jovial balladeer Burl Ives was a memorable presence in 30 movies and a dozen Broadway productions, recorded over 100 albums, and gave countless radio and television performances.

As a child, he had performed in public for change, but his real start in the business came in 1929 when he dropped out of teachers' college to wander the country like a vagabond, playing banjo and singing to keep himself fed. His first professional roles came in theater—Burl's high-watermark there came later, though, in 1958, when he originated the role of Big Daddy in *Cat on a Hot*

Tin Roof. By 1940 Burl had moved into radio with his own show, *The Wayfarin' Stranger.*

At the same time, with his especially sweet and mournful method of singing folk ballads, Burl was putting his stamp on standards from *Jimmy Crack Corn* to *I Know an Old Lady (Who Swallowed a Fly)* as well as on such children's songs as *Frosty the Snowman* and *Rudolph the Red-Nosed Reindeer.* His role as the narrator in the TV version of that annual holiday classic has endeared him to several generations of young people.

Burl was an imposing figure who loved to smoke, eat, and drink. For most of his life, he carried more than 300 pounds on his frame. Despite his size, Burl lived to be 85, when he died of mouth cancer. He was buried at Mound Church Cemetery in Willow Hill, Illinois.

GRAVE DIRECTIONS: Halfway between Newton and Oblong, turn north onto CR 2100, then east onto CR 1200, and you'll see Burl's stone behind the church.

WAYLON JENNINGS

JUNE 15, 1937 — FEBRUARY 13, 2002

WITH LONG HAIR, a black hat, and a bearded, scowling face, Waylon Jennings was one of the first musicians to bring real attitude to country music. By the time he came along in the mid-1960s, country had already had its share of rogues, from Hank Williams to Johnny Cash, but Waylon institutionalized the unapologetic swagger and menacing overtones of "Outlaw" country music and helped sow the seeds for the country megastars who would burst onto the scene two decades later.

Having already formed his own band at age 12, Waylon dropped out of school two years later (he eventually earned his GED at age 51) to pursue an opportunity as a disc jockey. When he was 17, Waylon met rising rock star Buddy Holly at the radio station and the two became fast friends; Buddy produced Waylon's first record. "Mainly what I learned from Buddy," Waylon said, "was an attitude. He loved music, and he taught me that it shouldn't have any barriers to it."

Buddy later employed Waylon as a bass player, taking him on his 1959 Winter Dance Party tour. In Clear Lake, Iowa, an exhausted Buddy chartered a small plane to get to the next gig and invited Waylon to join him, but Waylon gave his seat to J.P. "Big Bopper" Richardson, who was suffering from the flu. The plane crashed soon after takeoff in the early hours of February 3, 1959, killing everyone aboard—Buddy, the Big Bopper, Ritchie Valens, and the pilot. For years, Waylon was haunted by a joking exchange they'd had just before Buddy left to meet the plane. "Buddy says, 'You're not going on the plane tonight, huh?' I said, 'No.' He said, 'Well, I hope your bus freezes up.' And I said, 'Well, I hope your plane crashes.' I was awful young, and it took me a long time to get over that."

By the mid-'60s, Waylon had cultivated an instantly identifiable country-rockabilly style that featured a thudding, walk-all-over-you bass, a "chicken-pickin'" guitar technique, and rough-edged, plain-spoken lyrics. His rowdy image made him almost as famous as his music and, for a while, he shared a Nashville apartment with Johnny Cash after their respective marriages broke up. The pair lived high on methamphetamines and general destruction, and after Johnny remarried and got sober, Waylon complained that he'd "sold out to religion." Waylon also eventually gave up drugs, but he never gave in to religion. Despite his offstage behavior, he became a sought-after club headliner and recorded more than 60 albums and had dozens of hits, including "Walk On Out Of My Mind" and "Are You Sure Hank Done It This Way?"

In the 1980s, the original country-music legends fell from favor as the genre reverted to slick stylings, but Waylon, along with Willie Nelson, Johnny Cash, and Kris Kristofferson, shrewdly formed a superstar quartet and, as the Highwaymen, the musicians found success anew. But Waylon still remained an outlaw, blowing off his induction into the Country Music Hall of Fame. "It means absolutely nothing," he said, "if you want to know the truth."

Waylon was a lifelong sufferer of diabetes and in 2001 had a foot amputated. At 64, he died of the disease and was buried at the City of Mesa Cemetery in Mesa, Arizona.

GRAVE DIRECTIONS: Enter the cemetery at 1212 North Center Street and then turn left on Ninth Street, stopping at the sixth tree on the left, where you'll find Waylon tucked into the fourth row.

GEORGE JONES
SEPTEMBER 12, 1931 – APRIL 26, 2013

THOUGH HIS START was austere, busking for spare pennies and nickels on the streets of Beaumont, Texas, the hard-living baritone George Jones became a champion and symbol of traditional country music, eventually recording more than 150 albums.

At 19, George was forging his style on a daily radio show, performing six nights a week at a local country show for $17.50, and then had a brief fling with rockabilly, recording as Thumper Jones. But after a stint in the Marine Corps, he found his center, scored his first Top 5 hit with 1955's rousing "Why Baby Why," and began racking up a string of country-classic hits like "White Lightning" and "Window Up Above."

Universally respected and just as widely imitated, his precise baritone found vulnerability and doubt behind the cheerful drive of honky-tonk. But his up-tempo melodies had undercurrents of solitude, the ballads that were his specialty were suffused with stoic desolation, and even his memorable songs of the pleasures of a down-home Saturday night never seemed to free him from his private pains. Nicknamed "Possum" for his close-set eyes and pointed nose, and later "No-Show Jones" for the scores of concerts he missed during drinking binges, he bought, sold, and traded dozens of houses and hundreds of cars, he earned millions of dollars but losing much of it to drug use, mismanagement, and three divorce settlements. And through it all, George still kept recording; as his troubles increased, so did his fame and his album sales. "I was country music's national drunk and drug addict," he said.

After rehab in 1969 it seemed he had turned a corner, and that same year George married country music queen Tammy Wynette and quit the road to open the country-themed Old Plantation Music Park around his Florida mansion. The seemingly happy couple recorded elaborately arranged duets, three of which— "We're Gonna Hold On," "Golden Ring," and "Near You"—were number one country hits. But George's drinking and amphetamine addictions soon rekindled and, though they toured the nation in a bus adorned with a *Mr. and Mrs. Country Music* mural, the singers' marriage was falling apart, becoming a sort of public soap opera, with their audience following each new single as if they were news reports. In 1975, after a fight in which George was put in a straitjacket and hospitalized for a week, the couple divorced and the music park was shut down.

After the divorce, George grew even more erratic. At times he would sing in a Donald Duck voice onstage, his band members' paychecks bounced, and he began brandishing a gun. He led police on a televised chase through Nashville. When scheduled to play a series of sold-out gigs, he disappeared and rambled around Texas for three weeks instead. As his No-Show Jones nickname gained national circulation his singles slipped lower on the charts and he ended up declaring bankruptcy. Though he blamed his trajectory on everything

from bad management to the IRS, it was apparent that his troubles stemmed from abuse of cocaine and whiskey. At one point his wife hid the keys to all his cars, so he drove his lawn mower eight miles to a liquor store. They too were divorced not long afterward.

Yet, though he never bothered to wear a cowboy hat, George came to stand for country tradition and despite his travails he still had hits. "He Stopped Loving Her Today," a song about a man whose love ends only when his life does, is considered by many to be the greatest country song of all time.

In 1985, doctors gave George this choice: Dry out or die. He chose to turn his life around in a four-week program. "I did a lot of thinking," he said. "And I made up my mind—enough of that."

George stayed clean and, though his hit making slowed down, he became a revered elder statesman, often credited as an influence by generations that followed. "Through it all I kept reading articles that said I was the greatest country singer alive," he wrote in his 1996 memoir. "My talent, though it brought me fame and fortune, never brought me peace of mind."

At 81, George died of a respiratory infection. He was buried at Woodlawn Memorial Park in Nashville, the same cemetery in which his ex-wife Tammy Wynette rests.

GRAVE DIRECTIONS: Enter at the main entrance at 660 Thompson Lane, proceed to the four-way stop, and turn right at which point you'll clearly see the tall "Possum Kingdom" monument in the distance.

SCOTT JOPLIN
NOVEMBER 24, 1868 – APRIL 1, 1917

WHEN SCOTT JOPLIN settled in St. Louis in 1890 he was just an anonymous pianist, but by the time he left for New York 15 years later, he'd singlehandedly developed an entirely new musical genre. Scott created the form known as ragtime by blending European classical styles with African American harmonies and rhythms, and by the turn of the century had published 50 compositions in the vein, including "The Ragtime Dance," "The Easy Winners," and "The Entertainer."

In 1905 Scott settled in Harlem in the hope of elevating his new music to greater popularity. Having already successfully incorporated waltz and habanera dance beats into the style, Scott now sought to develop a ragtime opera. By 1910 his opera *Treemonisha* was complete and he turned it over to Irving Berlin for publication, though Berlin rejected it. The following spring Irving published a new hit song, "Alexander's Ragtime Band," and Scott was shocked to hear that Berlin had stolen the song's verse from a section of his own *Treemonisha*. This prompted Scott to alter that section of the opera so he himself couldn't be accused of plagiarizing Berlin, and to publish the opera himself the next year.

Unfortunately, there was no interest in Scott's opera. He was never able to raise any funds for the production of his masterpiece and he died without his *Treemonisha* ever having been performed. As further insult, within a decade after his 1917 death, Scott and his ragtime music were largely forgotten as a new improvisational style of jazz stole center stage. But in 1973, several of Scott's "rags" were selected for the soundtrack of a new movie, *The Sting*, which led to renewed interest in Scott's music. Two years later, Scott posthumously received his due when his magnum opus *Treemonisha*, after having lain dormant for more than 60 years, received its first professional production and earned a Pulitzer to boot.

After he'd suffered the effects of syphilis for the better part of a decade, the disease eventually got the better of Scott's mental capacities and, following a few months in a mental institution, he died there at 48.

Buried in an unmarked pauper's plot at Saint Michael's Cemetery in East Elmhurst, New York, Scott received an appropriate memorial 57 years later, an engraved stone donated by a group of admirers.

GRAVE DIRECTIONS: Enter the cemetery at 7202 Astoria Boulevard and proceed past the office. At the second intersection, on the left corner near the curb, you'll find Scott's grave.

PEGGY LEE
MAY 26, 1920 – JANUARY 21, 2002

NORMA DELORIS ENGSTROM grew up milking cows on a North Dakota farm and, after singing with the high school glee club, she made her singing debut on a local radio show. The manager there branded her "Peggy Lee," and she soon began singing with the dance bands of the late 1930s. During a gig at a Palm Springs nightspot, Peggy was unable to shout above the clamor of the audience, so she tried to garner attention by lowering her voice; the softer she sang, the more attentive the audience grew, and that soft and cool style, punctuated by seductive purrs, became her trademark.

After recording "Why Don't You Do Right?" with Benny Goodman's band in 1942, Peggy catapulted to fame and eventually wrote or collaborated on more than 500 songs. Today, it is common for singers to write their own songs, but in the 1940s, when there was a proliferation of music coming out of Tin Pan Alley, Broadway, and Hollywood, it was not; Peggy was among the first to pen and sing her own songs. In the 1950s, Peggy began making featured appearances in movies and was especially praised for her 1955 role opposite Danny Thomas in *The Jazz Singer*. However, Peggy is best remembered for her sultry simplicity and slow finger-snaps in the song "Fever," released in 1958.

Generations of children were introduced to Peggy's talents via the 1955 Disney animated feature, *Lady and the Tramp*. Peggy provided multiple character voices for the film and sang a half-dozen of its songs, including the cartoon's showstopper, "He's a Tramp." Peggy had retained all the rights and royalties of her *Tramp* work, but her contract—like the contracts of all performers of the day—didn't cover video residuals, since video technology was unknown in 1955. In 1988, after Disney trotted the feature out in video but failed to pay residuals, she sued. In 1991 she won her case in a landmark decision, prompting hundreds of other performers to claim their own video residuals.

After suffering a fall, undergoing double-bypass heart surgery, experiencing a serious stroke, and coping with her diabetes through all of this besides, Peggy had just about had it and was confined to a wheelchair. At 81, she died of a heart attack and was buried at Westwood Memorial Park in Los Angeles.

GRAVE DIRECTIONS: Behind the office complex at 10850 Wilshire Boulevard, enter the cemetery, turn left at the office, and walk into the Garden of Serenity area adjacent to the chapel. Near a bench dedicated to her memory in front of the triple fountain are Peggy's remains.

WOLFGANG AMADEUS MOZART
JANUARY 25, 1756 – DECEMBER 5, 1791

MOZART WAS A celebrated child prodigy who at age six delighted Salzburg audiences with his astounding ability to read difficult music perfectly and play an entire tune from memory after hearing it just once. By age 10 he had grown even more accomplished, equal in talent to that of his older contemporaries, and, as a teenager, he outstripped them.

Despite his reputation, Mozart could find no suitable post open to him, so in 1769 he set off for Italy and there produced his first large-scale opera series, including *Mitridate* and *Lucio Silla* all before the age of 18. After prolonged stays in Munich and Paris, Mozart ended up in Vienna at 25, where he would remain for the rest of his life, and there had one of the most prolific careers in the history of music.

In the 10 years before his premature death, Mozart's music rapidly grew beyond the comprehension of many of his contemporaries. Through dozens of works including symphonies and chamber music of the highest levels of imagination, he exhibited gifts that few could appreciate. Even more remarkable, Mozart produced his three greatest operas, *Figaro*, *Don Giovanni*, and *Cosi fan Tutte*, during the last three years of his life.

Finally, Mozart began work on what was to be his last project, the *Requiem*. This mass had been commissioned by a benefactor unknown to Mozart, and he became obsessed with the project for, in effect, he was writing it for himself. Ill and exhausted, he managed to finish the first two movements before being confined to his bed, suffering from blinding headaches, skin eruptions, and fainting spells. He finally became partially paralyzed and, after last rites were given, died quietly at only 35. Today it's believed that Mozart died either of rheumatic fever or uremia following chronic kidney disease.

For all his musical genius, Mozart was close to destitute at his time of death, received a third-class funeral, and was buried in a pauper's grave at Saint Marx Cemetery in Vienna, Austria. There's a monument there now, but it was erected in 1859 at the approximate location of his grave.

About 10 years after Mozart's death, the area where he was buried was dug up to make room for more burials, and the bones from those graves were crushed to reduce their size. After another hundred years, more or less, the Salzburg Mozarteum was presented with an unusual gift: Mozart's skull. Allegedly, a gravedigger rescued the skull during the "reorganization," and his descendants, finally tired of dusting the knick-knack, decided to let others enjoy it too. It's still on display there, but there's no evidence that it's really the master's.

BUCK OWENS
AUGUST 12, 1929 – MARCH 25, 2006

THE SHARECROPPING FAMILY of Alvis Owens once owned a mule named Buck, and one day six-year-old Alvis announced that from that day forward his name too was Buck. It stuck and nobody called him Alvis again.

The Texas farming family headed west in 1937 as part of the Dust Bowl migration but ended up settling in Arizona because of a busted truck. After he received a mandolin for Christmas at 13, music quickly consumed him and Buck hooked up with a honky-tonk band, Mac's Skillet Lickers. Throughout the 1950s Buck, who was married with a couple children by now, supported his family with session work and produced a number of singles, but they all fizzled. As his music aspirations foundered, Buck bought a one-third share of a tiny Washington State radio station and resorted to selling advertising and spinning records to keep food on the table. "If you had a really good radio, you could pick us up in the station parking lot," he recalled years later.

In time, though, a persistent Buck perfected his songwriting ability and a parade of classics followed, including "I've Got a Tiger by the Tail" and "Together Again." By the time the Beatles recorded a version of his "Act Naturally" and Ray Charles weighed in with a rendition of Buck's own "Cryin' Time," Buck wasn't looking back. Crafting a Telecaster-driven, rawer, and edgier structure than the refined and string-heavy traditional country sound of the day, Buck's new "Bakersfield sound" reshaped the country scene. With his streamlined, fresh yet unadorned style, he became the leading country music star of the 1960s, at one point releasing 15 consecutive number one singles.

Opposite Roy Clark, Buck co-hosted the *Hee-Haw* variety television show from 1969 to 1986, which he later acknowledged as a colossal professional blunder. The hokey and dim-witted program of cornball humor completely sullied his hard-earned reputation as a serious songwriter and performer and, perhaps even worse, younger audiences grew up knowing Buck as nothing more than a comedic country rube clad in overalls, strumming a red-white-and-blue guitar in a fake cornfield. In 1978, a few years after his beloved friend and bandmate Don Rich was killed in a motorcycle accident, the devastated artist quit the music business entirely except for the *Hee-Haw* tapings. "I think my music life ended when Rich did. Oh yeah, I carried on and I existed, but the real joy and love, the real lightning and thunder was gone forever," he confessed 25 years later. In those spare years Buck indulged in a slew of business interests including TV and radio stations, until a new enthusiasm was forged and neo-traditionalist Dwight Yoakam coaxed him back to recording and touring. In 1988 the pair recorded a chart-topping duet version of "Streets of Bakersfield."

A venture of which Buck was particularly proud was Crystal Palace, his own restaurant, nightclub, and museum, which opened in 1996 and where he performed dozens of impromptu gigs a year.

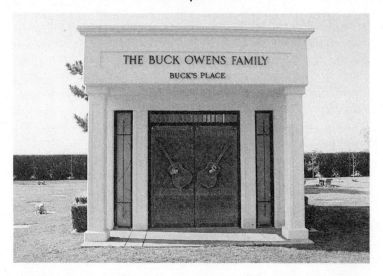

On a Friday night, after enjoying a favorite meal of chicken-fried steak, he declined to sit in on the night's music show after explaining to band members he wasn't feeling well. But before leaving the premises, a group of fans introduced themselves and explained they'd traveled all the way from Oregon on the chance that perhaps he would be joining the house band onstage that night. Predictably, the 76-year-old returned inside and performed an hour-long set, telling the audience, "If somebody comes all that way, I'm gonna give it my best shot. I might groan and squeak, but I'll see what I can do." Returning home later that night, Buck died in his sleep of heart failure.

Buck rests at Greenlawn Southwest Cemetery in Bakersfield, California.

GRAVE DIRECTIONS: Enter the cemetery at 2739 Panama Lane, turn at the first right, and proceed past the maintenance shed. Buck's beautiful family mausoleum will be on your right, and you won't miss it.

THE RAT PACK

IN THE LATE 1950s, well before Las Vegas was a Corporate America theme park, Frank Sinatra summoned four cronies to the Sands Hotel and Casino. Its Copa Room was promptly the hippest place in the universe.

With crooning lover-boy Frank as nominal "chairman," "the Rat Pack" became a cult of personalities living the high life of booze, broads, and bright lights. The group consisted of the chairman, himself; the easygoing singer Dean Martin; the one-eyed, singing and dancing wonder-boy Sammy Davis Jr.; the upper-crust, British pretty-boy Peter Lawford; and the stiff-shouldered comic Joey Bishop. They were the new American gods, and Las Vegas was their Mount Olympus.

Their "summit" meetings became the ultimate nightclub act and, while Las Vegas matured in their shadow, the quintet held court at their anything-goes playground. With a confidence and arrogance secured by seemingly all the money in the world, Frank and his swingin' pals, the culmination of cool, roasted one another with one-liners and belted out the hits of the day, and of days past. Reveling in their heady, bourbon-filled presence, drop-dead gorgeous women squirmed in their midst while starstruck common folk basked in the privilege of proximity.

The Rat Pack even conquered celluloid in such films as the casino-heist caper *Ocean's Eleven*, so everyone could share in their obvious fun. One of the Pack, Peter Lawford, was married to a woman whose brother happened to be named John F. Kennedy and, after the boys staged concerts to raise money for his 1960 presidential bid, the Oval Office got in on the gambol, initiating the trendy association of politics and celebrity.

But the carefree days didn't last, and after a few glory years, the Rat Pack dissolved. Relations between Frank and Peter soured when the president frowned on their mob-associated fraternity, and Joey soon rightfully returned to his own lightweight gigs. By 1964, as the nation struggled with a presidential assassination, a looming war in Vietnam, and turbulence brought on by civil rights protests, the Rat Pack seemed hopelessly anachronous, and there was no longer room for their world without rules or consequences. The years of high living had taken their toll and the fun was done.

PETER LAWFORD
SEPTEMBER 7, 1923 – DECEMBER 24, 1984

THOUGH HE APPEARED in dozens of films, was the first to kiss Elizabeth Taylor on camera, and counted himself among Marilyn Monroe's playmates, the debonair Peter Lawford was never a real Hollywood player. His membership in the Rat Pack was among the most tenuous and, in the first place, his ticket into Frank's golden circle seems to have been predicated on his standing with the Kennedy family. In 1962, after a row over Kennedy's objections to alleged Mafia connections, the two men never spoke again.

Peter peaked with the Rat Pack and after, in quick sequence, Frank snubbed him, Marilyn overdosed, and JFK was assassinated, Peter's career went south. It was briefly rejuvenated when he teamed with Sammy Davis Jr. in 1968's *Salt and Pepper* and its 1970 *One More Time* sequel, but, by the end of his life, the jet-setting playboy was broke, divorced three times, and his health had been destroyed by years of vodka, painkillers, and cocaine.

Peter was reduced to selling his life story to the tabloids and, at 61, he died of cardiac arrest complicated by kidney and liver failure. He was cremated and his ashes entombed but, three years later, it was learned that nobody had ever paid for the crypt maintenance. His children and wife at the time, Patricia Seaton, couldn't agree on who should pay the outstanding charges, so the tabloids were contacted again. In return for a photo spread of Peter's ashes being scattered at sea, *The National Enquirer* settled the balance with the cemetery.

SAMMY DAVIS JR.
DECEMBER 8, 1925 – MAY 16, 1990

SAMMY GOT HIS showbiz start at age three as Silent Sam, the Dancing Midget, alongside his father and uncle in vaudeville productions. Consequently, though it never seemed to matter, he *never* went to any kind of school. Sammy's tap-dancing film debut came in 1932 and, after serving during World War II, he returned to his father's troupe. In 1946, at 21, he recorded "The Way You Look Tonight," which was named Record of the Year.

By the mid-1950s Sammy was riding high as a mime, comedian, drummer, actor, singer, and dancer, but he faced a sudden setback in 1954 when he lost his left eye in a near-fatal auto accident. During his hospital recovery, he converted to Judaism, causing a press-sponsored hullabaloo. Undaunted, Sammy soon returned to the stage, wearing an eye patch until he could be fitted with a prosthetic, and within a year he enjoyed new hit singles, including "That Old Black Magic" and "Love Me or Leave Me." The next year he made his Broadway debut in the musical "Mr. Wonderful," which ran for some 400 performances.

A friendship that would last a lifetime ignited between Sammy and Frank Sinatra in 1949 and, 10 years later, Sammy counted himself as a charter member of Frank's Rat Pack. Barbed reproach was nothing new to Sammy and he was undaunted by criticism levied by many of his own race, who accused him of selling out as the token black in the white boys' pack. Those idle heckles paled against the public outcry and death threats that would follow his 1960 interracial marriage to Swedish actress May Britt.

But though he also later came under fire for his compulsive carousing and reckless gambling, and even for an admitted love for pornography and his 1972 support of Nixon, Sammy stuck to his art and rose above it all. Bedecked in heavy jewelry and clad in a snug jumpsuit or tuxedo, the slight showman with the crooked smile energized audiences and became one of America's most beloved entertainers.

By the late 1970s, though, after his chart-topping pop hit "Candy Man" and his own television variety show, Sammy's popularity waned, and he was primarily relegated to the casino circuit and second-rate films. With many from the entertainment world at his side, Sammy, a lifelong smoker, died of throat cancer at 64.

Wearing a pair of trademark Bojangles cuff links and a watch given him on his deathbed by Sinatra, Sammy was buried at Forest Lawn Memorial Park in Glendale, California.

GRAVE DIRECTIONS: Enter the park at 1712 South Glendale Avenue, stop at the booth for a cemetery map, then drive to the Freedom Mausoleum. Walk into the courtyards in front of the Freedom Mausoleum and you'll see two closed sections, the Gardens of Honor. Within the Garden of Honor section closer to the Freedom Mausoleum, Sammy lies two rows in front of the white Davis family statue.

DEAN MARTIN
JUNE 7, 1917 – DECEMBER 25, 1995

DINO PAUL CROCETTI sweated in steel mills, boxed under the name Kid Crochet, and smuggled bootleg liquor before making a go as a crooner and mutating into Dean Martin. By 1946, he was kibitzing onstage with a nasal comedian named Jerry Lewis, and within two years, they had the industry in their hands. Thirteen hugely popular straight-man-Martin and manic-fool-Lewis comedy films followed, but while Jerry's comedic ambitions ballooned, Dean's musical spirit simmered, despite the 1953 hit "That's Amore." By 1956, tired of breakups and make-ups prompted by Jerry's insecurities, Dean permanently dissolved the team. He never looked back and rarely even acknowledged Jerry's existence.

No one thought Dean would make it on his own, and he didn't. Instead the Rat Pack came calling and, in movies and Vegas nightclubs, Dean's persona was elevated to that of a most lovable and lecherous lush. Dean, with highball and cigarette firmly in hand, serenely floated above the fray, projecting a sense of utter detachment while audiences flocked to breathe the same rarefied air.

In 1964, Dean's deification was completed when "Everybody Loves Somebody" knocked the Beatles out of the number one spot. The next year saw the debut of the leering *Dean Martin Show*, but by the time of its cancelation nine seasons later, pop culture had inexorably shifted, and even Dean's workaday records no longer quite had a place. When playboy nihilism was finally shelved in the late 1970s, Dean's one-of-the-boys charisma made him seem absurdly passé and he loped through half-hearted singing gigs and celebrity roasts for the remainder of his life.

In 1987 his fighter-pilot son, Dino Jr., died in a plane crash and Dean completely removed himself from public life, spending his final quiet years haunting Hollywood restaurants alone. "I'm just waiting to die," he told Paul Anka one night.

On Christmas Day 1995, Dean's wait ended and he died of acute respiratory failure at 78.

He rests at Westwood Village Memorial Park in Los Angeles, California.

GRAVE DIRECTIONS: Behind the office complex at 10850 Wilshire Boulevard, enter the cemetery and look toward the cemetery office, on your far left is a series of alcoves. Dean's crypt is in the Sanctuary of Love alcove, third row from the bottom. His nameplate reminds us that "Everybody Loves Somebody Sometime."

FRANK SINATRA
DECEMBER 12, 1915 – MAY 14, 1998

BELIEVE IT OR NOT, Frank Sinatra once aspired to be a journalist. He was a copyboy at the *Jersey Observer* newspaper and, after enrolling in secretarial school where he studied English, typing, and shorthand, he was promoted to cub sports reporter. But as a self-taught singer, Frank was also working for $25 a week at a country roadhouse as a maitre d', singer, and comedian. It was there that he was discovered by Harry James in 1939.

After touring with James' band, Frank rose to prominence recording more than 90 songs with Tommy Dorsey's orchestra. By 1943 he was a film star as well, debuting in *Higher and Higher*, and his live performances were disrupted by the hysterical commotion of "bobby-soxer" fans. In 1949, though, Ol' Blue Eyes hit a soft spot; record sales stalled, concerts flopped due to his vocal cord hemorrhages, he was released from his film contract, and, on the personal front, an affair with Ava Gardner was an open scandal. At 34, the Voice seemed washed up.

Down but not out, Frank pulled himself out of the slump. With help from Ava, who was now his wife, Frank landed the role of the tough Italian, Angelo Maggio, in *From Here to Eternity* and, in 1953, he won an Academy Award for his efforts. A natural actor, Frank turned in top-notch performances in many more films, most notably *The Man With the Golden Arm* two years later and *The Manchurian Candidate* in 1962.

After his Academy win, Frank took off running once again. He overcame his vocal-cord afflictions and, armed with a new recording contract, Frank turned out a string of hits including "Young at Heart," "Hey! Jealous Lover," and "All the Way." It was his own golden era. By the time he held court as chairman of the board over his Rat Pack brothers, Frank held all the cards and dealt them in inimitable style.

By the mid-1960s, a sea change came over Las Vegas and, as new money domesticated business, Frank had to make way for the newcomers. His popularity softened ever so slightly and, in 1971, as his famous voice began to waver, he announced his retirement. Over the next two decades Frank cut back on records and movies and only performed occasionally. His last public appearance came in 1994.

At 82, Frank died of heart failure and was buried at Desert Memorial Park Cemetery in Cathedral City, California.

GRAVE DIRECTIONS: At 31705 Da Vall Drive, enter the cemetery, turn left, and follow the main drive around, but don't bear left toward the office. Once you've turned around the right-hand hairpin and Ramon Road is directly behind you, begin counting the trees on your right. Stop between the third and fourth trees, and count four markers in from the curb on the right to find Frank's grave.

JOEY BISHOP
FEBRUARY 3, 1918 – OCTOBER 17, 2007

IN PUBLIC OPINION, the glum-faced comedian Joey Bishop seemed to barely fit in with the Rat Pack's more flamboyant members, but Sinatra himself referred to Joey as "Hub of the Big Wheel" for his quick wit and capacity for coming up with some of the most-revered one-liners. The two met in 1952, teaming up for a series of gigs at New York's Copacabana with Sinatra headlining (of course), and but for a brief spat between them in the early

'60s that resulted in Joey getting booted from the cast of the Pack's third film, they remained lifelong friends.

In 1961 Joey served as master of ceremonies at John F. Kennedy's inaugural gala and, after the Rat Pack disintegrated, he became a TV talk-show host. His 1967 program, appropriately titled *The Joey Bishop Show*, was launched specifically to compete against Johnny Carson's *Tonight Show* juggernaut, but even the hilarious bantering between Joey and his sidekick, Regis Philbin, couldn't dent Carson's ratings and Joey's show was canceled after two seasons. Nonetheless, Carson held no grudges against his former competitor and Joey ended up guest-hosting *The Tonight Show* more times than anyone else—177 times to be exact.

Nearly 10 years after the last of his Rat Pack pals expired, Joey succumbed to natural causes at 89. In passing he closed the door to the fabled Rat Pack era firmly and permanently behind him. Joey was cremated and his ashes scattered.

SELENA
APRIL 16, 1971 – MARCH 31, 1995

WITH A POUTING smile and suggestive clothing, singer Selena Quintanilla was the ruling diva of Tejano music—"La Reina de la Musica Tejana"—and for seven years in a row was voted its best female vocalist. Tejano's roots are in the bouncy and fast-paced polka rhythms that are popular in Texas, but Selena's added twists of salsa and merengue resulted in a new and irresistible form of Tejano that found overwhelming popularity.

Born and raised in Texas, Selena had an impressive fan base in her home state, but she was most popular south of the border, where she succeeded in becoming the first American to conquer the enormous Mexican and Latin American markets. In 1993, her eighth album, *Amor Prohibido*, spawned four number one Latin singles and sold millions. But despite her triumphs in the Latin markets, it became apparent that to gain true critical acceptance, Selena needed to develop a coast-to-coast fan base in the States, which required an album with lyrics sung in English. Work on such a crossover album began and expectations were high, but Selena would never see its release.

A rabid fan of Selena's named Yolanda Saldivar started a grassroots Selena fan club that grew to be recognized as the official fan organization. By 1993, when Selena was featuring a clothing line at her own Selena Etc. boutiques, the assertive Yolanda had gained access to the singer's inner circle and finagled a managerial position at the fledgling San Antonio store. But it turned out that

Yolanda had almost zero business acumen, and matters soured even further when Selena's father, through a casual audit of the business receipts, discovered that Yolanda had been embezzling funds.

Yolanda steadfastly maintained her innocence, and she drove to Selena's hometown of Corpus Christi to meet with Selena, supposedly to present bank statements that would exonerate her. Yolanda checked into Room 158 at the Day's Inn at Interstate 37 and Navigation Boulevard and, on a Friday morning at around 11:45, Selena arrived. No one is exactly sure what happened at the motel, but somehow Selena was mortally wounded by a gunshot to the back. Staggering into the lobby, a terrified Selena fingered Yolanda as the shooter and collapsed. Though Selena was pronounced dead an hour later, for all intents, she died on the floor of the motel's lobby; when paramedics arrived there within minutes, she lay in a massive pool of blood with no pulse and no blood pressure.

In her red pickup truck, Yolanda kept police at bay for more than nine hours until she was taken without further shots fired. She was sentenced to life in prison and won't be eligible for parole until 2026.

Meanwhile, Selena's legacy lives on in her music, biographies, a movie, and her namesakes—in the five months following her murder, 619 Texas newborns were named Selena, a 600 percent increase over previous periods.

At 23, Selena was buried at Seaside Memorial Park in Corpus Christi, Texas.

GRAVE DIRECTIONS: From the entrance at 4500 Gaines Street, enter the cemetery and drive straight to the end of the drive. Turn right and, after 150 feet, you'll see Selena's grave.

KATE SMITH
MAY 1, 1909 – JUNE 17, 1986

AFTER ACHIEVING SUCCESS on Broadway and in vaudeville, Kate Smith, "the Songbird of the South," made her radio debut in 1931 and, within a few years, had two shows of her own. *The Kate Smith Hour* was a weekly variety show that featured her perfectly pitched singing and new talent acts, while her number one daytime radio show, *Kate Smith Speaks*, offered news and homespun commentary that eased an emotionally fraught America through some of its most trying historical times. During World War II,

Kate's on-air appeals for war bonds yielded contributions topping $600 million.

Kate was enormously popular; she made more than 15,000 radio broadcasts, received more than 20 million fan letters, and sold countless millions of records—and her trademark song, "When the Moon Comes Over the Mountain," itself sold some 6 million copies. Kate starred in her own movie, *Hello Everybody!* and in 1950 moved her radio program to TV where it stayed, in various incarnations, until 1962.

But despite her long list of accomplishments, Kate Smith will forever be best remembered as the vibrantly brave and passionate singer who made "God Bless America" an unofficial national anthem. Kate introduced the Irving Berlin song to the country in 1938 and, when it became apparent that it had achieved significance beyond that of just another pop tune, she refused to profit from the song, instead donating the royalties from its performances to the Boy and Girl Scouts of America, an arrangement that remains in place. Once, President Roosevelt quite aptly introduced Kate to England's King George VI by stating, simply, "This is Kate Smith. Miss Smith is America."

Though Kate recorded well over 2,000 songs, fittingly, the last song she ever sang publicly was "God Bless America," on a bicentennial special for the Fourth of July, 1976.

At 77, Kate died of complications from diabetes and was buried at Saint Agnes Cemetery in Lake Placid, New York.

GRAVE DIRECTIONS: Near 5500 Sentinel Street, enter the cemetery between the stone pillars and turn left at the "T." You won't miss Kate's mausoleum on the back left lawn.

DUSTY SPRINGFIELD
APRIL 16, 1939 – MARCH 2, 1999

IN 1960 THE soulful British crooner Dusty Springfield was a third of a folksy vocal trio called the Springfields, and on the strength of her sensuously husky voice, the group topped the charts with several singles, the most recognizable of them being "Silver Thread and Golden Needles."

By 1963 the group parted ways, and Dusty, always experimenting, switched over from a simple folk alto to a sultry and intimate white-soul. With a fresh, raw sound of rare passion, towering beehive hairdo, and panda-eye black mascara, she burst back into the limelight releasing a solo album, *A Girl*

Called Dusty. In a short time, Dusty was the newest trailblazer of the fickle fashion and music scene that came to be known as "mod."

In 1969 she recorded a landmark album, *Dusty in Memphis*, which included the crowd-pleasing single "Son of a Preacher Man." Though the record was an enormous commercial success, Dusty's personal fortunes were on the decline; a decade of hard living and substance abuse had compromised facets of her health, including a voice permanently weakened by repeated bouts of laryngitis.

Weary of fame, Dusty retired to California, where, apart from an occasional guest-singing contribution and a half-hearted 1978 comeback, she was musically dormant, concentrating instead on gay rights and animal protection.

Ten days before being inducted into the Rock & Roll Hall of Fame, Dusty was felled by breast cancer at 59.

Cremated, some of her ashes were scattered at the Cliffs of Moher in Ireland, while the remainder were interred at St. Mary the Virgin Church in Henley-on-Thames, England. In the grass on the left side of the church is a prominent tablet dedicated to her memory.

DONNA SUMMER
DECEMBER 31, 1948 – MAY 17, 2012

THE "CONTROVERSY" OF disco is now ancient and irrelevant history, but the fact remains that if you were driving around the streets of New York City in the late 1970s and your eight-track wasn't playing Donna Summer, the original Disco Queen whose hits captured the giddy hedonism of the time, it was more than likely broken.

Born LaDonna Adrian Gaines, Donna grew up with gospel, soul, and rock music, and at the tender age of 10 became the soloist of her church choir. "There was no question I would be a singer, I just always knew. I had credit in my neighborhood, people would lend me money and tell me to pay it back when I got famous," she said. Deciding in her teens to make music her career, she joined the Munich company of the rock musical *Hair* and relocated to Germany. She married an Austrian actor named Hellmuth Sommer, then kept his name after they divorced, albeit with a modified spelling.

Returning stateside in 1974, she burst onto the pop scene almost by accident. While writing "Love to Love You Baby" for another artist, producer Giorgio Moroder suggested to Donna that she cut a demo. Obliging him, she recorded the song while lying on her back on the studio floor with the lights out, cooing her breathy, moaning vocals "the way Marilyn Monroe would have." When the Casablanca record label requested an extended dance version, she delivered a 17-minute remix of whispered vocals and orgasmic groans. Though the track was too risqué for many radio stations, it fueled the decade's disco mania and made her a club icon and sensation.

By 1977 Donna had released two more albums chock-full of seductive and sexy wailings including "I Feel Love" and "Hot Stuff," but quickly became uncomfortable with the sex-symbol persona that was being created for her. "I'm not just sex, sex, sex," she complained. So depressed that she attempted suicide in the latter part of that year, an attempt that was thwarted only by the chance entry of a pair of hotel maids, Donna received counseling and sought consolation in religion, becoming a born-again Christian in 1979.

Born-again or not, with her doe eyes, cascade of hair, and sinuous dance moves, Donna remained disco music's glamorous public face, though by the early 1980s some of her glitter had lost its luster and her releases were no longer automatic hits. Soldiering on, she failed at new wave rock and then R&B before finding success anew in pop rock with *She Works Hard for the Money*. Later came a Grammy for the Christian rock song "He's a Rebel," and then Donna wrote a chart-topping country single for Dolly Parton, "Starting Over Again." In 2008, she topped the dance-music charts again, three times actually, with singles from what would be her last album, *Crayons*.

As Donna was never a smoker, fans were shocked to learn of her death at 63 of lung cancer. She battled the ailment for more than a year, keeping her medical condition a secret known only to her doctors and a close circle of family. She was buried at Harpeth Hills Memory Gardens in Nashville, Tennessee.

GRAVE DIRECTIONS: Enter the cemetery at 9090 Highway 100, make a left at the first drive, and then take the next right. On the left will be the Faith section where you won't miss the oversized Nacarato family monument. Walk down the path to the left of Nacaratos', and there you'll find the bad girl doing her last dance, on the left at the iron-gated "S" plot.

BARRY WHITE
SEPTEMBER 12, 1944 – JULY 4, 2003

DURING A SEVEN-MONTH jail stint for stealing tires, Barry White vowed to give up on crime and concentrate instead on music after hearing Elvis Presley's hit "It's Now or Never." It was a wise move;

while Barry's lush baritone voice earned him credence—and millions of dollars—as the consummate crooner of lovers young and old, his brother, Darryl, was killed in a dispute over four bucks.

Barry started out working as a talent scout and spread his wings quickly; in 1972 he produced Love Unlimited's smash-hit "Walking in the Rain with the One I Love," and the next year began a solo career of his own. To the heartbeat of muffled drums, while strings hovered and guitars echoed in the distance, Barry reassured the sentiments of love with his bottomless bass in a series of erotic pop-soul hits including "You're the First, the Last, My Everything" and "Can't Get Enough of Your Love, Babe." Another signature of Barry's music was his steamy spoken introductions and interludes that created a fantasy world of opulence and desire and destined his smooth classics to countless bedrooms.

After lava lamps, crushed velvet, and water beds peaked in the late 1970s, Barry's career faded, though his image and hit songs proved durable. In the 1990s, children of his original fans discovered his sensuous magic when rappers and dance-music acts sampled his sounds, which initiated a career resurgence. In 1994 his *The Icon Is Love* album sold a couple million while 1999's *Staying Power* won two rhythm-and-blues Grammies. By that time, Barry's deep and rumbling voice had become synonymous with seduction and he was universally recognized as the supreme man of love. But despite his erotically charged music, Barry never made tabloid headlines and his private life was sedate. "People are always looking for me to be a freak," he said in an interview. "What does Barry White do when he relaxes? I play video games. I deal with my dogs. I spend time with my children. I'm not a party animal."

At 58, Barry died from complications of kidney failure. He was cremated and his ashes remain with his family.

HANK WILLIAMS
SEPTEMBER 17, 1923 – JANUARY 1, 1953

HIRAM "HANK" WILLIAMS wove gospel and blues, along with a healthy dose of country twangs, through his humble melodies and completed the package with an overlay of simple yet powerfully emotive lyrics. Dubbed the "Hillbilly Shakespeare," he's credited with breaking country music out to the masses.

As a kid, Hank shined shoes and sold peanuts on the street to bring home a few pennies for his poor Alabama family. But after somehow getting his hands on a guitar and teaching himself to play, by 14 he and his band, the Drifting Cowboys, were passing the hat at honky-tonks and square dances.

By 1944 the Drifting Cowboys were regulars on the *Louisiana Hayride* radio show and, after his version of "Lovesick Blues" topped the 1949 charts, Hank was soon performing regularly at the Grand Ole Opry. During the next couple years, he upped his game further and the hits "Cold, Cold Heart," "Hey, Good Lookin'," and "Your Cheatin' Heart" came in quick succession.

In contrast to his professional success, Hank's personal life was a disaster: His marriage was on the rocks, constant back pain resulted in an addiction to painkillers, and it seemed he was an alcoholic. After he arrived at one too many gigs too drunk to perform, or failed to show up at all, the Grand Ole Opry decided that the drinking overwhelmed his music and fired him.

While delivering Hank to a New Year's show in Ohio, Hank's driver pulled his Cadillac into a Virginia gas station and discovered that his well-known passenger wasn't drunk and asleep but rather drunk and dead.

At 29, Hank was buried at Oakwood Annex Cemetery in Montgomery, Alabama.

GRAVE DIRECTIONS: Enter the cemetery at 1304 Upper We-
tumpka Road and drive to the circle at the top of the hill, where
you won't miss the two monoliths marking the graves of Hank and
his wife, Audrey.

TAMMY WYNETTE

MAY 5, 1942 – APRIL 6, 1998

RAISED IN HER grandparents' log cabin without indoor plumb-
ing while chicken and grits simmered in the smoky fireplace that
passed for a stove, future country music star Tammy Wynette, at
17, married a sometime-bootlegger. The marriage, though short-
lived, resulted in three children, whom she later supported with a
turn as a hairdresser. Dreaming of making it big as a singer, after
10-hour days in the salon she'd perform late into the night at
rough Tennessee roadhouses.

Tammy's break came in 1965 when the *Country Boy Eddie
Show* signed her on as a regular act, which quickly led to a record deal with Epic. In 1968 she released her defining song; not
only was it her biggest hit, but 50 years and a fortune in royalties
later "Stand by Your Man" remains the biggest hit by any female
country singer ever. The chart-topper wasn't her last, however, and
Tammy went on to rack up 19 more number ones.

Though she collaborated with many country artists, her biggest
collaboration was with fellow country singer and third husband
(of five), George Jones. Dubbed the "King and Queen of Country
Music," the sometimes-happy couple recorded 10 powerhouse
albums and dozens of celebrated singles together, including "Take
Me" and "We Loved It Away." After their stormy union ended in
1975, they remained friendly and recorded together occasionally.

Much of Tammy's life was spent in poor health and she endured at least a dozen major surgeries for a variety of ailments,
including an appendectomy and a complicated hysterectomy, plus
operations on her gallbladder, a kidney, and the nodules of her
throat. In 1993, she was sent into a five-day coma by a bile duct
infection that required an intestinal bypass. Not surprisingly,
Tammy eventually battled painkiller addiction too.

One evening after taking a sedative, Tammy lay on her couch
and died of a blood clot in the lungs, according to the coroner.
However, after a wrongful death lawsuit was brought against
the sedative manufacturer, Tammy was exhumed a year after her
burial for a new autopsy, resulting in her cause of death to be
changed to a cardiac arrhythmia.

At 55, Tammy was buried at Woodlawn Memorial Park in Nashville.

GRAVE DIRECTIONS: Enter the cemetery at 660 Thompson Lane, turn at the second left, and park in front of the main building. Enter through the double-oak doors and go up the short flight of stairs on your left. Proceed down this corridor, turn right at the second hallway, and go through the glass doors. Tammy's crypt is about three-fourths of the way down this hall, at eye level, on the right.

BUCKWHEAT ZYDECO
NOVEMBER 14, 1947 – SEPTEMBER 24, 2016

ZYDECO MUSIC IS a raucous blend of Afro-Caribbean rhythms, standard R&B, and traditional country that's overlaid with the French fiddle incarnations prevalent in the Creole-speaking Louisiana bayous. The essential instruments are an amplified accordion, to provide a tootling propulsion, and a frottoir or scrub board, which is a corrugated sheet-metal vest played with bottle openers that affords a unique percussive edge. Standard guitars and drums fill in a dynamic groove, and the result is an easy-to-dance-to, party-till-you-drop, quirky and authentic American sound.

In 1979 Stanley "Buckwheat" Dural Jr. started a zydeco band that he called the Ils Sont Partis Band, from the French Creole announcement he'd heard at horse races: "They're off!" The band name soon became Buckwheat Zydeco—a moniker that eventually was associated with Stanley himself. Alternately singing in boisterous Creole and English with unbridled exuberance and childlike delight, Buckwheat led his musical team through energetic and animated two-steps, waltzes, and shuffles for 30 years.

Wearing a broad-brimmed black hat and glasses while jamming on a white piano accordion emblazoned with the word BUCK-WHEAT, Stanley created music that became the face of zydeco, and Buckwheat Zydeco's relentless conviction was instrumental (heh) in popularizing the style. After earning a reputation for must-see live shows, in 1987 they released their breakout LP, *On a Night Like This*, which they eventually followed with nearly two dozen more like-minded zydeco albums.

Playing festivals the world over and collaborating with a rainbow of artists ranging from Willie Nelson to U2, Buckwheat was known for a good humor and kind spirit that infected his devoted audience. "You get out there, play good music and make people happy," he said. "That's what I'm about."

Following a battle with lung cancer, Buckwheat died at 68 and was buried at Calvary Cemetery in Lafayette, Louisiana.

GRAVE DIRECTIONS: Enter the cemetery at 355 Teurlings Drive where, near its middle, Buckwheat lies under the grass in an as-yet unmarked grave, just steps from the Cortis stone.

FAMOUS
PERSONALITIES
& INFAMOUS
NEWSMAKERS

CHARLES ATLAS

OCTOBER 30, 1893 – DECEMBER 24, 1972

ANEMIC AND WEAK as a youth, Charles Atlas brought body-building into the mainstream. He developed a workout system of pitting muscle against muscle that he called "dynamic tension," and, using this system, built himself up to become "The World's Most Perfectly Developed Man" in the 1920s.

Later he would launch an enormously popular bodybuilding course that featured in its advertising the now-classic image of a 97-pound weakling who loses his girl to a bully at the beach, only to win her back after using the Atlas techniques.

Charles died at 79 of a heart attack and rests at Saint John's Cemetery in Middle Village, New York.

CEMETERY DIRECTIONS: Middle Village is a neighborhood of Queens, New York. From either I-495 or the Interboro Parkway, take Woodhaven Boulevard to Metropolitan Avenue. The cemetery is then just a few blocks west of Woodhaven Boulevard at Metropolitan Avenue and 80th Street.

GRAVE DIRECTIONS: Charles is interred in the enormous mausoleum that sits in the cemetery's center. Drive past the office, turn right, then take the next right and the next left to get to the mausoleum. Drive around to the side and park near the doors to the right of the entrance with a red awning. Enter the bronze doors and go up one flight of stairs. Down the long hall in front of you, the Atlas crypt is about 150 feet away at eye level on the right—Unit 5, Floor 3, Section 1, Crypt 3A.

TAMMY FAYE BAKKER

MARCH 7, 1942 – JULY 20, 2007

TAMMY FAYE BAKKER was the diminutive, elaborately coiffed gospel singer who, along with her first husband, Jim Bakker, built a commercial empire around television evangelism only to see it collapse in sex and money scandals.

Amid a strict religious upbringing, Tammy had an epiphany of sorts when she was 10: At her Pentecostal church she began speaking in tongues, prompting her to promise to devote her life to religion. At North Central Bible College in Minneapolis several years later, she went on a date with Jim, who was the night monitor at her dorm. He proposed to her that very night, and they married the following month.

In the early years of their marriage the happy couple worked as traveling evangelists; he preached while she sang and played the accordion. In 1966 they joined Pat Robertson's fledgling Christian Broadcasting Network as the original hosts of *The 700 Club*—but left Pat in 1974 and began *The PTL Club,* the initials standing for "Praise the Lord" or "People That Love." The PTL Network, and especially its *Jim and Tammy Show,* was tremendously popular with people who enjoy giving their money to self-righteous evangelists. Interestingly, Tammy and Jim never quite made clear what God was doing with the $100 million–plus in donations the PTL received annually.

Tammy Faye, who stood just 4-foot-11 and presented herself in overstated outfits and heavy makeup, became a caricature, a parody for dabbing at mascara-tinted tears while Jim prayed to the heavens for the salvation of sinners. Openly emotional, Tammy often broke down in tears, long black streaks of mascara on her face as she pleaded for the health of an ailing viewer or recognized a particularly generous financial contribution. Off camera, her spendthrift shopping sprees became as famous as her makeup and the Bakkers enjoyed matching Rolls-Royces and lavish homes— even Fido got in on their largess, sprawled in his air-conditioned dog house. Tammy hoped heaven would include a giant shopping center "where there's no limit on your charge card."

In 1987, cracks in the Bakker façade appeared when it was revealed that Jim not only had a sexual encounter with a church secretary named Jessica Hahn, but also paid her $265,000 in hush money. Two years later, Jim was convicted of defrauding PTL supporters of more than $150 million and was handed a 45-year prison sentence. Meanwhile Tammy, who had promised in tearstained news conferences during Jim's trial that she'd stand by her man forever no matter what the outcome, promptly divorced Jim and married one of his business associates within months of his being sent to the can.

After PTL was exposed as a sham and crashed, Tammy launched herself as a newer, more hip celebrity persona. Gay men had embraced her as a camp figure in their gender-bending look-alike contests for years, so Tammy embraced them back and began attending gay pride events. A film about her named *The Eyes of Tammy Faye* was made in 1999, and she later appeared in the offbeat reality series *The Surreal Life,* in which she lived with a group of other faded celebrities including rapper Vanilla Ice and porn star Ron Jeremy.

Dying of colon cancer that had spread to her lungs, and weighing just 65 pounds, Tammy appeared on *Larry King Live* in July 2007 to say goodbye to her fans. She told Larry she had instructed her doctors not to tell her how much time they believed she had left. "I don't have any date written on me anywhere that says I'm going to die at any time, and so I just give it to the Lord," she said. At 65, Tammy died the next day, just hours after the show was broadcast. She was cremated and her ashes buried at Waldron Cemetery in Waldron, Kansas.

CEMETERY DIRECTIONS: Even by Kansas' standards, Waldron is pretty small, with a population of 17. You'll about trip over the cemetery coming into "town."

GRAVE DIRECTIONS: Tammy's flat granite marker is easy to find, about halfway to the back and on the west side.

BONNIE & CLYDE

CLYDE BARROW
MARCH 24, 1909 – MAY 23, 1934

BONNIE PARKER
OCTOBER 1, 1910 – MAY 23, 1934

ONE HOT TEXAS day in July 1930, a small-time thief named Clyde Barrow visited a friend. While there he happened to meet his friend's neighbor, Bonnie Parker. The two quickly became inseparable, and when Clyde was incarcerated for robbery some months later, Bonnie smuggled a gun into the jail. And so began the infamous saga of Bonnie and Clyde.

Through several books and four movies, their exploits have been romanticized endlessly, taking on bigger-than-life status. But, actually, it's hard to find anything very romantic about Bonnie and Clyde. In short, the Barrow gang, made up of Bonnie, Clyde, and the other outlaws who drifted in and out of their circle, traced a violent path through the south-central United States. Preying not only on "rich" banks, they robbed service stations, hardware stores, and fruit stands as well. As police loops grew tighter and their situation became increasingly desperate, they stepped up their fury and, by the time they were themselves killed in a hail of bullets, 12 innocent people had died.

By November 1932 Bonnie and Clyde were wanted for the murder of two storekeepers and one policeman and, tiring of nickel-and-dime holdups, they robbed their first bank. By March Clyde's parolee brother, Buck, and his skeptical wife, Blanche, had joined them, and the Barrow gang stepped up their assaults. The law did too, and the next year was a succession of shootouts staged in dusty, Depression-weary towns. When the smoke cleared, Buck was dead and Blanche was in custody, but Bonnie and Clyde remained on the lam.

In February 1934 Texas authorities had had enough of the duo's crime spree, and they hired bounty-hunter Frank Hamer to end it. In May, Bonnie, Clyde, and a new gang member, Henry Methvin, began a stay with Methvin's father, Iverson, at his farm near Gibsland, Louisiana. Hamer, who was hot on their trail, soon pulled into town and, in a secret meeting, hatched a plan with Iverson: In return for a reduced sentence for his son, Iverson would direct Bonnie and Clyde into the crosshairs of an ambush led by Hamer.

While staying with Iverson, Bonnie and Clyde had fallen into a routine. Early each day they drove to the nearby town of Sailes to gather a few supplies, always returning by 10:00 a.m. In setting up an ambush for the outlaws, Iverson's distinctive, beat-up lumber truck was parked along the route to Sailes as if it had broken down, while across the street a half-dozen shooters and an unarmed Iverson concealed themselves in the overhanging moss of the dense woodland. Right on schedule at 9:15 a.m., Bonnie and Clyde ambled up the road, first slowing and then stopping at Iverson's curiously parked truck. Once they were plainly identified, Hamer calmly gave orders to fire, and 167 bullets ended the lives of Bonnie and Clyde.

Inside the car, red-dressed Bonnie's lifeless hand held a bloody pack of cigarettes, Clyde's jaw dangled precariously, and, among the weapons in the back seat, Hamer found a saxophone. With the bodies still in it, the car was towed to an undertaker.

Contrary to popular myth, Bonnie and Clyde were not buried in the same casket, nor do they share a plot. In fact, they're not even buried in the same cemetery, though both are interred in Dallas, Texas. At 23, Bonnie was buried at Crown Hill Memorial Park, while 25-year-old Clyde was interred alongside his brother, Buck, at Western Heights Cemetery.

DIRECTIONS TO BONNIE'S GRAVE: At 9700 Webb Chapel Road, enter the cemetery at the green steel gates and bear left at the first drive. After a hundred feet, stop. Off to the right is a hedgerow, and Bonnie's flat marker can be found against the hedgerow, just a dozen stones from the hedge's end.

DIRECTIONS TO CLYDE'S AND BUCK'S GRAVES: These wise guys are buried in a small and defunct old relic of a cemetery on a main thoroughfare, hidden in plain sight. It's interesting that thousands of commuters pass by every day and it gets nary a glance. The cemetery can be seen at 1617 Fort Worth Avenue, but it's easier to access from the pedestrian gate on Neal Street. In the back, just in front of two overgrown bushes are the Barrow boys' markers.

DIRECTIONS TO THE BONNIE AND CLYDE AMBUSH SITE: On Route 154 about eight miles south of Gibsland, Louisiana, is a stone tablet that marks the spot where Bonnie and Clyde were ambushed. The fugitive duo was driving north and the police posse hid in the bushes on the east side.

Henry Methvin received his pardon from Texas as promised, but not from Oklahoma. He was arrested for murder and sentenced to death, though it was later commuted to life, and he was released after serving 12 years. In 1948 Henry was run over by a train.

LIZZIE BORDEN
JULY 19, 1860 – JUNE 1, 1927

ONE HOT AFTERNOON in August 1892 someone savagely murdered Andrew and Abby Borden with an ax in their home but, after more than a century of speculation, nobody can say for certain who really did it. Lizzie, their youngest daughter, was acquitted of the crime following a sensational trial whose high point came when both of the victims' heads were produced as exhibits. She lived the remainder of her life as a recluse, ostracized by a community that believed her to be guilty as charged (a kind of precursor to O.J. Simpson). In any case, she'll not be forgotten as long this familiar jump-rope jingle is still sung by children:

Lizzie Borden took an ax and gave her mother forty whacks;
When she saw what she had done, she gave her father forty-one.

Lizzie died of natural causes at 66 and is buried at Oak Grove Cemetery in Fall River, Massachusetts.

GRAVE DIRECTIONS: Enter the cemetery at 765 Prospect Street and bear left at the Turner mausoleum. Then make a left at the four corners, and after another 75 yards the Borden plot is on the left.

The house where the murders took place is at 92 Second St. in Fall River. It's now a museum and, if you dare, a bed and breakfast.

LENNY BRUCE
OCTOBER 13, 1925 – AUGUST 3, 1966

AS A STAND-UP nightclub entertainer, Lenny Bruce's monologues on race relations, sexual mores, and organized religion are today admired for their trailblazing qualities—but in his heyday, from the late 1950s to his death in 1966, Lenny was more commonly denounced as a "sick comic." He was also one of America's most visible victims of censorship and was arrested five times on obscenity charges, though appeals courts overturned all of his convictions.

Before his legal problems began, Lenny was a fast-talking purveyor of biting political and social comedic commentary; afterward he fell victim to his own cult of personality and validated himself, exulting, "I'm not a comedian, I'm Lenny Bruce." He became obsessed with his own arrests and grew more and more paranoid and less and less funny. His act often became just one long harangue, a recitation of court documents, or an endless stream of obscenities. Club owners refused to book him, Lenny's professional career spiraled sharply downward, and his personal life soon followed.

In 1964 Lenny woke up in a frenzy in the middle of the night and leapt, or fell, out of his San Francisco hotel window, breaking both ankles and a leg. After insisting that his casts be removed early, he was left partly crippled. With his body now wasted, he obsessed over his mortality, and began to lose his mind as well. Lenny became flabby and sickly, he secluded himself in his home, and injected more and more drugs to ease both his real and imagined pains.

Lenny contended that he most enjoyed shooting up while seated on the toilet. At 40, he was found lying dead in his bathroom, face down and naked. His bathrobe's sash was cinched tightly above the tracks in his arm, a hypodermic needle was nearby on the tile floor, and the white throne from which he'd toppled stood as sole witness.

Today, Lenny lies at Eden Memorial Park in Mission Hills, California.

GRAVE DIRECTIONS: Enter the park at 11500 Sepulveda Boulevard and start up the hill. After the mausoleum, make a right onto Mount of Olives Drive and stop at about the halfway point. Lenny's flat marker is on the right, six rows down the hill.

AL CAPONE & ELIOT NESS

AL CAPONE
JANUARY 17, 1899 – JANUARY 25, 1947

ELIOT NESS
APRIL 19, 1903 – MAY 7, 1957

THE ORIGINAL SCARFACE, Al Capone was a notorious mobster who rose through the syndicate hierarchy to eventually control the bootleg liquor industry of Chicago and beyond. Crafty and cautious, he kept his criminal activities at arm's length; he never owned property in his own name, never had a bank account, and, though he was responsible for dozens of murders, was most careful when ordering a killing and would never be present for it. His attentiveness to these particulars, despite his existence within such an obviously lawless lifestyle, frustrated and stymied prosecutors who struggled to nail Capone on charges of any real consequence.

In 1929 federal agent Eliot Ness assembled a crack squad of 10 top-notch agents, who came to be known as the Untouchables, and his team executed a relentless and vigorous strategy of raiding Capone's speakeasies, destroying his suppliers' stills, disrupting his transport network, and putting away his triggermen. Despite the Untouchables' dogged determination, time and time again the only real untouchable was proving to be the slippery kingpin Capone.

But then agent Eddie O'Hare pointed out that Capone had failed to pay income taxes—ever. At first, it seemed like a ridiculously worthless observation: Big deal, the most wanted criminal in the nation also owes the government a few bucks? Ooh, that's a big surprise, so what? But this was the dawn of the IRS' far-reaching powers and, in 1931, probably nobody was more surprised than Capone, who was handed an 11-year ticket to Alcatraz for tax evasion.

Admitting during his prison medical exam that he'd once had syphilis but insisting it had been cured, and declining a spinal tap to determine if he was still infected, America's most famous criminal was sent off to the big house. After five unremarkable years, Capone was one day found staring at a wall and it was soon determined he was suffering from the disease's advanced stages.

In 1939, judged to be harmlessly insane, he was released and retired to a Miami Beach estate. Physically uncoordinated, his speech garbled and confused, the now-paranoid kook spent hours fishing off his dock, clad in his jammies.

At 48, Capone was finally done in by a brain hemorrhage and was buried at Mount Carmel Cemetery in Hillside, Illinois.

GRAVE DIRECTIONS: Enter the cemetery at 11900 Roosevelt Road and, once inside, take an immediate right and stop after 100 feet. On the right is the eight-foot-tall Capone plot marker, as well as Al's personal ground-level stone.

Eliot Ness later became Cleveland's director of public safety, and at 54 the lawman died of a heart attack. For 40 years his cremains were tucked away at his family's home, but in 1997 at a special city ceremony, they were scattered in the lake at Cleveland's Lake View Cemetery.

GEORGE CARLIN

MAY 12, 1937 – JUNE 22, 2008

AS GEORGE CARLIN himself said, he was always swimming against the tide and always out of step. Not only did he quit school in the ninth grade, but he got kicked out of three other schools along the way. Kicked off the altar boys, kicked off the choirboys, kicked out of the Boy Scouts, kicked out of summer camp, and kicked out of the Air Force, the perennial nonconformist never fit in.

After working a fairly straitlaced comedy act and even wearing suit coats—but in his own estimation, not doing much more than shuffling along and keeping the bill collectors at bay—George took stock of his surroundings in his early thirties. It dawned on him that his friends, especially the ultra-successful ones in the music business such as Bob Dylan and Buffalo Springfield, had transitioned their dress and every facet of their being to express themselves politically and socially. This insight emboldened George to stop doing shtick, change his image to grungy jeans, shaggy beard and ponytail, and begin verbalizing a uniquely fearless attitude that became more authentic to audiences and more comfortable for himself. Whereas before he was saying funny things and "people-pleasing," his new persona of a disappointed yet idealistic antiauthoritarian who smartly criticized every aspect of our culture resonated sharply with the nation's cynical post-Vietnam mood. And his career soared.

George became a counterculture touchstone; he hosted the very first episode of *Saturday Night Live*, appeared on *The Tonight Show* 130 times, and put out a couple dozen albums—plus three best-selling books—while constantly touring. During the 1970s, when his wild comedic style accelerated and then permeated his offstage lifestyle, his drug use became excessive to the point of initiating a heart condition. By the '80s George had evolved into more of a curmudgeonly uncle whose humor was observational and in the next decade he tacked to the political side. Later, he grew increasingly dark. "I sort of gave up on this whole human adventure a long time ago," he said. "I think the human race has squandered its gift, and I think this country has squandered its promise. I think people in America sold out very cheaply, for sneakers and cheeseburgers. And I don't think it's fixable."

Nonetheless, his humor could never be categorized as a bummer and he proved that no subject was off-limits for insightful comedy. George Carlin legitimized the medium of humor for every social and intellectual tier, and when he passed of heart disease at 71, all of America noticed.

George was cremated and his ashes entrusted to his daughter.

BILLY CARTER
MARCH 29, 1937 – SEPTEMBER 25, 1988

GAS STATION PROPRIETOR and peanut farmer Billy Carter was vaulted to national celebrity in 1976 when his brother, Jimmy, was elected president of the United States.

Caring little for convention, he proved incapable of handling his sudden fame and became the butt of jokes for business dealings that were politically embarrassing to his brother, including a Libyan loan fiasco and his short-lived Billy Beer venture. Billy alternately courted and denounced the media, depending on the occasion, but was rather consistently skewered as a buffoon, a boob, and a wacko. In his own defense, with a sister who was a faith healer and a brother who was president, he once observed that he "was probably the only sane member of the family."

At 51, Billy died of pancreatic cancer and was buried at Lebanon Cemetery in Plains, Georgia.

GRAVE DIRECTIONS: Enter the cemetery on Old Plains Highway, make a right onto the first paved drive, then bear left. Stop a short distance on the right when you see a Carter plot (though you're not quite there yet). Another 50 feet behind this Carter plot is a second Carter plot, and it's there you'll find Billy's grave.

JACQUES COUSTEAU
JUNE 11, 1910 – JUNE 25, 1997

AS CO-INVENTOR of the world's first underwater breathing apparatus, the Aqualung, Jacques Cousteau cleared mines from French ports during WWII. Later forming a series of organizations through which he financed underwater expeditions, in 1953 he first gained celebrity with his documentary *The Silent World*, an account of the allure of a brand-new activity called scuba diving. During the 1960s, his Conshelf experiments—wherein "oceanauts" tried to demonstrate that humans could live and work on the ocean floor—competed for public attention with NASA's space program.

Though he held no scientific degree, Cousteau soon evolved into a revered scientist for bringing the wonders of Earth's oceans—sharks and whales, sunken treasure and coral reefs—into people's homes through his television series, *The Underwater World of Jacques Cousteau*. His show more or less invented the nature documentary as a distinct form but, no matter which sea creature cavorted before the lenses, there was hardly ever a doubt that the show's real star was Captain Cousteau himself. On zigzag voyages from Alaska to Africa to Antarctica aboard his research vessel *Calypso*, Jacques narrated in a highly personal Gallic-flavored English and, bundled under a red woolen watch cap, his deeply lined face with a dazzling smile became recognized as that of the world's leading sea explorer.

At 87, Jacques died of a heart attack and was buried in the cemetery of his hometown, Saint Andre-de-Cubzac, France.

RODNEY DANGERFIELD
NOVEMBER 22, 1921 – OCTOBER 5, 2004

AT 19, JACOB Cohen adopted the name Jack Roy and began bouncing around dingy New York–area gin joints as a singing waiter and comedian. Tales of his hard-knock experiences became fodder for his later routines and, after a particularly humiliating experience at a Catskills hotel in the 1950s, he quit show business. "To give you an idea of how well I was doing at the time," he recalled later, "when I quit, I was the only one who knew I quit."

Retreating to a middle-class lifestyle, he married and worked selling aluminum siding, but the idyllic suburban life soured and, as middle age approached, the paunchy, goggle-eyed comedian returned to the stage with an absurd name dreamed up by a New York nightclub owner: Rodney Dangerfield. In a rumpled suit and one hand perpetually loosening his trademark red necktie, he took the stage as a hapless, self-deprecating everyman slapped around by life and searching in vain for acceptance. "Last week my house was on fire. My wife told the kids, 'Be quiet, you'll wake up Daddy,'" he quipped.

Rodney's popularity grew steadily, and in 1969 he opened his own comedy club. With its namesake owner as a regular headliner, Dangerfield's soon became one of the city's hottest comedy showcases. In 1972, after seeing *The Godfather*, he made the final adjustment to his persona. "All I heard was the word 'respect,'" he recalled. "'You've got to give me respect,' or 'Respect him.' I thought to myself, it sounds like a funny image—a guy who gets no respect." The perennial loser, fidgety, and with a too-tight collar who elicited "no respect," struck a chord with fans and Rodney's career launched to the stratosphere. "Even the doorman gives me no respect. Every time I get in the elevator he asks, 'Basement?'"

With his image firmly established, it was one laugh after another for the next three decades. Rodney became a talk-show favorite, and appeared in several movies from a nouveau-rich boor in *Caddyshack* to a belligerent and sadistic father in *Natural Born Killers*. Despite good reviews, Rodney claimed he didn't like doing movies. "Too much waiting around, too much memorizing; I need that immediate feedback of people laughing." And probably their immediate respect too.

After a stroke and infectious abdominal complications from which not even his fictitious doctor friend Dr. Vinny Boombatz would've been able to save him, Rodney died at 82 and was buried at Westwood Memorial Park in Los Angeles.

GRAVE DIRECTIONS: Behind the office complex at 10850 Wilshire Boulevard, enter the cemetery, turn left at the office and, just after the chapel on the right, you'll see Rodney's stone along the drive.

JOHN DILLINGER & MELVIN PURVIS

JOHN DILLINGER
JUNE 28, 1902 – JULY 22, 1934

MELVIN PURVIS
OCTOBER 24, 1900 – FEBRUARY 29, 1960

FOR ALL THE notoriety enjoyed by bank robber John Dillinger, his life of crime was exceedingly short, and until he went to prison at age 20 for assault, he had no criminal record at all. But it seems that prison soured him, and after his release at 29, he orchestrated the escape of 10 of his inmate cronies, and with them established a potent gang. In a seven-month Midwest crime spree, they were responsible for 11 bank robberies and 15 deaths before their capture in Arizona.

But much to the embarrassment of law enforcement officials, Dillinger quickly escaped from prison using a wooden gun covered with black shoe polish and resumed his violent ways. A foiled

Wisconsin ambush killed three more innocents and Dillinger managed to escape the law's grasp yet again. J. Edgar Hoover, then director of the FBI, tagged him as "Public Enemy Number One," thus assuring his status as a kind of folk hero.

Dillinger's capture became the top priority for the agency and especially for Melvin Purvis, head of the FBI's Chicago office. After the Romanian landlady of Dillinger's girlfriend contacted Purvis and agreed to betray Dillinger in return for leniency in her own upcoming deportation hearing, a plan was devised to apprehend him as he and the two women were leaving a Chicago movie theater. As planned, Dillinger walked out of the theater and Purvis lit a cigar to signal the surrounding agents that the man was in fact him. As the agents approached, Dillinger was spooked and pulled a .38-caliber pistol from his belt. But before he could fire a shot he was hit by four bullets, three in his chest and one that entered the back of his neck and exited through his face. When agents arrived at a hospital with the very-dead Dillinger, the hospital refused to allow the gangster inside and he was laid on the lawn to await the coroner.

At 32, Dillinger was buried at Crown Hill Cemetery in Indianapolis, Indiana.

GRAVE DIRECTIONS: At 700 38th Street, enter the cemetery at the funeral home entrance, bear left at the mausoleum, go under the stone bridge, then turn at the next left. Stay on this road for almost a half-mile, then turn right immediately before Section 44. After about 150 feet the Dillinger plot is to the left, visible from the roadway.

After Dillinger's death, Purvis and his agents concentrated on capturing the remaining gang members, and within months most were either behind bars or dead. But Purvis himself got into a stew with Hoover, and soon after left the agency.

When he left the FBI, his fellow agents presented him with a nickel-plated Colt .45 and, 25 years later, Purvis may have committed suicide with the weapon. He certainly shot himself to death with it, but it's unclear whether it was intentional or if the gun accidentally went off as he tried to dislodge an odd-sized tracer round from its chamber.

At 59, Purvis was buried at Mount Hope Cemetery in Florence, South Carolina.

GRAVE DIRECTIONS: Enter the cemetery at 100 Cherokee Road, drive past the office, and go to the end of the drive in front of the mausoleum. Turn left, then left again, then make an immediate right and stop. On the left is the tall granite Purvis marker. His epitaph reads *"Saepe Timui Sed Numquam Curri*—Always Be Afraid, Never Run."

MORTON DOWNEY JR.

DECEMBER 9, 1933 – MARCH 12, 2001

MORTON DOWNEY JR. was a singer and songwriter who recorded "Boulevard of Broken Dreams" in 1959, which was accompanied by a before-its-time video featuring Morton wandering said boulevard in a trench coat. In the next couple of decades, he was a sometime–music producer and recorder who had a hand in writing the benchmark surf-rock tune "Wipeout," and during the 1970s Morton emerged as a loud-mouth know-it-all deejay. But in 1987 his ship came in and his entertainment career crystallized when he surfaced as the bombastic host of a confrontational television show that set viewers on their heads.

Running for just three seasons beginning in 1987, *The Morton Downey Jr. Show* was widely vilified as trash, but it *was* groundbreaking and transformed him into a pop culture phenomenon. Raising the volume on a persona he had cultivated over years on radio, Morton was an opinionated and growling, chain-smoking bully who openly abused his guests and whipped the studio audience into a frenzy that, more often than not, turned physical. Ostensibly debating religious, political, and social topics, Downey became better known for a catalog of put-downs and angry gestures. The show, dubbed "part TV talk show, part public lynching," spawned countless like-minded programs and created a genre of talk shows that paralleled blood sport.

By 1989 the show had peaked and, to revive his livelihood, Morton released a novelty album featuring the likes of "Hey Mr. Dealer," a denunciation of the drug trade, and "Zip It," a pithy command to his detractors. Tumbling even farther from the limelight, Morton executed a last-ditch effort to resuscitate his ratings by claiming that neo-Nazi skinheads roughed him up in an airport bathroom, cut off his hair, and painted a swastika on his head. Authorities could never verify the attack, Downey's critics pounced, calling it a publicity stunt, and in a short time one could stick a fork in his celebrity—it was done.

An impenitent four-pack-a-day smoker, Morton delighted in blatantly blowing smoke in the faces of his guests during arguments, but changed his tune after losing a lung to cancer. But railing against the habit's evils in public service spots proved to be too little too late for Morty, as the cancer claimed him at 67 and he was cremated.

BOBBY FISCHER

MARCH 9, 1943 – JANUARY 17, 2008

BROOKLYN-BRED GENIUS BOBBY Fischer made history in 1972 when he wrested the world chess title from four decades of Soviet domination, beating world champion Boris Spassky in the "Match of the Century" that came to be seen as a proxy for the Cold War.

A petulant and loutish Bobby pitted against an elegant Spassky made for an unforgettable spectacle and captured headlines around the world. Incensed by every condition under which the match was played, particularly offended by the whirr of television cameras, Bobby lost the first game and boycotted the second, insisting the remaining three games be played in an isolated room the size of a janitor's closet. Roaring back from what is a sizable deficit in chess, Bobby trounced Spassky and his small army of master strategists, 12½ to 8½.

His victory was widely seen as a symbolic triumph for Democracy over Communism, and it turned the tantrum-prone rebel into an unlikely American hero. Capturing the world's imagination, the public recognized that chess at its highest level was as thrilling as a duel to the death or as intellectually demanding as any scientific conundrum and, for the first time in the United States, the game became cool. Sales of chess sets skyrocketed along with the prestige of scores of formerly poverty-stricken chess teachers.

But Bobby was incapable of sustaining himself in the limelight and soon withdrew into a weird, contrarian solitude that he maintained for the remainder of his life. Tithing to a fringe church, he spent his days locked in a room playing chess against himself and reading Nazi literature. Offered huge financial incentives to defend his title, Bobby made ridiculously extravagant demands that, when met, were countered with even more preposterous terms. Becoming violently anti-American and a vicious anti-Semite (though his mother was Jewish), he spent years in far-flung countries alienated from all but a small band of friends and chess enthusiasts.

He finally emerged from his mysterious two-decade-long seclusion in 1992 and played a $5 million match against his old nemesis, Spassky. After Bobby won handily he dropped out of sight again, emerging now and then on scattered foreign radio stations to rant in increasingly belligerent terms against the United States and Jews. After the attacks of September 11, 2001, he rang up a Filipino radio station to hail the "wonderful news" and launch a profanity-laden tirade.

In chess circles, rumors surfaced intermittently that he was playing, that he was training, or that he was about to make a comeback, but it was all nonsense. Instead, Bobby Fischer became a poster boy for the adage about that fine line between genius and madman and, it seems, ultimately the burden of his 181 IQ permanently blurred that line.

Swearing off Western medicine to the end, Bobby died of degenerative renal failure at 64 and his last words were said to be, "Nothing soothes pain like the touch of a person." He was buried in the Cemetery of Laugardaelir Church in Laugardaelir, Iceland.

GRAVE DIRECTIONS: From Selfoss, follow Biskupstungnabraut Road north along the river for a few miles until you see the church and cemetery. Bobby's grave is near the gate in front of the church.

JIM FIXX
APRIL 23, 1932 – JULY 20, 1984

CONCERNED ABOUT A family history of heart disease, Jim Fixx took up jogging at 35 and, after losing 60 pounds and feeling physically and spiritually stronger, he wrote *The Complete Book of Running*. The book spurred the jogging craze of the late '70s and, as a self-styled guru of running, Jim became popular on talk shows and the lecture circuit, spreading the gospel that active people live longer and healthier lives.

After so adamantly extolling the virtues of jogging, Jim dropped dead of a heart attack at 52—while jogging. His death was an all-too-convenient defense for couch potatoes who choose to continue sedentary lifestyles but, after his autopsy, doctors agreed that if Jim had never jogged at all he'd still have died of a heart attack, many years earlier.

Jim was cremated and his ashes entrusted to his family.

At the place where Jim collapsed, a memorial has been erected in his honor. It's on Route 15 in Hardwick, Vermont, just 50 feet north of the Village Motel.

RON GOLDMAN & NICOLE BROWN SIMPSON

RON GOLDMAN
JULY 2, 1968 – JUNE 12, 1994

NICOLE BROWN SIMPSON
MAY 19, 1959 – JUNE 12, 1994

IN THE WHOLE sordid mess of the Simpson murder case, there seems to be only one thing on which everyone agrees: on June 12, 1994, *somebody* brutally stabbed and slashed Nicole Brown Simpson and her sometime-lover Ron Goldman to death at Nicole's posh Brentwood nest.

Nicole was the estranged wife of former football star O.J. Simpson, and soon nearly everyone in America would be pointing at him, convinced for many good reasons that he was the murderer. First of all, O.J. was insanely jealous, thus giving him a motive. Prior to the murders, he had purchased a knife from a cutlery shop that would've caused wounds compatible with those suffered by the victims, and he was never able to locate it later. DNA tests whose margin of error was in the neighborhood of one in a billion linked blood found at the scene to O.J., and blood found on his car and his socks to the victims. Missing gloves and bloody shoe prints were linked to O.J. Furthermore, he never established a verifiable alibi. Instead he jumped from one story to another as

LOVING SON, BROTHER AND FRIEND

RONALD LYLE GOLDMAN

JULY 2   JUNE 12
1968   1994

they crumbled beneath his inconsistencies. Immediately after the murders took place, O.J. boarded a flight to Chicago.

At this moment, thousands of people are in prison after being tried and convicted of murder, beyond a reasonable doubt, on much less than half of the evidence that was accumulated against O.J. But in October 1995 the millionaire hotshot walked away from his destiny, having been found not guilty.

The next year, the Goldman and Brown families pursued O.J. in a civil suit in which the burden of proof is lower than in criminal proceedings. In a civil case, guilt need only be proven according to a "preponderance of the evidence" rather than "beyond a reasonable doubt." After hearing four months of testimony, including O.J.'s (during the criminal trial he had invoked the Fifth Amendment, which is not an option in a civil trial), the jury found O.J. liable for the deaths of Ron and Nicole. The Goldman family was awarded $8.5 million in compensatory damages, while another $25 million in punitive damages was to be shared between both families.

Justice was served, except that the money was never paid. O.J. was "broke" and he retreated to Florida, where the law does not allow the seizure of future income. For a while, he lived in his $1.5 million house in Kendall collecting some $20,000 per month from a football pension, but in 2007 O.J. found himself again in the headlines after breaking into a Nevada hotel room and stealing some of his own memorabilia from a group of collectors at gunpoint. The following year karma prevailed, finally, when The Juice was sentenced to 33 years of hard time, though he was released for good behavior after serving just nine.

At their deaths, Ron and Nicole were 25 and 35, respectively. Ron was buried at Valley Oaks Cemetery in Westlake Village, California, while Nicole is at Ascension Cemetery in Lake Forest.

DIRECTIONS TO RON'S GRAVE: Drive into the cemetery at 5600 Lindero Canyon Road. Turn at the first left, and beneath the pine tree on the right is Ron's grave.

DIRECTIONS TO NICOLE'S GRAVE: At 24754 Trabuco Road, Nicole's grave is directly behind the office, three rows from the hedges.

JOHN GOTTI
OCTOBER 27, 1940 – JUNE 10, 2002

AFTER QUITTING SCHOOL in the 10th grade, John Gotti pursued a career as a professional thief and, after a relatively tame decade of burglary and stick-ups, he hooked up with the Gambino crime family and graduated to murder and other mayhem. After working his way up the ranks over the next two decades, in December 1985 Gotti masterminded the murder of his own mob family's boss, Paul Castellano. While Gotti and co-conspirator Sammy "the Bull" Gravano watched from their car parked across the Manhattan street, Gotti's hired hands greeted Castellano with a hail of bullets as he arrived at Sparks Steak House. With Castellano gone, Gotti assumed leadership of the Gambino family but, to his chagrin, his criminal enterprise was stamped out less than a decade later.

By the mid-1980s, law-enforcement agencies had finally begun to dismantle the foundations of organized crime with the help of technological advances in listening and tracking, tougher new laws, and a flush of appropriations set aside by the federal sector. Unfortunately for Gotti, his ascent to power coincided with the government's new efforts, and he unwittingly placed himself directly in the crosshairs of prosecutors.

Gotti was the classic gangster, and for the next half-dozen years, the government was obsessed with putting him away. But Gotti beat all the charges during three different trials and, for his habit of coming through criminal prosecutions unscathed, as well as for the air of importance he exuded in his expensive attire and fashionable pinky ring, he earned two monikers, "Teflon Don" and "Dapper Don."

But in 1992 his second-in-command, Sammy, cut a deal and switched teams. In exchange for immunity in a confessed 19 murders, Gravano was the star witness for the case fingering Gotti as the crime family's mastermind. His fate sealed, Gotti was sentenced to life in federal prison.

After 10 years of living alone in a 6-by-8-foot cell in Marion, Illinois, Gotti died of a cancer that had ravaged his neck and head. At 61, he was laid to rest alongside his son Frank at Saint John's Cemetery in Middle Village, New York.

Twelve-year-old Frank had been killed in March 1980 when he was struck by a car after darting into the street on a minibike. The driver of the vehicle, Gotti's neighbor John Favara, was hustled into a van four months after Frank's death and hasn't been heard from since. How's that for bad luck?

GRAVE DIRECTIONS: Enter the cemetery at 80-01 Metropolitan Avenue and make your way to the enormous mausoleum in the cemetery's center called St. John's Cloister. Enter at the entrance with the red awnings, go up the two short flights of stairs, then turn left and go up to the next floor. At the top of the stairs, turn right and then immediately left and there, on the bottom row on the right, are the wooden-faced crypts of John and Frank.

DOUG HENNING

MAY 3, 1947 – FEBRUARY 7, 2000

DOUG HENNING BECAME fascinated with magic after watching a levitation act on *The Ed Sullivan Show*. At 14 he placed a classified ad that read, "Magician: Have rabbit, will travel," and was soon performing at parties as "the Great Hendoo."

In 1974 Doug brought his Toronto-based rock-opera magic show called *Spellbound* to Broadway, where its success resulted in an offer of his own television special. The next year, a tie-dye-clad and long-haired Doug waved hello from his inaugural "World of Magic" TV spectacular where, annually for the next seven years, viewers were enthralled as Doug turned himself into a shark, walked through a brick wall, and made a horse disappear. Singlehandedly reviving the public's flagging interest in magic, Doug paved the way for the art's next generation; in fact, when Doug changed his focus in 1987, he sold some of his most famous illusions to David Copperfield.

In the late '80s, Doug exited the illusional magic business for a lifetime study of what he called "real magic"—Transcendental Meditation and levitation. With Maharishi Mahesh Yogi, Doug spent the remainder of his life trying to develop a Transcendental Meditation theme park in India where, he promised, one of the buildings would levitate. Unfortunately, the project never got off the ground (heh).

Dead of liver cancer at 52, Doug achieved levitation when his family scattered his ashes.

ABBIE HOFFMAN & JERRY RUBIN

ABBIE HOFFMAN
NOVEMBER 30, 1936 – APRIL 12, 1989

JERRY RUBIN
JULY 14, 1938 – NOVEMBER 28, 1994

THE CIVIL RIGHTS and antiwar movements of the 1960s were the first social revolutions to be televised and sharp-tongued Abbie Hoffman was the clown prince who held center court for the era's theatrics.

A member of the transitional 1950s generation between the beatniks and the hippies, Abbie expressed his rebellious teenage angst with ducktail haircuts and smoking in the boys' room. But after ferrying civil rights volunteers around Mississippi in 1963, he began toying with the idea of a full-on cultural revolution. Rejecting capitalism and the emptiness of American life, he and fellow rebel Jerry Rubin founded the Youth International Party, or Yippies, an anarchist group espousing political revolution, as well as sexual and drug freedom, "just for the hell of it."

With a legion of Yippies cheering from the sidelines, Abbie and Jerry engaged in a series of stunts meant to embarrass the Establishment. They disrupted the floor of the New York Stock Exchange by dropping fistfuls of dollars from the balcony; rallied thousands of Vietnam War protesters to exorcise the Pentagon; and appeared before a congressional committee wearing Revolutionary War costumes. Although the pranks were often comical, Abbie's motivation was deeply serious: "I grew up thinking democracy is not some place you hang your hat…It's something you do," he wrote.

In 1968 the Yippies nominated a pig for president, and later that year their theater reached a crescendo when thousands of protestors converged on the Democratic National Convention. Violence in the streets led to the arrests of Abbie and Jerry plus five of their minions. The Chicago Seven, as they came to be known, soon found themselves in the midst of a national political trial, defending themselves against charges of inciting a riot. In the famously unruly trial, the defendants blew kisses to the jury, answered questions while chewing gobs of jelly beans, and one day arrived in court dressed in judicial robes under which they wore blue Chicago police uniforms. Ultimately, the seven were acquitted.

In the late 1960s, Abbie began putting his ideas into books. *Revolution for the Hell of It, Woodstock Nation,* and *Steal this Book* together sold more than a million copies. In 1973 he was arrested for cocaine trafficking and, under threat of a 15-year-to-life sentence, went underground, had plastic surgery, and emerged as an ecological activist named Barry Freed. In 1980 on national television with Barbara Walters, Abbie came out of hiding and, after pleading guilty, served time on lesser charges.

Abbie maintained that he never considered himself as anything more than a good community organizer, but by the 1980s, the radical community had shrunk and, where once his every word was deemed significant, Abbie now spoke to small and often unenthusiastic audiences. Even his old rebel buddy, Jerry, had renounced radicalism and gone to work for a Wall Street firm, marketing a nutritional drink named Wow!

In 1989 Abbie was living in a spartan Pennsylvania apartment and working with an environmental group battling the diversion of Delaware River water to cool a nuclear reactor, but future plans and purpose seemed to elude him. Not fully recovered from a car accident some months earlier too, he may well have reminded him of an old fear he once wrote about of "growing old…alone and broke." In any event, at some point he decided to ingest a lethal mix of alcohol and the equivalent of 150 phenobarbital pills. Found cold and dead some days later by his landlord, Abbie was cremated at 52 and his ashes given to a friend, who keeps them on her mantel.

At 56, after a prolonged round of self-improvement that included meditation, acupuncture, and hypnotism in a search for a "new consciousness," Jerry met his end after being struck by a car while jaywalking in Los Angeles. For someone who all his life tweaked authority, it's fitting that what led to his death was one final act of nonconformity.

Jerry was buried at Hillside Memorial Park in Los Angeles.

GRAVE DIRECTIONS: At 6001 West Centinela Avenue, make your way to the Mount of Olives section, which is the grassy area on the hill to the left. Jerry's grave is under a tree at the end of the row directly behind the 7-14 curb marking.

HARRY HOUDINI

MARCH 24, 1874 – OCTOBER 31, 1926

AFTER CONCOCTING THE name "Houdini" from the famous French illusionist Jean Eugene Robert Houdin, the Hungarian-born Ehrich Weiss began his professional life as an entertainer at county fairs before becoming the foremost conjuring magician and escape artist of his day.

In 1894 Houdini met and married a struggling actress named Bess and, with her promotional acumen, Houdini's fledgling magic show grew quickly. He did card manipulations and run-of-the-mill illusions, but when the pair realized that his particularly macabre and dangerous tricks were the real crowd-pleasers, Houdini adjusted his act accordingly. First came the Needle Trick, a grisly effect involving the swallowing of needles and thread, followed by their regurgitation with the thread neatly looped through the needles' eyes. By 1898 Houdini was escaping from any pair of handcuffs the audience could produce in his Handcuff Challenge Act, which led to his renown as an escape artist.

In full view of audiences, Houdini was soon escaping from leg irons, straitjackets, and prison cells, and, when those routines became too easy, the drama and difficulty were ratcheted upward. Houdini was thrown into rivers in padlocked crates and locked canvas mailbags, he jumped from bridges in handcuffs, he was buried alive in sealed coffins and, onstage, his Upside-Down Water Torture Cell and Milk Can Escape illusions enthralled audiences, their jaws hanging open in astonishment. For more than two decades Harry remained in the limelight, and in later years he became a relentless exposer of unscrupulous spiritual mediums and a proud debunker of psychic frauds.

In 1926, at 52 years old, Houdini was still packing people in by the thousands, and his reputation was unparalleled. During a tour in the fall of that year, Houdini began experiencing stomach pains, but stubbornly refused to see a doctor. After an appearance at the Princess Theatre in Montreal, a college student, J. Gordon Whitehead, asked Houdini if the legend that he could sustain punches to his midsection without injury was true. Preoccupied with other conversation, Houdini more or less sidestepped the question, but he should also have sidestepped the blows that were to follow. Without warning, Whitehead pummeled Houdini at least three times in the abdomen, after which Houdini, grimacing in obvious pain, politely excused himself.

He struggled through the next day's show and, after arriving in London, Ontario, for the tour's next stop, a doctor informed

Houdini he was suffering from acute appendicitis. But the showbiz veteran refused to cancel that night's sold-out performance, which turned out to be his last. When Houdini's ruptured appendix was removed at three o'clock the next morning, the poison had already entered his bloodstream and he died in Detroit six days later, on Halloween.

Though the oft-repeated Houdini legend holds that Whitehead's punches were solely responsible for his death, that's not entirely true. It seems Houdini was already suffering from appendicitis and, even if Whitehead had never struck him, Houdini's appendix would have soon ruptured on its own. Nonetheless, his wife, Bess, was able to collect double indemnity on his life insurance policy claiming that the blows were equivalent to "an accident directly causing the premature death of Harry Houdini."

At Machpelah Cemetery in Ridgewood, New York, Houdini was buried in the very bronze coffin from which he had many times previously escaped. His rather large tombstone originally was topped with an imposing Houdini bust, but it was stolen many years later and never replaced.

GRAVE DIRECTIONS: Enter the cemetery at 8230 Cypress Hills Street and you won't miss Harry's tomb behind the office.

As an ultimate test of spiritualism, Houdini and Bess arranged a series of coded messages by which the first to die would—if possible—communicate with the other. After 12 years of trying to communicate with her deceased husband through the code, Bess finally declared the experiment a failure; though, every Halloween since, others have made their own attempts.

HOWARD HUGHES

NOVEMBER 24, 1905 – APRIL 5, 1976

HOWARD HUGHES, AN orphaned only child of millionaire parents, at 18 took over the family's business of manufacturing rotary drill bits used by the burgeoning oil industry. Shrewdly purchasing his competitors, by 1928 he boasted a then-unheard-of $2 million yearly income.

Howard later shifted his interest to making Hollywood movies, buying RKO Pictures and earning an Academy Award for producing *Two Arabian Knights*. All the while, of course, he sampled Hollywood's café society beauties and biggest stars, and became a symbol of Movieland's excesses and eccentricities.

In the midst of his hectic schedule, Howard became intrigued with the still-young field of aviation. In typical bigger-than-life Hughes fashion, not only did he learn to fly, Howard designed his own planes, formed a company that made experimental aircraft, and personally set air-speed records. During World War II, when metal was at a premium, his company built a plane of birch wood, the *Hercules,* also known by the nickname *Spruce Goose.* In 1938 he flew around the world in 91 hours, a feat for which he earned a Congressional Medal of Honor. (Howard never bothered to pick up the prize. After FDR's death, Harry Truman found the medal in a desk and mailed it to Hughes.)

But after a near-fatal airplane crash in 1946, Howard became addicted to opiates, and from then on began to unravel. By 1950, Howard was in complete seclusion, and only a few select Mormon nursemaids were allowed to see him. His enormous business enterprise was somehow directed by memo, and business meetings were often held in hotel washrooms, Howard in a stall while his associates gathered at the sinks. After 1956 Howard was not seen in public or photographed again for the rest of his life. In 1970, when the FBI investigated the possibility that he'd been murdered and his billions were in the process of being heisted, Howard confirmed through a telephone call that he was just fine, thank you.

In November 1966, clad in blue pajamas, Howard was stretchered off his private train and brought to the Desert Inn Hotel in Las Vegas, where he rented the entire top two floors. As New Year's Eve approached, the management of the hotel demanded that Howard leave to make way for vacationing high rollers, so Howard bought the whole place. When Howard's complaints about Las Vegas TV station KLAS going off the air after midnight went unanswered, he bought the broadcaster and had his favorite movies shown all night.

Through all of this, Howard *never* left the ninth-floor penthouse suite of his Desert Inn. Almost all of his time was spent sitting naked in a white leather chair in the center of the living room, an area he called the "germ-free zone," watching one film after another, while the windows remained covered by black curtains lest sunlight inadvertently fall on Howard's body. He was protected by guards who never caught a glimpse of their boss, and his staff awaited orders in the parlor around the clock. Due to his germ phobias, Howard slept atop sheets that were covered with a layer of paper towels, and he wrote his aides meticulous memos about how to wrap Kleenex around his eating utensils.

Finally, on Thanksgiving Day 1970, the bundle of neuroses called Howard, with his corkscrewing toenails, greasy, shoulder-length hair, and rotting teeth, was spirited onto a waiting jet and whisked to the Bahamas. The man obsessed with avoiding germs had, ironically, not allowed maids into the suite, and it had become disgustingly filthy and fetid. His aides stayed behind to clean up.

Howard's final years were spent abruptly moving from place to place: the Bahamas, London, Mexico, Panama, and, probably, other locations. By 1976 Howard was a living cadaver: His 6-foot-4 frame had shrunk by two inches and had wasted to 100 pounds, his face was gaunt and his dark eyes sunken, and his hair had turned a ghostly gray. As death enveloped him, Howard was boarded onto his jet and flown to Methodist Hospital in Houston for emergency care but, 30,000 feet in the air, Howard expired at 70 of kidney failure. The treasury department, which stood to reap over a billion dollars in estate taxes, required his identity be verified by fingerprints. An autopsy revealed broken hypodermic needles in his arms.

Howard had parlayed a small fortune from a revolutionary oil-drilling bit into a business empire than made him one of the richest men in the world, his estate estimated at $2 billion. Without an heir or an official will, 400 prospective beneficiaries tried to lay claim, but his assets eventually went to 22 cousins on both sides of his family.

Howard was buried at Glenwood Cemetery in Houston.

GRAVE DIRECTIONS: Enter the cemetery at 2525 Washington Avenue, turn right beyond the circle and bridge, and stay to the right on this drive. After a couple hundred yards, the Hughes plot is on the right, surrounded by an off-green steel fence.

STEVE IRWIN

FEBRUARY 22, 1962 – SEPTEMBER 4, 2006

STEVE IRWIN'S FEARLESSNESS of up-close encounters with varmints and beasts of every stripe originated from a childhood spent at a Queensland wildlife park operated by his parents. In due course, the effervescent environmentalist won global fame as the "Crocodile Hunter," on a television program on which he starred as a khaki-clad wildlife stalker who pushed the personal-space envelope with exotic animals while delivering mile-a-minute commentary in a ripe Australian twang.

Punctuated by a signature "Crikey!" exclamation whenever there was a close call, viewers were enlightened by his high-energy elucidations and came away from his shows with knowledge of lifestyle facts and figures for the scores of outlandish creatures that costarred with him. But it was Steve's high-energy stunts (that some critics categorized as "stupid," among other things), including leaping on the backs of huge crocodiles and grabbing deadly snakes by the tail, that gained him genuine notoriety. Ultimately, his proclivity for too-close-for-comfort danger cost Steve his life.

At Australia's Great Barrier Reef, Steve was snorkeling above a large stingray while filming segments for a show named "Oceans' Deadliest." The ray flicked his tail upward and the barb of its serrated and poisonous spine struck Steve squarely in the chest, piercing his heart before breaking off. Videotaped pulling the barb from his chest, a surprised and frightened Steve lost consciousness moments later and was dead within minutes.

In the days following his death it was reported that Steve was buried at the Australia Zoo in Beerwah—and that would make an endearing follow-up (as well as a boon to the zoo's business)—but you'll be disappointed if you try to visit him there. Administrators of the zoo are tight-lipped about the subject and I've been dead-ended after a series of other goose chases too. What's the world coming to when the day's preeminent grave researcher throws up his hands and admits he's flummoxed?

B. K. S. IYENGAR

DECEMBER 14, 1918 – AUGUST 20, 2014

MORE THAN ANY other practitioner of yoga, Bellur Krishnamachar Sundararaja Iyengar was responsible for its modern proliferation.

Born in the midst of an influenza outbreak, Iyengar survived a childhood marked by illness after illness—tuberculosis, typhoid fever, and malaria—and by the time he began studying yoga at 16 he was painfully frail. "My arms were thin, my legs were spindly, and my stomach protruded in an ungainly manner," he recalled, but in short order Iyengar was demonstrating "the most impressive and bewildering" positions in the court of the Maharaja of Mysore in his native India, and he credited yoga with saving his life.

For the next 15 years Iyengar headed a yoga institute in Pune where he hosted and honed his *asana*s (postures) and *pranayama* (breathing) so that he could attain a penetration beyond the physical body and access the inner *kosa*s (layers) of mind, energy, and spirit, to gain vitality, clarity, and calm. In 1952 came a turning point that transformed him from a relatively obscure yoga practitioner and teacher into an international guru, when the violinist Yehudi Menuhin attended an Iyengar clinic and came to recognize that his playing was improved by an invigorated mind-body connection as well as by the discipline inherent to the posture sequences and breathing exercises. In short order Menuhin introduced Iyengar to other prominent and inquisitive pupils and, as alternative explorations of body and mind flourished in the West, so too did hundreds of Iyengar yoga centers.

Formidable eyebrows, a flowing mane of white hair, and an out-of-proportion frame lent Iyengar an exaggerated stern and intimidating presence that he advantageously wielded in demanding absolute precision from his students. Off the mat, however, he was known to be warm, attentive, and nurturing, going so far as to design and initiate the use of various improvisations including blocks and straps to help those who are challenged by limited range of motion or different anatomies or physiologies attain the positions of Iyengar's strict asanas. Such assistive apparatuses were key to the advance of modern therapeutic yoga.

Upon its publication, his 1966 book, *Light on Yoga*, was speedily recognized as *the* definitive text of yoga for its step-by-step instruction and explanation of the benefits of asanas and pranayama in a clear and understandable format that was heretofore unavailable. Other works include 2005's *Light on Life*, which featured a more complete description of the emotional, intellectual, and spiritual developments that yogic traditions can offer.

As to the wider benefits of yoga, Iyengar opined that "before peace between the nations we have to find peace inside that small nation which is our own being." Too, he wondered, "How can you know God if you don't know your big toe?" Preaching that "practice is my feast and I do yoga from the self towards the body, not the other way around," Iyengar honored that maxim by keeping himself supremely fit, and even into his nineties could easily hold a headstand for many minutes. After lying immobile for a long period, he once offered his thoughts: "Nothing. But though I remain thoughtfully thoughtless, it is not an empty mind."

Following kidney problems, Iyengar died at 95 and was cremated, his ashes scattered to the wind.

STEVE JOBS

FEBRUARY 24, 1955 – OCTOBER 5, 2011

NEITHER A HARDWARE engineer nor a software programmer, Steve Jobs was a visionary who accelerated the integration of computer technology into society. Obsessed, arrogant, and tenacious, he was blessed with an intuitive understanding of the way in which the mass market might best integrate computing power into daily life. And then, melding the skills of a natural-born leader, tireless manager, and master salesman, he prodded and cajoled and inspired thousands of minds at his Apple computer company to develop his visions into easy-to-use, aesthetically pleasing, well-built, and yes, even fun, consumer-ready electronic devices.

His worldview was shaped by the 1960s counterculture of the San Francisco Bay Area where he grew up, the adopted son of a mechanic and an accountant who tinkered with him in the garage and taught him to read before going to school. After a short stay at a college his parents could ill afford, Jobs worked briefly as a video-game designer for Atari before backpacking around India for seven months, furthering teenage experiments with psychedelic drugs and seeking spiritual enlightenment.

But by 1975, Jobs was spending much of his time hanging around with a high school friend, Steve Wozniak, at the Homebrew Computer Club, an informal collection of geeks who gathered to trade know-how and parts for do-it-yourself computing devices, which at that time just barely existed. In 1976, "the two Steves," as they had become known in that circle, co-founded Apple Computer with a shop in the suburban garage of Jobs' parents. The following year they built and offered for sale— for $666.66 through an ad placed in *Scientific American*—the Apple II, which is considered to be the world's first commercially available personal computer. Instead of the boxy wooden affairs that hobbyists offered, the Apple II was a breakthrough sleek plastic affair intended for the den or kitchen that was offered as a digital lifestyle. Seven years later, Apple again set the industry on its head when it released its Macintosh, featuring a graphical user interface and mouse, which further popularized PCs for the masses. The computer revolution was on!

In 1985, after a corporate power struggle, Apple's board stripped Jobs of managerial duties and he left his own company. "I don't wear the right kind of pants to run this company," he told a gathering of Apple employees before he left. He was barefoot as he spoke, and wearing blue jeans. Soon he announced a new venture, NeXT, which also had a huge impact—in 1990 a NeXT machine was used to develop the first version of the World Wide Web. In 1986, Steve built a team that became Pixar Animation Studios, which produced a string of full-length computer-animated films starting with *Toy Story*.

It had taken a while for the world to realize what an amazing treasure Steve Jobs was, though he knew it all along. By 1996, his beloved Apple was in a shambles, losing money left and right, and its market share declined as key employees left for greener pastures. Selling NeXT to Apple, Jobs triumphantly returned to the company and, by quickly introducing the iMac, ending Apple's feud with archrival Microsoft, and demonstrating true leadership during such presentations as those at MacWorld, the company soon regained its buzz. Once in control of Apple again, Jobs set the company on the path to becoming a consumer-electronics powerhouse; in 2001 he pushed the company into the digital music business by introducing iTunes and the iPod MP3 player; in 2007 the iPhone and its touch-screen interface set the standard for the mobile computing market, while 2010's iPad culminated his vision for a more personal computing device.

In 2004 Apple announced that he had a rare but curable form of pancreatic cancer, and Jobs waged a long and public struggle with the disease. Remaining the face of the company even as he underwent treatment, Steve finally stepped down from his duties in 2009 after receiving a liver transplant.

"No one wants to die," he said in a 2005 commencement speech at Stanford University. "And yet death is the destination we all share. No one has ever escaped it." In closing, Jobs described how *The Whole Earth Catalog* deeply influenced him as a young man and how it ends with the admonition "Stay Hungry. Stay Foolish." "I have always wished that for myself," he said.

At 56, Steve Jobs died of his cancer, leaving his family, millions of devotees, and 49,000 Apple employees behind. Though some like to believe he was cremated and his ashes scattered in accordance with Eastern spiritual beliefs, it seems he was buried in an unmarked grave at Alta Mesa Memorial Park in Palo Alto, California.

CASEY KASEM

APRIL 27, 1932 – JUNE 15, 2014

ON THE FOURTH of July in 1970, disc jockey Casey Kasem and his producer friend Don Bustany premiered a radio show they named *American Top 40*. The show's exceedingly simple format consisted merely of Casey counting down *Billboard* magazine's most popular singles from the previous week amid a liberal sprinkling of colorful trivia about the artists and homey, feel-good anecdotes during the song breaks. Only five stations carried the show's debut, but within five years there were more than a thousand "coast to coast," as Casey liked to say, making him the best-known DJ in the country for four decades.

Interestingly, Casey confessed to never really caring for any type of music much; he knew his subject and kept up with it in a professional way, but when home, "I find myself just wanting to sit in my office and make it as quiet as possible." In the end, it seemed that perhaps the music didn't matter much to his program's longevity either. Hit singles in rock and pop, soul, country, and hip-hop came and went, but it was Casey's down-home delivery and regular-guy appeal that glued listeners to their radios. "If I were doing a rock show," he said, "then it would matter to know how I felt about what I was playing. But I'm just counting them down as they appear on the chart, one through forty. What really matters is what I say between the songs." Indeed, many likened Casey's comfortable on-air persona of homespun sentiment and assurance to the radio equivalent of comfort food, his relentlessly upbeat outlook embodied in the touchstone if not corny sign-off that he used to close every show: "Keep your feet on the ground, and keep reaching for the stars."

In 2004 Casey handed hosting duties to radio and television personality Ryan Seacrest while remaining in the background writing and producing. On the 39th anniversary of his first Top 40 program, Casey quietly retired.

In 2007 Casey had been diagnosed with Lewy body dementia, a degenerative disorder of the central nervous system similar to Parkinson's disease. When Casey's health had deteriorated to a point where he was unable to care for himself, a bizarre feud between Casey's second wife, Jean, and the children of Casey's first marriage emerged as Jean prevented any contact with her husband by anyone for months. Over Jean's vehement protests, in May 2014 a court granted Casey's daughter Kerri conservatorship over him, which included the right to make medical decisions on his behalf.

The only problem was that nobody knew where Casey was, as Jean had spirited him from a nursing home days earlier, saying only that "he was no longer in the United States." Days later, however, Casey was located in Washington State, though it hardly mattered, as he was unresponsive by then and died two weeks later.

Then things got really weird. A judge granted Kerri a restraining order to prevent Jean from cremating Casey so that an autopsy could be performed, but when Kerri went to hand deliver the order to the funeral home, she learned that Jean had had Casey moved to a Canadian funeral home, where the restraining order fell on deaf ears due to lack of jurisdiction. Finally, for completely unexplained reasons, Jean had Casey buried in an unmarked grave at Oslo Western Civil Cemetery in Norway, a country where Casey had no relations, ties, or heritage and that, in fact, he had never even visited. He lies alone there today in the cold ground, where he most probably will spend eternity. The whole thing makes one wonder.

EVEL KNIEVEL
OCTOBER 17, 1938 – NOVEMBER 30, 2007

FLYING HIGH THROUGH the air must have been hard-wired in stuntman Robert "Evel" Knievel's psyche; in 1959 he was the Northern Rocky Mountains Men's Ski Jumping champion, and during a later stint in the Army, he pole vaulted for their track team. But his true calling originated in 1965 when he announced, in a bid to attract customers to his Washington State motorcycle shop, that he'd jump his motorcycle 40 feet over parked cars and a box of rattlesnakes. Before 1,000 people, he did the stunt as promised, but failed to fly far enough. His bike landed hard on the rattlesnakes but the audience was completely thrilled. "Right then," he said, "I knew I could draw a big crowd by jumping over weird stuff."

So began his red-white-and-blue-spangled motorcycle daredevil career as the showman barnstormed the West, riding through fire walls, jumping over live mountain lions, and being towed at 200 mph behind dragster race cars with his own Evel Knievel Motorcycle Daredevil Touring Show. At first he'd jump over a couple cars, but the stakes and the obstacles grew exponentially higher until he was nearly killed when he jumped 151 feet across the fountains in front of Caesar's Palace in 1968. He cleared the fountains but, flung like a rag doll after crash landing, he suffered 17 broken bones and spent a month in a coma. "It was terrible," he said afterward. "I lost control of the

bike. Everything seemed to come apart. I kept smashing over and over and ended up against a brick wall, 165 feet away." Nonetheless, the jump, and especially the ensuing crash, made Evel bigger-than-life, a 1970s cultural icon who picked up where Houdini and Superman left off.

After recovery, when a lesser man (or a saner one) may have considered a different career, Evel hit the jump circuit anew. Jumping a dozen cars for $25,000 became weekly routine and, as imitators edged into his celebrity, Evel raised the stakes with bigger and bigger jumps. When cars got boring there were Pepsi delivery trucks followed by buses, then double-decker buses and, predictably, a shark-filled tank. After a failed attempt on Idaho's Snake River Canyon, he planned to launch his rocket-powered motorcycle over the Grand Canyon, but the Department of the Interior nixed the harebrained scheme.

By 1976 Knievel was done jumping motorcycles, the baton passed to his son, and the remainder of his life was spent wistfully enjoying the memories of his daredevil days. That is, whenever he could find time for lazy nostalgia what with the charges of soliciting an undercover policewoman for immoral purposes, hepatitis, a liver transplant, serving six months for assault on his former press agent with a baseball bat, bankruptcy, diabetes, and a divorce.

At 71 he died of pulmonary failure which, after all the high-flying crashes and broken bones, and concussions, is quite remarkable: Evel Knievel died, more or less, of old age.

He is buried at Mountain View Cemetery in Butte, Montana.

GRAVE DIRECTIONS: Enter the cemetery at 3910 Harrison Avenue (Route 2) and at the first crossroad turn left. After a few hundred feet, on the right, a spruce tree wrapped in red, white, and blue stands guard over Evel's headstone.

RAY KROC

OCTOBER 5, 1902 – JANUARY 14, 1984

AFTER A 17-YEAR career selling cups to restaurants in the Midwest, high school dropout Ray Kroc felt it was time to get out on his own, so he became the exclusive sales agent for a five-spindle multimixer. In 1953 Dick and Mac McDonald's fast-food emporium in San Bernardino, California, bought eight of the mixing machines from Ray. His curiosity piqued, Ray later explained: "I had to see what kind of an operation was making 40 milkshakes at a time."

When Ray went to see the restaurant the next year, he was entranced by the efficiency of the operation. There was only a very limited, low-priced menu and, though it was a hamburger restaurant, it was not of the popular drive-in variety; people had to get out of their cars to be served. A dyed-in-the-wool capitalist, Ray started dreaming about additional McDonald's stores, each equipped with eight multimixers churning up a steady stream of cash. The following day he pitched the idea of opening several restaurants to the brothers, and when asked, "Who could we get to open them for us?" Ray was ready.

"Well, what about me?" he replied.

Eventually a deal was struck whereby Ray gave the McDonalds a small percentage of the gross, and in 1955 he opened his first McDonald's restaurant in Des Plaines, Illinois. Business proved excellent, and by the time Ray bought the brothers out in 1961 for a paltry $2.7 million, there were 273 locations.

Free to run the business his own way, Ray never changed the fundamental format, but added his own wrinkles. First, from the parking lot to the kitchen floor to the bathrooms, everything was clean. Next, he applied team techniques to the food's preparation. New restaurants were located in swiftly growing suburban areas, where family visits to the local McDonald's became something of a tribal ritual. Finally, millions of dollars were poured into advertising, to the point where consumers were so preconditioned by the McDonald's promotional blanket that, as one industry wag flippantly pointed out, "the hamburger would taste good even if they left the meat out."

In choosing a franchise owner to manage a new outlet, Ray looked for someone who was good with people. "We'd rather get a salesman than a chef," Ray explained. And when it came to

479

training these franchise owners, Ray was unremittingly intense: At his own "Hamburger University," a training course led to a "Bachelor of Hamburgerology with a minor in French Fries." Ray's fastidious attention and passion paid off; by 1963 more than 1 billion hamburgers had been sold, and that same year, the 500th restaurant opened. Today there are more than 37,000 McDonald's restaurants in 120 countries.

Ray sensed that a nation of people who ate on the go wanted something different. He changed American business and eating habits by giving them what they wanted or, perhaps what *he* wanted. The ultimate salesman, Ray defined salesmanship as "the gentle art of letting the customer have it *your* way."

Ray served as senior chairman of McDonald's until his death at 81 after a series of strokes.

He was buried at El Camino Memorial Park in La Jolla, California.

GRAVE DIRECTIONS: Enter the cemetery at 5600 Carroll Canyon Road, turn at the first left, and go all the way up the hill. Turn left at the "T," follow this drive all the way to its end, and park at the loop. Walk toward the three big bells and turn into the mausoleum on the right. Proceed all the way through the mausoleum, exit the rear door and, once you're back outside, turn right and look up to see Ray's crypt.

JACK LALANNE
SEPTEMBER 26, 1914 – JANUARY 23, 2011

LONG BEFORE RICHARD Simmons, Jane Fonda, or the Atkins diet, Jack LaLanne popularized the idea that folks should exercise regularly and maintain a proper diet to retain youthfulness and vigor. He started working out with weights when they were an oddity, opened what is considered the first-ever health spa complete with its own juice bar and health food store in 1936, and launched the then-laughable idea of a television exercise program in 1951. He invented the forerunners of modern exercise machines, like leg-extension and pulley devices, and sold exercise videos and fitness books. He even proposed what was once a radical idea: Women, the elderly, and the disabled should work out to retain strength. "People thought I was a nut," Jack remembered. "When I started, it was believed there were health benefits to smoking, and even doctors were against me, saying that working with weights would give people heart attacks and cause them to lose their sex drive."

Growing up, Jack himself was in poor shape, a self-described "sugarholic" with a violent temper and suicidal thoughts. And that was only the beginning: He was failing in school, he was nearsighted and had terrible headaches, he was weak and skinny, and he had pimples and boils on his body. But his mother took him to a talk by Paul Bragg, a well-known speaker on nutrition, and that talk turned Jack's life around at 15. He took Bragg's message fully to heart and, by his own testimony and that of everyone around him, he never had any sweet of any kind from that day forward, nor did he drink a single cup of coffee or tea. He also lifted weights and performed calisthenics relentlessly. Within months all of Jack's maladies disappeared, he became a varsity athlete, and he even stopped wearing glasses.

After high school Jack became a pitchman for good health, starting a business selling his mother's healthful bread and cookies, and setting up a rudimentary gym training police officers and firefighters, "the fat and skinny ones who couldn't pass their physicals," he recalled. Word of his success spread, and business was good enough for him to open other gyms, eventually more than a hundred of them. The gyms led to *The Jack LaLanne Show*; when the exercise program debuted, his props consisted of merely a broomstick, a chair, and a rubber cord, though Jack characteristically offset his frugal set by employing a rapid-fire banter full of exuberance and good cheer. In his signature belted jumpsuit that showed off his impressive biceps, he tirelessly pranced through routines that ran the gamut from jumping jacks to fingertip push-ups. The program lasted 34 years, airing more than 3,000 episodes.

Jack saw himself as a combination cheerleader, rescuer, and savior, but he felt too that many people viewed him as an imposter, so in 1954 he decided to perform a variety of "feats of strength" stunts that ended up making him a household name. "I had to get people believing in me," he said. His first feat, performed in 1954 when he was 40, was to prove he wasn't "over the hill" and consisted of swimming the length of the Golden Gate Bridge, underwater, while carrying 140 pounds of air-tank equipment. Future feats included swimming from Alcatraz to shore wearing handcuffs, pulling a paddleboard 30 miles from the Farallon Islands to San Francisco, and completing a thousand push-ups in 21 minutes.

Though his feats tapered off after his 70th birthday, Jack retained a high level of energy well into what many would consider "old age," beginning each day at 5:00 a.m. with two hours of workouts: weight lifting followed by a swim against an artificial current. Promoting both himself and his calling into his final years, the seemingly eternal master of health and fitness brimmed with optimism and restated a host of aphorisms for an active and fit life. "I can't die," he most famously liked to say. "It would ruin my image."

But Jack finally did ruin his image: he died of respiratory failure at age 96 and was buried at Forest Lawn Memorial Park in Hollywood Hills, California.

GRAVE DIRECTIONS: Enter the park at 6300 Forest Lawn Drive, get a map at the information booth, and drive to God's Acre, which is the lawn in front of the Old North Church. Jack is buried there in Section 2019, Grave 1, though that area isn't marked very well. If you stand in front of the church and, with your back to it, walk in the ten-o'clock direction for about 150 feet, you'll be getting close to his flat tablet.

TIMOTHY LEARY
OCTOBER 22, 1920 – MAY 31, 1996

TIMOTHY LEARY'S NAME is synonymous with 1960s counterculture as the key polarizer who extended the generational distance from a gap to a chasm. Disillusioned young people saw Timothy as a harbinger of social change, while their parents viewed the Harvard University psychologist as an anti-establishment corrupter of youth.

Until his Harvard days when he met Richard Alpert, Timothy's life was conventional, and he even attended West Point before entering the Army during World War II. In 1961, though, Timothy and Alpert (today known as Baba Ram Dass) began experimenting with lysergic acid diethylamide, or LSD. Timothy went one step farther and publicly extolled the virtues of taking LSD as a vehicle for personal growth, and the "turn on, tune in, drop out" insurrection began.

By the time Timothy was fired from Harvard four years later, his psychopharmacological revolution, the Psychedelic Movement, was in full swing. At some point came the unspoken realization that LSD itself was not the key to spiritual or intellectual nirvana after all, and the psychedelic experience was then redirected into the Humanistic Revolution: an empowering ethereal movement emphasizing interpersonal relationships, multilevel personality assessments, group therapy, and body/mind interaction that ultimately fed into the enduring New Age movement.

While all of these revolutions and movements were finding their balance, Timothy was performing a balancing act of his own with the authorities. In January 1970, he was finally sentenced to up to 20 years on marijuana convictions. Nine months later, though, he escaped with help from the underground group The Weathermen and, after joining Black Panther fugitives, eluded captivity for three years before being caught in Afghanistan.

In 1976 Timothy had a change of heart and was paroled after he cooperated with federal authorities; unbelievably, after having preached against the establishment all his adult life, he informed on the very Weathermen who had helped him bust out of jail.

He had survived the '60s, the drugs, and the busts, but after his release Timothy never again had quite the same impact on the world. In the following decades, as attitudes hardened toward recreational drugs, he maintained a legal income source from his many books, dabbled as a stand-up comedian and a software developer, consorted with Hollywood friends, and made sporadic talk-show appearances.

In 1995 he was diagnosed with inoperable prostate cancer and, ever preoccupied with being Timothy Leary, he managed to turn his protracted death into a media event. After announcing that his death was imminent, he spun this "most fascinating experience in life" into something about which he was "eager and enthusiastic." For a while, Timothy even contemplated committing suicide in real time; in this period when the Internet was not even yet a mainstream gadget, his idea was to develop a Web page wherein fans and well-wishers—or adversaries, for that matter—could watch as he set sail on a final and most profound, far-out trip.

In due time, though, in private and in the still moments as the cancer began to assume control of his body, Timothy's enthusiasm for his death waned and his friends knew it was a trip he feared. Talking about taking one's own life and actually doing it are two very different things and, in the end, there was no last act of defiance.

Instead, at 75, Timothy died in his sleep at home. He died with dignity, and he was not logged on or spaced out.

Space would have to wait just a little longer; Timothy still had one last "far-out trip" to experience. In April of 1997, about seven grams of the psychedelic cosmonaut's ashes, along with those of Gene Roddenberry and 22 other space enthusiasts, were attached to the final booster stage of a rocket and blasted from the planet by a Texas-based company named Celestis, in the world's first space funeral. On May 20, 2002, after 28,132 orbits around the earth, the capsules of ashes reentered the atmosphere over New Guinea and burned up in a fiery finale.

LIBERACE
MAY 16, 1919 – FEBRUARY 4, 1987

BEST REMEMBERED FOR his extravagant costumes and the trademark giant candelabrum atop his piano, Wladziu Valentino Liberace was loved by his audiences for his musical talent and his unique showmanship. Throughout his long and lucrative career—much of it spent in ridiculously glitzy costumes consisting of jeweled capes, sequins, bright beads, and even hot pants—the critics found it hard to make fun of him because he always seemed to be having so much fun performing what he called "*Reader's Digest* versions" of familiar classic melodies. Liberace whipped through Chopin's "Minute Waltz" in 37 seconds, while Tchaikovsky's 45-minute Piano Concerto No. 1 took him just four minutes. His secret, he said, was "cutting out the dull parts."

But Liberace wasn't without classical credentials: He attended Wisconsin College of Music, followed by a three-year stint in the Chicago Symphony. During a chancy encore after a 1939 recital, he stumbled upon the musical formula that made him famous by breaking with concert tradition and performing the popular novelty song "Three Little Fishes." It drove the audience wild and Liberace later recognized that as the defining moment on his road to rhinestones and Rolls-Royces. In 1952 the *Liberace Television Hour* introduced him to middle America, and for the rest of his career he sold out dozens of shows each year as an American music icon and Las Vegas fixture.

By 1986, though, Liberace had lost significant weight and was in exceedingly poor health. Tabloids soon screamed that he was suffering of AIDS and, as expected, Liberace's camp denied it. But after his death at 67, his death certificate stated that Liberace had died of "cytomegalic virus pneumonia and human immunodeficiency viral disease."

Pictures of his most-recent boyfriend, and of his dog, Wrinkles, were placed in Liberace's casket and, wearing a white tuxedo and full makeup, he was entombed at Forest Lawn Memorial Park in Hollywood Hills, California.

GRAVE DIRECTIONS: Enter the park at 6300 Forest Lawn Drive, stop at the booth, and after getting a park map, go to the Courts of Remembrance. Walk into the courtyard and you won't miss Liberace's large white tomb against the wall on the right.

THE LINDBERGHS

CHARLES LINDBERGH, JR.
JUNE 22, 1930 – MARCH 1, 1932

CHARLES LINDBERGH
FEBRUARY 4, 1902 – AUGUST 26, 1974

ANNE MORROW LINDBERGH
JUNE 22, 1906 – FEBRUARY 7, 2001

IN 1926 CHARLES Lindbergh was flying a regular mail route between Chicago and St. Louis and, in those lonely hours, resolved to pursue the yet unclaimed $25,000 prize that had been offered in 1919 to the first aviator who flew nonstop between New York and Paris. Since its inception, the well-publicized challenge had been a sort of national obsession, and had captured the imagination of the American public. But, frustratingly, though there were plenty of front-page accounts glorifying the pioneers who set off to claim the prize, there had never been an exciting story of success. French aviators would fly out of Paris and crash-land in England, American fliers would be forced back to New York after encountering bad weather, and many pilots from both sides of the Atlantic simply took off and were never heard from again.

Charles had his own ideas about how to successfully cross the Atlantic. Unlike most of his contemporaries, he believed the passage should be flown alone, and he was also convinced that an airplane capable of crossing the Atlantic Ocean simply did not exist—it would have to be built. After enlisting the financial aid of a few St. Louis businessmen, he hired the Ryan Airplane company in San Diego to build him a plane for the crossing, and when it was ready two months later, Charles flew it to New York in preparation for his Paris flight.

Charles' plane, the *Spirit of St. Louis*, was designed expressly to fly across the Atlantic. Described as a "two-ton flying gas tank," every possible accommodation was sacrificed for better fuel economy: There was no radio and no brakes, a small periscope replaced a forward-facing windshield, and Charles wore no parachute. For food, he brought five sandwiches. "If I get to Paris, I won't need any more and if I don't get to Paris, I won't need any more, either," he noted dryly. There was no room for error.

May 21, 1927, the *Spirit of St. Louis* landed in Paris. Charles' singular accomplishment electrified the world, and he immediately embarked on a goodwill tour of some two dozen countries. During a visit to Mexico he met aspiring writer Anne Morrow and in 1929 the two were wed.

In 1932 the Lindberghs made headlines anew when their toddler son, Charles Jr., was snatched from his nursery at their Hopewell, New Jersey, home. A kidnapper left a note demanding $50,000 and after corresponding through newspaper classifieds and an intermediary, the ransom money was delivered to

a Bronx cemetery. But their baby was never returned. Instead he was found two months later, dead, near the Lindbergh home. Bruno Hauptmann was eventually arrested for the crime after he passed some of the ransom money at a gas station, and he went to the electric chair in 1936.

In 1939 Charles became spokesperson for the America First Committee, a group that opposed American entry into World War II, and his position put him at odds with President Roosevelt and ordinary Americans who questioned his loyalty. They were particularly repelled by his vocal anti-Semitic stance. In response, Charles resigned his Air Corps commission. After Pearl Harbor he asked for it back, but Roosevelt staunchly refused, so Charles spent the war years as an advisor at Henry Ford's B-24 bomber plant instead. After the war, the public generally forgot about, or at least overlooked, Charles' pre-war shenanigans.

During their marriage, Anne had come into fame of her own. In the 1930s the couple had worked together as commercial air flight surveyors and, during a pioneering flight from Canada to China, she had served as Charles' copilot. A meticulous documentarian, Anne related the story of that adventure in her first book, *North to the Orient*, which became a bestseller, as did the other dozen titles she'd write. In 1954 Charles' book, *Spirit of St. Louis*, detailing his famous transatlantic flight and largely written by Anne, won a Pulitzer Prize. In 1956, Anne authored one of the landmark bestsellers of the century, *Gift From the Sea*, a reflection on women's lives and their struggle for identity.

In their twilight years, the Lindberghs continued to fly, though mostly for pleasure. At 72, Charles died of cancer at their Maui home. After Charles' death, Anne began publishing her journals, letters, and memoirs, in part to provide a historical record of aviation and also to end the many misconceptions and fallacies about herself and her husband. After suffering a series of strokes, Anne died at 94 in the company of her family at her daughter's Vermont home.

Today, Charles' *Spirit of St. Louis* airplane hangs in the atrium of the National Air and Space Museum in Washington D.C.

Before Charles died, he sketched a simple design for his coffin and grave. He was buried under the shade of a java plum tree at Palapala Ho'omau Congregational Church Cemetery in Kipahulu on the Hawaiian island of Maui. His epitaph, Psalm 139:9, reads, "If I take the wings of the morning, and dwell in the uttermost parts of the sea."

GRAVE DIRECTIONS: On Route 360 near mile marker 41, look for the church's small sign directing you onto a small drive alongside a meadow. Park in front of the church and walk over to the cemetery on the ocean side of the church. Charles' grave is located approximately in the cemetery center surrounded by a simple iron chain.

Anne was cremated, and, in accordance with her wishes, her ashes were "scattered over the places she loved."

Charles Lindbergh Jr., who died at 18 months, was cremated and his ashes scattered over the Atlantic Ocean.

MARCEL MARCEAU
MARCH 22, 1923 – SEPTEMBER 22, 2007

THE ROOTS OF pantomime stretch back to the Greeks 500 years before Christ, and the Romans later used the art to depict current events or mock the gods. Mime also had its heydays during the Renaissance but, with the advent of the talkies, its future looked grim. However, in 1947, after escaping deportation to a Nazi death camp by altering his Mangel surname and thereby surviving to fight alongside fellow French resistors during WWII, Marcel Marceau initiated his dreamy harlequin-inspired clown named Bip and, in the nick of time, rescued the art form from history's dust bin.

Though some cynics may sneer, "Thanks for nuthin'," legions of admirers praised Marcel, clad as Bip in an ill-fitting striped shirt, too-long pants, and smashed hat topped with a jaunty red carnation, through more than 15,000 performances. Marcel created dozens of situations for his little white-faced character through the years, ranging from taming a lion to being stuck in an elevator to characterizing an old gossipy woman knitting a sweater. There were also "mimodramas," including "The Overcoat," the story of a Russian clerk who works for a decade to buy a coat only to have it stolen, as well as innumerable sketches like "The Creation of the World" and, his most revered, one showing the four stages of life—youth, maturity, old age, and death—all communicated beyond the barrier of language.

Delighted by those who emulated him well, such as Michael Jackson, who famously borrowed his moonwalk from Marcel's "Walking Against the Wind" sketch, Marcel also lamented that some of his less talented copycats had given mime a bad name, especially ruing street mimes who work popular tourist areas. After a long-winded disparagement of their skills when a reporter once asked his opinion, Marcel caught himself and concluded the exchange with, "Never get a mime talking. He won't stop."

At 84, Marcel was buried at Paris' Père Lachaise Cemetery.

MINNESOTA FATS
JANUARY 19, 1913 – JANUARY 15, 1996

THOUGH HE NEVER won a major professional pool tournament, Rudolf Wanderone Jr. was—and still is—the best-known player of all time.

A fast-talking hustler with no regular income, Rudolf carved an erratic living in Brooklyn's darkened pool halls by betting on his own prowess and winning more games than he lost. Making the rounds for 30 years, the consummate gambler with a colorful demeanor and hulking frame earned a reputation in increasingly greater circles and along the way picked up the moniker "New York Fats" or usually just "Fats." In time, almost *nobody* of the legions who professed knowledge of his smoky backroom exploits actually knew his real name.

In 1959 Walter Tevis wrote *The Hustler*, a fictitious account of a skillful player who roams from town to town conning people into thinking he's an easy mark until he meets his match in a player named Minnesota Fats. The book was made into a well-received movie by the same name two years later and it was then that Rudolph Wanderone Jr., ever the cocky huckster, capitalized on the movie and "became" Minnesota Fats.

While pool and billiard professionals and their supporters howled, Minnesota Fats snatched the limelight, passed himself off as the greatest ever, and soon became a household name. To be sure, Fats was an excellent player but his skills paled in comparison to the game's true champions and his critics' disparagements included pointing out that he'd never even *been* to Minnesota.

With one excuse after another, Fats wisely avoided national competitions that would reveal his charade to the generally unknowing public but, eventually, he was cornered into competing in a series of televised matches against pool star Willie Mosconi. The expert Mosconi took him apart with surgical precision but the audience hardly noticed because Fats stole the show with humorous banter and trash talk. Fats never did yield his pretense as "the greatest player ever" and, in a fitting twist, the man derided by purists for decades became the game's greatest publicity mechanism ever. In 1984 the Billiard Congress of America relented and inducted Minnesota Fats into its Hall of Fame for "Meritorious Service."

At 82, he died of congestive heart failure and was buried at Hermitage Memorial Gardens in Old Hickory, Tennessee. His epitaph reads, "Beat every living creature on Earth. St. Peter, rack 'em up!"

GRAVE DIRECTIONS: At 535 Shute Lane, drive straight into the cemetery, go halfway around the circle, turn right, then make a left at the "T" and stop after about a hundred feet. The Garden of Peace is the lawn on the left and Fats' flat stone can be found here in Section C, six rows from the road.

BRIAN PICCOLO
OCTOBER 31, 1943 – JUNE 16, 1970

THOUGH HE WAS the nation's leading rusher in college football during the 1964 season, Brian Piccolo was not even drafted by the NFL after his final year at Wake Forest University. Brian instead joined the Chicago Bears as a free agent and spent the next few seasons on the team's practice squad, watching from the sidelines as his roommate Gale Sayers put together consecutive seasons as the team's star running back.

But in 1968 Gale suffered a knee injury and Brian tenderly assisted him through rehab—and played in Gale's starting position for the season's final five games. During the off-season, Gale was cleared to return for the 1969 season and Brian was relegated to his familiar second-string position, but after a starting fullback was injured, Brian was called up again and, in a storybook scenario, started alongside his best friend, Gale.

After just one game together, Brian developed breathing problems and doctors soon diagnosed him with embryonal cell cancer. After surgery and chemotherapy it seemed he'd beaten the disease, but it returned the following winter. By summertime the cancer claimed Brian Piccolo at the age of 26.

A movie of his life, *Brian's Song*, was released in 1971, and its touching story of courage and humanity is an enduring tearjerker. The embryonal cell carcinoma that was almost always fatal 30 years ago is now often curable, partly through the generosity of the Brian Piccolo Cancer Research Fund, which was established after his death.

Brian is buried at Saint Mary's Catholic Cemetery in Evergreen Park, Illinois.

GRAVE DIRECTIONS: Enter the cemetery at 8700 South Hamlin Street and take the first right turn behind the office. A hundred feet on the left, stop in front of the Tarantino mausoleum and you'll find Brian's flat stone just to the left.

WILEY POST
NOVEMBER 22, 1898 – AUGUST 15, 1935

FOR AS LONG as he could remember, Wiley Post was entranced by flying machines, and he came to be one of the most colorful figures in aviation.

After World War I, Wiley was a roughneck on an Oklahoma oil rig, but he turned to highway robbery and in 1921 was sentenced to 10 years in the state penitentiary. Fortunate enough to be paroled the following year, Wiley eased into aviation as a parachutist and worked for a flying circus, where he learned the rudiments of flying from show-pilot friends.

In 1926 Wiley returned to the oil rigs to earn enough money to buy his own plane but during his first day on the job he lost his left eye. He soon regarded this as a blessing because the $1,800 insurance settlement helped purchase his first airplane. The next few years found Wiley traveling to county fairs and carnivals in exhibitions of stunt flying, or barnstorming, as it was known, and in 1930 he achieved national prominence when he won the National Air Race Derby and its $7,500 prize. The following year, with navigator Harold Gatty, he set an around-the-world record, circumnavigating the globe in eight days, and, in 1933 after adding an automatic pilot and a radio compass to his plane, Wiley bested the time by more than 20 hours and became the first solo flier to circle the earth.

Wiley then turned to high-altitude experiments and, together with the BF Goodrich Company, built the first pressurized flying suit. In this suit, Wiley flew into the stratosphere and discovered the jet stream. He's regarded as one of space flight's pioneers, though he lived more than two decades before the establishment of a United States space program.

Back when he was working for the flying circus, Wiley met the famous humorist Will Rogers and through the years the two had become fast friends; while Wiley was employed as the personal pilot of a wealthy Oklahoma oilman he had the opportunity to borrow a plane, and he would sometimes shuttle Will between engagements. By 1935 Wiley had become interested in surveying

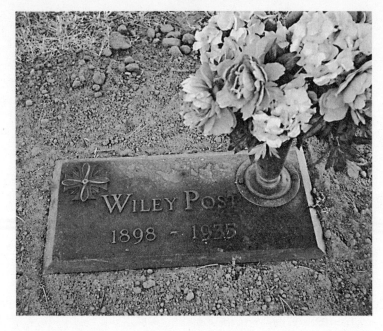

a mail-and-passenger air route from Seattle to Russia, and the pair planned to scout the route together.

All went as planned until they became lost in bad weather near Point Barrow, Alaska, and were forced to land the pontoon-equipped plane in a lagoon. After asking directions, Wiley tried to take off again, but the engine stalled. The plane plunged into the water and both men were killed instantly.

At 36, Wiley was buried at Memorial Park in Edmond, Oklahoma.

GRAVE DIRECTIONS: Enter the cemetery at 13313 North Kelly Avenue, go around the office, and proceed back to the flag and mirror pool. Make a right onto the drive after the pool, then stop after another hundred feet. On your left is an opening between two cedar trees, and there you'll find Wiley's plot, 30 feet from the drive.

RICHARD PRYOR

DECEMBER 1, 1940 – DECEMBER 10, 2005

GROWING UP IN the shadow of an Illinois bordello, Richard Pryor was raised among an assortment of drunks, whores, hustlers, and losers. Though the whole sorry and sordid upbringing did yield a lifetime of comedic material, the antics he picked up early didn't translate well to the classroom and he was expelled in the eighth grade.

From 1958 to 1960 Richard served in the Army but, aside from boot camp, almost his entire stint was spent in a military prison after he and a few brothers beat a particularly racist white serviceman. Upon returning home, Richard cut his teeth on the "chitlin' circuit," a string of wrong-side-of-the-track venues catering to black entertainers during segregation, and he quickly earned notoriety for an expletive-laced routine. Toning his act down to secure bookings at fancier clubs and on television, he forged a more vanilla-flavored format and by the mid-1960s was a reasonably successful mainstream comic.

Despite his success, he expressed frustration. "I made a lot of money being Bill Cosby," he recalled. "But I was hiding my personality and being a robot comic, repeating the same lines." The dam finally broke in the middle of a 1967 gig when, without any apparent provocation, Richard slammed the microphone to the floor and screamed, "What am I doing here?!"

Casting off the chains of his white-bread act, Richard took on a new persona and steered a fresh course straight into uncharted comedic waters. He summoned from memory the galaxy of nefarious characters he'd known from his youth and reincarnated them as his own. Embracing the stereotypes and adopting the blunt cadences and lingo of the street, he explored all conceivable embarrassments of every societal posture and unleashed an act chock-full of uproarious monologues. With socially and politically conscious opinions woven into his innovative "comedy without jokes," Richard's retelling of escapades and street characters culled from the misadventures of the black experience were side-splittingly hilarious and transcended traditional boundaries.

Richard's newfound skin lent him a fresh confidence and a self-assured stage presence overtook him. Hollywood took notice of the streetwise yet diffident funnyman who was alternately volatile then vulnerable, or crass one minute and sensitive the next. Hit comedies and concert films followed, including *Stir Crazy*, *Silver Streak*, and *Richard Pryor Live on the Sunset Strip*, making Richard one of the highest-paid stars of the day.

But he didn't tone things down after he became famous, and episodes of self-destructive behavior dogged him, jeopardizing his career as well as his life. In 1974 he spent 10 days in jail for an income tax quandary; four years later he rammed his Mercedes into a car containing his wife's friends and then pulled out a gun and shot it. After a marathon drug binge in 1980, paramedics found him walking in a daze, strung-out and seemingly oblivious to third-degree burns covering more than half his body. Widely reported as a cocaine free-basing accident, Richard later confessed he had poured 151-proof rum on his body and lit it afire in an effort to commit suicide.

Following the suicide attempt, Richard got clean by an extended visit at drug rehab and soon after mellowed considerably. In 1981 he even swore off use of the word "nigger" after an epiphany during a trip to Africa when he saw black people running governments and businesses. "I realized that I did not see anyone there I could call by that name," he recalled. Mellowing is one thing, but a complete metamorphosis eventually enveloped him and by the mid-'80s Richard was just plain lazy. After inking a five-year $40 million contract with Columbia Pictures, his robust film catalog work gave way to such dogs as *Brewster's Millions* and *See No Evil, Hear No Evil.* "I knew *Brewster's Millions* was no good to begin with," Pryor confessed. "But I was a pig, I got greedy."

The softening of his character may have been attributable to a middle-aged maturity or a realization he was driving too fast down a wrong-way street, but a 1986 diagnosis of multiple sclerosis was certainly a factor too. Owing a few films to Columbia, he directed himself in a semi-autobiography named *Jo Jo Dancer, Your Life is Calling*, a film he said refused to be written as a comedy. But the nervous system disease's cruelest symptoms—vertigo, tremors, and muscle weakness—slowly encroached and by the time of 1992's *Another You*, a frail and hesitant shell of the former Richard Pryor struggled to deliver his lines. No longer able to stand onstage, he tried delivering his monologue from an easy chair during a tour the following year, but ultimately was forced to cancel.

"I had some great things and I had some bad things. The best and the worst," he said in 1995. "In other words, I had a life." Richard passed away at 65 and was cremated.

BUFORD PUSSER
DECEMBER 12, 1937 – AUGUST 21, 1974

IN THE EARLY 1970s, the *Walking Tall* true-life movie series lent Hollywood romance to the exploits of a Tennessee sheriff, Buford Pusser. He was canonized as a friend of every honest man and a true-grit peacemaker who levied a brand of personal justice against any who might attempt to upset bucolic Southern tradition. Though entertaining, the *Walking Tall* features didn't let the facts get in the way of a good story, and Buford's larger-than-life legend thrived.

Before his career in law enforcement, Buford was discharged from Marine boot camp for an asthma condition, and he followed that stint with a short-lived career as "Buford the Bull" on the Chicago professional wrestling circuit. In 1962 he became the police chief of Adamsville, Tennessee, after his father arranged for Buford to succeed him upon his own retirement. In 1964 he won the seat of McNairy County Sheriff when the favored incumbent was killed in an auto accident before the voting day. It was shortly thereafter that Buford and his trademark Big Stick waged a campaign to rid the county of moonshiners and mobsters. His unorthodox law enforcement practices won him a number of enemies.

In 1967 Buford was called out on a middle-of-the-night emergency that turned out to be bogus and instead, he found himself in an ambush, presumably by folks who were unimpressed by his manner of applying the law. For reasons unexplained, his wife, Pauline, had accompanied him on the call, and she was killed in a hail of bullets while Buford was lucky to escape with just two bullet holes in his face and jaw. After the attack, Buford redoubled his efforts to clean up the county and sought to avenge his wife's death and, though no one was ever arrested for the ambush, at least one prime suspect soon wound up dead.

In 1970 Buford stepped down from his post as sheriff, as state law prohibited anyone from holding an elected office for more than three consecutive terms, and he later lost a reelection bid. In 1973, *Walking Tall*, starring Joe Don Baker, was released, and on its heels came a sequel and a song, *The Ballad of Buford Pusser*. Buford's exaggerated exploits soon became bartalk legend.

On the day it was announced that Buford would star as himself in a third *Walking Tall* movie he was killed in a single-car crash. Just that day, Buford had taken delivery of a new Corvette and, while on his way home, lost control at over 100 mph. He was killed instantly.

Buford was 36 at his death, and was buried next to his wife, Pauline, at the Adamsville War Memorial Park in Adamsville, Tennessee.

GRAVE DIRECTIONS: At the cemetery on Route 64 just west of the Route 22 junction, the Pusser plot is easy to find, marked by a tall granite slab in the cemetery's northwest corner.

❖

JOAN RIVERS
JUNE 8, 1933 — SEPTEMBER 4, 2014

WIELDING HER CATCHPHRASE "Can we talk?" Joan Rivers, the feisty and raspy comic who publicly lampooned her neurotic personal life for half a century, originally entered show business with the dream of a theatrical career. From Greenwich Village cafés to Catskills resorts, the rough-voiced firebrand honed a style of confrontational banter during a time when funny women were expected to only be kooky, in the way of Lucille Ball. Her freshly aggressive approach was risky, and risqué, and audiences were often appalled at her off-color jokes. Her bravura was decidedly not a sure-thing springboard to success; instead, it many times set her back. Ultimately, though, Joan's courage paved the way for a generation of women stand-up comics to stand toe-to-toe with men.

In 1965 Joan broke into the big time with a hilarious routine during her first appearance on Johnny Carson's *Tonight Show*, and the two hit it off famously. Joan told gags that ranged from the tale of her mother's struggle to marry her off to a story about a motorist who ran over her wig and apologized for killing her dog, and television's late-night king validated her shtick, saying at program's end, "God, you're funny!" Appearing on the show dozens of times, she toned down her acidity for the national audience and came to rely upon a self-deprecating theme: "A Peeping Tom looked in my window and pulled down the shade."

By 1983 Joan had been named permanent guest host for whenever Carson took a night off, which was often, and the exposure made her a superstar. But just three years later her star crested and she faced both professional and personal crises. First, after learning she was not being considered to replace Carson when he retired, she accepted an offer in 1986 from the fledgling Fox network to host her own late-night program, which would run opposite the *Tonight Show*. She phoned Carson to break the news, which he had already heard, but he refused her call, and according to Joan, they never spoke again: A friendship was shattered.

After the briefest of honeymoons, the ratings for Joan's show slumped and her relationship with Fox soured when erratic behavior by her husband and manager, Edgar Rosenberg, caused him to be banned from the set. In less than a year her show was canceled, Edgar spiraled into depression and took his own life, showbiz contracts dried up, Joan became bulimic, and she grew estranged from her only child, Melissa.

Devastated, Joan went into seclusion for a time but bounced back in 1989 with a new daytime talk show. She patched her relationship with Melissa, and they starred together in the TV docudrama *Tears and Laughter: The Joan and Melissa Rivers Story*, then began a prolific and profitable association as red-carpet commentators who poked a microphone into the freshly Botoxed faces of stars and asked, "Who are you wearing?"

Never again far from the spotlight, Joan flitted from coast to coast and from stage to studio in a whirl of activity and publicity, selling clothes and jewelry on TV shopping channels, appearing on reality shows, gossiping and skewering celebrities as a star of *Fashion Police*, and, always, relentlessly touring from Vegas to the heartland. She was the ultimate yenta, and her sheer moxie and ability to ad-lib effortlessly endeared her to millions. Were some offended? Sure, but to them Joan would advise, "Oh, grow up!"

At an outpatient surgery clinic where the much-nipped-and-tucked octogenarian lay anesthetized on a gurney for a reasonably routine scoping of her throat, a pair of doctors made a spur-of-the-moment decision to take a scalpel to a polyp-like growth on her vocal cords. The biopsy's incision triggered a seizing of Joan's vocal cords, and her airway was blocked, which led to brain damage and ultimately her death at 81. She was cremated and her ashes remain with her family.

WILL ROGERS
NOVEMBER 4, 1879 – AUGUST 15, 1935

AROUND THE TURN of the century, the part-Cherokee Oklahoman Will Rogers joined a traveling Wild West production as a trick roper; Will had especially keen lariat skills and developed a signature stunt of throwing three lassos at once, landing one around a running horse's neck, another around the rider, and the last under the horse to loop all four legs. He moved his routine along with a cracker-barrel wit, and before long, his folksy observations and homespun philosophies became more prized by audiences than his expert roping.

Americans adored his perceptive satire, which never crossed the line to mockery, and Will's persona became a pervasive cultural charm. He was a fixture and a favorite of the Ziegfeld Follies, appeared in dozens of movies and, in 1928, even ran for president on the Anti-Bunk ticket. Through some 4,000 syndicated newspaper columns and his own radio show, Will showcased an endless supply of sensibly sage, off-the-cuff quips and comments, like "I never met a man I didn't like" and "All I know is what I read in the papers." He remains a certified American folk hero.

Among Will's many friends and acquaintances was Wiley Post, a one-eyed record-setting aviator, who in 1935 was exploring a new air route between Seattle and Russia. The pair decided to scout the route together; Wiley needed to fly the course to determine whether it was practical, and Will was eager to document a trip with a maverick aviator to his faithful readers in newspaper columns banged out from faraway ports of call.

But a few days after leaving Seattle, the friends' adventure turned grim. With few landmarks to go by, Wiley had gotten his directions a little mixed up. After realizing he'd strayed from his planned course, he touched the pontoon-equipped plane down on an inlet near the tiny outpost of Point Barrow, Alaska. After getting their bearings from the locals, the pair was again on its way but, shortly after taking off from the water, the plane's engine quit. It fell straight down, and both Will and Wiley were killed.

Will was 55 at his death and is buried at his own Memorial and Museum in Claremore, Oklahoma.

GRAVE DIRECTIONS: At 1720 Will Rogers Boulevard, Will's tomb, complete with a statue of a horse, overlooks the expansive lawn.

ANDY ROONEY
JANUARY 14, 1919 – NOVEMBER 4, 2011

ANDY ROONEY WAS known best as the prickly witted, inquisitive, but cranky philosopher who delivered homespun commentary on *60 Minutes* each Sunday night for 33 years, but he was also a newspaper columnist and author and enjoyed considering himself a writer rather than a talking head—a role in which he was never comfortable, he said.

Drafted into the Army during his junior year at Colgate University, he was part of a generation of reporters who got their start as military correspondents during World War II. Though he did not know much about reporting, Andy managed to get himself assigned to the G.I. newspaper *Stars and Stripes* and for three years covered the war from the front, flying with the Army's Eighth Air Force on bombing raids over Germany and covering the Allied invasion of Europe.

After his discharge, Andy one day happened to encounter Arthur Godfrey in an elevator and, with atypical bluntness, told the biggest radio star of the day that his show needed better writing. Andy's nerve moved Godfrey to hire him and, by the time the show moved to television, Andy was the show's only writer. In 1964, challenged to write a piece on the most ordinary and boring object he could think of, he wrote "An Essay on Doors" and continued with award-winning contemplations on bridges, hotels, and chairs. The television essay genre was born.

In fall 1978, "A Few Minutes with Andy Rooney" was a regular *60 Minutes* segment, and the next season Andy had the end of the broadcast to himself, the last word on the most-watched television program in history. Delivered from behind a desk that he hewed himself, his frequently parodied essays and humorous soliloquies about aspects of the modern world he found bothersome brought forth tears of laughter, and occasionally, even tears of rage or sadness.

With his jowls, bushy eyebrows, deeply circled eyes, and advancing years, he addressed mostly mundane subjects with varying degrees of befuddlement, vexation, and sometimes pleasure. He admitted to loving football, Christmas, tennis, woodworking, and Dwight D. Eisenhower. He also claimed to like shined shoes and properly pressed pants and had machines in his office to take care of those functions, although somehow he always managed to look rumpled.

But he was better known for the things he did not like. He railed against "two-prong plugs in a three-prong society," the incomprehensibility of road maps, New Year's Eve, waiting in line for any reason, wash-and-wear shirts "that you can wash but not wear," and the uselessness of keys and locks. He observed that "there are more beauty parlors than there are beauties" and that "if dogs could talk, it would take a lot of the fun out of owning one." He made clear that he thought General George S. Patton and Ernest Hemingway, both of whom he had known personally, were gasbags and, on the subject of higher education, he declared that most college catalogs "rank among the great works of fiction of all time." Mainly, his essays struck a chord in viewers by pointing out life's unspoken truths or complaining about its subtle lies.

Andy so dreaded the day he had to end his signature commentaries that he kept going until he was 92. For his final essay, he said that he'd lived a life luckier than most. "I wish I could do this forever, but I can't," he said. And then, "I've done a lot of complaining here, but of all the things I've complained about, I can't complain about my life."

Only a month after delivering his 1,097th and final commentary, Andy died after complications from an unspecified operation. He was buried at Rensselaerville Cemetery in Rensselaerville, New York.

GRAVE DIRECTIONS: Drive through the stone-pillared entrance on Methodist Hill Road, turn at the first left, and proceed until the stone wall is on your left. Andy's flat stone is just in front of the Vane stone that's along the wall.

CARL SAGAN
NOVEMBER 9, 1934 – DECEMBER 20, 1996

TRAINED AT THE University of Chicago in both astronomy and biology, Carl Sagan taught at Harvard while working as an astrophysicist at the Smithsonian Observatory before settling in as Professor of Astronomy and Director for Planetary Studies at Cornell University in 1970.

From there, Carl used his natural gift for storytelling to extol the grandeur and mystery of the universe and to stimulate public enthusiasm for space science; his PBS television series, *Cosmos*, became the most-watched series in public-television history. Carl was perhaps the world's greatest popularizer of science and shared his lifelong passion in more than 600 scientific papers and eight books, including the Pulitzer Prize–winning *Dragons of Eden*.

Carl played a leading role in the Mariner, Viking, Voyager, and Galileo expeditions to other planets through his research on topics such as the greenhouse effect on Venus and windblown dust as an explanation for seasonal changes on Mars. He even detoured from space-based considerations to study what might be the long-term environmental consequences of nuclear war on our own Earth. But Carl's unbridled enthusiasm was reserved for searches for intelligent life elsewhere in the universe.

"Are we an exceptionally unlikely accident or is the universe brimming over with intelligence?" he asked as radio telescopes funded by a program close to his heart listened for signs of life in the billions of stars and galaxies.

So far, no response is forthcoming, but Carl offered that "it says something about the rarity and preciousness of life on this planet. The flip side of not finding life on another planet is appreciating life on Earth."

Despite receiving three bone marrow transplants from his sister, Cari, he died of a blood cancer called myelodysplasia. At 62, Carl was buried at Lakeview Cemetery in Ithaca, New York.

GRAVE DIRECTIONS: Enter the cemetery at the Wyckoff Road entrance and park on the right, immediately after the Temple Bethel section. Down the hill on the left, on the other side of the short chain fence, is Carl's flat marker.

COLONEL SANDERS
SEPTEMBER 9, 1890 – DECEMBER 16, 1980

HARLAND SANDERS GREW up in the backwoods of southern Indiana and learned to cook while still a child. His father had died before Harland was three, and by the time he was six it was his responsibility to prepare the meals while his mother worked. After the sixth grade he dropped out of school to supplement the family's meager income, and from his first job he brought home the bacon to the tune of $2 a week. By 12 he had left home to live and work on a farm, and from there he was able to provide the family with a more substantial amount of money.

During his adult years, Harland toiled as a streetcar conductor and an insurance agent, a tire salesman and a railroad fireman. He operated an Ohio River steamboat ferry and, after a law correspondence course, he practiced as a justice of the peace before taking a turn as a Corbin, Kentucky service station owner.

To augment the station's sparse gas receipts, Harland began cooking for hungry travelers. He didn't actually have a restaurant, so he served folks in his family's dining room. When more people began dropping by for the food than the gasoline, he knew he was onto something. In 1930, he bought the motel across the street and converted it into a 142-seat restaurant, Sanders Court.

Over the next decade, Harland perfected his secret recipe of "11 herbs and spices" used in the preparation of his Kentucky Fried Chicken, and his Sanders Court restaurant became known for having the best food, and especially the best chicken, for miles around. Business boomed, and the governor even named Harland an honorary Kentucky "Colonel" to recognize his contributions to the state's cuisine.

In the 1950s, though, a new interstate highway was built bypassing Corbin, business dried up, and the value of his property plummeted. At 65, the dejected Colonel auctioned everything off and, after paying the bills, found himself penniless and reduced to living on a $105 monthly Social Security check. But remarkably, in the twilight of his life, Harland decided that instead of sitting in a rocking chair feeling sorry for himself while waiting for government checks, he'd start anew.

The Colonel and his wife, Claudia, hit the road. Traveling around the countryside by car, they visited roadside eateries and cooked batches of chicken for the restaurant owners and their employees. If the reaction to the chicken was favorable, the Colonel entered into a handshake agreement that stipulated a payment to him of a nickel for each chicken the restaurant sold.

By 1964, when he sold his interest in the company for $2 million, the Colonel had more than 600 franchised outlets for his chicken. He stayed on with the new Kentucky Fried Chicken corporation as a spokesman and advisor for the next decade, but in 1975 the relationship strained when he publicly denounced some of KFC's fare, especially its gravy, which he derided as "sludge with a wallpaper taste." Nonetheless, his spectacled caricature today watches over each of the 5 million people who eat in one of KFC's 18,000 restaurants every day.

Colonel Sanders died of leukemia at 90 and was buried at Cave Hill Cemetery in Louisville, Kentucky.

GRAVE DIRECTIONS: Enter the cemetery at 701 Baxter Avenue and follow the yellow line that's painted in the road to the Colonel's grave.

SISKEL & EBERT

GENE SISKEL
JANUARY 26, 1946 – FEBRUARY 20, 1999

ROGER EBERT
JUNE 18, 1942 – APRIL 4, 2013

IN 1975, GENE Siskel and Roger Ebert were film critics at rival crosstown Chicago newspapers when they were asked to collaborate as co-hosts on a new movie-review program for the local public broadcasting station. Years later, both of them confessed that neither of them had any desire to team up with the other, but they did, and the show, originally titled *Sneak Previews*, was a hit. By 1986 the duo had inked a mega-deal with an arm of Disney for the format that eventually became known as *Siskel & Ebert*, and the award-winning show was among the most-watched entertainment series for more than a decade.

On set, the pair purposely dressed in casual clothes just as most people do when they go to the movies. The men perfectly balanced each other—Siskel was trim and balding while Ebert was larger with owlish glasses—and the show featured them as intellectually engaged but often contentious friends, sitting in cozy armchairs and ad-libbing about current films.

Typically, one or the other would introduce a clip and give his opinion, and then the other would weigh in. Their disagreements were more entertaining than their agreements, complete with knitted brows, are-you-serious headshakes, and humorous barbs. For all their combativeness, however, they actually agreed on a movie's worth much more often than they differed. Finally came their signature denouement: both thumbs up, both down, or, in a split decision, one of each. Ebert was the one who had come up with the all-or-nothing gestures, and Siskel thought of trademarking them, which they did. The highly coveted endorsement that had the power to lift or sink the fortunes of a film inevitably ran at the top of movie advertisements, while Siskel and Ebert's fortunes soared.

In May 1998 Siskel underwent surgery to remove a cancerous tumor from his brain and returned to the show soon afterward. Eight months later he announced he was taking time off for additional recuperation but soon died of complications at 53. He was buried at Westlawn Cemetery in Norridge, Illinois.

GRAVE DIRECTIONS: Enter the cemetery at 7801 West Montrose Avenue and get a map at the office. In the Memorial section at street marking 22-24, about halfway down, look for Arthur Gitler's grave along the curb. Siskel's flat bronze marker is in the same column as Arthur's, 18 rows back.

In 2009, Ebert estimated that since 1967, which is the year he began reviewing movies for the *Chicago Sun-Times*, he had viewed an average of perhaps 500 movies per year and written reviews for about half of them—some 10,000(!) movie reviews. But besides that overwhelming volume of accomplishment, he also published more than 20 books on a variety of subjects ranging from a book about rice cookers, *The Pot and How to Use It*, to a tome about being a pedestrian in his favorite city: *The Perfect London Walk*. In 1999 he created a film festival of his own: the Overlooked Film Festival, or just "Ebertfest," which was dedicated to highlighting neglected classics.

In a difficult battle with cancer, by 2006 Ebert had lost the ability to eat, drink, and speak, and he became a gaunter version of his once-portly self. Doubling down, he began a new chapter in his career, chronicling the journey of his illness on Facebook,

Twitter, and his blog, and gaining for himself a slew of new fans. Never a defeatist, he analyzed his medical struggles courageously. "No point in denying it," he wrote.

The last year of Ebert's life was his most prolific as he wrote 306 movie reviews and a blog post or two a week. But after fracturing a hip, he announced he was "taking a leave of presence" and died two days later at 70. His last blog post closed with "I'll see you at the movies.

He was cremated and his ashes entrusted to his family.

Three years before his death he wrote: "I know it is coming, and I do not fear it, because I believe there is nothing on the other side of death to fear. I hope to be spared as much pain as possible on the approach path. I was perfectly content before I was born, and I think of death as the same state. What I am grateful for is the gifts of intelligence, love, wonder, and laughter. You can't say it wasn't interesting. My lifetime's memories are what I have brought home from the trip. I will require them for eternity no more than that little souvenir of the Eiffel Tower I brought home from Paris."

ANNA NICOLE SMITH
NOVEMBER 28, 1967 – FEBRUARY 8, 2007

FAMOUS FOR BEING famous by virtue of a ditzy-blonde persona and exaggerated Marilyn Monroe looks and curves, Anna Nicole Smith played out the train wreck that was her life in made-for-reality-TV style.

A married mom by 18, Anna fell into topless dancing and the not-quite-natural blonde made the cover of *Playboy* in 1992. With Madison Avenue in hot pursuit, Anna became America's favorite new bombshell overnight.

Two years later, Anna married a man almost four times her age, Texas billionaire J. Howard Marshall II. As she never actually lived with Howard, married life amounted to little more than an overflowing stream of cash but, alas, after just 14 months of bliss the newlyweds' dreams were shattered when 90-year-old Howard was called to the great gig in the sky. As Howard had not yet written Anna into his will, his death set off a feud with her deceased husband's 67-year-old son, E. Pierce Marshall (who held the illogical distinction of being stepson to a 26-year-old model), concerning Anna's right to inherit half of his father's estate. After 20 mind-numbing years of court victories and reversals, it was finally decreed in 2015 that the Smith family was entitled to exactly zero percent of the Marshall fortune.

After being newly widowed, Anna became marginally famous for her over-the-top revealing outfits that strained to contain an ever-expanding circumference and, in 2002, she enjoyed true celebrity status with the premiere of *The Anna Nicole Show*, an unwatchable reality-TV program chronicling the minutiae of her daily life. Lucky viewers watched her miniature poodle hump everything in sight while her impoverished and toothless cousin Shelly appeared at the doorstep begging for a handout. As spaced-out Anna slurred that she "suffered" from celibacy because willing victims were turned off by her obesity, her calculating attorney offered comfort while a purple-haired assistant hinted at a lesbian hookup.

In 2006 relief washed over the tabloid-buying public when they learned Anna's celibacy had been cured; she soon gave birth to a daughter, Dannielynn. But the joy of the girl's birth was tempered three days later by the death of Anna's son, Daniel. While visiting his mother and newborn sister in their Bahamian hospital room, the 20-year-old collapsed and died from a lethal combination of Zoloft, Lexapro, and methadone.

To the delight of keyed-up gossip columnists, the identity of Dannielynn's father had been unclear since the day Anna announced her pregnancy and a three-ring circus of would-be fathers stepped forward to claim paternity. Anna's attorney, Howard K. Stern, was recorded as the father on the birth certificate but, though the two claimed a longtime secret affair, not too many were buying it. Following years brought a whirlwind of litigation as various parties sought to align themselves for the assumed windfall awaiting J. Howard Marshall II's not-quite granddaughter, Dannielynn, a payday that never arrived.

Five months after her daughter's birth, Anna was found unconscious in Room 607 of the Hard Rock Hotel in Seminole, Florida. Whisked through the lobby on a gurney by responding paramedics, one of whom rode atop her while frantically pumping her chest, Anna was nonetheless DOA at the hospital. After finding a variety of muscle relaxants and pain relievers in her body, the medical examiner declared that the 39-year-old died of combined drug intoxication, the primary drug being a sedative called chloral hydrate.

From behind steel barricades, hundreds of fans watched Anna's funeral ceremony. Later, her mahogany coffin, topped by a pink satin cloth with rhinestones spelling her name, with Anna inside in a pink gown and tiara, was lowered next to Daniel at Lakeview

Memorial Gardens in Nassau, Bahamas. After the services, as camera crews packed up, an onlooker recalled Anna's response about whether the trappings of fame ever troubled her. "Oh, no, I like it," she said. "I've always liked attention. I didn't get very much growing up, and I always wanted to be, you know, noticed."

For a time, the most popular tour on New Providence Island was the Anna Nicole Tour, which included the hospital where Daniel died, the church where her funeral took place, her seaside Horizons estate, and the cemetery. But a decade on, it seems that's all come to pass.

GRAVE DIRECTIONS: Off of Gladstone Road, in the cemetery's Garden of Eternal Peace near the northwest corner of the white Citadel gazebo, is Anna's polished black tablet.

DAVE THOMAS
JULY 2, 1932 – JANUARY 8, 2002

IN 1956 DAVE Thomas was working at a Fort Wayne, Indiana, barbecue restaurant when a bespectacled, white-haired gentleman stopped in and offered Dave's boss the opportunity to participate in a new chicken franchising deal he was cooking up. The gentleman turned out to be Colonel Harland Sanders, and the franchise was, of course, Kentucky Fried Chicken. But in 1956 neither of those names carried any weight. Still, Dave's boss entered into an agreement with the Colonel and added his chicken to the menu.

Six years later, when four failing Kentucky Fried Chicken outlets in Columbus, Ohio, desperately needed an experienced manager to turn them around, Dave jumped at the opportunity, cutting a deal in which he gained ownership of the locations to boot. In 1968, just another six years later, Dave sold the revitalized restaurants back to the KFC company and pocketed a cool $1.1 million.

Ever the entrepreneur, Dave a year later opened his first Wendy's Old Fashioned Hamburgers, naming the restaurant after his eight-year-old daughter, Melinda Lou, who had been nicknamed Wendy by her siblings. By lending the KFC restaurant strategies to the burgeoning fast-food hamburger business and always focusing on the customer, Dave grew that single restaurant into a chain of more than 6,000 with sales of over $7 billion.

A shrewd marketer—Wendy's "Where's the beef?" advertising campaign is still a classic—Dave became a household name when he began personally pitching his burgers and fries in television commercials in 1989. At the time, the company was in a difficult period and its earnings had tanked. But the humorous, homespun ads featuring a smiling, portly Dave in a Wendy's apron lent the company a fresh, down-home, unsophisticated image and launched Wendy's to unexpected success.

Dave had been adopted as a child, and in 1990 President George H.W. Bush asked him to be a national advocate for adoption. He accepted the challenge and encouraged people to consider adopting older children, not just babies. In 1992 he established the Dave Thomas Foundation for Adoption, which helps make adoption more affordable. "I know firsthand how important it is for every child to have a home and loving family," he said. "Without a family, I would not be where I am today."

Dave had a carcinoid tumor in his liver for more than a decade, he underwent quadruple heart-bypass surgery in 1996, and began undergoing dialysis for a kidney problem in early 2001. Finally, at 69, Dave's body gave out and he expired of the liver condition.

He was buried at Union Cemetery in Columbus, Ohio.

GRAVE DIRECTIONS: Drive into the cemetery at 3349 Olentangy River Road and you'll see three mausoleum buildings off to the right. Walk in through the middle doors of the building with rust-colored awnings and, immediately inside, look left. There's Dave!

TINY TIM
APRIL 12, 1932 – NOVEMBER 30, 1996

TINY TIM WAS the ukulele-strumming crooner who amused millions by trilling "Tiptoe Through the Tulips," a whimsical love ditty he appropriated on behalf of the flower generation. Born Herbert Khaury, the frizzy-haired, goofy-looking, offbeat entertainer built a career on this single hit song, his stratospheric falsetto, and an asexual and childlike stage persona.

Tiny found his fame on Johnny Carson's *Tonight Show*, and his 1969 on-air marriage to Vicki Budinger ("Miss Vicki," as he always called her), whom he met at a promotional event for his book, *Beautiful Thoughts*, drew an audience of 40 million. In later years he found fans within the retro-music crowd and always got an enthusiastic welcome at his off-center appearances, where, in fascinating interviews, he divulged numerous eccentricities: He'd never learned to drive; after showering, he dried himself with paper towels; to avoid using public bathrooms, Tiny wore adult diapers when he was away from home;

and he applied Oil of Olay lotion to his body eight times a day. Yep, Tiny had his issues.

By 1996 Tiny was on his third marriage (this time to Miss Sue), he was performing some 300 days a year, and he was in terrible health, suffering from congestive heart failure and diabetes. In September, after he became dizzy and fell from a stage, doctors informed Tiny that, though he might live a few more years, he could also die at any moment and should immediately discontinue performing. For a time, Tiny convalesced, but by November he was appearing at a few gigs. At the Women's Club of Minneapolis, Tiny and his ukulele took the stage but, partway into his signature "Tiptoe Through the Tulips," Tiny was looking shaky. Asked by his concerned Miss Sue if he was feeling all right, Tiny spoke his last words, "No, I'm not."

Tiny often fibbed about his age, but at 64, he was laid to rest, with a ukulele in his casket, at Lakewood Cemetery in Minneapolis, Minnesota.

GRAVE DIRECTIONS: Enter the cemetery at 3600 Hennepin Avenue, turn right, and follow the drive to the mausoleum. Enter the mausoleum, turn to the right, and get on the elevator. Take the elevator to the ground floor, then turn left out of the elevator. Proceed to the last alcove on the left and you'll see Tiny's crypt on the left wall.

THE VON TRAPP FAMILY

BARON GEORG VON Trapp was a distinguished Austrian naval commander, but when the Austro-Hungarian empire collapsed after World War I, his country lost its seacoast, and this captain's naval career promptly ended. After Georg's wife died a few years later, a 20-year-old Jesuit novitiate named Maria Kutschera joined his household to care for the seven children. A romance blossomed and in 1927 the 47-year-old ex-sailor married Maria the ex-nun. The happy couple would themselves have three children, but in the interim, the banks in Austria crashed and Georg's fortune was wiped out, leaving the von Trapp family destitute.

The von Trapps took the most logical course of action: The musically inclined Maria, all of the children, and their religious mentor, Monsignor Franz Wasner, polished their singing hobby into a stage act that became the family profession. Though Georg didn't participate in the singing, his stature as a baron (though a bankrupt one) and a naval commander (without a navy) opened doors, and the von Trapp family was soon performing Gregorian chants and English madrigals all over Europe.

In March 1938 the Nazis goose-stepped into Salzburg and the von Trapps fled Hitler's war machine, leaving their home and material possessions behind, never to return. In contrast to the romanticized version of their story in *The Sound of Music*, the von Trapps did not escape Austria by strolling across the Alps. Instead, they rode a train to Italy and boarded a ship to America without incident.

Stateside, the German-speaking von Trapps struggled to reestablish themselves. The enterprising Maria persisted and the family singing group again found success. For almost two decades the von Trapps spent eight months a year touring America, and every summer ran a music camp at their Vermont farm, until the frenetic pace took its toll; one of Maria's daughter's eloped in 1948 while her eldest daughter suffered a nervous breakdown and was administered electroshock therapy. Maria was eventually forced to hire non-family members for the singing group and finally, in 1957, when the oldest children were in their forties, the von Trapps stopped performing.

Maria later signed away all of the stage and film rights to her book, *The Trapp Family Singers*, for a paltry $9,000, and the story made its Broadway debut as *The Sound of Music* in 1959. The hit musical by Rodgers and Hammerstein enjoyed a run of more than 1,400 performances before it closed, and it's Oscar-winning movie clone starring Julie Andrews as Maria replicated that success.

Meanwhile, after a year-long stint as a New Guinea missionary, Maria toiled in the day-to-day operations of the Trapp Family Lodge until expiring of kidney disease at 82. Georg had died years earlier, at age 67, and most of their children have since gone over the rainbow as well.

GRAVE DIRECTIONS: At the 2,500-acre Trapp Family Lodge grounds in Stowe, Vermont, park next to the hotel. There you'll be happy to find that a variety of von Trapps have been interred in a garden conveniently located behind the gift shop.

SAM WALTON
MARCH 29, 1918 – APRIL 5, 1992

AS A FRANCHISEE of the Ben Franklin variety store chain, in 1960 Sam Walton presented its executives with a concept he envisioned for a new sort of discount store. Seeking to tweak the existing discount model, Sam looked to open bigger stores on the fringes of population centers that profited on smaller margins and bigger volumes. Not surprisingly, in the staid 1960s retail world, where change occurred glacially, the execs were not impressed with his revolutionary idea and declined to pursue it. Undeterred, Sam confidently went it alone and opened his first Wal-Mart on July 2, 1962.

Now committed to discounting, Sam crusaded to drive costs from the merchandising system and he doggedly drove his prices down and down and down. With his margins cut to the bone, it was imperative that Wal-Mart grow sales at a relentless pace and, boy, did it ever.

As the chain began to take off, Sam continually managed the growth, and at every turn seemed to make the right decision. As early as 1966 he understood the need to computerize his merchandise controls, and Wal-Mart went on to become the icon of just-in-time inventory. To keep merchandise resupply logistics streamlined, no stores were built more than a day's drive from a distribution center, and today Wal-Mart can fill merchandise orders overnight, compared with a week or more for its rivals. Also, Sam worked hard indoctrinating his employees, whom he always called associates; profit-sharing plans were installed, scholarships were established in the names of associates who crafted particularly useful business improvement ideas, and cheers and songs helped build a team atmosphere.

As Wal-Mart's influence grew, however, Sam was vilified by some, especially beleaguered small-town merchants. A nostalgic national press eulogized the lost graces of small-town America and the blame was put squarely on Sam's shoulders. Sam viewed all these arguments as foolishness, though, because *he* had once been a small-town merchant who had seen the future coming and chosen to eat rather than be eaten. Perhaps he did clutter

America's countryside, ruin its Main Street, and force a lot of people to change the way they made a living, but he merely hastened such inevitable changes. The consumer had chosen Wal-Mart because it gave America what it really wanted—friendly service, clean and organized stores, enormous selection and, above all, low prices. Capitalism had worked again.

Sam died at 74 of complications due to cancer and was buried at Bentonville Cemetery in Bentonville, Arkansas.

GRAVE DIRECTIONS: Enter the cemetery at 400 SW F Street and the Walton plot is just left of Lane 10.

NOTABLE
FIGURES
FROM
HISTORY

ALCOHOLICS ANONYMOUS FOUNDERS

ROBERT "DR. BOB" SMITH
AUGUST 8, 1879 – NOVEMBER 16, 1950

BILL "BILL W." WILSON
NOVEMBER 26, 1895 – JANUARY 24, 1971

AT THE TASTE of his first alcoholic drink Bill Wilson was convinced he had found the elixir of life, but after 17 years of hard drinking, alcohol had served only to destroy his health and career. From the rubble of that wasted life, Wilson overcame alcoholism and founded the Alcoholics Anonymous 12-step program that has helped millions of others do the same. Influenced by AA, alcoholism has been medically redefined as a chronic disease and, as AA has inspired numerous mirror programs for a host of addictions, Bill is regarded as a profoundly influential social architect.

In 1934 Bill's last drink precipitated an epiphany—a spiritually awakening flash of white light—and the former stockbroker who'd been reduced to an unemployable drunk came to believe that the key to sobriety was a change of heart. Five sober months later, while in Akron, Ohio, on business, Bill was tempted by the sounds and clamor of the hotel bar. Suddenly, at that moment, he realized that the only way he could save himself was to help another alcoholic. Through a series of desperate telephone calls in a strange town far from his home, he was able to find a skeptical drunk named Robert Smith, who agreed to meet him that night. One month later, on June 10, 1935, Bob, who happened to be a doctor, had his last drink, and that date is regarded as the official birth of AA, which is based on the idea that an alcoholic can only be helped by another alcoholic.

Dr. Bob (AA members use first names only) immediately began working with alcoholics at Akron hospitals while Bill codified their principles into "Twelve Traditions," an enduring blueprint for the Alcoholics Anonymous fellowship that has no formal or political organization, no governing officers, no rules or regulations, and no fees or dues. The chain reaction of "one drunk helping another" has resulted in mass-produced sobriety, and AA today has more than 3 million members in 150 countries.

Dr. Bob died of heart failure at 71 and was buried at Mount Peace Cemetery in Akron, Ohio.

GRAVE DIRECTIONS: At 183 Aqueduct Street, enter the cemetery at the drive with the brick columns, and after 50 feet, stop. Dr. Bob rests 200 feet to the left and six rows from the chain-link fence.

Bill died at 75 of emphysema and was buried at South Village Cemetery in East Dorset, Vermont.

GRAVE DIRECTIONS: On Route 7A, just north of Harmony Lane, enter the cemetery, turn right, and follow the road up the hill. Fifty feet past the hairpin turn, on the left, are two white footstones marking the graves of Bill and his wife, Lois.

NEIL ARMSTRONG

AUGUST 5, 1930 – AUGUST 25, 2012

IN THE STRICT and official terms of NASA-speak, Neil Armstrong was the "first human to set foot on a celestial body beyond Earth." But in his own words, the hero was more reticent about his accomplishment, merely finding the moon "an interesting place to be, and I recommend it."

Armstrong began his aerospace career as a Navy fighter pilot serving in the Korean War. He became a test pilot and flew hundreds of the hottest aircraft around, including a sleek X-15 rocket plane that he took to 38 miles above the surface of the earth, right to the edge of space. But as a NASA astronaut, he actually took just two trips into space. His first journey came in 1966 as commander of the Gemini 8 mission, which nearly ended in disaster when a thruster rocket malfunctioned and caused the landing capsule to spin wildly out of control. Armstrong kept his cool and brought the craft safely home.

His next space trip came in July 1969 when Armstrong and fellow astronauts Buzz Aldrin and Michael Collins journeyed 250,000 miles on Apollo 11 for a visit to the moon that went down in the history books. Four days after the trio blasted off from Cape Canaveral in Florida, the world watched and waited as their lunar module *Eagle* separated from the command module and began its descent to the moon's surface. Minutes later came the words from Armstrong: "Tranquility Base here, the *Eagle* has landed." About six and a half hours later at 10:56 p.m. ET on July 20, 1969, Armstrong, at 38, became the first person to set foot on the moon, uttering the now-famous "That's one small step for a man, one giant leap for mankind."

Aldrin followed him 15 minutes later and, before returning to the spacecraft, the two spent two and a half hours setting up an American flag, scooping up moon rocks, and installing a stainless steel plaque inscribed "We came in peace for all mankind." After returning home from the mission, Armstrong took a low profile and became what his son called a "reluctant American hero who always believed he was just doing his job." He left NASA in 1971.

Just after his 82nd birthday, Armstrong underwent quadruple-bypass heart surgery and died two weeks later from surgery complications. He was cremated, his ashes given to his wife.

In a statement his family said, "For those who may ask what they can do to honor Neil, we have a simple request. Honor his example of service, accomplishment, and modesty, and the next time you walk outside on a clear night and see the moon smiling down at you, think of Neil Armstrong and give him a wink."

DANIEL BOONE

NOVEMBER 2, 1734 – SEPTEMBER 26, 1820

PROBABLY AMERICA'S MOST famous pioneer, Daniel Boone first ventured into the Cumberland Gap region of the Blue Ridge Mountains around 1760. Although the location of the pass had been mapped more than 15 years earlier, the French and Indian War had discouraged exploration of the Kentucky wilderness. The British later prohibited western migration into the area, but Daniel and others ignored the crown's ban and crossed the gap to find what lay beyond.

In 1775, the Wilderness Road was built by Daniel and two dozen axmen, and it soon became the primary route to the West. He founded Boonesborough and, during the Revolutionary War, Kentucky was organized as a Virginia county.

Though they may not have been quite as romantic as his legend suggests, Daniel did have numerous encounters with the native people of Kentucky. In 1776, after Shawnee warriors kidnapped his daughter and two others, Daniel made a daring rescue by mounting a surprise nighttime attack. In 1778, after he was himself captured by another band of Shawnee who were planning an attack on Boonesborough, he negotiated a settlement with Chief Blackfish, preventing the onslaught. Admired for his leadership and his

woodsman skills, Daniel was later adopted into the tribe as a son of Blackfish.

In 1792, when Kentucky was admitted into the Union as the 15th state, litigation questioning settlers' title to their lands arose and Daniel lost all his property due to his lack of clear title. Undaunted, the inveterate pioneer continued west and settled in Missouri. In 1800 Daniel was appointed magistrate of the Femme Osage District in St. Charles County, Missouri, and received a large tract of land for his services. But when Missouri was transferred to the United States as part of the Louisiana Purchase, he once again lost all his land.

Daniel spent his remaining years at his son's Missouri home and passed away at 85.

He was buried in Marthasville, Missouri, near his wife, Rebecca, who had died seven years previously.

From there, the story gets muddled. In 1845 a delegation from Kentucky honored their pioneer hero with a monument in the capital city's cemetery, and Daniel and Rebecca were exhumed and reinterred in Frankfort. But mistakes happen easily in the grave-switching business, and it seems that someone dug up the wrong body. The grave next to Rebecca's was already occupied when Daniel died, so he was buried at her feet. Daniel's relatives, who were upset that he was being moved at all, didn't inform the diggers of his true location and they allowed Rebecca's bones to be carted off along with someone else's—not Daniel's. In 1983 a forensic anthropologist studied a plaster cast of the skull in the Frankfort grave and concluded that it belonged to "a large black man." Not surprisingly, proponents of the Frankfort locale dismissed the anthropologist's credentials and his findings.

Oh well. Both graves have worthy monuments; Frankfort's is bigger, but rural Marthasville seems more suited to a frontiersman.

DIRECTIONS TO GRAVE IN FRANKFORT, KENTUCKY: Enter the cemetery at 215 East Main Street and follow the line that's painted on the road. After a short distance, you can't miss his monument on the right.

DIRECTIONS TO GRAVE IN MARTHASVILLE, MISSOURI: On Route 94 just west of Dutzow, a sign points the way to the grave, which is atop a knoll overlooking Duque Creek.

JOHN WILKES BOOTH
MAY 10, 1838 – APRIL 26, 1865

IN 1863 A Southern sympathizer named John Wilkes Booth hatched a preposterous scheme to abduct President Abraham Lincoln and ransom him in exchange for Confederacy peace. Remarkably, Booth was actually able to enlist a half-dozen other conspirators in his harebrained scheme, but their plot was foiled when Lincoln changed plans just before they were set to capture him. A few weeks later, General Lee surrendered to the Union, and Booth's bunch quickly changed gears, plotting instead to assassinate Lincoln, Vice President Andrew Johnson, and Secretary of State William Seward simultaneously. Booth hoped the resulting chaos and weakness in the government would lead to a comeback for the South.

When Booth learned that Lincoln would be attending a performance at Ford's Theatre in Washington, his plan was set in motion. The conspirators agreed that the three murders would occur at about ten o'clock that evening. At the prescribed time, Booth sneaked into the theater and shot Lincoln in the back of the head at point-blank range. Meanwhile, the half-hearted attempts his co-conspirators made against their targets failed miserably.

After shooting Lincoln, Booth jumped down to the stage shouting, "*Sic semper tyrannis!* (Thus ever to tyrants!) The South is avenged!" He snapped the fibula bone in his left leg during his leap, then limped out the theater's back door to a waiting horse. He fled first to the tavern of sympathizer Mary Surratt, where he met up with David Herold, then to the home of another conspirator, Dr. Samuel Mudd, who splinted his leg.

For the next 12 days Booth and Herold traveled south under cover of night until federal authorities caught up with them near Port Royal, Virginia, surrounding them in a tobacco barn. Herold surrendered, but Booth refused to give up and the barn was set afire. In the ensuing confusion Booth was shot through the neck by Sergeant Boston Corbett. Though the orders had been to take the assassin alive, Booth died a few hours later at sunrise. According to a popular account Booth repeatedly muttered, "useless, useless," as he lay dying, but some historians now believe that the garbled, barely whispered sounds may have instead been "Lucy, Lucy," for his betrothed, Lucy Hale. In any event, his final words, supposedly, were "Tell Mother I died for my country." He was 26.

Booth's remains were sewn up in a horse blanket, wagoned to Belle Plain, then transported aboard the warship *Montauk* to Washington. Though some have maintained that the feds got the wrong man and the corpse was not Booth at all, his body was positively identified by a doctor who knew Booth and was able to confirm an old surgical scar. He also recorded that the corpse's left fibula had been recently broken. The "J.W.B." tattoo on his wrist should have erased any remaining doubts, but skeptics remain.

Booth was buried in a cell of the Old Penitentiary in what is now Fort Lesley J. McNair. Two years later the body was exhumed and reburied in a locked storeroom in Warehouse I at the prison. In 1869, Booth was again exhumed and released to his family, who buried him at Green Mount Cemetery in Baltimore, Maryland, where it's expected he'll remain for a long time to come.

GRAVE DIRECTIONS: Drive under the stone arch at 1501 Green Mount Avenue and turn immediately right. Follow this drive past the long staircase on the left and, as the drive bends right, the vault of a Richard Hardesty Thompson is on the left. Park here and walk up the cement path between the Hardesty and Sherman vaults. After 75 feet, the Booth plot is on the right marked by a tall obelisk. John's name is engraved into the obelisk, but his grave within the plot is unmarked.

CESAR CHAVEZ
MARCH 31, 1927 – APRIL 23, 1993

MIGRANT FARM WORKER Cesar Chavez captured worldwide attention by leading the battle to unionize the fields and orchards of California. In a life story that mirrored Steinbeck's *Grapes of*

Wrath, he poignantly represented the hardship of migrant farm-worker families and founded the United Farm Workers, which sought to end the exploitation of its members. Largely because of his efforts, California in 1975 passed the nation's first collective bargaining act for farm workers.

Cesar's early years were spent on his family's 160-acre farm in Arizona. But after the farm was lost during the Great Depression, the Chavez family, along with thousands of others, picked crops in the arid valleys of California at virtual slave-labor pay rates. In the 1950s Cesar began organizing Mexican-Americans into a political bloc, and by 1965 his fledgling union of 1,700 families had persuaded two growers to raise wages moderately. Cesar's union joined another, less-successful strike alongside a separate group of workers, and that was the beginning of five years of *La Huelga*—"the strike"—in which the frail labor leader became familiar worldwide as he battled the economic powers of California's San Joaquin Valley.

Cesar's style was akin to the methods of Gandhi and Martin Luther King Jr.: He fasted or invited arrest to call attention to his battle; he organized protest marches; he held lively rallies and organized boycotts. Church groups, college students, and other unionists supported the exploited farm workers, and in 1970, after losing millions of dollars, growers agreed to union contracts.

Though other successful boycotts and unionizations followed, Cesar ultimately failed to realize his dream of forging a nationwide organization, and the 1970 victory was probably the high point in the union's history. When some farm workers started organizing under the Teamster umbrella, their plight ceased to be recognized as a social cause and, by the 1980s, farm-worker unions were essentially nonexistent.

At a friend's Arizona home, Cesar died of natural causes in his sleep. His coffin, which was carried four miles to a UFW field office after a funeral mass, had been built by his brother and was so heavy that teams of eight pallbearers rotated every few minutes, while some 25,000 people gathered to say goodbye.

At 66, Cesar was buried at the commune-style headquarters of the former union, now the LaPaz Educational Retreat Center, in Keene, California.

GRAVE DIRECTIONS: Take the Keene exit off of Route 58 and follow Main Street east for a half-mile to a cement drive on the left. Go down the hill and you'll see Cesar's grave in the central courtyard.

WILLIAM "BUFFALO BILL" CODY

FEBRUARY 26, 1846 – JANUARY 10, 1917

THE LEGENDARY LIFE experiences of Buffalo Bill, some real and others imagined or exaggerated, embody the spirit of the West and fed the national grandiose tradition of frontier life that endures today. Though he certainly led an incredibly interesting and exciting life, over the years his biography has been increasingly romanticized, making it difficult to separate the fact from the fiction. With that, you've reached the interactive part of this book; I'll offer the chronological version of Bill's life that's generally accepted, and you can pencil in or scratch out the "facts" as you see fit.

William Cody was born in Iowa and, while still a child, worked for a wagon-freight company as a mounted messenger and wrangler, crossing the Great Plains several times. After his father died when Bill was 12, he became a trapper and then a prospector during the Pikes Peak gold rush of 1859. At 14, Bill began working for the Pony Express after the company advertised for "skinny, expert riders willing to risk death daily. Orphans preferred."

During the Civil War he served as a scout for the Union Army, and later he supplied buffalo meat to the Kansas Pacific Railroad, a job from which he gained the "Buffalo Bill" moniker. When the Fifth Cavalry was fighting the Sioux and Cheyenne tribes during the 1870s, Bill served as their civilian scout.

Beginning in 1869, a series of dime novels featuring Buffalo Bill were published and, while Bill was earning a real-life reputation, he was also becoming a national folk hero in the popular imagination. There would eventually be some 1,700 of these frontier tales, authored by at least seven different writers. In 1872 and for the following 11 years, Bill played himself in a stage production, *The Scouts of the Plains*, winning enthusiastic acclaim.

In 1883 Bill further capitalized on his fame and organized *Buffalo Bill's Wild West Show*, an outdoor extravaganza that dramatized some of the most picturesque elements of frontier life, including Pony Express rides, buffalo hunts, and Indian attacks. Half circus and half history lesson, the show proved an enormous success and toured for 30 years. Though Bill amassed a small fortune from his show business success, it was lost to mismanagement and his weakness for dubious investments and, in the end, even the *Wild West* show became the property of creditors.

Since 1885 Bill had maintained a ranch on an enormous tract outside of Yellowstone Park given him by the State of Wyoming. Today that land is the town of Cody and, as Buffalo Bill is its founding father, you'd expect he'd be buried there. But he's not. At 70 he died of natural causes while in Denver, and his wife, Louisa, maintained that Bill had indeed desired to be buried near Denver, atop a promontory with spectacular views of both the mountains and plains where he had spent the happiest times of his life. So there Bill rests, in a tomb blasted from solid rock at the summit of Lookout Mountain in Golden, Colorado.

GRAVE DIRECTIONS: Bill's grave is on the private property of the Buffalo Bill Memorial Museum, located at 987 Lookout Mountain Road, which is secured by a gate that doesn't open until about nine in the morning. When the gate is closed, people have been known to park outside the gate and visit his grave by strolling up the hill and following the signs.

CHRISTOPHER COLUMBUS
1451 – MAY 20, 1506

THERE SEEMS TO be a sort of movement afoot to discredit Christopher Columbus' discovery of America. Its proponents contend that Native Americans had considered the continent home for who-knows-how-many millennia, and anyway, the Vikings from northern Europe visited North America as early as the eleventh century. Though both contentions are true, the overall argument is tenuous and based on semantics.

Native Americans merely happened to have migrated to America over the eons; they had no broad understanding of the land mass and, alternately, no knowledge of Europe—and they weren't on track to "discover" it in kind any time soon. And the Vikings, for their part, had found only the cold, rocky, wind-swept coast of what's now Canada and, having enough of that back home in Greenland, they left, uninterested. On the other hand, Columbus found the lush islands and warm waters of the Caribbean. Though it's true he wasn't the first human to know of its existence, he was certainly the guy who leaked the news of it to Europe's fifteenth-century power club, setting up the endgame for European colonization and migration.

It was Columbus' plan to reach Asia by sailing west across the Atlantic, and therein lies a misconception. It's generally taught that Columbus had difficulty receiving financial backing for his plan because it was believed that the Earth was flat. Though that may have been a popular notion among the uneducated masses, it was evident to the informed people of his day, including other sailors and navigators, that the Earth was spherical. The problem was that nobody agreed with Columbus' estimate of the westward distance to Asia; he calculated it to be 2,700 miles, while King Ferdinand's and Queen Isabella's experts insisted it was about 5,000 miles.

In fact, everyone was quite wrong; the westward distance from Spain to Asia would've proven to be about 13,000 miles. But— luckily for Columbus—the Americas were in the way, making his miscalculation more or less irrelevant.

After aiming for Asia, Columbus' three fabled vessels most likely made their first landfall at what is now Watling Island in the Bahamas. A couple months later they headed back to Spain with the good news. Word of his discovery of new Asian lands rapidly spread, and Spain's new hero led dozens of ships and thousands of settlers back to the Caribbean over the next decade. In some of his logs Columbus described the new lands as belonging to a previously unknown continent, but later he retreated to his initial position that they belonged to Asia, and held that conviction to his death.

Of course, Spain was interested in colonizing these new lands, reaping their riches, and populating them with Christians; whether they happened to be part of eastern Asia or an entirely new continent was irrelevant. Columbus appointed himself "Vice King and General Governor of the Islands and Terra Firma of Asia and India," and it seems that, for a while anyway, Spanish royalty went along with it. But though Columbus might've been a pretty good sailor, he was a terribly cruel administrator. Ferdinand and Isabella had specifically instructed Columbus but, ever the renegade, he initiated European imperialism and embarked on a campaign of slavery and genocide, pilfering the natives' gold treasures.

In 1500, after Spanish settlers accused him of mismanagement, he was returned to Spain in shackles, stripped of his appointment.

Columbus next promised the king and queen that he had figured out exactly where the strait to India lay, and he finagled a final voyage in 1502. Heading farther west of the new Spanish colonies, he searched vainly for a passage along Central America's mosquito coast, but he returned empty-handed in 1504, and was no longer welcome in the royal court. Two years later, Columbus died from some manner of heart disease at 55.

But even in death, Columbus has never been able to stay in one place, and his postmortem journeys have prompted doubts over his final resting place, with rival tombs claimed by authorities in Seville, Spain, and Santo Domingo, Dominican Republic. He was first interred for three years in Valladolid, Spain, and then in Seville, but in 1542 his son's will had his cadaver transferred to the Cathedral of Santo Domingo. In 1795 the French took over the Dominican Republic and the world's most-active bag of bones was moved to Spanish-controlled Havana. Finally, after Cuba became independent in 1898, Columbus used the last of his frequent-boater miles and was interred at the church of La Cartuja in Seville.

But an 1877 excavation at the Cathedral of Santo Domingo unearthed a lead box inscribed, "Illustrious and distinguished male, don Cristobal Colon," Columbus' given Spanish name. Dominicans suggested that during the move to Havana the wrong body was selected, sparking an international squabble that simmered for more than a century. Finally in 2006, a forensic team led by Spanish geneticist Jose Antonio Lorente compared DNA from the bone fragments buried in the Seville church to DNA extracted from remains known to be from Columbus' brother Diego. After an absolute matchup between the two mitochondrial DNA samples, the case was closed and it's now apparent with 100 percent certainty that Columbus rests in Seville, Spain.

GENERAL GEORGE ARMSTRONG CUSTER

DECEMBER 5, 1839 – JUNE 25, 1876

AFTER GRADUATING LAST in his West Point class, George Custer surprised his mentors and established a reputation as a hard-fighting (if flamboyant) officer in the Union cavalry. Throughout the Civil War, he led his men in nearly every battle fought by the Army of the Potomac and, by battlefield commission, attained the rank of general.

After the war ended, though, Custer was busted back down to his regular rank of lieutenant colonel, and as commander of the 7th Calvary was charged with bringing renegade Sioux tribes back to their reservation. One fine summer day, upon discovering an Indian camp along Montana's Little Bighorn River, Custer divided his regiment into three columns in an effort to surround the camp and cut off the Indians' escape route. But unfortunately, the Indians didn't stick to the script and Custer and his column of 267 men were annihilated. He was dead at 36.

Three days later the bodies were given a hasty battlefield burial, and the following year what may have been Custer's remains were disinterred, given a military funeral, and reinterred in the Post Cemetery at the West Point Military Academy in New York.

GRAVE DIRECTIONS: Due to every conceivable variety of security concern, it's no longer possible to just show up and freely stroll around the grounds of West Point or its cemetery. The guided tours that are available do an excellent job of removing any vestige of enjoyment or spontaneity, but to each his own.

On the other hand, the Little Bighorn Battlefield national monument is very interesting and well worth a visit the next time you happen to be hanging around Crow Agency, Montana.

CHARLES DARWIN
FEBRUARY 12, 1809 – APRIL 19, 1882

IN 1859 CHARLES Darwin defined his theory of organic evolution in his book *The Origin of Species*, and in one fell swoop became both a well-respected and much-reviled figure. His theory of evolution is considered to be contrary to some biblical teachings and destructive to religion so, with his book's publication, Darwin sparked a controversy that still rages today.

But contrary to popular belief, Darwin was not the first person to propose evolution. In scientific circles it was widely discussed long before Darwin published his theory. Rather, the question was, *how* did evolution occur? Darwin proposed a viable mechanism for evolution (natural selection), and here's how it works: Individuals born with certain beneficial characteristics enjoy an advantage over their peers, and their offspring enjoy the same advantages. Over time, the individuals with the advantageous characteristics do better, live longer, and produce more offspring until, eventually, the population looks very different from its original version. In other words, new species arise when the environment favors certain characteristics over others.

What sounds fairly simple was quite controversial, and it remains so today, due in part to the erroneous simplification that
natural selection amounts to man being descended from apes.
Still, Darwin stood by his theory and spent the remainder of his
life defending it, carefully and methodically working over his copious research notes. He never swayed in the doctrine of his theory,
and it is accepted today by scientists worldwide.

After months of chest pains and seizures, Darwin died of heart
failure at 73.

Westminster Abbey in London functions as neither a cathedral nor a parish church, but is controlled by the royal crown and
has been used as the site for the Royal Coronation since 1066.
Burial there is one of the rarest and greatest of British honors,
and Darwin was so honored; he rests there in the area known as
"Scientists' Corner."

His family erected a bronze memorial with a life-sized relief
bust near the grave in 1888, but there's also an interesting sequel
to this account. His actual burial place is beneath the flagstone
in the center of the north aisle, at the precise spot where exists an
ornamental iron screen with a gate and a ticket booth. Darwin's
grave is at this gate, and every one of the thousands of visitors who
file past to pay their admission fee steps on his grave.

THOMAS EDISON
FEBRUARY 11, 1847 – OCTOBER 18, 1931

BUT FOR THE internal combustion engine and the airplane, it's
difficult to name any common Industrial Revolution–era invention for which Thomas Edison cannot claim considerable credit
or, more likely, the original patent. Having had just three weeks of
public schooling and a few years of home schooling by his mother,
Edison patented 1,093 inventions, which, in total, revolutionized
the fabric of modern civilization.

At 15, he started work as a telegraph operator, which led to his
first inventions: the automatic telegraph and the message printer,
which in turn led to his new career as full-time inventor. The
vote recorder and stock ticker came quickly, and sale of those
patents provided funds for Tom's own invention factory, first in
Newark and later in Menlo Park, where a staff of technicians collaborated on "invention to order." The vast New Jersey factory was
an antecedent of modern research and development laboratories,
and over the course of 50 years, churned out ideas that led to the
development or improvement of everything from cement plants
to plate glass, typewriters to dry-cell batteries, mimeographs to

phonographs, and talking motion pictures. He also made a significant discovery in pure science, the "Edison effect" that led to the electron tube and the underlying technology for radio broadcasting, television, and x-rays.

To research incandescence, Edison Electric Light Company (today's General Electric) was formed, the incandescent lightbulb was introduced in 1879, and central municipal power systems under Edison Electric Company soon followed. As consultant to the U.S. Navy during World War I, Tom contributed another 45 inventions, including navigating equipment, ship-to-shore telephones, and defensive systems against U-boats. With Henry Ford and the Firestone Company he developed a process to provide a domestic rubber source, which, in 1930, proved to be his last patent.

At 84 he died from complications of diabetes and is buried behind his home, Glenmont House, at 211 Main Street in West Orange, New Jersey. The home is now part of the Edison National Historic Site, which also includes the Edison Laboratory Museum where, among other memorabilia, you can peruse some of his 3,400 notebooks containing records of his ideas and research.

ALBERT EINSTEIN
MARCH 14, 1879 – APRIL 18, 1955

TO AVOID COMPULSORY military service, the German-born Albert Einstein gained Swiss citizenship and found employment there at a patent office. In 1905, working alone without the benefit of scientific literature or colleagues, he released a series of theoretical physics publications. Particularly astonishing among these was a paper on the theory of relativity, which, if correct, would overturn classical physics and set the scientific community on its head.

Basing his new theory on a reinterpretation of the classical principle of relativity, namely that the laws of physics had to have the same form in any frame of reference, and dismissing the traditional notion that time and space were absolute concepts, "special relativity" suggested instead that both time and space vary with circumstances; it was the speed of light that remained constant in all frames of reference.

Over the next decade, Einstein perfected his general theory of relativity and summed it up with the famous equation $E=mc^2$. Further, he predicted how a ray of light from a distant star, passing near the sun, would appear to be slightly bent in the direction of the sun. When this prediction was verified by the Royal Society of London, essentially proving relativity and overthrowing

Newtonian physics, Einstein earned the international acclaim he deserved.

A confirmed giant of science, Einstein spent the remainder of his life working toward a "grand unified theory of physics" that would integrate the properties of gravity, matter, and energy into a single, universal formula. His quest was unfulfilled, however, and continues to elude the best minds still.

In 1932 he accepted a post at Princeton University and in 1940 became a United States citizen. In a letter he later regarded as his life's biggest mistake, Einstein urged President Roosevelt to step up nuclear fission research, and though he played no direct part in the development of the atomic bomb, his name has been inextricably linked to the atomic age.

After the war, Einstein threw himself into political activism and joined other scientists in efforts to prevent the use of atomic weapons, including a proposal for the establishment of a world government system that would provide "the binding authority necessary for world security."

Albert Einstein died at 76 in his sleep. He was cremated the same day and his ashes scattered in New Jersey's Delaware River.

MEDGAR EVERS
JULY 2, 1925 – JUNE 12, 1963

MEDGAR EVERS GREW up in the Deep South during the Depression, and as soon as he turned 18, like many others of that era, promptly joined the Army. In 1944 he found himself on the beaches of Normandy, but little did he know that the biggest battle of his life was yet to be fought.

In 1954 Medgar decided to make a difference in the growing civil rights movement and in a short while was made Mississippi's first NAACP field secretary. The next years found him organizing voter-registration drives and, at times, boycotts in areas where the local populace was most obstinate. During the early 1960s the increased tempo of desegregation activities in the South created high and constant tensions, and the situation routinely reached the breaking point.

One hot night in 1963, President Kennedy made a broadcast on national television describing a bill he was sending to Congress that later became the Civil Rights Act of 1964. A few hours later, just after midnight, while stepping out of his Oldsmobile with an armload of "Jim Crow Must Go" T-shirts, Medgar was felled by a shotgun blast fired by an assailant who had lurked in the shadows outside his home. Fifteen minutes later, Medgar died at a local hospital.

At 37, he was buried with full military honors at Arlington National Cemetery in Arlington, Virginia.

GRAVE DIRECTIONS: Park in one of the lots off of Memorial Avenue, get a map at the booth, and, across the drive from the visitors' center in Section 36, you'll find Medgar at Grave 1431.

After Medgar's death the shotgun that was used to kill him was found in the bushes nearby, with the owner's fingerprints still fresh on it. Staunch white supremacist Byron De La Beckwith was soon arrested, stating then that "I didn't kill the nigra, but he's gone and he ain't coming back." Three decades and three trials later, he was convicted of the murder, though the verdict was tainted by what newspapers called an "O.J. jury," comprised of eight minorities, three white women, and one white man.

In 2001, suffering from a variety of health problems, Beckwith died in prison at 80. We don't really care where he's buried.

HENRY FORD
JULY 30, 1863 – APRIL 7, 1947

HENRY FORD HOLDS credit for the proliferation of the automobile, for better or for worse, but it's not because he built the first gasoline-powered vehicle (he didn't), nor is it due to his initiation of the assembly line and interchangeable parts. What really matters is that Henry Ford developed mass consumption. Ford's vision helped create a middle class, one marked by urbanization, rising wages, and some free time in which to spend them. If not for his drive to create a mass market for his cars, the American powerhouse economy that emerged, based on the buying power of an enormous middle class, more than likely would have developed much less vigorously.

In 1905, when Ford Motor Company had 50 competitors, the conventional wisdom was to build cars for the rich. But Ford recognized that if he were to build an automobile affordable to the common man, and an automotive infrastructure were to develop along with it, the world would beat a path to his door. To that end, Ford streamlined his facilities to produce a simple and reliable car, the Model T. Further, he campaigned in Washington for better roads and pushed for gas stations everywhere.

In 1914 Ford shocked the industrial world by paying his workers a $5-a-day minimum wage that more than doubled the prevailing wage. *The Wall Street Journal* called it an "economic crime," and his competitors expected that he had just expensed himself out of business; they couldn't fathom how low Ford had driven his cost per car and that, by making it feasible for more people to buy cars, his high labor costs were insignificant. Ford figured that if he paid his workers a real living wage, everyone would buy a car. And he was right. Within just two years, sales of the Model T increased to 720,000. People flocked to jobs in Ford's factories—more than 100,000 worked at his gigantic River Rouge plant—and they invariably bought one of his cars. By the time the Model T ceased production in 1927, more than 15 million had been sold.

Henry Ford was a complex personality who exhibited a variety of enthusiasms and prejudices. In 1915, adamant that "history is more or less bunk," he chartered an ocean-going "Peace Ship" in an attempt to end World War I by means of "continuous mediation." Three years later, Ford bought the *Dearborn Independent*, and for seven years published a series of attacks on the "International Jew," a mythical figure he blamed for society's ills. Anti-immigrant, anti-labor, and anti-liquor, he opposed social and cultural change, decrying Hollywood movies, out-of-home childcare, and new styles in dress and music. Worried that his workers would go crazy with their five bucks a day, he set up a "Sociological Department" to insure that they didn't blow their "wealth" on vices. He introduced European royalty and company executives to peculiar dances like the *mazurka* and the *quadrille* at old-fashioned social outings. He sponsored the reading of quaint essays to "plain folks" on a weekly radio hour, and experimented with soybeans for food and durable goods. Ford also constructed the rural Greenfield Village and its companion Henry Ford Museum, filling them with artifacts from when America was almost wholly countrified.

By the late 1920s, Ford's vertically integrated, automobile-building juggernaut was a model of self-sufficiency, boasting Brazilian rubber plantations and Minnesota iron ore mines. Ford became arrogantly convinced that auto buyers needed Ford more than Ford needed them and the stage was set for decline. Trusting in what he believed was an unerring instinct for the marketplace, he refused to offer any innovative features, even color, famously adding that "customers could have any color they wanted as long as it's black." He drove out subordinates who bucked his philosophies. Violently opposed to labor organizers, he employed company police to prevent unionization. By 1936 Ford Motor Company was third in sales in the industry and, if World War II hadn't come along and exploited the company's manufacturing prowess in the business of building bombers, tanks, and jeeps, it's entirely possible that Ford's 1932 V-8 engine might have been its last innovation.

A known pacifist, Ford opposed America's entry into World War II, but agreed to build airplane engines for the British in May 1940. After Pearl Harbor was attacked, Ford began a tremendous, all-out manufacturing effort, including the production of B-24 Liberator bombers at the rate of one an hour on a mile-long assembly line. By the end of the war, some 86,000 complete aircraft, 277,000 Willys jeeps, 57,000 airplane engines, and more than a million other fighting vehicles had been built at Ford factories from India to California to New Zealand.

At 83, the cantankerous innovator died in bed at his 1,300-acre Fair Lane mansion and was buried at Saint Martha's Episcopal Church in Detroit, Michigan.

GRAVE DIRECTIONS: At 15801 Joy Road, Henry's grave is easy to find in the Ford section of the cemetery.

SIGMUND FREUD
MAY 6, 1856 – SEPTEMBER 23, 1939

AROUND 1888, THE Austrian doctor Sigmund Freud began to develop a cluster of theories he would give the name of "psychoanalysis." His fundamental idea was that all humans are endowed with an unconscious, one in which potent sexual and aggressive drives, and defenses against them, struggle for supremacy. This idea has struck many as a romantic but scientifically unverifiable notion. His contention that the catalog of neurotic ailments to which humans are susceptible is nearly always the work of sexual maladjustments, and that erotic desire starts not in puberty but in infancy, seemed to many at the time nothing less than obscene. His dramatic evocation of a universal Oedipus complex, in which a little boy loves his mother and hates his father, seems to some more like a literary conceit than a thesis worthy of a scientist of the mind.

Freudian theory was built upon the foundations of both medical science and philosophy. As a scientist, Freud was interested in seeing how the human mind affected the body, particularly in cases of paranoia, hysteria, and other mental illnesses. As a theorist, he explored basic truths about how personalities are formed. In 1923 Freud ventured so far as to develop a model of the human mind consisting of three elements—the ego, the id, and the superego.

But the book that made Freud's reputation was his turn-of-the-century work *The Interpretation of Dreams*, an indefinable masterpiece of dream analysis, autobiography, mind theory, and even history. The principle underlying this work is that mental experiences and entities, like physical ones, are part of nature, and there are no mere accidents in mental procedures. The most nonsensical notion, the most casual slip of the tongue, the most fantastic dream, must have a meaning and can be used to demystify our often incomprehensible thoughts and actions.

For good or ill, Sigmund Freud, more than any other explorer of the psyche, shaped the notions of the twentieth century and the methods of contemporary psychoanalysis. The very vehemence and persistence of his detractors are a wry tribute to the staying power of his ideas.

In 1923 Freud was diagnosed with cancer of the jaw, but he continued to smoke heavily, insisting it was the tobacco that gave him his creativity and great capacity to work. By 1938, though, he had undergone 31 operations to remove tumors, and had been fit and refit with an extensive prosthesis to replace half his mouth. By the following summer, the 83-year-old couldn't eat, and he was surrounded by a mosquito net to keep the flies from his open wounds. At Freud's request, his doctor injected him with two lethal doses of morphine, and he was done.

Freud was cremated and his ashes interred in a Greek vase at the Ernest George Mausoleum of Golders Green Crematorium in London.

SIR EDMUND HILLARY
JULY 20, 1919 – JANUARY 11, 2008

PREFERRING TO BE called Ed and considering himself "an ordinary person with ordinary qualities," Sir Edmund Hillary was a gangling and unpretentious New Zealander who became the first person to summit Mount Everest, winning renown as one of the century's greatest adventurers. Part of a British climbing expedition, Ed and Sherpa mountaineer Tenzing Norgay scaled the mountain on May 29, 1953. Reaching the summit of Everest four days before Elizabeth II was crowned Queen of the British Empire, 33-year-old Ed was immediately knighted by the new queen.

"Awe, wonder, humility, pride, exaltation—these surely ought to be the confused emotions of the first men to stand on the highest peak on Earth, after so many others had failed," he noted. "But my dominant reactions were relief and surprise. Relief because the long grind was over and the unattainable had been attained. And surprise, because it had happened to me, old Ed Hillary, the beekeeper, once the star pupil of the Tuakau District School, but no great shakes at Auckland Grammar and a no-hoper at university, first to the top of Everest. I just didn't believe it."

Before Norgay's death in 1986, Ed consistently refused to confirm he was the first to the top, saying he and the Sherpa had climbed as a team. But in his 1999 book, *View from the Summit*, Ed finally admitted that he was the first to step atop Everest. "We drew closer together as Tenzing brought in the slack on the rope. I continued cutting a line of steps upwards. Next moment I had moved onto a flattish exposed area of snow with nothing but space in every direction," he wrote. "Tenzing quickly joined me and we looked round in wonder. To our immense satisfaction we realized we had reached the top of the world."

Ed later climbed 10 other neighboring Himalayan peaks and led a highly publicized, though ultimately unsuccessful, search for the Abominable Snowman in the 1960s. In 1958 he guided a group in a three-year Antarctic expedition that culminated with their crossing of the South Pole, and he wrote or co-authored 13 books. Still, he always maintained that he was most proud of his campaign to set up schools and health clinics in Nepal. Known as "burra sahib" (big man) by the Nepalese, Ed funded and helped build hospitals, health clinics, airfields, and schools in the small mountainous country through the Himalayan Trust he founded in 1962.

At 88, Ed died of natural causes. He was cremated and his ashes spread over New Zealand's Haruaki Gulf.

J. EDGAR HOOVER
JANUARY 1, 1895 – MAY 2, 1972

TWO YEARS AFTER earning a law degree from George Washington University, J. Edgar Hoover began working for the Department of Justice and, in 1924, before he was even 30 years old, was named the director of the Federal Bureau of Investigation. Hoover held the prized position for 48 years, through eight different presidential administrations, until his death in 1972. Through politics, publicity, and a strong record in law enforcement bolstered by underhanded manipulations and outright blackmail, Hoover became

one of Washington's most powerful figures, taking the free rein of a renegade, all but immune to control by his superiors.

Hoover was, by turns, admired and vilified, both his strengths and weaknesses larger than life. On the one hand, as America's top policeman, Hoover took a corrupt, inefficient, and dysfunctional organization, top-heavy with political hacks, and whipped it into shape in record time, building the basis of the world's most celebrated arm of law enforcement. Under Hoover's direction, a sense of decorum and professionalism was applied to crime fighting; appointments were based on merits, promotions were made on proven ability, and the round-'em-up, shoot-'em-up traditions were, eventually, abandoned. Hoover also oversaw the application of science to police work; he promoted the creation of police training facilities as well as the National Crime Information Center, its centralized fingerprint cataloging system, and its state-of-the-art laboratories. In the 1930s Hoover's agents rounded up the notorious gangsters and seedy drifters of his 10 Most Wanted list, in the war years they arrested German saboteurs and secret agents, in the postwar period the bureau established itself as the bulwark against communism, and during the turbulent 1960s the FBI disrupted and destroyed the KKK's murderous network. For certain, the FBI has demonstrated that it is not perfect or infallible, but, in the majority, the organization is an elite, professional, and incorruptible corps that exists to some degree as a result of J. Edgar Hoover's tyrannical determination.

But, of course, there's still the "other hand" to discuss. Hoover's shortcomings as an individual were many and, as would be expected because the Bureau was his life, these foibles infected his performance as its director. And, many contend, his faults transcended his accomplishments.

A paranoid who held virtually unchecked public power, he manipulated presidents from Roosevelt to Nixon, and kept extensive files on everyone from Groucho Marx to Bess Truman. Casting aside constitutional protections, Hoover used federal agents as his exclusive henchmen to destroy personal enemies, either real or imagined, through illegal wiretaps and hidden microphones. Hoover did not tolerate dissent or failure, and he directed agents to concentrate on areas that catapulted both his own and the Bureau's public reputations to a fraudulent level of invincibility. Though Hoover was himself a closet homosexual, he was obsessed with the crimes and failings of society's liberal orders and, with straitlaced morality, hypocritically sideswiped any attempts to advance progressive causes. He helped create McCarthyism, blackmailed the Kennedy brothers, forged connections with mobsters, and condoned and planned the systematic harassment of Martin Luther King Jr., retarding the civil rights movement. Indeed, a biographical study of J. Edgar Hoover's life is a contradictory study of observations and speculations blurred by hyperbolized facts and out-and-out lies.

Hoover successfully avoided independent investigations of both his and the FBI's conduct during his tenure. And, upon Hoover's death, Clyde Tolson, who enjoyed triple duty as the FBI's second-ranking officer, Hoover's gay lover, and the primary heir to the Hoover estate, destroyed many of Hoover's personal files, derailing future attempts at sorting out the truths of the Hoover administration. Congress later enacted legislation requiring Senate confirmation of future FBI directors and limiting their power to 10 years.

Hoover died of undiagnosed heart disease at 77, while still in the role of FBI director, and was buried at Congressional Cemetery in Washington, D.C.

GRAVE DIRECTIONS: Enter the cemetery at 1801 E Street SE, drive straight to the chapel, turn left, then turn left again. After 100 feet, stop. On the left, you won't miss his grave.

Upon Tolson's death at 74 in 1975, he was also buried at Congressional Cemetery, just a few yards away from Hoover.

IWO JIMA MARINES

DURING WORLD WAR II, the Japanese controlled the tiny South Pacific island of Iwo Jima, which, due to its strategic position just 700 miles off the Japanese mainland, was imperative for the American military to seize in order for an invasion of the mainland to occur.

The Japanese had buttressed the island with hundreds of machine-gun blockhouses and pillboxes and, in an effort to weaken the Japanese position, the United States Navy and Army Air Force subjected the fortifications to a massive, 74-day bombing campaign. Then, on February 19, 1945, American Marines scrambled from their carriers and waded through ankle-deep volcanic ash to establish a beachhead. Although the beaches had been captured after only minor resistance, the Japanese later emerged from underground shelters to unleash extensive firepower and wage one of the war's fiercest and bloodiest battles.

Four days after storming the beach, a 40-man American combat patrol reached the top of the island's 550-foot high Mount Suribachi and raised there a small United States flag. Later, a larger flag was located, and photographer Joe Rosenthal, recognizing a photographic opportunity, followed its bearer up the hill. As six men struggled on the rugged terrain to raise this larger Stars and Stripes, Rosenthal snapped a picture, perhaps the single most recognizable ever taken, for which he was awarded the Pulitzer Prize.

Although the flag-raising inspired the forces that were still trying to take the island, it could not minimize the heavy casualties suffered and, by March 25, when the clashes finally ended, 5,931 American servicemen lay dead, including three of the six flag-raisers. President Roosevelt ordered that the men in the picture be identified, and the three surviving flag-raisers were called home to make public appearances in connection with the Seventh War Loan Drive.

Starting at the bottom of the flagpole and working upward and left, the six men caught on film are: Corporal Harlan Block, PFC Rene Gagnon, PM2/C John Bradley, Sergeant Michael Strank, PFC Franklin Sousley, and PFC Ira Hayes.

HARLAN BLOCK
NOVEMBER 6, 1924 – MARCH 1, 1945

HARLAN BLOCK GRADUATED from Weslaco High School in 1942 and was drafted into the Marines the following year, where he qualified as a parachutist. After participating in the Bougainville Island campaign, Harlan was among the first of those who stormed Iwo Jima's beaches. His death, at 20 years old, occurred during an attack on the island's Nishi Ridge, just six days after the triumphant stand atop Mount Suribachi. Initially buried in the Marine Cemetery on Iwo Jima, his body was later returned to Texas, and he now rests at the Iwo Jima Monument and Museum in Harlingen.

DIRECTIONS TO HARLAN BLOCK'S GRAVE: Harlan is buried next to the enormous monument at 320 Iwo Jima Boulevard.

MICHAEL STRANK
NOVEMBER 10, 1919 – MARCH 1, 1945

AT JUST 25, Michael Strank was the oldest of the six men in the photograph. A Pennsylvania native, Michael worked for the Civilian Conservation Corps, joined the Marines in 1939, and had participated in campaigns on Wallis, Russell, and Bougainville Islands before storming ashore at Iwo Jima. Just six days after his claim to perpetuity atop Mount Suribachi, Michael was killed by enemy artillery fire. Initially buried in the Marine Cemetery on Iwo Jima, he was reinterred in Arlington National Cemetery in 1949.

DIRECTIONS TO MICHAEL STRANK'S GRAVE: Michael is buried in Lot 7179 of Section 12, down the hill from the Tomb of the Unknown Soldier.

FRANKLIN SOUSLEY
SEPTEMBER 19, 1925 – MARCH 21, 1945

AFTER GRADUATING FROM high school, Kentucky-native Franklin Sousley was drafted into the Marine Corps Reserve in January 1944. Thirteen months later he landed on Iwo Jima, and he was killed during fighting around the island's Kitano Point. He was only 19 years old. Initially buried in the Marine Cemetery on Iwo Jima, Franklin was later reinterred at Elizaville Cemetery in Elizaville, Kentucky.

DIRECTIONS TO FRANKLIN SOUSLEY'S GRAVE: On Route 170 just south of the Route 57 intersection, Franklin's grand monument is this cemetery's centerpiece.

IRA HAYES

JANUARY 12, 1923 – JANUARY 24, 1955

IRA HAYES WAS a Pima Indian on the Gila River Indian Reservation in Arizona, and in 1942 enlisted in the Marines and was assigned to the Parachute Training School. Inordinately shy, he hated the notoriety that the flag-raising brought him and even tried to conceal his participation when President Roosevelt ordered the flag-raisers identified. Despite his reluctance, Ira became the best known of the six flag-raisers, as his Native American heritage added a dimension that intrigued an already very interested public. In 1955, suffering from alcoholism at 32, Ira was found dead of exposure near his home. Before he was buried with honors at Arlington National Cemetery, his body lay in state at the Arizona State Capitol and, later, Johnny Cash memorialized him in a song, "The Ballad of Ira Hayes."

DIRECTIONS TO IRA HAYES' GRAVE: Ira is buried in Lot 479 of Section 34.

RENE GAGNON

MARCH 7, 1925 – OCTOBER 12, 1979

RENE GAGNON LEFT high school to work in a textile mill near Manchester, New Hampshire, and was inducted into the Marine Corps Reserve in May 1943. After the loan-drive tour, Rene was sent back overseas and he served in China until his 1946 discharge. He returned to New Hampshire and died unexpectedly at 54. Because Rene hadn't died while on active duty, he didn't meet Arlington National Cemetery burial requirements, and was interred at the Mount Calvary Mausoleum in Manchester. In 1981, two years after his death, a waiver request was approved and he was moved to Arlington.

DIRECTIONS TO RENE GAGNON'S GRAVE: Park in one of the lots off of Memorial Avenue, get a map at the booth, and you can find Rene's marker at Lot 343 in Section 51, which is adjacent to Arlington's own bronze sculpture of that Iwo Jima moment.

JOHN BRADLEY

JULY 10, 1923 – JANUARY 11, 1994

AFTER ENLISTING IN the Navy in 1943, John Bradley attended Field Medical School and was assigned to the 28th Marines in

1944. After the appearances in connection with the loan drive, John returned to action and, after being wounded in March 1945, returned home to Wisconsin, where he ran a funeral home until his death at 70 in 1994. John was buried at the Queen of Peace Cemetery in Antigo, Wisconsin.

DIRECTIONS TO JOHN BRADLEY'S GRAVE: In the left rear of the cemetery at 501 Park Street is a large mausoleum, across from which stands the proud Bradley stone.

THE KENNEDYS

JOHN F. KENNEDY
MAY 29, 1917 – NOVEMBER 22, 1963

ROBERT F. KENNEDY
NOVEMBER 20, 1925 – JUNE 6, 1968

JACQUELINE KENNEDY
JULY 28, 1929 – MAY 19, 1994

THE KENNEDYS ARE embedded in the American political culture of the past half-century like no other family. During the 1920s, the patriarch of the Kennedy family, Joe Kennedy Sr., amassed a fortune through banking and shipbuilding ventures and, most especially, by smuggling liquor into the country during Prohibition. Though he had presidential aspirations, he was an outspoken isolationist, so that dream died the day Pearl Harbor was bombed. Instead, Joe's ambitions were assumed by his second-oldest son, John F. Kennedy. Besides the fact that John came from a wealthy and prominent family, he was an excellent candidate for other reasons; he was Harvard educated, well spoken, good-looking, and his war record was distinguished by brave leadership. As the commander of the Navy torpedo boat PT-109, John had swum his crewmen to safety after their vessel was rammed by a Japanese destroyer.

In 1946 John was elected Democratic congressman from Boston, and in 1952 he easily advanced to the Senate. The following year John married the elegant Jacqueline Bouvier and, while recovering from back surgery in 1956, wrote *Profiles in Courage*, a study of eight bold political leaders. His book won the Pulitzer Prize. If John had been an excellent candidate before, he was now the perfect one, and a legitimate run for the presidency would shortly commence.

With his brother Robert as campaign manager, in 1960 John F. Kennedy beat Republican nominee Richard M. Nixon in a fantastically close election to become the 35th president of the United States. At 43, he was the first Roman Catholic ever elected to the office. President Kennedy's inaugural address set a tone of youthful idealism that raised the nation's hopes: "Ask not what your country can do for you, ask what you can do for your country," he exhorted. With the New Frontier, as his administration called itself, it was apparent that a change had come.

Kennedy's economic programs launched the country on its longest sustained expansion since World War II. He promoted social legislation, including Civil Rights reform, and in forming the Alliance for Progress and the Peace Corps, he brought Americans to the aid of developing nations. In the height of the Cold War period, Kennedy displayed moderation and a firm hand in foreign policy. He accepted responsibility for the Bay of Pigs fiasco and later, at the risk of all-out nuclear war, Kennedy engaged in a showdown with the Soviet Union over its missile installations in Cuba. Attempting to slow the arms race, he negotiated a partial nuclear test–ban treaty with the Soviets in 1963.

Kennedy's wit and charm earned him tremendous popularity and his entire family captivated America. This was Camelot and there was magic in the air. The nation's dashing chief executive gave eloquent speeches while glamorous Jackie sat purposefully beside him in a pillbox hat, hushed and unyieldingly in love. Meanwhile, the first couple's camera-ready children cavorted through the White House; bookish daughter Caroline rode a pony on the lawn, while her energetic, toddler brother, John Jr., played with toy trucks in his daddy's Oval Office.

But just after noon on a breezy Thursday in Dallas, the magic ran out. While Abraham Zapruder rolled tape, three bullets were fired as Kennedy's motorcade idled slowly down Elm Street and within the hour, America's 46-year-old leader was pronounced dead at Parkland Memorial Hospital.

The memorial site at Arlington National Cemetery consists of a circular walkway paved with irregular stones of Cape Cod granite. On an elevated terrace, Kennedy's grave is marked with a simple marble tablet, at the head of which an eternal flame burns from the center of a circular stone.

After its president's assassination, and after its Warren Commission concluded that the assassin, Lee Harvey Oswald, had acted alone, the stunned nation moved slowly forward, albeit with permanent scars. Jackie Kennedy remained in the public eye as John's widow, and a few years later became involved with Robert F. Kennedy's own presidential bid. But tragedy struck again when a Jordanian immigrant named Sirhan Sirhan shot Bobby three times as he walked through the kitchen of the Ambassador Hotel in Los Angeles after a rousing campaign speech. Dying the next day at 42, Bobby was laid to rest near John, his grave marked with a plain white cross.

In October 1968, Jackie became "Jackie O" when she married shipping magnate Aristotle Onassis. The marriage seemed rocky, the couple spent almost all of their time apart, and when Jackie became a widow again in 1975, a weight seemed to be lifted from her shoulders. Just before Aristotle's death, Jackie began working as a book editor, an endeavor she continued for most of the remainder of her life. As Jackie was relentlessly pursued by tabloid photographers, she became a familiar Manhattan sight, camouflaging herself in dark sunglasses and turned-up collar, her signature mane hidden beneath a kerchief. Stricken with non-Hodgkin's lymphoma, Jackie died at 64 and was buried alongside John.

GRAVE DIRECTIONS: John, Jackie, and Bobby are buried on a knoll near the main gate, where plenty of signs point the way.

JOHN CONNALLY
FEBRUARY 27, 1917 – JUNE 15, 1993

SITTING IN THE jump seat in front of the Kennedys on that dark day in Dallas were Texas governor John Connally and his wife, Nellie. Just as the president's Lincoln, its bubbletop off, approached an underpass near the intersection of Elm, Main, and Commerce streets, Nellie turned to the president and said laughingly, "You can't say that Dallas doesn't love you today." As he started to reply, a sharp rifle crack filled the air and a bullet crashed into Kennedy's head. John Connally turned to see what the commotion was, and a bullet then caught him in the back. It plowed down into his chest, went through a lung, fractured his right wrist, and lodged in his left thigh. Though Kennedy never knew what hit him, Connally remained conscious until he was anesthetized for surgery. He made a full recovery and later egocentrically speculated that he was the assassin's real target.

Connally left the governor's post in 1969 and in 1973, after Spiro Agnew resigned, declared himself a Republican in order to gain an appointment to the newly vacated vice-presidential seat from his friend Richard M. Nixon. But after a firestorm of protest, the plan was nixed and Connally slunk back to Texas. As it turns out, he may have been more perfectly suited to partner with Nixon than anyone ever guessed; in 1975 he was tried and acquitted in a milk-price bribery scandal, in 1977 he entered into a shady bank partnership with two Arab sheiks, and, after he got a bit too acquisitive during Texas' dizzying oil and real-estate heyday, Connally declared bankruptcy in 1987.

At 76, Connally died of pulmonary fibrosis and was buried at the Texas State Cemetery in Austin, Texas.

GRAVE DIRECTIONS: At 909 Navasota Street, Connally's tall black monument is easy to find in the Republic Hill section.

LEE HARVEY OSWALD

OCTOBER 18, 1939 – NOVEMBER 24, 1963

IT SEEMS APPARENT that Lee Harvey Oswald shot John F. Kennedy from the sixth floor of the Texas School Book Depository building. Beyond that, however, everything about him is up for grabs. Every conceivable possibility and impossibility concerning his life, whereabouts, motives, connections, and identity has been endlessly debated and examined by an army of government investigators, millions of truth-seeking citizens, and God knows how many conspiracy buffs—some of them flat-out nuts, others just passionate about the truth.

Despite the Warren Report's conclusions, it *is* very difficult to accept that Oswald alone killed Kennedy, and it seems certain that it will never be known exactly what happened and who was, or was not, involved.

For good reason, many are convinced there was at least one accomplice. If Oswald was the lone gunman, sound and film as well as ballistic evidence dictate one or another sequence of events, but forensics fail to support either of these sequences. Supporters of one particular "lone gunman" camp believe that Oswald fired three shots. But if that were true, one of those bullets must have inflicted seven wounds in two bodies—some nearly at right angles to one another—according to ballistic evidence. And, after those gymnastics, the evidence further stipulates that that bullet was the one found in near pristine condition lying atop Kennedy's stretcher—a clear impossibility. Supporters of the other "lone gunman" camp insist that Oswald fired four shots, but this scenario is also unfeasible simply because Oswald couldn't have squeezed four rounds out of his bolt-action rifle in the six seconds of shooting, as exhibited in Zapruder's infamous film—never mind that he would have had to train those shots on a moving target 75 yards away.

The forensic evidence of the Kennedy assassination does not seem to support any conceivable sequence of events in which there is only a single gunman and it appears that it was physically impossible for Oswald to have acted alone. However, the only person who could definitively say what really happened has been pushing up daisies at Shannon Rose Hill Memorial Park in Fort Worth, Texas, for more than five decades.

GRAVE DIRECTIONS: At 7301 East Lancaster Avenue, enter the cemetery, drive up the road that runs directly behind the funeral home, and stop at the brown Shannon mausoleum. Just behind and to the left of this mausoleum, along the road, is a flat marker for Skelton. Oswald lies in the grass, waiting, just 20 feet behind the Skelton marker. The inscription on his gravestone reads simply, "Oswald."

JEFFERSON DAVIS TIPPIT
SEPTEMBER 18, 1924 – NOVEMBER 22, 1963

IN ANY EVENT, after Oswald fired at Kennedy, he ditched his rifle between some boxes, ran out of the depository building, jumped on a bus and then into a cab, and then walked the remaining few blocks to his rooming house. He left his room after just a few minutes and, at 1:18 p.m., a caller radioed to the Dallas police that one of its own had been gunned down. The fallen policeman was Officer Jefferson Davis Tippit, and his assailant, as you may have guessed, turned out to be Oswald. Apparently, Tippit had stopped to question a suspicious-looking Oswald and, after exchanging a few words, Oswald felled him with revolver shots to the head and chest.

At his funeral, of course, 39-year-old Officer Tippit was afforded all the ceremony that befits one killed in the line of duty and, in light of the circumstances, he was deservedly honored by the public at large. However, in the eyes of conspiracy theorists, nobody is beyond reproach, and a number of them directly accuse Tippit of being "the other gunman." In these scenarios, Tippit didn't just happen to cross paths with Oswald. Instead, they were discussing their next move minutes after the assassination when Oswald double-crossed Tippit, ostensibly to eliminate a witness. Well, anything's possible, I guess.

GRAVE DIRECTIONS: At 6000 South R. L. Thornton Freeway near Exit 420 off I-35, Tippet is buried in Section 62, a distinguished area reserved for those whose lives were dedicated to some special service.

JACK RUBY
APRIL 25, 1911 – JANUARY 3, 1967

TWO DAYS AFTER Kennedy and Tippit died, Oswald was transferred from police headquarters to the Dallas County jail and a crowd gathered to witness his departure. Oswald was escorted through the basement of the Dallas police building by a black-hatted detective, Lyle Cassidy Graves, who gripped Oswald's upper arm tightly while a phalanx of police provided the illusion of security. Then, while live television cameras rolled, a strip-club owner, Jack Ruby, emerged from the crowd, stabbed a .38 revolver at Oswald's abdomen, and fired. Two hours later Oswald was dead at 24.

Some call Ruby a hero, while others believe that Ruby, a shady operator who had minor connections to organized crime and the Dallas Police Department, killed Oswald to keep him from revealing a larger conspiracy. During his trial Ruby claimed that his rage at Kennedy's murder was the sole motive for his action but, whatever his motives, he certainly helped propel the cottage

business of conspiracy theorists. Ruby was convicted of "murder with malice" and sentenced to death, but the verdict was overturned on the grounds that he could not have received a fair trial in Dallas at the time. While awaiting a second trial, Ruby died of lung cancer at 55.

GRAVE DIRECTIONS: Enter the cemetery at 7801 West Montrose Avenue; turn at the first left and then again at the next right. At the Violet section on your left, stop at the "2" and Ruby's grave is 18 rows back.

L.C. GRAVES
OCTOBER 8, 1918 – FEBRUARY 11, 1995

SOME BUFFS PAINT a conspiracy of the Kennedy assassination that even encompasses members of the Dallas police force, and especially Lyle Cassidy Graves, or L.C. as he was commonly known, because of the amateurish protection offered to Oswald. Graves left the force in 1970 and worked as a bank-fraud investigator for the next dozen years. Though he had plenty of opportunities, he never cashed in on his link to history. At 76, he died of cardiac arrest.

GRAVE DIRECTIONS: Enter the cemetery at 3920 Samuell Boulevard and park wherever you can. You'll find L.C.'s flat marker on the left, 30 feet in front of the Wolff mausoleum.

MARTIN LUTHER KING JR.
JANUARY 15, 1929 – APRIL 4, 1968

AFTER RECEIVING HIS doctorate in theology from Boston University, Martin Luther King Jr. moved to Montgomery, Alabama, in 1955, where he was to be a preacher at a Baptist church. Having grown up in Atlanta, he was no stranger to Southern prejudice, but the scale of racial bigotry in Montgomery was so outrageous that Martin's ambitions were refocused, and he dedicated his life to amending those inequities and presenting his race with a fair chance at the American Dream.

In 1957, Martin founded the Southern Christian Leadership Conference and became a figure with a national platform. The civil rights movement had begun and, after years of nonviolent protests, the movement reached its zenith when the Civil Rights Act of 1964 was passed. The broad-reaching legislation guaranteed equal rights in all areas of the public domain, and a civil rights commission would ensure that these laws were enforced. Though Martin and his thousands of followers had not struggled in vain, the victory had come at a cost. They had endured high-pressure fire hoses, midnight cross burnings, and backwoods lynchings. But Martin had remained peaceful throughout, and in biblical cadence assured his followers that their fight could be victorious if they did not resort to bloodshed.

While standing on the balcony of the Lorraine Motel in Memphis, Martin was killed at 39 by a single bullet fired at him from the bathroom of a flophouse across the parking lot. A rifle and a pair of binoculars marked with the fingerprints of one of the house's residents, James Earl Ray, were found nearby and he was arrested in London two months later. Pleading guilty in order to avoid the death penalty, he died of hepatitis in prison at 70.

In a magnificent crypt atop a reflecting pool, Martin lies at his own Martin Luther King Jr. National Historic Site, established in Atlanta in 1970.

GENERAL DOUGLAS MacARTHUR

JANUARY 26, 1880 – APRIL 5, 1964

DOUGLAS MacARTHUR WAS the son of a Union army hero, and he and his father remain the only such pair ever to receive the Congressional Medal of Honor.

After graduating at the top of his West Point class in 1903, he rose through the Army's ranks, eventually becoming its first public-relations officer, and is largely credited with selling the American people on the Selective Service Act of 1917. Upon the entry of the United States into World War I, MacArthur commanded a combat brigade in France and became the war's most decorated American soldier.

While his peers were demoted to their pre-war ranks, MacArthur received a plum new assignment as superintendent of West Point and dragged the moribund academy into the twentieth century, enabling it to produce officers fit to lead the country in the type of modern war he had just experienced firsthand.

By 1941, MacArthur was commander of forces in the Far East, heading a military mission preparing the Philippines for independence. But with the attack on Pearl Harbor and the onset of war, and without enough time to build a force capable of resisting the Japanese, his soldiers retreated to the Bataan peninsula while Mac-Arthur himself was ordered to Australia. MacArthur left his men to face almost-certain destruction, comforted only by the belief that he would later lead an army back to rescue them. For the next three years, his personal quest—"I shall return"—became almost synonymous with the war in the Pacific. Although MacArthur's path through the dense South Pacific island jungles could hardly have been foreseen in the initial war plans, the offensive under his command returned U.S. forces to the Philippines in October of 1944, and MacArthur dramatically waded ashore at Leyte during its liberation. The next year, as supreme commander of the Allied powers, MacArthur presided over the Japanese surrender aboard the USS Missouri, which brought an end to World War II.

His place as a leading figure of the twentieth century secure, MacArthur may have made his greatest contribution to history in the next five years as supreme commander of the allied powers in Japan. As its military governor, he implemented policies that purged Japan of its militarism, and through the successful occupation of a devastated Japan, he saw it rebuild, institute a democratic government, and chart a course that has made it one of the world's leading industrial powers.

Commanding an American-led coalition of United Nations forces during the Korean War, MacArthur forced the North Koreans to surrender most of the gains they had won during their surprise invasion. But when Chinese forces began fighting alongside the North Koreans, he advocated an extension of the war into China and President Truman relieved him of command.

As the last great general of World War II to come home, MacArthur received a hero's welcome and concluded his address to Congress with his citation of an old military song, "Old soldiers never die, they just fade away." True to his word, the old soldier faded from the public eye and quietly lived out the remainder of his years in New York until his death of natural causes at 84.

He is buried at his own MacArthur Memorial at 198 Bank Street in Norfolk, Virginia.

JOSEPH McCARTHY
NOVEMBER 14, 1909 – MAY 2, 1957

JOE McCARTHY WAS an undistinguished first-term senator from Wisconsin when he found his cause in February 1950. Appearing at a Republican Women's Club meeting in West Virginia, McCarthy announced that by clandestine effort he had collected a "list of 205 cases of individuals who appear to be either card-carrying members or certainly loyal to the Communist Party" working within the state department.

In spite of the fact that it was not a crime to be a member of the Communist Party, despite McCarthy's refusal to disclose exactly how he had arrived at this list, and, even though McCarthy couldn't nail down the number of infiltrators that existed—in a Salt Lake City speech the following week there were only 57, and on the Senate floor five days later there were 81—the assertion was like gasoline tossed on the smoldering coals of Cold War anxiety.

The furor should have been extinguished in July 1950 when, after McCarthy failed to produce a single name of an actual Communist, the Tydings Senate subcommittee concluded that his campaign was a "hoax and a fraud." But by then, McCarthy's fantastic controversy had gained the momentum of a runaway train, and it certainly wasn't going to be derailed by a mere subcommittee's opinion. Instead, McCarthy rallied anxious supporters with inflammatory speeches and subpoenaed prominent citizens to Washington, where he demanded "the naming of names." Regularly usurping executive and judicial authority, McCarthy cast suspicion on anyone he pleased. To question his character or the motivations of his witch-hunt could result in being blackballed, which was "as good as Red."

His coffers overflowing with donations from frenzied supporters, McCarthy won his 1952 reelection and became chairman of the Permanent Subcommittee on Investigations of Governmental Operations. In 1954 he pressed to convene hearings to investigate the extent of communist espionage activity in the Army. His own Republican party resisted the hearings, as they knew full well that nothing would be found. But Democrats pushed the hearings ahead to allow McCarthy the opportunity to commit political suicide and, with any luck, kill his party.

On April 23, 1954, the hearings began and McCarthy's flagrant disregard for proper investigative procedure and reckless interrogative tactics were quickly exposed to some 20 million television viewers. After 36 days of testimony, the Army was vindicated and Senator McCarthy became immediately irrelevant. In July a resolution accusing McCarthy of conduct "unbecoming a member of the United States Senate" was introduced, and in December 1954 the Senate voted to censure him.

Even before his professional reputation was destroyed there were whisperings that McCarthy suffered from alcoholism, and after his censure, though still a senator, he stayed home and watched soap operas while drinking continuously. In the summer of 1956 he was hospitalized for detoxification, where he suffered fits of delirium screaming that snakes were attacking him. The treatment helped, but McCarthy soon resumed drinking and his face grew bloated, his body drawn, and his skin yellow.

When he was again admitted to the Navy Medical Center in Bethesda, Maryland, his wife said he was undergoing treatment for an old knee injury, but when he died four days later at 47, the hospital reported it was from "acute hepatitis, origin unknown." It was later acknowledged that McCarthy was being treated in the neurology ward for alcohol abuse, which caused his liver failure.

He is buried at Saint Mary's Church Cemetery in Appleton, Wisconsin.

GRAVE DIRECTIONS: Enter the cemetery at 2121 Prospect Street, go over the bridge, and stop after the chapel. Joe's stone is on the right, adjacent to the river.

J. ROBERT OPPENHEIMER

APRIL 22, 1904 – FEBRUARY 18, 1967

IN 1939, NIELS Bohr brought to the United States the news that German scientists had succeeded at nuclear fission; they'd split the atom. This meant that the Nazis were on their way to developing an atomic bomb and, once President Roosevelt absorbed the terrible implications, he ordered the initiation of a scientific program aimed at developing such a weapon before the enemy did.

Splintered research had been ongoing at Columbia University, the University of Chicago, and at an emerging facility in Oak Ridge, Tennessee, but now there was a new urgency to the atomic project; to realize the objective, no expense would be spared and no sacrifice could be considered too great. The country's top theoretical physicists and a few thousand support staff began working together on the so-called Manhattan Project in Los Alamos, New Mexico. The resident genius, J. Robert Oppenheimer, was appointed technical director.

Under his direction the best minds in physics worked to solve the riddles of the atomic bomb challenge and their efforts were rewarded on July 16, 1945, when the first nuclear detonation occurred at the Trinity Bomb site in the New Mexico desert. As Oppenheimer stood watching the mushroom cloud on that grimly historic day, the gravity of the accomplishment weighed on him, and he later recalled that a phrase of Hindu scripture floated through his mind, "I have become death, the destroyer of worlds."

A few weeks later atomic bombs were detonated over the Japanese cities of Hiroshima and Nagasaki, prompting the unconditional surrender of Japan and the end of World War II.

After the war, Oppenheimer chaired the Advisory Committee to the Atomic Energy Commission and there voiced his opposition to the development of the next generation of atomic bomb, the hydrogen bomb. Later, at the height of the hysterical Communist witch-hunts in 1953, Oppenheimer's security clearance was revoked and his advisor role terminated in light of his opposition to new mass-destruction weapons and his increasing support for liberal philosophies.

Oppenheimer served as director of the Institute for Advanced Study at Princeton University for the remainder of his days and died of throat cancer at 62.

He was cremated and his ashes scattered off the Virgin Islands.

ROSA PARKS
FEBRUARY 4, 1913 – OCTOBER 24, 2005

BOYCOTTS ARE NOTORIOUSLY ineffective but in 1955 a defiant act by a seemingly run-of-the-mill seamstress who had "just had enough" led to a boycott that perhaps made up for every other fruitless protest that had ever come before, or since.

The 14th Amendment to the Constitution adopted shortly after the Civil War requires states to provide equal protection to all citizens. Nonetheless, deep racial inequalities existed in many areas of the country for much of the twentieth century, most notably in the Deep South, where blacks were treated as less than second-class citizens, a practice that, more often than not, was supported by law and decree.

As recently as the 1950s in Montgomery, Alabama, black people were required to sit in the "colored" rearward sections of city buses and, as the front white sections filled, they had to give up their seats and stand in the rear or get off. Blacks could not stand in the aisle where a white was seated and, perhaps most humiliating, if a white was on the bus and a black wished to embark or disembark, he had to use the rear door so as to not walk past the white. Finally, if it so happened that a crowd of whites got on and occupied all the seats, the blacks were obligated to get off and walk.

On her way home from work one day in 1955, Rosa Parks, a 42-year-old black woman, took a seat in the "colored" section of a Montgomery bus and as it filled up the driver demanded that she move so a white male passenger could have her seat. When Rosa refused to give up her seat, a police officer arrested her and as the officer took her away, she asked, "Why do you push us around?" The officer's response: "I don't know, but the law's the law, and you're under arrest." Rosa was convicted of disorderly conduct and fined $14.

Four days later, the NAACP proposed a lawsuit to Mrs. Parks naming her as plaintiff in a case arguing the constitutionality of Montgomery's bus segregation laws and, though her husband pleaded with her to drop the matter because of the very real possibility that angry whites would kill her, she agreed to the suit. In support of Rosa's cause and in protest of all Jim Crow segregation laws, blacks boycotted city buses, crippling the transit company's finances. The boycott was finally ended 381 days later when the U.S. Supreme Court found in favor of Mrs. Parks; the bus segregation laws were unconstitutional. That successful challenge to segregation empowered the fledgling civil rights movement, which begat a decade of turmoil in the nation's history, but ultimately resulted in social justice via the Civil Rights Act of 1964.

As for Rosa, her work was done. But for participating in a few peaceful marches during the movement and giving an occasional short speech in the years after, she settled in Detroit and avoided the limelight. In 1996 her place in history was universally acknowledged as she was awarded the nation's highest civilian honor, the Presidential Medal of Freedom.

At 92, she died of natural causes and was buried at Woodlawn Cemetery in Detroit.

GRAVE DIRECTIONS: Enter the cemetery at 19975 Woodward Avenue and, parking immediately on the left, you'll see the Rosa L. Parks Freedom Chapel behind the office.

JULIUS & ETHEL ROSENBERG

JULIUS ROSENBERG
MAY 12, 1918 – JUNE 19, 1953

ETHEL ROSENBERG
SEPTEMBER 28, 1915 – JUNE 19, 1953

IN JULY OF 1950 Ethel and Julius Rosenberg were arrested on charges of espionage on behalf of the Soviet Union. The trial and subsequent conviction of the Rosenbergs in 1951 led to one of the most controversial sentences ever handed down in the United States, as many felt that they were the victims of the era's Communist witch-hunt atmosphere.

Witch-hunt or not, it does seem to have been proven in court, and is generally agreed, that while employed as an engineer by the U.S. Army Signal Corps, Julius stole military technology and passed along atomic secrets through an intermediary to the Soviet vice consul. However, Ethel's prosecution may have been particularly unfair because, though she knew of her husband's role and the role of her brother, David Greenglass, who testified for the prosecution to save his own life, Ethel had not actively spied.

Nonetheless, both Rosenbergs were convicted and sentenced to death under the Espionage Act of 1917 and, despite worldwide pleas that their lives be spared, President Eisenhower refused to commute their sentences.

On a hot June night at the Sing Sing death house in Ossining, New York, in 1953, Julius was led into the death chamber and

killed in the electric chair by three shocks of 2,000 volts each. While thousands of people gathered in protest around the country, Ethel was placed in the chair next. The top of her head had been shaved to ensure a good contact with the electrodes, she wore a green print dress with white polka dots, and she was stoic and defiant. It took five jolts before Ethel was declared dead at 8:16 p.m. Julius was 35 and Ethel was 37 at the time of their deaths.

They now lie side by side at Wellwood Cemetery in Farmingdale, New York.

GRAVE DIRECTIONS: At 1400 Wellwood Avenue, turn into the first entrance, which is North Avenue. Follow North Avenue for a short distance and then, between Akiba and Bialik roads, there will be a marking on the left curb for Walkway F-G. Fifty feet along this walk is the Rosenberg plot.

OSKAR SCHINDLER
APRIL 28, 1908 – OCTOBER 9, 1974

OSKAR SCHINDLER GREW up the son of a wealthy family in what is now the Czech Republic, but during the deep economic depression that gripped Europe before World War II, the family business was lost and the Schindler family went bankrupt. In 1939 the first German divisions marched into Czechoslovakia and Oskar was inclined to join the Nazi Party. In a short time, Poland fell to the Germans and Oskar immigrated to Krakow in search of opportunity.

In Poland, after developing a rapport with the local Gestapo chiefs, he was recruited by the German Intelligence Agency to collect information about Poles who might not be sympathetic to the Nazi cause. Through the status he acquired in that post, Oskar was able to acquire two factories, previously Jewish-owned, that had recently become "available."

Oskar ran his new pot-making business exactly as his fellow usurping Nazi industrialists did. Employing neighborhood Jews, the cheapest labor he could find, Oskar turned a profit and disregarded the realities that were responsible for his newfound business success.

But soon Oskar had misgivings, and he began to manipulate Nazi officials to prevent his Jewish workers from being carted off to the death camps. Oskar's protection of his Jewish workers became increasingly aggressive but covert until he realized, in 1942, after witnessing a particular raid on a Jewish ghetto, that the Nazis wanted nothing less than the complete extermination of every Jew. While watching innocent people being packed onto trains bound for certain death, something awakened in him. "Beyond this day, no thinking person could fail to see what would happen," he said later. "I was now resolved to do everything in my power to defeat the system."

Soon, Oskar had convinced officials to allow him to house part of the Plazow labor camp in his factory by deeming the detainees "necessary" workers. The old were registered as 20 years younger and the children were registered as adults. Lawyers, doctors, and artists were registered as metal workers and mechanics, all so they might survive.

By the fall of 1944 the Germans were frantically trying to complete their extermination of Poland's Jews before the Russians arrived to liberate them, and it seemed certain that Schindler's Jews' time had run out. But instead of giving them up, Oskar desperately exerted his influence on contacts from Krakow to Warsaw to Berlin in an effort to spare his factory and, most importantly, his workers. And, where no one would have believed it possible, he succeeded. Oskar was granted permission to move the whole of his factory to occupied Bruennlitz, Czechoslovakia, and to take all his workers with him. The 1,098 workers who had been written on Schindler's list of employees avoided the fate of countless others who were sent to the Nazi gas chambers.

In May 1945 it was all over. The Russians moved into Bruennlitz, but in an ironic twist, though Schindler's Jews were now free, Schindler, himself a Nazi, became a fugitive. With his wife and a handful of workers, Schindler fled to Argentina, where he lived until 1958 before returning to Germany. He spent the remaining years of his life dividing his time between Germany and Israel, where he was honored and taken care of by his "*Schindlerjuden*"—Schindler Jews. Pressed for an explanation of his heroism, Schindler later offered, "I am the conscience of all those who knew something, but did nothing."

In 1962, Schindler was recognized by Yad Vashem, Israel's Holocaust memorial located on the Hill of Remembrance near Mount Herzl on the western outskirts of Jerusalem. Along the avenue of trees where "Righteous Gentiles" are remembered, he was invited to plant a carob tree and, in 1967 when Schindler finally planted the tree, it was adorned with a Talmudic inscription: "Whoever saves a single soul, it is as if he saved the whole world."

Schindler died of liver failure in Hildersheim, Germany, at the age of 66. He was buried in the Catholic section of the Mount Zion Cemetery in Jerusalem. Located atop Mount Zion, the cemetery and grave are easy to locate.

BUGSY SIEGEL
FEBRUARY 28, 1906 – JUNE 20, 1947

THOUGH BENJAMIN "BUGSY" Siegel didn't invent Las Vegas (and, contrary to popular belief, he didn't even build its first casino), the Las Vegas narrative will be forever linked to the Bugsy Siegel legend.

Bugsy and his pal Meyer Lansky headed a Brooklyn gang and amassed a minor fortune through bootlegging during Prohibition. When the liquor revenue stream dried up with Prohibition's 1933 repeal, Lansky (who by this time had emerged as the boss) sought to replace the income by expanding into Nevada, where gambling had been recently legalized, and he tapped Bugsy to develop a casino operation in the dusty railroad junction town of Las Vegas. After failing to buy a couple of existing gambling joints in the downtown area, Bugsy eventually bought a controlling interest in a venture headed by Billy Wilkerson, who had a vision of a luxurious gaming paradise in the desert six miles outside of town. Wilkerson soon ran out of money and was pushed out, and the Flamingo Hotel and Casino became Bugsy's baby.

Bugsy had estimated that it would cost just over a million dollars to build the lavish facility, but the costs inevitably escalated and Lansky was forced to seek fellow racketeer investors. The price tag topped $6 million before the hotel section was completed, and Lansky's investor buddies were convinced that Bugsy had skimmed money from the construction funds. They voted for a contract on Bugsy's life. However, Lansky recommended that the execution of his childhood friend be

stayed until after the casino opened. If Bugsy's desert dream proved as successful as had been promised, there would be ways for him to repay the money. If not, the contract could be fulfilled.

On the day after Christmas 1946, the Flamingo opened and flopped. A tremendous West Coast storm grounded flights that Bugsy had chartered for his Hollywood friends and, because there were yet no rooms to stay in, regular customers who trekked to the gala shortly left. Lansky's cronies again called for Bugsy's execution, but Lansky was convinced that the casino would become profitable and won his old friend another stay. Meanwhile, Bugsy remained ignorant of the ongoing scheme and devoted all of his waking hours to turning the operation around.

The Flamingo Hotel was completed in March 1947, and within two months the business was in the black—but by then it was too late. On a June evening, Bugsy was reading the evening papers on the sofa of his girlfriend's Beverly Hills home when, at about 10:30 p.m., eight bullets flew through the living room window. Five of them hit their marks, and Bugsy was killed.

Even though his gangland slaying was front-page news, Bugsy's funeral was attended by only five people, all of them relatives. Neither his old buddy Meyer Lansky nor any of his Hollywood acquaintances, not even his girlfriend, Virginia Hill, made time for the service.

At 41, Bugsy was buried at Hollywood Forever in Hollywood, California.

GRAVE DIRECTIONS: Enter the cemetery at 6000 Santa Monica Boulevard turn right after the information booth, then make a left and go all the way to the end of the drive, parking in front of the Beth Olam Mausoleum. Walk into the mausoleum and turn right at the second hall, which is labeled "M2." Bugsy's crypt is about halfway down this hall, on the left-hand side, third row from the bottom, Number 3087.

Say what you will about Bugsy Siegel, but he must have done something right. God knows I've seen a lot of celebrity resting places, but his crypt is the first I've ever seen peppered with lipstick impressions.

The Las Vegas that Bugsy knew doesn't really exist anymore, and in 1993 the last of the original Flamingo buildings were torn down. Today, the only homage to Bugsy is a plaque in the garden near the Flamingo's pool.

TOKYO ROSE

JULY 4, 1916 – SEPTEMBER 26, 2006

IN THE SUMMER of 1941 Iva Toguri D'Aquino, a daughter of Japanese immigrants, graduated from UCLA with a degree in zoology and then went to Tokyo to care for an ailing aunt. But when Pearl Harbor was attacked in December she became stranded in Japan and, refusing to renounce her U.S. citizenship, was labeled as an enemy alien and fell under constant surveillance by military police. Estranged and evicted from her aunt and uncle's home for voicing pro-American sentiments, Iva soon found herself on the streets, knowing virtually no Japanese and without a food ration card but, nonetheless, finagled herself an office job at the Domei News Agency.

Meanwhile, an Australian POW named Charles Cousens was dispensing half-truths on a Radio Tokyo propaganda program called *Zero Hour*, a Japanese psychological warfare campaign designed to lower the morale of Allied servicemen stationed throughout the Pacific. In 1943 his captors hit upon the idea of using an American woman disc jockey to further taunt and humiliate the Allies, and Iva joined Cousens on the show.

Iva took the post and, though she introduced herself on *Zero Hour* every day as "Orphan Ann," American servicemen invented and indelibly attached to her the famous moniker of Tokyo Rose. Six days a week, Orphan Ann or, if you prefer, Tokyo Rose, taunted servicemen with made-up stories of infidelity on the home front and issued false reports of battle outcomes while spinning popular and romantic records of the day in an effort to demoralize and make lonely the millions of listening soldiers and sailors.

Most Americans' knowledge of Tokyo Rose ends right about here and, were there not a corollary to the story, she wouldn't be included in this book. A clear traitor in a time of war, she'd be relegated to the dust bin of history, an interesting aside for historians. But as we know, it's not often that history is exactly black or white...

The rest of the story is that through the subtle efforts of Iva and Cousens and others, *Zero Hour* became a farce. Japanese officials in charge of the show, though fluent in English, were clueless to sarcasm, inflections, and double entendres of the language, and Iva made a mockery of their propaganda bulletins. Though the Radio Tokyo broadcasts gained notoriety back home in the States as yet another way in which the devilishly cruel Japanese debased Allied fighting forces, most sailors and soldiers actually found the broadcasts ridiculous and silly. And after the war as the narrative of Tokyo Rose was propped up by books and film, the story developed into exaggerated folklore despite some veterans who acknowledged their memories of gathering around the radio with wartime buddies to snicker at her sham misinformation broadcasts. Though there were traitors that used the radio waves during World War II (Axis Sally and Lord Haw Haw, most famously), it today seems apparent that Tokyo Rose's loyalties were always with the Allies.

When the war ended Iva was arrested for treason and spent a year in a six-by-nine-foot cell, but was released once it was concluded there were no grounds for her prosecution. But loyalty issues soon became a public flashpoint and as particular broadcast personalities doggedly vilified her as a traitor, clamor for charges against her raised traction and in 1948 she was charged with seven crimes against the United States. Ultimately convicted on a single count of treason for a broadcast in which she said, "Orphans of the Pacific, you really are orphans now. How will you get home now that all your ships are lost?" Iva was sentenced to 10 years in federal prison. In 1977 Iva was exonerated by a pardon from President Ford.

At 90, Iva died of natural causes and was buried at Montrose Cemetery in Chicago, Illinois.

GRAVE DIRECTIONS: Enter the cemetery at 5400 North Pulaski Road, take the middle road at the three-way "Y," and then make your next left. After about 150 feet, Iva is buried in the section on the left. Her grassy grave is unmarked, but it's just a few paces from the Brady stone.

HARRIET TUBMAN
1820(?) – MARCH 10, 1913

HARRIET TUBMAN'S ANCESTORS had been brought from Africa in shackles to slave over the broad farmlands of eastern Maryland, but Harriet escaped to the freedom of Pennsylvania in 1849 after learning that she was to be sold to a slave-owner in the Deep South. Upon reaching Philadelphia, where Harriet later reflected, "I was free, but there was no one to welcome me to the land of freedom," she was directed to the abolitionist William Still, who ran the General Vigilance Committee. Still disclosed to Harriet the existence of the underground railroad, a loose network of safe houses maintained by antislavery sympathizers that constituted a route to freedom in the North. For the next 16 years, until the

Thirteenth Amendment in 1865 freed blacks from indenture, Harriet made at least 18 trips to the South and led some 300 slaves, including seven members of her family, along the underground railroad, becoming its most celebrated "conductor." By Harriet's own admission, "I never run my train off the track and I never lost a passenger."

Harriet spent two of the Civil War years in South Carolina working for the Union Army as a nurse and helping blacks organize for their impending freedom. After the war, she settled in Auburn, New York, where the state government assisted her in acquiring a home. In 1896, when she was well into her seventies, Harriet acquired additional acreage and established the Harriet Tubman Home for the Aged, which provided shelter and services for the indigent freed blacks.

Harriet's last two years were spent as an in-patient of her own home for the aged, and she died there of pneumonia.

At about 93, Harriet was buried at Fort Hill Cemetery in Auburn, New York.

GRAVE DIRECTIONS: At 19 Fort Street, enter the cemetery by turning right immediately before the stone fort building. Follow the drive along the cemetery's chain-link fence perimeter and, a hundred feet after the drive turns hard to the left, look to the left for a big spruce tree. Just in front of the spruce tree, Harriet's gravestone is flanked by a pair of shrubs.

If you're interested, the Harriet Tubman home is now a museum, just 1½ miles farther south on Route 34.

THE WRIGHT BROTHERS

WILBUR WRIGHT
APRIL 16, 1867 – MAY 30, 1912

ORVILLE WRIGHT
AUGUST 19, 1871 – JANUARY 30, 1948

IN THE LATE 1800s Wilbur and Orville Wright took an interest in flying, which at that time only meant gliding, and within a short time they read all that had been written on the subject. Disagreeing with the manner in which most flying-machine tinkerers were approaching the problem, Wilbur started anew and defined what he felt were the essential elements of a flying machine. To wit, it would need wings to provide lift, a power source for propulsion, and a system of control. Of all the early aviators, Wilbur was the first to recognize that a flying machine must be controlled in all three axes of rotation, now known as pitch, roll, and yaw, and it seems that simple abstraction was his key advantage. This, and their dogged perseverance, led the brothers to build the first successful flying machine.

By 1902 the brothers had built a controllable glider, but to graduate to a self-propelled flying machine they'd need a lightweight internal combustion engine, which did not exist. Undaunted, within a year they had built a four-cylinder, 12-horsepower engine in their bicycle shop and fitted it with a propeller whose design was based on the same aeronautical principle as their wings. Orville and Wilbur understood that a propeller is essentially a rotating wing.

In the autumn of 1903 the brothers' flying machine was complete. They shipped it to Kitty Hawk, North Carolina, and, after winning a coin toss, Wilbur attempted to fly it. He stalled the engine on takeoff and caused some minor damage, so the next attempt would be Orville's. Three days later, on December 17, 1903, Orville Wright did for 12 seconds what no person had ever done before. He flew.

After two more years of fine-tuning their Flyer, they could stay aloft for as long as they liked, or until their fuel ran out, and their 1905 Wright Flyer became the world's first practical airplane. Surprisingly, their airplane was not an immediate commercial success.

The Wrights contacted the United States War Department, as well as foreign governments, and offered to sell them a flying machine, but they were turned down time and time again. Government bureaucrats thought they were crackpots, and others thought that if two Ohio bicycle mechanics could build an airplane, they could do it themselves. But the Wrights persisted and finally, in 1908, they sold their first aircraft to the United States government.

Unfortunately, Wilbur never witnessed the tremendous strides made in aviation over the next decades, as he died in 1912 of typhoid fever. He was 45. Orville lived to be 76, expiring of a heart attack while fixing the doorbell at his home in 1948.

Both lifelong bachelors, the brothers are buried together at Woodland Cemetery in Dayton, Ohio.

GRAVE DIRECTIONS: Enter the cemetery at 118 Woodland Avenue, bear left at the "T," and head up the hill. At the first intersection, bear left at the Lowes mausoleum and then turn right at the Staniland mausoleum. Stop at the Phillips mausoleum on the left. The Wrights are in this section, about 50 feet behind Phillips.

MALCOLM X & BETTY SHABAZZ

MALCOLM X
MAY 19, 1925 – FEBRUARY 21, 1965

BETTY SHABAZZ
MAY 28, 1936 – JUNE 23, 1997

MALCOLM X'S FATHER was an outspoken supporter of black leaders long before "civil rights" became a buzzword. As a result, the family was harassed by vigilante groups and Malcolm's father eventually ended up on streetcar tracks with a crushed skull and a body nearly severed in half, though the death was ruled accidental.

Malcolm was sent to prison for burglary in 1946, and it was there that he converted to the Black Muslim faith, the Nation of Islam. By the time of his 1952 parole, he wholeheartedly embraced the faith's beliefs and tirelessly championed its basic argument that evil is an inherent characteristic of the white man's world. He believed that in order to flourish, blacks had to completely separate themselves from white civilization. Malcolm was soon ordained a minister, and in 1956 he met his future wife, Betty, who had also taken the last name "X," as many Nation of Islam followers do—it represents an African family name that can never be known.

Malcolm developed a brilliant platform style and, with bitter eloquence, took the Nation of Islam from an insignificant splinter group to an organization that boasted thousands of official members and an untold number of sympathizers. By far the Nation of Islam's most effective and prominent preacher, Malcolm was in almost constant demand on college campuses, where he derided the civil-rights movement and rejected integration and racial equality, calling instead for black separatism and the taking up of arms against whites. This message was the opposite of the nonviolent approach that activists such as Dr. Martin Luther King Jr. preached and, as a result of this militant stance, many whites viewed Malcolm with fear and contempt, while many blacks distanced themselves from his tirades.

As Malcolm became increasingly famous, he provoked tension and jealousy among the Nation of Islam leaders. Its founder, Elijah Muhammad, sought to rid himself of the formidable threat to his own power. After Malcolm described John F. Kennedy's assassination as a "case of chickens coming home to roost," Muhammad suspended his protégé from the faith.

In 1964 Malcolm followed a pilgrimage to Mecca with a prolonged period of study in the Middle East, where he was impressed by the sight of people of all races coming together in the name of Islam. He returned to the United States a changed man, proclaimed himself a convert to orthodox Islam, adopted a new name, El-Hajj Malik El-Shabazz, and fostered a new philosophy known as Black Consciousness encouraging blacks to share their racial and cultural heritage.

Malcolm no longer accepted that white people were evil, and he became critical of the now-rival Nation of Islam, condemning its ideas as counterproductive; it was economics, not color, that kept blacks from succeeding, the new Malcolm insisted. Further, Malcolm raised questions about Nation of Islam financial irregularities, and denounced Elijah Muhammad as a fake and an immoral philanderer. As the two sides traded accusations, the conflict escalated into outright violence and death threats were recorded.

While preparing for an address at Harlem's Audubon Ballroom in February 1965, Malcolm X was ambushed and died after being shot more than a dozen times. Though his three assassins had ties to the Nation of Islam, they insisted someone else had paid them. Nonetheless, they were convicted of the murder and sentenced to life in prison.

After her husband's death, Betty Shabazz earned a doctorate in education and traveled widely to speak on civil rights and racial tolerance.

In June 1997 Betty died after being severely burned in a fire started by her 12-year-old grandson, reportedly set because he was unhappy that he had been sent to live with her.

Malcolm X and Betty are buried side by side at Ferncliff Cemetery in Hartsdale, New York.

GRAVE DIRECTIONS: Enter the cemetery at the third entrance on 280 Secor Road and bear right. On the left at the top of the paved loop is the Pinewood section. Drive about ¾ of the way around the loop and stop at the rough and narrow path on the left. Four rows from the road and 10 rows from the path are the graves of Malcolm X and Betty Shabazz at marker number 150.

ALVIN YORK
DECEMBER 13, 1887 – SEPTEMBER 2, 1964

ALVIN YORK HAILED from the backwaters of Tennessee, where he and his family scraped out a living and supplemented their dinner table through hunting. In his small world, Alvin was well known as a drinker and gambler and general nuisance, but after an epiphany at 26 he turned his life around. He became a member of the Church of Christ, a teacher in the Sunday school, and leader of the choir.

Three years later, in 1917, the United States joined the war against Germany and Alvin's faith was tested when he received a draft notice. Following the church's teachings, Alvin returned the notice with the words "Dont want to Fight" scrawled across the back. However, his case was denied because his church did not expressly prohibit killing during war, and Alvin reluctantly reported to basic training, where he distinguished himself as an expert marksman.

In the Argonne Forest in October of 1918, Alvin and 16 other soldiers mistakenly wound up behind enemy lines and surprised a number of German troops eating breakfast. A brief firefight ensued and resulted in the unexpected surrender of a superior German force to the 17 men. But once the Germans realized that the American contingent was limited, another squad of German machine-gunners on a nearby hill was alerted and opened fire on the Americans, as well as on their own troops, who had just surrendered. Ordered to silence the machine guns, the marksman Alvin picked off at least a dozen of the Germans on the hill, and in short order they too chose to surrender. By the time York and his men, now numbering just nine, reached the safety of the American lines they had captured 132 Germans. Word quickly spread that York had single-handedly "captured the whole German army."

Upon returning to America, Sergeant York was issued the Medal of Honor and showered with appearance and endorsement offers. He soon began using his popularity to raise money for a school for underprivileged children and, in 1927, the Alvin C. York Institute was established. It later became a special part of the Tennessee school system.

Alvin's hero status matured to its fullest in the years during World War II, when his story from the previous war was made into a top-grossing movie, *Sergeant York*. Twenty years later, such status mattered little when the Internal Revenue Service pursued him for some $170,000 in back taxes and interest owed from the movie royalty income. Partially paralyzed and almost completely blind from a stroke, Alvin was broke and unable to pay the debt, so the American public rallied behind him and established the York Relief Fund. After $130,000 was raised, President Kennedy called the matter "a national disgrace" and ordered it resolved. The IRS settled for $100,000, and the remainder was placed in a trust for the York family.

In a veteran's hospital, Alvin died at 76 from stroke complications and was buried at Wolf River Cemetery in Pall Mall, Tennessee.

GRAVE DIRECTIONS: Off Wolf River Loop Road, enter the cemetery at the second entrance and you'll see Alvin's grave under the American flag that flies proud.

INDEX

River Yamuna, 317 (scattered)

INDIANA
Fairmount, 86
Indianapolis, 458

IRELAND
Cliffs of Moher, 438

ISRAEL
Jerusalem, 554

ITALY
Florence, 244
Modena, 272

JAMAICA
Nine Mile, 360

KANSAS
Garden City, 246
Waldron, 448

KENTUCKY
Elizaville, 537
Frankfort, 517
Louisville, 19, 502

LOUISIANA
Lafayette, 444
Metarie, 366
Mooringsport, 353

MAINE
Brooklin, 297

MARYLAND
Baltimore, 275, 519
Rockville, 251
Sandyville, 103
Towson, 88

MASSACHUSETTS
Chilmark, 157
Concord, 233
Fall River, 451
Lowell, 237
Malden, 79
Provincetown, 267
Stockbridge, 279

MICHIGAN
Detroit, 531, 551
Warren, 396

MINNESOTA
Minneapolis, 508
Richfield, 217

MISSISSIPPI
Greenwood, 351
Wiggins, 26

MISSOURI
Mansfield, 200
Marthasville, 518
St. Louis, 239, 301

MONTANA
Butte, 478

NEVADA
Las Vegas, 95

NEW HAMPSHIRE
Concord, 219

NEW JERSEY
Collingswood, 299
Delaware River, 528 (scattered)
East Hanover, 53
Lyndhurst, 372
Newark, 238
Red Bank, 38
Scotch Plains, 139
West Orange, 527
Westfield, 419

NEW MEXICO
Abiquiu, 220 (scattered)
Ranchos de Taos, 111
Santa Fe, 104 (scattered)

NEW YORK
Auburn, 559
Bethel, 347 (scattered)
Bronx, 213, 396, 411
Brooklyn, 58, 185, 191
Buffalo, 349
East Elmhurst, 425
East Hampton, 257
Elmira, 294
Elmont, 117
Farmingdale, 407, 553
Fishkill, 223
Flushing, 395, 415
Hartsdale, 83, 165, 194, 563
Hastings-on-Hudson, 414
Hawthorne, 43, 46, 136
Huntington, 322
Interlaken, 163
Ithaca, 500
Jamestown, 115
Lake Placid, 437
Middle Village, 446, 465
Monticello, 389
New York City, 316
Putnam Valley, 17
Rensselaerville, 500
Ridgewood, 193, 469
Sag Harbor, 211
Sleepy Hollow, 261
Valhalla, 41, 195, 278
West Babylon, 276
West Point, 525
Westhampton, 25
Woodstock, 310, 311

NEW ZEALAND
Haruaki Gulf, 533 (scattered)

NORTH CAROLINA
Belvidere, 388
Chapel Hill, 122
Ellerbe, 19 (scattered)
Hertford, 50
Mooresville, 27
Raleigh, 62
Roanoke Island, 102
Smithfield, 99
Wilmington, 61

NORTH DAKOTA
Fargo, 45

NORWAY
Oslo, 477

OHIO
Akron, 515
Canton, 44
Cleveland, 453
Columbus, 507
Dayton, 204, 561
Peoli, 64
Rushtown, 59

OKLAHOMA
Claremore, 498
Edmond, 492
Tulsa, 119

OREGON
Coos Bay, 55
Pleasant Hill, 262

PENNSYLVANIA
Bensalem, 382
Bethel Park, 297
Dublin, 242
Frazer, 330
Lackawaxen, 254
Pen Argyl, 133
Philadelphia, 29

RUSSIA
Tula, 292

RWANDA
Karisoke Research Center, 209

SAMOA
Apia, 288

SOUTH CAROLINA
Beech Island, 321
Florence, 458
Greenville, 33

SPAIN
Figueres, 249